BERLITZ PHRASE BOOKS

World's bestselling phrase books feature not only expressions and vocabulary you'll need, but also travel tips, useful facts and pronunciation throughout. The handiest and most readable conversation aid available.

Arabic	French	Polish
Chinese	German	Portuguese
Danish	Greek	Russian
Dutch	Hebrew	Serbo-Croatian
European (14 languages)	Hungarian	Spanish
	Italian	Lat.-Am. Spanish
European Menu Reader	Japanese	Swahili
	Korean	Swedish
Finnish	Norwegian	Turkish

BERLITZ CASSETTEPAKS

The above-mentioned titles are also available combined with a cassette to help you improve your accent. A helpful miniscript is included containing the complete text of the dual language hi-fi recording.

Berlitz Dictionaries

Dansk	Engelsk, Fransk, Italiensk, Spansk, Tysk
Deutsch	Dänisch, Englisch, Finnisch, Französisch, Italienisch, Niederländisch, Norwegisch, Portugiesisch, Schwedisch, Spanisch
English	Danish, Dutch, Finnish, French, German, Italian, Norwegian, Portuguese, Spanish, Swedish
Español	Alemán, Danés, Finlandés, Francés, Holandés, Inglés, Noruego, Sueco
Français	Allemand, Anglais, Danois, Espagnol, Finnois, Italien, Néerlandais, Norvégien, Portugais, Suédois
Italiano	Danese, Finlandese, Francese, Inglese, Norvegese, Olandese, Svedese, Tedesco
Nederlands	Duits, Engels, Frans, Italiaans, Portugees, Spaans
Norsk	Engelsk, Fransk, Italiensk, Spansk, Tysk
Português	Alemão, Francês, Holandês, Inglês, Sueco
Suomi	Englanti, Espanja, Italia, Ranska, Ruotsi, Saksa
Svenska	Engelska, Finska, Franska, Italienska, Portugisiska, Spanska, Tyska

BERLITZ®

spanish-english
english-spanish
dictionary

Mulen Gage

diccionario
español-inglés
inglés-español

By the Staff of Berlitz Guides

Copyright © 1974, 1979 by Berlitz Guides,
a division of Macmillan S.A., Avenue d'Ouchy 61,
1000 Lausanne 6, Switzerland.

All rights reserved. No part of this book may be reproduced or trans-
mitted in any form or by any means, electronic or mechanical, including
photocopying, recording or by any information storage and retrieval
system without permission in writing from the publisher.

Revised edition 1979
Library of Congress Catalog Card Number: 78-78079

16th printing 1989
Printed in England

Berlitz Trademark Reg. U.S. Patent Office
and other countries—Marca Registrada.

Contents

Indice

Preface

In selecting the 12.500 word-concepts in each language for this dictionary, the editors have had the traveller's needs foremost in mind. This book will prove invaluable to all the millions of travellers, tourists and business people who appreciate the reassurance a small and practical dictionary can provide. It offers them—as it does beginners and students—all the basic vocabulary they are going to encounter and to have to use, giving the key words and expressions to allow them to cope in everyday situations.

Like our successful phrase books and travel guides, these dictionaries—created with the help of a computer data bank—are designed to slip into pocket or purse, and thus have a role as handy companions at all times.

Besides just about everything you normally find in dictionaries, there are these Berlitz bonuses:

● imitated pronunciation next to each foreign-word entry, making it easy to read and enunciate words whose spelling may look forbidding

● a unique, practical glossary to simplify reading a foreign restaurant menu and to take the mystery out of complicated dishes and indecipherable names on bills of fare

● useful information on how to tell the time and how to count, on conjugating irregular verbs, commonly seen abbreviations and converting to the metric system, in addition to basic phrases.

While no dictionary of this size can pretend to completeness, we expect the user of this book will feel well armed to affront foreign travel with confidence. We should, however, be very pleased to receive comments, criticism and suggestions that you think may be of help in preparing future editions.

Prefacio

Al seleccionar las 12 500 palabras-conceptos en cada una de las lenguas de este diccionario, los redactores han tenido muy en cuenta las necesidades del viajero. Esta obra es indispensable para millones de viajeros, turistas y hombres de negocios, quienes apreciarán la seguridad que aporta un diccionario pequeño y práctico. Tanto a ellos como a los principiantes y estudiantes les ofrece todo el vocabulario básico que encontrarán o deberán emplear en el lenguaje de todos los días; les proporciona las palabras clave y las expresiones que les permitirán enfrentarse a las situaciones de la vida diaria.

Al igual que nuestros conocidos manuales de conversación y guías turísticas, estos diccionarios – realizados en computadora con la ayuda de un banco de datos – han sido ideados para llevarse en el bolsillo o en un bolso de mano, asumiendo de este modo su papel de compañeros disponibles en todo momento.

Además de las nociones que de ordinario ofrece un diccionario, encontrará:

- una transcripción fonética tan sencilla que facilita la lectura, aun cuando la palabra extranjera parezca impronunciable
- un léxico gastronómico inédito que le hará «descifrar» los menús en un restaurante extranjero, revelándole el secreto de los platos complicados y los misterios de la cuenta
- informaciones prácticas que le ayudarán a comunicar la hora y a contar, así como a utilizar los verbos irregulares, las abreviaturas más comunes y algunas expresiones útiles.

Ningún diccionario de este formato puede tener la pretensión de ser completo, pero el fin de este libro es permitir que quien lo emplee posea un arma para enfrentarse con confianza al viaje en el extranjero. Sin embargo, recibiremos con gusto los comentarios, críticas y sugestiones que con toda seguridad nos permitirán preparar las futuras ediciones.

spanish-english

_____

español-inglés

Introduction

This dictionary has been designed to take account of your practical needs. Unnecessary linguistic information has been avoided. The entries are listed in alphabetical order regardless of whether the entry word is printed in a single word or in two or more separate words. As the only exception to this rule, a few idiomatic expressions are listed as main entries alphabetically according to the most significant word of the expression. When an entry is followed by sub-entries, such as expressions and locutions, these, too, have been listed in alphabetical order.[1]

Each main-entry word is followed by a phonetic transcription (see guide to pronunciation). Following the transcription is the part of speech of the entry word whenever applicable. When an entry word may be used as more than one part of speech, the translations are grouped together after the respective part of speech.

Whenever an entry word is repeated in sub-entries a tilde ($\sim$) is used to represent the full entry word.

An asterisk (*) in front of a verb indicates that the verb is irregular. For details you may refer to the lists of irregular verbs.

The dictionary is based on Castilian Spanish. All words and meanings of words that are exclusively Mexican have been marked as such (see list of abbreviations used in the text).

Abbreviations

adj	adjective	*n*	noun
adv	adverb	*nAm*	noun (American)
Am	American	*num*	numeral
art	article	*p*	past tense
conj	conjunction	*pl*	plural
f	feminine	*plAm*	plural (American)
fMe	feminine (Mexican)	*pp*	past participle
fpl	feminine plural	*pr*	present tense
fplMe	feminine plural (Mexican)	*pref*	prefix
m	masculine	*prep*	preposition
Me	Mexican	*pron*	pronoun
mMe	masculine (Mexican)	*v*	verb
mpl	masculine plural	*vAm*	verb (American)
mplMe	masculine plural (Mexican)	*vMe*	verb (Mexican)

---

[1] Note that the alphabetical order in Spanish differs from our own in three cases: *ch*, *ll* and *ñ* are considered independent letters and come after *c*, *l* and n, respectively.

Guide to Pronunciation

Each main entry in this part of the dictionary is followed by a phonetic transcription which shows you how to pronounce the words. This transcription should be read as if it were English. It is based on Standard British pronunciation, though we have tried to take account of General American pronunciation also. Below, only those letters and symbols are explained which we consider likely to be ambiguous or not immediately understood.

The syllables are separated by hyphens, and stressed syllables are printed in *italics*.

Of course, the sounds of any two languages are never exactly the same, but if you follow carefully our indications, you should be able to pronounce the foreign words in such a way that you'll be understood. To make your task easier, our transcriptions occasionally simplify slightly the sound system of the language while still reflecting the essential sound differences.

Consonants

bh	a rather indecisive **b**, i.e. one verging on **v**
dh	like **th** in **th**is, often rather indecisive, possibly quite like **d**
g	always hard, as in **g**o
ģ	a **g**-sound where the tongue doesn't quite close the air passage between itself and the roof of the mouth, so that the escaping air produces audible friction; it is also on occasions pronounced as an indecisive **g**
kh	like **ģ**, but based on a **k**-sound; therefore hard and voiceless, like **ch** in Scottish lo**ch**
lʸ	like **lli** in mi**lli**on
ñ	as in the Spanish se**ñ**or, or like **ni** in o**ni**on
r	slightly rolled in the front of the mouth
rr	strongly rolled **r**
s	always hard, as in **s**o

Vowels and Diphthongs

ah	a short version of the **a** in c**a**r, i.e. a sound between **a** in c**a**t and **u** in c**u**t
igh	as in s**igh**
ou	as in l**ou**d

1) Raised letters (e.g. **ay⁰⁰**, **ʸah**) should be pronounced only fleetingly.

2) Spanish vowels (i.e. not diphthongs) are pure and fairly short. There- fore, you should try to read a transcription like **oa** without moving tongue or lips while pronouncing the sound.

Latin-American Pronunciation

Our transcriptions reflect the pronunciation of Castilian, the official language of Spain. In Latin America, two of the Castilian sounds are practically unknown:

1) **ll** as in the word **calle** (which we represent by **lʸ**) is usually pronounced like Spanish **y** (as in English yet); in the Río de la Plata region, though, both **ll** and **y** are pronounced like **s** in pleasure.

2) The letters **c** (before **e** and **i**) and **z** are pronounced like **s** in **so** instead of **th** as in **thin**.

A

a (ah) *prep* to, on; at; **a las ...** at ... o'clock

abacería (ah-bhah-thay-*ree*-ah) *f* grocer's

abacero (ah-bhah-*thay*-roa) *m* grocer

abadía (ah-bhah-*dhee*-ah) *f* abbey

abajo (ah-*bhah*-khoa) *adv* downstairs; down; **hacia ~** downwards

abandonar (ah-bhahn-doa-*nahr*) *v* abandon

abanico (ah-bhah-*nee*-koa) *m* fan

abarrotería (ah-bhah-rroa-tay-*ree*-ah) *fMe* grocer's

abarrotero (ah-bhah-rroa-*tay*-roa) *mMe* grocer

abastecimiento (ah-bhahss-tay-thee-*m*ʸ*ayn*-toa) *m* supply

abatido (ah-bhah-*tee*-dhoa) *adj* down

abecedario (ah-bhay-thay-*dah*-rʸoa) *m* alphabet

abedul (ah-bhay-*dhool*) *m* birch

abeja (ah-*bhay*-khah) *f* bee

abertura (ah-bhayr-*too*-rah) *f* opening

abierto (ah-*bh*ʸ*ayr*-toa) *adj* open

abismo (ah-*bhee*-zmoa) *m* abyss

ablandador (ah-bhlahn-dah-*dhoar*) *m* water-softener

ablandar (ah-bhlahn-*dahr*) *v* soften

abogado (ah-bhoa-*gah*-dhoa) *m* barrister, lawyer, attorney; solicitor; advocate

abolir (ah-bhoa-*leer*) *v* abolish

abolladura (ah-bhoa-lʸah-*dhoo*-rah) *f* dent

abonado (ah-bhoa-*nah*-dhoa) *m* subscriber

abono (ah-*bhoa*-noa) *m* manure, dung

aborto (ah-*bhoar*-toa) *m* miscarriage; abortion

abrazar (ah-bhrah-*thahr*) *v* embrace; hug

abrazo (ah-*bhrah*-thoa) *m* hug; embrace

abrecartas (ah-bhray-*kahr*-tahss) *m* paper-knife

abrelatas (ah-bhray-*lah*-tahss) *m* can opener, tin-opener

abreviatura (ah-bhray-bhʸah-*too*-rah) *f* abbreviation

abrigar (ah-bhree-*gahr*) *v* shelter

abrigo (ah-*bhree*-goa) *m* coat, overcoat; **~ de pieles** fur coat

abril (ah-*bhreel*) April

abrir (ah-*bhreer*) *v* open; unlock; turn on

abrochar (ah-bhroa-*chahr*) *v* button

abrupto (ah-*bhroop*-toa) *adj* steep

absceso (ahbhs-*thay*-soa) *m* abscess

absolución (ahbh-soa-loo-*th*ʸ*oan*) *f* acquittal

absolutamente (ahbh-soa-loo-tah-*mayn*-tay) *adv* absolutely

absoluto (ahbh-soa-*loo*-toa) *adj* sheer; total

abstemio (ahbhs-*tay*-m^yoa) *m* teetotaller

*__abstenerse de__ (ahbhs-tay-*nayr*-say) abstain from

abstracto (ahbhs-*trahk*-toa) *adj* abstract

absurdo (ahbh-*soor*-dhoa) *adj* absurd; foolish

abuela (ah-*bhway*-lah) *f* grandmother

abuelo (ah-*bhway*-loa) *m* grandfather, granddad; **abuelos** *mpl* grandparents *pl*

abundancia (ah-bhoon-*dahn*-th^yah) *f* abundance, plenty

abundante (ah-bhoon-*dahn*-tay) *adj* abundant, plentiful

abundar (ah-bhoon-*dahr*) *v* abound

aburrido (ah-bhoo-*rree*-dhoa) *adj* boring, dull

aburrimiento (ah-bhoo-rree-*m^yayn*-toa) *m* annoyance

aburrir (ah-bhoo-*rreer*) *v* bore, annoy

abusar de (ah-bhoo-*sahr*) exploit

abuso (ah-*bhoo*-soa) *m* misuse, abuse

acá (ah-*kah*) *adv* here

acabar (ah-kah-*bhahr*) *v* end; **acabado** finished; over

academia (ah-kah-*dhay*-m^yah) *f* academy; ~ **de bellas artes** art school

acallar (ah-kah-*l^yahr*) *v* silence

acampador (ah-kahm-pah-*dhoar*) *m* camper

acampar (ah-kahm-*pahr*) *v* camp

acantilado (ah-kahn-tee-*lah*-dhoa) *m* cliff

acariciar (ah-kah-ree-*th^yahr*) *v* cuddle

acaso (ah-*kah*-soa) *adv* perhaps

accesible (ahk-thay-*see*-bhlay) *adj* accessible

acceso (ahk-*thay*-soa) *m* entrance, access; approach

accesorio (ahk-thay-*soa*-r^yoa) *adj* additional; **accesorios** *mpl* accessories *pl*

accidental (ahk-thee-dhayn-*tahl*) *adj* accidental

accidente (ahk-thee-*dhayn*-tay) *m* accident; ~ **aéreo** plane crash

acción (ahk-*th^yoan*) *f* share; action; deed; **acciones** *fpl* stocks and shares

acechar (ah-thay-*chahr*) *v* watch for

aceite (ah-*thay*-tay) *m* oil; ~ **bronceador** suntan oil; ~ **de mesa** salad oil; ~ **de oliva** olive oil; ~ **lubricante** lubrication oil; ~ **para el pelo** hair-oil

aceitoso (ah-thay-*toa*-soa) *adj* oily

aceituna (ah-thay-*too*-nah) *f* olive

acelerador (ah-thay-lay-rah-*dhoar*) *m* accelerator

acelerar (ah-thay-lay-*rahr*) *v* accelerate

acento (ah-*thayn*-toa) *m* accent

acentuar (ah-thayn-*twahr*) *v* emphasize, stress

aceptar (ah-thayp-*tahr*) *v* accept

acera (ah-*thay*-rah) *f* pavement; sidewalk *nAm*

acerca de (ah-*thayr*-kah day) about

acercarse (ah-thayr-*kahr*-say) *v* approach

acero (ah-*thay*-roa) *m* steel; ~ **inoxidable** stainless steel

*__acertar__ (ah-thayr-*tahr*) *v* *hit; guess right

acidez (ah-thee-*dhayth*) *f* heartburn

ácido (*ah*-thee-dhoa) *m* acid

aclamar (ah-klah-*mahr*) *v* cheer

aclaración (ah-klah-rah-*th^yoan*) *f* explanation

aclarar (ah-klah-*rahr*) *v* clarify

acné (ahk-*nay*) *m* acne

acogida (ah-koa-*khee*-dhah) *f* reception

acomodación (ah-koa-moa-dhah-*th^yoan*) *f* accommodation

acomodado (ah-koa-moa-*dhah*-dhoa) *adj* well-to-do

acomodador (ah-koa-moa-dhah-*dhoar*) *m* usher

acomodadora (ah-koa-moa-dhah-*dhoa*-rah) *f* usherette

acomodar (ah-koa-moa-*dhahr*) *v* accommodate

acompañar (ah-koam-pah-*ñahr*) *v* accompany; conduct

aconsejar (ah-koan-say-*khahr*) *v* recommend, advise

*acontecer (ah-koan-tay-*thayr*) *v* occur

acontecimiento (ah-koan-tay-thee-*mᵞayn*-toa) *m* event; happening, occurrence

*acordar (ah-koar-*dhahr*) *v* agree; ***acordarse** *v* remember, recollect, recall

acortar (ah-koar-*tahr*) *v* shorten

*acostar (ah-koass-*tahr*) *v* *lay down; ***acostarse** *v* *go to bed

acostumbrado (ah-koass-toom-*brah*-dhoa) *adj* accustomed; customary; ***estar ~ a** *be used to

acostumbrar (ah-koass-toom-*brahr*) *v* accustom

*acrecentarse (ah-kray-thayn-*tahr*-say) *v* increase

acreditar (ah-kray-dhee-*tahr*) *v* credit

acreedor (ah-kray-ay-*dhoar*) *m* creditor

acta (*ahk*-tah) *f* certificate; **actas** minutes

actitud (ahk-tee-*toodh*) *f* attitude; position

actividad (ahk-tee-bhee-*dhahdh*) *f* activity

activo (ahk-*tee*-bhoa) *adj* active

acto (*ahk*-toa) *m* act, deed

actor (ahk-*toar*) *m* actor

actriz (ahk-*treeth*) *f* actress

actual (ahk-*twahl*) *adj* present; topical

actualmente (ahk-twahl-*mayn*-tay) *adv* now

actuar (ahk-*twahr*) *v* act

acuarela (ah-kwah-*ray*-lah) *f* watercolour

acuerdo (ah-*kwayr*-dhoa) *m* approval; agreement, settlement; **¡de acuerdo!** all right!, okay!; ***estar de ~ con** approve of

acumulador (ah-koo-moo-lah-*dhoar*) *m* battery

acusación (ah-koo-sah-*thᵞoan*) *f* charge

acusado (ah-koo-*sah*-dhoa) *m* accused

acusar (ah-koo-*sahr*) *v* accuse; charge

adaptar (ah-dhahp-*tahr*) *v* adapt; suit

adecuado (ah-dhay-*kwah*-dhoa) *adj* adequate; convenient, appropriate

adelantar (ah-dhay-lahn-*tahr*) *v* *get on; **por adelantado** in advance; **prohibido ~** no overtaking

adelante (ah-dhay-*lahn*-tay) *adv* ahead, onwards, forward

adelanto (ah-dhay-*lahn*-toa) *m* advance

adelgazar (ah-dhayl-gah-*thahr*) *v* slim

además (ah-dhay-*mahss*) *adv* moreover, furthermore, besides; **~ de** beyond, besides

adentro (ah-*dhayn*-troa) *adv* inside, in; **hacia ~** inwards

adeudado (ah-dhayᵒᵒ-*dhah*-dhoa) *adj* due

adición (ah-dhee-*thᵞoan*) *f* addition

adicional (ah-dhee-thᵞoa-*nahl*) *adj* additional

adicionar (ah-dhee-thᵞoa-*nahr*) *v* add; count

¡adiós! (ah-*dhᵞoass*) good-bye!

adivinanza (ah-dhee-bhee-*nahn*-thah) *f* riddle

adivinar (ah-dhee-bhee-*nahr*) *v* guess

adjetivo (ahdh-khay-*tee*-bhoa) *m* adjective

administración (ahdh-mee-neess-trah-

th^yoan) *f* administration; direction

administrar (ahdh-mee-neess-*trahr*) *v* manage; direct; administer

administrativo (ahdh-mee-neess-trah-*tee*-bhoa) *adj* administrative

admirable (ahdh-mee-*rah*-bhlay) *adj* admirable

admiración (ahdh-mee-rah-*th^yoan*) *f* admiration

admirador (ahdh-mee-rah-*dhoar*) *m* fan

admirar (ahdh-mee-*rahr*) *v* admire

admisión (ahdh-mee-*s^yoan*) *f* admission; admittance

admitir (ahdh-mee-*teer*) *v* admit; acknowledge

adonde (ah-*dhoan*-day) *adv* where

adoptar (ah-dhoap-*tahr*) *v* adopt

adorable (ah-dhoa-*rah*-bhlay) *adj* adorable

adorar (ah-dhoa-*rahr*) *v* worship

adormidera (ah-dhoar-mee-*dhay*-rah) *f* poppy

adorno (ah-*dhoar*-noa) *m* ornament

adquirible (ahdh-kee-*ree*-bhlay) *adj* obtainable, available

*adquirir** (ahdh-kee-*reer*) *v* acquire; *buy

adquisición (ahdh-kee-see-*th^yoan*) *f* acquisition

aduana (ah-*dwah*-nah) *f* Customs *pl*

adulto (ah-*dhool*-toa) *adj* grown-up, adult; *m* grown-up, adult

adverbio (ahdh-*bhayr*-bh^yoa) *m* adverb

advertencia (ahdh-bhayr-*tayn*-th^yah) *f* warning

*advertir** (ahdh-bhayr-*teer*) *v* caution, warn; notice

aerolínea (ah-ay-roa-*lee*-nay-ah) *f* airline

aeropuerto (ah-ay-roa-*pwayr*-toa) *m* airport

aerosol (ah-ay-roa-*soal*) *m* atomizer

afamado (ah-fah-*mah*-dhoa) *adj* noted

afección (ah-fayk-*th^yoan*) *f* affection

afectado (ah-fayk-tah-dhoa) *adj* affected

afectar (ah-fayk-*tahr*) *v* affect; feign

afeitadora eléctrica (ah-fay-tah-*dhoa*-rah ay-*layk*-tree-kah) electric razor

afeitarse (ah-fay-*tahr*-say) *v* shave; **máquina de afeitar** safety-razor; shaver

afición (ah-fee-*th^yoan*) *f* hobby

aficionado (ah-fee-th^yoa-*nah*-dhoa) *m* supporter

afilar (ah-fee-*lahr*) *v* sharpen; **afilado** sharp

afiliación (ah-fee-l^yah-*th^yoan*) *f* membership

afiliado (ah-fee-*l^yah*-dhoa) *adj* affiliated

afirmación (ah-feer-mah-*th^yoan*) *f* statement

afirmar (ah-feer-*mahr*) *v* claim

afirmativo (ah-feer-mah-*tee*-bhoa) *adj* affirmative

aflicción (ah-fleek-*th^yoan*) *f* grief

afligido (ah-flee-*khee*-dhoa) *adj* sad; *estar ~ grieve

afluente (ah-*flwayn*-tay) *m* tributary

afortunado (ah-foar-too-*nah*-dhoa) *adj* fortunate, lucky

África (*ah*-free-kah) *f* Africa

África del Sur (*ah*-free-kah dayl soor) South Africa

africano (ah-free-*kah*-noa) *adj* African; *m* African

afuera (ah-*fway*-rah) *adv* outside, outdoors; **hacia ~** outwards

afueras (ah-*fway*-rahss) *fpl* outskirts *pl*

agarradero (ah-gah-rrah-*dhay*-roa) *m* grip

agarrar (ah-gah-*rrahr*) *v* grasp, seize; **agarrarse** *v* *hold on

agarre (ah-*gah*-rray) *m* grip, grasp

agencia (ah-*khayn*-th^yah) *f* agency; ~

de viajes travel agency

agenda (ah-*khayn*-dah) *f* diary

agente (ah-*khayn*-tay) *m* agent; ~ **de policía** policeman; ~ **de viajes** travel agent

ágil (*ah*-kheel) *adj* supple

agitación (ah-khee-tah-*th*ʸ*oan*) *f* excitement; bustle

agitar (ah-khee-*tahr*) *v* stir up

agosto (ah-*goass*-toa) August

agotado (ah-goa-*tah*-dhoa) *adj* sold out

agotar (ah-goa-*tahr*) *v* use up

agradable (ah-grah-*dhah*-bhlay) *adj* agreeable; enjoyable, pleasing, pleasant; nice

*agradecer (ah-grah-dhay-*thayr*) *v* thank

agradecido (ah-grah-dhay-*thee*-dhoa) *adj* grateful, thankful

agrario (ah-*grah*-rʸoa) *adj* agrarian

agraviar (ah-grah-*bh*ʸ*ahr*) *v* wrong

agregar (ah-gray-*gahr*) *v* add

agresivo (ah-gray-*see*-bhoa) *adj* aggressive

agrícola (ah-*gree*-koa-lah) *adj* agrarian

agricultura (ah-gree-kool-*too*-rah) *f* agriculture

agrio (*ah*-grʸoa) *adj* sour

agua (*ah*-gwah) *f* water; ~ **corriente** running water; ~ **de mar** sea-water; ~ **de soda** soda-water; ~ **dulce** fresh water; ~ **helada** iced water; ~ **mineral** mineral water; ~ **potable** drinking-water

aguacero (ah-gwah-*thay*-roa) *m* shower; downpour

aguafuerte (ah-gwah-*fwayr*-tay) *f* etching

aguanieve (ah-gwah-*n*ʸ*ay*-bhay) *f* slush

aguantar (ah-gwahn-*tahr*) *v* *bear

aguardado (ah-gwahr-*dhah*-dhoa) due

aguardar (ah-gwahr-*dahr*) *v* expect

agudo (ah-*goo*-dhoa) *adj* keen; acute

águila (*ah*-gee-lah) *m* eagle

aguja (ah-*goo*-khah) *f* needle; spire; **labor de ~** needlework

agujero (ah-goo-*khay*-roa) *m* hole

ahí (ah-*ee*) *adv* there

ahogar (ah-oa-*gahr*) *v* drown; **ahogarse** *v* *be drowned

ahora (ah-*oa*-rah) *adv* now; **de ~ en adelante** henceforth; **hasta ~** so far

ahorrar (ah-oa-*rrahr*) *v* save

ahorros (ah-*oa*-rroass) *mpl* savings *pl*; **caja de ~** savings bank

ahuyentar (ou-ʸ*ayn*-*tahr*) *v* chase

aire (*igh*-ray) *m* air; sky; breath; ~ **acondicionado** air-conditioning; **cámara de ~** inner tube; ***tener aires de** look

airear (igh-ray-*ahr*) *v* air, ventilate

aireo (igh-*ray*-oa) *m* ventilation

airoso (igh-*roa*-soa) *adj* airy

aislado (ighz-*lah*-dhoa) *adj* isolated

aislador (ighz-lah-*dhoar*) *m* insulator

aislamiento (ighz-lah-*m*ʸ*ayn*-toa) *m* isolation; insulation

aislar (ighz-*lahr*) *v* isolate; insulate

ajedrez (ah-khay-*dhrayth*) *m* chess

ajeno (ah-*khay*-noa) *adj* foreign

ajetrearse (ah-khay-tray-*ahr*-say) *v* labour

ajo (*ah*-khoa) *m* garlic

ajustar (ah-khooss-*tahr*) *v* adjust

ala (*ah*-lah) *f* wing

alabar (ah-lah-*bhahr*) *v* praise

alambre (ah-*lahm*-bray) *m* wire

alargar (ah-lahr-*gahr*) *v* lengthen; renew; hand

alarma (ah-*lahr*-mah) *f* alarm; ~ **de incendio** fire-alarm

alarmante (ah-lahr-*mahn*-tay) *adj* scary

alarmar (ah-lahr-*mahr*) *v* alarm

alba (*ahl*-bhah) *f* dawn

albañil (ahl-bhah-*ñeel*) *m* bricklayer

albaricoque (ahl-bhah-ree-*koa*-kay) *m* apricot

albergue para jóvenes (ahl-*bhayr*-gay pah-rah khoa-bhay-nayss) youth hostel

alborotador (ahl-bhoa-roa-tah-*dhoar*) *adj* rowdy

alboroto (ahl-bhoa-*roa*-toa) *m* noise, racket

álbum (*ahl*-bhoom) *m* album

alcachofa (ahl-kah-*choa*-fah) *f* artichoke

alcalde (ahl-*kahl*-dhay) *m* mayor

alcance (ahl-*kahn*-thay) *m* reach, range

alcanzable (ahl-kahn-*thah*-bhlay) *adj* attainable

alcanzar (ahl-kahn-*thahr*) *v* achieve, reach

alce (*ahl*-thay) *m* moose

alcohol (ahl-*koal*) *m* alcohol; ~ **de quemar** methylated spirits

alcohólico (ahl-*koa*-lee-koa) *adj* alcoholic

aldea (ahl-*day*-ah) *f* hamlet

alegrar (ah-lay-*grahr*) *v* cheer up

alegre (ah-*lay*-gray) *adj* cheerful, merry, joyful; glad, gay

alegría (ah-lay-*gree*-ah) *f* gaiety; gladness

alejar (ah-lay-*khahr*) *v* move away

alemán (ah-lay-*mahn*) *adj* German; *m* German

Alemania (ah-lay-*mah*-nᶜah) *f* Germany

***alentar** (ah-layn-*tahr*) *v* encourage

alergia (ah-*layr*-khᶜah) *f* allergy

alfiler (ahl-fee-*layr*) *m* pin

alfombra (ahl-*foam*-brah) *f* carpet

alfombrilla (ahl-foam-*bree*-lᶜah) *f* rug

álgebra (*ahl*-gay-bhrah) *f* algebra

algo (*ahl*-goa) *pron* something; *adv* somewhat

algodón (ahl-goa-*dhoan*) *m* cotton;

cotton-wool; **de** ~ cotton

alguien (*ahl*-gᵛayn) *pron* someone, somebody

alguno (ahl-*goo*-noa) *adj* any; **algunos** *adj* some; *pron* some

alhaja (ah-*lah*-hah) *f* gem

alharaca (ah-lah-*rah*-kah) *f* fuss

aliado (ah-*lᵛah*-dhoa) *m* associate; **Aliados** *mpl* Allies *pl*

alianza (ah-*lᵛahn*-thah) *f* alliance

alicates (ah-lee-*kah*-tayss) *mpl* pliers *pl*

alienado (ah-lᵛay-*nah*-dhoa) *m* lunatic

aliento (ah-*lᵛayn*-toa) *m* breath

alimentar (ah-lee-mayn-*tahr*) *v* *feed

alimento (ah-lee-*mayn*-toa) *m* fare; food

alivio (ah-*lee*-bhᵛoa) *m* relief

alma (*ahl*-mah) *f* soul

almacén (ahl-mah-*thayn*) *m* depot, warehouse, depository, store-house; store; ~ **de licores** off-licence; **grandes almacenes** department store

almacenaje (ahl-mah-thay-*nah*-khay) *m* storage

almacenar (ahl-mah-thay-*nahr*) *v* store

almanaque (ahl-mah-*nah*-kay) *m* almanac

almendra (ahl-*mayn*-drah) *f* almond

almidón (ahl-mee-*dhoan*) *m* starch

almidonar (ahl-mee-dhoa-*nahr*) *v* starch

almirante (ahl-mee-*rahn*-tay) *m* admiral

almohada (ahl-moa-*ah*-dhah) *f* pillow; ~ **eléctrica** heating pad

almohadilla (ahl-moa-ah-*dhee*-lᵛah) *f* pad

almohadón (ahl-moa-ah-*dhoan*) *m* cushion; pillow

almuerzo (ahl-*mwayr*-thoa) *m* lunch, luncheon

alojamiento (ah-loa-khah-*mᵛayn*-toa)

m accommodation, lodgings *pl*

alojar (ah-loa-*khahr*) *v* lodge

alondra (ah-*loan*-drah) *f* lark

alquilar (ahl-kee-*lahr*) *v* hire; rent, lease, *let

alquiler (ahl-kee-*layr*) *m* rent; ~ **de coches** car hire; **de** ~ for hire

alrededor de (ahl-ray-dhay-*dhoar* day) around, round; about

alrededores (ahl-ray-dhay-*dhoa*-rayss) *mpl* environment, surroundings *pl*

altar (ahl-*tahr*) *m* altar

altavoz (ahl-tah-*bhoath*) *m* loudspeaker

alteración (ahl-tay-rah-*thᵞoan*) *f* alteration

alterar (ahl-tay-*rahr*) *v* alter

alternar con (ahl-tayr-*nahr*) mix with

alternativa (ahl-tayr-nah-*tee*-bhah) *f* alternative

alternativo (ahl-tayr-nah-*tee*-bhoa) *adj* alternate

altiplano (ahl-tee-*plah*-noa) *m* uplands *pl*

altitud (ahl-tee-*toodh*) *f* altitude

altivo (ahl-*tee*-bhoa) *adj* haughty

alto (*ahl*-toa) *adj* high, tall; **en** ~ overhead

¡alto! (*ahl*-toa) stop!

altura (ahl-*too*-rah) *f* height

aludir a (ah-loo-*dheer*) allude to

alumbrado (ah-loom-*brah*-dhoa) *m* lighting

alumna (ah-*loom*-nah) *f* schoolgirl

alumno (ah-*loom*-noa) *m* scholar, pupil; schoolboy

alzar (ahl-*thahr*) *v* raise

allá (ah-*lᵞah*) *adv* over there; **más** ~ beyond; **más** ~ **de** past, beyond

allí (ah-*lᵞee*) *adv* there

amable (ah-*mah*-bhlay) *adj* kind, friendly

amado (ah-*mah*-dhoa) *adj* dear

amaestrar (ah-mah-ayss-*trahr*) *v* train

amamantar (ah-mah-mahn-*tahr*) *v* nurse

amanecer (ah-mah-nay-*thayr*) *m* sunrise, daybreak

amante (ah-*mahn*-tay) *m* lover

amapola (ah-mah-*poa*-lah) *f* poppy

amar (ah-*mahr*) *v* love

amargo (ah-*mahr*-goa) *adj* bitter

amarillo (ah-mah-*ree*-lᵞoa) *adj* yellow

amatista (ah-mah-*teess*-tah) *f* amethyst

ámbar (*ahm*-bahr) *m* amber

ambicioso (ahm-bee-*thᵞoa*-soa) *adj* ambitious

ambiente (ahm-*bᵞayn*-tay) *m* atmosphere

ambiguo (ahm-*bee*-gwoa) *adj* ambiguous

ambos (*ahm*-boass) *adj* both; either

ambulancia (ahm-boo-*lahn*-thᵞah) *f* ambulance

ambulante (ahm-boo-*lahn*-tay) *adj* itinerant

amenaza (ah-may-*nah*-thah) *f* threat

amenazador (ah-may-nah-thah-*dhoar*) *adj* threatening

amenazar (ah-may-nah-*thahr*) *v* threaten

ameno (ah-*may*-noa) *adj* nice

América (ah-*may*-ree-kah) *f* America; ~ **Latina** Latin America

americana (ah-may-ree-*kah*-nah) *f* jacket

americano (ah-may-ree-*kah*-noa) *adj* American; *m* American

amiga (ah-*mee*-gah) *f* friend

amígdalas (ah-*meeg*-dhah-lahss) *fpl* tonsils *pl*

amigdalitis (ah-meeg-dhah-*lee*-teess) *f* tonsilitis

amigo (ah-*mee*-goa) *m* friend

amistad (ah-meess-*tahdh*) *f* friendship

amistoso (ah-meess-*toa*-soa) *adj* friendly

amnistía (ahm-neess-*tee*-ah) *f* amnesty

amo (*ah*-moa) *m* master

amoníaco (ah-moa-*nee*-ah-koa) *m* ammonia

amontonar (ah-moan-toa-*nahr*) *v* pile

amor (ah-*moar*) *m* love; darling, sweetheart

amorío (ah-moa-*ree*-oa) *m* affair, romance

amortiguador (ah-moar-tee-gwah-*dhoar*) *m* shock absorber

amortizar (ah-moar-tee-*thahr*) *v* *pay off

amotinamiento (ah-moa-tee-nah-*mᵛayn*-toa) *m* mutiny

ampliación (ahm-plᵛah-*thᵛoan*) *f* enlargement; extension

ampliar (ahm-*plᵛahr*) *v* enlarge; extend

amplio (*ahm*-plᵛoa) *adj* broad

ampolla (ahm-*poa*-lᵛah) *f* blister

amueblar (ah-mway-*bhlahr*) *v* furnish

amuleto (ah-moo-*lay*-toa) *m* charm

analfabeto (ah-nahl-fah-*bhay*-toa) *m* illiterate

análisis (ah-*nah*-lee-seess) *f* analysis

analista (ah-nah-*leess*-tah) *m* analyst

analizar (ah-nah-lee-*thahr*) *v* analyse; *break down

análogo (ah-*nah*-loa-goa) *adj* similar

anarquía (ah-nahr-*kee*-ah) *f* anarchy

anatomía (ah-nah-toa-*mee*-ah) *f* anatomy

anciano (ahn-*thᵛah*-noa) *adj* aged; elderly

ancla (*ahng*-klah) *f* anchor

ancho (*ahn*-choa) *adj* broad; wide; *m* breadth

anchoa (ahn-*choa*-ah) *f* anchovy

anchura (ahn-*choo*-rah) *f* width

andadura (ahn-dah-*dhoo*-rah) *f* walk

andamio (ahn-*dah*-mᵛoa) *m* scaffolding

***andar** (ahn-*dahr*) *v* walk

andares (ahn-*dah*-rayss) *mpl* pace

andén (ahn-*dayn*) *m* platform

anemia (ah-*nay*-mᵛah) *f* anaemia

anestesia (ah-nayss-*tay*-sᵛah) *f* anaesthesia

anestésico (ah-nayss-*tay*-see-koa) *m* anaesthetic

anexar (ah-nayk-*sahr*) *v* annex

anexo (ah-*nayk*-soa) *m* annex, enclosure

anfitrión (ahn-fee-*trᵛoan*) *m* host

ángel (*ahng*-khayl) *m* angel

angosto (ahng-*goass*-toa) *adj* narrow, tight

anguila (ahng-*gee*-lah) *f* eel

ángulo (*ahng*-goo-loa) *m* angle

angustioso (ahng-gooss-*tᵛoa*-soa) *adj* afraid

anhelar (ah-nay-*lahr*) *v* desire, long for

anhelo (ah-*nay*-loa) *m* longing

anillo (ah-*nee*-lᵛoa) *m* ring; ~ **de boda** wedding-ring; ~ **de esponsales** engagement ring

animado (ah-nee-*mah*-dhoa) *adj* crowded

animal (ah-nee-*mahl*) *m* beast, animal; ~ **de presa** beast of prey; ~ **doméstico** pet

animar (ah-nee-*mahr*) *v* encourage, inspire; animate

ánimo (*ah*-nee-moa) *m* mind; courage

aniversario (ah-nee-bhayr-*sah*-rᵛoa) *m* anniversary; jubilee

anoche (ah-*noa*-chay) *adv* last night

anomalía (ah-noa-mah-*lee*-ah) *f* aberration

anónimo (ah-*noa*-nee-moa) *adj* anonymous

anormal (ah-noar-*mahl*) *adj* abnormal

anotación (ah-noa-tah-*thᵛoan*) *f* entry

anotar (ah-noa-*tahr*) *v* *write down

ansia (*ahn*-sᵛah) *f* anxiety

ansioso (ahn-*sᵛoa*-soa) *adj* anxious, eager

ante (*ahn*-tay) *prep* in front of

anteayer (ahn-tay-ah-ᵞ*ayr*) *adv* the day before yesterday

antecedentes (ahn-tay-thay-*dhayn*-tayss) *mpl* background

antena (ahn-tay-nah) *f* aerial

anteojos (ahn-tay-*oa*-khoass) *mpl* spectacles, glasses

antepasado (ahn-tay-pah-*sah*-dhoa) *m* ancestor

antepecho (ahn-tay-*pay*-choa) *m* window-sill

anterior (ahn-tay-rᵞ*oar*) *adj* former, prior, previous

antes (*ahn*-tayss) *adv* before; formerly; at first; ~ **de** before; ~ **de que** before

antibiótico (ahn-tee-*bh*ᵞ*oa*-tee-koa) *m* antibiotic

anticipar (ahn-tee-thee-*pahr*) *v* advance

anticipo (ahn-tee-*thee*-poa) *m* advance

anticonceptivo (ahn-tee-koan-thayp-*tee*-bhoa) *m* contraceptive

anticongelante (ahn-tee-koang-khay-*lahn*-tay) *m* antifreeze

anticuado (ahn-tee-*kwah*-dhoa) *adj* old-fashioned; ancient, out of date, quaint

anticuario (ahn-tee-*kwah*-rᵞoa) *m* antique dealer

antigualla (ahn-tee-*gwah*-lᵞah) *f* antique

Antigüedad (ahn-tee-gway-*dhahdh*) *f* antiquity

antigüedades (ahn-tee-gway-*dhah*-dhayss) *fpl* antiquities *pl*

antiguo (ahn-*tee*-gwoa) *adj* ancient, antique; former

antipatía (ahn-tee-pah-*tee*-ah) *f* antipathy, dislike

antipático (ahn-tee-*pah*-tee-koa) *adj* nasty, unpleasant

antiséptico (ahn-tee-*sayp*-tee-koa) *m* antiseptic

antojarse (ahn-toa-*khahr*-say) *v* fancy, *feel like

antojo (ahn-*toa*-khoa) *m* fad, whim

antología (ahn-toa-loa-*khee*-ah) *f* anthology

antorcha (ahn-*toar*-chah) *f* torch

anual (ah-*nwahl*) *adj* annual, yearly

anuario (ah-*nwah*-ree-oa) *m* annual

anudar (ah-noo-*dhahr*) *v* tie; knot

anular (ah-noo-*lahr*) *v* cancel

anunciar (ah-noon-thᵞ*ahr*) *v* announce

anuncio (ah-*noon*-thᵞoa) *m* announcement; advertisement

anzuelo (ahn-*thway*-loa) *m* fishing hook

añadir (ah-ñah-*dheer*) *v* add

año (*ah*-ñoa) *m* year; **al** ~ per annum; ~ **bisiesto** leap-year; ~ **nuevo** New Year

apagado (ah-pah-*gah*-dhoa) *adj* mat

apagar (ah-pah-*gahr*) *v* extinguish; *put out, switch off

aparato (ah-pah-*rah*-toa) *m* appliance, apparatus; machine

aparcamiento (ah-pahr-kah-mᵞ*ayn*-toa) *m* parking; **zona de** ~ parking zone

*aparecer** (ah-pah-*ray*-thayr) *v* appear

aparejo (ah-pah-*ray*-khoa) *m* gear; ~ **de pesca** fishing tackle

aparente (ah-pah-*rayn*-tay) *adj* apparent

aparición (ah-pah-ree-thᵞ*oan*) *f* apparition

apariencia (ah-pah-rᵞ*ayn*-thᵞah) *f* appearance, semblance

apartado (ah-pahr-*tah*-dhoa) *adj* out of the way

apartamento (ah-pahr-tah-*mayn*-toa) *m* suite; apartment *nAm*

apartar (ah-pahr-*tahr*) *v* separate

aparte (ah-*pahr*-tay) *adv* aside; *adj* individual

apasionado (ah-pah-sᵞoa-*nah*-dhoa)

adj passionate

apearse (ah-pay-*ahr*-say) *v* *get off

apelación (ah-pay-lah-*th^yoan*) *f* appeal

apelmazado (ah-pay-plah-*mah*-thah-dhoa) *adj* lumpy

apellido (ah-pay-*l^yee*-dhoa) *m* family name, surname; ~ **de soltera** maiden name

apenado (ah-pay-*nah*-dhoa) *adj* sorry

apenas (ah-*pay*-nahss) *adv* hardly, barely, scarcely; just

apéndice (ah-*payn*-dee-thay) *m* appendix

apendicitis (ah-payn-dee-*thee*-teess) *f* appendicitis

aperitivo (ah-pay-ree-*tee*-bhoa) *m* aperitif, drink

apertura (ah-payr-*too*-rah) *f* opening

apestar (ah-payss-*tahr*) *v* *stink

apetito (ah-pay-*tee*-toa) *m* appetite

apetitoso (ah-pay-tee-*toa*-soa) *adj* appetizing

apio (*ah*-p^yoa) *m* celery

aplaudir (ah-plou-*dheer*) *v* clap

aplauso (ah-*plou*-soa) *m* applause

aplazar (ah-plah-*thahr*) *v* postpone, adjourn, *put off

aplicación (ah-plee-kah-*s^yoan*) *f* application

aplicar (ah-plee-*kahr*) *v* apply; **aplicarse a** apply; *be valid for

apogeo (ah-poa-*khayoa*) *m* height; zenith; ~ **de la temporada** peak season

*apostar (ah-poass-*tahr*) *v* *bet

apoyar (ah-poa-*^yahr*) *v* support; **apoyarse** *v* *lean

apoyo (ah-*poa*-^yoa) *m* support; assistance

apreciar (ah-pray-*th^yahr*) *v* appreciate

aprecio (ah-*pray*-th^yoa) *m* appreciation

aprender (ah-prayn-*dayr*) *v* *learn; **aprenderse de memoria** memorize

apresar (ah-pray-*sahr*) *v* hijack

apresurado (ah-pray-soo-*rah*-dhoa) *adj* hasty

apresurarse (ah-pray-soo-*rahr*-say) *v* hasten, hurry

apretado (ah-pray-*tah*-dhoa) *adj* tight

*apretar (ah-pray-*tahr*) *v* press; tighten

apretón (ah-pray-*toan*) *m* clutch; ~ **de manos** handshake

aprobación (ah-proa-bhah-*th^yoan*) *f* approval

*aprobar (ah-proa-*bhahr*) *v* approve; pass

apropiado (ah-proa-*p^yah*-dhoa) *adj* appropriate, suitable, proper; fit

aprovechar (ah-proa-bhay-*chahr*) *v* profit, benefit

aproximadamente (ah-proak-see-mah-dhah-*mayn*-tay) *adv* about, approximately

aproximado (ah-proak-see-*mah*-dhoa) *adj* approximate

aptitud (ahp-tee-*toodh*) *f* qualification; faculty

apto (*ahp*-toa) *adj* suitable; ***ser ~ para** qualify

apuesta (ah-*pwayss*-tah) *f* bet

apuntar (ah-poon-*tahr*) *v* aim at; point out

apunte (ah-*poon*-tay) *m* note; memo; **libreta de apuntes** notebook

aquel (ah-*kayl*) *adj* that; **aquellos** *adj* those

aquél (ah-*kayl*) *pron* that; **aquéllos** *pron* those

aquí (ah-*kee*) *adv* here

árabe (*ah*-rah-bhay) *adj* Arab; *m* Arab

Arabia Saudí (ah-*rah*-bh^yah sou-*dhee*) Saudi Arabia

arado (ah-*rah*-dhoa) *m* plough

arancel (ah-rahn-*thayl*) *m* tariff; duty

araña (ah-*rah*-ñah) *f* spider; **tela de ~**

cobweb

arar (ah-*rahr*) v plough

arbitrario (ahr-bhee-*trah*-rʸoa) adj arbitrary

árbitro (*ahr*-bhee-troa) m umpire

árbol (*ahr*-bhoal) m tree; ~ **de levas** camshaft

arbolado (ahr-bhoa-*lah*-dhoa) m woodland

arbusto (ahr-*bhooss*-toa) m shrub

arca (*ahr*-kah) f chest

arcada (ahr-*kah*-dhah) f arcade

arce (*ahr*-thay) m maple

arcilla (ahr-*thee*-lʸah) f clay

arco (*ahr*-koa) m arch, bow; ~ **iris** rainbow

archivo (ahr-*chee*-bhoa) m archives pl

arder (ahr-*dhayr*) v *burn

ardilla (ahr-*dhee*-lʸah) f squirrel

área (*ah*-ray-ah) f area; are

arena (ah-*ray*-nah) f sand

arenoso (ah-ray-*noa*-soa) adj sandy

arenque (ah-*rayng*-kay) m herring

Argelia (ahr-*khay*-lʸah) f Algeria

argelino (ahr-khay-*lee*-noa) adj Algerian; m Algerian

Argentina (ahr-khayn-*tee*-nah) f Argentina

argentino (ahr-khayn-*tee*-noa) adj Argentinian; m Argentinian

argumentar (ahr-goo-mayn-*tahr*) v argue

argumento (ahr-goo-*mayn*-toa) m argument

árido (*ah*-ree-dhoa) adj arid

arisco (ah-*reess*-koa) adj unkind

aritmética (ah-reet-*may*-tee-kah) f arithmetic

arma (*ahr*-mah) f weapon, arm

armador (ahr-mah-*dhoar*) m shipowner

armadura (ahr-mah-*dhoo*-rah) f frame; armour

armar (ahr-*mahr*) v arm

armario (ahr-*mah*-rʸoa) m cupboard; closet

armonía (ahr-moa-*nee*-ah) f harmony

aroma (ah-*roa*-mah) m aroma

arpa (*ahr*-pah) f harp

arqueado (ahr-kay-*ah*-dhoa) adj arched

arqueología (ahr-kay-oa-loa-*khee*-ah) f archaeology

arqueólogo (ahr-kay-*oa*-loa-goa) m archaeologist

arquitecto (ahr-kee-*tayk*-toa) m architect

arquitectura (ahr-kee-tayk-*too*-rah) f architecture

arraigarse (ah-rrigh-*gahr*-say) v settle down

arrancar (ah-rrahng-*kahr*) v uproot, pull out; start off

arranque (ah-*rrahng*-kay) m starter motor

arrastrar (ah-rrahss-*trahr*) v haul, drag; *draw; **arrastrarse** v crawl

arrecife (ah-rray-*thee*-fay) m reef

arreglar (ah-rray-*glahr*) v settle; tidy up; repair, fix; **arreglarse con** *make do with

arreglo (ah-*rray*-gloa) m arrangement; settlement; **con ~ a** in accordance with

arrendamiento (ah-rrayn-dah-*mʸayn*-toa) m lease; **contrato de ~** lease

*arrendar** (ah-rrayn-*dahr*) v lease

arrepentimiento (ah-rray-payn-tee-*mʸayn*-toa) m regret, repentance

arrestar (ah-rrayss-*tahr*) v arrest

arresto (ah-*rrayss*-toa) m arrest

arriar (ah-*rʸahr*) v *strike, lower

arriate (ah-*rʸah*-tay) m flowerbed

arriba (ah-*rree*-bhah) adv upstairs; up

arriesgado (ah-rryayz-*gah*-dhoa) adj risky

arriesgar (ah-rrʸayz-*gahr*) v venture, risk

arrodillarse (ah-rroa-dhee-*l*ʸ*ahr*-say) v
*kneel

arrogante (ah-rroa-*gahn*-tay) adj
snooty

arrojar (ah-rroa-*khahr*) v *throw

arroyo (ah-rroa-ʸoa) m stream, brook

arroz (ah-*rroath*) m rice

arruga (ah-*rroo*-gah) f wrinkle

arrugar (ah-rroo-*gahr*) v wrinkle

arruinar (ah-rrwee-*nahr*) v ruin; **arruinado** broke

arte (*ahr*-tay) m/f art; **artes industriales** arts and crafts; **bellas artes**
fine arts

arteria (ahr-*tay*-rʸah) f artery; ~ **principal** thoroughfare

artesanía (ahr-tay-sah-*nee*-ah) f handicraft

articulación (ahr-tee-koo-lah-*th*ʸ*oan*) f
joint

artículo (ahr-*tee*-koo-loa) m article

artificial (ahr-tee-fee-*th*ʸ*ahl*) adj artificial

artificio (ahr-tee-*fee*-thʸoa) m artifice

artista (ahr-*teess*-tah) m/f artist

artístico (ahr-*teess*-tee-koa) adj artistic

arzobispo (ahr-thoa-*beess*-poa) m
archbishop

asamblea (ah-sahm-*blay*-ah) f assembly, meeting

asar (ah-*sahr*) v roast; ~ **en parrilla**
roast

asbesto (ahdh-*bhayss*-toa) m asbestos

ascensor (ah-thayn-*soar*) m lift; elevator nAm

aseado (ah-say-*ah*-dhoa) adj tidy

asegurar (ah-say-goo-*rahr*) v assure,
insure; **asegurarse de** ascertain

asemejarse (ah-say-may-*khahr*-say) v
resemble

asesinar (ah-say-see-*nahr*) v murder

asesinato (ah-say-see-*nah*-toa) m murder, assassination

asesino (ah-say-*see*-noa) m murderer

asfalto (ahss-*fahl*-toa) m asphalt

así (ah-*see*) adv thus, so; ~ **que** so
that

Asia (*ah*-sʸah) f Asia

asiático (ah-*s*ʸ*ah*-tee-koa) adj Asian;
m Asian

asiento (ah-*s*ʸ*ayn*-toa) m seat

asignación (ah-seeg-nah-*th*ʸ*oan*) f allowance

asignar (ah-seeg-*nahr*) v allot; ~ **a** assign to

asilo (ah-*see*-loa) m asylum

asimismo (ah-see-*meez*-moa) adv also,
likewise

***asir** (ah-*seer*) v grip

asistencia (ah-seess-*tayn*-thʸah) f attendance; assistance

asistente (ah-seess-*tayn*-tay) m assistant

asistir (ah-seess-*teer*) v assist, aid; ~ **a**
assist at, attend

asma (*ahz*-mah) f asthma

asociación (ah-soa-thʸah-*th*ʸ*oan*) f association; club, society

asociado (ah-soa-*th*ʸ*ah*-dhoa) m associate

asociar (ah-soa-*th*ʸ*ahr*) v associate;
asociarse a join

asombrar (ah-soam-*brahr*) v amaze,
astonish

asombro (ah-*soam*-broa) m amazement; wonder

asombroso (ah-soam-*broa*-soa) adj astonishing

aspecto (ahss-*payk*-toa) m aspect; appearance, look; sight

áspero (*ahss*-pay-roa) adj harsh;
rough

aspiración (ahss-pee-rah-*th*ʸ*oan*) f in-
halation; aspiration

aspirador (ahss-pee-rah-*dhoar*) m vacuum cleaner; **pasar el** ~ hoover

aspirar (ahss-pee-*rahr*) v aspire; ~ **a**
aim at

aspirina (ahss-pee-*ree*-nah) *f* aspirin

asqueroso (ahss-kay-*roa*-soa) *adj* disgusting

astilla (ahss-*tee*-l^yah) *f* splinter; chip

astillar (ahss-tee-*l^yahr*) *v* chip

astillero (ahss-tee-*l^yay*-roa) *m* shipyard

astronomía (ahss-troa-noa-*mee*-ah) *f* astronomy

astucia (ahss-*too*-th^yah) *f* ruse

astuto (ahss-*too*-toa) *adj* cunning; clever, sly

asunto (ah-*soon*-toa) *m* affair, matter; concern, business; topic

asustado (ah-sooss-*tah*-dhoa) *adj* afraid

asustar (ah-sooss-*tahr*) *v* scare; **asustarse** *v* *be frightened

atacar (ah-tah-*kahr*) *v* attack, assault; *strike

atadura (ah-tah-*dhoo*-rah) *f* binding

atañer (ah-tah-*ñayr*) *v* concern

ataque (ah-*tah*-kay) *m* attack, fit; stroke; ~ **cardíaco** heart attack

atar (ah-*tahr*) *v* tie, *bind; fasten; bundle

atareado (ah-tah-ray-*ah*-dhoa) *adj* busy

atención (ah-tayn-*th^yoan*) *f* attention; consideration, notice; **prestar** ~ *pay attention, look out

***atender a** (ah-tayn-*dayr*) attend to, see to; nurse

atento (ah-*tayn*-toa) *adj* attentive; thoughtful

ateo (ah-*tay*-oa) *m* atheist

aterido (ah-tay-*ree*-dhoa) *adj* numb

aterrador (ah-tay-rrah-*dhoar*) *adj* terrifying

aterrizar (ah-tay-rree-*thahr*) *v* land

aterrorizar (ah-tay-rroa-ree-*thahr*) *v* terrify

Atlántico (aht-*lahn*-tee-koa) *m* Atlantic

atleta (aht-*lay*-tah) *m* athlete

atletismo (aht-lay-*teez*-moa) *m* athletics *pl*

atmósfera (aht-*moass*-fay-rah) *f* atmosphere

atómico (ah-*toa*-mee-koa) *adj* atomic

átomo (*ah*-toa-moa) *m* atom

atónito (ah-*toa*-nee-toa) *adj* speechless

atontado (ah-toan-*tah*-dhoa) *adj* dumb

atormentar (ah-toar-mayn-*tahr*) *v* torment

atornillar (ah-toar-nee-*l^yahr*) *v* screw

atracar (ah-trah-*kahr*) *v* dock

atracción (ah-trahk-*th^yoan*) *f* attraction

atraco (ah-*trah*-koa) *m* hold-up

atractivo (ah-trahk-*tee*-bhoa) *adj* attractive

***atraer** (ah-trah-*ayr*) *v* attract

atrapar (ah-trah-*pahr*) *v* contract

atrás (ah-*trahss*) *adv* back

atrasado (ah-trah-*sah*-dhoa) *adj* overdue

***atravesar** (ah-trah-bhay-*sahr*) *v* cross, pass through

atreverse (ah-tray-*bhayr*-say) *v* dare

atrevido (ah-tray-*bhee*-dhoa) *adj* daring

***atribuir a** (ah-tree-*bhweer*) assign to

atroz (ah-*troath*) *adj* horrible

atún (ah-*toon*) *m* tuna

audacia (ou-*dhah*-th^yah) *f* nerve

audaz (ou-*dhahth*) *adj* bold

audible (ou-*dhee*-bhlay) *adj* audible

auditorio (ou-dhee-*toa*-r^yoa) *m* audience

aula (*ou*-lah) *f* auditorium

aumentar (ou-mayn-*tahr*) *v* increase, raise

aumento (ou-*mayn*-toa) *m* increase; rise; raise *nAm*

aun (ah-*oon*) *adv* (aún) yet; even

aunque (*oung*-kay) *conj* although, though

aurora (ou-*roa*-rah) f dawn
ausencia (ou-*sayn*-thᵛah) f absence
ausente (ou-*sayn*-tay) adj absent
Australia (ouss-*trah*-lᵛah) f Australia
australiano (ouss-trah-*lᵛah*-noa) adj Australian; m Australian
Austria (*ouss*-trᵛah) f Austria
austríaco (ouss-*tree*-ah-koa) adj Austrian; m Austrian
auténtico (ou-*tayn*-tee-koa) adj authentic; true, original
auto (*ou*-toa) m car
autobús (ou-toa-*bhooss*) m coach, bus
autoestopista (ou-toa-ayss-toa-*peess*-tah) m hitchhiker
automático (ou-toa-*mah*-tee-koa) adj automatic
automatización (ou-toa-mah-tee-thah-*thᵛoan*) f automation
automóvil (ou-toa-*moa*-bheel) m motor-car, automobile; ~ **club** automobile club
automovilismo (ou-toa-moa-bhee-*leez*-moa) m motoring
automovilista (ou-toa-moa-bhee-*leess*-tah) m motorist
autonomía (ou-toa-noa-*mee*-ah) f self-government
autónomo (ou-*toa*-noa-moa) adj independent, autonomous
autopista (ou-toa-*peess*-tah) f motorway; highway nAm; ~ **de peaje** turnpike nAm
autopsia (ou-*toap*-sᵛah) f autopsy
autor (ou-*toar*) m author
autoridad (ou-toa-ree-*dhahdh*) f authority
autoritario (ou-toa-ree-*tah*-rᵛoa) adj authoritarian
autorización (ou-toa-ree-thah-*thᵛoan*) f authorization; permission
autorizar (ou-toa-ree-*thahr*) v allow; license
autoservicio (ou-toa-sayr-*bhee*-thᵛoa) m self-service

***hacer autostop** (ah-*thayr* ou-toa-*stoap*) hitchhike
auxilio (ouk-*see*-lᵛoa) m assistance; **primeros auxilios** first-aid
avalancha (ah-bhah-*lahn*-chah) f avalanche
avanzar (ah-bhahn-*thahr*) v advance
avaro (ah-*bhah*-roa) adj avaricious
avefría (ah-bhay-*free*-ah) f pewit
avellana (ah-bhay-*lᵛah*-nah) f hazelnut
avena (ah-*bhay*-nah) f oats pl
avenida (ah-bhay-*nee*-dhah) f avenue
aventura (ah-bhayn-*too*-rah) f adventure
***avergonzarse** (ah-bhayr-goan-*thahr*-say) v *be ashamed
avería (ah-bhay-*ree*-ah) f breakdown
averiarse (ah-bhay-rᵛahr-say) v *break down; **averiado** adj out of order
aversión (ah-bhayr-*sᵛoan*) f aversion, dislike
avestruz (ah-bhayss-*trooth*) m ostrich
avión (ah-*bhᵛoan*) m aeroplane; aircraft, plane; airplane nAm; ~ **a reacción** jet; ~ **turborreactor** turbojet
avíos (ah-*bhee*-oass) mpl kit; ~ **de pesca** fishing gear
avisar (ah-bhee-*sahr*) v inform
aviso (ah-*bhee*-soa) m notice
avispa (ah-*bheess*-pah) f wasp
aya (*ah*-ᵛah) f governess
ayer (ah-ᵛayr) adv yesterday
ayuda (ah-ᵛoo-dhah) f help; relief; ~ **de cámara** valet
ayudante (ah-ᵛoo-*dhahn*-tay) m helper
ayudar (ah-ᵛoo-*dhahr*) v aid, help
ayuntamiento (ah-ᵛoon-tah-mᵛayn-toa) m town hall
azada (ah-*thah*-dhah) f spade
azafata (ah-thah-*fah*-tah) f hostess; stewardess
azar (ah-*thahr*) m chance, luck

azor (ah-*thoar*) *m* hawk

azote (ah-*thoa*-tay) *m* whip

azúcar (ah-*thoo*-kahr) *m/f* sugar; **te-rrón de** ~ lump of sugar

azucena (ah-thoo-*thay*-nah) *f* lily

azul (ah-*thool*) *adj* blue

azulejo (ah-thoo-*lay*-khoa) *m* tile

B

babor (bah-*bhoar*) *m* port

bacalao (bah-kah-*lah*-oa) *m* cod; had-dock

bacteria (bahk-*tay*-rʸah) *f* bacterium

bache (*bah*-chay) *m* hole

bahía (bah-*ee*-ah) *f* bay

bailar (bigh-*lahr*) *v* dance

baile (*bigh*-lay) *m* ball; dance

baja (*bah*-khah) *f* slump

bajada (bah-*khah*-dhah) *f* descent

bajamar (bah-khah-*mahr*) *f* low tide

bajar (bah-*khahr*) *v* lower; **bajarse** *v* *bend down

bajo (*bah*-khoa) *adj* low; short; *prep* under, below; *m* bass

bala (*bah*-lah) *f* bullet

baladí (bah-lah-*dhee*) *adj* insignificant

balance (bah-*lahn*-thay) *m* balance

balanza (bah-*lahn*-thah) *f* scales *pl*

balbucear (bahl-bhoo-thay-*ahr*) *v* falter

balcón (bahl-*koan*) *m* balcony; circle

balde (*bahl*-day) *m* pail, bucket

baldío (bahl-*dee*-oa) *adj* waste

balneario (bahl-nay-ah-*rʸoa*) *m* spa

ballena (bah-*lʸay*-nah) *f* whale

ballet (bah-*lay*) *m* ballet

bambú (bahm-*boo*) *m* bamboo

banco (*bahng*-koa) *m* bank; bench

banda (*bahn*-dah) *f* band; gang

bandeja (bahn-*day*-khah) *f* tray

bandera (bahn-*day*-rah) *f* flag; banner

bandido (bahn-*dee*-dhoa) *m* bandit

banquete (bahng-*kay*-tay) *m* banquet

bañador (bah-ñah-*dhoar*) *m* bathing-trunks

bañarse (bah-*ñahr*-say) *v* bathe

baño (*bah*-ñoa) *m* bath; *mMe* bath-room; ~ **turco** Turkish bath; **cal-zón de** ~ swimming-trunks; **traje de** ~ swim-suit

bar (bahr) *m* bar; saloon, café

barajar (bah-rah-*khahr*) *v* shuffle

baranda (bah-*rahn*-dah) *f* banisters *pl*

barandilla (bah-rahn-*dee*-lʸah) *f* rail; railing

barato (bah-*rah*-toa) *adj* inexpensive, cheap

barba (*bahr*-bhah) *f* beard

barbero (bahr-*bhay*-roa) *m* barber

barbilla (bahr-*bhee*-lʸah) *f* chin

barca (*bahr*-kah) *f* boat

barco (*bahr*-koa) *m* boat

barítono (bah-*ree*-toa-noa) *m* baritone

barman (*bahr*-mahn) *m* bartender, barman

barniz (bahr-*neeth*) *m* varnish; ~ **para las uñas** nail-polish

barnizar (bahr-nee-*thahr*) *v* varnish

barómetro (bah-*roa*-may-troa) *m* ba-rometer

barquillo (bahr-*kee*-lʸoa) *m* waffle

barra (*bah*-rrah) *f* bar, rod; counter

barrer (bah-*rrayr*) *v* *sweep

barrera (bah-*rray*-rah) *f* barrier, rail; ~ **de protección** crash barrier

barril (bah-*rreel*) *m* barrel, cask

barrilete (bah-rree-*lay*-tay) *m* keg

barrio (*bah*-rrʸoa) *m* quarter, district; ~ **bajo** slum

barroco (bah-*rroa*-koa) *adj* baroque

barrote (bah-*rroa*-tay) *m* bar

basar (bah-*sahr*) *v* base

báscula (*bahss*-koo-lah) *f* weighing-machine

base (*bah*-say) *f* basis, base

basílica (bah-*see*-lee-kah) *f* basilica

bastante (bahss-*tahn*-tay) *adv* enough, sufficient; fairly, pretty, rather, quite

bastar (bahss-*tahr*) *v* suffice

bastardo (bahss-*tahr*-dhoa) *m* bastard

bastón (bahss-*toan*) *m* cane; walking-stick; **bastones de esquí** ski sticks

basura (bah-*soo*-rah) *f* trash, rubbish, garbage; **cubo de la ~** rubbish-bin

bata (*bah*-tah) *f* dressing-gown; **~ de baño** bathrobe; **~ suelta** negligee

batalla (bah-*tah*-lᵞah) *f* battle

batería (bah-tay-*ree*-ah) *f* battery

batidora (bah-tee-*dhoa*-rah) *f* mixer

batir (bah-*teer*) *v* *beat, whip

baúl (bah-*ool*) *m* trunk

bautismo (bou-*teez*-moa) *m* baptism

bautizar (bou-tee-*thahr*) *v* christen, baptize

bautizo (bou-*tee*-thoa) *m* christening, baptism

baya (*bah*-ᵞah) *f* berry

bebé (bay-*bhay*) *m* baby

beber (bay-*bhayr*) *v* *drink

bebida (bay-*bhee*-dhah) *f* drink, beverage; **~ no alcohólica** soft drink; **bebidas espirituosas** spirits

beca (*bay*-kah) *f* grant, scholarship

becerro (bay-*thay*-rroa) *m* calf skin

beige (*bay*-khay) *adj* beige

béisbol (*bayz*-bhoal) *m* baseball

belga (*bayl*-gah) *adj* Belgian; *m* Belgian

Bélgica (*bayl*-khee-kah) *f* Belgium

belleza (bay-*lᵞay*-thah) *f* beauty; **salón de ~** beauty salon

bello (*bay*-lᵞoa) *adj* fine

bellota (bay-*lᵞoa*-tah) *f* acorn

***bendecir** (bayn-day-*theer*) *v* bless

bendición (bayn-dee-*thᵞoan*) *f* blessing

beneficio (bay-nay-*fee*-thᵞoa) *m* profit, benefit

berenjena (bay-rayng-*khay*-nah) *f* eggplant

berro (*bay*-rroa) *m* watercress

besar (bay-*sahr*) *v* kiss

beso (*bay*-soa) *m* kiss

betún (bay-*toon*) *m* shoe polish

biblia (*bee*-bhlᵞah) *f* bible

biblioteca (bee-bhlᵞoa-*tay*-kah) *f* library

bicicleta (bee-thee-*klay*-tah) *f* cycle, bicycle

biciclo (bee-*thee*-kloa) *m* cycle, bicycle

bicimotor (bee-thee-moa-*toar*) *m* moped

biela (*bᵞay*-lah) *f* piston-rod

bien (bᵞayn) *adv* well; **¡bien!** all right!; **bien ... bien** either ... or

bienes (*bᵞay*-nayss) *mpl* goods *pl*; possessions

bienestar (bᵞay-nayss-*tahr*) *m* ease; welfare

bienvenida (bᵞayn-bhay-*nee*-dhah) *f* welcome; ***dar la ~** welcome

bienvenido (bᵞayn-bhay-*nee*-dhoa) *adj* welcome

biftec (beef-*tayk*) *m* steak

bifurcación (bee-foor-kah-*thᵞoan*) *f* road fork, fork

bifurcarse (bee-foor-*kahr*-say) *v* fork

bigote (bee-*goatay*) *m* moustache

bilingüe (bee-*leeng*-gway) *adj* bilingual

bilis (*bee*-leess) *f* gall, bile

billar (bee-*lᵞahr*) *m* billiards *pl*

billete (bee-*lᵞay*-tay) *m* ticket; **~ de andén** platform ticket; **~ de banco** banknote; **~ gratuito** free ticket

biología (bᵞoa-loa-*khee*-ah) *f* biology

biológico (bᵞoa-*loa*-khee-koa) *adj* biological

bisagra (bee-*sah*-grah) *f* hinge

bizco (*beeth*-koa) *adj* cross-eyed

bizcocho (beeth-*koa*-choa) *m* cookie *nAm*

blanco¹ (*blahng*-koa) *adj* white; blank

blanco² (*blahng*-koa) *m* mark, target

blando (*blahn*-doa) *adj* soft
blanquear (blahng-kay-*ahr*) *v* bleach
bloc (bloak) *mMe* writing-pad
bloque (*bloa*-kay) *m* block; writing-pad
bloquear (bloa-kay-*ahr*) *v* block
blusa (*bloo*-sah) *f* blouse
bobina (boa-*bhee*-nah) *f* spool; ~ **del encendido** ignition coil
bobo (*boa*-bhoa) *adj* silly
boca (*boa*-kah) *f* mouth
bocadillo (boa-kah-*dhee*-lYoa) *m* sandwich
bocado (boa-*kah*-dhoa) *m* bite
bocina (boa-*thee*-nah) *f* horn, hooter; **tocar la** ~ hoot
boda (*boa*-dhah) *f* wedding
bodega (boa-*dhay*-gah) *f* hold
bofetada (boa-fay-*tah*-dhah) *f* smack, slap
boina (*boi*-nah) *f* beret
bolera (boa-*lay*-rah) *f* bowling alley
boletín meteorológico (boa-lay-*teen* may-tay-oa-roa-*loa*-khee-koa) weather forecast
boleto (boa-*lay*-toa) *mMe* ticket
bolígrafo (boa-*lee*-grah-foa) *m* ballpoint-pen, Biro
Bolivia (boa-*lee*-bhYah) *f* Bolivia
boliviano (boa-lee-*bhY ah*-noa) *adj* Bolivian; *m* Bolivian
bolsa (*boal*-sah) *f* bag; stock market, stock exchange; pocket-book, purse; ~ **de hielo** ice-bag; ~ **de papel** paper bag
bolsillo (boal-*see*-lYoa) *m* pocket
bolso (*boal*-soa) *m* handbag; bag
bollo (*boa*-lYoa) *m* bun
bomba (*boam*-bah) *f* pump; bomb; ~ **de agua** water pump; ~ **de gasolina** petrol pump; fuel pump *Am*
bombardear (boam-bahr-dhay-*ahr*) *v* bomb
bombear (boam-bay-*ahr*) *v* pump

bomberos (boam-*bay*-roass) *mpl* fire-brigade
bombilla (boam-*bee*-lYah) *f* light bulb; ~ **de flash** flash-bulb
bombón (boam-*boan*) *m* chocolate; candy *nAm*
bondad (boan-*dahdh*) *f* goodness
bondadoso (boan-dah-*dhoa*-soa) *adj* good-natured, kind
bonito (boa-*nee*-toa) *adj* pretty; fair, nice, lovely
boquerón (boa-kay-*roan*) *m* whitebait
boquilla (boa-kee-*lYah*) *f* cigarette-holder
bordado (boar-*dhah*-dhoa) *m* embroidery
bordar (boar-*dhahr*) *v* embroider
borde (*boar*-dhay) *m* edge, border; verge, rim, brim; ~ **del camino** wayside
bordillo (boar-*dhee*-lYoa) *m* curb
a bordo (ah *boar*-doa) aboard
borracho (boa-*rrah*-choa) *adj* drunk
borrar (boa-*rrahr*) *v* erase
borrascoso (boa-rrahss-*koa*-soa) *adj* gusty
borrón (boa-*rroan*) *m* blot
bosque (*boass*-kay) *m* wood, forest
bosquejar (boass-kay-*khahr*) *v* sketch
bosquejo (boass-*kay*-khoa) *m* sketch
bostezar (boass-tay-*thahr*) *v* yawn
bota (*boa*-tah) *f* boot; **botas de esquí** ski boots
botadura (boa-tah-*dhoo*-rah) *f* launching
botánica (boa-*tah*-nee-kah) *f* botany
bote (*boa*-tay) *m* rowing-boat; ~ **a motor** motor-boat
botella (boa-*tay*-lYah) *f* bottle
botón (boa-*toan*) *m* button; knob, push-button; ~ **del cuello** collar stud
botones (boa-*toa*-nayss) *mpl* bellboy
bóveda (boa-*bhay*-dhah) *f* vault, arch

boxear (boak-say-*ahr*) *v* box

boya (*boa*-Yah) *f* buoy

braga (*brah*-gah) *f* briefs *pl*; panties *pl*

bragueta (brah-*gay*-tah) *f* fly

branquia (*brahng*-kYah) *f* gill

Brasil (brah-*seel*) *m* Brazil

brasileño (brah-see-*lay*-ñoa) *adj* Brazilian; *m* Brazilian

braza (*brah*-thah) *f* breaststroke; ~ **de mariposa** butterfly stroke

brazo (*brah*-thoa) *m* arm; **del** ~ arm-in-arm

brea (*bray*-ah) *f* tar

brecha (*bray*-chah) *f* breach

bregar (bray-*gahr*) *v* labour

brema (*bray*-mah) *f* bream

breve (*bray*-bhay) *adj* brief; **en** ~ soon

brezal (bray-*thahl*) *m* moor

brezo (*bray*-thoa) *m* heather

brillante (bree-*l*Yahn-tay) *adj* brilliant

brillantina (bree-lYahn-*tee*-nah) *f* hair cream

brillar (bree-*l*Yahr) *v* glow, *shine

brillo (*bree*-lYoa) *m* glow, gloss

brincar (breeng-*kahr*) *v* hop; skip

brindis (*breen*-deess) *m* toast

brisa (*bree*-sah) *f* breeze

británico (bree-*tah*-nee-koa) *adj* British; *m* Briton

brocha (*broa*-chah) *f* brush; ~ **de afeitar** shaving-brush

broche (*broa*-chay) *m* brooch

broma (*broa*-mah) *f* joke

bronca (*broang*-kah) *f* row

bronce (*broan*-thay) *m* bronze; **de** ~ bronze

bronquitis (broang-*kee*-teess) *f* bronchitis

brotar (broa-*tahr*) *v* bud

bruja (*broo*-khah) *f* witch

brújula (*broo*-khoo-lah) *f* compass

brumoso (broo-*moa*-soa) *adj* foggy; hazy

brutal (broo-*tahl*) *adj* brutal

bruto (*broo*-toa) *adj* gross

bucear (boo-thay-*ahr*) *v* dive

bueno (*bway*-noa) *adj* good; kind; sound; ¡**bueno**! well!

buey (bway) *m* ox

bufanda (boo-*fahn*-dah) *f* scarf

buffet (boof-*fayt*) *m* buffet

buhardilla (bwahr-*dee*-lYah) *f* attic

buho (*boo*-oa) *m* owl

buitre (*bwee*-tray) *m* vulture

bujía (boo-*khee*-ah) *f* sparking-plug

bulbo (*bool*-bhoa) *m* bulb; light bulb

Bulgaria (bool-*gah*-rYah) *f* Bulgaria

búlgaro (*bool*-gah-roa) *adj* Bulgarian; *m* Bulgarian

bulto (*bool*-toa) *m* bulk

bulla (*boo*-lYah) *f* fuss

buque (*boo*-kay) *m* ship; vessel; ~ **a motor** launch; ~ **cisterna** tanker; ~ **de guerra** man-of-war; ~ **velero** sailing-boat

burbuja (boor-*boo*-khah) *f* bubble

burdel (boor-*dhayl*) *m* brothel

burdo (*boor*-dhoa) *adj* coarse

burgués (boor-*gayss*) *adj* middle-class, bourgeois

burla (*boor*-lah) *f* mockery

burlarse de (boor-*lahr*-say) mock

burocracia (boo-roa-*krah*-thYah) *f* bureaucracy

burro (*boo*-rroa) *m* ass, donkey

buscar (booss-*kahr*) *v* look for; look up, *seek, search; hunt for; *ir a ~ *get, pick up, fetch

búsqueda (*booss*-kay-dhah) *f* search

busto (*booss*-toa) *m* bust

butaca (boo-*tah*-kah) *f* armchair, easy chair; stall; orchestra seat *Am*

buzón (boo-*thoan*) *m* pillar-box, letter-box; mailbox *nAm*

C

caballero (kah-bhah-*l*^Yay-roa) *m* gentleman; knight

caballitos (kah-bhah-*l*^Yee-toass) *mpl* merry-go-round

caballo (kah-bhah-l^Yoa) *m* horse; ~ **de carrera** race-horse; ~ **de vapor** horsepower

cabaña (kah-bhah-ñah) *f* cabin, hut

cabaret (kah-bhah-*rayt*) *m* cabaret; nightclub

cabecear (kah-bhay-thay-*ahr*) *v* nod

cabeceo (kah-bhay-*thay*-oa) *m* nod

cabello (kah-*bhay*-l^Yoa) *m* hair

cabelludo (kah-bhay-l^Y*oo*-dhoa) *adj* hairy

cabeza (kah-*bhay*-thah) *f* head; ~ **de turco** scapegoat; **dolor de** ~ headache

cabezudo (kah-bhay-*thoo*-dhoa) *adj* head-strong

cabina (kah-*bhee*-nah) *f* cabin; booth; ~ **telefónica** telephone booth

cable (*kah*-bhlay) *m* cable

cablegrafiar (kah-bhlay-grah-f^Y*ahr*) *v* cable

cablegrama (kah-bhlay-*grah*-mah) *m* cable

cabo (*kah*-bhoa) *m* cape

cabra (*kah*-bhrah) *f* goat

cabritilla (kah-bhree-*tee*-l^Yah) *f* kid

cabrón (kah-*bhroan*) *m* goat

cacahuate (kah-kah-*wah*-tay) *mMe* peanut

cacahuete (kah-kah-*way*-tay) *m* peanut

cacerola (kah-thay-*roa*-lah) *f* saucepan

cachear (kah-chay-*ahr*) *v* search

cachivache (kah-chee-*bhah*-chay) *m* junk

cada (*kah*-dhah) *adj* every, each; ~ **uno** everyone

cadáver (kah-*dhah*-bhayr) *m* corpse

cadena (kah-*dhay*-nah) *f* chain

cadera (kah-*dhay*-rah) *f* hip

caducado (kah-dhoo-*kah*-dhoa) *adj* expired

*****caer** (kah-*ayr*) *v* *fall; **dejar** ~ drop

café (kah-*fay*) *m* coffee; public house

cafeína (kah-fay-*ee*-nah) *f* caffeine

cafetera filtradora (kah-fay-*tay*-rah feel-trah-*dhoa*-rah) percolator

cafetería (kah-fay-tay-*ree*-ah) *f* snack-bar, cafeteria

caída (kah-*ee*-dhah) *f* fall

caja (*kah*-khah) *f* box; crate; pay-desk; ~ **de cartón** carton; ~ **de caudales** safe, vault; ~ **de cerillas** match-box; ~ **de colores** paint-box; ~ **de velocidades** gear-box; ~ **fuerte** safe; ~ **metálica** canister

cajera (kah-*khay*-rah) *f* cashier

cajero (kah-*khay*-roa) *m* cashier

cajón (kah-*khoan*) *m* drawer

cal (kahl) *f* lime

calambre (kah-*lahm*-bray) *m* cramp

calamidad (kah-lah-mee-*dhahdh*) *f* disaster

calcetín (kahl-thay-*teen*) *m* sock

calcio (*kahl*-th^Yoa) *m* calcium

calculadora (kahl-koo-lah-*dhoa*-rah) *f* adding-machine

calcular (kahl-koo-*lahr*) *v* reckon, calculate

cálculo (*kahl*-koo-loa) *m* calculation; ~ **biliar** gallstone

calderilla (kahl-day-*ree*-l^Yah) *f* petty cash

calefacción (kah-lay-fahk-*th^Yoan*) *f* heating

calefactor (kah-lay-fahk-*toar*) *m* heater

calendario (kah-layn-*dah*-r^Yoa) *m* calendar

*****calentar** (kah-layn-*tahr*) *v* warm, heat

calidad (kah-lee-*dhahdh*) *f* quality; **de**

primera ~ first-class
caliente (kah-l^yayn-tay) *adj* warm, hot
calificado (kah-lee-fee-kah-dhoa) *adj* qualified
calina (kah-lee-nah) *f* haze
calinoso (kah-lee-noa-soa) *adj* hazy
calma (kahl-mah) *f* calm
calmante (kahl-mahn-tay) *m* tranquillizer, sedative
calmar (kahl-mahr) *v* calm down; **calmarse** *v* calm down
calor (kah-loar) *m* warmth, heat
caloría (kah-loa-ree-ah) *f* calorie
calorífero (kah-loa-ree-fay-roa) *m* hot-water bottle
calumnia (kah-loom-n^yah) *f* slander
calvinismo (kahl-bhee-neez-moa) *m* Calvinism
calvo (kahl-bhoa) *adj* bald
calzada (kahl-thah-dhah) *f* carriage-way, causeway; drive
calzado (kahl-thah-dhoa) *m* footwear
calzoncillos (kahl-thoan-thee-l^yoass) *mpl* pants *pl*, briefs *pl*, drawers; shorts *plAm*
callado (kah-l^yah-dhoa) *adj* silent
callarse (kah-l^yahr-say) *v* *be silent
calle (kah-l^yay) *f* street; road; ~ **lateral** side-street; ~ **mayor** main street
callejón (kah-l^yay-khoan) *m* alley, lane; ~ **sin salida** cul-de-sac
callo (kah-l^yoa) *m* callus; corn
cama (kah-mah) *f* bed; ~ **de tijera** camp-bed; cot *nAm*; **camas gemelas** twin beds; ~ **y desayuno** bed and breakfast
camafeo (kah-mah-fay-oa) *m* cameo
cámara (kah-mah-rah) *f* camera; ~ **fotográfica** camera
camarada (kah-mah-rah-dhah) *m* comrade
camarera (kah-mah-ray-rah) *f* waitress
camarero (kah-mah-ray-roa) *m* waiter; steward; **jefe de camareros** head-waiter

camarón (kah-mah-roan) *m* shrimp
camastro (kah-mahss-troa) *m* bunk
cambiar (kahm-b^yahr) *v* alter, change; vary; exchange, switch; ~ **de marcha** change gear
cambio (kahm-b^yoa) *m* alteration, change, variation; turn; exchange; exchange rate; **oficina de** ~ money exchange
camello (kah-may-l^yoa) *m* camel
caminar (kah-mee-nahr) *v* *go; hike
caminata (kah-mee-nah-tah) *f* walk
camino (kah-mee-noa) *m* way; road; **a mitad de** ~ halfway; **borde del** ~ roadside; ~ **de** bound for; ~ **en obras** road up; ~ **principal** main road
camión (kah-m^yoan) *m* lorry; truck *nAm*
camioneta (kah-m^yoa-nay-tah) *f* van
camisa (kah-mee-sah) *f* shirt
camiseta (kah-mee-say-tah) *f* undershirt; vest
camisón (kah-mee-soan) *m* nightdress
campamento (kahm-pah-mayn-toa) *m* camp
campana (kahm-pah-nah) *f* bell
campanario (kahm-pah-nah-r^yoa) *m* steeple
campaña (kahm-pah-ñah) *f* campaign; **catre de** ~ camp-bed
campeón (kahm-pay-oan) *m* champion
campesino (kahm-pay-see-noa) *m* peasant
camping (kahm-peeng) *m* camping site, camping
campo (kahm-poa) *m* countryside, country; field; ~ **de aviación** airfield; ~ **de golf** golf-course; ~ **de tenis** tennis-court; **día de** ~ picnic
Canadá (kah-nah-dhah) *m* Canada
canadiense (kah-nah-dh^yayn-say) *adj*

Canadian; *m* Canadian

canal (kah-*nahl*) *m* canal; channel; **Canal de la Mancha** English Channel

canario (kah-*nah*-r^yoa) *m* canary

cancelación (kahn-thay-lah-th^yoan) *f* cancellation

cancelar (kahn-thay-*lahr*) *v* cancel

cáncer (*kahn*-thayr) *m* cancer

canción (kahn-th^yoan) *f* song

cancha (*kahn*-chah) *f* tennis-court

candado (kahn-*dah*-dhoa) *m* padlock

candela (kahn-*day*-lah) *f* candle

candelabro (kahn-day-*lah*-bhroa) *m* candelabrum

candidato (kahn-dee-*dhah*-toa) *m* candidate

canela (kah-*nay*-lah) *f* cinnamon

cangrejo (kahng-*gray*-khoa) *m* crab

canguro (kahng-*goo*-roa) *m* kangaroo

canica (kah-*nee*-kah) *f* marble

canoa (kah-*noa*-ah) *f* canoe

cansancio (kahn-*sahn*-th^yoa) *m* fatigue

cansar (kahn-*sahr*) *v* tire; **cansado** tired, weary

cantadora (kahn-tah-*dhoa*-rah) *f* singer

cantante (kahn-*tahn*-tay) *m* singer

cantar (kahn-*tahr*) *v* *sing

cántaro (*kahn*-tah-roa) *m* pitcher; jug

cantera (kahn-*tay*-rah) *f* quarry

cantidad (kahn-tee-*dhahdh*) *f* amount, quantity; number; lot

cantina (kahn-*tee*-nah) *f* canteen; *fMe* saloon

canto (*kahn*-toa) *m* singing; edge

caña (*kah*-ñah) *f* cane; ~ **de pescar** fishing rod

cañada (kah-*ñah*-dhah) *f* glen

cáñamo (*kah*-ñah-moa) *m* hemp

cañón (kah-*ñoan*) *m* gun; gorge

caos (*kah*-oass) *m* chaos

caótico (kah-*oa*-tee-koa) *adj* chaotic

capa (*kah*-pah) *f* cloak, cape; layer, deposit

capacidad (kah-pah-thee-*dhahdh*) *f* capacity

capataz (kah-pah-*tahth*) *m* foreman

capaz (kah-*pahth*) *adj* able; capable; *ser ~ **de** *be able to; qualify

capellán (kah-pay-l^yahn) *m* chaplain

capilla (kah-pee-l^yah) *f* chapel

capital (kah-pee-*tahl*) *m* capital; *adj* capital

capitalismo (kah-pee-tah-*leez*-moa) *m* capitalism

capitán (kah-pee-*tahn*) *m* captain

capitulación (kah-pee-too-lah-th^yoan) *f* capitulation

capítulo (kah-*pee*-too-loa) *m* chapter

capó (kah-*poa*) *m* bonnet; hood *nAm*

capricho (kah-*pree*-choa) *m* fancy, whim

cápsula (*kahp*-soo-lah) *f* capsule

captura (kahp-*too*-rah) *f* capture

capturar (kahp-too-*rahr*) *v* capture

capucha (kah-*poo*-chah) *f* hood

capullo (kah-*poo*-l^yoa) *m* bud

caqui (*kah*-kee) *m* khaki

cara (*kah*-rah) *f* face

caracol (kah-rah-*koal*) *m* snail; ~ **marino** winkle

carácter (kah-*rahk*-tayr) *m* character

característica (kah-rahk-tay-*reess*-tee-kah) *f* characteristic, feature; quality

característico (kah-rahk-tay-*reess*-tee-koa) *adj* typical, characteristic

caracterizar (kah-rahk-tay-ree-*thahr*) *v* characterize, mark

caramelo (kah-rah-*may*-loa) *m* caramel, toffee, sweet

caravana (kah-rah-*bhah*-nah) *f* caravan; trailer *nAm*

carbón (kahr-*bhoan*) *m* coal; ~ **de leña** charcoal

carburador (kahr-bhoo-rah-*dhoar*) *m* carburettor

cárcel (*kahr*-thayl) *f* jail, gaol

carcelero (kahr-thay-*lay*-roa) m jailer
cardenal (kahr-dhay-*nahl*) m cardinal
cardinal (kahr-dhee-*nahl*) adj cardinal
cardo (*kahr*-dhoa) m thistle
*carecer (kah-ray-*thayr*) v lack
carencia (kah-*rayn*-thʸah) f want, shortage
carga (*kahr*-gah) f charge; cargo, freight, load; batch
cargar (kahr-*gahr*) v charge; load
cargo (*kahr*-goa) m office; freight
cari (*kah*-ree) m curry
caridad (kah-ree-*dhahdh*) f charity
carillón (kah-ree-*lʸoan*) m chimes pl
cariño (kah-*ree*-ñoa) m affection; pet
cariñoso (kah-ree-*ñoa*-soa) adj affectionate
carmesí (kahr-may-*see*) adj crimson
carnaval (kahr-nah-*bhahl*) m carnival
carne (*kahr*-nay) f meat; flesh; ~ **de cerdo** pork; ~ **de gallina** gooseflesh; ~ **de ternera** veal; ~ **de vaca** beef
carnero (kahr-*nay*-roa) m mutton
carnicero (kahr-nee-*thay*-roa) m butcher
caro (*kah*-roa) adj expensive, dear
carpa (*kahr*-pah) f carp
carpintero (kahr-peen-*tay*-roa) m carpenter
carrera (kah-*rray*-rah) f career; race; ~ **de caballos** horserace; **pista para carreras** race-track
carretera (kah-rray-*tay*-rah) f highway
carretilla (kah-rray-*tee*-lʸah) f wheelbarrow
carro (*kah*-rroa) m cart; mMe car; ~ **de gitanos** caravan
carrocería (kah-rroa-thay-*ree*-ah) f coachwork
carroza (*kah*-*rroa*-thah) f coach
carta (*kahr*-tah) f map; letter; ~ **certificada** registered letter; ~ **de crédito** letter of credit; ~ **de recomen-**

dación letter of recommendation; ~ **de vinos** wine-list; ~ **marina** chart
cartel (kahr-*tayl*) m poster, placard
cárter (*kahr*-tayr) m crankcase
cartera (kahr-*tay*-rah) f bag; satchel; wallet
cartero (kahr-*tay*-roa) m postman
cartílago (kahr-*tee*-lah-goa) m cartilage
cartón (kahr-*toan*) m cardboard; carton; **de** ~ cardboard
cartucho (kahr-*too*-choa) m cartridge
casa (*kah*-sah) f house; home; **a** ~ home; **ama de** ~ housewife; ~ **de campo** cottage; ~ **de correos** post-office; ~ **del párroco** vicarage; ~ **de pisos** block of flats; apartment house Am; ~ **de reposo** rest-home; ~ **flotante** houseboat; ~ **señorial** manor-house; **en** ~ at home; indoors, indoor, home; **gobierno de la** ~ housekeeping
casarse (kah-*sahr*-say) v marry
cascada (kahss-*kah*-dhah) f waterfall
cascanueces (kahss-kah-*nway*-thayss) m nutcrackers pl
cáscara (*kahss*-kah-rah) f shell; skin; ~ **de nuez** nutshell
casco (*kahss*-koa) m helmet; hoof
casero (kah-*say*-roa) adj home-made
casi (*kah*-see) adv almost, nearly
casimir (kah-see-*meer*) m cashmere
casino (kah-*see*-noa) m casino
caso (*kah*-soa) m event; case; instance; ~ **de urgencia** emergency; **en** ~ **de** in case of; **en ningún** ~ by no means; **en tal** ~ then; **en todo** ~ at any rate, anyway
caspa (*kahss*-pah) f dandruff
casquillo (kahss-*kee*-lʸoa) m socket
castaña (kahss-*tah*-ñah) f chestnut
astellano (kahss-tay-*lʸah*-noa) adj Castilian; m Castilian

castigar (kahss-tee-*gahr*) v punish

castigo (kahss-*tee*-goa) m penalty, punishment

castillo (kahss-tee-*l*Yoa) m castle

casto (*kahss*-toa) adj chaste; pure

castor (kahss-*toar*) m beaver

por casualidad (poar kah-swah-lee-*dhahdh*) by chance

catacumba (kah-tah-*koom*-bah) f catacomb

catálogo (kah-*tah*-loa-goa) m catalogue

catarro (kah-*tah*-rroa) m catarrh

catástrofe (kah-*tahss*-troa-fay) f disaster, catastrophe, calamity

catedral (kah-tay-*dhrahl*) f cathedral

catedrático (kah-tay-*dhrah*-tee-koa) m professor

categoría (kah-tay-goa-*ree*-ah) f category

católico (kah-*toa*-lee-koa) adj catholic, Roman Catholic

catorce (kah-*toar*-thay) num fourteen

catorceno (kah-toar-*thay*-noa) num fourteenth

caucho (*kou*-choa) m rubber

causa (*kou*-sah) f cause, reason; case; lawsuit; **a ~ de** because of, on account of, for, owing to

causar (kou-*sahr*) v cause

cautela (kou-*tay*-lah) f caution

cautivar (kou-tee-*bhahr*) v fascinate

cavar (kah-*bhahr*) v *dig

caviar (kah-*bh*Yahr) m caviar

cavidad (kah-bhee-*dhahdh*) f cavity

caza (*kah*-thah) f chase, hunt; game; **apeadero de ~** lodge

cazador (kah-thah-*dhoar*) m hunter

cazar (kah-*thahr*) v hunt; chase; **~ en vedado** poach

cebada (thay-*bhah*-dhah) f barley

cebo (*thay*-bhoa) m bait

cebolla (thay-*bhoa*-l*Y*ah) f onion

cebollino (thay-bhoa-*l*Yee-noa) m chives pl

cebra (*thay*-bhrah) f zebra

ceder (thay-*dhayr*) v indulge, *give in

*cegar (thay-*gahr*) v blind

ceja (*thay*-khah) f eyebrow

celda (*thayl*-dah) f cell

celebración (thay-lay-bhrah-*th*Yoan) f celebration

celebrar (thay-lay-*bhrahr*) v celebrate

célebre (*thay*-lay-bhray) adj famous

celebridad (thay-lay-bhree-*dhahdh*) f celebrity

celeste (thay-*layss*-tay) adj heavenly

celibato (thay-lee-*bhah*-toa) m celibacy

celo (*thay*-loa) m zeal, diligence; **celos** jealousy

celofán (thay-loa-*fahn*) m cellophane

celoso (thay-*loa*-soa) adj zealous, diligent; envious, jealous

célula (*thay*-loo-lah) f cell

cementerio (thay-mayn-*tay*-r*Y*oa) m churchyard, graveyard, cemetery

cemento (thay-*mayn*-toa) m cement

cena (*thay*-nah) f dinner, supper

cenar (thay-*nahr*) v dine, *eat

cenicero (thay-nee-*thay*-roa) m ashtray

cenit (thay-*neet*) m zenith

ceniza (thay-*nee*-thah) f ash

censura (thayn-*soo*-rah) f censorship

centelleante (thayn-tay-l*Y*ay-*ahn*-tay) adj sparkling

centígrado (thayn-*tee*-grah-dhoa) adj centigrade

centímetro (thayn-*tee*-may-troa) m centimetre; tape-measure

central (thayn-*trahl*) adj central; **central eléctrica** power-station; **central telefónica** telephone exchange

centralizar (thayn-trah-lee-*thahr*) v centralize

centro (*thayn*-troa) m centre; **~ comercial** shopping centre; **~ de la ciudad** town centre; **~ de recreo** recreation centre

cepillar (thay-pee-l Y ahr) v brush
cepillo (thay-pee-l Y oa) m brush; ~ **de dientes** toothbrush; ~ **de la ropa** clothes-brush; ~ **para el cabello** hairbrush; ~ **para las uñas** nailbrush
cera (thay-rah) f wax
cerámica (thay-rah-mee-kah) f ceramics pl; crockery, pottery
cerca (thayr-kah) f fence
cerca de (thayr-kah day) near, by; almost
cercano (thayr-kah-noa) adj close, nearby, near
cercar (thayr-kahr) v encircle, surround
cerdo (thayr-dhoa) m pig
cereales (thay-ray-ah-layss) mpl corn
cerebro (thay-ray-bhroa) m brain; **conmoción cerebral** concussion
ceremonia (thay-ray-moa-n Y ah) f ceremony
cereza (thay-ray-thah) f cherry
cerilla (thay-ree-l Y ah) f match
cerillo (thay-ree-l Y oa) mMe match
cero (thay-roa) m zero, nought
cerradura (thay-rrah-dhoo-rah) f lock; **ojo de la** ~ keyhole
***cerrar** (thay-rrahr) v close, *shut; fasten; turn off; ~ **con llave** lock
cerrojo (thay-rroa-khoa) m bolt
certificación (thayr-tee-fee-kah-th Y oan) f certificate
certificado (thayr-tee-fee-kah-dhoa) m certificate; ~ **de salud** health certificate
certificar (thayr-tee-fee-kahr) v register
cervato (thayr-bhah-toa) m fawn
cervecería (thayr-bhay-thay-ree-ah) f brewery
cerveza (thayr-bhay-thah) f beer; ale
cesar (thay-sahr) v cease, quit, stop, discontinue
césped (thayss-paydh) m lawn; grass

cesta (thayss-tah) f basket
cesto (thayss-toa) m hamper; ~ **para papeles** wastepaper-basket
cicatriz (thee-kah-treeth) f scar
ciclista (thee-kleess-tah) m cyclist
ciclo (thee-kloa) m cycle
ciego (th Y ay-goa) adj blind
cielo (th Y ay-loa) m heaven; sky; ~ **raso** ceiling
ciencia (th Y ayn-th Y ah) f science
científico (th Y ayn-tee-fee-koa) adj scientific; m scientist
ciento (th Y ayn-toa) num hundred; **por** ~ percent
cierre (th Y ay-rray) m fastener; ~ **relámpago** zipper
cierto (th Y ayr-toa) adj certain; **por** ~ indeed
ciervo (th Y ayr-bhoa) m deer
cifra (thee-frah) f number, figure
cigarrillo (thee-gah-rree-l Y oa) m cigarette
cigüeña (thee-gway-ñah) f stork
cigüeñal (thee-gway-ñahl) m crankshaft
cilindro (thee-leen-droa) m cylinder; **culata del** ~ cylinder head
cima (thee-mah) f top, summit; hilltop
cinc (theengk) m zinc
cincel (theen-thayl) m chisel
cinco (theeng-koa) num five
cincuenta (theeng-kwayn-tah) num fifty
cine (thee-nay) m pictures
cinematógrafo (thee-nay-mah-toa-grah-foa) m cinema
cinta (theen-tah) f ribbon, tape; ~ **adhesiva** scotch tape, adhesive tape; ~ **de goma** elastic band; ~ **métrica** tape-measure
cintura (theen-too-rah) f waist
cinturón (theen-too-roan) m belt; bypass; ~ **de seguridad** seat-belt

cipo (*thee*-poa) *m* milepost

circo (*theer*-koa) *m* circus

*** circuir** (theer-*kweer*) *v* encircle

circulación (theer-koo-lah-*th^yoan*) *f* circulation

circular (theer-koo-*lahr*) *v* circulate

círculo (*theer*-koo-loa) *m* circle, ring; club

circundante (theer-koon-*dahn*-tay) *adj* surrounding

circundar (theer-koon-*dahr*) *v* circle

circunstancia (theer-koons-*tahn*-th^yah) *f* circumstance, condition

ciruela (thee-*rway*-lah) *f* plum; **~ pasa** prune

cirujano (thee-roo-*khah*-noa) *m* surgeon

cisne (*theez*-nay) *m* swan

cistitis (theess-*tee*-teess) *f* cystitis

cita (*thee*-tah) *f* date, appointment; quotation

citación (thee-tah-*th^yoan*) *f* summons

citar (thee-*tahr*) *v* quote

ciudad (th^yoo-*dhahdh*) *f* city, town

ciudadanía (th^yoo-dhah-dhah-*nee*-ah) *f* citizenship

ciudadano (th^yoo-dhah-*dhah*-noa) *m* citizen

cívico (*thee*-bhee-koa) *adj* civic

civil (thee-*bheel*) *adj* civilian, civil

civilización (thee-bhee-lee-thah-*th^yoan*) *f* civilization

civilizado (thee-bhee-lee-*thah*-dhoa) *adj* civilized

claridad (klah-ree-*dhahdh*) *f* clarity

clarificar (klah-ree-fee-*kahr*) *v* clarify

claro (*klah*-roa) *adj* clear; plain, distinct; serene; *m* clearing

clase (*klah*-say) *f* class; sort; form; classroom; **~ media** middle class; **~ turista** tourist class; **de primera ~** first-rate; **toda ~ de** all sorts of

clásico (*klah*-see-koa) *adj* classical

clasificar (klah-see-fee-*kahr*) *v* classify, assort, sort, arrange

cláusula (*klou*-soo-lah) *f* clause

clavar (klah-*bhahr*) *v* pin

clavicémbalo (klah-bhee-*thaym*-bah-loa) *m* harpsichord

clavícula (klah-*bhee*-koo-lah) *f* collarbone

clavo (*klah*-bhoa) *m* nail

clemencia (klay-*mayn*-th^yah) *f* mercy

clérigo (*klay*-ree-goa) *m* clergyman, minister

cliente (kl^yayn-tay) *m* client, customer

clima (*klee*-mah) *m* climate

climatizado (klee-mah-tee-*thah*-dhoa) *adj* air-conditioned

clínica (*klee*-nee-kah) *f* clinic

cloro (*kloa*-roa) *m* chlorine

club de yates yacht-club

coagularse (koa-ah-goo-*lahr*-say) *v* coagulate

cobarde (koa-*bhahr*-dhay) *adj* cowardly; *m* coward

cobertizo (koa-bhayr-*tee*-thoa) *m* shed

cobrador (koa-bhrah-*dhoar*) *m* conductor

cobrar (koa-*bhrahr*) *v* cash

cobre (*koa*-bhray) *m* copper, brass; **cobres** *mpl* brassware

cocaína (koa-kah-*ee*-nah) *f* cocaine

cocina (koa-*thee*-nah) *f* kitchen; cooker, stove; **~ de gas** gas cooker

cocinar (koa-thee-*nahr*) *v* cook

cocinero (koa-thee-*nay*-roa) *m* cook

coco (*koa*-koa) *m* coconut

cocodrilo (koa-koa-*dhree*-l^yoa) *m* crocodile

cóctel (*koak*-tayl) *m* cocktail

coche (*koa*-chay) *m* car; carriage; **~ cama** sleeping-car; **~ comedor** dining-car; **~ de carreras** sports-car; **~ Pullman** Pullman

cochecillo (koa-chay-*thee*-l^yoa) *m* pram; baby carriage *Am*

cochinillo (koa-chee-*nee*-l^yoa) *m* piglet

codicia (koa-*dhee*-thᵞah) *f* greed

codicioso (koa-dhee-*thᵞoa*-soa) *adj* greedy

código (*koa*-dhee-goa) *m* code; ~ **postal** zip code *Am*

codo (*koa*-dhoa) *m* elbow

codorniz (koa-dhoar-*neeth*) *f* quail

coger (koa-*khayr*) *v* *catch; *take; **llegar a** ~ *catch

coherencia (koa-ay-*rayn*-thᵞah) *f* coherence

cohete (koa-*ay*-tay) *m* rocket

coincidencia (koa-een-thee-*dhayn*-thᵞah) *f* concurrence

coincidir (koa-een-thee-*dheer*) *v* coincide

cojear (koa-khay-*ahr*) *v* limp

cojo (*koa*-khoa) *adj* lame

col (koal) *m* cabbage; ~ **de Bruselas** sprouts *pl*

cola (*koa*-lah) *f* queue, file, line; tail; gum, glue; ***hacer** ~ queue

colaboración (koa-lah-bhoa-rah-*thᵞoan*) *f* co-operation

colcha (*koal*-chah) *f* counterpane, quilt

colchón (koal-*choan*) *m* mattress

colección (koa-layk-*thᵞoan*) *f* collection; ~ **de arte** art collection

coleccionar (koa-layk-thᵞoa-*nahr*) *v* gather

coleccionista (koa-layk-thᵞoa-*neess*-tah) *m* collector

colectivo (koa-layk-*tee*-bhoa) *adj* collective

colector (koa-layk-*toar*) *m* collector

colega (koa-*lay*-gah) *m* colleague

colegio (koa-*lay*-khᵞoa) *m* college

cólera (*koa*-lay-rah) *f* anger, passion, temper

colérico (koa-*lay*-ree-koa) *adj* hot-tempered

***colgar** (koal-*gahr*) *v* *hang

coliflor (koa-lee-*floar*) *f* cauliflower

colina (koa-*lee*-nah) *f* hill

colisión (koa-lee-sᵞoan) *f* collision

colmena (koa-*may*-nah) *f* beehive

colmo (*koal*-moa) *m* height

colocar (koa-loa-*kahr*) *v* *lay, place, *put

Colombia (koa-*loam*-bᵞah) *f* Colombia

colombiano (koa-loam-*bᵞah*-noa) *adj* Colombian; *m* Colombian

colonia (koa-*loa*-nᵞah) *f* colony; ~ **veraniega** holiday camp

color (koa-*loar*) *m* colour; ~ **de agua-da** water-colour; **de** ~ coloured

colorado (koa-loa-*rah*-dhoa) *adj* colourful

colorante (koa-loa-*rahn*-tay) *m* colourant

colorete (koa-loa-*ray*-tay) *m* rouge

columna (koa-*loom*-nah) *f* column, pillar; ~ **del volante** steering-column

columpiarse (koa-loom-*pᵞahr*-say) *v* *swing

columpio (koa-*loom*-pᵞoa) *m* swing; seesaw

collar (koa-*lᵞahr*) *m* beads *pl*, necklace; collar

coma (*koa*-mah) *f* comma; *m* coma

comadrona (koa-mah-*dhroa*-nah) *f* midwife

comandante (koa-mahn-*dahn*-tay) *m* commander; captain

comarca (koa-*mahr*-kah) *f* district

comba (*koam*-bah) *f* bend

combate (koam-*bah*-tay) *m* combat, battle, struggle, fight; ~ **de boxeo** boxing match

combatir (koam-bah-*teer*) *v* combat, battle, *fight

combinación (koam-bee-nah-*thᵞoan*) *f* combination; slip

combinar (koam-bee-*nahr*) *v* combine

combustible (koam-booss-*tee*-bhlay) *m* fuel; ~ **líquido** fuel oil

comedia (koa-*may*-dhᵞah) *f* comedy;

~ **musical** musical

comediante (koa-may-*dh^yahn*-tay) *m* comedian

comedor (koa-may-*dhoar*) *m* dining-room; ~ **de gala** banqueting-hall

comentar (koa-mayn-*tahr*) *v* comment

comentario (koa-mayn-*tah*-r^yoa) *m* comment

***comenzar** (koa-mayn-*thahr*) *v* commence, *begin

comer (koa-*mayr*) *v* *eat

comercial (koa-mayr-*th^yahl*) *adj* commercial

comerciante (koa-mayr-*th^yahn*-tay) *m* merchant; trader, dealer; ~ **al por menor** retailer

comerciar (koa-mayr-*th^yahr*) *v* trade

comercio (koa-*mayr*-th^yoa) *m* commerce, trade, business; ~ **al por menor** retail trade

comestible (koa-mayss-*tee*-bhlay) *adj* edible

comestibles (koa-mayss-*tee*-bhlayss) *mpl* groceries *pl*; **tienda de ~ finos** delicatessen

cometer (koa-may-*tayr*) *v* commit

cómico (*koa*-mee-koa) *adj* comic, funny; *m* comedian; entertainer

comida (koa-*mee*-dhah) *f* food; meal; ~ **principal** dinner

comidilla (koa-mee-*dhee*-l^yah) *f* hobby-horse

comienzo (koa-*m^yayn*-thoa) *m* beginning, start

comillas (koa-*mee*-l^yahss) *fpl* quotation marks

comisaría (koa-mee-sah-*ree*-ah) *f* police-station

comisión (koa-mee-*s^yoan*) *f* committee, commission

comité (koa-mee-*tay*) *m* committee

comitiva (koa-mee-*tee*-bhah) *f* procession

como (*koa*-moa) *adv* as, like, like; **así ~** as well as; ~ **máximo** at most; ~ **si** as if

cómo (*koa*-moa) *adv* how

cómoda (*koa*-moa-dhah) *f* chest of drawers; bureau *nAm*

comodidad (koa-moa-dhee-*dhahdh*) *f* comfort, leisure

cómodo (*koa*-moa-dhoa) *adj* convenient, easy

compacto (koam-*pahk*-toa) *adj* compact

compadecerse de (koam-pah-dhay-*thayr*-say) pity

compañero (koam-pah-*ñay*-roa) *m* companion; associate; ~ **de clase** class-mate

compañía (koam-pah-*ñee*-ah) *f* company; society

comparación (koam-pah-rah-*th^yoan*) *f* comparison

comparar (koam-pah-*rahr*) *v* compare

compartimento (koam-pahr-tee-*mayn*-toa) *m* compartment; ~ **para fumadores** smoking-compartment

compartir (koam-pahr-*teer*) *v* share

compasión (koam-pah-*s^yoan*) *f* sympathy

compasivo (koam-pah-*see*-bhoa) *adj* sympathetic

compatriota (koam-pah-*tr^yoa*-tah) *m* countryman

compeler (koam-pay-*layr*) *v* compel

compensación (koam-payn-sah-*th^yoan*) *f* compensation

compensar (koam-payn-*sahr*) *v* compensate; *make good

competencia (koam-pay-*tayn*-th^yah) *f* competition, rivalry; capacity

competente (koam-pay-*tayn*-tay) *adj* expert, qualified

competidor (koam-pay-tee-*dhoar*) *m* competitor, rival

***competir** (koam-pay-*teer*) *v* compete

compilar (koam-pee-*lahr*) *v* compile

*complacer (koam-plah-*thayr*) v please; *give satisfaction

complejo (koam-*play*-khoa) adj complex; m complex

completamente (koam-play-tah-*mayn*-tay) adv completely, quite

completar (koam-play-*tahr*) v complete; fill in; fill out Am

completo (koam-*play*-toa) adj complete; whole, total, utter; full up

complicado (koam-plee-*kah*-dhoa) adj complicated

cómplice (*koam*-plee-thay) m accessary

complot (koam-*ploat*) m plot

*componer (koam-poa-*nayr*) v compose

comportarse (koam-poar-*tahr*-say) v behave, act

composición (koam-poa-see-*th*^y*oan*) f composition; essay

compositor (koam-poa-see-*toar*) m composer

compra (*koam*-prah) f purchase; *ir de compras shop

comprador (koam-prah-*dhoar*) m purchaser, buyer

comprar (koam-*prahr*) v purchase, *buy

comprender (koam-prayn-*dayr*) v *understand; *see, *take; comprise, contain

comprensión (koam-prayn-*s*^y*oan*) m understanding

comprobante (koam-proa-*bhahn*-tay) m voucher

*comprobar (koam-proa-*bhahr*) v ascertain, diagnose, establish, note; prove

comprometerse (koam-proa-may-*tayr*-say) v engage

compromiso (koam-proa-*mee*-soa) m compromise; engagement

compuerta (koam-*pwayr*-tah) f sluice

común (koa-*moon*) adj common; ordinary; en ~ joint

comuna (koa-*moo*-nah) f commune

comunicación (koa-moo-nee-kah-*th*^y*oan*) f communication

comunicado (koa-moo-nee-*kah*-dhoa) m communiqué, information

comunicar (koa-moo-nee-*kahr*) v communicate, inform

comunidad (koa-moo-nee-*dhahdh*) f congregation

comunismo (koa-moo-*neez*-moa) m communism

comunista (koa-moo-*neess*-tah´) m communist

con (koan) prep with; by

*concebir (koan-thay-*bheer*) v conceive

conceder (koan-thay-*dhayr*) v extend, grant; award

concentración (koan-thayn-trah-*th*^y*oan*) f concentration

concentrarse (koan-thayn-*trahr*-say) v concentrate

concepción (koan-thayp-*th*^y*oan*) f conception

concepto (koan-*thayp*-toa) m idea

*concernir (koan-thayr-*neer*) v touch, concern; concerniente a concerning

concesión (koan-thay-*s*^y*oan*) f concession

conciencia (koan-*th*^y*ayn*-th^yah) f conscience; consciousness

concierto (koan-*th*^y*ayr*-toa) m concert

conciso (koan-*thee*-soa) adj concise

*concluir (koang-*klweer*) v conclude

conclusión (koang-kloo-*s*^y*oan*) f conclusion; issue, ending

*concordar (koang-koar-*dhahr*) v agree

concreto (koang-*kray*-toa) adj concrete

concupiscencia (koang-koo-pee-*thayn*-th^yah) f lust

concurrido (koang-koo-*rree*-dhoa) adj

busy

concurrir (koang-koo-*rreer*) *v* coincide; concur

concurso (koang-*koor*-soa) *m* competition, contest; quiz

concha (*koan*-chah) *f* shell; sea-shell

condado (koan-*dah*-dhoa) *m* county

conde (*koan*-day) *m* count, earl

condena (koan-*day*-nah) *f* conviction

condenado (koan-day-*nah*-dhoa) *m* convict

condesa (koan-*day*-sah) *f* countess

condición (koan-dee-th^yoan) *f* condition, term

condicional (koan-dee-th^yoa-*nahl*) *adj* conditional

condimentado (koan-dee-mayn-*tah*-dhoa) *adj* spiced

***conducir** (koan-doo-*theer*) *v* *lead, carry, conduct; *drive

conducta (koan-*dook*-tah) *f* behaviour, conduct

conducto (koan-*dook*-toa) *m* pipe

conductor (koan-dook-*toar*) *m* driver; *mMe* conductor

conectar (koa-nayk-*tahr*) *v* connect

conejo (koa-*nay*-khoa) *m* rabbit; **conejillo de Indias** guinea-pig

conexión (koa-nayk-s^yoan) *f* connection

confeccionado (koan-fayk-th^yoa-*nah*-dhoa) *adj* ready-made

confederación (koan-fay-day-day-rah-th^yoan) *f* union

conferencia (koan-fay-*rayn*-th^yah) *f* conference; lecture; ~ **interurbana** trunk-call

***confesarse** (koan-fay-*sahr*-say) *v* confess

confesión (koan-fay-s^yoan) *f* confession

confiable (koan-f^yah-bhlay) *adj* trustworthy

confianza (koan-f^yahn-thah) *f* faith,

trust, confidence; **indigno de** ~ untrustworthy

confiar (koan-f^yahr) *v* commit; ~ **en** trust

confidencial (koan-fee-dhayn-th^yahl) *adj* confidential

confirmación (koan-feer-mah-th^yoan) *f* confirmation

confirmar (koan-feer-*mahr*) *v* confirm, acknowledge

confiscar (koan-feess-*kahr*) *v* confiscate, impound

confitería (koan-fee-tay-*ree*-ah) *f* sweetshop

confitero (koan-fee-*tay*-roa) *m* confectioner

confitura (koan-fee-*too*-rah) *f* marmalade

conflicto (koan-*fleek*-toa) *m* conflict

conforme (koan-*foar*-may) *adj* alike; in agreement; ~ **a** according to, in agreement with

conformidad (koan-foar-mee-*dhahdh*) *f* agreement

confort (koan-*foart*) *m* comfort

confortable (koan-foar-*tah*-bhlay) *adj* comfortable; cosy

confundir (koan-foon-*deer*) *v* *mistake, confuse

confusión (koan-foo-s^yoan) *f* confusion; disturbance

confuso (koan-*foo*-soa) *adj* confused

congelado (koang-khay-*lah*-dhoa) *adj* frozen; **alimento** ~ frozen food

congelador (koang-khay-lah-*dhoar*) *m* deep-freeze

congelar (koang-khay-*lahr*) *v* *freeze

congestión (koang-khayss-t^yoan) *f* jam

congregación (koang-gray-gah-th^yoan) *f* congregation

congreso (koang-*gray*-soa) *m* congress

conjetura (koang-khay-*too*-rah) *f* guess

conjeturar (koang-khay-too-*rahr*) *v* guess

conjuración (koang-khoo-rah-*th^yoan*) *f* plot

conmemoración (koan-may-moa-rah-*th^yoan*) *f* commemoration

conmovedor (koan-moa-bhay-*dhoar*) *adj* touching

*__conmover__ (koan-moa-*bhayr*) *v* move

connotación (koan-noa-tah-*th^yoan*) *f* connotation

*__conocer__ (koa-noa-*thayr*) *v* *know

conocido (koa-noa-*thee*-dhoa) *m* acquaintance

conocimiento (koa-noa-thee-*m^yayn*-toa) *m* knowledge

conquista (koang-*keess*-tah) *f* conquest, capture

conquistador (koang-keess-tah-*dhoar*) *m* conqueror

conquistar (koang-keess-*tahr*) *v* conquer, capture

consciente (koan-*th^yayn*-tay) *adj* conscious, aware

consecuencia (koan-say-*kwayn*-th^yah) *f* consequence, result; issue

*__conseguir__ (koan-say-*geer*) *v* *get; *make, obtain

consejero (koan-say-*khay*-roa) *m* counsellor; councillor

consejo (koan-*say*-khoa) *m* advice, counsel; council, board

consentimiento (koan-sayn-tee-*m^yayn*-toa) *m* consent; approval

*__consentir__ (koan-sayn-*teer*) *v* agree, consent

conserje (koan-*sayr*-khay) *m* concierge, janitor

conservación (koan-sayr-bhah-*th^yoan*) *f* preservation

conservador (koan-sayr-bhah-*dhoar*) *adj* conservative

conservas (koan-sayr-*bhahr*) *v* preserve

conservas (koan-*sayr*-bhahss) *fpl* tinned food

conservatorio (koan-sayr-bhah-*toa-r^yoa*) *m* music academy

considerable (koan-see-dhay-*rah*-bhlay) *adj* considerable

consideración (koan-see-dhay-rah-*th^yoan*) *f* consideration

considerado (koan-see-dhay-*rah*-dhoa) *adj* considerate

considerando (koan-see-dhay-*rahn*-doa) *prep* considering

considerar (koan-see-dhay-*rahr*) *v* regard, consider; *think over; count, reckon

consigna (koan-*seeg*-nah) *f* left luggage office

por consiguiente (poar koan-see-*g^yayn*-tay) consequently

consistir en (koan-seess-*teer*) consist of

*__consolar__ (koan-soa-*lahr*) *v* comfort

consorcio (koan-*soar*-th^yoa) *m* concern

conspirar (koans-pee-*rahr*) *v* conspire

constante (koans-*tahn*-tay) *adj* even, constant; steadfast

constar de (koans-*tahr*) consist of

constitución (koans-tee-too-*th^yoan*) *f* constitution

*__constituir__ (koans-tee-*tweer*) *v* constitute; represent

construcción (koans-trook-*th^yoan*) *f* construction

*__construir__ (koans-*trweer*) *v* construct, *build

consuelo (koan-*sway*-loa) *m* comfort

cónsul (*koan*-sool) *m* consul

consulado (koan-soo-*lah*-dhoa) *m* consulate

consulta (koan-*sool*-tah) *f* consultation

consultar (koan-sool-*tahr*) *v* consult

consultorio (koan-sool-*toa-r^yoa*) *m* surgery

consumidor (koan-soo-mee-*dhoar*) *m* consumer

consumir (koan-soo-*meer*) *v* use up

contacto (koan-*tahk*-toa) *m* contact; touch

contador (koan-tah-*dhoar*) *m* meter

contagioso (koan-tah-kh^Yoa-soa) *adj* infectious, contagious

contaminación (koan-tah-mee-nah-th^Yoan) *f* pollution

***contar** (koan-*tahr*) *v* count; relate, *tell; ~ **con** rely on

contemplar (koan-taym-*plahr*) *v* contemplate

contemporáneo (koan-taym-poa-*rah*-nay-oa) *adj* contemporary; *m* contemporary

contenedor (koan-tay-nay-*dhoar*) *m* container

***contener** (koan-tay-*nayr*) *v* contain; restrain

contenido (koan-tay-*nee*-dhoa) *m* contents *pl*

contentar (koan-tayn-*tahr*) *v* satisfy

contento (koan-*tayn*-toa) *adj* happy, glad, content, joyful; pleased

contestar (koan-tayss-*tahr*) *v* answer

contienda (koan-t^Yayn-dah) *f* dispute

contiguo (koan-tee-gwoa) *adj* neighbouring

continental (koan-tee-nayn-*tahl*) *adj* continental

continente (koan-tee-*nayn*-tay) *m* continent

continuación (koan-tee-nwah-*th^Yoan*) *f* sequel

continuamente (koan-tee-nwah-*mayn*-tay) *adv* all the time, continually

continuar (koan-tee-*nwahr*) *v* *go on, *go ahead; carry on, continue, *keep on; *keep

continuo (koan-*tee*-nwoa) *adj* continuous, continual

contorno (koan-*toar*-noa) *m* outline, contour

contra (*koan*-trah) *prep* against, versus

contrabandear (koan-trah-bhahn-day-ahr) *v* smuggle

***contradecir** (koan-trah-dhay-*theer*) *v* contradict

contradictorio (koan-trah-dheek-*toa*-r^Yoa) *adj* contradictory

contrahecho (koan-trah-*ay*-choa) *adj* deformed

contralto (koan-*trahl*-toa) *m* alto

contrario (koan-trah-r^Yoa) *adj* opposite, contrary; *m* contrary, reverse; **al ~** on the contrary

contraste (koan-*trahss*-tay) *m* contrast

contratiempo (koan-trah-t^Yaym-poa) *m* misfortune

contratista (koan-trah-*teess*-tah) *m* contractor

contrato (koan-*trah*-toa) *m* agreement, contract

contribución (koan-tree-bhoo-*th^Yoan*) *f* contribution

***contribuir** (koan-tree-*bhweer*) *v* contribute

contrincante (koan-treeng-*kahn*-tay) *m* opponent

control (koan-*troal*) *m* inspection, control

controlar (koan-troa-*lahr*) *v* check, control

controvertible (koan-troa-bhayr-*tee*-bhlay) *adj* controversial

controvertido (koan-troa-bhayr-*tee*-dhoa) *adj* controversial

convencer (koam-bayn-*thayr*) *v* convince, persuade; convict

convencimiento (koam-bayn-thee-m^Yayn-toa) *m* conviction

conveniente (koam-bay-n^Yayn-tay) *adj* adequate, proper; convenient

convenio (koam-*bay*-n^Yoa) *m* settlement

***convenir** (koam-bay-*neer*) *v* agree; fit, suit

convento (koam-*bayn*-toa) *m* cloister,

convent; nunnery

conversación (koam-bayr-sah-*th*Voan) f conversation, talk, discussion

*convertir (koam-bayr-*teer*) v convert; *convertirse en turn into

convicción (koam-beek-*th*Voan) f persuasion

convidar (koam-bee-*dhahr*) v invite

convulsión (koam-bool-*s*Voan) f convulsion

cónyuges (koan-Voo-khayss) mpl married couple

coñac (koa-*ñahk*) m cognac

cooperación (koa-oa-pay-rah-*th*Voan) f co-operation

cooperador (koa-oa-pay-rah-*dhoar*) adj co-operative

cooperativa (koa-oa-pay-rah-*tee*-bhah) f co-operative

cooperativo (koa-oa-pay-rah-*tee*-bhoa) adj co-operative

coordinación (koa-oar-dhee-nah-*th*Voan) f co-ordination

coordinar (koa-oar-dhee-*nahr*) v co-ordinate

copa (*koa*-pah) f cup

copia (*koa*-pVah) f copy, carbon copy

copiar (koa-*p*Vahr) v copy

coraje (koa-*rah*-khay) m guts

coral (koa-*rahl*) m coral

corazón (koa-rah-*thoan*) m heart; core

corbata (koar-*bhah*-tah) f tie, necktie; ~ de lazo bow tie

corbatín (koar-bhah-*teen*) m bow tie

corcino (koar-*thee*-noa) m fawn

corcho (*koar*-choa) m cork

cordel (koar-*dhayl*) m string

cordero (koar-*dhay*-roa) m lamb

cordial (koar-*dh*Vahl) adj cordial, hearty, sympathetic

cordillera (koar-dhee-*l*Vay-rah) f mountain range

cordón (koar-*dhoan*) m cord, line; lace, shoe-lace; ~ de extensión ex-

tension cord; ~ flexible flex

cornamenta (koar-nah-*mayn*-tah) f antlers pl

corneja (koar-*nay*-khah) f crow

coro (*koa*-roa) m choir

corona (koa-*roa*-nah) f crown

coronar (koa-roa-*nahr*) v crown

coronel (koa-roa-*nayl*) m colonel

corpulento (koar-poo-*layn*-toa) adj corpulent, stout

corral (koa-*rrahl*) m yard; aves de ~ poultry

correa (koa-*rray*-ah) f leash, strap; ~ del ventilador fan belt; ~ de reloj watch-strap

corrección (koa-rrayk-*th*Voan) f correction

correcto (koa-*rrayk*-toa) adj correct; right

corredor (koa-rray-*dhoar*) m broker; bookmaker; ~ de casas house agent

*corregir (koa-rray-*kheer*) v correct

correo (koa-*rray*-oa) m post, mail; ~ aéreo airmail; enviar por ~ mail; sello de correos postage stamp

correr (koa-*rrayr*) v *run; dash; flow

correspondencia (koa-rrayss-poan-dayn-th Vah) f correspondence

corresponder (koa-rrayss-poan-*dayr*) v correspond; **corresponderse** v correspond

corresponsal (koa-rrayss-poan-*sahl*) m correspondent

corrida de toros (koa-*rree*-dhah day *toa*-roass) bullfight

corriente (koa-*rr*Vayn-tay) adj current; regular, customary, plain; f current; stream; ~ alterna alternating current; ~ continua direct current; ~ de aire draught

corromper (koa-rroam-*payr*) v corrupt

corrupción (koa-rroop-*th*Voan) f corruption

corrupto (koa-*rroop*-toa) *adj* corrupt

corsé (koar-*say*) *m* corset

cortadura (koar-tah-*dhoo*-rah) *f* cut

cortaplumas (koar-tah-*ploo*-mahss) *m* penknife

cortar (koar-*tahr*) *v* *cut; chip, *cut off

corte (*koar*-tay) *f* court

cortés (koar-*tayss*) *adj* civil, courteous, polite

corteza (koar-*tay*-thah) *f* bark; crust

cortijo (koar-*tee*-khoa) *m* farmhouse

cortina (koar-*tee*-nah) *f* curtain

corto (*koar*-toa) *adj* short

cortocircuito (koar-toa-theer-*kwee*-toa) *m* short circuit

cosa (*koa*-sah) *f* thing; **entre otras cosas** among other things

cosecha (koa-*say*-chah) *f* harvest, crop

coser (koa-*sayr*) *v* sew

cosméticos (koaz-*may*-tee-koass) *mpl* cosmetics *pl*

cosquillear (koass-kee-*lʸahr*) *v* tickle

costa (*koass*-tah) *f* coast

*costar (koass-*tahr*) *v* *cost

coste (*koass*-tay) *m* cost

costilla (koass-*tee*-lʸah) *f* rib

costoso (koass-*toa*-soa) *adj* expensive

costumbre (koass-*toom*-bray) *f* custom; **costumbres** morals

costura (koass-*too*-rah) *f* seam; **sin ~** seamless

cotidiano (koa-tee-dh*ʸah*-noa) *adj* everyday

cotorra (koa-*toa*-rrah) *f* parakeet

cráneo (*krah*-nay-oa) *m* skull

cráter (*krah*-tayr) *m* crater

creación (kray-ah-th*ʸoan*) *f* creation

crear (kray-*ahr*) *v* create

*crecer (kray-*thayr*) *v* *grow

crecimiento (kray-thee-m*ʸayn*-toa) *m* growth

crédito (*kray*-dhee-toa) *m* credit

crédulo (*kray*-dhoo-loa) *adj* credulous

creencia (kray-*ayn*-th*ʸ*ah) *f* belief

*creer (kray-*ayr*) *v* believe; guess, reckon

crema (*kray*-mah) *f* cream; **~ de afeitar** shaving-cream; **~ de base** foundation cream; **~ de noche** night-cream; **~ facial** face-cream; **~ hidratante** moisturizing cream; **~ para la piel** skin cream; **~ para las manos** hand cream

cremallera (kray-mah-*lʸay*-rah) *f* zip

cremoso (kray-*moa*-soa) *adj* creamy

crepúsculo (kray-*pooss*-koo-loa) *m* twilight, dusk

crespo (*krayss*-poa) *adj* curly

cresta (*krayss*-tah) *f* ridge

creta (*kray*-tah) *f* chalk

criada (kr*ʸ*ah-dhah) *f* housemaid

criado (kr*ʸ*ah-dhoa) *m* servant

criar (kr*ʸ*ahr) *v* rear; raise

criatura (kr*ʸ*ah-*too*-rah) *f* creature; infant

crimen (*kree*-mayn) *m* crime

criminal (kree-mee-*nahl*) *adj* criminal; *m* criminal

criminalidad (kree-mee-nah-lee-*dhahdh*) *f* criminality

crisis (*kree*-seess) *f* crisis

cristal (kreess-*tahl*) *m* crystal; pane; **de ~** crystal

cristiano (kreess-*tʸah*-noa) *adj* Christian; *m* Christian

Cristo (*kreess*-toa) Christ

criterio (kree-*tay*-r*ʸ*oa) *m* criterion

crítica (*kree*-tee-kah) *f* criticism

criticar (kree-tee-*kahr*) *v* criticize

crítico (*kree*-tee-koa) *adj* critical; *m* critic

cromo (*kroa*-moa) *m* chromium

crónica (*kroa*-nee-kah) *f* chronicle

crónico (*kroa*-nee-koa) *adj* chronic

cronológico (kroa-noa-*loa*-khee-koa) *adj* chronological

cruce (*kroo*-thay) *m* crossroads; **~ pa-**

ra peatones pedestrian crossing; crosswalk *nAm*

crucero (kroo-*thay*-roa) *m* cruise

crucificar (kroo-thee-fee-*kahr*) *v* crucify

crucifijo (kroo-thee-*fee*-khoa) *m* crucifix

crucifixión (kroo-thee-feek-sʸoan) *f* crucifixion

crudo (*kroo*-dhoa) *adj* raw

cruel (krwayl) *adj* harsh, cruel

crujido (kroo-*khee*-dhoa) *m* crack

crujiente (kroo-khʸayn-tay) *adj* crisp

crujir (kroo-*kheer*) *v* creak, crack

cruz (krooth) *f* cross

cruzada (kroo-*thah*-dhah) *f* crusade

cruzar (kroo-*thahr*) *v* cross

cuadrado (kwah-*dhrah*-dhoa) *adj* square; *m* square

cuadriculado (kwah-dhree-koo-*lah*-dhoa) *adj* chequered

cuadro (*kwah*-dhroa) *m* cadre; picture; **a cuadros** chequered; ~ **de distribución** switchboard

cuál (kwahl) *pron* which

cualidad (kwah-lee-*dhahdh*) *f* property

cualquiera (kwahl-*kʸay*-rah) *pron* anyone, anybody; whichever; **cualquier cosa** anything

cuando (*kwahn*-doa) *conj* when; ~ **quiera que** whenever

cuándo (*kwahn*-doa) *adv* when

cuánto (*kwahn*-toa) *adv* how much; how many; **cuanto más ... más** the ... the; **en cuanto a** as regards

cuarenta (kwah-*rayn*-tah) *num* forty

cuarentena (kwah-rayn-*tay*-nah) *f* quarantine

cuartel (kwahr-*tayl*) *m* barracks *pl*; ~ **general** headquarters *pl*

cuarterón (kwahr-tay-*roan*) *m* panel

cuarto¹ (*kwahr*-toa) *num* fourth; *m* quarter; ~ **de hora** quarter of an hour

cuarto² (*kwahr*-toa) *m* chamber; ~ **de aseo** lavatory; washroom *nAm*; ~ **de baño** bathroom; ~ **de niños** nursery; ~ **para huéspedes** spare room

cuatro (*kwah*-troa) *num* four

Cuba (*koo*-bhah) *f* Cuba

cubano (koo-*bhah*-noa) *adj* Cuban; *m* Cuban

cubierta (koo-*bhʸayr*-tah) *f* cover; deck

cubierto (koo-*bhʸayr*-toa) *adj* cloudy

cubiertos (koo-*bhʸayr*-toass) *mpl* cutlery

cubo (*koo*-bhoa) *m* cube; ~ **de la basura** dustbin

cubrir (koo-*bhreer*) *v* cover

cuclillo (koo-*klee*-lʸoa) *m* cuckoo

cuchara (koo-*chah*-rah) *f* spoon; soup-spoon, tablespoon

cucharada (koo-chah-*rah*-dhah) *f* spoonful

cucharadita (koo-chah-rah-*dhee*-tah) *f* teaspoonful

cucharilla (koo-chah-*ree*-lʸah) *f* teaspoon

cuchillo (koo-*chee*-lʸoa) *m* knife

cuello (*kway*-lʸoa) *m* neck; collar; ~ **de botella** bottleneck

cuenta (*kwayn*-tah) *f* account; bill; check *nAm*; bead; ~ **de banco** bank account; *darse* ~ *see

cuento (*kwayn*-toa) *m* story, tale

cuerda (*kwayr*-dhah) *f* cord; string; *dar ~ *wind

cuerno (*kwayr*-noa) *m* horn

cuero (*kway*-roa) *m* leather; ~ **vacuno** cow-hide

cuerpo (*kwayr*-poa) *m* body

cuervo (*kwayr*-bhoa) *m* raven

cuestión (kwayss-*tʸoan*) *f* matter, issue, question

cueva (*kway*-bhah) *f* cavern, cave; wine-cellar

cuidado (kwee-*dhah*-dhoa) *m* care;
   **tener ~ watch out, look out
cuidadoso (kwee-dhah-*dhoa*-soa) *adj*
   careful; diligent
cuidar de (kwee-*dhahr*) attend to, look
   after, tend, **take care of
culebra (koo-*lay*-bhrah) *f* snake
culpa (*kool*-pah) *f* guilt, fault, blame
culpable (kool-*pah*-bhlay) *adj* guilty
culpar (kool-*pahr*) *v* blame
cultivar (kool-tee-*bhahr*) *v* cultivate;
   **grow, raise
cultivo (kool-*tee*-bhoa) *m* cultivation
culto (*kool*-toa) *adj* cultured; *m* worship
cultura (kool-*too*-rah) *f* culture
cultural (kool-too-*rahl*) *adj* cultural
cumbre (*koom*-bray) *f* peak
cumpleaños (koom-play-*ah*-ñoass) *m*
   birthday
cumplimentar (koom-plee-mayn-*tahr*)
   v compliment
cumplimiento (koom-plee-*m*ʸ*ayn*-toa)
   m compliment
cumplir (koom-*pleer*) *v* accomplish
cuna (*koo*-nah) *f* cradle; ~ **de viaje**
   carry-cot
cuneta (koo-*nay*-tah) *f* ditch; gutter
cuña (*koo*-ñah) *f* wedge
cuñada (koo-*ñah*-dhah) *f* sister-in-law
cuñado (koo-*ñah*-dhoa) *m* brother-in-
   law
cuota (*kwoa*-tah) *f* quota
cupón (koo-*poan*) *m* coupon
cúpula (*koo*-poo-lah) *f* dome
cura (*koo*-rah) *m* priest; *f* cure
curación (koo-rah-*th*ʸ*oan*) *f* cure, recovery
curandero (koo-rahn-*day*-roa) *m* quack
curar (koo-*rahr*) *v* cure, heal; **curarse**
   v recover
curato (koo-*rah*-toa) *m* parsonage
curiosidad (koo-r*ʸ*oa-see-*dhahdh*) *f*
   curiosity; sight; curio

curioso (koo-r*ʸ*oa-soa) *adj* curious; inquisitive; quaint
cursiva (koor-*see*-bhah) *f* italics *pl*
curso (*koor*-soa) *m* course; lecture; ~
   intensivo intensive course
curva (koor-bhah) *f* turn, curve, bend
curvado (koor-*bhah*-dhoa) *adj* curved
curvo (*koor*-bhoa) *adj* crooked, bent
custodia (kooss-*toa*-dhʸah) *f* custody
cuyo (*koo*-ʸoa) *pron* whose; of which

CH

chabacano (chah-bhah-*kah*-noa) *mMe*
   apricot
chal (chahl) *m* shawl
chaleco (chah-*lay*-koa) *m* waistcoat;
   vest *nAm*; ~ **salvavidas** lifebelt
chalet (chah-*layt*) *m* chalet
champán (chahm-*pahn*) *m* champagne
champú (chahm-*poo*) *m* shampoo
chantaje (chahn-*tah*-khay) *m* blackmail; **hacer ~ blackmail
chapa (*chah*-pah) *f* plate, sheet
chaparrón (chah-pah-*rroan*) *m* cloud-
   burst
chapucero (chah-poo-*thay*-roa) *adj*
   sloppy
chaqueta (chah-*kay*-tah) *f* jacket; cardigan; ~ **ligera** blazer
charanga (chah-*rahng*-gah) *f* brass
   band
charco (*chahr*-koa) *m* puddle
charla (*chahr*-lah) *f* chat
charlar (chahr-*lahr*) *v* chat
charlatán (chahr-lah-*tahn*) *m* chatterbox; quack
charola (chah-*roa*-lah) *fMe* tray
chasis (chah-*seess*) *m* chassis
chatarra (chah-*tah*-rrah) *f* scrap-iron
checo (*chay*-koa) *adj* Czech; *m* Czech
Checoslovaquia (chay-koaz-loa-*bhah*-

kʸah) f Czechoslovakia

cheque (*chay*-kay) *m* cheque; check *nAm*; ~ **de viajero** traveller's cheque

chicle (*chee*-klay) *m* chewing-gum

chico (*chee*-koa) *m* boy; kid

chichón (chee-*choan*) *m* lump

Chile (*chee*-lay) *m* Chile

chileno (chee-*lay*-noa) *adj* Chilean; *m* Chilean

chillar (chee-*lʸahr*) *v* scream, shriek

chillido (chee-*lʸee*-dhoa) *m* scream, shriek

chimenea (chee-may-*nay*-ah) *f* chimney; fireplace

China (*chee*-nah) *f* China

chinche (*cheen*-chay) *f* bug; drawing-pin; thumbtack *nAm*

chinchorro (cheen-*choa*-rroa) *m* dinghy

chino (*chee*-noa) *adj* Chinese; *m* Chinese; *adjMe* curly

chisguete (cheez-*gay*-tay) *m* squirt

chisme (*cheez*-may) *m* gossip; ***contar chismes** gossip

chispa (*cheess*-pah) *f* spark

chistoso (cheess-*toa*-soa) *adj* witty, humorous

chocante (choa-*kahn*-tay) *adj* revolting, shocking

chocar (choa-*kahr*) *v* collide, crash, bump; shock; ~ **contra** knock against

chocolate (choa-koa-*lah*-tay) *m* chocolate

chófer (*choa*-fayr) *m* chauffeur

choque (*choa*-kay) *m* crash; shock

chorro (*choa*-rroa) *m* spout, jet

chuleta (choo-*lay*-tah) *f* chop, cutlet

chupar (choo-*pahr*) *v* suck

D

dactilógrafa (dahk-tee-*loa*-grah-fah) *f* typist

dadivoso (dah-dhee-*bhoa*-soa) *adj* liberal

daltoniano (dahl-toa-*nʸah*-noa) *adj* colour-blind

dama (*dah*-mah) *f* lady

danés (dah-*nayss*) *adj* Danish; *m* Dane

dañar (dah-*ñahr*) *v* damage; *hurt

daño (*dah*-ñoa) *m* mischief; harm; *hacer ~ *hurt

dañoso (dah-*ñoa*-soa) *adj* harmful

***dar** (dahr) *v* *give; **dado que** supposing that

dátil (*dah*-teel) *m* date

dato (*dah*-toa) *m* data *pl*

de (day) *prep* of; out of, from, off; with

debajo (day-*bhah*-khoa) *adv* underneath, beneath, below; ~ **de** under, beneath, below

debate (day-*bhah*-tay) *m* debate, discussion

debatir (day-bhah-*teer*) *v* discuss

debe (*day*-bhay) *m* debit

deber (day-*bhayr*) *m* duty; *v* *have to, need to, need; owe; ~ **de** *be bound to

debido (day-*bhee*-dhoa) *adj* due; proper; ~ **a** owing to

débil (*day*-bheel) *adj* faint, weak, feeble

debilidad (day-bhee-lee-*dhahdh*) *f* weakness

decencia (day-*thayn*-thʸah) *f* decency

decente (day-*thayn*-tay) *adj* decent

decepcionar (day-thayp-thʸoa-*nahr*) *v* *let down, disappoint

decidir (day-thee-*dheer*) *v* decide; **de-**

cidido resolute

décimo (day-thee-moa) num tenth

decimoctavo (day-thee-moak-tah-bhoa) num eighteenth

decimonono (day-thee-moa-noa-noa) num nineteenth

decimoséptimo (day-thee-moa-sayp-tee-moa) num seventeenth

decimosexto (day-thee-moa-sayks-toa) num sixteenth

***decir** (day-theer) v *say, *tell; ***querer** ~ *mean

decisión (day-thee-sʸoan) f decision

decisivo (day-thee-see-bhoa) adj decisive

declaración (day-klah-rah-thʸoan) f statement, declaration

declarar (day-klah-rahr) v state, declare

decoración (day-koa-rah-thʸoan) f decoration

decorativo (day-koa-rah-tee-bhoa) adj decorative

decreto (day-kray-toa) m decree

dedal (day-dhahl) m thimble

dédalo (day-dhah-loa) m muddle

dedicar (day-dhee-kahr) v devote, dedicate

dedo (day-dhoa) m finger; ~ **auricular** little finger; ~ **del pie** toe

***deducir** (day-dhoo-theer) v infer, deduce; deduct

defecto (day-fayk-toa) m fault

defectuoso (day-fayk-twoa-soa) adj defective, faulty

***defender** (day-fayn-dayr) v defend

defensa (day-fayn-sah) f defence; plea; fMe fender

defensor (day-fayn-soar) m champion

deficiencia (day-fee-thʸayn-thʸah) f deficiency, shortcoming

déficit (day-fee-theet) m deficit

definición (day-fee-nee-thʸoan) f definition

definir (day-fee-neer) v define; **definido** definite

definitivo (day-fee-nee-tee-bhoa) adj definitive

deforme (day-foar-may) adj deformed

dejar (day-khahr) v *let, *leave; *leave behind, desert; ~ **de** stop

delantal (day-lahn-tahl) m apron

delante de (day-lahn-tay day) before, in front of, ahead of

delegación (day-lay-gah-thʸoan) f delegation

delegado (day-lay-gah-dhoa) m delegate

deleitable (day-lay-tah-bhlay) adj enjoyable

deleite (day-lay-tay) m delight

deleitoso (day-lay-toa-soa) adj delightful

deletrear (day-lay-tray-ahr) v *spell

deletreo (day-lay-tray-oa) m spelling

delgado (dayl-gah-dhoa) adj thin

deliberación (day-lee-bhay-rah-thʸoan) f deliberation

deliberar (day-lee-bhay-rahr) v deliberate; **deliberado** adj deliberate

delicado (day-lee-kah-dhoa) adj delicate, tender

delicia (day-lee-thʸah) f joy, delight

delicioso (day-lee-thʸoa-soa) adj wonderful, delightful, delicious, lovely

delincuente (day-leeng-kwayn-tay) m criminal

delito (day-lee-toa) m crime

demanda (day-mahn-dah) f request; application; demand

demás (day-mahss) adj remaining

demasiado (day-mah-sʸah-dhoa) adv too

democracia (day-moa-krah-thʸah) f democracy

democrático (day-moa-krah-tee-koa) adj democratic

***demoler** (day-moa-layr) v demolish

demolición (day-moa-lee-*thᴠoan*) *f* demolition

demonio (day-*moa*-nᴠoa) *m* devil

demostración (day-moass-trah-*thᴠoan*) *f* demonstration

*demostrar** (day-moass-*trahr*) *v* demonstrate, *show, prove

*denegar** (day-nay-*gahr*) *v* deny

denominación (day-noa-mee-nah-*thᴠoan*) *f* denomination

denso (*dayn*-soa) *adj* thick, dense

dentadura postiza (dayn-tah-*dhoo*-rah poass-*tee*-thah) false teeth, denture

dentista (dayn-*teess*-tah) *m* dentist

dentro (*dayn*-troa) *adv* inside; **de ~** within; **~ de** inside, within; into; in

departamento (day-pahr-tah-*mayn*-toa) *m* department; section, division

depender de (day-payn-*dayr*) depend on

dependiente (day-payn-*dᴠayn*-tay) *adj* dependant; *m* shop assistant

deporte (day-*poar*-tay) *m* sport; **conjunto de ~** sportswear; **chaqueta de ~** sports-jacket

deportista (day-poar-*teess*-tah) *m* sportsman

depositar (day-poa-see-*tahr*) *v* bank

depósito (day-*poa*-see-toa) *m* deposit; **~ de gasolina** petrol tank

depresión (day-pray-sᴠoan) *f* depression

deprimente (day-pree-*mayn*-tay) *adj* depressing

deprimir (day-pree-*meer*) *v* depress; **deprimido** blue, depressed, low

derecho (day-*ray*-choa) *m* right; law, right, justice, straight; *adj* upright; right-hand; **~ administrativo** administrative law; **~ civil** civil law; **~ comercial** commercial law; **~ electoral** franchise, suffrage; **~ penal** criminal law

derivar de (day-ree-*bhahr*) *be derived from

derramar (day-rrah-*mahr*) *v* *shed

derribar (day-rree-*bhahr*) *v* knock down

derrochador (day-rroa-chah-*dhoar*) *adj* wasteful

derrota (day-*rroa*-tah) *f* defeat

derrotar (day-rroa-*tahr*) *v* defeat

derrumbarse (day-rroom-*bahr*-say) *v* collapse

desabotonar (day-sah-bhoa-toa-*nahr*) *v* unbutton

desacelerar (day-sah-thay-lay-*rahr*) *v* slow down

desacostumbrado (day-sah-koass-toom-*brah*-dhoa) *adj* unaccustomed

desacostumbrar (day-sah-koass-toom-*brahr*) *v* unlearn

desafiar (day-sah-*fᴠahr*) *v* dare; challenge

desafilado (day-sah-fee-*lah*-dhoa) *adj* blunt

desafortunado (day-sah-foar-too-*nah*-dhoa) *adj* unlucky, unfortunate

desagradable (day-sah-grah-*dhah*-bhlay) *adj* nasty, disagreeable, unpleasant; unkind

desagradar (day-sah-grah-*dhahr*) *v* displease

desagüe (day-*sah*-gway) *m* sewer, drain

desaliñado (day-sah-lee-*ñah*-doa) *adj* untidy

desamueblado (day-sah-mway-*bhlah*-dhoa) *adj* unfurnished

desánimo (day-*sah*-nee-moa) *m* depression

*desaparecer** (day-sah-pah-ray-*thayr*) *v* disappear; vanish

desaparecido (day-sah-pah-ray-*thee*-dhoa) *adj* lost; *m* missing person

desapasionado (day-sah-pah-sᴠoa-*nah*-dhoa) *adj* matter-of-fact

*desaprobar** (day-sah-proa-*bhahr*) *v*

disapprove

desarrollar (day-sah-rroa-*l*Υ*ahr*) v develop

desarrollo (day-sah-*rroa*-lΥoa) m development

desasosiego (day-sah-soa-sΥay-goa) m unrest

desastre (day-*sahss*-tray) m disaster, calamity

desastroso (day-sahss-*troa*-soa) adj disastrous

desatar (day-sah-*tahr*) v *undo, untie, unfasten

desautorizado (day-sou-toa-ree-*thah*-dhoa) adj unauthorized

desayuno (day-sah-Υoo-noa) m breakfast

descafeinado (dayss-kah-fay-*nah*-dhoa) adj decaffeinated

descansar (dayss-kahn-*sahr*) v rest; relax

descanso (dayss-*kahn*-soa) m rest; break; half-time

descarado (dayss-kah-*rah*-dhoa) adj bold, impertinent

descargar (dayss-kahr-*gahr*) v discharge, unload

descendencia (day-thayn-*dayn*-thΥah) f origin

* **descender** (day-thayn-*dhayr*) v *fall

descendiente (day-thayn-*d*Υ*ayn*-tay) m descendant

descolorido (dayss-koa-loa-*ree*-dhoa) adj discoloured

descompostura (dayss-koam-poass-*too*-rah) fMe breakdown

* **desconcertar** (dayss-koan-thayr-*tahr*) v overwhelm, embarrass

desconectar (dayss-koa-nayk-*tahr*) v disconnect

desconfiado (dayss-koan-fΥah-dhoa) adj suspicious

desconfianza (dayss-koan-fΥahn-thah) f suspicion

desconfiar de (dayss-koan-fΥahr) v mistrust

descongelarse (dayss-koang-khay-*lahr*-say) v thaw

* **desconocer** (dayss-koa-noa-*thayr*) v not to *know, fail to recognize

desconocido (dayss-koa-noa-*thee*-dhoa) adj unknown; unfamiliar

descontento (dayss-koan-*tayn*-toa) adj discontented

descorchar (dayss-koar-*chahr*) v uncork

descortés (dayss-koar-*tayss*) adj impolite

describir (dayss-kree-*bheer*) v describe

descripción (dayss-kreep-*th*Υ*oan*) f description

descubrimiento (dayss-koo-bhree-*m*Υ*ayn*-toa) m discovery

descubrir (dayss-koo-*bhreer*) v discover, detect

descuento (dayss-*kwayn*-toa) m discount; ~ **bancario** bank-rate

descuidar (dayss-kwee-*dhahr*) v neglect; **descuidado** slovenly

descuido (dayss-*kwee*-dhoa) m oversight

desde (*dayz*-dhay) prep from; since; ~ **entonces** since; ~ **que** since

desdén (dayz-*dhayn*) m disdain

desdichado (dayz-dhee-*chah*-dhoa) adj unhappy

deseable (day-say-ah-bhlay) adj desirable

desear (day-say-*ahr*) v desire; wish, want

desecar (day-say-*kahr*) v drain

desechable (day-say-*chah*-bhlay) adj disposable

desechar (day-say-*chahr*) v discard

desecho (day-*say*-choa) m refuse

desembarcar (day-saym-bahr-*kahr*) v disembark; land

desembocadura (day-saym-boa-kah-

dhoo-rah) *f* mouth

desempaquetar (day-saym-pah-kay-*tahr*) *v* unpack

desempeñar (day-saym-pay-*ñahr*) *v* perform

desempleo (day-saym-*play*-oa) *m* unemployment

desengaño (day-sayng-*gah*-ñoa) *m* disappointment

desenvoltura (day-saym-boal-*too*-rah) *f* ease

desenvolver (day-saym-boal-*bhayr*) *v* unwrap

deseo (day-*say*-oa) *m* wish, desire

desertar (day-sayr-*tahr*) *v* desert

desesperación (day-sayss-pay-rah-*th*ʸ*oan*) *f* despair

desesperado (day-sayss-pay-*rah*-dhoa) *adj* hopeless, desperate; **estar ~* despair

desfavorable (dayss-fah-bhoa-*rah*-bhlay) *adj* unfavourable

desfile (dayss-*fee*-lay) *m* parade

desgarrar (dayz-gah-*rrahr*) *v* *tear

desgracia (dayz-*grah*-th*ʸ*ah) *f* misfortune

desgraciadamente (dayz-grah-th*ʸ*ah-dhah-*mayn*-tay) *adv* unfortunately

deshacer (day-sah-*thayr*) *v* *undo

deshielo (day-s*ʸ*ay-loa) *m* thaw

deshilacharse (day-see-lah-*chahr*-say) *v* fray

deshonesto (day-soa-*nayss*-toa) *adj* crooked

deshonor (day-soa-*noar*) *m* disgrace

deshonra (day-*soan*-rah) *f* shame

deshuesar (day-sway-*sahr*) *v* bone

desierto (day-s*ʸ*ayr-toa) *adj* desert; *m* desert

designar (day-seeg-*nahr*) *v* designate; appoint

desigual (day-see-*gwahl*) *adj* unequal, uneven

desinclinado (day-seeng-klee-*nah*-dhoa) *adj* unwilling

desinfectante (day-seen-fayk-*tahn*-tay) *m* disinfectant

desinfectar (day-seen-fayk-*tahr*) *v* disinfect

desinteresado (day-seen-tay-ray-sah-dhoa) *adj* unselfish

desliz (dayz-*leeth*) *m* slide; slip

deslizarse (dayz-lee-*thahr*-say) *v* *slide; slip

deslucido (dayz-loo-*thee*-dhoa) *adj* dim

deslumbrador (dayz-loom-brah-*dhoar*) *adj* glaring

desmayarse (dayz-mah-ʸ*ahr*-say) *v* faint

desnudarse (dayz-noo-*dhahr*-say) *v* undress

desnudo (dayz-*noo*-dhoa) *adj* naked, nude, bare; *m* nude

desnutrición (dayz-noo-tree-th*ʸ*oan) *f* malnutrition

desocupado (day-soa-koo-*pah*-dhoa) *adj* unoccupied; unemployed

desodorante (day-soa-dhoa-*rahn*-tay) *m* deodorant

desorden (day-*soar*-dayn) *m* disorder; mess

despachar (dayss-pah-*chahr*) *v* dispatch, despatch, *send off

despacho (dayss-*pah*-choa) *m* study

despedida (dayss-pay-*dhee*-dhah) *f* parting; departure

despedir (dayss-pay-*dheer*) *v* dismiss; fire; **despedirse* v check out

despegar (dayss-pay-*gahr*) *v* *take off

despegue (dayss-pay-gay) *m* take-off

despensa (dayss-*payn*-sah) *f* larder

desperdicio (dayss-payr-*dhee*-th*ʸ*oa) *m* litter; waste

despertador (dayss-payr-tah-*dhoar*) *m* alarm-clock

despertar (dayss-payr-*tahr*) *v* *wake, *awake; **despertarse* v wake up

despierto (dayss-p*ʸ*ayr-toa) *adj*

awake; vigilant

*desplegar (dayss-play-*gahr*) v unfold; expand

desplomarse (dayss-ploa-*mahr*-say) v collapse

despreciar (dayss-pray-*th^yahr*) v scorn, despise

desprecio (dayss-*pray*-th^yoa) m scorn, contempt

despreocupado (dayss-pray-oa-koo-*pah*-dhoa) adj carefree

después (dayss-*pwayss*) adv afterwards; then; ~ de after; ~ de que after

destacado (dayss-tah-*kah*-dhoa) adj outstanding

destacarse (dayss-tah-*kahr*-say) v *stand out

destapar (dayss-tah-*pahr*) v uncover

destartalado (dayss-tahr-tah-*lah*-dhoa) adj ramshackle

destello (dayss-*tay*-l^yoa) m glare

*desteñirse (dayss-tay-*ñeer*-say) v fade, discolour; no destiñe fast-dyed

destinar (dayss-tee-*nahr*) v destine; address

destinatario (dayss-tee-nah-tah-r^yoa) m addressee

destino (dayss-*tee*-noa) m fate, destiny, lot; destination

destornillador (dayss-toar-nee-l^yah-dhoar) m screw-driver

destornillar (dayss-toar-nee-*l^yahr*) v unscrew

destrucción (dayss-trook-th^yoan) f destruction

*destruir (dayss-*trweer*) v destroy; wreck

desvalorización (dayz-bhah-loa-ree-thah-*th^yoan*) f devaluation

desvalorizar (dayz-bhah-loa-ree-*thahr*) v devalue

desvelado (dayz-bhay-*lah*-dhoa) adj

sleepless

desventaja (dayz-bhayn-*tah*-khah) f disadvantage

desviar (dayz-*bh^yahr*) v avert; desviarse v deviate

desvío (dayz-*bhee*-oa) m detour; diversion

detallado (day-tah-*l^yah*-dhoa) adj detailed

detalle (day-*tah*-l^yay) m detail; vender al ~ retail

detective (day-tayk-*tee*-bhay) m detective

detención (day-tayn-*th^yoan*) f custody

*detener (day-tay-*nayr*) v detain

detergente (day-tayr-*khayn*-tay) m detergent

determinar (day-tayr-mee-*nahr*) v define, determine; determinado definite

detestar (day-tayss-*tahr*) v hate, dislike

detrás (day-*trahss*) adv behind; ~ de behind, after

deuda (day^{oo}-dhah) f debt

*devolver (day-bhoal-*bhayr*) v *bring back; *send back

día (*dee*-ah) m day; ¡buenos días! hello!; de ~ by day; ~ de trabajo working day; ~ laborable weekday; el otro ~ recently

diabetes (d^yah-*bhay*-tayss) f diabetes

diabético (d^yah-*bhay*-tee-koa) m diabetic

diablo (*d^yah*-bhloa) m devil

diabluras (d^yah-*bhloo*-rahss) fpl mischief

diagnosis (d^yahg-*noa*-seess) m diagnosis

diagnosticar (d^yahg-noass-tee-*kahr*) v diagnose

diagonal (d^yah-goa-*nahl*) adj diagonal; f diagonal

dialecto (d^yah-*layk*-toa) m dialect

diamante (dᵛah-*mahn*-tay) *m* diamond

diapositiva (dᵛah-poa-see-*tee*-bhah) *f* slide

diario (dᵛah-rᵛoa) *adj* daily; *m* daily, newspaper; diary; **a ~** per day; **~ matutino** morning paper

diarrea (dᵛah-*rray*-ah) *f* diarrhoea

dibujar (dee-bhoo-*khahr*) *v* sketch, *draw

dibujo (dee-*bhoo*-khoa) *m* sketch, drawing; **dibujos animados** cartoon

diccionario (deek-thᵛoa-*nah*-rᵛoa) *m* dictionary

diciembre (dee-thᵛaym-bray) December

dictado (deek-*tah*-dhoa) *m* dictation

dictador (deek-tah-*dhoar*) *m* dictator

dictadura (deek-tah-*dhoo*-rah) *f* dictatorship

dictáfono (deek-*tah*-foa-noa) *m* dictaphone

dictar (deek-*tahr*) *v* dictate

dichoso (dee-*choa*-soa) *adj* happy

diecinueve (dᵛay-thee-*nway*-bhay) *num* nineteen

dieciocho (dᵛay-thᵛoa-choa) *num* eighteen

dieciséis (dᵛay-thee-*sayss*) *num* sixteen

diecisiete (dᵛay-thee-sᵛay-tay) *num* seventeen

diente (dᵛayn-tay) *m* tooth; **~ de león** dandelion

diesel (dee-sayl) *m* diesel

diestro (dᵛayss-troa) *adj* skilful

diez (dᵛayth) *num* ten

diferencia (dee-fay-*rayn*-thᵛah) *f* difference; contrast, distinction

diferente (dee-fay-*rayn*-tay) *adj* different; unlike

***diferir** (dee-fay-*reer*) *v* vary, differ; delay

difícil (dee-*fee*-theel) *adj* hard, difficult

dificultad (dee-fee-kool-*tahdh*) *f* difficulty

difteria (deef-*tay*-rᵛah) *f* diphtheria

difunto (dee-*foon*-toa) *adj* dead

difuso (dee-*foo*-soa) *adj* dim

digerible (dee-khayss-*tee*-bhlay) *adj* digestible

***digerir** (dee-khay-*reer*) *v* digest

digestión (dee-khayss-tᵛoan) *f* digestion

dignidad (deeg-nee-*dhahdh*) *f* dignity

digno de (*dee*-ñoa day) worthy of

dilación (dee-lah-*thᵛoan*) *f* delay, respite

diligencia (dee-lee-*khayn*-thᵛah) *f* diligence

diligente (dee-lee-*khayn*-tay) *adj* industrious

***diluir** (dee-*lweer*) *v* dilute

dimensión (dee-mayn-sᵛoan) *f* extent, size

Dinamarca (dee-nah-*mahr*-kah) *f* Denmark

dínamo (*dee*-nah-moa) *f* dynamo

dinero (dee-*nay*-roa) *m* money; **~ contante** cash

dios (dᵛoass) *m* god

diosa (dᵛoa-sah) *f* goddess

diploma (dee-*ploa*-mah) *m* diploma, certificate

diplomático (dee-ploa-*mah*-tee-koa) *m* diplomat

diputado (dee-poo-*tah*-dhoa) *m* deputy; Member of Parliament

dique (*dee*-kay) *m* dike, dam

dirección (dee-rayk-*thᵛoan*) *f* direction; way; address; leadership, lead; **~ de escena** direction; **~ única** one-way traffic

directamente (dee-rayk-tah-*mayn*-tay) *adv* straight; straight away

directo (dee-*rayk*-toa) *adj* direct

director (dee-rayk-*toar*) *m* director,

manager; conductor; **~ de escuela** head teacher, headmaster; principal

directorio telefónico (dee-rayk-*toa*-rʸoa tay-lay-*foa*-nee-koa) *Me* telephone directory

directriz (dee-rayk-*treeth*) *f* directive

dirigir (dee-ree-*kheer*) *v* head; direct; **dirigirse a** address

disciplina (dee-thee-*plee*-nah) *f* discipline

discípulo (deess-*thee*-poo-loa) *m* pupil

disco (*deess*-koa) *m* disc; record

discreto (deess-*kray*-toa) *adj* inconspicuous

disculpa (deess-*kool*-pah) *f* apology

disculpar (deess-kool-*pahr*) *v* excuse; **disculparse** *v* apologize; **¡disculpe!** sorry!

discurso (deess-*koor*-soa) *m* speech

discusión (deess-koo-*sʸoan*) *f* discussion, argument

discutir (deess-koo-*teer*) *v* discuss, deliberate, argue

disentería (dee-sayn-tay-*ree*-ah) *f* dysentery

***disentir** (dee-sayn-*teer*) *v* disagree

diseñar (dee-say-*ñahr*) *v* design

diseño (dee-*say*-ñoa) *m* design; pattern; **cuaderno de ~** sketch-book

disfraz (deess-*frahth*) *m* disguise

disfrazarse (deess-frah-*thahr*-say) *v* disguise

disfrutar (deess-froo-*tahr*) *v* enjoy

disgustar (deez-gooss-*tahr*) *v* displease

disimular (dee-see-moo-*lahr*) *v* conceal

dislocado (deez-loa-*kah*-dhoa) *adj* dislocated

dislocar (deez-loa-*kahr*) *v* wrench

disminución (deez-mee-noo-*thʸoan*) *f* decrease

***disminuir** (deez-mee-*nweer*) *v* reduce, lessen, decrease

***disolver** (dee-soal-*bhayr*) *v* dissolve

disparar (deess-pah-*rahr*) *v* fire

disparo (deess-*pah*-roa) *m* shot

dispensar (deess-payn-*sahr*) *v* exempt; **~ de** discharge of; **¡dispense usted!** sorry!

dispensario (deess-payn-*sah*-rʸoa) *m* health centre

***disponer** (deess-poa-*nayr*) *v* sort; **~ de** dispose of

disponible (deess-poa-*nee*-bhlay) *adj* available; spare

disposición (deess-poa-see-*thʸoan*) *f* disposal

dispuesto (deess-*pwayss*-toa) *adj* inclined, willing

disputa (deess-*poo*-tah) *f* dispute, argument, quarrel

disputar (deess-poo-*tahr*) *v* argue, quarrel; dispute

distancia (deess-*tahn*-thʸah) *f* distance; space, way

distinción (deess-teen-*thʸoan*) *f* distinction, difference

distinguido (deess-teeng-*gee*-dhoa) *adj* distinguished, dignified

distinguir (deess-teeng-*geer*) *v* distinguish; **distinguirse** *v* excel

distinto (deess-*teen*-toa) *adj* distinct

distracción (deess-trahk-*thʸoan*) *f* amusement

***distraer** (deess-trah-*ayr*) *v* distract

distribuidor (deess-tree-bhwee-*dhoar*) *m* distributor

***distribuir** (deess-tree-*bhweer*) *v* distribute; issue

distrito (deess-*tree*-toa) *m* district; **~ electoral** constituency

disturbio (deess-*toor*-bhʸoa) *m* disturbance

disuadir (dee-swah-*dheer*) *v* dissuade from

diván (dee-*bhahn*) *m* couch

diversión (dee-bhayr-*sʸoan*) *f* pleasure, fun; diversion, entertainment

diverso (dee-*bhayr*-soa) *adj* diverse

divertido (dee-bhayr-*tee*-dhoa) *adj* amusing, entertaining

*****divertir** (dee-bhayr-*teer*) *v* amuse, entertain

dividir (dee-bhee-*dheer*) *v* divide

divino (dee-*bhee*-noa) *adj* divine

división (dee-bhee-*s*y*oan*) *f* division; section

divorciar (dee-bhoar-*th*y*ahr*) *v* divorce

divorcio (dee-*bhoar*-th*y*oa) *m* divorce

dobladillo (doa-bhlah-*dhee*-l*y*oa) *m* hem

doblar (doa-*bhlahr*) *v* *bend; fold

doble (*doa*-bhlay) *adj* double

doce (*doa*-thay) *num* twelve

docena (doa-*thay*-nah) *f* dozen

doctor (doak-*toar*) *m* doctor

doctrina (doak-*tree*-nah) *f* doctrine

documento (doa-koo-*mayn*-toa) *m* document

*****doler** (doa-*layr*) *v* ache

dolor (doa-*loar*) *m* ache, pain; grief; **dolores** *mpl* labour; **sin ~** painless

dolorido (doa-loa-*ree*-dhoa) *adj* painful

doloroso (doa-loa-*roa*-soa) *adj* sore

domesticado (doa-mayss-tee-*kah*-dhoa) *adj* tame

domesticar (doa-mayss-tee-*kahr*) *v* tame

doméstico (doa-*mayss*-tee-koa) *adj* domestic; **faenas domésticas** housework

domicilio (doa-mee-*thee*-l*y*oa) *m* domicile

dominación (doa-mee-nah-*th*y*oan*) *f* domination

dominante (doa-mee-*nahn*-tay) *adj* leading

dominar (doa-mee-*nahr*) *v* master

domingo (doa-*meeng*-goa) *m* Sunday

dominio (doa-*mee*-n*y*oa) *m* dominion, rule

don (doan) *m* faculty

donación (doa-nah-*th*y*oan*) *f* donation

donante (doa-*nahn*-tay) *m* donor

donar (doa-*nahr*) *v* donate

doncella (doan-*thay*-l*y*ah) *f* chambermaid

donde (*doan*-day) *conj* where; **en ~ sea** anywhere

dónde (*doan*-day) *adv* where

dondequiera (doan-day-*k*y*ay*-rah) *adv* anywhere; **~ que** wherever

dorado (doa-*rah*-dhoa) *adj* gilt; golden

dormido (doar-*mee*-dhoa) *adj* asleep; **quedarse ~** *oversleep

*****dormir** (doar-*meer*) *v* *sleep

dormitorio (doar-mee-*toa*-r*y*oa) *m* bedroom; dormitory

dos (doass) *num* two; **~ veces** twice

dosis (*doa*-seess) *f* dose

dotado (doa-*tah*-dhoa) *adj* talented

dragón (drah-*goan*) *m* dragon

drama (*drah*-mah) *m* drama

dramático (drah-*mah*-tee-koa) *adj* dramatic

dramaturgo (drah-mah-*toor*-goa) *m* playwright, dramatist

drenar (dray-*nahr*) *v* drain

droguería (droa-gay-*ree*-ah) *f* chemist's, pharmacy; drugstore *nAm*

ducha (*doo*-chah) *f* shower

duda (*doo*-dhah) *f* doubt; *****poner en ~** query; **sin ~** undoubtedly, without doubt

dudar (doo-*dhahr*) *v* doubt

dudoso (doo-*dhoa*-soa) *adj* doubtful

duelo (*dway*-loa) *m* duel; grief

duende (*dwayn*-dhay) *m* elf

dueña (*dway*-ñah) *f* mistress

dueño (*dway*-ñoa) *m* landlord

dulce (*dool*-thay) *adj* sweet; smooth; *m* sweet; **dulces** cake; sweets; candy *nAm*

duna (*doo*-nah) *f* dune

duodécimo (dwoa-*day*-thee-moa) *num* twelfth

duque (*doo*-kay) *m* duke

duquesa (doo-*kay*-sah) *f* duchess

duración (doo-rah-*thʸoan*) *f* duration

duradero (doo-rah-*dhay*-roa) *adj* permanent, lasting

durante (doo-*rahn*-tay) *prep* for, during

durar (doo-*rahr*) *v* last; continue

duro (*doo*-roa) *adj* hard; tough

E

ébano (*ay*-bhah-noa) *m* ebony

eclipse (ay-*kleep*-say) *m* eclipse

eco (*ay*-koa) *m* echo

economía (ay-koa-noa-*mee*-ah) *f* economy

económico (ay-koa-*noa*-mee-koa) *adj* economic; thrifty, economical; cheap

economista (ay-koa-noa-*meess*-tah) *m* economist

economizar (ay-koa-noa-mee-*thahr*) *v* economize

Ecuador (ay-kwah-*dhoar*) *m* Ecuador

ecuador (ay-kwah-*dhoar*) *m* equator

ecuatoriano (ay-kwah-toa-*rʸah*-noa) *m* Ecuadorian

eczema (ayk-*thay*-mah) *m* eczema

echada (ay-*chah*-dhah) *f* cast

echar (ay-*chahr*) *v* toss; ~ **al correo** post; ~ **a perder** *spoil; ~ **la culpa** blame

edad (ay-*dhahdh*) *f* age; **mayor de** ~ of age; **menor de** ~ under age

Edad Media (ay-*dhahdh* may-dhʸah) Middle Ages

edición (ay-dhee-*thʸoan*) *f* issue, edition; ~ **de mañana** morning edition

edificar (ay-dhee-fee-*kahr*) *v* construct

edificio (ay-dhee-*fee*-thʸoa) *m* construction, building

editor (ay-dhee-*toar*) *m* publisher

edredón (ay-dhray-*dhoan*) *m* eiderdown

educación (ay-dhoo-kah-*thʸoan*) *f* education

educar (ay-dhoo-*kahr*) *v* educate, *bring up, raise

efectivamente (ay-fayk-tee-bhah-*mayn*-tay) *adv* as a matter of fact, in fact

efectivo (ay-fayk-*tee*-bhoa) *m* cash; *hacer ~ cash

efecto (ay-*fayk*-toa) *m* effect

efectuar (ay-fayk-*twahr*) *v* effect; implement

efervescencia (ay-fayr-bhay-*thaynthʸah*) *f* fizz

eficacia (ay-fee-*kah*-thʸah) *f* efficacy

eficaz (ay-fee-*kahth*) *adj* effective

eficiente (ay-fee-*thʸayn*-tay) *adj* efficient

egipcio (ay-*kheep*-thʸoa) *adj* Egyptian; *m* Egyptian

Egipto (ay-*kheep*-toa) *m* Egypt

egocéntrico (ay-goa-*thayn*-tree-koa) *adj* self-centred

egoísmo (ay-goa-*eez*-moa) *m* selfishness

egoísta (ay-goa-*eess*-tah) *adj* egoistic, selfish

eje (*ay*-khay) *m* axle

ejecución (ay-khay-koo-*thʸoan*) *f* execution

ejecutar (ay-khay-koo-*tahr*) *v* perform, execute

ejecutivo (ay-khay-koo-*tee*-bhoa) *adj* executive; *m* executive

ejemplar (ay-khaym-*plahr*) *m* copy

ejemplo (ay-*khaym*-ploa) *m* instance, example; **por** ~ for instance, for example

ejercer (ay-khayr-*thayr*) *v* exercise

ejercicio (ay-khayr-*thee*-thʸoa) *m* exercise

ejercitar (ay-khayr-thee-*tahr*) *v* exercise

ejército (ay-*khayr*-thee-toa) *m* army

ejote (ay-*khoa*-tay) *mMe* bean

el (ayl) *art* (f la; pl los, las) the

él (ayl) *pron* he

elaborar (ay-lah-boa-*rahr*) *v* elaborate

elasticidad (ay-lahss-tee-thee-*dhahdh*) *f* elasticity

elástico (ay-*lahss*-tee-koa) *adj* elastic; *m* rubber band

elección (ay-layk-*th*ᵛoan) *f* choice, pick, selection; election

electricidad (ay-layk-tree-thee-*dhahdh*) *f* electricity

electricista (ay-layk-tree-*theess*-tah) *m* electrician

eléctrico (ay-*layk*-tree-koa) *adj* electric

electrónico (ay-layk-*troa*-nee-koa) *adj* electronic

elefante (ay-lay-*fahn*-tay) *m* elephant

elegancia (ay-lay-*gahn*-th ᵛah) *f* elegance

elegante (ay-lay-*gahn*-tay) *adj* smart, elegant

* **elegir** (ay-lay-*kheer*) *v* elect, select

elemental (ay-lay-mayn-*tahl*) *adj* primary

elemento (ay-lay-*mayn*-toa) *m* element

elevador (ay-lay-bhah-*dhoar*) *mMe* lift; elevator *nAm*

elevar (ay-lay-*bhahr*) *v* elevate

eliminar (ay-lee-mee-*nahr*) *v* eliminate

elogio (ay-*loa*-kh ᵛoa) *m* praise, glory

elucidar (ay-loo-thee-*dhahr*) *v* elucidate

ella (*ay*-l ᵛah) *pron* she

ello (*ay*-l ᵛoa) *pron* it

ellos (*ay*-l ᵛoass) *pron* they

emancipación (ay-mahn-thee-pah-*th*ᵛoan) *f* emancipation

embajada (aym-bah-*khah*-dhah) *f* embassy

embajador (aym-bah-khah-*dhoar*) *m* ambassador

embalaje (aym-bah-*lah*-khay) *m* packing

embalar (aym-bah-*lahr*) *v* pack

embalse (aym-*bahl*-say) *m* reservoir

embarazada (aym-bah-rah-*thah*-dhah) *adj* pregnant

embarazoso (aym-bah-rah-*thoa*-soa) *adj* embarrassing, awkward; puzzling

embarcación (aym-bahr-kah-*th*ᵛoan) *f* vessel; embarkation

embarcar (aym-bahr-*kahr*) *v* embark

embargar (aym-bahr-*gahr*) *v* confiscate

embargo (aym-*bahr*-goa) *m* embargo; **sin ~** yet, however, though, still

emblema (aym-*blay*-mah) *m* emblem

emboscada (aym-boass-*kah*-dhah) *f* ambush

embotado (aym-boa-*tah*-dhoa) *adj* dull

embotellamiento (aym-boa-tay-l ᵛah-m ᵛayn-toa) *m* traffic jam

embrague (aym-*brah*-gay) *m* clutch

embriagado (aym-br ᵛah-*gah*-dhoa) *adj* intoxicated

embrollar (aym-broa-l ᵛahr) *v* muddle

embrollo (aym-*broa*-l ᵛoa) *m* muddle

embromar (aym-broa-*mahr*) *v* kid

embudo (aym-*boo*-dhoa) *m* funnel

emergencia (ay-mayr-*khayn*-th ᵛah) *f* emergency

emigración (ay-mee-grah-*th*ᵛoan) *f* emigration

emigrante (ay-mee-*grahn*-tay) *m* emigrant

emigrar (ay-mee-*grahr*) *v* emigrate

eminente (ay-mee-*nayn*-tay) *adj* outstanding

emisión (ay-mee-s ᵛoan) *f* issue

emisor (ay-mee-*soar*) *m* transmitter

emitir (ay-mee-*teer*) *v* *broadcast; utter

emoción (ay-moa-*th*ᵛoan) *f* emotion

empalme (aym-*pahl*-may) *m* junction

empapar (aym-pah-*pahr*) *v* soak

empaquetar (aym-pah-kay-*tahr*) *v* pack up

emparedado (aym-pah-ray-*dhah*-dhoa) *m* sandwich

emparentado (aym-pah-rayn-*tah*-dhoa) *adj* related

empaste (aym-*pahss*-tay) *m* filling

empeñar (aym-pay-*ñahr*) *v* pawn

empeño (aym-*pay*-ñoa) *m* pawn; determination

emperador (aym-pay-rah-*dhoar*) *m* emperor

emperatriz (aym-pay-rah-*treeth*) *f* empress

*empezar** (aym-pay-*thahr*) *v* *begin, start

empleado (aym-play-*ah*-dhoa) *m* employee; ~ de oficina clerk

emplear (aym-play-*ahr*) *v* employ; engage

empleo (aym-*play*-oa) *m* job, employment

emprender (aym-prayn-*dayr*) *v* *undertake

empresa (aym-*pray*-sah) *f* undertaking, enterprise; concern, business

empujar (aym-poo-*khahr*) *v* push; press

empujón (aym-poo-*khoan*) *m* push

en (ayn) *prep* at, in; inside, to

enamorado (ay-nah-moa-*rah*-dhoa) *adj* in love

enamorarse (aynah-moa-*rahr*-say) *v* *fall in love

enano (ay-*nah*-noa) *m* dwarf

encantado (ayng-kahn-*tah*-dhoa) *adj* delighted

encantador (ayng-kahn-tah-*dhoar*) *adj* glamorous; charming, enchanting

encantar (ayng-kahn-*tahr*) *v* delight; bewitch

encanto (ayng-*kahn*-toa) *m* glamour, charm; spell

encarcelamiento (ayng-kahr-thay-lah-mᵛayn-toa) *m* imprisonment

encarcelar (ayng-kahr-thay-*lahr*) *v* imprison

encargarse de (ayng-kahr-*gahr*-say) *take over, *take charge of

encargo (ayng-*kahr*-goa) *m* assignment

encariñado con (ayng-kah-ree-*ñah*-dhoa koan) attached to

encendedor (ayn-thayn-day-*dhoar*) *m* cigarette-lighter

*encender** (ayn-thayn-*dayr*) *v* *light; turn on, switch on

encendido (ayn-thayn-*dee*-dhoa) *m* ignition

*encerrar** (ayn-thay-*rrahr*) *v* *shut in; encircle

encía (ayn-*thee*-ah) *f* gum

enciclopedia (ayn-thee-kloa-*pay*-dhᵛah) *f* encyclopaedia

encima (ayn-*thee*-mah) *adv* above; over; ~ de over, above, on top of

encinta (ayn-*theen*-tah) *adj* pregnant

encogerse (ayng-koa-*khayr*-say) *v* *shrink; no encoge shrinkproof

*encontrar** (ayng-koan-*trahr*) *v* *come across, *find; *encontrarse con *meet, encounter, run into

encorvado (ayng-koar-*bhah*-dhoa) *adj* curved

encrucijada (ayng-kroo-thee-*khah*-dhah) *f* crossing, junction

encuentro (ayng-*kwayn*-troa) *m* meeting, encounter

encuesta (ayng-*kwayss*-tah) *f* inquiry; enquiry

encurtidos (ayng-koor-*tee*-dhoass) *mpl* pickles *pl*

enchufar (ayn-choo-*fahr*) *v* plug in

enchufe (ayn-*choo*-fay) *m* plug

endosar (ayn-doa-*sahr*) *v* endorse

endulzar (ayn-dool-*thahr*) *v* sweeten

enemigo (ay-nay-*mee*-goa) *m* enemy

energía (ay-nayr-*khee*-ah) *f* energy;

power; zest; ~ **nuclear** nuclear energy

enérgico (ay-*nayr*-khee-koa) *adj* energetic

enero (ay-*nay*-roa) January

enfadado (ayn-fah-*dhah*-dhoa) *adj* angry, cross

énfasis (*ayn*-fah-seess) *m* stress

enfatizar (ayn-fah-tee-*thahr*) *v* emphasize

enfermedad (ayn-fayr-may-*dhahdh*) *f* disease; ailment, sickness, illness; ~ **venérea** venereal disease

enfermera (ayn-fayr-*may*-rah) *f* nurse

enfermería (ayn-fayr-may-*ree*-ah) *f* infirmary

enfermizo (ayn-fayr-*mee*-thoa) *adj* unsound

enfermo (ayn-*fayr*-moa) *adj* sick, ill

enfoque (ayn-*foa*-kay) *m* approach

enfrentarse con (ayn-frayn-*tahr*-say) face

enfrente de (ayn-*frayn*-tay day) facing, opposite

engañar (ayng-gah-*ñahr*) *v* cheat, deceive; fool

engaño (ayng-*gah*-ñoa) *m* deceit

engrasar (ayng-grah-*sahr*) *v* grease

enhebrar (ay-nay-*bhrahr*) *v* thread

enigma (ay-*neeg*-mah) *m* mystery, enigma, puzzle

enjuagar (ayng-khwah-*gahr*) *v* rinse

enjuague (ayng-*khwah*-gay) *m* rinse; ~ **bucal** mouthwash

enjugar (ayng-khoo-*gahr*) *v* wipe

enlace (ayn-*lah*-thay) *m* connection, link

enlazar (ayn-lah-*thahr*) *v* link

enmaderado (ayn-mah-dhay-*rah*-dhoa) *m* panelling

enmohecido (ayn-moa-ay-*thee*-dhoa) *adj* mouldy

enojado (ay-noa-*khah*-doa) *adj* angry, cross

enojo (ay-*noa*-khoa) *m* anger

enorme (ay-*noar*-may) *adj* huge, enormous, immense

enrollar (ayn-roa-*lʸahr*) *v* *wind

ensalada (ayn-sah-*lah*-dhah) *f* salad

ensamblar (ayn-sahm-*blahr*) *v* join

ensanchar (ayn-sahn-*chahr*) *v* widen

ensayar (ayn-sah-*ʸahr*) *v* test; rehearse; **ensayarse** *v* practise

ensayo (ayn-*sah*-ʸoa) *m* test; rehearsal; essay

ensenada (ayn-say-*nah*-dhah) *f* inlet, creek

enseñanza (ayn-say-*ñahn*-thah) *f* tuition; teachings *pl*

enseñar (ayn-say-*ñahr*) *v* *teach; *show

ensueño (ayn-*sway*-ñoa) *m* day-dream

entallar (ayn-tah-*lʸahr*) *v* carve

*entender** (ayn-tayn-*dayr*) *v* conceive; *take

entendimiento (ayn-tayn-dee-*mʸayn*-toa) *m* insight; conception

enteramente (ayn-tay-rah-*mayn*-tay) *adv* completely, entirely, quite

enterar (ayn-tay-*rahr*) *v* inform

entero (ayn-*tay*-roa) *adj* whole, entire

*enterrar** (ayn-tay-*rrahr*) *v* bury

entierro (ayn-*tʸay*-rroa) *m* burial

entonces (ayn-*toan*-thayss) *adv* then; **de** ~ contemporary

entrada (ayn-*trah*-dhah) *f* entry, entrance, way in; admission; appearance; entrance-fee; **prohibida la** ~ no admittance

entrañas (ayn-*trah*-ñahss) *fpl* insides

entrar (ayn-*trahr*) *v* *go in, enter

entre (*ayn*-tray) *prep* among, amid; between

entreacto (ayn-tray-*ahk*-toa) *m* intermission

entrega (ayn-*tray*-gah) *f* delivery

entregar (ayn-tray-*gahr*) *v* *give; deliver; commit; extradite

entremeses (ayn-tray-*may*-sayss) *mpl* hors-d'œuvre

entrenador (ayn-tray-nah-*dhoar*) *m* coach

entrenamiento (ayn-tray-nah-*m*ʸayn-toa) *m* training

entrenar (ayn-tray-*nahr*) *v* train, drill

entresuelo (ayn-tray-*sway*-loa) *m* mezzanine

entretanto (ayn-tray-*tahn*-toa) *adv* meanwhile, in the meantime

* **entretener** (ayn-tray-tay-*nayr*) *v* amuse, entertain

entretenido (ayn-tray-tay-*nee*-dhoa) *adj* entertaining

entretenimiento (ayn-tray-tay-nee-mʸayn-toa) *m* amusement, entertainment

entrevista (ayn-tray-*bheess*-tah) *f* interview

entumecido (ayn-too-may-*thee*-dhoa) *adj* numb

entusiasmo (ayn-too-sʸahz-moa) *m* enthusiasm

entusiasta (ayn-too-sʸahss-tah) *adj* enthusiastic, keen

envenenar (aym-bay-nay-*nahr*) *v* poison

enviado (aym-bʸah-dhoa) *m* envoy

enviar (aym-bʸahr) *v* dispatch, *send

envidia (aym-bee-dhʸah) *f* envy

envidiar (aym-bee-*dhʸahr*) *v* grudge, envy

envidioso (aym-bee-dhʸoa-soa) *adj* envious

envío (aym-*bee*-oa) *m* expedition, consignment

* **envolver** (aym-boal-*bhayr*) *v* wrap; involve

épico (*ay*-pee-koa) *adj* epic

epidemia (ay-pee-*dhay*-mʸah) *f* epidemic

epilepsia (ay-pee-*layp*-sʸah) *f* epilepsy

epílogo (ay-*pee*-loa-goa) *m* epilogue

episodio (ay-pee-*soa*-dheeoa) *m* episode

época (*ay*-poa-kah) *f* period

equilibrio (ay-kee-*lee*-bhrʸoa) *m* balance

equipaje (ay-kee-*pah*-khay) *m* baggage, luggage; ~ **de mano** hand luggage; hand baggage *Am*; **furgón de equipajes** luggage van

equipar (ay-kee-*pahr*) *v* equip

equipo (ay-*kee*-poa) *m* outfit, equipment; gang; team; crew; soccer team

equitación (ay-kee-tah-*thʸoan*) *f* riding

equivalente (ay-kee-bhah-*layn*-tay) *adj* equivalent

equivocación (ay-kee-bhoa-kah-*thʸoan*) *f* misunderstanding, mistake

equivocado (ay-kee-bhoa-*kah*-dhoa) *adj* mistaken

equivocarse (ay-kee-bhoa-*kahr*-say) *v* *be mistaken

equívoco (ay-*kee*-bhoa-koa) *adj* ambiguous

era (*ay*-rah) *f* era

erguido (ayr-*gee*-dhoa) *adj* erect

erigir (ay-ree-*kheer*) *v* erect

erizo (ay-*ree*-thoa) *m* hedgehog; ~ **de mar** sea-urchin

* **errar** (ay-*rrahr*) *v* err; wander

erróneo (ay-*rroa*-nay-oa) *adj* wrong

error (ay-*rroar*) *m* mistake, error

erudito (ay-roo-*dhee*-toa) *m* scholar

esbelto (ayz-*bhayl*-toa) *adj* slim, slender

escala (ayss-*kah*-lah) *f* scale; ~ **de incendios** fire-escape; ~ **musical** scale

escalar (ayss-kah-*lahr*) *v* ascend

escalera (ayss-kah-*lay*-rah) *f* stairs *pl*, staircase; ~ **de mano** ladder; ~ **móvil** escalator

escalofrío (ayss-kah-loa-*free*-oa) *m* chill, shiver

escama (ayss-*kah*-mah) *f* scale

escándalo (ayss-*kahn*-dah-loa) *m* scandal; offence

Escandinavia (ayss-kahn-dee-*nah*-bhYah) *f* Scandinavia

escandinavo (ayss-kahn-dee-*nah*-bhoa) *adj* Scandinavian; *m* Scandinavian

escapar (ayss-kah-*pahr*) *v* escape

escaparate (ayss-kah-pah-*rah*-tay) *m* shop-window

escape (ayss-*kah*-pay) *m* exhaust; **gases de** ~ exhaust gases

escaque (ayss-*kah*-kay) *m* check

escarabajo (ayss-kah-rah-*bhah*-khoa) *m* beetle, bug

escarcha (ayss-*kahr*-chah) *f* frost

escarcho (ayss-*kahr*-choa) *m* roach

escarlata (ayss-kahr-*lah*-tah) *adj* scarlet

escarnio (ayss-*kahr*-nYoa) *m* scorn

escasez (ayss-kah-*sayth*) *f* scarcity, shortage

escaso (ayss-*kah*-soa) *adj* scarce; minor

escena (ay-*thay*-nah) *f* scene; setting

escenario (ayss-thay-*nah*-rYoa) *m* stage

esclavo (ayss-*klah*-bhoa) *m* slave

esclusa (ayss-*kloo*-sah) *f* lock

escoba (ayss-*koa*-bhah) *f* broom

escocés (ayss-koa-*thayss*) *adj* Scottish, Scotch; *m* Scot

Escocia (ayss-*koa*-thYah) *f* Scotland

escoger (ayss-koa-*khayr*) *v* *choose, pick

escolta (ayss-*koal*-tah) *f* escort

escoltar (ayss-koal-*tahr*) *v* escort

escombro (ayss-*koam*-broa) *m* mackerel

esconder (ayss-koan-*dayr*) *v* *hide

escribano (ayss-kree-*bhah*-noa) *m* clerk

escribir (ayss-kree-*bheer*) *v* *write; ~ **a máquina** type; **papel de** ~ notepaper; **por escrito** written, in writ-

ing

escrito (ayss-*kree*-toa) *m* writing

escritor (ayss-kree-*toar*) *m* writer

escritorio (ayss-kree-*toa*-rYoa) *m* desk, bureau

escritura (ayss-kree-*too*-rah) *f* handwriting

escrupuloso (ayss-kroo-poo-*loa*-soa) *adj* careful

escuadrilla (ayss-kwah-*dhree*-lYah) *f* squadron

escuchar (ayss-koo-*chahr*) *v* listen; eavesdrop

escuela (ayss-*kway*-lah) *f* school; **director de** ~ head teacher, headmaster; ~ **secundaria** secondary school

escultor (ayss-kool-*toar*) *m* sculptor

escultura (ayss-kool-*too*-rah) *f* sculpture

escupir (ayss-koo-*peer*) *v* *spit

escurridor (ayss-koo-rree-*dhoar*) *m* strainer

ese (*ay*-say) *adj* that; **ése** *pron* that

esencia (ay-*sayn*-thYah) *f* essence

esencial (ay-sayn-*thYahl*) *adj* essential; vital

esfera (ayss-*fay*-rah) *f* sphere; atmosphere

*esforzarse (ayss-foar-*thahr*-say) *v* try, bother

esfuerzo (ayss-*fwayr*-thoa) *m* effort; strain; stress

esgrimir (ayss-gree-*meer*) *v* fence

eslabón (ayz-lah-*bhoan*) *m* link

esmaltado (ayz-mahl-*tah*-dhoa) *adj* enamelled

esmaltar (ayz-mahl-*tahr*) *v* glaze

esmalte (ayz-*mahl*-tay) *m* enamel

esmeralda (ayz-may-*rahl*-dah) *f* emerald

esnórquel (ayz-*noar*-kayl) *m* snorkel

eso (*ay*-soa) *pron* that

espaciar (ayss-pah-*thYahr*) *v* space

espacio (ayss-*pah*-thYoa) *m* room;

space

espacioso (ayss-pah-*th*ʸ*oa*-soa) *adj* spacious, roomy, large

espada (ayss-*pah*-dhah) *f* sword

espalda (ayss-*pahl*-dah) *f* back; **dolor de ~** backache

espantado (ayss-pahn-*tah*-dhoa) *adj* frightened

espantar (ayss-pahn-*tahr*) *v* frighten

espanto (ayss-*pahn*-toa) *m* fright; horror

espantoso (ayss-pahn-*toa*-soa) *adj* dreadful

España (ayss-*pah*-ñah) *f* Spain

español (ayss-pah-*ñoal*) *adj* Spanish; *m* Spaniard

esparadrapo (ayss-pah-rah-*dhrah*-poa) *m* adhesive tape, plaster

esparcir (ayss-pahr-*theer*) *v* scatter, *shed

espárrago (ayss-*pah*-rrah-goa) *m* asparagus

especia (ayss-*pay*-th ʸah) *f* spice

especial (ayss-pay-*th*ʸ*ahl*) *adj* special; peculiar, particular

especialidad (ayss-pay-th ʸah-lee-*dhahdh*) *f* speciality

especialista (ayss-pay-th ʸah-*leess*-tah) *m* specialist

especializarse (ayss-pay-th ʸah-lee-*thahr*-say) *v* specialize; **especializado** skilled

especialmente (ayss-pay-th ʸahl-*mayn*-tay) *adv* especially

especie (ayss-*payth*ʸ*ay*) *f* species, breed

específico (ayss-pay-*thee*-fee-koa) *adj* specific

espécimen (ayss-*pay*-thee-mayn) *m* specimen

espectáculo (ayss-payk-*tah*-koo-loa) *m* spectacle, show; **~ de variedades** floor show

espectador (ayss-payk-tah-*dhoar*) *m* spectator

espectro (ayss-*payk*-troa) *m* ghost; spectrum

especular (ayss-pay-koo-*lahr*) *v* speculate

espejo (ayss-*pay*-khoa) *m* mirror, looking-glass

espeluznante (ayss-pay-looth-*nahn*-tay) *adj* creepy

espera (ayss-*pay*-rah) *f* waiting

esperanza (ayss-pay-*rahn*-thah) *f* hope; expectation

esperanzado (ayss-pay-rahn-*thah*-dhoa) *adj* hopeful

esperar (ayss-pay-*rahr*) *v* hope; wait; expect, await

espesar (ayss-pay-*sahr*) *v* thicken

espeso (ayss-*pay*-soa) *adj* thick

espesor (ayss-pay-*soar*) *m* thickness

espetón (ayss-pay-*toan*) *m* spit

espía (ayss-*pee*-ah) *m* spy

espiar (ayss-*p*ʸ*ahr*) *v* peep

espina (ayss-*pee*-nah) *f* thorn; fishbone; **~ dorsal** backbone

espinacas (ayss-pee-*nah*-kahss) *fpl* spinach

espinazo (ayss-pee-*nah*-thoa) *m* spine

espirar (ayss-pee-*rahr*) *v* expire

espíritu (ayss-*pee*-ree-too) *m* spirit; ghost

espiritual (ayss-pee-ree-*twahl*) *adj* spiritual

espléndido (ayss-*playn*-dee-dhoa) *adj* splendid; glorious, enchanting, magnificent

esplendor (ayss-playn-*doar*) *m* splendour

esponja (ayss-*poang*-khah) *f* sponge

esposa (ayss-*poa*-sah) *f* wife; **esposas** *fpl* handcuffs *pl*

esposo (ayss-*poa*-soa) *m* husband

espuma (ayss-*poo*-mah) *f* froth, foam, lather

espumante (ayss-poo-*mahn*-tay) *adj*

sparkling
espumar (ayss-poo-*mahr*) *v* foam
esputo (ayss-*poo*-toa) *m* spit
esquela (ayss-*kay*-lah) *f* note
esqueleto (ayss-kay-*lay*-toa) *m* skeleton
esquema (ayss-*kay*-mah) *m* diagram; scheme
esquí (ayss-*kee*) *m* ski; skiing; ~ **acuático** water ski; **salto de** ~ skijump
esquiador (ayss-k^yah-*dhoar*) *m* skier
esquiar (ayss-k^y*ahr*) *v* ski
esquina (ayss-*kee*-nah) *f* corner
esquivo (ayss-*kee*-bhoa) *adj* shy
estable (ayss-*tah*-bhlay) *adj* permanent, stable
***establecer** (ayss-tah-bhlay-*thayr*) *v* establish
establo (ayss-*tah*-bhloa) *m* stable
estación (ayss-tah-*th*^y*oan*) *f* season; station; depot *nAm*; ~ **central** central station; ~ **de servicio** filling station; ~ **terminal** terminal
estacionamiento (ayss-tah-th^yoa-nah-m^yayn-toa) *m* parking lot *Am*; **derechos de** ~ parking fee
estacionar (ayss-tah-th^yoa-*nahr*) *v* park; **prohibido estacionarse** no parking
estacionario (ayss-tah-th^yoa-*nah*-r^yoa) *adj* stationary
estadio (ayss-*tah*-dh^yoa) *m* stadium
estadista (ayss-tah-*dheess*-tah) *m* statesman
estadística (ayss-tah-*dheess*-tee-kah) *f* statistics *pl*
Estado (ayss-*tah*-doa) *m* state
estado (ayss-*tah*-dhoa) *m* state, condition
Estados Unidos (ayss-*tah*-dhoass oo-*nee*-dhoass) the States, United States
estafa (ayss-*tah*-fah) *f* swindle
estafador (ayss-tah-fah-*dhoar*) *m* swindler

estafar (ayss-tah-*fahr*) *v* cheat, swindle
estallar (ayss-tah-*l*^y*ahr*) *v* explode
estambre (ayss-*tahm*-bray) *m/f* worsted
estampa (ayss-*tahm*-pah) *f* engraving
estampilla (ayss-tahm-*pee*-l^yah) *fMe* stamp
estancia (ayss-*tahn*-th^yah) *f* stay
estanco (ayss-*tahng*-koa) *m* cigar shop, tobacconist's
estanque (ayss-*tahng*-kay) *m* pond
estanquero (ayss-tahng-*kay*-roa) *m* tobacconist
estante (ayss-*tahn*-tay) *m* shelf
estaño (ayss-*tah*-ñoa) *m* tin; pewter
***estar** (ayss-*tahr*) *v* *be
estatua (ayss-*tah*-twah) *f* statue
estatura (ayss-tah-*too*-rah) *f* figure
este[1] (*ayss*-tay) *m* east
este[2] (*ayss*-tay) *adj* this; **éste** *pron* this
estera (ayss-*tay*-rah) *f* mat
estercolero (ayss-tayr-koa-*lay*-roa) *m* dunghill
estéril (ayss-*tay*-reel) *adj* sterile
esterilizar (ayss-tay-ree-lee-*thahr*) *v* sterilize
estético (ayss-*tay*-tee-koa) *adj* aesthetic
estilo (ayss-*tee*-loa) *m* style
estilográfica (ayss-tee-loa-*grah*-fee-kah) *f* fountain-pen
estima (ayss-*tee*-mah) *f* esteem
estimación (ayss-tee-mah-*th*^y*oan*) *f* respect; estimate
estimar (ayss-tee-*mahr*) *v* esteem; estimate
estimulante (ayss-tee-moo-*lahn*-tay) *m* stimulant
estimular (ayss-tee-moo-*lahr*) *v* stimulate; urge
estímulo (ayss-*tee*-moo-loa) *m* impulse
estipulación (ayss-tee-poo-lah-*th*^y*oan*)

f stipulation

estipular (ayss-tee-poo-*lahr*) *v* stipulate

estirar (ayss-tee-*rahr*) *v* stretch

estirón (ayss-tee-*roan*) *m* tug

esto (*ayss*-toa) *adj* this

estola (ayss-*toa*-lah) *f* stole

estómago (ayss-*toa*-mah-goa) *m* stomach; **dolor de ~** stomach-ache

estorbar (ayss-toar-*bhahr*) *v* disturb, embarrass

estornino (ayss-toar-*nee*-noa) *m* starling

estornudar (ayss-toar-noo-*dhahr*) *v* sneeze

estrangular (ayss-trahng-goo-*lahr*) *v* choke, strangle

estrato (ayss-*trah*-toa) *m* layer

estrechar (ayss-tray-*chahr*) *v* tighten

estrecho (ayss-*tray*-choa) *adj* narrow; tight

estrella (ayss-*tray*-l^yah) *f* star

estremecido (ayss-tray-may-*thee*-dhoa) *adj* shivery

estremecimiento (ayss-tray-may-thee-m^y*ayn*-toa) *m* shudder

estreñido (ayss-tray-*ñee*-dhoa) *adj* constipated

estreñimiento (ayss-tray-ñee-m^y*ayn*-toa) *m* constipation

estribo (ayss-*tree*-bhoa) *m* stirrup

estribor (ayss-tree-*bhoar*) *m* starboard

estricto (ayss-*treek*-toa) *adj* strict

estrofa (ayss-*troa*-fah) *f* stanza

estropeado (ayss-troa-pay-*ah*-dhoa) *adj* broken; crippled

estropear (ayss-troa-pay-*ahr*) *v* mess up

estructura (ayss-trook-*too*-rah) *f* structure; fabric

estuario (ayss-*twah*-r^yoa) *m* estuary

estuco (ayss-*too*-koa) *m* plaster

estuche (ayss-*too*-chay) *m* case

estudiante (ayss-too-dh^y*ahn*-tay) *m* student

estudiar (ayss-too-dh^y*ahr*) *v* study

estudio (ayss-*too*-dh^yoa) *m* study

estufa (ayss-*too*-fah) *f* stove; **~ de gas** gas stove

estupefaciente (ayss-too-pay-fah-th^y*ayn*-tay) *m* drug

estupendo (ayss-too-*payn*-doa) *adj* wonderful

estúpido (ayss-*too*-pee-dhoa) *adj* stupid; dumb

etapa (ay-*tah*-pah) *f* stage

etcétera (ayt-*thay*-tay-rah) and so on, etcetera

éter (*ay*-tayr) *m* ether

eternidad (ay-tayr-nee-*dhahdh*) *f* eternity

eterno (ay-*tayr*-noa) *adj* eternal

etíope (ay-*tee*-oa-pay) *adj* Ethiopian; *m* Ethiopian

Etiopía (ay-t^yoa-p^yah) *f* Ethiopia

etiqueta (ay-tee-*kay*-tah) *f* tag

Europa (ay^{oo}-*roa*-pah) *f* Europe

europeo (ay^{oo}-roa-*pay*-oa) *adj* European; *m* European

evacuar (ay-bhah-*kwahr*) *v* evacuate

evaluar (ay-bhah-*lwahr*) *v* evaluate, estimate

evangelio (ay-bhahng-*khay*-l^yoa) *m* gospel

evaporar (ay-bhah-poa-*rahr*) *v* evaporate

evasión (ay-bhah-*s^yoan*) *f* escape

eventual (ay-bhayn-*twahl*) *adj* eventual; possible

evidente (ay-bhee-*dhayn*-tay) *adj* evident; self-evident

evidentemente (ay-bhee-dhayn-tay-*mayn*-tay) *adv* apparently

evitar (ay-bhee-*tahr*) *v* avoid

evolución (ay-bhoa-loo-*th^yoan*) *f* evolution

exactamente (ayk-sahk-tah-*mayn*-tay) *adv* exactly

exactitud (ayk-sahk-tee-*toodh*) *f* correctness

exacto (ayk-*sahk*-toa) *adj* precise, exact, accurate

exagerar (ayk-sah-khay-*rahr*) *v* exaggerate

examen (ayk-*sah*-mayn) *m* examination

examinar (ayk-sah-mee-*nahr*) *v* examine

excavación (ayks-kah-bhah-*th^yoan*) *f* excavation

exceder (ayk-thay-*dhayr*) *v* exceed

excelencia (ayk-thay-*layn*-th^yah) *f* excellence

excelente (ayk-thay-*layn*-tay) *adj* excellent, fine

excéntrico (ayk-*thayn*-tree-koa) *adj* eccentric

excepción (ayk-thayp-*th^yoan*) *f* exception

excepcional (ayk-thayp-th^yoa-*nahl*) *adj* exceptional

excepto (ayk-*thayp*-toa) *prep* except

excesivo (ayk-thay-*see*-bhoa) *adj* excessive

exceso (ayk-*thay*-soa) *m* excess; ~ **de velocidad** speeding

excitación (ayk-thee-tah-*th^yoan*) *f* excitement

excitante (ayk-thee-*tahn*-tay) *adj* exciting

excitar (ayk-thee-*tahr*) *v* excite

exclamación (ayks-klah-mah-*th^yoan*) *f* exclamation

exclamar (ayks-klah-*mahr*) *v* exclaim

***excluir** (ayks-*klweer*) *v* exclude

exclusivamente (ayks-kloo-see-bhah-*mayn*-tay) *adv* exclusively, solely

exclusivo (ayks-kloo-*see*-bhoa) *adj* exclusive

excursión (ayks-koor-*s^yoan*) *f* trip, excursion

excusa (ayks-*koo*-sah) *f* apology, excuse

excusar (ayks-koo-*sahr*) *v* excuse

exención (ayk-sayn-*th^yoan*) *f* exemption

exento (ayk-*sayn*-toa) *adj* exempt; ~ **de impuestos** duty-free

exhalar (ayk-sah-*lahr*) *v* exhale

exhausto (ayk-*souss*-toa) *adj* overtired

exhibir (ayk-see-*bheer*) *v* exhibit, display

exigencia (ayk-see-*khayn*-th^yah) *f* demand

exigente (ayk-see-*khayn*-tay) *adj* particular

exigir (ayk-see-*kheer*) *v* demand

exiliado (ayk-see-*l^yah*-dhoa) *m* exile

exilio (ayk-*see*-l^yoa) *m* exile

eximir (ayk-see-*meer*) *v* exempt

existencia (ayk-seess-*tayn*-th^yah) *f* existence; **existencias** *fpl* supply, stock; ***tener en** ~ stock

existir (ayk-seess-*teer*) *v* exist

éxito (*ayk*-see-toa) *m* success, luck; hit; **de** ~ successful; ***tener** ~ manage, succeed

exorbitante (ayk-soar-bhee-*tahn*-tay) *adj* prohibitive

exótico (ayk-*soa*-tee-koa) *adj* exotic

expansión (ayks-pahn-*s^yoan*) *f* expansion

expedición (ayks-pay-dhee-*th^yoan*) *f* expedition

expediente (ayks-pay-*dh^yayn*-tay) *m* file

experiencia (ayks-pay-*r^yayn*-th^yah) *f* experience

experimentar (ayks-pay-ree-mayn-*tahr*) *v* experiment; experience; **experimentado** experienced

experimento (ayks-pay-ree-*mayn*-toa) *m* experiment

experto (ayks-*payr*-toa) *m* expert

expirar (ayks-pee-*rahr*) *v* expire

explanada (ayks-plah-*nah*-dhah) f esplanade

explicable (ayks-plee-*kah*-bhlay) adj accountable

explicación (ayks-plee-kah-*th*ʸoan) f explanation

explicar (ayks-plee-*kahr*) v explain; account for

explícito (ayks-*plee*-thee-toa) adj express, explicit

explorador (ayks-ploa-rah-*dhoar*) m scout, boy scout

exploradora (ayks-ploa-rah-*dhoa*-rah) f girl guide

explorar (ayks-ploa-*rahr*) v explore

explosión (ayks-ploa-s*ʸ*oan) f explosion, blast; outbreak

explosivo (ayks-ploa-*see*-bhoa) adj explosive; m explosive

explotar (ayks-ploa-*tahr*) v exploit

*exponer (ayks-poa-*nayr*) v exhibit

exportación (ayks-poar-tah-*th*ʸoan) f exportation, export

exportar (ayks-poar-*tahr*) v export

exposición (ayks-poa-see-*th*ʸoan) f exposition, exhibition, display, show; exposure; ~ **de arte** art exhibition

exposímetro (ayks-poa-*see*-may-troa) m exposure meter

expresar (ayks-pray-*sahr*) v express

expresión (ayks-pray-s*ʸ*oan) f expression

expresivo (ayks-pray-*see*-bhoa) adj expressive

expreso (ayks-*pray*-soa) adj explicit; express; **por** ~ special delivery

expulsar (ayks-pool-*sahr*) v chase; expel

exquisito (ayks-kee-*see*-toa) adj exquisite; delicious

éxtasis (*ayks*-tah-seess) m ecstasy

*extender (ayks-tayn-*dayr*) v *spread, expand

extenso (ayks-*tayn*-soa) adj compre-

hensive, extensive

extenuar (ayks-tay-*nwahr*) v exhaust

exterior (ayks-tay-r*ʸ*oar) adj external, exterior; m exterior, outside

externo (ayks-*tayr*-noa) adj outward

extinguir (ayks-teeng-*geer*) v extinguish

extintor (ayks-teen-*toar*) m fire-extinguisher

extorsión (ayks-toar-s*ʸ*oan) f extortion

extorsionar (ayks-toar-s*ʸ*oa-*nahr*) v extort

extra (*ayks*-trah) adj extra

extracto (ayks-*trahk*-toa) m excerpt

*extraer (ayks-trah-*ayr*) v extract

extranjero (ayks-trahng-*khay*-roa) adj alien, foreign; m alien, foreigner; stranger; **en el** ~ abroad

extrañar (ayks-trah-*ñahr*) v amaze, surprise; banish

extraño (ayks-*trah*-ñoa) adj foreign, strange; peculiar, queer, funny

extraoficial (ayks-trah-oa-fee-*th*ʸahl) adj unofficial

extraordinario (ayks-trah-oar-dhee-*nah*-rʸoa) adj extraordinary, exceptional

extravagante (ayks-trah-bhah-*gahn*-tay) adj extravagant

extraviar (ayks-trah-*bh*ʸahr) v *mislay

extremo (ayks-*tray*-moa) adj extreme; very, utmost; m extreme; end

exuberante (ayk-soo-bhay-*rahn*-tay) adj exuberant

F

fábrica (*fah*-bhree-kah) f factory; works pl, mill; ~ **de gas** gasworks

fabricante (fah-bhree-*kahn*-tay) m manufacturer

fabricar (fah-bhree-*kahr*) v manufacture

fábula (*fah*-bhoo-lah) f fable

fácil (*fah*-theel) adj easy

facilidad (fah-thee-lee-*dhahdh*) f ease; facility

facilitar (fah-thee-lee-*tahr*) v facilitate

factible (fahk-*tee*-bhlay) adj attainable

factor (fahk-*toar*) m factor

factura (fahk-*too*-rah) f invoice

facturar (fahk-too-*rahr*) v bill

facultad (fah-kool-*tahdh*) f faculty

fachada (fah-*chah*-dhah) f façade

faisán (figh-*sahn*) m pheasant

faja (*fah*-khah) f strip; girdle

falda (*fahl*-dah) f skirt

faldón (fahl-*doan*) m gable

falsificación (fahl-see-fee-kah-*th*ʸ*oan*) f fake

falsificar (fahl-see-fee-*kahr*) v forge, counterfeit

falso (*fahl*-soa) adj false; untrue

falta (*fahl*-tah) f error; want, lack; offence; **sin ~** without fail

faltar (fahl-*tahr*) v fail

fallar (fah-*l*ʸ*ahr*) v fail

*****fallecer** (fah-l*ʸ*ay-*thayr*) v depart

fama (*fah*-mah) f fame; **de ~ mundial** world-famous; **de mala ~** notorious

familia (fah-*mee*-l*ʸ*ah) f family

familiar (fah-mee-*l*ʸ*ahr*) adj familiar

famoso (fah-*moa*-soa) adj famous

fanal (fah-*nahl*) m headlamp

fanático (fah-*nah*-tee-koa) adj fanatical

fantasía (fahn-tah-*see*-ah) f fantasy

fantasma (fahn-*tahz*-mah) m spook, phantom, ghost

fantástico (fahn-*tahss*-tee-koa) adj fantastic

farallón (fah-rah-*l*ʸ*oan*) m cliff

fardo (*fahr*-dhoa) m load

farmacéutico (fahr-mah-*thay*ᵒᵒ-tee-koa) m chemist

farmacia (fahr-*mah*-th*ʸ*ah) f chemist's,

pharmacy; drugstore *nAm*

farmacología (fahr-mah-koa-loa-*khee*-ah) f pharmacology

faro (*fah*-roa) m headlight; lighthouse

farol trasero (fah-*roal* trah-*say*-roa) tail-light

farsa (*fahr*-sah) f farce

fascismo (fah-*theez*-moa) m fascism

fascista (fah-*theess*-tah) adj fascist; m fascist

fase (*fah*-say) f stage, phase

fastidiar (fahss-tee-*dh*ʸ*ahr*) v annoy, bother

fastidioso (fahss-tee-*dh*ʸ*oa*-soa) adj difficult

fatal (fah-*tahl*) adj fatal; mortal

favor (fah-*bhoar*) m favour; **a ~ de** on behalf of; **por ~** please

favorable (fah-bhoa-*rah*-bhlay) adj favourable

*****favorecer** (fah-bhoa-ray-*thayr*) v favour

favorecido (fah-bhoa-ray-*thee*-dhoa) m payee

favorito (fah-bhoa-*ree*-toa) adj pet; m favourite

fe (fay) f faith

febrero (fay-*bhray*-roa) February

febril (fay-*bhreel*) adj feverish

fecundo (fay-*koon*-doa) adj fertile

fecha (*fay*-chah) f date

federación (fay-dhay-rah-*th*ʸ*oan*) f federation

federal (fay-dhay-*rahl*) adj federal

felicidad (fay-lee-thee-*dhahdh*) f happiness

felicitación (fay-lee-thee-tah-*th*ʸ*oan*) f congratulation

felicitar (fay-lee-thee-*tahr*) v congratulate

feliz (fay-*leeth*) adj happy

femenino (fay-may-*nee*-noa) adj feminine; female

fenómeno (fay-*noa*-may-noa) m phenomenon

feo (fay-oa) adj ugly

feria (fay-rˠah) f fair

fermentar (fayr-mayn-tahr) v ferment

feroz (fay-roath) adj wild

ferretería (fay-rray-tay-ree-ah) f hardware store

ferrocarril (fay-rroa-kah-rreel) m railway; railroad nAm

fértil (fayr-teel) adj fertile

fertilidad (fayr-tee-lee-dhahdh) f fertility

festival (fayss-tee-bhahl) m festival

festivo (fayss-tee-bhoa) adj festive

feudal (fayᵒᵒ-dhahl) adj feudal

fiable (fˠah-bhlay) adj reliable

fianza (fˠahn-thah) f security; bail; deposit

fiasco (fˠahss-koa) m failure

fibra (fee-bhrah) f fibre

ficción (feek-thˠoan) f fiction

ficha (fee-chah) f chip, token

fiebre (fˠay-bhray) f fever; ~ **del heno** hay fever

fiel (fˠayl) adj faithful, true

fieltro (fˠayl-troa) m felt

fiero (fˠay-roa) adj fierce

fiesta (fˠayss-tah) f feast; party; holiday

figura (fee-goo-rah) f figure

figurarse (fee-goo-rahr-say) v imagine

fijador (fee-khah-dhoar) m setting lotion

fijar (fee-khahr) v attach; **fijarse en** mind

fijo (fee-khoa) adj fixed; permanent

fila (fee-lah) f row, rank

Filipinas (fee-lee-pee-nahss) fpl Philippines pl

filipino (fee-lee-pee-noa) adj Philippine; m Filipino

filmar (feel-mahr) v film

filme (feel-may) m movie

filosofía (fee-loa-soa-fee-ah) f philosophy

filosófico (fee-loa-soa-fee-koa) adj philosophical

filósofo (fee-loa-soa-foa) m philosopher

filtrar (feel-trahr) v strain

filtro (feel-troa) m filter; ~ **de aire** air-filter; ~ **del aceite** oil filter

fin (feen) m end; aim, purpose; **a** ~ **de** so that; **al** ~ at last

final (fee-nahl) adj eventual, final; m end; **al** ~ at last

financiar (fee-nahn-thˠahr) v finance

financiero (fee-nahn-thˠay-roa) adj financial

finanzas (fee-nahn-thahss) fpl finances pl

finca (feeng-kah) f premises pl

fingir (feeng-kheer) v pretend

finlandés (feen-lahn-dayss) adj Finnish; m Finn

Finlandia (feen-lahn-dˠah) f Finland

fino (fee-noa) adj delicate, fine; sheer

firma (feer-mah) f signature; firm

firmar (feer-mahr) v sign

firme (feer-may) adj steady, firm; secure

física (fee-see-kah) f physics

físico (fee-see-koa) adj physical; m physicist

fisiología (fee-sˠoa-loa-khee-ah) f physiology

flaco (flah-koa) adj thin

flamenco (flah-mayng-koa) m flamingo

flauta (flou-tah) f flute

flecha (flay-chah) f arrow

flexible (flayk-see-bhlay) adj flexible; supple, elastic

flojel (floa-khayl) m down

flojo (floa-khoa) adj weak

flor (floar) f flower

florista (floa-reess-tah) m florist

floristería (floa-reess-tay-ree-ah) f

flower-shop

flota (floa-tah) f fleet

flotador (floa-tah-dhoar) m float

flotar (floa-tahr) v float

fluido (floo-ee-dhoa) adj fluid; m fluid

fluir (flweer) v flow, stream

foca (foa-kah) f seal

foco (foa-koa) m focus; mMe light bulb

folklore (foal-kloa-ray) m folklore

folleto (foa-lᵞay-toa) m brochure

fondo (foan-doa) m background; ground, bottom; mMe slip; **fondos** mpl fund

fonético (foa-nay-tee-koa) adj phonetic

foque (foa-kay) m foresail

forastero (foa-rahss-tay-roa) m foreigner; stranger

forma (foar-mah) f form, shape

formación (foar-mah-thᵞoan) f formation

formal (foar-mahl) adj formal

formalidad (foar-mah-lee-dhahdh) f formality

formar (foar-mahr) v form, shape; educate

formato (foar-mah-toa) m size

formidable (foar-mee-dhah-bhlay) adj huge

fórmula (foar-moo-lah) f formula

formulario (foar-moo-lah-rᵞoa) m form; ~ **de matriculación** registration form

forro (foa-rroa) m lining

fortaleza (foar-tah-lay-thah) f fortress, fort

fortuna (foar-too-nah) f fortune

forúnculo (foa-roong-koo-loa) m boil

forzar (foar-thahr) v force; strain

forzosamente (foar-thoa-sah-mayn-tay) adv by force

foso (foa-soa) m moat

foto (foa-toa) f photo

fotocopia (foa-toa-koa-pᵞah) f photostat

fotografía (foa-toa-grah-fee-ah) f photograph; photography; ~ **de pasaporte** passport photograph

fotografiar (foa-toa-grah-fᵞahr) v photograph

fotógrafo (foa-toa-grah-foa) m photographer

fracasado (frah-kah-sah-dhoa) adj unsuccessful

fracaso (frah-kah-soa) m failure

fracción (frahk-thᵞoan) f fraction

fractura (frahk-too-rah) f fracture, break

fracturar (frahk-too-rahr) v fracture

frágil (frah-kheel) adj fragile

fragmento (frahg-mayn-toa) m fragment, piece; extract

frambuesa (frahm-bway-sah) f raspberry

francés (frahn-thayss) adj French; m Frenchman

Francia (frahn-thᵞah) f France

franco (frahng-koa) adj postage paid, post-paid

francotirador (frahng-koa-tee-rah-dhoar) m sniper

franela (frah-nay-lah) f flannel

franja (frahng-khah) f fringe

franqueo (frahng-kay-oa) m postage

frasco (frahss-koa) m flask

frase (frah-say) f sentence; phrase

fraternidad (frah-tayr-nee-dhahdh) f fraternity

fraude (frou-dhay) m fraud

frecuencia (fray-kwayn-thᵞah) f frequency

frecuentar (fray-kwayn-tahr) v associate with

frecuente (fray-kwayn-tay) adj frequent

frecuentemente (fray-kwayn-tay-mayn-tay) adv frequently, often

*fregar (fray-*gahr*) v wash up; scrub
*freír (fray-*eer*) f fry
frenar (fray-*nahr*) v slow down
freno (*fray*-noa) m brake; ~ **de mano** hand-brake; ~ **de pie** foot-brake
frente (*frayn*-tay) f forehead; m front
fresa (*fray*-sah) f strawberry
fresco (*frayss*-koa) adj fresh; chilly, cool
fricción (freek-*th^yoan*) f friction
frigorífico (free-goa-*ree*-fee-koa) m fridge
frío (*free*-oa) adj cold; m cold
frontera (froan-*tay*-rah) f frontier, border; boundary, bound
frotar (froa-*tahr*) v rub
fruta (*froo*-tah) f fruit
fruto (*froo*-toa) m fruit
fuego (*fway*-goa) m fire
fuente (*fwayn*-tay) f source, fountain; dish
fuera (*fway*-rah) adv out; off, away; ~ **de** outside, out of; ~ **de lugar** misplaced; ~ **de temporada** off season
fuerte (*fwayr*-tay) adj powerful, strong; mighty; loud
fuerza (*fwayr*-thah) f force; power, might, energy; strength; ~ **de voluntad** will-power; ~ **motriz** driving force; **fuerzas armadas** military force, armed forces
fugitivo (foo-khee-*tee*-bhoa) m runaway
fumador (foo-mah-*dhoar*) m smoker; **compartimento para fumadores** smoker
fumar (foo-*mahr*) v smoke; **prohibido** ~ no smoking
función (foon-*th^yoan*) f function
funcionamiento (foon-th^yoa-nah-*m^yayn*-toa) m working, operation
funcionar (foon-th^yoa-*nahr*) v work, operate

funcionario (foon-th^yoa-nah-*r^yoa*) m civil servant
funda (*foon*-dah) f sleeve; ~ **de almohada** pillow-case
fundación (foon-dah-*th^yoan*) f foundation
fundamentado (foon-dah-mayn-*tah*-dhoa) adj well-founded
fundamental (foon-dah-mayn-*tahl*) adj fundamental, basic
fundamento (foon-dah-*mayn*-toa) m basis, base
fundar (foon-*dahr*) v found
fundir (foon-*deer*) v melt
funerales (foo-nay-*rah*-layss) mpl funeral
furgoneta (foor-goa-*nay*-tah) f delivery van
furioso (foo-*r^yoa*-soa) adj furious
furor (foo-*roar*) m anger, rage
fusible (foo-*see*-bhlay) m fuse
fusil (foo-*seel*) m gun
fusión (foo-*s^yoan*) f merger
fútbol (*foot*-bhoal) m soccer; football
fútil (*foo*-teel) adj petty
futuro (foo-*too*-roa) adj future

G

gabinete (gah-bhee-*nay*-tay) m cabinet
gafas (*gah*-fahss) fpl goggles pl; ~ **de sol** sun-glasses pl
gaitero (gigh-*tay*-roa) adj gay
galería (gah-lay-*ree*-ah) f gallery; ~ **de arte** art gallery
galgo (*gahl*-goa) m greyhound
galope (gah-*loa*-pay) m gallop
galleta (gah-*l^yay*-tah) f biscuit
gallina (gah-*l^yee*-nah) f hen
gallo (*gah*-l^yoa) m cock; ~ **de bosque** grouse
gamba (*gahm*-bah) f prawn

gamuza (gah-*moo*-thah) *f* suede

gana (*gah*-nah) *f* fancy; appetite

ganado (gah-*nah*-dhoa) *m* cattle *pl*

ganador (gah-nah-*dhoar*) *adj* winning

ganancia (gah-*nahn*-thʸah) *f* gain, profit

ganar (gah-*nahr*) *v* gain; *make, earn

ganas (*gah*-nahss) *fpl* desire

gancho (*gahn*-choa) *m* hook

ganga (*gahng*-gah) *f* bargain

garaje (gah-*rah*-khay) *m* garage; **dejar en ~** garage

garante (gah-*rahn*-tay) *m* guarantor

garantía (gah-rahn-*tee*-ah) *f* guarantee

garantizar (gah-rahn-tee-*thahr*) *v* guarantee

garganta (gahr-*gahn*-tah) *f* throat; **dolor de ~** sore throat

garra (*gah*-rrah) *f* claw

garrafa (gah-*rrah*-fah) *f* carafe

garrote (gah-*rroa*-tay) *m* club, cudgel

garza (*gahr*-thah) *f* heron

gas (gahss) *m* gas; **cocina de ~** gas cooker

gasa (*gah*-sah) *f* gauze

gasolina (gah-soa-*lee*-nah) *f* petrol; gasoline *nAm*, gas *nAm*; **puesto de ~** petrol station

gastado (gahss-*tah*-dhoa) *adj* worn-out, worn, threadbare

gastar (gahss-*tahr*) *v* *spend; wear out

gasto (*gahss*-toa) *m* expense, expenditure; **gastos de viaje** fare, travelling expenses

gástrico (*gahss*-tree-koa) *adj* gastric

gastrónomo (gahss-*troa*-noa-moa) *m* gourmet

gatear (gah-tay-*ahr*) *v* *creep

gatillo (gah-*tee*-lʸoa) *m* trigger

gato (*gah*-toa) *m* cat; jack

gaviota (gah-*bhʸoa*-tah) *f* gull, seagull

gema (*khay*-mah) *f* gem

gemelos (khay-*may*-loass) *mpl* twins

pl; binoculars *pl*; cuff-links *pl*; **~ de campaña** field glasses

* **gemir** (khay-*meer*) *v* groan, moan

generación (khay-nay-rah-thʸoan) *f* generation

generador (khay-nay-rah-*dhoar*) *m* generator

general (khay-nay-*rahl*) *adj* general; universal, public, broad; *m* general; **en ~** in general

generalmente (khay-nay-rahl-*mayn*-tay) *adv* mostly, as a rule

generar (khay-nay-*rahr*) *v* generate

género (*khay*-nay-roa) *m* gender; kind

generosidad (khay-nay-roa-see-*dhahdh*) *f* generosity

generoso (khay-nay-*roa*-soa) *adj* generous, liberal

genial (khay-nʸahl) *adj* genial

genio (*khay*-nʸoa) *m* genius

genital (khay-nee-*tahl*) *adj* genital

gente (*khayn*-tay) *f* folk; people *pl*

gentil (khayn-*teel*) *adj* gentle

genuino (khay-*nwee*-noa) *adj* genuine

geografía (khay-oa-grah-*fee*-ah) *f* geography

geográfico (khay-oa-*grah*-fee-koa) *adj* geographical

geología (khay-oa-loa-*khee*-ah) *f* geology

geometría (khay-oa-may-*tree*-ah) *f* geometry

gerencial (khay-rayn-thʸahl) *adj* administrative

germen (*khayr*-mayn) *m* germ

gesticular (khayss-tee-koo-*lahr*) *v* gesticulate

gestión (khayss-tʸoan) *f* administration, management

gesto (*khayss*-toa) *m* sign

gigante (khee-*gahn*-tay) *m* giant

gigantesco (khee-gahn-*tayss*-koa) *adj* enormous, gigantic

gimnasia (kheem-*nah*-sʸah) *f* gymnastics *pl*

gimnasio (kheem-*nah*-s^yoa) *m* gymnasium

gimnasta (kheem-*nahss*-tah) *m* gymnast

ginecólogo (khee-nay-*koa*-loa-goa) *m* gynaecologist

girar (khee-*rahr*) *v* turn

giro (*khee*-roa) *m* draft; **~ postal** postal order

gitano (khee-*tah*-noa) *m* gipsy

glaciar (glah-th^y*ahr*) *m* glacier

glándula (*glahn*-doo-lah) *f* gland

globo (*gloa*-bhoa) *m* globe; balloon

gloria (*gloa*-r^yah) *f* glory

glorieta (gloa-r^y*ay*-tah) *f* roundabout

glosario (gloa-*sah*-r^yoa) *m* vocabulary

glotón (gloa-*toan*) *adj* greedy

gobernador (goa-bhayr-nah-*dhoar*) *m* governor

gobernante (goa-bhayr-*nahn*-tay) *m* ruler

***gobernar** (goa-bhayr-*nahr*) *v* reign, rule

gobierno (goa-*bh^yayr*-noa) *m* government, rule; **~ de la casa** housekeeping

goce (*goa*-thay) *m* enjoyment

gol (goal) *m* goal

golf (goalf) *m* golf; **campo de ~** golf-links

golfo (*goal*-foa) *m* gulf

golondrina (goa-loan-*dree*-nah) *f* swallow

golosina (goa-loa-*see*-nah) *f* delicacy; **golosinas** sweets; candy *nAm*

golpe (*goal*-pay) *m* blow; knock, bump; ***dar golpes** bump

golpear (goal-pay-*ahr*) *v* *beat, knock, *strike; thump, tap

golpecito (goal-pay-*thee*-toa) *m* tap

gollerías (goa-l^yay-*ree*-ahss) *fpl* delicatessen

goma (*goa*-mah) *f* gum; **~ de borrar** eraser, rubber; **~ de mascar** chewing-gum; **~ espumada** foam-rubber

góndola (*goan*-doa-lah) *f* gondola

gordo (*goar*-dhoa) *adj* big; fat, stout

gorra (*goa*-rrah) *f* cap

gorrión (goa-rr^y*oan*) *m* sparrow

gorro (*goa*-rroa) *m* cap; **~ de baño** bathing-cap

gota (*goa*-tah) *f* drop; gout

gotear (goa-tay-*ahr*) *v* leak

goteo (goa-*tay*-oa) *m* leak

gozar (goa-*thahr*) *v* enjoy

grabación (grah-bhah-*th^yoan*) *f* recording

grabado (grah-*bhah*-dhoa) *m* engraving; picture, print

grabador (grah-bhah-*dhoar*) *m* engraver

grabar (grah-*bhahr*) *v* engrave

gracia (*grah*-th^yah) *f* grace

gracias (*grah*-th^yahss) thank you

gracioso (grah-th^y*oa*-soa) *adj* funny, humorous; graceful

grado (*grah*-dhoa) *m* degree; grade; **a tal ~** so

gradual (grah-*dhwahl*) *adj* gradual

graduar (grah-*dhwahr*) *v* grade; **graduarse** *v* graduate

gráfico (*grah*-fee-koa) *adj* graphic; *m* graph, chart, diagram

gramática (grah-*mah*-tee-kah) *f* grammar

gramatical (grah-mah-tee-*kahl*) *adj* grammatical

gramo (*grah*-moa) *m* gram

gramófono (grah-*moa*-foa-noa) *m* gramophone

Gran Bretaña (grahn bray-*tah*-ñah) Great Britain

grande (*grahn*-day) *adj* big; great, large, major

grandeza (grahn-*day*-thah) *f* greatness; grandness

grandioso (grahn-*d^yoa*-soa) *adj* superb, magnificent

granero (grah-*nay*-roa) *m* barn

granito (grah-*nee*-toa) *m* granite

granizo (grah-*nee*-thoa) *m* hail

granja (*grahng*-khah) *f* farm

granjera (grahng-*khay*-rah) *f* farmer's wife

granjero (grahng-*khay*-roa) *m* farmer

grano (*grah*-noa) *m* grain; corn; pimple

grapa (*grah*-pah) *f* clamp; staple

grasa (*grah*-sah) *f* fat, grease; *fMe* shoe polish

grasiento (grah-*s^yayn*-toa) *adj* fatty, greasy

graso (*grah*-soa) *adj* fat

grasoso (grah-*soa*-soa) *adj* greasy

gratis (*grah*-teess) *adv* free of charge

gratitud (grah-tee-*toodh*) *f* gratitude

grato (*grah*-toa) *adj* enjoyable

gratuito (grah-*twee*-toa) *adj* gratis, free of charge, free

grava (*grah*-bhah) *f* gravel

grave (*grah*-bhay) *adj* grave; bad

gravedad (grah-bhay-*dhahdh*) *f* gravity

Grecia (*gray*-th^yah) *f* Greece

griego (*gr^yay*-goa) *adj* Greek; *m* Greek

grieta (*gr^yay*-tah) *f* cleft, chasm; cave

grifo (*gree*-foa) *m* tap; faucet *nAm*

grillo (*gree*-l^yoa) *m* cricket

gripe (*gree*-pay) *f* influenza, flu

gris (greess) *adj* grey

gritar (gree-*tahr*) *v* cry; yell, scream, shout

grito (*gree*-toa) *m* cry; yell, scream, shout

grosella (groa-*say*-l^yah) *f* currant; ~ **espinosa** gooseberry; ~ **negra** black-currant

grosero (groa-*say*-roa) *adj* gross; coarse, rude, impertinent

grotesco (groa-*tayss*-koa) *adj* ludicrous

grúa (*groo*-ah) *f* crane

gruesa (*grway*-sah) *f* gross

grueso (*grway*-soa) *adj* corpulent

grumo (*groo*-moa) *m* lump

*****gruñir** (groo-*ñeer*) *v* growl

grupo (*groo*-poa) *m* group; party, set, bunch

gruta (*groo*-tah) *f* grotto

guante (*gwahn*-tay) *m* glove

guapo (*gwah*-poa) *adj* handsome

guarda (gwahr-dhah) *m* custodian

guardabarros (gwahr-dhah-*bhah*-rroass) *m* mud-guard

guardabosques (gwahr-dhah-*bhoass*-kayss) *m* forester

guardar (gwahr-*dhahr*) *v* *keep, *put away; guard; ~ **con llave** lock up; **guardarse** *v* beware

guardarropa (gwahr-dhah-*rroa*-pah) *m* wardrobe; cloakroom; checkroom *nAm*

guardería (gwahr-dhay-*ree*-ah) *f* nursery

guardia (*gwahr*-dh^yah) *f* guard; *m* policeman; ~ **personal** bodyguard

guardián (gwahr-*dh^yahn*) *m* attendant, warden; caretaker

guateque (gwah-*tay*-kay) *m* party

guerra (*gay*-rrah) *f* war; ~ **mundial** world war

guía (*gee*-ah) *m* guide; *f* guidebook; ~ **telefónica** telephone directory; telephone book *Am*

guiar (g^yahr) *v* guide

guijarro (gee-*khah*-rroa) *m* pebble

guión (g^yoan) *m* dash; hyphen

guisante (gee-*sahn*-tay) *m* pea

guisar (gee-*sahr*) *v* cook

guiso (*gee*-soa) *m* dish

guitarra (gee-*tah*-rrah) *f* guitar

gusano (goo-*sah*-noa) *m* worm

gustar (gooss-*tahr*) *v* care for, like; fancy

gusto (*gooss*-toa) *m* taste; **con mucho ~** gladly

gustosamente (gooss-toa-sah-*mayn*-tay) *adv* willingly, gladly

H

*haber (ah-*bhayr*) *v* *have

hábil (ah-bheel) *adj* able, skilful, skilled

habilidad (ah-bhee-lee-*dhahdh*) *f* ability; skill, art

habitable (ah-bhee-*tah*-bhlay) *adj* inhabitable, habitable

habitación (ah-bhee-tah-*th*^yoan) *f* room; **~ para huéspedes** guest-room

habitante (ah-bhee-*tahn*-tay) *m* inhabitant

habitar (ah-bhee-*tahr*) *v* inhabit

hábito (*ah*-bhee-toa) *m* habit

habitual (ah-bhee-*twahl*) *adj* habitual

habitualmente (ah-bhee-twahl-*mayn*-tay) *adv* usually

habla (*ah*-bhlah) *f* speech

habladuría (ah-bhlah-dhoo-*ree*-ah) *f* rubbish

hablar (ah-*bhlahr*) *v* *speak, talk

*hacer (ah-*thayr*) *v* act; *do; *have, cause to, *make; **hace** ago; ***hacerse** *v* *become; *grow, *go, *get

hacia (*ah*-th^yah) *prep* at, towards, to; about; **~ abajo** down; **~ adelante** forward; **~ arriba** upwards, up; **~ atrás** backwards

hacienda (ah-*th*^yayn-dah) *f* estate

hacha (*ah*-chah) *f* axe

hada (*ah*-dhah) *f* fairy; **cuento de hadas** fairytale

halcón (ahl-*koan*) *m* hawk

halibut (ah-lee-*bhoot*) *m* halibut

hallar (ah-*l^yahr*) *v* *come across

hallazgo (ah-*l^yahdh*-goa) *m* finding

hamaca (ah-*mah*-kah) *f* hammock

hambre (*ahm*-bray) *f* hunger

hambriento (ahm-*br^yayn*-toa) *adj* hungry

harina (ah-*ree*-nah) *f* flour

harto de (*ahr*-toa day) fed up with, tired of

hasta (*ahss*-tah) *prep* to, till, until; **~ ahora** so far; **~ que** till

haya (*ah*-^yah) *f* beech

hebilla (ay-*bhee*-l^yah) *f* buckle

hebreo (ay-*bhray*-oa) *m* Hebrew

hechizar (ay-chee-*thahr*) *v* bewitch

hecho (*ay*-choa) *m* fact

*heder (ay-*dhayr*) *v* *smell

hediondo (ay-*dh*^yoan-doa) *adj* smelly

helado (ay-*lah*-dhoa) *adj* freezing; *m* ice-cream

*helar (ay-*lahr*) *v* *freeze

hélice (*ay*-lee-thay) *f* propeller

hemorragia (ay-moa-*rrah*-kh^yah) *f* haemorrhage; **~ nasal** nosebleed

hemorroides (ay-moa-*rroi*-dhayss) *fpl* haemorrhoids *pl*, piles *pl*

*hender (ayn-*dayr*) *v* *split

hendidura (ayn-dee-*dhoo*-rah) *f* chink, crack

heno (*ay*-noa) *m* hay

heredar (ay-ray-*dhahr*) *v* inherit

hereditario (ay-ray-dhee-*tah*-r^yoa) *adj* hereditary

herencia (ay-*rayn*-th^yah) *f* inheritance, legacy

herida (ay-*ree*-dhah) *f* injury, wound

*herir (ay-*reer*) *v* injure, wound

hermana (ayr-*mah*-nah) *f* sister

hermano (ayr-*mah*-noa) *m* brother

hermético (ayr-*may*-tee-koa) *adj* airtight

hermoso (ayr-*moa*-soa) *adj* beautiful

hernia (*ayr*-n^yah) *f* hernia; **~ intervertebral** slipped disc

héroe (*ay*-roa-ay) *m* hero

heroico (ay-*roi*-koa) *adj* heroic

heroísmo (ay-roa-*eez*-moa) *m* heroism

herradura (ay-rrah-*dhoo*-rah) *f* horse-shoe

herramienta (ay-rrah-*mᵞayn*-tah) *f* tool, utensil, implement; **bolsa de herramientas** tool kit

herrería (ay-rray-*ree*-ah) *f* ironworks

herrero (ay-*rray*-roa) *m* smith, blacksmith

herrumbre (ay-*rroom*-bray) *f* rust

*****hervir** (ayr-*bheer*) *v* boil

heterosexual (ay-tay-roa-sayk-*swahl*) *adj* heterosexual

hidalgo (ee-*dhahl*-goa) *m* nobleman

hidrógeno (ee-*dhroa*-khay-noa) *m* hydrogen

hiedra (ᵞay-dhrah) *f* ivy

hielo (ᵞay-loa) *m* ice

hierba (ᵞayr-bhah) *f* herb; **brizna de ~** blade of grass; **mala ~** weed

hierro (ᵞay-rroa) *m* iron; **de ~** iron; **~ fundido** cast iron

hígado (ee-gah-dhoa) *m* liver

higiene (ee-*khᵞay*-nay) *f* hygiene

higiénico (ee-*khᵞay*-nee-koa) *adj* hygienic; **papel ~** toilet-paper

higo (ee-goa) *m* fig

hija (ee-khah) *f* daughter

hijastro (ee-*khahss*-troa) *m* stepchild

hijo (ee-khoa) *m* son

hilar (ee-*lahr*) *v* *spin

hilo (ee-loa) *m* yarn, thread; **~ de zurcir** darning wool

himno (eem-noa) *m* hymn; **~ nacional** national anthem

hinchar (een-*noar*) *v* inflate; **hincharse** *v* *swell

hinchazón (een-chah-*thoan*) *f* swelling

hipo (ee-poa) *m* hiccup

hipocresía (ee-poa-kray-*see*-ah) *f* hypocrisy

hipócrita (ee-*poa*-kree-tah) *adj* hypocritical; *m* hypocrite

hipódromo (ee-*poa*-dhroa-moa) *m* race-course

hipoteca (ee-poa-*tay*-kah) *f* mortgage

hispanoamericano (eess-pah-noa-ah-may-ree-*kah*-noa) *adj* Spanish-American

histérico (eess-*tay*-ree-koa) *adj* hysterical

historia (eess-*toa*-rᵞah) *f* history; **~ de amor** love-story; **~ del arte** art history

historiador (eess-toa-rᵞah-*dhoar*) *m* historian

histórico (eess-*toa*-ree-koa) *adj* historical, historic

hocico (oa-*thee*-koa) *m* mouth, snout

hogar (oa-*gahr*) *m* hearth

hoja (oa-khah) *f* leaf; sheet; blade; **~ de afeitar** razor-blade; **~ de pedido** order-form; **hojas de oro** gold leaf

¡hola! (oa-lah) hello!

Holanda (oa-*lahn*-dah) *f* Holland

holandés (oa-lahn-*dayss*) *adj* Dutch; *m* Dutchman

hombre (oam-bray) *m* man

hombro (oam-broa) *m* shoulder

homenaje (oa-may-*nah*-khay) *m* tribute, homage

homosexual (oa-moa-sayk-*swahl*) *adj* homosexual

hondo (oan-doa) *adj* deep

honesto (oa-*nayss*-toa) *adj* honest; honourable, straight

hongo (oang-goa) *m* mushroom; toadstool

honor (oa-*noar*) *m* honour; glory

honorable (oa-noa-*rah*-bhlay) *adj* honourable

honorarios (oa-noa-*rah*-rᵞoass) *mpl* fee

honra (oan-rrah) *f* honour

honradez (oan-rah-*dhayth*) *f* honesty

honrado (oan-*rrah*-dhoa) *adj* honest

honrar (oan-*rahr*) *v* honour

hora (*oa*-rah) *f* hour; ~ **de afluencia** rush-hour; ~ **de llegada** time of arrival; ~ **de salida** time of departure; ~ **punta** peak hour; **horas de consulta** consultation hours; **horas de oficina** office hours, business hours; **horas de visita** visiting hours; **horas hábiles** business hours

horario (oa-*rah*-rʸoa) *m* schedule; timetable; ~ **de verano** summer time

horca (*oar*-kah) *f* gallows *pl*

horizontal (oa-ree-thoan-*tahl*) *adj* horizontal

horizonte (oa-ree-*thoan*-tay) *m* horizon

hormiga (oar-*mee*-gah) *f* ant

hormigón (oar-mee-*goan*) *m* concrete

hornear (oar-nay-*ahr*) *v* bake

horno (*oar*-noa) *m* oven; furnace

horquilla (oar-*kee*-lʸah) *f* hairpin, hair-grip; bobby pin *Am*

horrible (oa-*rree*-bhlay) *adj* horrible; hideous

horror (oa-*rroar*) *m* horror

horticultura (oar-tee-kool-*too*-rah) *f* horticulture

hospedar (oass-pay-*dhahr*) *v* entertain; **hospedarse** *v* stay

hospedería (oass-pay-dhay-*ree*-ah) *f* hostel

hospicio (oass-*pee*-thʸoa) *m* home

hospital (oass-pee-*tahl*) *m* hospital

hospitalario (oass-pee-tah-*lah*-rʸoa) *adj* hospitable

hospitalidad (oass-pee-tah-lee-*dhahdh*) *f* hospitality

hostil (oass-*teel*) *adj* hostile

hotel (oa-*tayl*) *m* hotel

hoy (oi) *adv* today; ~ **en día** nowadays

hoyo (*oa*-ʸoa) *m* pit

hueco (*way*-koa) *adj* hollow; *m* gap

huelga (*wayl*-gah) *f* strike; ***estar en** ~ *strike

huella (*way*-lʸah) *f* trace

huérfano (*wayr*-fah-noa) *m* orphan

huerto (*wayr*-toa) *m* kitchen garden

hueso (*way*-soa) *m* bone; stone

huésped (*wayss*-paydh) *m* guest; lodger, boarder

hueva (*way*-bhah) *f* roe

huevera (way-*bhay*-rah) *f* egg-cup

huevo (*way*-bhoa) *m* egg; **yema de** ~ egg-yolk

***huir** (weer) *v* escape

hule (*oo*-lay) *mMe* rubber

humanidad (oo-mah-nee-*dhahdh*) *f* humanity, mankind

humano (oo-*mah*-noa) *adj* human

humedad (oo-may-*dhahdh*) *f* moisture, humidity, damp

***humedecer** (oo-may-dhay-*thayr*) *v* moisten, damp

húmedo (*oo*-may-dhoa) *adj* moist, humid, damp; wet

humilde (oo-*meel*-day) *adj* humble

humo (*oo*-moa) *m* smoke

humor (oo-*moar*) *m* spirit, mood; humour; **de buen** ~ good-tempered, good-humoured

humorístico (oo-moa-*reess*-tee-koa) *adj* humorous

hundimiento (oon-dee-*mʸayn*-toa) *m* ruination

hundirse (oon-*deer*-say) *v* *sink

húngaro (*oong*-gah-roa) *adj* Hungarian; *m* Hungarian

Hungría (oong-*gree*-ah) *m* Hungary

huracán (oo-rah-*kahn*) *m* hurricane

hurtar (oor-*tahr*) *v* *steal

hurto (*oor*-toa) *m* theft

husmear (oos-may-*ahr*) *v* scent, *get wind of

I

ibérico (eek-*bhay*-ree-koa) *adj* Iberian
icono (ee-*koa*-noa) *m* icon
ictericia (eek-tay-*ree*-thʸah) *f* jaundice
idea (ee-*dhay*-ah) *f* idea
ideal (ee-dhay-*ahl*) *adj* ideal; *m* ideal
idear (ee-dhay-*ahr*) *v* devise
idéntico (ee-*dhayn*-tee-koa) *adj* identical
identidad (ee-dhayn-tee-*dhahdh*) *f* identity; **carnet de ~** identity card
identificación (ee-dhayn-tee-fee-kah-*thʸoan*) *f* identification
identificar (ee-dhayn-tee-fee-*kahr*) *v* identify
idioma (ee-*dhʸoa*-mah) *m* language
idiomático (ee-dhʸoa-*mah*-tee-koa) *adj* idiomatic
idiota (ee-*dhʸoa*-tah) *adj* idiotic; *m* idiot, fool
ídolo (*ee*-dhoa-loa) *m* idol
iglesia (ee-*glay*-sʸah) *f* chapel, church
ignorancia (eeg-noa-*rahn*-thʸah) *f* ignorance
ignorante (eeg-noa-*rahn*-tay) *adj* ignorant
ignorar (eeg-noa-*rahr*) *v* ignore
igual (ee-*gwahl*) *adj* equal, alike; level, even; **sin ~** unsurpassed
igualar (ee-gwah-*lahr*) *v* level, equalize; equal
igualdad (ee-gwahl-*dahdh*) *f* equality
igualmente (ee-gwahl-*mayn*-tay) *adv* alike; equally
ilegal (ee-lay-*gahl*) *adj* illegal, unlawful
ilegible (ee-lay-*khee*-bhlay) *adj* illegible
ileso (ee-*lay*-soa) *adj* unhurt
ilimitado (ee-lee-mee-*tah*-dhoa) *adj* unlimited

iluminación (ee-loo-mee-nah-*thʸoan*) *f* illumination
iluminar (ee-loo-mee-*nahr*) *v* illuminate
ilusión (ee-loo-*sʸoan*) *f* illusion
ilustración (ee-looss-trah-*thʸoan*) *f* illustration; picture
ilustrar (ee-looss-*trahr*) *v* illustrate
ilustre (ee-*looss*-tray) *adj* illustrious
imagen (ee-*mah*-khayn) *f* image, picture; **~ reflejada** reflection
imaginación (ee-mah-khee-nah-*thʸoan*) *f* fancy, imagination
imaginar (ee-mah-khee-*nahr*) *v* conceive; **imaginarse** *v* fancy, imagine
imaginario (ee-mah-khee-*nah*-rʸoa) *adj* imaginary
imitación (ee-mee-tah-*thʸoan*) *f* imitation
imitar (ee-mee-*tahr*) *v* imitate, copy
impaciente (eem-pah-*thʸayn*-tay) *adj* eager, impatient
impar (eem-*pahr*) *adj* odd
imparcial (eem-pahr-*thʸahl*) *adj* impartial
impecable (eem-pay-*kah*-bhlay) *adj* faultless
impedimento (eem-pay-dhee-*mayn*-toa) *m* impediment
*****impedir** (eem-pay-*dheer*) *v* hinder, impede; restrain, prevent
impeler (eem-pay-*layr*) *v* propel
imperdible (eem-payr-*dhee*-bhlay) *m* safety-pin
imperfección (eem-payr-fayk-*thʸoan*) *f* fault
imperfecto (eem-payr-*fayk*-toa) *adj* imperfect
imperial (eem-pay-*rʸahl*) *adj* imperial
imperio (eem-*pay*-rʸoa) *m* empire
impermeable (eem-payr-may-*ah*-bhlay) *adj* waterproof, rainproof; *m* raincoat, mackintosh
impersonal (eem-payr-soa-*nahl*) *adj*

impersonal

impertinencia (eem-payr-tee-*nayn*-th**Y**ah) *f* impertinence

impertinente (eem-payr-tee-*nayn*-tay) *adj* bold, impertinent

impetuoso (eem-pay-*twoa*-soa) *adj* violent

implicar (eem-plee-*kahr*) *v* imply; **implicado** involved

imponente (eem-poa-*nayn*-tay) *adj* grand, imposing

imponible (eem-poa-*nee*-bhlay) *adj* dutiable

impopular (eem-poa-poo-*lahr*) *adj* unpopular

importación (eem-poar-tah-*th**Y**oan*) *f* import

importador (eem-poar-tah-*dhoar*) *m* importer

importancia (eem-poar-*tahn*-th**Y**ah) *f* importance; *****tener ~** matter

importante (eem-poar-*tahn*-tay) *adj* important; considerable, capital, big

importar (eem-poar-*tahr*) *v* import

importuno (eem-poar-*too*-noa) *adj* annoying

imposible (eem-poa-*see*-bhlay) *adj* impossible

impotencia (eem-poa-*tayn*-th**Y**ah) *f* impotence

impotente (eem-poa-*tayn*-tay) *adj* powerless; impotent

impresión (eem-pray-*s**Y**oan*) *f* impression; **~ digital** fingerprint

impresionante (eem-pray-s**Y**oa-*nahn*-tay) *adj* impressive; striking

impresionar (eem-pray-s**Y**oa-*nahr*) *v* *****strike, impress

impreso (eem-*pray*-soa) *m* printed matter

imprevisto (eem-pray-*bheess*-toa) *adj* unexpected, incidental

*****imprimir** (eem-pree-*meer*) *v* print

improbable (eem-proa-*bhah*-bhlay) *adj* unlikely, improbable

ímprobo (*eem*-proa-bhoa) *adj* unfair, dishonest

impropio (eem-*proa*-p**Y**oa) *adj* improper; wrong

improvisar (eem-proa-bhee-*sahr*) *v* improvise

imprudente (eem-proo-*dhayn*-tay) *adj* unwise

impudente (eem-poo-*dhayn*-tay) *adj* impudent

impuesto (eem-*pwayss*-toa) *m* taxation, tax; Customs duty; **~ de aduana** Customs duty; **impuestos de importación** import duty; **libre de impuestos** tax-free

impulsivo (eem-pool-*see*-bhoa) *adj* impulsive

impulso (eem-*pool*-soa) *m* urge, impulse

inaccesible (ee-nahk-thay-*see*-bhlay) *adj* inaccessible

inaceptable (ee-nah-thayp-*tah*-bhlay) *adj* unacceptable

inadecuado (ee-nah-dhay-*kwah*-dhoa) *adj* inadequate; unfit, unsuitable

inapreciable (ee-nah-pray-*th**Y**ah*-bhlay) *adj* priceless

incapaz (eeng-kah-*pahth*) *adj* unable, incapable

incendio (een-*thayn*-d**Y**oa) *m* fire

incidente (een-thee-*dhayn*-tay) *m* incident

incienso (een-*th**Y**ayn*-soa) *m* incense

incierto (een-*th**Y**ayr*-toa) *adj* uncertain

incineración (een-thee-nay-rah-*th**Y**oan*) *f* cremation

incinerar (een-thee-nay-*rahr*) *v* cremate

incisión (een-thee-*s**Y**oan*) *f* cut

incitar (een-thee-*tahr*) *v* incite

inclinación (eeng-klee-nah-*th**Y**oan*) *f* tendency, inclination; incline

inclinar (eeng-klee-*nahr*) *v* bow; **inclinado** inclined; sloping, slanting; **inclinarse** *v* *be inclined to; slope, slant

***incluir** (eeng-*klweer*) *v* include; enclose; count; **todo incluido** all in

incluso (eeng-*kloo*-soa) *adj* inclusive, included

incombustible (eeng-koam-booss-*tee*-bhlay) *adj* fireproof

incomible (eeng-koa-*mee*-bhlay) *adj* inedible

incomodidad (eeng-koa-moa-dhee-*dhahdh*) *f* inconvenience

incómodo (eeng-*koa*-moa-dhoa) *adj* uncomfortable

incompetente (eeng-koam-pay-*tayn*-tay) *adj* incompetent; unqualified

incompleto (eeng-koam-*play*-toa) *adj* incomplete

inconcebible (eeng-koan-thay-*bhee*-bhlay) *adj* inconceivable

incondicional (eeng-koan-dee-th^yoa-nahl) *adj* unconditional

inconsciente (eeng-koan-*th^yayn*-tay) *adj* unaware; unconscious

inconveniencia (eeng-koam-bay-n^yayn-th^yah) *f* inconvenience

incorrecto (eeng-koa-*rrayk*-toa) *adj* incorrect

increíble (eeng-kray-*ee*-bhlay) *adj* incredible

incrementar (eeng-kray-mayn-*tahr*) *v* increase

inculto (eeng-*kool*-toa) *adj* uncultivated; uneducated

incurable (eeng-koo-*rah*-bhlay) *adj* incurable

indagación (een-dah-gah-*th^yoan*) *f* inquiry

indagar (een-dah-*gahr*) *v* query

indecente (een-day-*thayn*-tay) *adj* indecent

indefenso (een-day-*fayn*-soa) *adj* un-

protected

indefinido (een-day-fee-*nee*-dhoa) *adj* indefinite

indemnización (een-daym-nee-thah-*th^yoan*) *f* compensation, indemnity

independencia (een-day-payn-*dayn*-th^yah) *f* independence

independiente (een-day-payn-*d^yayn*-tay) *adj* self-employed, independent

indeseable (een-day-say-*ah*-bhlay) *adj* undesirable

India (*een*-d^yah) *f* India

indicación (een-dee-kah-*th^yoan*) *f* indication

indicador (een-dee-kah-*dhoar*) *m* trafficator, indicator

indicar (een-dee-*kahr*) *v* indicate; declare

indicativo (een-dee-kah-*tee*-bhoa) *m* area code

índice (*een*-dee-thay) *m* index, table of contents; index finger

indiferencia (een-dee-fay-*rayn*-th^yah) *f* indifference

indiferente (een-dee-fay-*rayn*-tay) *adj* indifferent; careless

indígena (een-*dee*-khay-nah) *m* native

indigestión (een-dee-khayss-*t^yoan*) *f* indigestion

indignación (een-deeg-nah-*th^yoan*) *f* indignation

indio (*een*-d^yoa) *adj* Indian; *m* Indian

indirecto (een-dee-*rayk*-toa) *adj* indirect

indispensable (een-deess-payn-*sah*-bhlay) *adj* essential

indispuesto (een-deess-*pwayss*-toa) *adj* unwell

individual (een-dee-bhee-*dhwahl*) *adj* individual

individuo (een-dee-*bhee*-dhwoa) *m* individual

Indonesia (een-doa-*nay*-s^yah) *f* Indonesia

indonesio (een-doa-*nay*-s^yoa) *adj* Indonesian; *m* Indonesian

indudable (een-doo-*dhah*-bhlay) *adj* undoubted

indulto (een-*dool*-toa) *m* pardon

industria (een-*dooss*-tr^yah) *f* industry; ingenuity

ineficiente (ee-nay-fee-*th^yayn*-tay) *adj* inefficient

inerte (ee-*nayr*-tay) *adj* limp

inesperado (ee-nayss-pay-*rah*-dhoa) *adj* unexpected

inestable (ee-nayss-*tah*-bhlay) *adj* unsteady, unstable

inevitable (ee-nay-bhee-*tah*-bhlay) *adj* unavoidable, inevitable

inexacto (ee-nayk-*sahk*-toa) *adj* incorrect, inaccurate; false

inexperto (ee-nayks-*payr*-toa) *adj* inexperienced

inexplicable (ee-nayks-plee-*kah*-bhlay) *adj* unaccountable

infancia (een-*fahn*-th^yah) *f* infancy

infantería (een-fahn-tay-*ree*-ah) *f* infantry

infantil (een-fahn-*teel*) *adj* childlike

infección (een-fayk-*th^yoan*) *f* infection

infectar (een-fayk-*tahr*) *v* infect; **infectarse** *v* *become septic

inferior (een-fay-*r^yoar*) *adj* inferior; bottom

infiel (een-*f^yayl*) *adj* unfaithful

infierno (een-*f^yayr*-noa) *m* hell

infinidad (een-fee-nee-*dhahdh*) *f* infinity

infinitivo (een-fee-nee-*tee*-bhoa) *m* infinitive

infinito (een-fee-*nee*-toa) *adj* endless, infinite

inflable (een-*flah*-bhlay) *adj* inflatable

inflación (een-flah-*th^yoan*) *f* inflation

inflamable (een-flah-*mah*-bhlay) *adj* inflammable

inflamación (een-flah-mah-*th^yoan*) *f* inflammation

influencia (een-*flwayn*-th^yah) *f* influence

*****influir** (een-*flweer*) *v* influence

influjo (een-*floo*-khoa) *m* influence

influyente (een-floo-*^yayn*-tay) *adj* influential

información (een-foar-mah-*th^yoan*) *f* enquiry, information; **oficina de informaciones** inquiry office

informal (een-foar-*mahl*) *adj* informal; casual

informar (een-foar-*mahr*) *v* report, inform; plead; **informarse** *v* inquire

informe (een-*foar*-may) *m* report; **informes** *mpl* information; *****pedir informes** inquire

infortunio (een-foar-*too*-n^yoa) *m* misfortune

infrarrojo (een-frah-*rroa*-khoa) *adj* infra-red

infrecuente (een-fray-*kwayn*-tay) *adj* infrequent

infringir (een-freeng-*kheer*) *v* trespass

ingeniero (eeng-khay-*n^yay*-roa) *m* engineer

ingenioso (eeng-khay-*n^yoa*-soa) *adj* ingenious

ingenuo (eeng-*khay*-nwoa) *adj* naïve; simple

Inglaterra (eeng-glah-*tay*-rrah) *f* England; Britain

ingle (*eeng*-glay) *f* groin

inglés (eeng-*glayss*) *adj* English; *m* Englishman; Briton

ingrato (eeng-*grah*-toa) *adj* ungrateful

ingrediente (eeng-gray-*dh^yayn*-tay) *m* ingredient

ingresar (eeng-gray-*sahr*) *v* deposit

ingreso (eenggray-soa) *m* entry

ingresos (eeng-*gray*-soass) *mpl* revenue, earnings *pl*; income; **impuesto sobre los ~** income-tax

inhabitable (ee-nah-bhee-*tah*-bhlay) *adj* uninhabitable

inhabitado (ee-nah-bhee-*tah*-dhoa) *adj* uninhabited

inhalar (ee-nah-*lahr*) *v* inhale

inicial (ee-nee-*th*ʸ*ahl*) *adj* initial; *f* initial

iniciar (ee-nee-*th*ʸ*ahr*) *v* initiate

iniciativa (ee-nee-th*ʸ*ah-tee-bhah) *f* initiative

ininterrumpido (ee-neen-tay-rroom-*pee*-dhoa) *adj* continuous

injusticia (eeng-khooss-*tee*-th*ʸ*ah) *f* injustice

injusto (eeng-*khooss*-toa) *adj* unfair, unjust

inmaculado (een-mah-koo-*lah*-dhoa) *adj* stainless, spotless

inmediatamente (een-may-dh*ʸ*ah-tah-*mayn*-tay) *adv* instantly, immediately

inmediato (een-may-*dh*ʸ*ah*-toa) *adj* immediate, prompt; **de ~** immediately

inmenso (een-*mayn*-soa) *adj* immense

inmerecido (een-may-ray-*thee*-dhoa) *adj* unearned

inmigración (een-mee-grah-*th*ʸ*oan*) *f* immigration

inmigrante (een-mee-*grahn*-tay) *m* immigrant

inmigrar (een-mee-*grahr*) *v* immigrate

inmodesto (een-moa-*dhayss*-toa) *adj* immodest

inmueble (een-*mway*-bhlay) *m* house

inmundo (een-*moon*-doa) *adj* filthy

inmunidad (een-moo-nee-*dhahdh*) *f* immunity

inmunizar (een-moo-nee-*thahr*) *v* immunize

innato (een-*nah*-toa) *adj* natural

innecesario (een-nay-thay-*sah*-r*ʸ*oa) *adj* unnecessary

innumerable (een-noo-may-*rah*-bhlay) *adj* innumerable

inocencia (ee-noa-*thayn*-th*ʸ*ah) *f* innocence

inocente (ee-noa-*thayn*-tay) *adj* innocent

inoculación (ee-noa-koo-lah-*th*ʸ*oan*) *f* inoculation

inocuo (ee-*noa*-kwoa) *adj* harmless

inoportuno (ee-noa-poar-*too*-noa) *adj* inconvenient; misplaced

inquietarse (eeng-k*ʸ*ay-*tahr*-say) *v* worry

inquieto (een-*k*ʸ*ay*-toa) *adj* restless; uneasy, worried

inquietud (eeng-k*ʸ*ay-*toodh*) *f* unrest; worry

inquilino (eeng-kee-*lee*-noa) *m* tenant

insalubre (een-sah-*loo*-bhray) *adj* unhealthy

insatisfecho (een-sah-teess-*fay*-choa) *adj* dissatisfied

inscribir (eens-kree-*bheer*) *v* enter, book, list; **inscribirse** *v* register, check in

inscripción (eens-kreep-*th*ʸ*oan*) *f* inscription; registration

insecticida (een-sayk-tee-*thee*-dhah) *m* insecticide

insectífugo (een-sayk-*tee*-foo-goa) *m* insect repellent

insecto (een-*sayk*-toa) *m* insect; bug *nAm*

inseguro (een-say-*goo*-roa) *adj* unsafe; doubtful

insensato (een-sayn-*sah*-toa) *adj* senseless

insensible (een-sayn-*see*-bhlay) *adj* insensitive; heartless

insertar (een-sayr-*tahr*) *v* insert

insignificante (een-seeg-nee-fee-*kahn*-tay) *adj* unimportant, petty, insignificant

insípido (een-*see*-pee-dhoa) *adj* tasteless

insistir (een-seess-*teer*) v insist

insolación (een-soa-lah-*th^yoan*) f sunstroke

insolencia (een-soa-*layn*-th^yah) f insolence

insolente (een-soa-*layn*-tay) adj insolent

insólito (een-*soa*-lee-toa) adj uncommon, unusual

insomnio (een-*soam*-n^yoa) m insomnia

insonorizado (een-soa-noa-ree-*thah*-dhoa) adj soundproof

insoportable (een-soa-poar-*tah*-bhlay) adj intolerable

inspección (eens-payk-*th^yoan*) f inspection; ~ **de pasaportes** passport control

inspeccionar (eens-payk-th^yoa-*nahr*) v inspect

inspector (eens-payk-*toar*) m inspector

inspirar (een-spee-*rahr*) v inspire

instalación (eens-tah-lah-*th^yoan*) f installation; plant

instalar (eens-tah-*lahr*) v install; furnish

instantánea (eens-tahn-*tah*-nay-ah) f snapshot

instantáneamente (eens-tahn-tah-nay-ah-*mayn*-tay) adv instantly

instante (eens-*tahn*-tay) m instant; second; **al ~** instantly

instinto (een-*steen*-toa) m instinct

institución (eens-tee-too-*th^yoan*) f institution, institute

__instituir__ (eens-tee-*tweer*) v institute

instituto (eens-tee-*too*-toa) m institution, institute

institutor (eens-tee-too-*toar*) m teacher

instrucción (eens-trook-*th^yoan*) f instruction; direction

instructivo (eens-trook-*tee*-bhoa) adj instructive

instructor (eens-trook-*toar*) m instructor

__instruir__ (eens-*trweer*) v instruct

instrumento (eens-troo-*mayn*-toa) m instrument; ~ **músico** musical instrument

insuficiente (een-soo-fee-*th^yayn*-tay) adj insufficient

insufrible (een-soo-*free*-bhlay) adj unbearable

insultante (een-sool-*tahn*-tay) adj offensive

insultar (een-sool-*tahr*) v insult; scold, call names

insulto (een-*sool*-toa) m insult

intacto (een-*tahk*-toa) adj intact; unbroken, whole

integral (een-tay-*grahl*) adj integral

integrar (een-tay-*grahr*) v integrate

intelecto (een-tay-*layk*-toa) m intellect

intelectual (een-tay-layk-*twahl*) adj intellectual

inteligencia (een-tay-lee-*khayn*-th^yah) f intelligence, brain

inteligente (een-tay-lee-*khayn*-tay) adj intelligent; clever, smart

intención (een-tayn-*th^yoan*) f intention, purpose; *__tener la ~ de__* intend

intencionado (een-tayn-th^yoa-*nah*-dhoa) adj on purpose

intencional (een-tayn-th^yoa-*nahl*) adj intentional

intensidad (een-tayn-see-*dhahdh*) f intensity

intenso (een-*tayn*-soa) adj intense

intentar (een-tayn-*tahr*) v attempt, try; intend

intercambiar (een-tayr-kahm-*b^yahr*) v exchange

interés (een-tay-*rayss*) m interest

interesado (een-tay-ray-*sah*-dhoa) adj interested; concerned; m candidate

interesante (een-tay-ray-*sahn*-tay) adj

interesting

interesar (een-tay-ray-*sahr*) *v* interest

interferencia (een-tayr-fay-*rayn*-th^yah) *f* interference

interferir (een-tayr-fay-*reer*) *v* interfere

ínterin (*een*-tay-reen) *m* interim

interior (een-tay-*r^yoar*) *adj* inside, inner; domestic; *m* interior, inside

intermediario (een-tayr-may-*dh^yah*-r^yoa) *m* intermediary

intermedio (een-tayr-*may*-dh^yoa) *m* interlude

internacional (een-tayr-nah-th^yoa-*nahl*) *adj* international

internado (een-tayr-*nah*-dhoa) *m* boarding-school

interno (een-*tayr*-noa) *adj* internal; resident

interpretar (een-tayr-pray-*tahr*) *v* interpret

intérprete (een-*tayr*-pray-tay) *m* interpreter

interrogar (een-tay-rroa-*gahr*) *v* interrogate

interrogativo (een-tay-rroa-gah-*tee*-bhoa) *adj* interrogative

interrogatorio (een-tay-rroa-gah-*toa*-r^yoa) *m* interrogation, examination

interrumpir (een-tay-rroom-*peer*) *v* interrupt

interrupción (een-tay-rroop-th^yoan) *f* interruption

interruptor (een-tay-rroop-*toar*) *m* switch

intersección (een-tayr-sayk-th^yoan) *f* intersection

intervalo (een-tayr-*bhah*-loa) *m* interval

intervención (een-tayr-bhayn-th^yoan) *f* intervention

***intervenir** (een-tayr-bhay-*neer*) *v* intervene

intestino (een-tayss-*tee*-noa) *m* intestine, gut; ~ **recto** rectum; **intesti-**

nos intestines *pl*, bowels *pl*

intimidad (een-tee-mee-*dhahdh*) *f* privacy

íntimo (*een*-tee-moa) *adj* intimate; cosy

intoxicación alimentaria (een-toak-see-kah-*th^yoan* ah-lee-mayn-*tah*-r^yah) food poisoning

intransitable (een-trahn-see-*tah*-bhlay) *adj* impassable

intriga (een-*tree*-gah) *f* intrigue

introducción (een-troa-dhook-*th^yoan*) *f* introduction

***introducir** (een-troa-dhoo-*theer*) *v* introduce; *bring up

intruso (een-*troo*-soa) *m* trespasser

inundación (ee-noon-dah-*th^yoan*) *f* flood

inusitado (ee-noo-see-*tah*-dhoa) *adj* unusual

inútil (ee-*noo*-teel) *adj* useless

inútilmente (ee-noo-teel-*mayn*-tay) *adv* in vain

invadir (eem-bah-*dheer*) *v* invade

inválido (eem-*bah*-lee-dhoa) *adj* invalid, disabled; *m* invalid

invasión (eem-bah-*s^yoan*) *f* invasion

invención (eem-bayn-*th^yoan*) *f* invention

inventar (eem-bayn-*tahr*) *v* invent

inventario (eem-bayn-tah-r^yoa) *m* inventory

inventivo (eem-bayn-*tee*-bhoa) *adj* inventive

inventor (eem-bayn-*toar*) *m* inventor

invernáculo (eem-bayr-*nah*-koo-loa) *m* greenhouse

invernadero (eem-bayr-nah-*dhay*-roa) *m* greenhouse

inversión (eem-bayr-*s^yoan*) *f* investment

inversionista (eem-bayr-s^yoa-*neess*-tah) *m* investor

inverso (eem-*bayr*-soa) *adj* reverse

*invertir (eem-bayr-*teer*) *v* invert; invest

investigación (eem-bayss-tee-gah-*th^yoan*) *f* research; investigation, enquiry

investigador (eem-bhayss-tee-gah-*dhoar*) *m* research worker

investigar (eem-bayss-tee-*gahr*) *v* investigate, enquire

invierno (eem-*b^yayr*-noa) *m* winter; **deportes de ~** winter sports

invisible (eem-bee-*see*-bhlay) *adj* invisible

invitación (eem-bee-tah-*th^yoan*) *f* invitation

invitado (eem-bee-*tah*-dhoa) *m* guest

invitar (eem-bee-*tahr*) *v* invite; ask

inyección (een-^yayk-*th^yoan*) *f* shot, injection

inyectar (een-^yayk-*tahr*) *v* inject

*ir (eer) *v* *go; **~ por** fetch; ***irse** *v* *go away

Irak (ee-*rahk*) *m* Iraq

Irán (ee-*rahn*) *m* Iran

iraní (ee-rah-*nee*) *adj* Iranian; *m* Iranian

iraquí (ee-rah-*kee*) *adj* Iraqi; *m* Iraqi

irascible (ee-rahss-*thee*-bhlay) *adj* irascible, quick-tempered

Irlanda (eer-*lahn*-dah) *f* Ireland

irlandés (eer-lahn-*dayss*) *adj* Irish; *m* Irishman

ironía (ee-roa-*nee*-ah) *f* irony

irónico (ee-*roa*-nee-koa) *adj* ironical

irrazonable (ee-rrah-thoa-*nah*-bhlay) *adj* unreasonable

irreal (ee-rray-*ahl*) *adj* unreal

irreflexivo (ee-rray-flayk-*see*-bhoa) *adj* rash

irregular (ee-rray-goo-*lahr*) *adj* irregular; uneven

irrelevante (ee-rray-lay-*bhahn*-tay) *adj* insignificant

irreparable (ee-rray-pah-*rah*-bhlay) *adj* irreparable

irrevocable (ee-rray-bhoa-*kah*-bhlay) *adj* irrevocable

irritable (ee-rree-*tah*-bhlay) *adj* irritable

irritante (ee-rree-*tahn*-tay) *adj* annoying

irritar (ee-rree-*tahr*) *v* annoy, irritate

irrompible (ee-rroam-*pee*-bhlay) *adj* unbreakable

irrupción (ee-rroop-*th^yoan*) *f* invasion, raid

isla (*eez*-lah) *f* island

islandés (eez-lahn-*dayss*) *adj* Icelandic; *m* Icelander

Islandia (eez-*lahn*-d^yah) *f* Iceland

Israel (eess-rah-*ayl*) *m* Israel

israelí (eess-rah-ay-*lee*) *adj* Israeli; *m* Israeli

istmo (*eest*-moa) *m* isthmus

Italia (ee-*tah*-l^yah) *f* Italy

italiano (ee-tah-*l^yah*-noa) *adj* Italian; *m* Italian

ítem (*ee*-taym) *m* item

itinerario (ee-tee-nay-*rah*-r^yoa) *m* itinerary

izar (ee-*thahr*) *v* hoist

izquierdo (eeth-*k^yayr*-dhoa) *adj* left; left-hand

J

jabón (khah-*bhoan*) *m* soap; **~ de afeitar** shaving-soap; **~ en polvo** soap powder, washing-powder

jade (*khah*-dhay) *m* jade

jadear (khah-dhay-*ahr*) *v* pant

jalar (khah-*lahr*) *vMe* *draw

jalea (khah-*lay*-ah) *f* jelly

jamás (khah-*mahss*) *adv* ever

jamón (khah-*moan*) *m* ham

Japón (khah-*poan*) *m* Japan

japonés (khah-poa-*nayss*) *adj* Japanese; *m* Japanese

¡jaque! (*khah*-kay) check!

jarabe (khah-*rah*-bhay) *m* syrup

jardín (khahr-*dheen*) *m* garden; ~ **de infancia** kindergarten; ~ **público** public garden; ~ **zoológico** zoological gardens, zoo

jardinero (khahr-dhee-*nay*-roa) *m* gardener

jarra (*khah*-rrah) *f* jar

jaula (*khou*-lah) *f* cage

jefe (*khay*-fay) *m* chief, manager, boss; leader; chieftain; ~ **de cocina** chef; ~ **de estación** stationmaster; ~ **de Estado** head of state; ~ **de gobierno** premier

jengibre (khayng-*khee*-bhray) *m* ginger

jerarquía (khay-rahr-*kee*-ah) *f* hierarchy

jeringa (khay-*reeng*-gah) *f* syringe

jersey (khayr-*say*) *m* jersey; jumper

jinete (khee-*nay*-tay) *m* horseman, rider

jitomate (khee-toa-*mah*-tay) *mMe* tomato

Jordania (khoar-*dhah*-nⁱah) *f* Jordan

jordano (khoar-*dhah*-noa) *adj* Jordanian; *m* Jordanian

jornada (khoar-*nah*-dhah) *f* day trip

joven (*khoa*-bhayn) *adj* young; *m* lad

jovencito (khoa-bhayn-*thee*-toa) *m* teenager

jovial (khoa-*bhⁱahl*) *adj* jolly

joya (*khoa*-ⁱah) *f* jewel, gem

joyería (khoa-ⁱay-*ree*-ah) *f* jewellery

joyero (khoa-*ⁱay*-roa) *m* jeweller

jubilado (khoo-bhee-*lah*-dhoa) *adj* retired

judía (khoo-*dhee*-ah) *f* bean

judío (khoo-*dhee*-oa) *adj* Jewish; *m* Jew

juego (*khway*-goa) *m* game, play; set; *hacer ~ con** match; ~ **de bolos** bowling; ~ **de damas** draughts; ~ **de té** tea-set

jueves (*khway*-bhayss) *m* Thursday

juez (khwayth) *m* judge

jugada (khoo-*gah*-dhah) *f* move

jugador (khoo-gah-*dhoar*) *m* player

*jugar (khoo-*gahr*) *v* play

juguete (khoo-*gay*-tay) *m* toy

juguetería (khoo-gay-tay-*ree*-ah) *f* toyshop

juicio (khwee-*th*ⁱoa) *m* sense; judgment

julio (*khoo*-lⁱoa) July

junco (*khoong*-koa) *m* rush

jungla (*khoong*-glah) *f* jungle

junio (*khoo*-nⁱoa) June

junquillo (khoong-*kee*-lⁱoa) *m* reed

junta (*khoon*-tah) *f* meeting

juntamente (khoon-tah-*mayn*-tay) *adv* jointly

juntar (khoon-*tahr*) *v* attach; collect; join; **juntarse** *v* gather

junto a (*khoon*-toa ah) beside; next to

juntos (*khoon*-toass) *adv* together

jurado (khoo-*rah*-dhoa) *m* jury

juramento (khoo-rah-*mayn*-toa) *m* vow, oath; *prestar ~* vow

jurar (khoo-*rahr*) *v* *swear

jurídico (khoo-*ree*-dhee-koa) *adj* legal

jurista (khoo-*reess*-tah) *m* lawyer

justamente (khooss-tah-*mayn*-tay) *adv* rightly; just

justicia (khooss-*tee*-thⁱah) *f* justice

justificar (khooss-tee-fee-*kahr*) *v* justify

justo (*khooss*-toa) *adj* fair, just, righteous, right; correct, appropriate, proper

juvenil (khoo-bhay-*neel*) *adj* juvenile

juventud (khoo-bhayn-*toodh*) *f* youth

juzgar (khoodh-*gahr*) *v* judge

K

Kenya (kay-n^yah) m Kenya

kilogramo (kee-loa-grah-moa) m kilogram

kilometraje (kee-loa-may-trah-khay) m distance in kilometres

kilómetro (kee-loa-may-troa) m kilometre

L

la (lah) pron her

laberinto (lah-bhay-reen-toa) m maze, labyrinth

labio (lah-bh^yoa) m lip

labor (lah-bhoar) f labour

laboratorio (lah-bhoa-rah-toa-r^yoa) m laboratory; ~ **de lenguas** language laboratory

laca (lah-kah) f lacquer; ~ **para el cabello** hair-spray

ladera (lah-dhay-rah) f hillside

lado (lah-dhoa) m side; way; **al** ~ next-door; **al otro** ~ across; **al otro** ~ **de** across

ladrar (lah-dhrahr) v bay, bark

ladrillo (lah-dhree-l^yoa) m brick

ladrón (lah-dhroan) m thief, robber; burglar

lago (lah-goa) m lake

lágrima (lah-gree-mah) f tear

laguna (lah-goo-nah) f lagoon

lamentable (lah-mayn-tah-bhlay) adj lamentable

lamentar (lah-mayn-tahr) v lament; grieve

lamer (lah-mayr) v lick

lámpara (lahm-pah-rah) f lamp; ~ **para lectura** reading-lamp; ~ **sorda** hurricane lamp

lana (lah-nah) f wool; **de** ~ woollen

landa (lahn-dhah) f heath

langosta (lahng-goass-tah) f lobster

lanza (lahn-thah) f spear

lanzamiento (lahn-thah-m^yayn-toa) m throw

lanzar (lahn-thahr) v *cast; launch

lápida (lah-pee-dhah) f gravestone, tombstone

lápiz (lah-peeth) m pencil; ~ **labial** lipstick; ~ **para las cejas** eye-pencil

largo (lahr-goa) adj long; **a lo** ~ **de** along, past; **pasar de** ~ pass by

laringitis (lah-reeng-khee-teess) f laryngitis

¡qué lástima! (kay lahss-tee-mah) what a pity!

lata (lah-tah) f tin, canister, can

lateralmente (lah-tay-rahl-mayn-tay) adv sideways

latín (lah-teen) m Latin

latinoamericano (lah-tee-noa-ah-may-ree-kah-noa) adj Latin-American

latitud (lah-tee-toodh) f latitude

latón (lah-toan) m brass

lavable (lah-bhah-bhlay) adj washable; fast-dyed

lavabo (lah-bhah-bhoa) m wash-stand

lavabos (lah-bhah-bhoass) mpl bathroom; ~ **para caballeros** men's room; ~ **para señoras** ladies' room

lavado (lah-bhah-dhoa) m washing

lavandería (lah-bhahn-day-ree-ah) f laundry; ~ **de autoservicio** launderette

lavar (lah-bhahr) v wash

laxante (lahk-sahn-tay) m laxative

le (lay) pron him; her

leal (lay-ahl) adj true, loyal

lección (layk-th^yoan) f lesson

lectura (layk-too-rah) f reading

leche (lay-chay) f milk; **batido de** ~ milk-shake

lechería (lay-chay-*ree*-ah) *f* dairy

lechero (lay-*chay*-roa) *m* milkman

lechigada (lay-chee-*gah*-dhah) *f* litter

lechoso (lay-*choa*-soa) *adj* milky

lechuga (lay-*choo*-gah) *f* lettuce

*** leer** (lay-*ayr*) *v* *read

legación (lay-gah-*th^y oan*) *f* legation

legal (lay-*gahl*) *adj* legal

legalización (lay-gah-lee-thah-*th^y oan*) *f* legalization

legible (lay-*khee*-bhlay) *adj* legible

legítimo (lay-*khee*-tee-moa) *adj* legitimate, legal

legumbre (lay-*goom*-bray) *f* vegetable

lejano (lay-*khah*-noa) *adj* remote, far, distant

lejos (*lay*-khoass) *adv* far

lema (*lay*-mah) *f* motto, slogan

lengua (*layng*-gwah) *f* tongue; language; ~ **materna** native language, mother tongue

lenguado (layng-*gwah*-dhoa) *m* sole

lenguaje (layng-*gwah*-khay) *m* speech

lente (*layn*-tay) *m/f* lens; ~ **de aumento** magnifying glass; **lentillas** *fpl* contact lenses

lento (*layn*-toa) *adj* slow; slack

león (lay-*oan*) *m* lion

lepra (*lay*-prah) *f* leprosy

lerdo (*layr*-dhoa) *adj* slow

les (layss) *pron* them

lesión (lay-s^y oan) *f* injury

letra (*lay*-trah) *f* letter

levadura (lay-bhah-*dhoo*-rah) *f* yeast

levantamiento (lay-bhahn-tah-*m^y ayn*-toa) *m* rise; rising

levantar (lay-bhahn-*tahr*) *v* lift; *bring up; **levantarse** *v* *rise, *get up

leve (*lay*-bhay) *adj* slight

ley (lay) *f* law

leyenda (lay-*y ayn*-dah) *f* legend

liar (l^y ahr) *v* bundle

libanés (lee-bhah-*nayss*) *adj* Lebanese; *m* Lebanese

Líbano (*lee*-bhah-noa) *m* Lebanon

liberación (lee-bhay-rah-*th^y oan*) *f* liberation; delivery

liberal (lee-bhay-*rahl*) *adj* liberal

liberalismo (lee-bhay-rah-*leez*-moa) *m* liberalism

Liberia (lee-*bhay*-r^y ah) *f* Liberia

liberiano (lee-bhay-*r^y ah*-noa) *adj* Liberian; *m* Liberian

libertad (lee-bhayr-*tahdh*) *f* liberty, freedom

libra (*lee*-bhrah) *f* pound

libranza (lee-*bhrahn*-thah) *f* money order

librar (lee-*bhrahr*) *v* deliver

libre (*lee*-bhray) *adj* free

librería (lee-bhay-*ree*-ah) *f* bookstore

librero (lee-*bhray*-roa) *m* bookseller

libro (*lee*-bhroa) *m* book; ~ **de bolsillo** paperback; ~ **de cocina** cookery-book; ~ **de reclamaciones** complaints book; ~ **de texto** textbook

licencia (lee-*thayn*-th^y ah) *f* permission, licence; leave

lícito (*lee*-thee-toa) *adj* lawful

licor (lee-*koar*) *m* liqueur

líder (*lee*-dhayr) *m* leader

liebre (*l^y ay*-bhray) *f* hare

liga (*lee*-gah) *f* union, league

ligero (lee-*khay*-roa) *adj* light; slight

lima (*lee*-mah) *f* file; lime; ~ **para las uñas** nail-file

limitar (lee-mee-*tahr*) *v* limit

límite (*lee*-mee-tay) *m* boundary, limit; ~ **de velocidad** speed limit

limón (lee-*moan*) *m* lemon

limonada (lee-moa-*nah*-dhah) *f* lemonade

limpiaparabrisas (leem-p^y ah-pah-rah-*bhree*-sahss) *m* windscreen wiper

limpiapipas (leem-p^y ah-*pee*-pahss) *m* pipe cleaner

limpiar (leem-*p^y ahr*) *v* clean; ~ **en se-**

co dry-clean
limpieza (leem-*p*ʸ*ay*-thah) *f* cleaning
limpio (*leem*-pʸoa) *adj* clean
lindo (*leen*-doa) *adj* sweet
línea (*lee*-nay-ah) *f* line; **~ de navegación** shipping line; **~ de pesca** fishing line; **~ principal** main line
lino (*lee*-noa) *m* linen
linterna (leen-*tayr*-nah) *f* lantern; torch, flash-light
liquidación (lee-kee-dhah-*th*ʸ*oan*) *f* clearance sale
líquido (*lee*-kee-dhoa) *adj* liquid
liso (*lee*-soa) *adj* smooth
lista (*leess*-tah) *f* list; **~ de correos** poste restante; **~ de espera** waiting-list; **~ de precios** price-list
listín telefónico (leess-*teen* tay-lay-*foa*-nee-koa) telephone directory; telephone book *Am*
listo (*leess*-toa) *adj* bright; clever, smart; ready
litera (lee-*tay*-rah) *f* berth
literario (lee-tay-*rah*-rʸoa) *adj* literary
literatura (lee-tay-rah-*too*-rah) *f* literature
litoral (lee-toa-*rahl*) *m* sea-coast
litro (*lee*-troa) *m* litre
lo (loa) *pron* it; **~ que** what
lobo (*loa*-bhoa) *m* wolf
local (loa-*kahl*) *adj* local
localidad (loa-kah-lee-*dhahdh*) *f* locality; seat
localizar (loa-kah-lee-*thahr*) *v* locate
loción (loa-*th*ʸ*oan*) *f* lotion
loco (*loa*-koa) *adj* crazy; mad
locomotora (loa-koa-moa-*toa*-rah) *f* engine, locomotive
locuaz (loa-*kwahth*) *adj* talkative
locura (loa-*koo*-rah) *f* madness, lunacy
lodo (*loa*-dhoa) *m* mud
lodoso (loa-*dhoa*-soa) *adj* muddy
lógica (*loa*-khee-kah) *f* logic
lógico (*loa*-khee-koa) *adj* logical

lograr (loa-*grahr*) *v* achieve; secure
lona (*loa*-nah) *f* canvas; **~ impermeable** tarpaulin
longitud (loang-khee-*toodh*) *f* length; longitude; **~ de onda** wave-length
longitudinalmente (loang-khee-too-dhee-nahl-*mayn*-tay) *adv* lengthways
loro (*loa*-roa) *m* parrot
lotería (loa-tay-*ree*-ah) *f* lottery
loza (*loa*-thah) *f* earthenware; pottery, faience, crockery
lubricación (loo-bhree-kah-*th*ʸ*oan*) *f* lubrication
lubricar (loo-bhree-*kahr*) *v* lubricate
lubrificar (loo-bhree-fee-*kahr*) *v* lubricate
lucio (*loo*-thʸoa) *m* pike
*****lucir** (loo-*theer*) *v* *shine
lucha (*loo*-chah) *f* combat, fight; contest, strife; struggle
luchar (loo-*chahr*) *v* struggle, *fight
luego (*lway*-goa) *adv* later; **¡hasta luego!** so long!
lugar (loo-*gahr*) *m* place; spot; **en ~ de** instead of; **~ de camping** camping site; **~ de descanso** holiday resort; **~ de nacimiento** place of birth; **~ de reunión** meeting-place; *****tener ~** *take place
lúgubre (*loo*-goo-bhray) *adj* creepy
lujo (*loo*-khoa) *m* luxury
lujoso (loo-*khoa*-soa) *adj* luxurious
lumbago (loom-*bah*-goa) *m* lumbago
luminoso (loo-mee-*noa*-soa) *adj* luminous
luna (*loo*-nah) *f* moon; **~ de miel** honeymoon
lunático (loo-*nah*-tee-koa) *adj* insane, lunatic
lunes (*loo*-nayss) *m* Monday
lúpulo (*loo*-poo-loa) *m* hop
lustroso (looss-*troa*-soa) *adj* glossy
luto (*loo*-toa) *m* mourning
luz (looth) *f* light; **luces de freno**

brake lights; ~ **de estacionamiento** parking light; ~ **de la luna** moonlight; ~ **del día** daylight; ~ **del sol** sunlight; ~ **lateral** sidelight; ~ **trasera** rear-light

LL

llaga (lʸah-gah) f sore
llama (lʸah-mah) f flame
llamada (lʸah-mah-dhah) f call; ~ **local** local call; ~ **telefónica** telephone call
llamar (lʸah-mahr) v cry, call; **así llamado** so-called; ~ **por teléfono** phone; **llamarse** v *be called
llano (lʸah-noa) adj flat; level, even, smooth; m plain
llanta (lʸahn-tah) f rim; fMe tire
llave (lʸah-bhay) f key; **ama de llaves** housekeeper; **guardar con** ~ lock up; ~ **de la casa** latchkey; ~ **inglesa** spanner
llegada (lʸay-gah-dhah) f arrival; coming
llegar (lʸay-gahr) v arrive; ~ **a** attain
llenar (lʸay-nahr) v fill; fill in; fill out Am; fill up
lleno (lʸay-noa) adj full
llevar (lʸay-bhahr) v *take; *bear, carry; *wear; **llevarse** v *take away
llorar (lʸoa-rahr) v cry, *weep
*llover (lʸoa-bhayr) v rain
llovizna (lʸoa-bheeth-nah) f drizzle
lluvia (lʸoo-bhʸah) f rain
lluvioso (lʸoo-bhʸoa-soa) adj rainy

M

macizo (mah-thee-thoa) adj solid, massive
machacar (mah-chah-kahr) v mash
macho (mah-choa) adj male
madera (mah-dhay-rah) f wood; **de** ~ wooden; ~ **de construcción** timber
madero (mah-dhay-roa) m log
madrastra (mah-dhrahss-trah) f stepmother
madre (mah-dhray) f mother
madriguera (mah-dhree-gay-rah) f den
madrugada (mah-dhroo-gah-dhah) f daybreak
madrugar (mah-dhroo-gahr) v *rise early
madurez (mah-dhoo-rayth) f maturity
maduro (mah-dhoo-roa) adj mature, ripe
maestro (mah-ayss-troa) m master; schoolteacher, schoolmaster, teacher; ~ **particular** tutor
magia (mah-khʸah) f magic
mágico (mah-khee-koa) adj magic
magistrado (mah-kheess-trah-dhoa) m magistrate
magnético (mahg-nay-tee-koa) adj magnetic
magneto (mahg-nay-toa) m magneto
magnetófono (mahg-nay-toa-foa-noa) m tape-recorder
magnífico (mahg-nee-fee-koa) adj splendid, gorgeous, magnificent, swell
magro (mah-groa) adj lean
magulladura (mah-goo-lʸah-dhoo-rah) f bruise
magullar (mah-goo-lʸahr) v bruise
maíz (mah-eeth) m maize; ~ **en la mazorca** corn on the cob
majestad (mah-khayss-tahdh) f majes-

ty
mal (mahl) *m* harm, evil; wrong; mischief
malaria (mah-*lah*-rʸah) *f* malaria
Malasia (mah-*lah*-sʸah) *f* Malaysia
malayo (mah-*lah*-ʸoa) *adj* Malaysian; *m* Malay
*****maldecir** (mahl-day-*theer*) *v* curse
maldición (mahl-dee-*th*ʸoan) *f* curse
maleta (mah-*lay*-tah) *f* suitcase, bag
maletín (mah-lay-*teen*) *m* grip *nAm*
malévolo (mah-*lay*-bhoa-loa) *adj* spiteful
malicia (mah-lee-th*ʸah) *f* mischief
malicioso (mah-lee-*th*ʸoa-soa) *adj* malicious
maligno (mah-*leeg*-noa) *adj* malignant; ill
malo (*mah*-loa) *adj* bad; evil, ill
malva (*mahl*-bhah) *adj* mauve
malvado (mahl-*bhah*-dhoa) *adj* wicked, evil
malla (*mah*-lʸah) *f* mesh
mamífero (mah-*mee*-fay-roa) *m* mammal
mampara (mahm-*pah*-rah) *f* screen
mampostear (mahm-poass-tay-*ahr*) *v* *lay bricks
mamut (mah-*moot*) *m* mammoth
manada (mah-*nah*-dhah) *f* herd
manantial (mah-nahn-t*ʸahl*) *m* spring
mancuernillas (mahn-kwayr-nee-lʸahss) *fplMe* cuff-links *pl*
mancha (*mahn*-chah) *f* stain, spot, speck; blot
manchado (mahn-*chah*-dhoa) *adj* soiled
manchar (mahn-*chahr*) *v* stain
mandar (mahn-*dahr*) *v* command; *send; ~ a buscar *send for
mandarina (mahn-dah-*ree*-nah) *f* mandarin, tangerine
mandato (mahn-*dah*-toa) *m* mandate; order

mandíbula (mahn-*dee*-bhoo-lah) *f* jaw
mando (*mahn*-doa) *m* command
manejable (mah-nay-*khah*-bhlay) *adj* handy; manageable
manejar (mah-nay-*khahr*) *v* handle
manejo (mah-*nay*-khoa) *m* management
manera (mah-*nay*-rah) *f* way, manner; **de otra ~** otherwise
manga (*mahng*-gah) *f* sleeve
mango (*mahng*-goa) *m* handle
manía (mah-*nee*-ah) *f* craze
manicura (mah-nee-*koo*-rah) *f* manicure; *****hacer la ~** manicure
manifestación (mah-nee-fayss-tah-th*ʸoan) *f* demonstration; *****hacer una ~** demonstrate
*****manifestar** (mah-nee-fayss-*tahr*) *v* reveal
maniquí (mah-nee-*kee*) *m* model, mannequin
mano (*mah*-noa) *f* hand; **de segunda ~** second-hand; **hecho a ~** handmade
mansión (mahn-s*ʸoan) *f* mansion
manso (*mahn*-soa) *adj* tame
manta (*mahn*-tah) *f* blanket
mantel (mahn-*tayl*) *m* table-cloth
*****mantener** (mahn-tay-*nayr*) *v* maintain
mantenimiento (mahn-tay-nee-m*ʸayn-toa) *m* maintenance
mantequilla (mahn-tay-kee-lʸah) *f* butter
manual (mah-*nwahl*) *adj* manual; *m* handbook; **~ de conversación** phrase-book
manuscrito (mah-nooss-*kree*-toa) *m* manuscript
manutención (mah-noo-tayn-th*ʸoan) *f* upkeep
manzana (mahn-*thah*-nah) *f* apple; **~ de casas** house block *Am*
mañana (mah-*ñah*-nah) *f* morning;

adv tomorrow; **esta ~** this morning

mapa (*mah*-pah) *m* map; **~ de carreteras** road map

maquillaje (mah-kee-*lᵞah*-khay) *m* make-up

máquina (*mah*-kee-nah) *f* engine, machine; **~ de afeitar** razor; **~ de billetes** ticket machine; **~ de coser** sewing-machine; **~ de escribir** typewriter; **~ de lavar** washing-machine; **~ tragamonedas** slot-machine

maquinaria (mah-kee-*nah*-rᵞah) *f* machinery

mar (mahr) *m* sea; **orilla del ~** seaside, seashore

maravilla (mah-rah-*bhee*-lᵞah) *f* marvel

maravillarse (mah-rah-bhee-*lᵞahr*-say) *v* marvel

maravilloso (mah-rah-bhee-*lᵞoa*-soa) *adj* wonderful, marvellous, fine

marca (*mahr*-kah) *f* brand; mark; **~ de fábrica** trademark

marcar (mahr-*kahr*) *v* mark; score

marco (*mahr*-koa) *m* frame

marcha (*mahr*-chah) *f* march; ***dar ~ atrás** reverse; **~ atrás** reverse

marchar (mahr-*chahr*) *v* march

marea (mah-*ray*-ah) *f* tide

mareado (mah-ray-*ah*-dhoa) *adj* dizzy, giddy; seasick

mareo (mah-*ray*-oa) *m* giddiness; seasickness

marfil (mahr-*feel*) *m* ivory

margarina (mahr-gah-*ree*-nah) *f* margarine

margen (*mahr*-khayn) *m* margin

marido (mah-*ree*-dhoa) *m* husband

marina (mah-*ree*-nah) *f* navy; seascape

marinero (mah-ree-*nay*-roa) *m* sailor

marino (mah-*ree*-noa) *m* seaman

mariposa (mah-ree-*poa*-sah) *f* butterfly

marisco (mah-*reess*-koa) *m* shellfish

marisma (mah-*reez*-mah) *f* swamp

marítimo (mah-*ree*-tee-moa) *adj* maritime

mármol (*mahr*-moal) *m* marble

marqués (mahr-*kayss*) *m* marquis

marroquí (mah-rroa-*kee*) *adj* Moroccan; *m* Moroccan

Marruecos (mah-*rway*-koass) *m* Morocco

martes (*mahr*-tayss) *m* Tuesday

martillo (mahr-*tee*-lᵞoa) *m* hammer

mártir (*mahr*-teer) *m* martyr

marzo (*mahr*-thoa) March

mas (mahss) *conj* but

más (mahss) *adv* more; plus; **algo ~** some more; **el ~** most; **~ de** over

masa (*mah*-sah) *f* mass; crowd, lot; dough, batter

masaje (mah-*sah*-khay) *m* massage; ***dar ~** massage; **~ facial** face massage

masajista (mah-sah-*kheess*-tah) *m* masseur

máscara (*mahss*-kah-rah) *f* mask; **~ facial** face-pack

masculino (mahss-koo-*lee*-noa) *adj* masculine

masticar (mahss-tee-*kahr*) *v* chew

mástil (*mahss*-teel) *m* mast

matar (mah-*tahr*) *v* kill

mate (*mah*-tay) *adj* mat, dim, dull

matemáticas (mah-tay-*mah*-tee-kahss) *fpl* mathematics

matemático (mah-tay-*mah*-tee-koa) *adj* mathematical

materia (mah-*tay*-rᵞah) *f* matter; **~ prima** raw material

material (mah-tay-*rᵞahl*) *adj* material, substantial; *m* material

matiz (mah-*teeth*) *m* nuance

matorral (mah-toa-*rrahl*) *m* scrub, bush

matrícula (mah-*tree*-koo-lah) f registration number

matrimonial (mah-tree-moa-*n*ʸ*ahl*) adj matrimonial

matrimonio (mah-tree-*moa*-nʸoa) m wedding, marriage; matrimony

matriz (mah-*treeth*) f womb

mausoleo (mou-soa-*lay*-oa) m mausoleum

máximo (*mahk*-see-moa) m maximum

mayo (*mah*-ʸoa) May

mayor (mah-*ʸoar*) adj superior, major; main, eldest; m major

mayoría (mah-ʸoa-*ree*-ah) f majority; bulk

mayorista (mah-ʸoa-*reess*-tah) m wholesale dealer

mayúscula (mah-*ʸooss*-koo-lah) f capital letter

mazo (*mah*-thoa) m mallet

me (may) pron me; myself

mecánico (may-kah-nee-koa) adj mechanical; m mechanic

mecanismo (may-kah-*neez*-moa) m mechanism, machinery

mecanografiar (may-kah-noa-grah-*f*ʸ*ahr*) v type

mecer (may-*thayr*) v rock

mecha (*may*-chah) f fuse

medalla (may-*dhah*-lʸah) f medal

media (*may*-dhʸah) f stocking; ~ **pantalón** panty-hose; **medias elásticas** support hose

mediador (may-dhʸah-*dhoar*) m mediator

medianamente (may-dhʸah-nah-*mayn*-tay) adv fairly

mediano (may-*dhʸah*-noa) adj medium

medianoche (may-dhʸah-*noa*-chay) f midnight

mediante (may-*dhʸahn*-tay) adv by means of

mediar (may-*dhʸahr*) v mediate

medicamento (may-dhee-kah-*mayn*-toa) m medicine, drug

medicina (may-dhee-*thee*-nah) f medicine

médico (*may*-dhee-koa) adj medical; m doctor, physician; ~ **de cabecera** general practitioner

medida (may-*dhee*-dhah) f measure; **hecho a la** ~ made to order, tailor-made

medidor (may-dhee-*dhoar*) m gauge

medieval (may-dhʸay-*bhahl*) adj mediaeval

medio (*may*-dhʸoa) adj half; medium; middle; m midst, middle; means; **en** ~ **de** amid; ~ **ambiente** milieu, environment

mediocre (may-*dhʸoa*-kray) adj moderate, poor

mediodía (may-dhʸoa-*dhee*-ah) m midday, noon

***medir** (may-*dheer*) v measure

meditación (may-dhee-tah-*th*ʸ*oan*) f meditation

meditar (may-dhee-*tahr*) v meditate

Mediterráneo (may-dhee-tay-*rrah*-nay-oa) Mediterranean

médula (*may*-dhoo-lah) f marrow

medusa (may-*dhoo*-sah) f jelly-fish

mejicano (may-khee-*kah*-noa) adj Mexican; m Mexican

Méjico (*may*-khee-koa) m Mexico

mejilla (may-*khee*-lʸah) f cheek

mejillón (may-khee-*l*ʸ*oan*) m mussel

mejor (may-*khoar*) adj better; superior

mejora (may-*khoa*-rah) f improvement

mejorar (may-khoa-*rahr*) v improve

melancolía (may-lahng-koa-*lee*-ah) f melancholy

melancólico (may-lahng-*koa*-lee-koa) adj sad

melocotón (may-loa-koa-*toan*) m peach

melodía (may-loa-*dhee*-ah) f melody

melodioso (may-loa-*dh*ʸoa-soa) adj tuneful

melodrama (may-loa-*dhrah*-mah) m melodrama

melón (may-*loan*) m melon

membrana (maym-*brah*-nah) f diaphragm

memorable (may-moa-*rah*-bhlay) adj memorable

memoria (may-*moa*-rʸah) f memory; **de ~** by heart

menaje (may-*nah*-khay) m household

mención (mayn-*th*ʸoan) f mention

mencionar (mayn-th*ʸoa*-nahr) v mention

mendigar (mayn-dee-*gahr*) v beg

mendigo (mayn-*dee*-goa) m beggar

menor (may-*noar*) adj minor; junior

menos (*may*-noass) adv less; minus; but; **a ~ que** unless; **por lo ~** at least

menosprecio (may-noass-*pray*-thʸoa) m contempt

mensaje (mayn-*sah*-khay) m message

mensajero (mayn-sah-*khay*-roa) m messenger

menstruación (mayns-trwah-*th*ʸoan) f menstruation

mensual (mayn-*swahl*) adj monthly

menta (*mayn*-tah) f mint; peppermint

mental (mayn-*tahl*) adj mental

mente (*mayn*-tay) f mind

***mentir** (mayn-*teer*) v lie

mentira (mayn-*tee*-rah) f lie

menú (may-*noo*) m menu

menudo (may-*noo*-dhoa) adj minute, small, tiny; **a ~** often

mercado (mayr-*kah*-dhoa) m market; **~ negro** black market

mercancía (mayr-kahn-*thee*-ah) f merchandise

mercería (mayr-thay-*ree*-ah) f haberdashery

mercurio (mayr-*koo*-rʸoa) m mercury

***merecer** (may-ray-*thayr*) v merit, deserve

meridional (may-ree-dhʸoa-*nahl*) adj southern, southerly

merienda (may-*r*ʸ*ayn*-dah) f tea

mérito (*may*-ree-toa) m merit

merluza (mayr-*loo*-thah) f whiting

mermelada (mayr-may-*lah*-dhah) f jam

mes (mayss) m month

mesa (*may*-sah) f table

mesera (may-*say*-rah) fMe waitress

mesero (may-*say*-roa) mMe waiter

meseta (may-*say*-tah) f plateau

meta (*may*-tah) f goal; finish

metal (may-*tahl*) m metal

metálico (may-*tah*-lee-koa) adj metal

meter (may-*tayr*) v *put

meticuloso (may-tee-koo-*loa*-soa) adj precise

metódico (may-*toa*-dhee-koa) adj methodical

método (*may*-toa-dhoa) m method

métrico (*may*-tree-koa) adj metric

metro (*may*-troa) m metre; underground; subway nAm

mezcla (*mayth*-klah) f mixture

mezclar (mayth-*klahr*) v mix; **mezclarse en** interfere with

mezquino (mayth-*kee*-noa) adj narrow-minded, stingy; mean

mezquita (mayth-*kee*-tah) f mosque

mi (mee) adj my

micrófono (mee-*kroa*-foa-noa) m microphone

microscopio (mee-kroass-*koa*-pʸoa) m microscope

microsurco (mee-kroa-*soor*-koa) m long-playing record

miedo (*m*ʸ*ay*-dhoa) m fear, fright; ***tener ~** *be afraid

miel (*m*ʸ*ayl*) f honey

miembro (*m*ʸ*aym*-broa) m limb; member

mientras (m^yayn-trahss) *conj* whilst, while

miércoles (m^yayr-koa-layss) *m* Wednesday

migaja (mee-*gah*-khah) *f* crumb

migraña (mee-*grah*-ñah) *f* migraine

mil (meel) *num* thousand

milagro (mee-*lah*-groa) *m* wonder, miracle

milagroso (mee-lah-*groa*-soa) *adj* miraculous

militar (mee-lee-*tahr*) *adj* military; *m* soldier

milla (*mee*-l^yah) *f* mile

millaje (mee-*l^yah*-khay) *m* mileage

millón (mee-*l^yoan*) *m* million

millonario (mee-l^yoa-nah-r^yoa) *m* millionaire

mimar (mee-*mahr*) *v* *spoil

mina (*mee*-nah) *f* mine; pit; ~ **de oro** goldmine

mineral (mee-nay-*rahl*) *m* mineral; ore

minería (mee-nay-*ree*-ah) *f* mining

minero (mee-*nay*-roa) *m* miner

miniatura (mee-n^yah-*too*-rah) *f* miniature

mínimo (*mee*-nee-moa) *adj* least

mínimum (*mee*-nee-moom) *m* minimum

ministerio (mee-neess-*tay*-r^yoa) *m* ministry

ministro (mee-*neess*-troa) *m* minister

minoría (mee-noa-*ree*-ah) *f* minority

minorista (mee-noa-*reess*-tah) *m* retailer

minucioso (mee-noo-*th^yoa*-soa) *adj* thorough

minusválido (mee-nooz-*bhah*-lee-*dhoa*) *adj* disabled

minuto (mee-*noo*-toa) *m* minute

mío (*mee*-oa) *pron* mine

miope (m^yoa-pay) *adj* short-sighted

mirada (mee-*rah*-dhah) *f* look

mirar (mee-*rahr*) *v* look; watch, view; look at; stare, gaze

mirlo (*meer*-loa) *m* blackbird

misa (*mee*-sah) *f* Mass

misceláneo (mee-thay-*lah*-nay-oa) *adj* miscellaneous

miserable (mee-say-*rah*-bhlay) *adj* miserable

miseria (mee-*say*-r^yah) *f* misery

misericordia (mee-say-ree-*koar*-d^yah) *f* mercy

misericordioso (mee-say-ree-koar-*d^yoa*-soa) *adj* merciful

misión (mee-s^yoan) *f* mission

mismo (*meez*-moa) *adj* same

misterio (meess-*tay*-r^yoa) *m* mystery

misterioso (meess-tay-*r^yoa*-soa) *adj* mysterious; obscure

mitad (mee-*tahdh*) *f* half; **partir por la** ~ halve

mito (*mee*-toa) *m* myth

moción (moa-*th^yoan*) *f* motion

mochila (moa-*chee*-lah) *f* rucksack, knapsack

moda (*moa*-dhah) *f* fashion; **a la** ~ fashionable

modales (moa-*dah*-layss) *mpl* manners *pl*

modelar (moa-dhay-*lahr*) *v* model

modelo (moa-*dhay*-loa) *m* model

moderado (moa-dhay-*rah*-dhoa) *adj* moderate

moderno (moa-*dhayr*-noa) *adj* modern

modestia (moa-*dhayss*-t^yah) *f* modesty

modesto (moa-*dhayss*-toa) *adj* modest

modificación (moa-dhee-fee-kah-*th^yoan*) *f* change

modificar (moa-dhee-fee-*kahr*) *v* change, modify

modismo (moa-*dheez*-moa) *m* idiom

modista (moa-*dheess*-tah) *f* dressmaker

modo (*moa*-dhoa) *m* fashion, manner; **de cualquier** ~ anyhow; **de ningún** ~ by no means; **de todos modos**

any way; at any rate; **en ~ alguno** at all; **~ de empleo** directions for use

mohair (moa-ayr) m mohair

moho (moa-oa) m mildew

mojado (moa-khah-dhoa) adj wet; moist, damp

mojigato (moa-khee-gah-toa) adj hypocritical

mojón (moa-khoan) m landmark

*moler (moa-layr) v *grind

molestar (moa-layss-tahr) v disturb, trouble, bother

molestia (moa-layss-tʸah) f trouble, nuisance, bother

molesto (moa-layss-toa) adj troublesome, inconvenient

molinero (moa-lee-nay-roa) m miller

molino (moa-lee-noa) m mill; **~ de viento** windmill

momentáneo (moa-mayn-tah-nay-oa) adj momentary

momento (moa-mayn-toa) m moment

monarca (moa-nahr-kah) m monarch, ruler

monarquía (moa-nahr-kee-ah) f monarchy

monasterio (moa-nahss-tay-rʸoa) m monastery

moneda (moa-nay-dhah) f currency; coin; change; **~ extranjera** foreign currency

monedero (moa-nay-dhay-roa) m purse

monetario (moa-nay-tah-rʸoa) adj monetary; **unidad monetaria** monetary unit

monja (moang-khah) f nun

monje (moang-khay) m monk

mono (moa-noa) m monkey; overalls pl

monólogo (moa-noa-loa-goa) m monologue

monopolio (moa-noa-poa-lʸoa) m monopoly

monótono (moa-noa-toa-noa) adj monotonous

monstruo (moans-trwoa) m monster

montaña (moan-tah-ñah) f mountain

montañismo (moan-tah-ñeez-moa) m mountaineering

montañoso (moan-tah-ñoa-soa) adj mountainous

montar (moan-tahr) v mount, *get on; assemble; *ride

monte (moan-tay) m mount

montículo (moan-tee-koo-loa) m mound

montón (moan-toan) m heap, stack, pile

montuoso (moan-twoa-soa) adj hilly

monumento (moa-noo-mayn-toa) m monument; memorial

mora (moa-rah) f mulberry; blackberry

morado (moa-rah-dhoa) adj violet

moral (moa-rahl) adj moral; f moral; spirits

moralidad (moa-rah-lee-dhahdh) f morality

mordaza (moar-dhah-thah) f clamp

mordedura (moar-dhay-dhoo-rah) f bite

*morder (moar-dhayr) v *bite

morena (moa-ray-nah) f brunette

moreno (moa-ray-noa) adj brown

moretón (moa-ray-toan) m bruise

morfina (moar-fee-nah) f morphine, morphia

*morir (moa-reer) v die

moro (moa-roa) m Moor

morral (moa-rrahl) m haversack

morro (moa-rroa) m pussy-cat

mortal (moar-tahl) adj mortal; fatal

mosaico (moa-sigh-koa) m mosaic

mosca (moass-kah) f fly

mosquitero (moass-kee-tay-roa) m mosquito-net

mosquito (moass-kee-toa) m mosquito

mostaza (moass-tah-thah) f mustard

mostrador (moass-trah-dhoar) m counter

*mostrar (moass-trahr) v display, *show

mote (moa-tay) m nickname

moteado (moa-tay-ah-dhoa) adj spotted

motel (moa-tayl) m motel

motín (moa-teen) m riot

motivo (moa-tee-bhoa) m motive; cause, occasion

motocicleta (moa-toa-thee-klay-tah) f motor-cycle; motorbike nAm

motoneta (moa-toa-nay-tah) f scooter

motor (moa-toar) m motor, engine; ~ de arranque starter motor

*mover (moa-bhayr) v move; stir

movible (moa-bhee-bhlay) adj movable

móvil (moa-bheel) adj mobile

movimiento (moa-bhee-mᵛayn-toa) m movement, motion

mozo (moa-thoa) m boy; porter

muchacha (moo-chah-chah) f girl; maid

muchacho (moo-chah-choa) m boy; lad

muchedumbre (moo-chay-dhoom-bray) f crowd

mucho (moo-choa) adv much; far, very; adj much; con ~ by far; muchos adj many

mudanza (moo-dhahn-thah) f move

mudarse (moo-dhahr-say) v move; change

mudo (moo-dhoa) adj mute, dumb

muebles (mway-bhlayss) mpl furniture

muela (mway-lah) f molar; dolor de muelas toothache

muelle (mway-lᵛay) m dock, wharf, quay, pier, jetty; spring

muerte (mwayr-tay) f death

muerto (mwayr-toa) adj dead

muestra (mwayss-trah) f sample

mugir (moo-kheer) v roar

mujer (moo-khayr) f woman; wife

mújol (moo-khoal) m mullet

muleta (moo-lay-tah) f crutch

mulo (moo-loa) m mule

multa (mool-tah) f fine; ticket

multiplicación (mool-tee-plee-kah-thᵛoan) f multiplication

multiplicar (mool-tee-plee-kahr) v multiply

multitud (mool-tee-toodh) f crowd

mundial (moon-dᵛahl) adj world-wide, global

mundo (moon-doa) m world; todo el ~ everyone

municipal (moo-nee-thee-pahl) adj municipal

municipalidad (moo-nee-thee-pah-lee-dhahdh) f municipality

muñeca (moo-ñay-kah) f doll; wrist

muralla (moo-rah-lᵛah) f wall

muro (moo-roa) m wall

músculo (mooss-koo-loa) m muscle

musculoso (mooss-koo-loa-soa) adj muscular

muselina (moo-say-lee-nah) f muslin

museo (moo-say-oa) m museum; ~ de figuras de cera waxworks pl

musgo (mooz-goa) m moss

música (moo-see-kah) f music

musical (moo-see-kahl) adj musical; comedia ~ musical comedy

músico (moo-see-koa) m musician

muslo (mooz-loa) m thigh

musulmán (moo-sool-mahn) m Muslim

mutuo (moo-twoa) adj mutual

muy (moo ee) adv very, quite

N

nácar (*nah*-kahr) *m* mother-of-pearl

*nacer (nah-*thayr*) *v* *be born

nacido (nah-*thee*-dhoa) *adj* born

nacimiento (nah-thee-*m*ʸ*ayn*-toa) *m* birth; rise

nación (nah-*th*ʸ*oan*) *f* nation

nacional (nah-thʸoa-*nahl*) *adj* national

nacionalidad (nah-thʸoa-nah-lee-*dhahdh*) *f* nationality

nacionalizar (nah-thʸoa-nah-lee-*thahr*) *v* nationalize

nada (*nah*-dhah) nothing; nil

nadador (nah-dhah-*dhoar*) *m* swimmer

nadar (nah-*dhahr*) *v* *swim

nadie (*nah*-dhʸay) *pron* nobody, no one

naipe (*nigh*-pay) *m* playing-card

nalga (*nahl*-gah) *m* buttock

naranja (nah-*rahng*-khah) *f* orange

narciso (nahr-*thee*-soa) *m* daffodil

narcosis (nahr-*koa*-seess) *f* narcosis

narcótico (nahr-*koa*-tee-koa) *m* narcotic

nariz (nah-*reeth*) *f* nose

narración (nah-rrah-*th*ʸ*oan*) *f* account

nata (*nah*-tah) *f* cream

natación (nah-tah-*th*ʸ*oan*) *f* swimming

nativo (nah-*tee*-bhoa) *adj* native

natural (nah-too-*rahl*) *adj* natural; *m* nature

naturaleza (nah-too-rah-*lay*-thah) *f* nature

naturalmente (nah-too-rahl-*mayn*-tay) *adv* naturally

náusea (*nou*-say-ah) *f* nausea, sickness

navaja (nah-*bhah*-khah) *f* pocket-knife

naval (nah-*bhahl*) *adj* naval

navegable (nah-bhay-*gah*-bhlay) *adj* navigable

navegación (nah-bhay-gah-*th*ʸ*oan*) *f* navigation

navegar (nah-bhay-*gahr*) *v* sail; navigate

Navidad (nah-bhee-*dhahdh*) *f* Xmas, Christmas

nebuloso (nay-bhoo-*loa*-soa) *adj* misty

necesario (nay-thay-*sah*-rʸoa) *adj* necessary; requisite

neceser (nay-thay-*sayr*) *m* toilet case

necesidad (nay-thay-see-*dhahdh*) *f* need, necessity; want; misery

necesitar (nay-thay-see-*tahr*) *v* need

necio (*nay*-thʸoa) *adj* foolish, silly

*negar (nay-*gahr*) *v* deny

negativa (nay-gah-*tee*-bhah) *f* refusal

negativo (nay-gah-*tee*-bhoa) *adj* negative; *m* negative

negligencia (nay-glee-*khayn*-thʸah) *f* neglect

negligente (nay-glee-*khayn*-tay) *adj* neglectful, careless

negociación (nay-goa-thʸah-*th*ʸ*oan*) *f* negotiation

negociante (nay-goa-*th*ʸ*ahn*-tay) *m* dealer

negociar (nay-goa-*th*ʸ*ahr*) *v* negotiate

negocio (nay-*goa*-thʸoa) *m* business; ***hacer negocios con** *deal with; **hombre de negocios** businessman; ~ **fotográfico** camera shop; **viaje de negocios** business trip

negro (*nay*-groa) *adj* black; *m* Negro

neón (*nay*-oan) *m* neon

nervio (*nayr*-bhʸoa) *m* nerve

nervioso (nayr-*bh*ʸ*oa*-soa) *adj* nervous

neto (*nay*-toa) *adj* net

neumático (nayºº-*mah*-tee-koa) *adj* pneumatic; *m* tyre, tire; ~ **de repuesto** spare tyre; ~ **desinflado** flat tyre

neumonía (nayºº-moa-*nee*-ah) *f* pneumonia

neuralgia (nayºº-*rahl*-khʸah) *f* neuralgia

neurosis (nay⁰⁰-*roa*-seess) f neurosis

neutral (nay⁰⁰-*trahl*) adj neutral

neutro (nay⁰⁰-troa) adj neuter

*****nevar** (nay-*bhahr*) v snow

nevasca (nay-*bhahss*-kah) f snowstorm

nevoso (nay-*bhoa*-soa) adj snowy

ni … ni (nee) neither … nor

nicotina (nee-koa-*tee*-nah) f nicotine

nido (*nee*-dhoa) m nest

niebla (nʸay-bhlah) f mist, fog; haze; **faro de ~** foglamp

nieta (nʸay-tah) f granddaughter

nieto (nʸay-toa) m grandson

nieve (nʸay-bhay) f snow

Nigeria (nee-*khay*-rʸah) f Nigeria

nigeriano (nee-khay-*rʸah*-noa) adj Nigerian; m Nigerian

ninguno (neeng-*goo*-noa) adj no; pron none; **~ de los dos** neither

niñera (nee-*ñay*-rah) f nurse

niño (*nee*-ñoa) m child; kid

níquel (*nee*-kayl) m nickel

nitrógeno (nee-*troa*-khay-noa) m nitrogen

nivel (nee-*bhayl*) m level; **~ de vida** standard of living; **paso a ~** level crossing

nivelar (nee-bhay-*lahr*) v level

no (noa) not; no; **si ~** otherwise, else

noble (*noa*-bhlay) adj noble

nobleza (noa-*bhlay*-thah) f nobility

noción (noa-*thʸoan*) f notion; idea

nocturno (noak-*toor*-noa) adj nightly

noche (*noa*-chay) f night; **de ~** overnight, by night; **esta ~** tonight

nogal (noa-*gahl*) m walnut

nombramiento (noam-brah-*mʸayn*-toa) m appointment, nomination

nombrar (noam-*brahr*) v name, mention; appoint, nominate

nombre (*noam*-bray) m noun; name; denomination; **en ~ de** on behalf of, in the name of; **~ de pila** Christian name, first name

nominación (noa-mee-nah-*thʸoan*) f nomination

nominal (noa-mee-*nahl*) adj nominal

nordeste (noar-*dhayss*-tay) m northeast

norma (*noar*-mah) f standard

normal (noar-*mahl*) adj normal; regular, standard

noroeste (noa-roa-*ayss*-tay) m northwest

norte (*noar*-tay) m north; **del ~** northerly; **polo ~** North Pole

norteño (noar-*tay*-ñoa) adj northern

Noruega (noa-*rway*-gah) f Norway

noruego (noa-*rway*-goa) adj Norwegian; m Norwegian

nos (noass) pron ourselves

nosotros (noa-*soa*-troass) pron we; us

nostalgia (noass-*tahl*-khʸah) f homesickness

nota (*noa*-tah) f ticket; note; mark

notable (noa-*tah*-bhlay) adj considerable; remarkable, striking, noticeable

notar (noa-*tahr*) v notice; note

notario (noa-*tah*-rʸoa) m notary

noticia (noa-*tee*-thʸah) f news, notice; **noticias** fpl news, tidings pl

noticiario (noa-tee-*thʸah*-rʸoa) m news; newsreel

notificar (noa-tee-fee-*kahr*) v notify

notorio (noa-*toa*-rʸoa) adj well-known

novedad (noa-bhay-*dhahdh*) f novelty

novela (noa-*bhay*-lah) f novel; **~ policíaca** detective story; **~ por entregas** serial

novelista (noa-bhay-*leess*-tah) f novelist

noveno (noa-*bhay*-noa) num ninth

noventa (noa-*bhayn*-tah) num ninety

novia (*noa*-bhʸah) f fiancée; bride

noviazgo (noa-*bhʸahth*-goa) m engagement

noviembre (noa-bhᵞaym-bray) November

***hacer novillos** (ah-thayr noa-bhee-lᵞoass) play truant

novio (noa-bhᵞoa) m fiancé; bridegroom

nube (noo-bhay) f cloud

nublado (noo-bhlah-dhoa) adj cloudy, overcast

nuca (noo-kah) f nape of the neck

nuclear (noo-klay-ahr) adj nuclear

núcleo (noo-klay-oa) m nucleus; heart, essence, core

nudillo (noo-dhee-lᵞoa) m knuckle

nudo (noo-dhoa) m knot; lump; ~ **corredizo** loop

nuestro (nwayss-troa) adj our

Nueva Zelanda (nway-bhah thay-lahn-dah) New Zealand

nueve (nway-bhay) num nine

nuevo (nway-bhoa) adj new; **de** ~ again

nuez (nwayth) f nut; ~ **moscada** nutmeg

nulo (noo-loa) adj invalid, void

numeral (noo-may-rahl) m numeral

número (noo-may-roa) m number; digit; quantity; size; act

numeroso (noo-may-roa-soa) adj numerous

nunca (noong-kah) adv never

nutritivo (noo-tree-tee-bhoa) adj nutritious, nourishing

nylon (nigh-loan) m nylon

O

o (oa) conj or; **o ... o** either ... or

oasis (oa-ah-seess) f oasis

***obedecer** (oa-bhay-dhay-thayr) v obey

obediencia (oa-bhay-dhᵞayn-thᵞah) f obedience

obediente (oa-bhay-dhᵞayn-tay) adj obedient

obertura (oa-bhayr-too-rah) f overture

obesidad (oa-bhay-see-dhahdh) f fatness

obeso (oa-bhay-soa) adj corpulent

obispo (oa-bheess-poa) m bishop

objeción (oabh-khay-thᵞoan) f objection; ***hacer** ~ **a** mind

objetar (oabh-khay-tahr) v object

objetivo (oabh-khay-tee-bhoa) adj objective; m design, objective, target

objeto (oabh-khay-toa) m object; **objetos de valor** valuables pl; **objetos perdidos** lost and found

oblea (oa-bhlay-ah) f wafer

oblicuo (oa-bhlee-kwoa) adj slanting

obligar (oa-bhlee-gahr) v oblige; force

obligatorio (oa-bhlee-gah-toa-rᵞoa) adj compulsory, obligatory

oblongo (oa-bhloang-goa) adj oblong

obra (oa-bhrah) f work; ~ **de arte** work of art; ~ **de teatro** play; ~ **hecha a mano** handwork; ~ **maestra** masterpiece

obrar (oa-bhrahr) v work; perform

obrero (oa-bhray-roa) m workman, worker, labourer; ~ **portuario** docker

obsceno (oabh-thay-noa) adj obscene

obscuridad (oabhs-koo-ree-dhahdh) f gloom

obscuro (oabhs-koo-roa) adj dark, obscure

observación (oabh-sayr-bhah-thᵞoan) f observation; remark; ***hacer una** ~ remark

observar (oabh-sayr-bhahr) v watch, observe, notice, note

observatorio (oabh-sayr-bhah-toa-rᵞoa) m observatory

obsesión (oabh-say-sᵞoan) f obsession

obstáculo (oabhs-tah-koo-loa) m obstacle

no obstante (noa oabhs-*tahn*-tay) nevertheless

obstinado (oabhs-tee-*nah*-dhoa) *adj* dogged, obstinate

*__obstruir__ (oabhs-*trweer*) *v* block

*__obtener__ (oabh-tay-*nayr*) *v* obtain

obtenible (oabh-tay-*nee*-bhlay) *adj* available

obtuso (oabh-*too*-soa) *adj* blunt

obvio (*oabh*-bh^yoa) *adj* apparent, obvious

oca (*oa*-kah) *f* goose

ocasión (oa-kah-s^yoan) *f* occasion; chance

ocasionalmente (oa-kah-s^yoa-nahl-*mayn*-tay) *adv* occasionally

ocaso (oa-*kah*-soa) *m* sunset

occidental (oak-thee-dhayn-*tahl*) *adj* westerly; western

occidente (oak-thee-*dhayn*-tay) *m* west

océano (oa-*thay*-ah-noa) *m* ocean; **Océano Pacífico** Pacific Ocean

ocio (*oa*-th^yoa) *m* leisure

ocioso (oa-th^yoa-soa) *adj* idle

octavo (oak-*tah*-bhoa) *num* eighth

octubre (oak-*too*-bhray) October

oculista (oa-koo-*leess*-tah) *m* oculist

ocultar (oa-kool-*tahr*) *v* *hide

ocupación (oa-koo-pah-*th^yoan*) *f* occupation; business

ocupante (oa-koo-*pahn*-tay) *m* occupant

ocupar (oa-koo-*pahr*) *v* occupy; *take up; **ocupado** *adj* engaged, busy; occupied; **ocuparse de** look after

ocurrencia (oa-koo-*rrayn*-th^yah) *f* idea

ocurrir (oa-koo-*rreer*) *v* occur

ochenta (oa-*chayn*-tah) *num* eighty

ocho (*oa*-choa) *num* eight

odiar (oa-*dh^yahr*) *v* hate

odio (*oa*-dh^yoa) *m* hatred, hate

oeste (oa-*ayss*-tay) *m* west

ofender (oa-fayn-*dayr*) *v* wound,

*hurt, offend, injure

ofensa (oa-*fayn*-sah) *f* offence

ofensivo (oa-fayn-*see*-bhoa) *adj* offensive; *m* offensive

oferta (oa-*fayr*-tah) *f* offer, supply

oficial (oa-fee-*th^yahl*) *adj* official; *m* officer; ~ **de aduanas** Customs officer

oficina (oa-fee-*thee*-nah) *f* office; ~ **de cambio** exchange office; ~ **de colocación** employment exchange; ~ **de informaciones** information bureau; ~ **de objetos perdidos** lost property office

oficinista (oa-fee-thee-*neess*-tah) *m* clerk

oficio (oa-*fee*-th^yoa) *m* trade

*__ofrecer__ (oa-fray-*thayr*) *v* offer

oído (oa-*ee*-dhoa) *m* hearing; **dolor de oídos** earache

*__oír__ (oa-*eer*) *v* *hear

ojal (oa-*khahl*) *m* buttonhole

ojeada (oa-khay-*ah*-dhah) *f* glimpse, glance; look

ojear (oa-khay-*ahr*) *v* glance

ojo (*oa*-khoa) *m* eye

ola (*oa*-lah) *f* wave

*__oler__ (oa-*layr*) *v* *smell

olmo (*oal*-moa) *m* elm

olor (oa-*loar*) *m* smell, odour

olvidadizo (oal-bhee-dhah-*dhee*-thoa) *adj* forgetful

olvidar (oal-bhee-*dhahr*) *v* *forget

olla (*oa*-l^yah) *f* pot; kettle; ~ **a presión** pressure-cooker

ombligo (oam-*blee*-goa) *m* navel

omitir (oa-mee-*teer*) *v* *leave out, omit; fail

omnipotente (oam-nee-poa-*tayn*-tay) *adj* omnipotent

once (*oan*-thay) *num* eleven

onceno (oan-*thay*-noa) *num* eleventh

onda (*oan*-dah) *f* wave

ondulación (oan-doo-lah-*th^yoan*) *f*

wave; ~ **permanente** permanent wave

ondulado (oan-doo-*lah*-dhoa) *adj* wavy

ondulante (oan-doo-*lahn*-tay) *adj* undulating

ónix (*oa*-neeks) *m* onyx

ópalo (*oa*-pah-loa) *m* opal

opcional (oap-th^yoa-*nahl*) *adj* optional

ópera (*oa*-pay-rah) *f* opera

operación (oa-pay-rah-th^yoan) *f* operation, surgery

operar (oa-pay-*rahr*) *v* operate

opereta (oa-pay-*ray*-tah) *f* operetta

opinar (oa-pee-*nahr*) *v* consider

opinión (oa-pee-*n^yoan*) *f* view, opinion

*oponerse (oa-poa-*nayr*-say) *v* oppose; ~ **a** object to

oportunidad (oa-poar-too-nee-*dhahdh*) *f* chance, opportunity

oportuno (oa-poar-*too*-noa) *adj* convenient

oposición (oa-poa-see-*th^yoan*) *f* opposition

oprimir (oa-pree-*meer*) *v* oppress

óptico (*oap*-tee-koa) *m* optician

optimismo (oap-tee-*meez*-moa) *m* optimism

optimista (oap-tee-*meess*-tah) *adj* optimistic; *m* optimist

óptimo (*oap*-tee-moa) *adj* best

opuesto (oa-*pwayss*-toa) *adj* opposite; averse

oración (oa-rah-th^yoan) *f* prayer

oral (oa-*rahl*) *adj* oral

orar (oa-*rahr*) *v* pray

orden (*oar*-dhayn) *f* command; order; *m* method; **de primer** ~ first-rate; ~ **del día** agenda

ordenar (oar-dhay-*nahr*) *v* arrange; order

ordinario (oar-dhee-*nah*-r^yoa) *adj* simple, ordinary; common, vulgar

oreja (oa-*ray*-khah) *f* ear

orfebre (oar-*fay*-bhray) *m* goldsmith

orgánico (oar-*gah*-nee-koa) *adj* organic

organillo (oar-gah-*nee*-l^yoa) *m* streetorgan

organismo (oar-gah-*neez*-moa) *m* organism

organización (oar-gah-nee-thah-*th^yoan*) *f* organization

organizar (oa;-gah-nee-*thahr*) *v* organize; arrange

órgano (*oar*-gah-noa) *m* organ

orgullo (oar-*goo*-l^yoa) *m* pride

orgulloso (oar-goo-*l^yoa*-soa) *adj* proud

orientación (oa-r^yayn-tah-*th^yoan*) *f* orientation

oriental (oa-r^yayn-*tahl*) *adj* eastern, easterly; oriental

orientarse (oa-r^yayn-*tahr*-say) *v* orientate

oriente (oa-r^yayn-tay) *m* Orient

origen (oa-*ree*-khayn) *m* origin

original (oa-ree-khee-*nahl*) *adj* original

originalmente (oa-ree-khee-nahl-*mayn*-tay) *adv* originally

originar (oa-ree-khee-*nahr*) *v* originate

orilla (oa-*ree*-l^yah) *f* bank; shore

orina (oa-*ree*-nah) *f* urine

orlón (oar-*loan*) *m* orlon

ornamental (oar-nah-mayn-*tahl*) *adj* ornamental

oro (*oa*-roa) *m* gold

orquesta (oar-*kayss*-tah) *f* orchestra; band

ortodoxo (oar-toa-*dhoak*-soa) *adj* orthodox

os (oass) *pron* you

osar (oa-*sahr*) *v* dare

oscilar (oa-thee-*lahr*) *v* *swing

oscuridad (oass-koo-ree-*dhahdh*) *f* dark

oscuro (oass-*koo*-roa) *adj* dark, dim, obscure

oso (*oa*-soa) *m* bear

ostentación (oass-tayn-tah-th^yoan) *f* fuss

ostra (oass-trah) *f* oyster

otoño (oa-toa-ñoa) *m* autumn; fall *nAm*

otro (oa-troa) *adj* other, different; another; ~ **más** another

ovalado (oa-bhah-lah-dhoa) *adj* oval

oveja (oa-bhay-khah) *f* sheep

overol (oa-bhay-roal) *mMe* overalls *pl*

oxidado (oak-see-dhah-dhoa) *adj* rusty

oxígeno (oak-see-khay-noa) *m* oxygen

oyente (oa-^yayn-tay) *m* auditor, listener

P

pabellón (pah-bhay-l^yoan) *m* pavilion

***pacer** (pah-thayr) *v* graze

paciencia (pah-th^yayn-th^yah) *f* patience

paciente (pah-th^yayn-tay) *adj* patient; *m* patient

pacifismo (pah-thee-feez-moa) *m* pacifism

pacifista (pah-thee-feess-tah) *adj* pacifist; *m* pacifist

***padecer** (pah-dhay-thayr) *v* suffer

padrastro (pah-dhrahss-troa) *m* stepfather

padre (pah-dhray) *m* father

padres (pah-dhrayss) *mpl* parents *pl*; ~ **adoptivos** foster-parents *pl*; ~ **políticos** parents-in-law *pl*

padrino (pah-dhree-noa) *m* godfather

paga (pah-gah) *f* wages *pl*

pagano (pah-gah-noa) *adj* heathen, pagan; *m* heathen, pagan

pagar (pah-gahr) *v* *pay; **pagado por adelantado** prepaid; ~ **a plazos** *pay on account

página (pah-khee-nah) *f* page

pago (pah-goa) *m* payment; **primer ~** down payment

painel (pigh-nayl) *m* panel

país (pah-eess) *m* country, land; ~ **natal** native country

paisaje (pigh-sah-khay) *m* scenery, landscape

paisano (pigh-sah-noa) *m* civilian

Países Bajos (pah-ee-sayss -bah-khoass) *mpl* the Netherlands

paja (pah-khah) *f* straw

pájaro (pah-khah-roa) *m* bird

paje (pah-khay) *m* page-boy

pala (pah-lah) *f* spade, shovel

palabra (pah-lah-bhrah) *f* word

palacio (pah-lah-th^yoa) *m* palace

palanca (pah-lahng-kah) *f* lever; ~ **de cambios** gear lever

palangana (pah-lahng-gah-nah) *f* basin; wash-basin

pálido (pah-lee-dhoa) *adj* pale; dull; light

palillo (pah-lee-l^yoa) *m* toothpick

palma (pahl-mah) *f* palm

palo (pah-loa) *m* stick; ~ **de golf** golf-club

paloma (pah-loa-mah) *f* pigeon

palpable (pahl-pah-bhlay) *adj* palpable

palpar (pahl-pahr) *v* *feel

palpitación (pahl-pee-tah-th^yoan) *f* palpitation

pan (pahn) *m* bread, loaf; ~ **integral** wholemeal bread; ~ **tostado** toast

pana (pah-nah) *f* corduroy, velveteen

panadería (pah-nah-dhay-ree-ah) *f* bakery

panadero (pah-nah-dhay-roa) *m* baker

panecillo (pah-nay-thee-l^yoa) *m* roll

pánico (pah-nee-koa) *m* panic

pantalones (pahn-tah-loa-nayss) *mpl* trousers *pl*; slacks *pl*; pants *plAm*; ~ **cortos** shorts *pl*; ~ **de esquí** ski pants *pl*; ~ **de gimnasia** trunks *pl*

pantalla (pahn-tah-l^yah) *f* lampshade;

screen

pantano (pahn-*tah*-noa) *m* marsh, bog

pantanoso (pahn-tah-*noa*-soa) *adj* marshy

pantorrilla (pahn-toa-*rree*-l^yah) *f* calf

pañal (pah-*ñahl*) *m* nappy; diaper *nAm*

pañería (pah-ñay-*ree*-ah) *f* drapery

pañero (pah-*ñay*-roa) *m* draper

paño (*pah*-ñoa) *m* cloth; ~ **higiénico** sanitary towel

pañuelo (pah-*ñway*-loa) *m* handkerchief; ~ **de papel** tissue, Kleenex®

Papa (*pah*-pah) *m* pope

papa (*pah*-pah) *fMe* potato

papá (pah-*pah*) *m* dad

papaíto (pah-pah-*ee*-toa) *m* daddy

papel (pah-*payl*) *m* paper; **de** ~ paper; ~ **carbón** carbon paper; ~ **de envolver** wrapping paper; ~ **de escribir** writing-paper; ~ **de estaño** tinfoil; ~ **de lija** sandpaper; ~ **higiénico** toilet-paper; ~ **para cartas** notepaper; ~ **para mecanografiar** typing paper; ~ **pintado** wallpaper; ~ **secante** blotting paper

papelería (pah-pay-lay-*ree*-ah) *f* stationery; stationer's

paperas (pah-*pay*-rahss) *fpl* mumps

paquete (pah-*kay*-tay) *m* packet, package, parcel; bundle

Paquistán (pah-keess-*tahn*) *m* Pakistan

paquistaní (pah-keess-tah-*nee*) *adj* Pakistani; *m* Pakistani

par (pahr) *adj* even; *m* pair

para (*pah*-rah) *prep* to, for; to, in order to; ~ **con** towards; ~ **que** what for

parabrisas (pah-rah-*bhree*-sahss) *m* windscreen; windshield *nAm*

parachoques (pah-rah-*choa*-kayss) *m* fender, bumper

parada (pah-*rah*-dhah) *f* parade; stop;

~ **de taxis** taxi rank; taxi stand *Am*

parado (pah-*rah*-dhoa) *adjMe* erect

parador (pah-rah-*dhoar*) *m* roadhouse

parafina (pah-rah-*fee*-nah) *f* paraffin

paraguas (pah-*rah*-gwahss) *m* umbrella

paraíso (pah-rah-*ee*-soa) *m* paradise

paralelo (pah-rah-*lay*-loa) *adj* parallel; *m* parallel

paralítico (pah-rah-*lee*-tee-koa) *adj* lame

paralizar (pah-rah-lee-*thahr*) *v* paralise

pararse (pah-*rahr*-say) *v* halt; pull up

parcela (pahr-*thay*-lah) *f* plot

parcial (pahr-th^yahl) *adj* partial

parecer (pah-ray-*thayr*) *m* view, opinion

***parecer** (pah-ray-*thayr*) *v* appear, seem, look

parecido (pah-ray-*thee*-dhoa) *adj* alike; **bien** ~ good-looking

pared (pah-*raydh*) *f* wall

pareja (pah-*ray*-khah) *f* couple; partner

pariente (pah-r^yayn-tay) *m* relative, relation

parlamentario (pahr-lah-mayn-*tah*-r^yoa) *adj* parliamentary

parlamento (pahr-lah-*mayn*-toa) *m* parliament

párpado (*pahr*-pah-dhoa) *m* eyelid

parque (*pahr*-kay) *m* park; ~ **de estacionamiento** car park; ~ **de reserva zoológica** game reserve; ~ **nacional** national park

parquímetro (pahr-*kee*-may-troa) *m* parking meter

párrafo (*pahr*-rrah-foa) *m* paragraph

parrilla (pah-*ree*-l^yah) *f* grill; grillroom; **asar en** ~ grill

parroquia (pah-*rroa*-k^yah) *f* parish

parsimonioso (pahr-see-moa-n^yoa-soa) *adj* economical

parte (*pahr*-tay) *f* part; share; **en al-**

guna ~ somewhere; **en ninguna** ~ nowhere; **en** ~ partly; **otra** ~ elsewhere; ~ **posterior** rear; ~ **superior** top, top side; **por otra** ~ besides; **por todas partes** everywhere, throughout

participante (pahr-tee-thee-*pahn*-tay) *m* participant

participar (pahr-tee-thee-*pahr*) *v* participate

particular (pahr-tee-koo-*lahr*) *adj* private; particular; **en** ~ specially, in particular

particularidad (pahr-tee-koo-lah-ree-*dhahdh*) *f* detail; peculiarity

partida (pahr-tee-dhah) *f* departure

partido (pahr-*tee*-dhoa) *m* side, party; match; ~ **de fútbol** football match

partir (pahr-*teer*) *v* *leave, depart, pull out, *set out; **a** ~ **de** as from; from

parto (*pahr*-toa) *m* childbirth, delivery

párvulo (*pahr*-bhoo-loa) *m* toddler; **escuela de párvulos** kindergarten

pasa (*pah*-sah) *f* raisin; ~ **de Corinto** currant

pasado (pah-*sah*-dhoa) *adj* past; *m* past

pasaje (pah-*sah*-khay) *m* passage

pasajero (pah-sah-*khay*-roa) *m* passenger

pasaporte (pah-sah-*poar*-tay) *m* passport

pasar (pah-*sahr*) *v* happen; *go through; pass; *spend; ~ **por alto** overlook; **pasarse sin** spare

pasarela (pah-sah-*ray*-lah) *f* gangway

Pascua (*pahss*-kwah) *f* Easter

paseante (pah-say-*ahn*-tay) *m* walker

pasear (pah-say-*ahr*) *v* walk, stroll

paseo (pah-*say*-oa) *m* stroll; ride; promenade

pasillo (pah-*see*-lʸoa) *m* corridor; aisle

pasión (pah-*sʸoan*) *f* passion

pasivo (pah-*see*-bhoa) *adj* passive

paso (*pah*-soa) *m* step, pace; move, gait; crossing; mountain pass; **de** ~ **casual**; ~ **a nivel** crossing; **prioridad de** ~ right of way; **prohibido el** ~ no entry

pasta (*pahss*-tah) *f* paste; ~ **dentífrica** toothpaste

pastel (pahss-*tayl*) *m* cake

pastelería (pahss-tay-lay-*ree*-ah) *f* pastry, cake; pastry shop

pastilla (pahss-*tee*-lʸah) *f* tablet

pastor (pahss-*toar*) *m* shepherd; clergyman, parson, rector

pata (*pah*-tah) *f* paw; leg

patada (pah-*tah*-dhah) *f* kick

patata (pah-*tah*-tah) *f* potato; **patatas fritas** chips

patear (pah-tay-*ahr*) *v* kick; stamp

patente (pah-*tayn*-tay) *f* patent

patillas (pah-*tee*-lʸahss) *fpl* whiskers *pl*, sideburns *pl*

patín (pah-*teen*) *m* skate; scooter

patinaje (pah-tee-*nah*-khay) *m* skating

patinar (pah-tee-*nahr*) *v* skate; skid

pato (*pah*-toa) *m* duck

patria (*pah*-trʸah) *f* native country, fatherland

patriota (pah-*trʸoa*-tah) *m* patriot

patrón (pah-*troan*) *m* boss, master; employer; landlord

patrona (pah-*troa*-nah) *f* landlady

patrulla (pah-*troo*-lʸah) *f* patrol

patrullar (pah-troo-*lʸahr*) *v* patrol

paulatinamente (pou-lah-tee-nah-*mayn*-tay) *adv* gradually

pausa (*pou*-sah) *f* pause; *hacer una ~ pause

pavimentar (pah-bhee-mayn-*tahr*) *v* pave

pavimento (pah-bhee-*mayn*-toa) *m* pavement

pavo (*pah*-bhoa) *m* peacock; turkey

payaso (pah-*ʸah*-soa) *m* clown

paz (pahth) f peace; quiet

peaje (pay-ah-khay) m toll

peatón (pay-ah-toan) m pedestrian; **prohibido para los peatones** no pedestrians

pecado (pay-kah-dhoa) m sin

pecio (pay-th^yoa) m wreck

peculiar (pay-koo-l^yahr) adj peculiar

pecho (pay-choa) m chest; bosom

pedal (pay-dhahl) m pedal

pedazo (pay-dhah-thoa) m piece; scrap

pedernal (pay-dhayr-nahl) m flint

pedicuro (pay-dhee-koo-roa) m chiropodist, pedicure

pedido (pay-dhee-dhoa) m order

*****pedir** (pay-dheer) v beg; order; charge

pegajoso (pay-gah-khoa-soa) adj sticky

pegar (pay-gahr) v smack, slap, *hit; *stick, paste; **pegarse** v *burn

peinado (pay-nah-dhoa) m hair-do

peinar (pay-nahr) v comb

peine (pay-nay) m comb; ~ **de bolsillo** pocket-comb

pelar (pay-lahr) v peel

peldaño (payl-dah-ñoa) m step

pelea (pay-lay-ah) f battle

peletero (pay-lay-tay-roa) m furrier

pelícano (pay-lee-kah-noa) m pelican

película (pay-lee-koo-lah) f film; ~ **en colores** colour film

peligro (pay-lee-groa) m danger; peril; risk; distress

peligroso (pay-lee-groa-soa) adj dangerous; perilous

pelmazo (payl-mah-thoa) m bore

pelota (pay-loa-tah) f ball

peluca (pay-loo-kah) f wig

peluquero (pay-loo-kay-roa) m hairdresser

pelvis (payl-bheess) m pelvis

pellizcar (pay-l^yeeth-kahr) v pinch

pena (pay-nah) f sorrow; pains; penalty; ~ **de muerte** death penalty

pendiente (payn-d^yayn-tay) adj slanting; m earring, pendant; f gradient, slope

penetrar (pay-nay-trahr) v penetrate

penicilina (pay-nee-thee-lee-nah) f penicillin

península (pay-neen-soo-lah) f peninsula

pensador (payn-sah-dhoar) m thinker

pensamiento (payn-sah-m^yayn-toa) m idea, thought

*****pensar** (payn-sahr) v *think; ~ **en** *think of

pensativo (payn-sah-tee-bhoa) adj thoughtful

pensión (payn-s^yoan) f guest-house, pension, boarding-house; board; ~ **alimenticia** alimony; ~ **completa** full board, board and lodging

Pentecostés (payn-tay-koass-tayss) m Whitsun

peña (pay-ñah) f boulder

peón (pay-oan) m pawn

peor (pay-oar) adj worse; adv worse

pepino (pay-pee-noa) m cucumber

pepita (pay-pee-tah) f pip

pequeño (pay-kay-ñoa) adj small, little; petty, minor

pera (pay-rah) f pear

perca (payr-kah) f perch, bass

percepción (payr-thayp-th^yoan) f perception

perceptible (payr-thayp-tee-bhlay) adj perceptible, noticeable

percibir (payr-thee-bheer) v perceive

percha (payr-chah) f hanger, coathanger, peg; hat rack

*****perder** (payr-dhayr) v *lose; miss; waste

pérdida (payr-dhee-dhah) f loss

perdiz (payr-dheeth) f partridge

perdón (payr-dhoan) m pardon;

grace; **¡perdón!** sorry!

erdonar (payr-dhoa-*nahr*) *v* *forgive

erecedero (pay-ray-thay-*dhay*-roa) *adj* perishable

perecer (pay-ray-*thayr*) *v* perish

eregrinación (pay-ray-gree-nah-*th^Yoan*) *f* pilgrimage

eregrino (pay-ray-*gree*-noa) *m* pilgrim

erejil (pay-ray-*kheel*) *m* parsley

erezoso (pay-ray-*thoa*-soa) *adj* lazy

erfección (payr-fayk-*th^Yoan*) *f* perfection

erfecto (payr-*fayk*-toa) *adj* perfect; faultless

erfil (payr-*feel*) *m* profile

erfume (payr-*foo*-may) *m* perfume; scent

eriódico (pay-r^Yoa-dhee-koa) *adj* periodical; *m* periodical, paper; **vendedor de periódicos** newsagent

eriodismo (pay-r^Yoa-*deez*-moa) *m* journalism

eriodista (pay-r^Yoa-*dheess*-tah) *m* journalist

eríodo (pay-*ree*-oa-dhoa) *m* period, term

erito (pay-*ree*-toa) *m* expert, connoisseur

erjudicar (payr-khoo-dhee-*kahr*) *v* harm

erjudicial (payr-khoo-dhee-*th^Yahl*) *adj* harmful, hurtful

erjuicio (payr-*khwee*-th^Yoa) *m* harm, damage

erjurio (payr-*khoo*-r^Yoa) *m* perjury

erla (*payr*-lah) *f* pearl

permanecer (payr-mah-nay-*thayr*) *v* remain

ermanente (payr-mah-*nayn*-tay) *adj* permanent; **planchado ~** permanent press

ermiso (payr-*mee*-soa) *m* permission, authorization; permit, licence; **~ de**

conducir driving licence; **~ de pesca** fishing licence; **~ de residencia** residence permit; **~ de trabajo** work permit; labor permit *Am*

permitir (payr-mee-*teer*) *v* permit, allow; enable; **permitirse** *v* afford

perno (*payr*-noa) *m* bolt

pero (*pay*-roa) *conj* yet, only, but

peróxido (pay-*roak*-see-dhoa) *m* peroxide

perpendicular (payr-payn-dee-koo-*lahr*) *adj* perpendicular

perpetuo (payr-*pay*-twoa) *adj* perpetual

perra (*pay*-rrah) *f* bitch

perrera (pay-*rray*-rah) *f* kennel

perro (*pay*-rroa) *m* dog; **~ lazarillo** guide-dog

persa (*payr*-sah) *adj* Persian; *m* Persian

***perseguir** (payr-say-*geer*) *v* pursue

perseverar (payr-say-bhay-*rahr*) *v* *keep up

Persia (*payr*-s^Yah) *f* Persia

persiana (payr-s^Y*ah*-nah) *f* shutter, blind

persistir (payr-seess-*teer*) *v* insist

persona (payr-*soa*-nah) *f* person; **por ~** per person

personal (payr-soa-*nahl*) *adj* personal, private; *m* personnel, staff

personalidad (payr-soa-nah-lee-*dhahdh*) *f* personality

perspectiva (payrs-payk-*tee*-bhah) *f* perspective; prospect

persuadir (payr-swah-*dheer*) *v* persuade

***pertenecer** (payr-tay-nay-*thayr*) *v* belong

pertenencias (payr-tay-*nayn*-th^Yahss) *fpl* belongings *pl*

pertinaz (payr-tee-*nahth*) *adj* obstinate

pesado (pay-*sah*-dhoa) *adj* heavy

pesadumbre (pay-sah-*dhoom*-bray) *f*

grief

pesar (pay-*sahr*) v weigh; **a ~ de** despite, in spite of

pesca (*payss*-kah) f fishing; fishing industry

pescadería (payss-kah-dhay-*ree*-ah) f fish shop

pescador (payss-kah-*dhoar*) m fisherman

pescar (payss-*kahr*) v fish; **~ con caña** angle

pesebre (pay-*say*-bhray) m manger

pesimismo (pay-see-*meez*-moa) m pessimism

pesimista (pay-see-*meess*-tah) adj pessimistic; m pessimist

pésimo (*pay*-see-moa) adj worst; terrible

peso (*pay*-soa) m weight; burden

pestaña (payss-*tah*-ñah) f eyelash

petaca (pay-*tah*-kah) f pouch; tobacco pouch

pétalo (*pay*-tah-loa) m petal

petición (pay-tee-*th*ʸ*oan*) f petition

petirrojo (pay-tee-*rroa*-khoa) m robin

petróleo (pay-*troa*-lay-oa) m petroleum, oil; **~ lampante** kerosene; **pozo de ~** oil-well; **refinería de ~** oil-refinery

pez (payth) m fish

piadoso (pʸah-*dhoa*-soa) adj pious

pianista (pʸah-*neess*-tah) m pianist

piano (*p*ʸ*ah*-noa) m piano; **~ de cola** grand piano

picadero (pee-kah-*dhay*-roa) m riding-school

picadura (pee-kah-*dhoo*-rah) f sting, bite; cigarette tobacco

picante (pee-*kahn*-tay) adj spicy, savoury

picar (pee-*kahr*) v itch; mince; *sting

pícaro (*pee*-kah-roa) m rascal

picazón (pee-kah-*thoan*) f itch

pico (*pee*-koa) m beak; peak; pick-

pie (pʸay) m foot; **a ~** on foot; walking; **de ~** upright; ***estar de ~** *stand; **~ de cabra** crowbar

piedad (pʸay-*dhahdh*) f pity; ***tener ~ de** pity

piedra (*p*ʸ*ay*-dhrah) f stone; **de ~** stone; **~ miliar** milestone; **~ pómez** pumice stone; **~ preciosa** stone

piel (pʸayl) f skin; fur, hide; peel; **de ~** leather; **~ de cerdo** pigskin

pierna (*p*ʸ*ayr*-nah) f leg

pieza (*p*ʸ*ay*-thah) f part; **de dos piezas** two-piece; **~ de repuesto** spare part; **~ en un acto** one-act play

pijama (pee-*khah*-mah) m pyjamas pl

pilar (pee-*lahr*) m pillar

píldora (*peel*-doa-rah) f pill

pileta (pee-*lay*-tah) f sink

piloto (pee-*loa*-toa) m pilot

pillo (*pee*-lʸoa) m rascal

pimienta (pee-*m*ʸ*ayn*-tah) f pepper

pincel (peen-*thayl*) m paint-brush

pinchado (peen-*chah*-dhoa) adj punctured

pinchar (peen-*chahr*) v prick

pinchazo (peen-*chah*-thoa) m puncture

pingüino (peeng-*gwee*-noa) m penguin

pino (*pee*-noa) m fir-tree

pintar (peen-*tahr*) v paint

pintor (peen-*toar*) m painter

pintoresco (peen-toa-*rayss*-koa) adj picturesque, scenic

pintura (peen-*too*-rah) f paint; painting; **~ al óleo** oil-painting

pinzas (*peen*-thahss) fpl tweezers pl

pinzón (peen-*thoan*) m finch

piña (*pee*-ñah) f pineapple

pío (*pee*-oa) adj pious

piojo (*p*ʸ*oa*-khoa) m louse

pionero (pʸoa-*nay*-roa) m pioneer

pipa (*pee*-pah) f pipe

pirata (pee-*rah*-tah) m pirate

isar (pee-*sahr*) v step

iscina (pee-*thee*-nah) f swimming pool

iso (*pee*-soa) m storey, floor; flat; apartment *nAm*; ~ **bajo** ground floor

ista (*peess*-tah) f ring; track; lane; ~ **de aterrizaje** runway; ~ **de patinaje** skating-rink; ~ **para carreras** race-course

istola (peess-*toa*-lah) f pistol

istón (peess-*toan*) m piston

itillera (pee-tee-lʸay-rah) f cigarette-case

izarra (pee-*thah*-rrah) f slate; blackboard

laca (*plah*-kah) f registration plate

lacer (plah-*thayr*) m pleasure

* placer (plah-*thayr*) v please

laga (*plah*-gah) f plague

lan (plahn) m plan, project

lancha (*plahn*-chah) f iron; **no precisa** ~ wash and wear, drip-dry

lanchar (plahn-*chahr*) v iron; press

laneador (plah-nay-ah-*dhoar*) m glider

lanear (plah-nay-*ahr*) v plan

laneta (plah-*nay*-tah) m planet

lanetario (plah-nay-*tah*-rʸoa) m planetarium

lano (*plah*-noa) adj level, even, plane; m plan, map; **primer** ~ foreground

lanta (*plahn*-tah) f plant

lantación (plahn-tah-thʸoan) f plantation

lantar (plahn-*tahr*) v plant

lantear (plahn-tay-*ahr*) v *put

lástico (*plahss*-tee-koa) m plastic; **de** ~ plastic

lata (*plah*-tah) f silver; **de** ~ silver; ~ **labrada** silverware

látano (*plah*-tah-noa) m banana

latero (plah-*tay*-roa) m silversmith

platija (plah-*tee*-khah) f plaice

platillo (plah-*tee*-lʸoa) m saucer

platino (plah-*tee*-noa) m platinum

plato (*plah*-toa) m dish, plate; course; ~ **para sopa** soup-plate

playa (*plah*-ʸah) f beach; ~ **de veraneo** seaside resort; ~ **para nudistas** nudist beach

plaza (*plah*-thah) f square; ~ **de mercado** market-place; ~ **de toros** bullring; ~ **fuerte** stronghold

plazo (*plah*-thoa) m term; instalment; **compra a plazos** hire-purchase

pleamar (play-ah-*mahr*) f high tide

* plegar (play-*gahr*) v crease

pliegue (*plʸay*-gay) m crease, fold

plomero (ploa-*may*-roa) m plumber

plomo (*ploa*-moa) m lead

pluma (*ploo*-mah) f feather; pen

plural (ploo-*rahl*) m plural

población (poa-bhlah-thʸoan) f population

pobre (*poa*-bhray) adj poor

pobreza (poa-*bhray*-thah) f poverty

poco (*poa*-koa) adj little; m bit; **dentro de** ~ presently; **pocos** adj few; **un** ~ some

poder (poa-*dhayr*) m power; authority

* poder (poa-*dhayr*) v *be able to, *can; *might; *may

poderoso (poa-dhay-*roa*-soa) adj powerful

podrido (poa-*dhree*-dhoa) adj rotten

poema (poa-*ay*-mah) m poem; ~ **épico** epic

poesía (poa-ay-*see*-ah) f poetry

poeta (poa-*ay*-tah) m poet

poético (poa-*ay*-tee-koa) adj poetic

polaco (poa-*lah*-koa) adj Polish; m Pole

polea (poa-*lay*-ah) f pulley

policía (poa-lee-*thee*-ah) f police pl

polifacético (poa-lee-fah-*thay*-tee-koa) adj all-round

polilla (poa-*lee*-l^yah) *f* moth

polio (*poa*-l^yoa) *f* polio

poliomielitis (poa-l^yoa-m^yay-*lee*-teess) *f* polio

política (poa-*lee*-tee-kah) *f* policy; politics

político (poa-*lee*-tee-koa) *adj* political; *m* politician

póliza (*poa*-lee-thah) *f* policy

Polonia (poa-*loa*-n^yah) *f* Poland

polución (poa-loo-*th^yoan*) *f* pollution

polvera (poal-*bhay*-rah) *f* powder compact

polvo (*poal*-bhoa) *m* dust; powder; grit; ~ **facial** face-powder; ~ **para los dientes** toothpowder; ~ **para los pies** foot powder

pólvora (*poal*-bhoa-rah) *f* gunpowder

polvoriento (poal-bhoa-*r^yayn*-toa) *adj* dusty

pollero (poa-*l^yay*-roa) *m* poulterer

pollo (*poa*-l^yoa) *m* chicken

pomelo (poa-*may*-loa) *m* grapefruit

pómulo (*poa*-moo-loa) *m* cheek-bone

ponderado (poan-day-*rah*-dhoa) *adj* sober

***poner** (poa-*nayr*) *v* place, *lay, *put, *set; ***ponerse** *v* *put on

pony (*poa*-nee) *m* pony

popelín (poa-pay-*leen*) *m* poplin

popular (poa-poo-*lahr*) *adj* popular; vulgar; **canción** ~ folk song; **danza** ~ folk-dance

populoso (poa-poo-*loa*-soa) *adj* populous

por (*poar*) *prep* by; for; via; times

porcelana (poar-thay-*lah*-nah) *f* china, porcelain

porcentaje (poar-thayn-*tah*-khay) *m* percentage

porción (poar-*th^yoan*) *f* portion, helping

porque (*poar*-kay) *conj* because, for, as; **por qué** why

porra (*poa*-rrah) *f* club

portabagajes (poar-tah-bah-*khah*-gayss) *m* luggage rack

portador (poar-tah-*dhoar*) *m* bearer

portaequipajes (poar-tah-ay-kee-*pah*-khayss) *m* boot; trunk *nAm*

portafolio (poar-tah-*foa*-l^yoa) *m* attaché case, briefcase

portaligas (poar-tah-*lee*-gahss) *m* suspender belt

portátil (poar-*tah*-teel) *adj* portable

portero (poar-*tay*-roa) *m* doorman, door-keeper, porter; goalkeeper

pórtico (*poar*-tee-koa) *m* arcade

portilla (poar-*tee*-l^yah) *f* porthole

portón (poar-*toan*) *m* gate

Portugal (poar-too-*gahl*) *m* Portugal

portugués (poar-too-*gayss*) *adj* Portuguese; *m* Portuguese

porvenir (poar-bhay-*neer*) *m* future

posada (poa-*sah*-dhah) *f* inn

posadero (poa-sah-*dhay*-roa) *m* innkeeper

***poseer** (poa-say-*ayr*) *v* own, possess

posesión (poa-say-*s^yoan*) *f* possession

posibilidad (poa-see-bhee-lee-*dhahdh*) *f* possibility

posible (poa-*see*-bhlay) *adj* possible

posición (poa-see-*th^yoan*) *f* position

positiva (poa-see-*tee*-bhah) *f* positive, print

positivo (poa-see-*tee*-bhoa) *adj* positive

postal ilustrada (poass-*tahl* ee-looss-*trah*-dhah) picture postcard

poste (*poass*-tay) *m* post, pole; ~ **de farol** lamp-post; ~ **de indicador** signpost

posterior (poass-tay-*r^yoar*) *adj* subsequent

postizo (poass-*tee*-thoa) *m* hair piece

postre (*poass*-tray) *m* dessert

potable (poa-*tah*-bhlay) *adj* for drinking

potencia (poa-*tayn*-thʸah) f capacity; power

pozo (*poa*-thoa) m well; **~ de petróleo** oil-well

práctica (*prahk*-tee-kah) f practice

prácticamente (*prahk*-tee-kah-mayn-tay) adv practically

practicar (prahk-tee-*kahr*) v practise

práctico (*prahk*-tee-koa) adj practical; business-like; m pilot

prado (*prah*-dhoa) m meadow, pasture

precario (pray-*kah*-rʸoa) adj critical, precarious

precaución (pray-kou-*thʸoan*) f precaution

precaverse (pray-kah-*bhayr*-say) v beware

precedente (pray-thay-*dhayn*-tay) adj previous, preceding, last

preceder (pray-thay-*dhayr*) v precede

precio (*pray*-thʸoa) m price; charge, cost, rate; **~ de compra** purchase price; **~ del billete** fare

precioso (pray-*thʸoa*-soa) adj precious; lovely

precipicio (pray-thee-*pee*-thʸoa) m precipice

precipitación (pray-thee-pee-tah-*thʸoan*) f precipitation

precipitarse (pray-thee-pee-*tahr*-say) v rush; crash; **precipitado** adj rash

preciso (pray-*thee*-soa) adj precise; very

predecesor (pray-dhay-thay-*soar*) m predecessor

* **predecir** (pray-dhay-*theer*) v predict

predicar (pray-dhee-*kahr*) v preach

preferencia (pray-fay-*rayn*-thʸah) f preference

preferible (pray-fay-*ree*-bhlay) adj preferable

* **preferir** (pray-fay-*reer*) v prefer; **preferido** adj favourite

prefijo (pray-*fee*-khoa) m prefix

pregunta (pray-*goon*-tah) f question; query, inquiry

preguntar (pray-goon-*tahr*) v ask; enquire; **preguntarse** v wonder

prejuicio (pray-*khwee*-thʸoa) m prejudice

preliminar (pray-lee-mee-*nahr*) adj preliminary

prematuro (pray-mah-*too*-roa) adj premature

premio (*pray*-mʸoa) m award, prize; **~ de consolación** consolation prize

prender (prayn-*dayr*) v attach

prensa (*prayn*-sah) f press; **conferencia de ~** press conference

preocupación (pray-oa-koo-pah-*thʸoan*) f concern, anxiety, worry; trouble

preocupado (pray-oa-koo-*pah*-dhoa) adj concerned, anxious

preocuparse de (pray-oa-koo-*pahr*-say) care about

preparación (pray-pah-rah-*thʸoan*) f preparation

preparado (pray-pah-*rah*-dhoa) adj prepared, ready

preparar (pray-pah-*rahr*) v prepare; cook

preposición (pray-poa-see-*thʸoan*) f preposition

presa (*pray*-sah) f dam

prescindir (pray-theen-*deer*) v omit; disregard; **prescindiendo de** apart from

prescribir (prayss-kree-*bheer*) v prescribe

prescripción (prayss-kreep-*thʸoan*) f prescription

presencia (pray-*sayn*-thʸah) f presence

presenciar (pray-sayn-*thʸahr*) v witness

presentación (pray-sayn-tah-*thʸoan*) f introduction

presentar (pray-sayn-*tahr*) v introduce,

present; offer; **presentarse** *v* report

presente (pray-*sayn*-tay) *adj* present; *m* present

preservar (pray-sayr-*bhahr*) *v* preserve

presidente (pray-see-*dhayn*-tay) *m* president, chairman

presidir (pray-see-*dheer*) *v* preside at

presión (pray-*s^yoan*) *f* pressure; ~ **atmosférica** atmospheric pressure; ~ **del aceite** oil pressure; ~ **del neumático** tyre pressure

preso (*pray*-soa) *m* prisoner; **coger** ~ capture

prestamista (prayss-tah-*meess*-tah) *m* pawnbroker

préstamo (*prayss*-tah-moa) *m* loan

prestar (prayss-*tahr*) *v* *lend; ~ **atención a** attend to, *pay attention to; **tomar prestado** borrow

prestidigitador (prayss-tee-dhee-khee-tah-*dhoar*) *m* magician

prestigio (prayss-*tee*-kh^yoa) *m* prestige

presumible (pray-soo-*mee*-bhlay) *adj* presumable

presumido (pray-soo-*mee*-dhoa) *adj* presumptuous

presumir (pray-soo-*meer*) *v* assume; boast

presuntuoso (pray-soon-*twoa*-soa) *adj* conceited; presumptuous

presupuesto (pray-soo-*pwayss*-toa) *m* budget

pretender (pray-tayn-*dayr*) *v* claim

pretensión (pray-tayn-*s^yoan*) *f* claim

pretexto (pray-*tayks*-toa) *m* pretext, pretence

*prevenir (pray-bhay-*neer*) *v* anticipate, prevent

preventivo (pray-bhayn-*tee*-bhoa) *adj* preventive

*prever (pray-*bhayr*) *v* anticipate

previo (*pray*-bh^yoa) *adj* previous

previsión (pray-bhee-*s^yoan*) *f* outlook, forecast

prima (*pree*-mah) *f* cousin; premium

primario (pree-*mah*-r^yoa) *adj* primary

primavera (pree-mah-*bhay*-rah) *f* springtime, spring

primero (pree-*may*-roa) *num* first; *adj* foremost; primary

primitivo (pree-mee-*tee*-bhoa) *adj* primitive

primo (*pree*-moa) *m* cousin

primordial (pree-moar-*dh^yahl*) *adj* primary

princesa (preen-*thay*-sah) *f* princess

principal (preen-thee-*pahl*) *adj* principal; chief, main, cardinal; *m* principal

principalmente (preen-thee-pahl-*mayn*-tay) *adv* mainly

príncipe (*preen*-thee-pay) *m* prince

principiante (preen-thee-*p^yahn*-tay) *m* beginner, learner

principio (preen-*thee*-p^yoa) *m* principle; **al** ~ at first

prioridad (pr^yoa-ree-*dhahdh*) *f* priority

prisa (*pree*-sah) *f* haste, speed, hurry; ***dar** ~ *speed; ***darse** ~ hurry; **de** ~ in a hurry

prisión (pree-*s^yoan*) *f* prison

prisionero (pree-s^yoa-*nay*-roa) *m* prisoner; ~ **de guerra** prisoner of war

prismáticos (preez-*mah*-tee-koass) *mpl* binoculars *pl*

privado (pree-*bhah*-dhoa) *adj* private

privar de (pree-*bhahr*) deprive of

privilegio (pree-bhee-*lay*-kh^yoa) *m* privilege

probable (proa-*bhah*-bhlay) *adj* probable; likely

probablemente (proa-bhah-bhlay-*mayn*-tay) *adv* probably

probador (proa-bhah-*dhoar*) *m* fitting room

*probar (proa-*bhahr*) *v* attempt; test; taste; ***probarse** *v* try on

problema (proa-*bhlay*-mah) *m* problem, question

procedencia (proa-thay-*dhayn*-thʸah) *f* origin

proceder (proa-thay-*dhayr*) *v* proceed

procedimiento (proa-thay-dhee-*m*ʸ*ayn*-toa) *m* procedure; process

procesión (proa-thay-sʸ*oan*) *f* procession

proceso (proa-*thay*-soa) *m* process, trial, lawsuit

proclamar (proa-klah-*mahr*) *v* proclaim

procurador (proa-koo-rah-*dhoar*) *m* solicitor

procurar (proa-koo-*rahr*) *v* furnish

pródigo (*proa*-dhee-goa) *adj* lavish

producción (proa-dhook-thʸ*oan*) *f* production, output; ~ **en serie** mass production

***producir** (proa-dhoo-*theer*) *v* produce

producto (proa-*dhook*-toa) *m* product, produce

productor (proa-dhook-*toar*) *m* producer

profano (proa-*fah*-noa) *m* layman

profesar (proa-fay-*sahr*) *v* confess

profesión (proa-fay-sʸ*oan*) *f* profession

profesional (proa-fay-sʸoa-*nahl*) *adj* professional

profesor (proa-fay-*soar*) *m* master, teacher; professor

profesora (proa-fay-*soa*-rah) *f* teacher

profeta (proa-*fay*-tah) *m* prophet

profundidad (proa-foon-dee-*dhahdh*) *f* depth

profundo (proa-*foon*-doa) *adj* low; profound

programa (proa-*grah*-mah) *m* programme

progresista (proa-gray-*seess*-tah) *adj* progressive

progresivo (proa-gray-*see*-bhoa) *adj* progressive

progreso (proa-*gray*-soa) *m* progress

prohibición (proa-ee-bhee-thʸ*oan*) *f* prohibition

prohibido (proa-ee-*bhee*-dhoa) *adj* prohibited

***prohibir** (proa-ee-*bheer*) *v* prohibit, *forbid

prolongación (proa-loang-gah-thʸ*oan*) *f* prolongation

prolongar (proa-loang-*gahr*) *v* extend

promedio (proa-*may*-dhʸoa) *adj* average; *m* average, mean; **en** ~ on the average

promesa (proa-*may*-sah) *f* promise

prometer (proa-may-*tayr*) *v* promise

prometido (proa-may-*tee*-dhoa) *adj* engaged

promoción (proa-moa-thʸ*oan*) *f* promotion

promontorio (proa-moan-*toa*-rʸoa) *m* headland

***promover** (proa-moa-*bhayr*) *v* promote

pronombre (proa-*noam*-bray) *m* pronoun

pronosticar (proa-noass-tee-*kahr*) *v* forecast

pronto (*proan*-toa) *adj* prompt; *adv* soon, shortly; **tan** ~ **como** as soon as

pronunciación (proa-noon-thʸah-thʸ*oan*) *f* pronunciation

pronunciar (proa-noon-thʸ*ahr*) *v* pronounce

propaganda (proa-pah-*gahn*-dah) *f* propaganda

propicio (proa-*pee*-thʸoa) *adj* favourable; well-disposed

propiedad (proa-pʸay-*dhahdh*) *f* property; estate

propietario (proa-pʸay-tah-rʸoa) *m* owner, proprietor; landlord

propina (proa-*pee*-nah) *f* gratuity, tip

propio (*proa*-pʸoa) *adj* own

*proponer (proa-poa-*nayr*) *v* propose

proporción (proa-poar-*th^yoan*) *f* proportion

proporcional (proa-poar-th^yoa-*nahl*) *adj* proportional

proporcionar (proa-poar-th^yoa-*nahr*) *v* adjust; procure

propósito (proa-*poa*-see-toa) *m* purpose; **a ~** by the way

propuesta (proa-*pwayss*-tah) *f* proposition, proposal

prórroga (*proa*-rroa-gah) *f* extension

prosa (*proa*-sah) *f* prose

*proseguir (proa-say-*geer*) *v* proceed, continue, carry on

prospecto (proass-*payk*-toa) *m* prospectus

prosperidad (proass-pay-ree-*dhahdh*) *f* prosperity

próspero (*proass*-pay-roa) *adj* prosperous

prostituta (proass-tee-*too*-tah) *f* prostitute

protección (proa-tayk-*th^yoan*) *f* protection

proteger (proa-tay-*khayr*) *v* protect

proteína (proa-tay-*ee*-nah) *f* protein

protesta (proa-*tayss*-tah) *f* protest

protestante (proa-tayss-*tahn*-tay) *adj* Protestant

protestar (proa-tayss-*tahr*) *v* protest

provechoso (proa-bhay-*choa*-soa) *adj* profitable

*proveer (proa-bhay-*ayr*) *v* provide; **~ de** furnish with

proverbio (proa-*bhayr*-bh^yoa) *m* proverb

provincia (proa-*bheen*-th^yah) *f* province

provincial (proa-bheen-*th^yahl*) *adj* provincial

provisional (proa-bhee-s^yoa-*nahl*) *adj* provisional, temporary

provisiones (proa-bhee-s^yoa-nayss) *fpl* provisions *pl*

provocar (proa-bhoa-*kahr*) *v* cause

próximamente (*proak*-see-mah-mayn-tay) *adv* shortly

próximo (*proak*-see-moa) *adj* next

proyectar (proa-^yayk-*tahr*) *v* project

proyecto (proa-^yayk-toa) *m* project, scheme

proyector (proa-^yayk-*toar*) *m* spotlight

prudente (proo-*dhayn*-tay) *adj* cautious, wary, gentle

prueba (*prway*-bhah) *f* experiment, trial, test; proof, token, evidence; **a ~** on approval

prurito (proo-*ree*-toa) *m* itch

psicoanalista (see-koa-ah-nah-*leess*-tah) *m* analyst, psychoanalyst

psicología (see-koa-loa-*khee*-ah) *f* psychology

psicológico (see-koa-*loa*-khee-koa) *adj* psychological

psicólogo (see-*koa*-loa-goa) *m* psychologist

psiquiatra (see-*k^yah*-trah) *m* psychiatrist

psíquico (*see*-kee-koa) *adj* psychic

publicación (poo-bhlee-kah-*th^yoan*) *f* publication

publicar (poo-bhlee-*kahr*) *v* publish

publicidad (poo-bhlee-thee-*dhahdh*) *f* advertising, publicity

público (*poo*-bhlee-koa) *adj* public; *m* public

pueblo (*pway*-bhloa) *m* nation, people; village

puente (*pwayn*-tay) *m* bridge; **~ colgante** suspension bridge; **~ levadizo** drawbridge; **~ superior** main deck

puerta (*pwayr*-tah) *f* door; **~ corrediza** sliding door; **~ giratoria** revolving door

puerto (*pwayr*-toa) *m* harbour, port; **~ de mar** seaport

pues (pwayss) *conj* since

puesta (*pwayss*-tah) *f* bet

puesto (loo-*gahr*) *m* spot; job, post, position; stand, stall, booth; ~ **de gasolina** service station; gas station *Am*; ~ **de libros** bookstand

puesto que (*pwayss*-toa kay) because, since

pulcro (*pool*-kroa) *adj* neat

pulgar (pool-*gahr*) *m* thumb

pulir (poo-*leer*) *v* polish

pulmón (pool-*moan*) *m* lung

pulóver (poo-*loa*-bhayr) *m* pullover

púlpito (*pool*-pee-toa) *m* pulpit

pulpo (*pool*-poa) *m* octopus

pulsera (pool-*say*-rah) *f* bracelet, bangle

pulso (*pool*-soa) *m* pulse

pulverizador (pool-bhay-ree-thah-*dhoar*) *m* atomizer

punta (*poon*-tah) *f* tip, point

puntiagudo (poon-tᶌah-*goo*-dhoa) *adj* pointed

puntilla (poon-*tee*-lᶌah) *f* lace

punto (*poon*-toa) *m* point; item, issue; period, full stop; stitch; **géneros de** ~ hosiery; *hacer* ~ *knit; ~ **de congelación** freezing-point; ~ **de partida** starting-point; ~ **de vista** point of view; ~ **y coma** semi-colon

puntual (poon-*twahl*) *adj* punctual

punzada (poon-*thah*-dhah) *f* stitch

punzar (poon-*thahr*) *v* pierce

puñado (poo-*ñah*-dhoa) *m* handful

puñetazo (poo-ñay-*tah*-thoa) *m* punch; *dar puñetazos* punch

puño (*poo*-ñoa) *m* fist; cuff

pupitre (poo-*pee*-tray) *m* desk

purasangre (poo-rah-*sahng*-gray) *adj* thoroughbred

puro (*poo*-roa) *adj* pure; clean, neat, sheer; *m* cigar

purpúreo (poor-*poo*-ray-oa) *adj* purple

pus (pooss) *f* pus

Q

que (kay) *pron* who, which, that; *conj* that; as, than

qué (kay) *pron* what; *adv* how

quebradizo (kay-bhrah-*dhee*-thoa) *adj* crisp

quebrantar (kay-bhrahn-*tahr*) *v* *break

*quebrar** (kay-*bhrahr*) *v* crack, *break, *burst

quedar (kay-*dhahr*) *v* remain; **quedarse** *v* remain, stay

queja (*kay*-khah) *f* complaint

quejarse (kay-*khahr*-say) *v* complain

quemadura (kay-mah-*dhoo*-rah) *f* burn; ~ **del sol** sunburn

quemar (kay-*mahr*) *v* *burn

*querer** (kay-*rayr*) *v* *will, want; like, *be fond of

querida (kay-*ree*-dhah) *f* sweetheart; mistress

querido (kay-*ree*-dhoa) *adj* beloved, dear; precious; *m* darling

queso (*kay*-soa) *m* cheese

quien (kᶌayn) *pron* who; **a** ~ whom

quienquiera (kᶌayng-*kᶌay*-rah) *pron* whoever

quieto (*kᶌay*-toa) *adj* still, quiet; *estarse* ~ *keep quiet

quilate (kee-*lah*-tay) *m* carat

quilla (*kee*-lᶌah) *f* keel

química (*kee*-mee-kah) *f* chemistry

químico (*kee*-mee-koa) *adj* chemical

quincalla (keeng-*kah*-lᶌah) *f* hardware

quince (*keen*-thay) *num* fifteen

quincena (keen-*thay*-nah) *f* fortnight

quinceno (keen-*thay*-noa) *num* fifteenth

quinina (kee-*nee*-nah) *f* quinine

quinta (*keen*-tah) *f* country house

quinto¹ (*keen*-toa) *num* fifth

quinto² (*keen*-toa) *m* conscript

quiosco (kᵛoass-koa) *m* kiosk; ~ **de periódicos** newsstand

quitamanchas (kee-tah-*mahn*-chahss) *m* cleaning fluid, stain remover

quitar (kee-*tahr*) *v* *take away

quitasol (kee-tah-*soal*) *m* sunshade

quizás (kee-*thahss*) *adv* maybe, perhaps

R

rábano (*rah*-bhah-noa) *m* radish; ~ **picante** horseradish

rabia (*rah*-bhᵛah) *f* rage; rabies

rabiar (rah-*bhᵛahr*) *v* rage

rabioso (rah-*bhᵛoa*-soa) *adj* mad

racial (rah-*thᵛahl*) *adj* racial

ración (rah-*thᵛoan*) *f* ration

radiador (rah-dhᵛah-*dhoar*) *m* radiator

radical (rah-dhee-*kahl*) *adj* radical

radio (*rah*-dhᵛoa) *m* radius; spoke; *f* wireless, radio

radiografía (rah-dhᵛoa-grah-*fee*-ah) *f* X-ray

radiografiar (rah-dhᵛoa-grah-*fᵛahr*) *v* X-ray

raedura (rah-ay-*dhoo*-rah) *f* scratch; ***hacer raeduras** scratch

ráfaga (*rah*-fah-gah) *f* gust, blow

raíz (rah-*eeth*) *f* root

rallar (rah-*lᵛahr*) *v* grate

rama (*rah*-mah) *f* branch, bough

ramita (rah-*mee*-tah) *f* twig

ramo (*rah*-moa) *m* bouquet, bunch

rampa (*rahm*-pah) *f* ramp

rana (*rah*-nah) *f* frog

rancio (*rahn*-thᵛoa) *adj* rancid

rancho (*rahn*-choa) *mMe* farmhouse

rango (*rahng*-goa) *m* rank

ranura (rah-*noo*-rah) *f* slot

rápidamente (*rah*-pee-dah-mayn-tay) *adv* soon

rapidez (rah-pee-*dhayth*) *f* speed

rápido (*rah*-pee-dhoa) *adj* fast, rapid, quick; **rápidos de río** rapids *pl*

raqueta (rah-*kay*-tah) *f* racquet

raro (*rah*-roa) *adj* uncommon, rare; strange, odd; **raras veces** rarely

rascacielos (rahss-kah-*thᵛay*-loass) *m* skyscraper

rascar (rahss-*kahr*) *v* scratch

rasgar (rahz-*gahr*) *v* rip

rasgo (*rahz*-goa) *m* trait; feature; ~ **característico** characteristic

rasgón (rahz-*goan*) *m* tear

rasguño (rahz-*goo*-ño-a) *m* scratch

raso (*rah*-soa) *adj* bare; *m* satin

raspar (rahss-*pahr*) *v* scrape

rastrear (rahss-tray-*ahr*) *v* trace

rastrillo (rahss-*tree*-lᵛoa) *m* rake

rastro (*rahss*-troa) *m* trail

rasurarse (rah-soo-*rahr*-say) *v* shave

rata (*rah*-tah) *f* rat

rato (*rah*-toa) *m* while

ratón (rah-*toan*) *m* mouse

raya (*rah*-ᵛah) *f* line, stripe; crease; parting

rayado (rah-ᵛah-dhoa) *adj* striped

rayador (rah-ᵛah-*dhoar*) *m* grater

rayo (*rah*-ᵛoa) *m* beam, ray

rayón (rah-ᵛoan) *m* rayon

raza (*rah*-thah) *f* race; breed

razón (rah-*thoan*) *f* wits *pl*, sense, reason; **no** ***tener** ~ *be wrong; ***tener** ~ * be right

razonable (rah-thoa-*nah*-bhlay) *adj* reasonable

razonar (rah-thoa-*nahr*) *v* reason

reacción (ray-ahk-*thᵛoan*) *f* reaction

reaccionar (ray-ahk-thᵛoa-*nahr*) *v* react

real (ray-*ahl*) *adj* factual, true, substantial; royal

realidad (ray-ah-lee-*dhahdh*) *f* reality;

en ~ actually, as a matter of fact, really, in effect

realizable (ray-ah-lee-*thah*-bhlay) *adj* feasible, realizable

realización (ray-ah-lee-thah-*th^yoan*) *f* achievement

realizar (ray-ah-lee-*thahr*) *v* realize; carry out

rebaja (ray-*bhah*-khah) *f* reduction, rebate; **rebajas** *fpl* sales

rebajar (ray-bhah-*khahr*) *v* lower, reduce

rebaño (ray-*bhah*-ño͞a) *m* flock

rebelde (ray-*bhayl*-day) *m* rebel

rebelión (ray-bhay-*l^yoan*) *f* revolt, rebellion

recado (ray-*kah*-dhoa) *m* errand

recambio (ray-*kahm*-b^yoa) *m* spare part

recaudar (ray-kou-*dhahr*) *v* raise

recepción (ray-thayp-*th^yoan*) *f* reception

recepcionista (ray-thayp-th^yoa-*neess*-tah) *f* receptionist

receptáculo (ray-thayp-*tah*-koo-loa) *m* container

receptor (ray-thayp-*toar*) *m* receiver

receta (ray-*thay*-tah) *f* recipe

recibir (ray-thee-*bheer*) *v* receive

recibo (ray-*thee*-bhoa) *m* voucher, receipt; **oficina de** ~ reception office

recién (ray-*th^yayn*) *adv* recently

reciente (ray-*th^yayn*-tay) *adj* recent

recientemente (ray-th^yayn-tay-*mayn*-tay) *adv* lately, recently

recio (*ray*-th^yoa) *adj* strong

recíproco (ray-*thee*-proa-koa) *adj* mutual

recital (ray-thee-*tahl*) *m* recital

reclamar (ray-klah-*mahr*) *v* claim

recluta (ray-*kloo*-tah) *m* recruit

recoger (ray-koa-*khayr*) *v* pick up, pick; collect, gather; *overtake

recogida (ray-koa-*khee*-dhah) *f* collec-

tion

recomendación (ray-koa-mayn-dah-*th^yoan*) *f* recommendation

* **recomendar** (ray-koa-mayn-*dahr*) *v* recommend

* **recomenzar** (ray-koa-mayn-*thahr*) *v* recommence

recompensa (ray-koam-*payn*-sah) *f* prize, reward

recompensar (ray-koam-payn-*sahr*) *v* reward

reconciliación (ray-koan-thee-l^yah-*th^yoan*) *f* reconciliation

* **reconocer** (ray-koa-noa-*thayr*) *v* recognize; admit, confess, acknowledge; realize

reconocimiento (ray-koa-noa-thee-*m^yayn*-toa) *m* recognition; check-up

récord (*ray*-koardh) *m* record

* **recordar** (ray-koar-*dhahr*) *v* remind; *think of

recorrer (ray-koa-*rrayr*) *v* cross

recortar (ray-koar-*tahr*) *v* trim

recreación (ray-kray-ah-*th^yoan*) *f* recreation

recreo (ray-*kray*-oa) *m* recreation; **patio de** ~ playground

recriar (ray-kr^y*ahr*) *v* *breed

rectangular (rayk-tahng-goo-*lahr*) *adj* rectangular

rectángulo (rayk-*tahng*-goo-loa) *m* oblong, rectangle

rectificación (rayk-tee-fee-kah-*th^yoan*) *f* correction

recto (*rayk*-toa) *adj* erect

rector (rayk-*toar*) *m* rector

rectoría (rayk-toa-*ree*-ah) *f* rectory

recuerdo (ray-*kwayr*-dhoa) *m* remembrance, memory; souvenir

recuperación (ray-koo-pay-rah-*th^yoan*) *f* revival

recuperar (ray-koo-pay-*rahr*) *v* recover

rechazar (ray-chah-*thahr*) *v* reject, turn down

red (raydh) f net; network; ~ **de carreteras** road system; ~ **de pescar** fishing net

redacción (ray-dhahk-thᵞoan) f wording; editorial staff

redactar (ray-dhahk-tahr) v *make up; *draw up

redactor (ray-dhahk-toar) m editor

redecilla (ray-dhay-thee-lᵞah) f hairnet

redimir (ray-dhee-meer) v redeem

rédito (ray-dhee-toa) m interest

redondeado (ray-dhoan-day-ah-dhoa) adj rounded

redondo (ray-dhoan-doa) adj round

reducción (ray-dhook-thᵞoan) f reduction, rebate

*****reducir** (ray-dhoo-theer) v *cut, decrease, reduce

reembolsar (ray-aym-boal-sahr) v reimburse

reemplazar (ray-aym-plah-thahr) v replace

reemprender (ray-aym-prayn-dayr) v resume

reexpedir (ray-ayks-pay-dheer) v forward

referencia (ray-fay-rayn-thᵞah) f reference; **punto de** ~ landmark

*****referir** (ray-fay-reer) v refer; narrate

refinería (ray-fee-nay-ree-ah) f refinery

reflector (ray-flayk-toar) m reflector; searchlight

reflejar (ray-flay-khahr) v reflect

reflejo (ray-flay-khoa) m reflection

reflexionar (ray-flayk-sᵞoa-nahr) v *think

Reforma (ray-foar-mah) f reformation

refractario (ray-frahk-tah-rᵞoa) adj fireproof

refrenar (ray-fray-nahr) v curb

refrescar (ray-frayss-kahr) v refresh

refresco (ray-frayss-koa) m refreshment

refrigerador (ray-free-khay-rah-dhoar) m fridge, refrigerator

refugio (ray-foo-khᵞoa) m cover, shelter

refunfuñar (ray-foon-foo-ñahr) v grumble

regalar (ray-gah-lahr) v present

regaliz (ray-gah-leeth) m liquorice

regalo (ray-gah-loa) m present, gift

regata (ray-gah-tah) f regatta

regatear (ray-gah-tay-ahr) v bargain

régimen (ray-khee-mayn) m (pl regimenes) régime; government, rule; diet

regimiento (ray-khee-mᵞayn-toa) m regiment

región (ray-khᵞoan) f region; zone, country, area

regional (ray-khᵞoa-nahl) adj regional

*****regir** (ray-kheer) v govern, rule

registrar (ray-kheess-trahr) v book, record

registro (ray-kheess-troa) m record

regla (ray-glah) f rule; regulation; ruler; **en** ~ in order; **por** ~ **general** as a rule

reglamento (ray-glah-mayn-toa) m regulation

regocijo (ray-goa-thee-khoa) m joy

regordete (ray-goar-dhay-tay) adj plump

regresar (ray-gray-sahr) v *go back, *get back

regreso (ray-gray-soa) m return; **viaje de** ~ return journey; **vuelo de** ~ return flight

regulación (ray-goo-lah-thᵞoan) f regulation

regular (ray-goo-lahr) v regulate; adj regular

rehabilitación (ray-ah-bhee-lee-tah-thᵞoan) f rehabilitation

rehén (ray-ayn) m hostage

rehusar (rayᵒᵒ-sahr) v refuse; reject

reina (*ray*-nah) *f* queen

reinado (ray-*nah*-dhoa) *m* reign

reino (*ray*-noa) *m* kingdom

reintegrar (rayn-tay-*grahr*) *v* *repay, refund

reintegro (rayn-*tay*-groa) *m* repayment, refund

*reír (ray-*eer*) *v* laugh

reivindicación (ray-bheen-dee-kah-*th^yoan*) *f* claim

reivindicar (ray-bheen-dee-*kahr*) *v* claim

reja (*ray*-khah) *f* grate; fence, gate

rejilla (ray-*khee*-l^yah) *f* luggage rack

relación (ray-lah-*th^yoan*) *f* connection, relation; reference; report

relacionar (ray-lah-th^yoa-*nahr*) *v* relate

relajación (ray-lah-khah-*th^yoan*) *f* relaxation

relajado (ray-lah-*khah*-dhoa) *adj* easygoing

relámpago (ray-*lahm*-pah-goa) *m* lightning; flash

relatar (ray-lah-*tahr*) *v* report

relativo (ray-lah-*tee*-bhoa) *adj* comparative, relative; ~ **a** regarding

relato (ray-*lah*-toa) *m* tale

relevar (ray-lay-*bhahr*) *v* relieve

relieve (ray-*l^yay*-bhay) *m* relief

religión (ray-lee-*kh^yoan*) *f* religion

religioso (ray-lee-*kh^yoa*-soa) *adj* religious

reliquia (ray-*lee*-k^yah) *f* relic

reloj (ray-*loakh*) *m* clock; watch; ~ **de bolsillo** pocket-watch; ~ **de pulsera** wrist-watch

relojero (ray-loa-*khay*-roa) *m* watchmaker

reluciente (ray-loo-*th^yayn*-tay) *adj* bright

*relucir (ray-loo-*theer*) *v* *shine

rellenado (ray-l^yay-*nah*-doa) *adj* stuffed

relleno (ray-*l^yay*-noa) *m* stuffing; filling

remanente (ray-mah-*nayn*-tay) *m* remnant

remar (ray-*mahr*) *v* row

remedio (ray-*may*-dh^yoa) *m* remedy

*remendar (ray-mayn-*dahr*) *v* mend; patch

remesa (ray-*may*-sah) *f* remittance

remitir (ray-mee-*teer*) *v* remit; ~ **a** refer to

remo (*ray*-moa) *m* paddle, oar

remoción (ray-moa-*th^yoan*) *f* removal

remojar (ray-moa-*khahr*) *v* soak

remolacha (ray-moa-*lah*-chah) *f* beetroot, beet

remolcador (ray-moal-kah-*dhoar*) *m* tug

remolcar (ray-moal-*kahr*) *v* tug, tow

remolque (ray-*moal*-kay) *m* trailer

remoto (ray-*moa*-toa) *adj* remote, faraway, far-off

*remover (ray-moa-*bhayr*) *v* remove

remuneración (ray-moo-nay-rah-*th^yoan*) *f* remuneration

remunerar (ray-moo-nay-*rahr*) *v* remunerate

Renacimiento (ray-nah-thee-*m^yayn*-toa) *m* Renaissance

rendición (rayn-dee-*th^yoan*) *f* surrender

*rendir (rayn-*deer*) *v* *pay; ~ **homenaje** honour; ***rendirse** *v* surrender

renglón (rayng-*gloan*) *m* line

reno (*ray*-noa) *m* reindeer

renombre (ray-*noam*-bray) *m* reputation

*renovar (ray-noa-*bhahr*) *v* renew

renta (*rayn*-tah) *f* revenue

rentable (rayn-*tah*-bhlay) *adj* paying

renunciar (ray-noon-*th^yahr*) *v* *give up

*reñir (ray-*ñeer*) *v* dispute, quarrel

reparación (ray-pah-rah-*th^yoan*) *f* reparation; repair

reparar (ray-pah-*rahr*) *v* repair, mend

repartir (ray-pahr-*teer*) *v* divide, *deal

reparto (ray-*pahr*-toa) *m* delivery; **camioneta de ~** pick-up van

repelente (ray-pay-*layn*-tay) *adj* repellent, revolting

repentinamente (ray-payn-tee-nah-*mayn*-tay) *adv* suddenly

repertorio (ray-payr-*toa*-r^yoa) *m* repertory

repetición (ray-pay-tee-*th^yoan*) *f* repetition

repetidamente (ray-pay-tee-dhah-*mayn*-tay) *adv* again and again

*****repetir** (ray-pay-*teer*) *v* repeat

repleto (ray-*play*-toa) *adj* chock-full, crowded

reportero (ray-poar-*tay*-roa) *m* reporter

reposado (ray-poa-*sah*-dhoa) *adj* restful

reposo (ray-*poa*-soa) *m* rest

reprender (ray-prayn-*dayr*) *v* reprimand, scold

representación (ray-pray-sayn-tah-*th^yoan*) *f* representation; show, performance

representante (ray-pray-sayn-*tahn*-tay) *m* agent

representar (ray-pray-sayn-*tahr*) *v* represent

representativo (ray-pray-sayn-tah-tee-bhoa) *adj* representative

reprimir (ray-pree-*meer*) *v* suppress

*****reprobar** (ray-proa-*bhahr*) *v* reject

reprochar (ray-proa-*chahr*) *v* reproach

reproche (ray-*proa*-chay) *m* reproach, blame

reproducción (ray-proa-dhook-*th^yoan*) *f* reproduction

*****reproducir** (ray-proa-dhoo-*theer*) *v* reproduce

reptil (rayp-*teel*) *m* reptile

república (ray-*poo*-bhlee-kah) *f* republic

republicano (ray-poo-bhlee-*kah*-noa) *adj* republican

repuesto (ray-*pwayss*-toa) *m* store; refill

repugnancia (ray-poog-*nahn*-th^yah) *f* dislike

repugnante (ray-poog-*nahn*-tay) *adj* repellent, disgusting, revolting

repulsivo (ray-pool-*see*-bhoa) *adj* repulsive

reputación (ray-poo-tah-*th^yoan*) *f* reputation, fame

requerimiento (ray-kay-ree-*m^yayn*-toa) *m* requirement

*****requerir** (ray-kay-*reer*) *v* require, demand

resaca (ray-*sah*-kah) *f* undercurrent; hangover

resbaladizo (rayz-bhah-lah-*dhee*-thoa) *adj* slippery

resbalar (rayz-bhah-*lahr*) *v* slip, glide

rescatar (rayss-kah-*tahr*) *v* rescue

rescate (rayss-*kah*-tay) *m* rescue; ransom

*****resentirse por** (ray-sayn-*teer*-say) resent

reseña (ray-*say*-ñah) *f* review

reserva (ray-*sayr*-bhah) *f* qualification; reserve; booking; **de ~** spare

reservación (ray-sayr-bhah-*th^yoan*) *f* reservation, booking

reservar (ray-sayr-*bhahr*) *v* engage; reserve, book

resfriado (rayss-*fr^yah*-dhoa) *m* cold

resfriarse (rayss-*fr^yahr*-say) *v* catch a cold

residencia (ray-see-*dhayn*-th^yah) *f* residence

residente (ray-see-*dhayn*-tay) *adj* resident; *m* resident

residir (ray-see-*dheer*) *v* reside

residuo (ray-*see*-dhwoa) *m* remnant

resignación (ray-seeg-nah-*th^yoan*) *f* resignation

resignar (ray-seeg-*nahr*) v resign

resina (ray-*see*-nah) f resin

resistencia (ray-seess-*tayn*-thʸah) f resistance

resistir (ray-seess-*teer*) v resist

resolución (ray-soa-loo-*thʸoan*) f resolution

* **resolver** (ray-soal-*bhayr*) v solve

* **resonar** (ray-soa-*nahr*) v sound

respectivo (rayss-payk-*tee*-bhoa) adj respective

respecto a (rayss-*payk*-toa ah) about, regarding

respetable (rayss-pay-*tah*-bhlay) adj respectable

respetar (rayss-pay-*tahr*) v respect

respeto (rayss-*pay*-toa) m respect, esteem, regard

respetuoso (rayss-pay-*twoa*-soa) adj respectful

respiración (rayss-pee-rah-*thʸoan*) f respiration, breathing

respirar (rayss-pee-*rahr*) v breathe

* **resplandecer** (rayss-plahn-day-*thayr*) v *shine

resplandor (rayss-plahn-*doar*) m glare

responder (rayss-poan-*dayr*) v reply, answer

responsabilidad (rayss-poan-sah-bhee-lee-*dhahdh*) f responsibility; liability

responsable (rayss-poan-*sah*-bhlay) adj responsible; liable

respuesta (rayss-*pwayss*-tah) f reply, answer

* **restablecerse** (rayss-tah-bhlay-*thayr*-say) v recover

restablecimiento (rayss-tah-bhlay-thee-mʸayn-toa) m recovery

restante (rayss-*tahn*-tay) adj remaining

restar (rayss-*tahr*) v subtract

restaurante (rayss-tou-*rahn*-tay) m restaurant; ~ **de autoservicio** self-service restaurant

resto (*rayss*-toa) m rest; remnant, remainder

restricción (rayss-treek-*thʸoan*) f restriction; qualification

resuelto (ray-*swayl*-toa) adj resolute, determined

resultado (ray-sool-*tah*-dhoa) m result; issue, outcome, effect

resultar (ray-sool-*tahr*) v result; prove

resumen (ray-*soo*-mayn) m résumé, survey, summary

retardar (ray-tahr-*dhahr*) v delay

* **retener** (ray-tay-*nayr*) v *hold

retina (ray-*tee*-nah) f retina

retirar (ray-tee-*rahr*) v *withdraw

reto (*ray*-toa) m challenge

retrasado (ray-trah-*sah*-dhoa) adj late

retraso (ray-*trah*-soa) m delay

retrato (ray-*trah*-toa) m portrait

retrete (ray-*tray*-tay) m toilet

retroceso (ray-troa-*thay*-soa) m recession

retumbo (ray-*toom*-boa) m roar

reumatismo (rayᵒᵒ-mah-*teez*-moa) m rheumatism

reunión (rayᵒᵒ-*nʸoan*) f meeting, assembly, rally

reunir (rayᵒᵒ-*neer*) v join, assemble; reunite

revelación (ray-bhay-lah-*thʸoan*) f revelation

revelar (ray-bhay-*lahr*) v reveal; *give away; develop

revendedor (ray-bhayn-day-*dhoar*) m retailer

* **reventar** (ray-bhayn-*tahr*) v crack, *burst

reventón (ray-bhayn-*toan*) m blow-out

reverencia (ray-bhay-*rayn*-thʸah) f respect

reverso (ray-*bhayr*-soa) m reverse

revés (ray-*bhayss*) m reverse; **al** ~ the other way round; upside-down; inside out

revisar (ray-bhee-*sahr*) v revise, over-haul

revisión (ray-bhee-s^y*oan*) f revision

revisor (ray-bhee-*soar*) m ticket collector

revista (ray-*bheess*-tah) f journal; review, magazine; revue; ~ **mensual** monthly magazine

revocar (ray-bhoa-*kahr*) v recall

revolución (ray-bhoa-loo-th^y*oan*) f revolution

revolucionar (ray-bhoa-loo-th^yoa-*nahr*) v rebel

revolucionario (ray-bhoa-loo-th^yoa-nah-r^yoa) adj revolutionary

*****revolver** (ray-bhoal-*bhayr*) v stir

revólver (ray-*bhoal*-bhayr) m revolver, gun

revuelta (ray-*bhwayl*-tah) f revolt

rey (ray) m king

rezar (ray-*thahr*) v pray

riada (r^y*ah*-dhah) f flood

ribera (ree-*bhay*-rah) f riverside, river bank, shore

rico (*ree*-koa) adj rich; wealthy; nice, enjoyable, tasty

ridiculizar (ree-dhee-koo-lee-*thahr*) v ridicule

ridículo (ree-*dhee*-koo-loa) adj ridiculous, ludicrous

riesgo (r^y*ayz*-goa) m hazard, chance, risk

rigoroso (ree-goa-*roa*-soa) adj severe

riguroso (ree-goo-*roa*-soa) adj bleak

rima (*ree*-mah) f rhyme

rímel (*ree*-mayl) m mascara

rincón (reeng-*koan*) m angle

rinoceronte (ree-noa-thay-*roan*-tay) m rhinoceros

riña (*ree*-ñah) f dispute

riñón (ree-*ñoan*) m kidney

río (*ree*-oa) m river; ~ **abajo** downstream; ~ **arriba** upstream

riqueza (ree-*kay*-thah) f riches pl, wealth

risa (*ree*-sah) f laughter, laugh

ritmo (*reet*-moa) m rhythm; pace

rival (ree-*bhahl*) m rival

rivalidad (ree-bhah-lee-*dhahdh*) f rivalry

rivalizar (ree-bhah-lee-*thahr*) v rival

rizador (ree-thah-*dhoar*) m curling-tongs pl; **rizadores** mpl hair rollers

rizar (ree-*thahr*) v curl

rizo (*ree*-thoa) m curl

robar (roa-*bhahr*) v rob; burgle

roble (*roa*-bhlay) m oak

robo (*roa*-bhoa) m robbery, theft

robusto (roa-*bhooss*-toa) adj solid, robust

roca (*roa*-kah) f rock

rocío (roa-*thee*-oa) m dew

rocoso (roa-*koa*-soa) adj rocky

rodaballo (roa-dhah-*bhah*-l^yoa) m brill

*****rodar** (roa-*dhahr*) v roll

rodear (roa-dhay-*ahr*) v cirele, surround; by-pass

rodilla (roa-*dhee*-l^yah) f knee

*****rogar** (roa-*gahr*) v ask

rojo (*roa*-khoa) adj red

rollo (*roa*-l^yoa) m roll

romano (roa-*mah*-noa) adj Roman

Romanticismo (roa-mahn-tee-*theez*-moa) m Romanticism

romántico (roa-*mahn*-tee-koa) adj romantic

rompecabezas (roam-pay-kah-*bhay*-thahss) m puzzle; jigsaw puzzle

romper (roam-*payr*) v *break

roncar (roang-*kahr*) v snore

ronco (*roang*-koa) adj hoarse

ropa (*roa*-pah) f clothes pl; ~ **blanca** linen; ~ **de cama** bedding; ~ **interior** underwear; ~ **interior de mujer** lingerie; ~ **sucia** washing, laundry

rosa (*roa*-sah) f rose; adj rose

rosado (roa-*sah*-dhoa) adj pink

rosario (roa-*sah*-r^yoa) *m* beads *pl*, rosary

rostro (*roas*-troa) *m* face

rota (*roa*-tah) *f* rattan

roto (*roa*-toa) *adj* broken

rótula (*roa*-too-lah) *f* kneecap

rotular (roa-too-*lahr*) *v* label

rótulo (*roa*-too-loa) *m* label

rozadura (roa-thah-*dhoo*-rah) *f* graze

rubí (roo-*bhee*) *m* ruby

rubia (*roo*-bh^yah) *f* blonde

rubio (*roo*-bh^yoa) *adj* fair

ruborizarse (roo-bhoa-ree-*thahr*-say) blush

rubricar (roo-bhree-*kahr*) *v* initial

rueda (*rway*-dhah) *f* wheel; **patinaje de ruedas** roller-skating; ~ **de repuesto** spare wheel

ruego (*rway*-goa) *m* request

rugido (roo-*khee*-dhoa) *m* roar

rugir (roo-*kheer*) *v* roar

ruibarbo (rwee-*bhahr*-bhoa) *m* rhubarb

ruido (*rwee*-dhoa) *m* noise

ruidoso (rwee-*dhoa*-soa) *adj* noisy

ruina (*rwee*-nah) *f* ruins; ruin, destruction

ruinoso (rwee-*noa*-soa) *adj* dilapidated

ruiseñor (rwee-say-*ñoar*) *m* nightingale

ruleta (roo-*lay*-tah) *f* roulette

rulo (*roo*-loa) *m* curler

Rumania (roo-*mah*-n^yah) *f* Rumania

rumano (roo-*mah*-noa) *adj* Rumanian; *m* Rumanian

rumbo (*room*-boa) *m* course

rumor (roo-*moar*) *m* rumour

rural (roo-*rahl*) *adj* rural

Rusia (*roo*-s^yah) *f* Russia

ruso (*roo*-soa) *adj* Russian; *m* Russian

rústico (*rooss*-tee-koa) *adj* rustic

ruta (*roo*-tah) *f* route; ~ **principal** thoroughfare

rutina (roo-*tee*-nah) *f* routine

S

sábado (*sah*-bhah-dhoa) *m* Saturday

sábana (*sah*-bhah-nah) *f* sheet

sabañón (sah-bhah-*ñoan*) *m* chilblain

*saber** (sah-*bhayr*) *v* *know; *be able to; **a** ~ namely; ~ **a** taste

sabiduría (sah-bhee-dhoo-*ree*-ah) *f* wisdom

sabio (*sah*-bh^yoa) *adj* wise

sabor (sah-*bhoar*) *m* flavour

sabroso (sah-*bhroa*-soa) *adj* savoury, tasty

sacacorchos (sah-kah-*koar*-choass) *mpl* corkscrew

sacapuntas (sah-kah-*poon*-tahss) *m* pencil-sharpener

sacar (sah-*kahr*) *v* *take out; *draw; ~ **brillo** brush

sacarina (sah-kah-*ree*-nah) *f* saccharin

sacerdote (sah-thayr-*dhoa*-tay) *m* priest

saco (*sah*-koa) *m* sack; *mMe* jacket; ~ **de compras** shopping bag; ~ **de dormir** sleeping-bag

sacrificar (sah-kree-fee-*kahr*) *v* sacrifice

sacrificio (sah-kree-*fee*-th^yoa) *m* sacrifice

sacrilegio (sah-kree-*lay*-kh^yoa) *m* sacrilege

sacristán (sah-kreess-*tahn*) *m* sexton

sacudir (sah-koo-*dheer*) *v* *shake

sagrado (sah-*grah*-dhoa) *adj* sacred

sainete (sigh-*nay*-tay) *m* farce

sal (sahl) *f* salt; **sales de baño** bath salts

sala (*sah*-lah) *f* hall; ~ **de conciertos** concert hall; ~ **de espera** waiting-room; ~ **de estar** sitting-room, living-room; ~ **de lectura** reading-room; ~ **para fumar** smoking-room

salado (sah-*lah*-dhoa) *adj* salty

salario (sah-*lah*-rʸoa) *m* pay

salchicha (sahl-*chee*-chah) *f* sausage

saldo (*sahl*-doa) *m* balance

salero (sah-*lay*-roa) *m* salt-cellar

salida (sah-*lee*-dhah) *f* issue, exit, way out; ~ **de emergencia** emergency exit

****salir** (sah-*leer*) *v* *go out; appear

saliva (sah-*lee*-bhah) *f* spit

salmón (sahl-*moan*) *m* salmon

salón (sah-*loan*) *m* salon, lounge, drawing-room; ~ **de baile** ballroom; ~ **de belleza** beauty parlour; ~ **de demostraciones** showroom; ~ **de té** tea-shop

salpicadera (sahl-pee-kah-*dhay*-rah) *f* Me mud-guard

salpicar (sahl-pee-*kahr*) *v* splash

salsa (*sahl*-sah) *f* sauce; gravy

saltamontes (sahl-tah-*moan*-tayss) *m* grasshopper

saltar (sahl-*tahr*) *v* jump, *leap; skip

salto (*sahl*-toa) *m* jump, leap, hop

salud (sah-*loodh*) *f* health

saludable (sah-loo-*dhah*-bhlay) *adj* wholesome

saludar (sah-loo-*dhahr*) *v* greet; salute

saludo (sah-*loo*-dhoa) *m* greeting

salvador (sahl-bhah-*dhoar*) *m* saviour

salvaje (sahl-*bhah*-khay) *adj* wild, savage; fierce, desert

salvar (sahl-*bhahr*) *v* save

sanatorio (sah-nah-*toa*-rʸoa) *m* sanatorium

sandalia (sahn-*dah*-lʸah) *f* sandal; **sandalias de gimnasia** gym shoes

sandía (sahn-*dee*-ah) *f* watermelon

sangrar (sahng-*grahr*) *v* *bleed

sangre (*sahng*-gray) *f* blood

sangriento (sahng-*grʸayn*-toa) *adj* bloody

sanitario (sah-nee-*tah*-rʸoa) *adj* sanitary

sano (*sah*-noa) *adj* healthy, well

santo (*sahn*-toa) *adj* holy; *m* saint; ~ **y seña** password

santuario (sahn-*twah*-rʸoa) *m* shrine

sapo (*sah*-poa) *m* toad

sarampión (sah-rahm-*pʸoan*) *m* measles

sardina (sahr-*dhee*-nah) *f* sardine

sartén (sahr-*tayn*) *f* pan; frying-pan

sastre (*sahss*-tray) *m* tailor

satélite (sah-*tay*-lee-tay) *m* satellite

satisfacción (sah-teess-fahk-*thʸoan*) *f* satisfaction

****satisfacer** (sah-teess-fah-*thayr*) *v* satisfy; **satisfecho** satisfied

saudí (sou-*dhee*) *adj* Saudi Arabian

sauna (*sou*-nah) *f* sauna

sazonar (sah-thoa-*nahr*) *v* flavour

se (say) *pron* himself; herself; yourselves; themselves

secadora (say-kah-*dhoa*-rah) *f* dryer

secar (say-*kahr*) *v* dry

sección (sayk-*thʸoan*) *f* section; agency

seco (*say*-koa) *adj* dry

secretaria (say-kray-*tah*-rʸah) *f* secretary

secretario (say-kray-*tah*-rʸoa) *m* secretary; clerk

secreto (say-*kray*-toa) *adj* secret; *m* secret

sector (sayk-*toar*) *m* sector

secuencia (say-*kwayn*-thʸah) *f* shot

secuestrador (say-kwayss-trah-*dhoar*) *m* hijacker

secundario (say-koon-*dah*-rʸoa) *adj* secondary; minor

sed (saydh) *f* thirst

seda (*say*-dhah) *f* silk

sede (*say*-dhay) *f* seat

sediento (say-*dhʸayn*-toa) *adj* thirsty

sedoso (say-*dhoa*-soa) *adj* silken

* **seducir** (say-dhoo-*theer*) v seduce

en seguida (ayn say-*gee*-dhah) straight away, at once, presently

* **seguir** (say-*geer*) v follow; ~ **el paso** *keep up with; **todo seguido** straight on, straight ahead

según (say-*goon*) prep according to

segundo (say-*goon*-doa) num second; m second

seguramente (say-goo-rah-*mayn*-tay) adv surely

seguridad (say-goo-ree-*dhahdh*) f security, safety; **cinturón de ~** safety-belt

seguro (say-*goo*-roa) adj safe; sure; m insurance; **póliza de ~** insurance policy; ~ **de viaje** travel insurance; ~ **de vida** life insurance

seis (sayss) num six

selección (say-layk-*th*ᵞ*oan*) f selection; choice

seleccionado (say-layk-th*ᵞ*oa-*nah*-dhoa) adj select

seleccionar (say-layk-th*ᵞ*oa-*nahr*) v select

selecto (say-*layk*-toa) adj select

selva (*sayl*-bhah) f jungle, forest

selvoso (sayl-*bhoa*-soa) adj wooded

sellar (say-*l*ᵞ*ahr*) v stamp

sello (*say*-l*ᵞ*oa) m stamp; seal

semáforo (say-*mah*-foa-roa) m traffic light

semana (say-*mah*-nah) f week; **fin de ~** weekend

semanal (say-mah-*nahl*) adj weekly

* **sembrar** (saym-*brahr*) v *sow

semejante (say-may-*khahn*-tay) adj like

semejanza (say-may-*khahn*-thah) f resemblance, similarity

semi- (*say*-mee) semi-

semicírculo (say-mee-*theer*-koo-loa) m semicircle

semilla (say-*mee*-l*ᵞ*ah) f seed

senado (say-*nah*-dhoa) m senate

senador (say-nah-*dhoar*) m senator

sencillo (sayn-*thee*-l*ᵞ*oa) adj plain

senda (*sayn*-dah) f footpath

sendero (sayn-*day*-roa) m trail

senil (say-*neel*) adj senile

seno (*say*-noa) m bosom; breast

sensación (sayn-sah-*th*ᵞ*oan*) f sensation; feeling

sensacional (sayn-sah-th*ᵞ*oa-*nahl*) adj sensational

sensato (sayn-*sah*-toa) adj sensible; down-to-earth

sensibilidad (sayn-see-bhee-lee-*dhahdh*) f sensibility

sensible (sayn-*see*-bhlay) adj sensitive; perceptible

sensitivo (sayn-see-*tee*-bhoa) adj sensitive

* **sentarse** (sayn-*tahr*-say) v *sit down; * **estar sentado** *sit; * **sentar bien** *become

sentencia (sayn-*tayn*-th*ᵞ*ah) f sentence, verdict

sentenciar (sayn-tayn-*th*ᵞ*ahr*) v sentence

sentido (sayn-*tee*-dhoa) m sense; reason; ~ **del honor** sense of honour; **sin ~** meaningless

sentimental (sayn-tee-mayn-*tahl*) adj sentimental

sentimiento (sayn-tee-*m*ᵞ*ayn*-toa) m sentiment

* **sentir** (sayn-*teer*) v *feel, sense; regret

seña (*say*-ñah) f sign; **señas personales** description

señal (say-*ñahl*) f signal, sign, indication; m token, tick; * **hacer señales** signal; wave; ~ **de alarma** distress signal

señalar (say-ñah-*lahr*) v tick off, indicate

señor (say-*ñoar*) m mister; sir

señora (say-*ñoa*-rah) *f* lady; mistress; madam

señorita (say-ñoa-*ree*-tah) *f* miss

separación (say-pah-rah-*th*ᵛ*oan*) *f* division

separadamente (say-pah-rah-dhah-*mayn*-tay) *adv* apart

separado (say-pah-*rah*-dhoa) *adj* separate; **por ~** apart, separately

separar (say-pah-*rahr*) *v* separate, part; divide; detach

septentrional (sayp-tayn-tr*ᵛ*oa-*nahl*) *adj* north

septicemia (sayp-tee-*thay*-mᵛah) *f* blood-poisoning

séptico (*sayp*-tee-koa) *adj* septic

septiembre (sayp-*t*ᵛ*aym*-bray) September

séptimo (*sayp*-tee-moa) *num* seventh

sepulcro (say-*pool*-kroa) *m* sepulchre

sepultura (say-pool-*too*-rah) *f* grave

sequía (say-*kee*-ah) *f* drought

ser (sayr) *m* being, creature; **~ humano** human being

*****ser** (sayr) *v* *be

sereno (say-*ray*-noa) *adj* serene

serie (*say*-rᵛay) *f* series; sequence

seriedad (say-rᵛay-*dhahdh*) *f* seriousness, gravity

serio (*say*-rᵛoa) *adj* serious

sermón (sayr-*moan*) *m* sermon

serpentear (sayr-payn-tay-*ahr*) *v* *wind

serrín (say-*rreen*) *m* sawdust

servicial (sayr-bhee-*th*ᵛ*ahl*) *adj* helpful

servicio (sayr-bhee-th*ᵛ*oa) *m* service; service charge; **~ de habitación** room service; **~ de mesa** dinnerservice; **~ postal** postal service

servilleta (sayr-bhee-*l*ᵛ*ay*-tah) *f* napkin, serviette; **~ de papel** paper napkin

*****servir** (sayr-*bheer*) *v* serve; attend on, wait on; *be of use

sesenta (say-*sayn*-tah) *num* sixty

sesión (say-s*ᵛoan*) *f* session

seta (*say*-tah) *f* mushroom

setenta (say-*tayn*-tah) *num* seventy

seto (*say*-toa) *m* hedge

severo (say-*bhay*-roa) *adj* harsh, strict, severe

sexo (*sayk*-soa) *m* sex

sexto (*sayks*-toa) *num* sixth

sexual (sayk-*swahl*) *adj* sexual

sexualidad (sayk-swah-lee-*dhahdh*) *f* sexuality; sex

si (see) *conj* if; in case; whether; **si ... o** whether ... or; **~ bien** though

sí (see) yes

Siam (sᵛahm) *m* Siam

siamés (sᵛah-*mayss*) *adj* Siamese; *m* Siamese

siempre (s*ᵛaym*-pray) *adv* ever, always

sien (sᵛayn) *f* temple

sierra (s*ᵛay*-rrah) *f* saw

siesta (s*ᵛayss*-tah) *f* nap

siete (s*ᵛay*-tay) *num* seven

sifón (see-*foan*) *m* siphon, syphon

siglo (*see*-gloa) *m* century

significado (seeg-nee-fee-*kah*-dhoa) *m* meaning

significar (seeg-nee-fee-*kahr*) *v* *mean

significativo (seeg-nee-fee-kah-*tee*-bhoa) *adj* significant

signo (*seeg*-noa) *m* sign; **~ de interrogación** question mark

siguiente (see-g*ᵛayn*-tay) *adj* following

sílaba (*see*-lah-bhah) *f* syllable

silbar (seel-*bhahr*) *v* whistle

silbato (seel-*bhah*-toa) *m* whistle

silenciador (see-layn-th*ᵛah-dhoar*) *m* silencer

silencio (see-*layn*-th*ᵛoa*) *m* stillness, quiet, silence

silencioso (see-layn-th*ᵛoa*-soa) *adj* silent

silla (*see*-l*ᵛah*) *f* chair; saddle; **~ de ruedas** wheelchair; **~ de tijera**

deck chair

sillón (see-*l^yoan*) *m* armchair

simbólico (seem-*boa*-lee-koa) *adj* symbolic

símbolo (*seem*-boa-loa) *m* symbol

similar (see-mee-*lahr*) *adj* similar

simpatía (seem-pah-*tee*-ah) *f* sympathy

simpático (seem-*pah*-tee-koa) *adj* nice, pleasant; obliging

simple (*seem*-play) *adj* simple

simular (see-moo-*lahr*) *v* simulate

simultáneo (see-mool-*tah*-nay-oa) *adj* simultaneous

sin (seen) *prep* without

sinagoga (see-nah-*goa*-gah) *f* synagogue

sincero (seen-*thay*-roa) *adj* sincere; open, honest

sindicato (seen-dee-*kah*-toa) *m* trade-union

sinfonía (seen-foa-*nee*-ah) *f* symphony

singular (seeng-goo-*lahr*) *adj* singular, queer; *m* singular

siniestro (see-*n^yayss*-troa) *adj* ominous, sinister

sino (*see*-noa) *conj* but

sinónimo (see-*noa*-nee-moa) *m* synonym

sintético (seen-*tay*-tee-koa) *adj* synthetic

síntoma (*seen*-toa-mah) *m* symptom

sintonizar (seen-toa-nee-*thahr*) *v* tune in

siquiera (see-*k^yay*-rah) *adv* at least; *conj* even though

sirena (see-*ray*-nah) *f* siren; mermaid

Siria (*see*-r^yah) *f* Syria

sirio (*see*-r^yoa) *adj* Syrian; *m* Syrian

sirviente (seer-*bh^yayn*-tay) *m* domestic; boy

sistema (seess-*tay*-mah) *m* system; ~ **decimal** decimal system; ~ **de lubricación** lubrication system; ~ **de**

refrigeración cooling system

sistemático (seess-tay-*mah*-tee-koa) *adj* systematic

sitio (*see*-t^yoa) *m* site; seat, room; siege

situación (see-twah-*th^yoan*) *f* situation

situado (see-*twah*-dhoa) *adj* situated

situar (see-*twahr*) *v* locate

slogan (*sloa*-gahn) *m* slogan

smoking (*smoa*-keeng) *m* dinner-jacket; tuxedo *nAm*

soberano (soa-bhay-*rah*-noa) *m* sovereign

soberbio (soa-*bhayr*-bh^yoa) *adj* superb

sobornar (soa-bhoar-*nahr*) *v* bribe

soborno (soa-*bhoar*-noa) *m* bribery

sobra (*soa*-bhrah) *f* surplus

sobrar (soa-*bhrahr*) *v* *be left over; *be in plenty

sobre (*soa*-bhray) *prep* on, upon; *m* envelope

sobrecubierta (soa-bhray-koo-*bh^yayr*-tah) *f* jacket

sobreexcitado (soa-bhray-ayk-thee-*tah*-dhoa) *adj* overstrung

sobrepeso (soa-bhray-*pay*-soa) *m* overweight

sobretasa (soa-bhray-*tah*-sah) *f* surcharge

sobretodo (soa-bhray-*toa*-dhoa) *m* coat, topcoat

sobrevivir (soa-bhray-bhee-*bheer*) *v* survive

sobrina (soa-*bhree*-nah) *f* niece

sobrino (soa-*bhree*-noa) *m* nephew

sobrio (*soa*-bhr^yoa) *adj* sober

social (soa-*th^yahl*) *adj* social

socialismo (soa-th^yah-*leez*-moa) *m* socialism

socialista (soa-th^yah-*leess*-tah) *adj* socialist; *m* socialist

sociedad (soa-th^yay-*dhahdh*) *f* community, society; company

socio (*soa*-th^yoa) *m* associate; partner

socorro (soa-*koa*-rroa) *m* aid; **puesto de** ~ first-aid post
soda (*soa*-dhah) *f* soda-water
sofá (soa-*fah*) *m* sofa
sofocante (soa-foa-*kahn*-tay) *adj* stuffy
sofocarse (soa-foa-*kahr*-say) *v* choke
soga (*soa*-gah) *f* rope
sol (soal) *m* sun; **tomar el** ~ sunbathe
solamente (soa-lah-*mayn*-tay) *adv* merely, only
solapa (soa-*lah*-pah) *f* lapel
soldado (soal-*dah*-dhoa) *m* soldier
soldador (soal-dah-*dhoar*) *m* soldering-iron
soldadura (soal-dah-*dhoo*-rah) *f* joint
***soldar** (soal-*dahr*) *v* solder; weld
soleado (soa-lay-*ah*-dhoa) *adj* sunny
soledad (soa-lay-*dhahdh*) *f* solitude
solemne (soa-*laym*-nay) *adj* solemn
***soler** (soa-*layr*) *v* would
solicitar (soa-lee-thee-*tahr*) *v* request; ~ **un puesto** apply
solicitud (soa-lee-thee-*toodh*) *f* application
sólido (*soa*-lee-dhoa) *adj* solid, firm; *m* solid
solitario (soa-lee-*tah*-r^{y}oa) *adj* lonely
solo (*soa*-loa) *adj* only, single
sólo (*soa*-loa) *adv* alone; only
***soltar** (soal-*tahr*) *v* loosen
soltero (soal-*tay*-roa) *adj* single; *m* bachelor
solterona (soal-tay-*roa*-nah) *f* spinster
soluble (soa-*loo*-bhlay) *adj* soluble
solución (soa-loo-*th^{y}oan*) *f* solution
sombra (*soam*-brah) *f* shade; shadow; ~ **para los ojos** eye-shadow
sombreado (soam-bray-*ah*-dhoa) *adj* shady
sombrerera (soam-bray-*ray*-rah) *f* milliner
sombrero (soam-*bray*-roa) *m* hat
sombrío (soam-*bree*-oa) *adj* sombre, gloomy
someter (soa-may-*tayr*) *v* subject; **someterse** *v* submit
somnífero (soam-*nee*-fay-roa) *m* sleeping-pill
***sonar** (soa-*nahr*) *v* sound; *ring
sonido (soa-*nee*-dhoa) *m* sound
sonreír (soan-ray-*eer*) *v* smile
sonrisa (soan-*ree*-sah) *f* smile
***soñar** (soa-*ñahr*) *v* *dream
soñoliento (soa-ñoa-*l^{y}ayn*-toa) *adj* sleepy
sopa (*soa*-pah) *f* soup
soplar (soa-*plahr*) *v* *blow
soportar (soa-poar-*tahr*) *v* *bear, endure, sustain; support
sóquet (*soa*-kayt) *mMe* socket
sorbo (*soar*-bhoa) *m* sip
sórdido (*soar*-dhee-dhoa) *adj* filthy
sordo (*soar*-dhoa) *adj* deaf
sorprender (soar-prayn-*dayr*) *v* surprise; *catch
sorpresa (soar-*pray*-sah) *f* surprise; astonishment
sorteo (soar-*tay*-oa) *m* draw
sosegado (soa-say-*gah*-dhoa) *adj* sedate
sospecha (soass-*pay*-chah) *f* suspicion
sospechar (soass-pay-*chahr*) *v* suspect
sospechoso (soass-pay-*choa*-soa) *adj* suspicious; **persona sospechosa** suspect
sostén (soass-*tayn*) *m* brassiere, bra
***sostener** (soass-tay-*nayr*) *v* support, *hold up
sota (*soa*-tah) *f* knave
sótano (*soa*-tah-noa) *m* basement; cellar
soto (*soa*-toa) *m* grove
soviético (soa-*bh^{y}ay*-tee-koa) *adj* Soviet
starter (*stahr*-tayr) *m* choke
su (soo) *adj* his; her; their
suahili (swah-*ee*-lee) *m* Swahili

suave (*swah*-bhay) *adj* mild, mellow; gentle

subacuático (soo-bhah-*kwah*-tee-koa) *adj* underwater

subalterno (soo-bhahl-*tayr*-noa) *adj* subordinate

subasta (soo-*bhahss*-tah) *f* auction

súbdito (*soobh*-dhee-toa) *m* subject

subestimar (soo-bhayss-tee-*mahr*) *v* underestimate

subida (soo-*bhee*-dhah) *f* climb, rise, ascent

subir (soo-*bheer*) *v* *rise, ascend; *get on

súbito (*soo*-bhee-toa) *adj* sudden

sublevación (soo-bhlay-bhah-*th^yoan*) *f* rebellion

sublevarse (soo-bhlay-*bhahr*-say) *v* revolt

subordinado (soo-bhoar-dhee-*nah*-dhoa) *adj* subordinate

subrayar (soobh-rah-*^yahr*) *v* underline

subsidio (soobh-*see*-dh^yoa) *m* subsidy

substancia (soobh-*tahn*-th^yah) *f* substance

substantivo (soobh-stahn-*tee*-bhoa) *m* noun

***substituir** (soobhs-tee-*tweer*) *v* replace

subterráneo (soobh-tay-*rrah*-nay-oa) *adj* underground

subtítulo (soobh-*tee*-too-loa) *m* subtitle

suburbano (soo-bhoor-*bhah*-noa) *adj* suburban; *m* commuter

suburbio (soo-*bhoor*-bh^yoa) *m* suburb

subvención (soobh-bhayn-*th^yoan*) *f* grant

subyugar (soobh-*^yoo*-gahr) *v* overwhelm

suceder (soo-thay-*dhayr*) *v* happen, occur; succeed

sucesión (soo-thay-*s^yoan*) *f* sequence

suceso (soo-*thay*-soa) *m* event

suciedad (soo-th^yay-*dhahdh*) *f* dirt; muck

sucio (*soo*-th^yoa) *adj* dirty; unclean, foul

sucumbir (soo-koom-*beer*) *v* succumb

sucursal (soo-koor-*sahl*) *f* branch

sudar (soo-*dhahr*) *v* perspire, sweat

sudeste (soo-*dhayss*-tay) *m* south-east

sudoeste (soo-dhoa-*ayss*-tay) *m* south-west

sudor (soo-*dhoar*) *m* perspiration, sweat

Suecia (sway-*th^yah*) *f* Sweden

sueco (*sway*-koa) *adj* Swedish; *m* Swede

suegra (*sway*-grah) *f* mother-in-law

suegro (*sway*-groa) *m* father-in-law

suela (*sway*-lah) *f* sole

sueldo (*swayl*-doa) *m* salary, pay; **aumento de ~** rise; raise *nAm*

suelo (*sway*-loa) *m* soil, earth; floor

suelto (*swayl*-toa) *adj* loose

sueño (*sway*-ño) *m* sleep; dream

suero (*sway*-roa) *m* serum

suerte (*swayr*-tay) *f* luck; fortune, lot; chance; **mala ~** bad luck

suéter (*sway*-tayr) *m* sweater

suficiente (soo-fee-*th^yayn*-tay) *adj* enough, sufficient; ***ser ~** *do

sufragio (soo-*frah*-kh^yoa) *m* suffrage

sufrimiento (soo-free-*m^yayn*-toa) *m* affliction, sorrow, suffering

sufrir (soo-*freer*) *v* suffer

***sugerir** (soo-khay-*reer*) *v* suggest

sugestión (soo-khayss-*t^yoan*) *f* suggestion

suicidio (swee-*thee*-dh^yoa) *m* suicide

Suiza (swee-*thah*) *f* Switzerland

suizo (*swee*-thoa) *adj* Swiss; *m* Swiss

sujetador (soo-khay-tah-*dhoar*) *m* brassiere, bra

sujeto (soo-*khay*-toa) *m* subject; theme

sujeto a (soo-*khay*-toa ah) liable to,

subject to

suma (*soo*-mah) *f* amount, sum

sumar (soo-*mahr*) *v* add; amount to

sumario (soo-*mah*-rᵞoa) *m* summary

suministrar (soo-mee-neess-*trahr*) *v* furnish, supply

suministro (soo-mee-*neess*-troa) *m* supply

a lo sumo (*soo*-moa) at most

superar (soo-pay-*rahr*) *v* exceed, *out-do

superficial (soo-payr-fee-*thᵞahl*) *adj* superficial

superficie (soo-payr-fee-*thᵞay*) *f* surface; area

superfluo (soo-*payr*-flwoa) *adj* super-fluous, redundant

superior (soo-pay-*rᵞoar*) *adj* superior, upper; top

superlativo (soo-payr-lah-*tee*-bhoa) *adj* superlative; *m* superlative

supermercado (soo-payr-mayr-*kah*-dhoa) *m* supermarket

superstición (soo-payrs-tee-*thᵞoan*) *f* superstition

supervisar (soo-payr-bhee-*sahr*) *v* supervise

supervisión (soo-payr-bhee-*sᵞoan*) *f* supervision

supervisor (soo-payr-bhee-*soar*) *m* supervisor

supervivencia (soo-payr-bhee-*bhayn*-thᵞah) *f* survival

suplemento (soo-play-*mayn*-toa) *m* supplement

suplicar (soo-plee-*kahr*) *v* beg

***suponer** (soo-poa-*nayr*) *v* assume, suppose

supositorio (soo-poa-see-*toa*-rᵞoa) *m* suppository

supremo (soo-*pray*-moa) *adj* supreme

suprimir (soo-pree-*meer*) *v* discon-tinue

por supuesto (poar soo-*pwayss*-toa)

naturally, of course

sur (soor) *m* south; **polo** ~ South Pole

surco (*soor*-koa) *m* groove

surgir (soor-*kheer*) *v* *arise

surtido (soor-*tee*-dhoa) *m* assortment

suscribir (sooss-kree-*bheer*) *v* sign

suscripción (sooss-kreep-*thᵞoan*) *f* subscription

suscrito (sooss-*kree*-toa) *m* under-signed

suspender (sooss-payn-*dayr*) *v* sus-pend; ***ser suspendido** fail

suspensión (sooss-payn-*sᵞoan*) *f* sus-pension

suspicacia (sooss-pee-*kah*-thᵞah) *f* sus-picion

suspicaz (sooss-pee-*kahth*) *adj* suspi-cious

sustancia (sooss-*tahn*-thᵞah) *f* sub-stance

sustancial (sooss-tahn-*thᵞahl*) *adj* sub-stantial

sustento (sooss-*tayn*-toa) *m* livelihood

***sustituir** (sooss-tee-*tweer*) *v* substi-tute

sustituto (sooss-tee-*too*-toa) *m* deputy, substitute

susto (*sooss*-toa) *m* scare

susurrar (soo-soo-*rrahr*) *v* whisper

susurro (soo-*soo*-rroa) *m* whisper

sutil (soo-*teel*) *adj* subtle

sutura (soo-*too*-rah) *f* stitch; ***hacer una** ~ sew up

suyo (*soo*-ᵞoa) *pron* his

T

tabaco (tah-*bhah*-koa) *m* tobacco; ~ **de pipa** pipe tobacco

taberna (tah-*bhayr*-nah) *f* public house, pub; tavern; **moza de** ~

barmaid

tabique (tah-*bhee*-kay) *m* partition

tabla (*tah*-bhlah) *f* board; chart, table; ~ **de conversión** conversion chart; ~ **para surf** surf-board

tablero (tah-*bhlay*-roa) *m* board; ~ **de ajedrez** checkerboard *nAm*; ~ **de damas** draught-board; ~ **de instrumentos** dashboard

tablón (tah-*bhloan*) *m* plank

tabú (tah-*bhoo*) *m* taboo

tacón (tah-*koan*) *m* heel

táctica (*tahk*-tee-kah) *f* tactics *pl*

tacto (*tahk*-toa) *m* touch

tailandés (tigh-lahn-*dayss*) *adj* Thai; *m* Thai

Tailandia (tigh-*lahn*-dʸah) *f* Thailand

tajada (tah-*khah*-dhah) *f* slice

tajar (tah-*khahr*) *v* chop

tal (tahl) *adj* such; **con** ~ **que** provided that; ~ **como** such as

taladrar (tah-lah-*dhrahr*) drill, bore

taladro (tah-*lah*-dhroa) *m* drill

talco (*tahl*-koa) *m* talc powder

talento (tah-*layn*-toa) *m* gift, talent

talentoso (tah-layn-*toa*-soa) *adj* gifted

talismán (tah-leez-*mahn*) *m* lucky charm

talón (tah-*loan*) *m* heel; counterfoil, stub

talonario (tah-loa-*nah*-rʸoa) *m* chequebook; check-book *nAm*

talla (*tah*-lʸah) *f* wood-carving, carving

tallar (tah-*lʸahr*) *v* carve

taller (tah-*lʸayr*) *m* workshop

tallo (*tah*-lʸoa) *m* stem

tamaño (tah-*mah*-ñoa) *m* size; ~ **extraordinario** outsize

también (tahm-*bʸayn*) *adv* too, also, as well; **así** ~ likewise

tambor (tahm-*boar*) *m* drum; ~ **del freno** brake drum

tamiz (tah-*meeth*) *m* sieve

tamizar (tah-mee-*thahr*) *v* sift, sieve

tampoco (tahm-*poa*-koa) *adv* not ... either

tan (tahn) *adv* so, such

tangible (tahng-*khee*-bhlay) *adj* tangible

tanque (*tahng*-kay) *m* tank

tanteo (tahn-*tay*-oa) *m* score

tanto (*tahn*-toa) *adv* as much; as; **por lo** ~ therefore; **por** ~ so; **tanto ... como** both ... and

tapa (*tah*-pah) *f* lid, top, cover; appetizer

tapiz (tah-*peeth*) *m* tapestry

tapizar (tah-pee-*thahr*) *v* upholster

tapón (tah-*poan*) *m* stopper, cork; tampon

taquigrafía (tah-kee-grah-*fee*-ah) *f* shorthand

taquígrafo (tah-*kee*-grah-foa) *m* stenographer

taquilla (tah-*kee*-lʸah) *f* box-office

tararear (tah-rah-ray-*ahr*) *v* hum

tardanza (tahr-*dhahn*-thah) *f* delay

tarde (*tahr*-dhay) *f* afternoon; evening

tardío (tahr-*dhee*-oa) *adj* late

tarea (tah-*ray*-ah) *f* duty, task; job

tarifa (tah-*ree*-fah) *f* rate; ~ **nocturna** night rate

tarjeta (tahr-*khay*-tah) *f* card; ~ **de crédito** credit card; charge plate *Am*; ~ **de temporada** season-ticket; ~ **de visita** visiting-card; ~ **postal** postcard, card; ~ **postal ilustrada** picture postcard; ~ **verde** green card

tarta (*tahr*-tah) *f* cake

taxi (*tahk*-see) *m* cab, taxi

taxímetro (tahk-*see*-may-troa) *m* taximeter

taxista (tahk-*seess*-tah) *m* cab-driver, taxi-driver

taza (*tah*-thah) *f* cup; mug; ~ **de té** teacup

tazón (tah-*thoan*) *m* bowl, basin

te (tay) *pron* yourself

té (tay) *m* tea

teatro (tay-*ah*-troa) *m* drama; theatre; ~ **de la ópera** opera house; ~ **de variedades** music-hall, variety theatre; ~ **guiñol** puppet-show

tebeo (tay-*bhay*-oa) *m* comics *pl*

técnica (*tayk*-nee-kah) *f* technique

técnico (*tayk*-nee-koa) *adj* technical; *m* technician

tecnología (tayk-noa-loa-*khee*-ah) *f* technology

techo (*tay*-choa) *m* roof; ~ **de paja** thatched roof

teja (*tay*-khah) *f* tile

tejedor (tay-khay-*dhoar*) *m* weaver

tejer (tay-*khayr*) *v* *weave

tejido (tay-*khee*-dhoa) *m* fabric, tissue, material

tela (*tay*-lah) *f* cloth; ~ **para toallas** towelling

telaraña (tay-lah-*rah*-ñah) *f* spider's web

telefonear (tay-lay-foa-nay-*ahr*) *v* phone; call up *Am*

telefonista (tay-lay-foa-*neess*-tah) *f* telephonist, telephone operator

teléfono (tay-*lay*-foa-noa) *m* phone, telephone; **llamar por ~** ring up

telegrafiar (tay-lay-grah-*f*ʸ*ahr*) *v* telegraph

telegrama (tay-lay-*grah*-mah) *m* telegram

telémetro (tay-*lay*-may-troa) *m* rangefinder

teleobjetivo (tay-lay-oabh-khay-*tee*-bhoa) *m* telephoto lens

telepatía (tay-lay-pah-*tee*-ah) *f* telepathy

telesilla (tay-lay-*see*-lʸah) *m* ski-lift

televisión (tay-lay-bhee-*s*ʸ*oan*) *f* television

televisor (tay-lay-bhee-*soar*) *m* television set

télex (*tay*-layks) *m* telex

telón (tay-*loan*) *m* curtain

tema (*tay*-mah) *m* theme

*temblar** (taym-*bhlahr*) *v* tremble, shiver

temer (tay-*mayr*) *v* fear, dread

temor (tay-*moar*) *m* fear, dread

temperamento (taym-pay-rah-*mayn*-toa) *m* temperament

temperatura (taym-pay-rah-*too*-rah) *f* temperature; ~ **ambiente** room temperature

tempestad (taym-payss-*tahdh*) *f* tempest

tempestuoso (taym-payss-*twoa*-soa) *adj* stormy

templo (*taym*-ploa) *m* temple

temporada (taym-poa-*rah*-dhah) *f* season; **apogeo de la ~** high season; ~ **baja** low season

temporal (taym-poa-*rahl*) *adj* temporary

temprano (taym-*prah*-noa) *adj* early

tenazas (tay-*nah*-thahss) *f* tongs *pl*, pincers *pl*

tendencia (tayn-*dayn*-thʸah) *f* tendency

*tender a** (tayn-*dayr*) tend; *tender-se** *v* *lie down

tendero (tayn-*day*-roa) *m* shopkeeper; tradesman

tendón (tayn-*doan*) *m* sinew, tendon

tenedor (tay-nay-*dhoar*) *m* fork

*tener** (tay-*nayr*) *v* *have; *keep, *hold; ~ **que** *must; *ought to, *should, *shall; *be obliged to; **tenga usted** here you are

teniente (tay-*n*ʸ*ayn*-tay) *m* lieutenant

tenis (*tay*-neess) *m* tennis; ~ **de mesa** ping-pong, table tennis

tensión (tayn-*s*ʸ*oan*) *f* strain, pressure, tension; ~ **arterial** blood pressure

tenso (*tayn*-soa) *adj* tense

tentación (tayn-tah-*th*ʸoan) f temptation

***tentar** (tayn-*tahr*) v tempt

tentativa (tayn-tah-*tee*-bhah) f attempt, try

tentempié (tayn-taym-*p*ʸay) m snack

***teñir** (tay-*ñeer*) v dye

teología (tay-oa-loa-*khee*-ah) f theology

teoría (tay-oa-*ree*-ah) f theory

teórico (tay-*oa*-ree-koa) adj theoretical

terapia (tay-rah-pʸah) f therapy

tercero (tayr-*thay*-roa) num third

terciopelo (tayr-thʸoa-*pay*-loa) m velvet

terilene (tay-ree-*lay*-nay) m terylene

terminación (tayr-mee-nah-*th*ʸoan) f finish

terminar (tayr-mee-*nahr*) v end, finish; accomplish; **terminarse** v expire, end

término (*tayr*-mee-noa) m term; issue

termo (*tayr*-moa) m vacuum flask, thermos flask

termómetro (tayr-*moa*-may-troa) m thermometer

termostato (tayr-moass-*tah*-toa) m thermostat

ternero (tayr-*nay*-roa) m calf

ternura (tayr-*noo*-rah) f tenderness

terraplén (tay-rrah-*playn*) m embankment

terraza (tay-*rrah*-thah) f terrace

terremoto (tay-rray-*moa*-toa) m earthquake

terreno (tay-*rray*-noa) m terrain; field, grounds

terrible (tay-*rree*-bhlay) adj frightful; awful, horrible, terrible, dreadful

territorio (tay-rree-*toa*-rʸoa) m territory

terrón (tay-*rroan*) m lump

terror (tay-*rroar*) m terror; terrorism

terrorismo (tay-rroa-*reez*-moa) m terrorism

terrorista (tay-rroa-*reess*-tah) m terrorist

tesis (*tay*-seess) f thesis

Tesorería (tay-soa-ray-*ree*-ah) f treasury

tesorero (tay-soa-*ray*-roa) m treasurer

tesoro (tay-*soa*-roa) m treasure

testamento (tayss-tah-*mayn*-toa) m will

testarudo (tayss-tah-*roo*-dhoa) adj pigheaded, stubborn

testigo (tayss-*tee*-goa) m witness; ~ **de vista** eye-witness

testimoniar (tayss-tee-moa-*n*ʸahr) v testify

testimonio (tayss-tee-*moa*-nʸoa) m testimony

tetera (tay-*tay*-rah) f teapot

textil (tayks-*teel*) m textile

texto (*tayks*-toa) m text

textura (tayks-*too*-rah) f texture

tez (tayth) f complexion

ti (tee) pron you

tía (*tee*-ah) f aunt

tibio (*tee*-bhʸoa) adj tepid, lukewarm

tiburón (tee-bhoo-*roan*) m shark

tiempo (*t*ʸaym-poa) m time; weather; **a** ~ in time; ~ **libre** spare time

tienda (*t*ʸayn-dah) f shop; tent

tierno (*t*ʸayr-noa) adj gentle, tender

tierra (*t*ʸay-rrah) f earth; ground, soil; land; **en** ~ ashore; ~ **baja** lowlands pl; ~ **firme** mainland

tieso (*t*ʸay-soa) adj stiff

tifus (*tee*-fooss) m typhoid

tigre (*tee*-gray) m tiger

tijeras (tee-*khay*-rahss) fpl scissors pl; ~ **para las uñas** nail-scissors pl

tilo (*tee*-loa) m limetree, lime

timbre (*teem*-bray) m tone; bell; doorbell; mMe postage stamp

timidez (tee-mee-*dhayth*) f timidity, shyness

tímido (tee-mee-dhoa) *adj* timid, embarrassed, shy

timón (tee-*moan*) *m* helm, rudder

timonel (tee-moa-*nayl*) *m* steersman

timonero (tee-moa-*nay*-roa) *m* helmsman

tímpano (teem-pah-noa) *m* ear-drum

tinta (*teen*-tah) *f* ink

tintorería (teen-toa-ray-*ree*-ah) *f* dry-cleaner's

tintura (teen-*too*-rah) *f* dye

tío (*tee*-oa) *m* uncle

típico (*tee*-pee-koa) *adj* typical, characteristic

tipo (*tee*-poa) *m* type; fellow, guy

tirada (tee-*rah*-dhah) *f* issue

tirano (tee-*rah*-noa) *m* tyrant

tirantes (tee-*rahn*-tayss) *mpl* braces *pl*; suspenders *plAm*

tirar (tee-*rahr*) *v* pull; *throw; *shoot

tiritar (tee-ree-*tahr*) *v* shiver

tiro (*tee*-roa) *m* shot

tirón (tee-*roan*) *m* wrench

titular (tee-too-*lahr*) *m* headline

título (tee-too-loa) *m* heading, title; degree

toalla (toa-*ah*-lᶴah) *f* towel; ~ **de baño** bath towel

tobera (toa-*bhay*-rah) *f* nozzle

tobillo (toa-*bhee*-lᶴoa) *m* ankle

tobogán (toa-bhoa-*gahn*) *m* slide

tocadiscos (toa-kah-*deess*-koass) *m* record-player

tocador (toa-kah-*dhoar*) *m* dressing-table; powder-room; **artículos de ~** toiletry

tocante a (toa-*kahn*-tay ah) regarding

tocar (toa-*kahr*) *v* touch, *hit; play; **no ~** *keep off

tocino (toa-*thee*-noa) *m* bacon

todavía (toa-dhah-*bhee*-ah) *adv* still, however

todo (*toa*-dhoa) *adj* all; entire; *pron* everything; **sobre ~** most of all, essentially, especially; **todos** *pron* everybody

toldo (*toal*-doa) *m* awning

tolerable (toa-lay-*rah*-bhlay) *adj* tolerable

tomar (toa-*mahr*) *v* *catch; *take; ~ **el pelo** tease

tomate (toa-*mah*-tay) *m* tomato

tomillo (toa-*mee*-lᶴoa) *m* thyme

tomo (*toa*-moa) *m* volume

tonada (toa-*nah*-dhah) *f* tune

tonel (toa-*nayl*) *m* barrel, cask

tonelada (toa-nay-*lah*-dhah) *f* ton

tónico (*toa*-nee-koa) *m* tonic; ~ **para el cabello** hair tonic

tono (*toa*-noa) *m* tone; note; shade

tontería (toan-tay-*ree*-ah) *f* nonsense, rubbish; *decir tonterías** talk rubbish

tonto (*toan*-toa) *adj* foolish; *m* fool

topetar (toa-pay-*tahr*) *v* bump

topetón (toa-pay-*toan*) *m* bump

toque (*toa*-kay) *m* touch

torcedura (toar-thay-*dhoo*-rah) *f* sprain

torcer (toar-*thayr*) *v* twist; *torcerse** *v* sprain

tordo (*toar*-dhoa) *m* thrush

tormenta (toar-*mayn*-tah) *f* storm

tormento (toar-*mayn*-toa) *m* torment

tormentoso (toar-mayn-*toa*-soa) *adj* thundery

tornar (toar-*nahr*) *v* return

torneo (toar-*nay*-oa) *m* tournament

tornillo (toar-*nee*-lᶴoa) *m* screw

en torno (ayn *toar*-noa) about, around

en torno de (ayn *toar*-noa day) round, around

toro (*toa*-roa) *m* bull

toronja (toa-*roan*-khah) *fMe* grapefruit

torpe (*toar*-pay) *adj* clumsy, awkward

torre (*toa*-rray) *f* tower

torsión (toar-sᶴoan) *f* twist

tortilla (toar-*tee*-lᶴah) *f* omelette

tortuga (toar-*too*-gah) *f* turtle

tortuoso (toar-*twoa*-soa) *adj* winding

tortura (toar-*too*-rah) *f* torture

torturar (toar-too-*rahr*) *v* torture

tos (toass) *f* cough

toser (toa-*sayr*) *v* cough

tostado (toass-*tah*-dhoa) *adj* tanned

total (toa-*tahl*) *adj* total; overall, utter; *m* total; whole; **en ~** altogether

totalitario (toa-tah-lee-*tah*-r^yoa) *adj* totalitarian

totalizador (toa-tah-lee-thah-*dhoar*) *m* totalizator

totalmente (toa-tahl-*mayn*-tay) *adv* completely, altogether, wholly

tóxico (*toak*-see-koa) *adj* toxic

trabajar (trah-bhah-*khahr*) *v* work

trabajo (trah-*bhah*-khoa) *m* work, labour; difficulty; **~ manual** handicraft

tractor (trahk-*toar*) *m* tractor

tradición (trah-dhee-*th^yoan*) *f* tradition

tradicional (trah-dhee-th^yoa-*nahl*) *adj* traditional

traducción (trah-dhook-*th^yoan*) *f* translation

*traducir (trah-dhoo-*theer*) *v* translate

traductor (trah-dhook-*toar*) *m* translator

*traer (trah-*ayr*) *v* *bring

tragar (trah-*gahr*) *v* swallow

tragedia (trah-*khay*-dh^yah) *f* drama, tragedy

trágico (*trah*-khee-koa) *adj* tragic

traición (trigh-*th^yoan*) *f* treason

traicionar (trigh-th^yoa-*nahr*) *v* betray

traidor (trigh-*dhoar*) *m* traitor

traílla (trah-ee-l^yah) *f* lead

traje (*trah*-khay) *m* suit; gown; robe; **~ de baño** bathing-suit; **~ de etiqueta** evening dress; **~ del país** national dress; **~ de malla** tights *pl*; **~ pantalón** pant-suit

trama (*trah*-mah) *f* plot

trampa (*trahm*-pah) *f* trap; hatch

tranquilidad (trahng-kee-lee-*dhahdh*) *f* tranquillity

tranquilizar (trahng-kee-lee-*thahr*) *v* reassure

tranquilo (trahng-*kee*-loa) *adj* tranquil, quiet, calm; peaceful

transacción (trahn-sahk-*th^yoan*) *f* transaction, deal; **volumen de transacciones** turnover

transatlántico (trahn-saht-*lahn*-tee-koa) *adj* transatlantic

transbordador (trahnz-bhoar-dhah-*dhoar*) *m* ferry-boat; **~ de trenes** train ferry

transcurrir (trahns-koo-*rrer*) *v* pass

transeúnte (trahn-say-*oon*-tay) *m* passer-by

*transferir (trahns-fay-*reer*) *v* transfer

transformador (trahns-foar-mah-*dhoar*) *m* transformer

transformar (trahns-foar-*mahr*) *v* transform

transgredir (trahnz-gray-*deer*) *v* offend

transición (trahn-see-*th^yoan*) *f* transition

tránsito (*trahn*-see-toa) *m* traffic

transmisión (trahnz-mee-s^yoan) *f* transmission, broadcast

transmitir (trahnz-mee-*teer*) *v* transmit

transparente (trahns-pah-*rayn*-tay) *adj* transparent

transpiración (trahns-pee-rah-*th^yoan*) *f* perspiration

transpirar (trahns-pee-*rahr*) *v* perspire

transportar (trahns-poar-*tahr*) *v* transport; ship

transporte (trahns-*poar*-tay) *m* transportation, transport

tranvía (trahm-*bee*-ah) *m* tram; streetcar *nAm*

trapo (*trah*-poa) *m* rag; **~ de cocina** tea-cloth

tras (trahss) *prep* behind

*** hacer trasbordo** (ah-*thayr* trahz-*bhoar*-dhoa) change

trasero (trah-*say*-roa) *m* bottom

trasladar (trahz-lah-*dhahr*) *v* move

traslúcido (trahz-*loo*-thee-dhoa) *adj* sheer

trastornado (trahss-toar-*nah*-dhoa) *adj* upset

trastornar (trahss-toar-*nahr*) *v* upset

trastos (*trahss*-toass) *mpl* litter

tratado (trah-*tah*-dhoa) *m* essay; treaty

tratamiento (trah-tah-*m^yayn*-toa) *m* treatment; ~ **de belleza** beauty treatment

tratar (trah-*tahr*) *v* handle, treat; ~ **con** *deal with

trato (*trah*-toa) *m* intercourse

a través de (ah trah-*bhayss* day) across, through

travesía (trah-bhay-*see*-ah) *f* crossing, passage

travieso (trah-*bh^yay*-soa) *adj* naughty, bad; mischievous

trazar (trah-*thahr*) *v* sketch

trébol (*tray*-bhoal) *m* clover, shamrock

trece (*tray*-thay) *num* thirteen

treceno (tray-*thay*-noa) *num* thirteenth

trecho (*tray*-choa) *m* stretch

treinta (*trayn*-tah) *num* thirty

treintavo (trayn-*tah*-bhoa) *num* thirtieth

tremendo (tray-*mayn*-doa) *adj* awful, terrible; tremendous, terrific

trementina (tray-mayn-*tee*-nah) *f* turpentine

tren (trayn) *m* train; ~ **de cercanías** stopping train; ~ **de mercancías** goods train; ~ **de pasajeros** passenger train; ~ **directo** through train; ~ **expreso** express train; ~ **nocturno** night train; ~ **ómnibus** local train

trenza (*trayn*-thah) *f* twine

trepar (tray-*pahr*) *v* climb

tres (trayss) *num* three

triangular (tr^yahng-goo-*lahr*) *adj* triangular

triángulo (*tr^yahng*-goo-loa) *m* triangle

tribu (*tree*-bhoo) *m* tribe

tribuna (tree-*bhoo*-nah) *f* stand

tribunal (tree-bhoo-*nahl*) *m* court, law court

trigal (tree-*gahl*) *m* cornfield

trigo (*tree*-goa) *m* grain, corn; wheat

trimestral (tree-mayss-*trahl*) *adj* quarterly

trimestre (tree-*mayss*-tray) *m* quarter

trinchar (treen-*chahr*) *v* carve

trineo (tree-*nay*-oa) *m* sleigh, sledge

triste (*treess*-tay) *adj* sad

tristeza (treess-*tay*-thah) *f* sorrow, sadness

triturar (tree-too-*rahr*) *v* *grind

triunfante (tr^yoon-*fahn*-tay) *adj* triumphant

triunfar (tr^yoon-*fahr*) *v* triumph

triunfo (*tr^yoon*-foa) *m* triumph

*** trocar** (troa-*kahr*) *v* swap

trolebús (troa-lay-*bhooss*) *m* trolleybus

trompeta (troam-*pay*-tah) *f* trumpet

tronada (troa-*nah*-dhah) *f* thunderstorm

*** tronar** (troa-*nahr*) *v* thunder

tronco (*troang*-koa) *m* trunk

trono (*troa*-noa) *m* throne

tropas (*troa*-pahss) *fpl* troops *pl*

*** tropezarse** (troa-pay-*thahr*-say) *v* stumble

tropical (troa-pee-*kahl*) *adj* tropical

trópicos (*troa*-pee-koass) *mpl* tropics *pl*

trozo (*troa*-thoa) *m* chunk, morsel, bit; fragment, passage

truco (*troo*-koa) *m* trick

trucha (*troo*-chah) *f* trout

trueno (*trway*-noa) *m* thunder

tu (too) *adj* your

tú (too) *pron* you

tuberculosis (too-bhayr-koo-*loa*-seess) *f* tuberculosis

tubo (*too*-bhoa) *m* tube

tuerca (*twayr*-kah) *f* nut

tulipán (too-lee-*pahn*) *m* tulip

tumba (*toom*-bah) *f* tomb

tumor (too-*moar*) *m* growth, tumour

tunecino (too-nay-*thee*-noa) *adj* Tunisian; *m* Tunisian

túnel (*too*-nayl) *m* tunnel

Túnez (*too*-nayth) *m* Tunisia

túnica (*too*-nee-kah) *f* tunic

turbar (toor-*bhahr*) *v* embarrass

turbera (toor-*bhay*-rah) *f* moor

turbina (toor-*bhee*-nah) *f* turbine

turco (*toor*-koa) *adj* Turkish; *m* Turk

turismo (too-*reez*-moa) *m* tourism

turista (too-*reess*-tah) *m* tourist; **oficina para turistas** tourist office

turno (*toor*-noa) *m* turn; shift

turrón (too-*rroan*) *m* nougat

Turquía (toor-*kee*-ah) *f* Turkey

tutela (too-*tay*-lah) *f* custody

tutor (too-*toar*) *m* tutor; guardian

tuyos (*too*-Yoass) *adj* your

U

ubicación (oo-bhee-kah-*th*Yoan) *f* situation, location

ujier (oo-*kh*Yayr) *m* bailiff

úlcera (*ool*-thay-rah) *f* ulcer, sore; ~ **gástrica** gastric ulcer

ulterior (ool-tay-*r*Yoar) *adj* further

últimamente (*ool*-tee-mah-mayn-tay) *adv* lately

último (*ool*-tee-moa) *adj* ultimate; last

ultraje (ool-*trah*-khay) *m* outrage

ultramar (ool-trah-*mahr*) *adv* overseas

ultravioleta (ool-trah-bh Yoa-*lay*-tah) *adj* ultraviolet

umbral (oom-*brahl*) *m* threshold

un (oon) *art* a **art**

unánime (oo-*nah*-nee-may) *adj* like-minded, unanimous

ungüento (oong-*gwayn*-toa) *m* ointment, salve

únicamente (*oo*-nee-kah-mayn-tay) *adv* exclusively

único (*oo*-nee-koa) *adj* unique, sole

unidad (oo-nee-*dhahdh*) *f* unity; unit

unido (oo-*nee*-dhoa) *adj* joint

uniforme (oo-nee-*foar*-may) *adj* uniform; *m* uniform

unilateral (oo-nee-lah-tay-*rahl*) *adj* one-sided

unión (oo-*n*Yoan) *f* union

Unión Soviética (oo-*n*Yoan soa-bh Yaytee-kah) Soviet Union

unir (oo-*neer*) *v* unite; combine; **unirse a** join

universal (oo-nee-bhayr-*sahl*) *adj* universal

universidad (oo-nee-bhayr-see-*dhahdh*) *f* university

universo (oo-nee-*bhayr*-soa) *m* universe

uno (*oo*-noa) *num* one; *pron* one; **unos** *adj* some; *pron* some

uña (*oo*-ñah) *f* nail

urbano (oor-*bhah*-noa) *adj* urban

urgencia (oor-*khayn*-th Yah) *f* urgency; emergency; **botiquín de** ~ first-aid kit

urgente (oor-*khayn*-tay) *adj* pressing, urgent

urraca (oo-*rrah*-kah) *f* magpie

Uruguay (oo-roo-*gwigh*) *m* Uruguay

uruguayo (oo-roo-*gwah*-Yoa) *adj* Uruguayan; *m* Uruguayan

usar (oo-*sahr*) *v* use

uso (*oo*-soa) *m* use, usage

usted (ooss-*taydh*) *pron* you; **a** ~

you; **de ~** your

usual (oo-*swahl*) *adj* common, customary, usual

usuario (oo-swah-*r*Yoa) *m* user

utensilio (oo-tayn-*see*-lYoa) *m* utensil

útil (*oo*-teel) *adj* useful

utilidad (oo-tee-lee-*dhahdh*) *f* utility, use

utilizable (oo-tee-lee-*thah*-bhlay) *adj* usable

utilizar (oo-tee-lee-*thahr*) *v* utilize

uvas (*oo*-bhahss) *fpl* grapes *pl*

V

vaca (*bah*-kah) *f* cow

vacaciones (bah-kah-*th*Yoa-nayss) *fpl* holiday, vacation; **de ~** on holiday

vacante (bah-*kahn*-tay) *adj* vacant; *f* vacancy

vaciar (bah-*th*Yahr) *v* empty; vacate

vacilante (bah-thee-*lahn*-tay) *adj* unsteady, shaky

vacilar (bah-thee-*lahr*) *v* hesitate; falter

vacío (bah-*thee*-oa) *adj* empty; *m* vacuum

vacunación (bah-koo-nah-*th*Yoan) *f* vaccination

vacunar (bah-koo-*nahr*) *v* vaccinate, inoculate

vadear (bah-dhay-*ahr*) *v* wade

vado (*bah*-dhoa) *m* ford

vagabundear (bah-gah-bhoon-day-*ahr*) *v* tramp, roam

vagabundo (bah-gah-*bhoon*-doa) *m* tramp

vagancia (bah-*gahn*-thYah) *f* vagrancy

vagar (bah-*gahr*) *v* wander

vago (*bah*-goa) *adj* vague; faint, dim; idle

vagón (bah-*goan*) *m* waggon, carriage; coach

vainilla (bigh-*nee*-lYah) *f* vanilla

vale (*bah*-lay) *m* banknote

***valer** (bah-*layr*) *v* *be worth; **~ la pena** *be worth-while

valiente (bah-*l*Yayn-tay) *adj* courageous, plucky, brave

valija (bah-*lee*-khah) *f* case

valioso (bah-*l*Yoa-soa) *adj* valuable

valor (bah-*loar*) *m* worth, value; courage; **bolsa de valores** stock exchange; **sin ~** worthless

vals (bahls) *m* waltz

valuar (bah-*l*Wahr) *v* value; appreciate

válvula (*bahl*-bhoo-lah) *f* valve

valle (*bah*-lYay) *m* valley

vanidoso (bah-nee-*dhoa*-soa) *adj* vain

vano (*bah*-noa) *adj* idle, vain; **en ~** in vain

vapor (bah-*poar*) *m* steam, vapour; steamer; **~ de línea** liner

vaporizador (bah-poa-ree-thah-*dhoar*) *m* atomizer

vaqueros (bah-*kay*-roass) *mpl* jeans *pl*

variable (bah-*r*Yah-bhlay) *adj* variable

variación (bah-rYah-*th*Yoan) *f* variation

variado (bah-*r*Yah-dhoa) *adj* varied

variar (bah-*r*Yahr) *v* vary

varice (*bah*-ree-thay) *f* varicose vein

varicela (bah-ree-*thay*-lah) *f* chickenpox

variedad (bah-rYay-*dhahdh*) *f* variety; **espectáculo de variedades** variety show

varios (*bah*-rYoass) *adj* various, several

vaselina (bah-say-*lee*-nah) *f* vaseline

vasija (bah-*see*-khah) *f* vessel

vaso (*bah*-soa) *m* glass; mug, tumbler; vase; **~ sanguíneo** bloodvessel

vasto (*bahss*-toa) *adj* wide, vast; extensive

vatio (*bah*-tYoa) *m* watt

vecindad (bay-theen-*dahdh*) f neighbourhood, vicinity

vecindario (bay-theen-*dah*-r^Yoa) m community

vecino (bay-*thee*-noa) adj neighbouring; m neighbour

vegetación (bay-khay-tah-*th^Yoan*) f vegetation

vegetariano (bay-khay-tah-r^Y*ah*-noa) m vegetarian

vehículo (bay-ee-koo-loa) m vehicle

veinte (*bayn*-tay) num twenty

vejez (bay-*khayth*) f old age

vejiga (bay-*khee*-gah) f bladder

vela (*bay*-lah) f sail; **deporte de ~** yachting

velo (*bay*-loa) m veil

velocidad (bay-loa-thee-*dhahdh*) f speed; rate; gear; **límite de ~** speed limit; **~ de cruce** cruising speed

velocímetro (bay-loa-*thee*-may-troa) m speedometer

veloz (bay-*loath*) adj swift

vena (*bay*-nah) f vein

vencedor (bayn-thay-*dhoar*) m winner

vencer (bayn-*thayr*) v *overcome, conquer; *win

vencimiento (bayn-thee-m^Y*ayn*-toa) m expiry

vendaje (bayn-*dah*-khay) m bandage

vendar (bayn-*dahr*) v dress

vendedor (bayn-day-*dhoar*) m salesman

vendedora (bayn-day-*dhoa*-rah) f salesgirl

vender (bayn-*dayr*) v *sell; **~ al detalle** retail

vendible (bayn-dee-*bhlay*) adj saleable

vendimia (bayn-dee-m^Yah) f vintage

veneno (bay-*nay*-noa) m poison

venenoso (bay-nay-*noa*-soa) adj poisonous

venerable (bay-nay-*rah*-bhlay) adj venerable

venerar (bay-nay-*rahr*) v worship

venezolano (bay-nay-thoa-*lah*-noa) adj Venezuelan; m Venezuelan

Venezuela (bay-nay-*thway*-lah) f Venezuela

venganza (bayng-*gahn*-thah) f revenge

venidero (bay-nee-*dhay*-roa) adj oncoming

***venir** (bay-*neer*) v *come

venta (*bayn*-tah) f sale; **de ~** for sale; **~ al por mayor** wholesale

ventaja (bayn-*tah*-khah) f benefit, advantage; profit; lead

ventajoso (bayn-tah-*khoa*-soa) adj advantageous

ventana (bayn-*tah*-nah) f window; **~ de la nariz** nostril

ventarrón (bayn-tah-*rroan*) m gale

ventilación (bayn-tee-lah-*th^Yoan*) f ventilation

ventilador (bayn-tee-lah-*dhoar*) m fan, ventilator

ventilar (bayn-tee-*lahr*) v ventilate

ventisca (bhayn-*teess*-kah) f blizzard

ventoso (bayn-*toa*-soa) adj windy

***ver** (bayr) v *see, notice

veranda (bay-*rahn*-dah) f veranda

verano (bay-*rah*-noa) m summer; **pleno ~** midsummer

verbal (bayr-*bhahl*) adj verbal

verbo (*bayr*-bhoa) m verb

verdad (bayr-*dhahdh*) f truth

verdaderamente (bayr-dhah-dhay-rah-*mayn*-tay) adv really

verdadero (bayr-dhah-*dhay*-roa) adj true; real, very; actual

verde (*bayr*-dhay) adj green

verdulero (bayr-dhoo-*lay*-roa) m greengrocer

veredicto (bay-ray-*dheek*-toa) m verdict

vergel (bayr-gayl) m orchard

vergüenza (bayr-*gwayn*-thah) f shame;

¡qué vergüenza! shame!

verídico (bay-ree-dhee-koa) *adj* truthful

verificar (bay-ree-fee-*kahr*) *v* check, verify

verosímil (bay-roa-see-meel) *adj* credible

versión (bayr-s*y*oan) *f* version

verso (*bayr*-soa) *m* verse

*verter (bayr-*tayr*) *v* pour; *spill

vertical (bayr-tee-*kahl*) *adj* vertical

vértigo (*bayr*-tee-goa) *m* dizziness, vertigo

vestíbulo (bayss-*tee*-bhoo-loa) *m* hall, lobby; foyer

vestido (bayss-*tee*-dhoa) *m* frock, dress; **vestidos** *mpl* clothes *pl*

*vestir (bayss-*teer*) *v* dress; ***vestirse** *v* dress

vestuario (bayss-*twah*-r*y*oa) *m* wardrobe; dressing-room

veterinario (bay-tay-ree-*nah*-r*y*oa) *m* veterinary surgeon

vez (bayth) *f* time; **alguna ~** some time; **a veces** sometimes; **de ~ en cuando** occasionally, now and then; **otra ~** again, once more; **pocas veces** seldom; **una ~** once

vía (*bee*-ah) *f* track; **~ del tren** railroad *nAm*; **~ navegable** waterway

viaducto (b*y*ah-*dhook*-toa) *m* viaduct

viajar (b*y*ah-*khahr*) *v* travel

viaje (*b*yah-khay) *m* journey; trip, voyage

viajero (b*y*ah-*khay*-roa) *m* traveller

vibración (bee-bhrah-*th*y*oan*) *f* vibration

vibrar (bee-*bhrahr*) *v* tremble, vibrate

vicario (bee-*kah*-r*y*oa) *m* vicar

vicepresidente (bee-thay-pray-see-*dhayn*-tay) *m* vice-president

vicioso (bee-*th*y*oa*-soa) *adj* vicious

víctima (*beek*-tee-mah) *f* casualty, victim

victoria (beek-*toa*-r*y*ah) *f* victory

vid (beedh) *f* vine

vida (*bee*-dhah) *f* life; lifetime; **en ~** alive; **~ privada** privacy

vidrio (bee-dhr*y*oa) *m* glass; **de ~** glass; **~ de color** stained glass

viejo (*b*y*ay*-khoa) *adj* old; ancient, aged; stale

viento (*b*y*ayn*-toa) *m* wind

vientre (*b*y*ayn*-tray) *m* belly

viernes (*b*y*ayr*-nayss) *m* Friday

viga (*bee*-gah) *f* beam

vigente (bee-*khayn*-tay) *adj* valid

vigésimo (bee-*khay*-see-moa) *num* twentieth

vigilar (bee-khee-*lahr*) *v* watch, patrol

vigor (bee-*goar*) *m* strength; stamina

vil (beel) *adj* foul

villa (*bee*-l*y*ah) *f* villa

villano (bee-*l*y*ah*-noa) *m* villain

vinagre (bee-*nah*-gray) *m* vinegar

vinatero (bee-nah-*tay*-roa) *m* wine-merchant

vino (*bee*-noa) *m* wine

viña (*bee*-ñah) *f* vineyard

violación (b*y*oa-lah-*th*y*oan*) *f* violation

violar (b*y*oa-*lahr*) *v* assault, rape

violencia (b*y*oa-*layn*-th*y*ah) *f* violence

violento (b*y*oa-*layn*-toa) *adj* violent; fierce, severe

violeta (b*y*oa-*lay*-tah) *f* violet

violín (b*y*oa-*leen*) *m* violin

virgen (*beer*-khayn) *f* virgin

virtud (beer-*toodh*) *f* virtue

viruelas (bee-*rway*-lahss) *fpl* smallpox

visado (bee-*sah*-dhoa) *m* visa

visar (bee-*sahr*) *v* endorse

visibilidad (bee-see-bhee-lee-*dhahdh*) *f* visibility

visible (bee-*see*-bhlay) *adj* visible

visión (bee-s*y*oan) *f* vision

visita (bee-*see*-tah) *f* visit, call

visitante (bee-see-*tahn*-tay) *m* visitor

visitar (bee-see-*tahr*) *v* visit, call on

vislumbrar (beez-loom-*brahr*) *v* glimpse

vislumbre (beez-*loom*-bray) *m* glimpse

visón (bee-*soan*) *m* mink

visor (bee-*soar*) *m* view-finder

vista (*beess*-tah) *f* sight; view; **punto de ∼** outlook

vistoso (beess-*toa*-soa) *adj* striking

vital (bee-*tahl*) *adj* vital

vitamina (bee-tah-*mee*-nah) *f* vitamin

vitrina (bee-*tree*-nah) *f* show-case

viuda (b^yoo-dhah) *f* widow

viudo (b^yoo-dhoa) *m* widower

vivaz (bee-*bhahth*) *adj* active

vivero (bee-*bhay*-roa) *m* nursery

vivienda (bee-*bh^yayn*-dah) *f* house

vivir (bee-*bheer*) *v* live; experience

vivo (*bee*-bhoa) *adj* alive, live; brisk, vivid, lively

vocabulario (boa-kah-bhoo-*lah*-r^yoa) *m* vocabulary

vocación (boa-kah-*th^yoan*) *f* vocation

vocal (boa-*kahl*) *f* vowel; *adj* vocal

vocalista (boa-kah-*leess*-tah) *m* vocalist

volante (boa-*lahn*-tay) *m* steering-wheel

*****volar** (boa-*lahr*) *v* *fly

volatería (boa-lah-tay-*ree*-ah) *f* fowl

volcán (boal-*kahn*) *m* volcano

voltaje (boal-*tah*-khay) *m* voltage

voltio (*boal*-t^yoa) *m* volt

volumen (boa-*loo*-mayn) *m* volume

voluminoso (boa-loo-mee-*noa*-soa) *adj* bulky; big

voluntad (boa-loon-*tahdh*) *f* will; **buena ∼** goodwill

voluntario (boa-loon-tah-*r^yoa*) *adj* voluntary; *m* volunteer

*****volver** (boal-*bhayr*) *v* return, turn back; turn over, turn, turn round; **∼ a casa** *go home; *****volverse** *v* turn round

vomitar (boa-mee-*tahr*) *v* vomit

vosotros (boa-*soa*-troass) *pron* you

votación (boa-tah-*th^yoan*) *f* vote

votar (boa-*tahr*) *v* vote

voto (*boa*-toa) *m* vote; vow

voz (boath) *f* voice; cry; **en ∼ alta** aloud

vuelo (*bway*-loa) *m* flight; **∼ fletado** charter flight; **∼ nocturno** night flight

vuelta (*bwayl*-tah) *f* return journey, way back; tour; turning, turn; round; **ida y ∼** round trip *Am*

vuestro (*bwayss*-troa) *adj* your

vulgar (bool-*gahr*) *adj* vulgar

vulnerable (bool-nay-*rah*-bhlay) *adj* vulnerable

Y

y (ee) *conj* and

ya (^yah) *adv* already; **∼ no** no longer; **∼ que** as

*****yacer** (^yah-*thayr*) *v* *lie

yacimiento (^yah-thee-*m^yayn*-toa) *m* deposit

yate (^yah-tay) *m* yacht

yegua (^yay-gwah) *f* mare

yema (^yay-mah) *f* yolk

yerno (^yayr-noa) *m* son-in-law

yeso (^yay-soa) *m* plaster

yo (^yoa) *pron* I

yodo (^yoa-dhoa) *m* iodine

yugo (^yoo-goa) *m* yoke

Yugoslavia (^yoo-goaz-*lah*-bh^yah) *f* Yugoslavia, Jugoslavia

yugoslavo (^yoo-goaz-*lah*-bhoa) *adj* Jugoslav; *m* Yugoslav, Jugoslav

Z

zafiro (thah-*fee*-roa) *m* sapphire

zanahoria (thah-nah-*oa*-rʸah) *f* carrot

zanja (*thahng*-khah) *f* ditch

zapatería (thah-pah-tay-*ree*-ah) *f* shoe-shop

zapatero (thah-pah-*tay*-roa) *m* shoe-maker

zapatilla (thah-pah-*tee*-lʸah) *f* slipper

zapato (thah-*pah*-toa) *m* shoe; **zapatos de gimnasia** plimsolls *pl*; sneakers *plAm*; **zapatos de tenis** tennis shoes

zatara (thah-*tah*-rah) *f* raft

zodíaco (thoa-*dhee*-ah-koa) *m* zodiac

zona (*thoa*-nah) *f* zone; area; **~ industrial** industrial area

zoología (thoa-oa-loa-*khee*-ah) *f* zoology

zorro (*thoa*-rroa) *m* fox

zueco (*thway*-koa) *m* wooden shoe

zumo (*thoo*-moa) *m* juice; squash

zumoso (thoo-*moa*-soa) *adj* juicy

zurcir (thoor-*theer*) *v* darn

zurdo (*thoor*-dhoa) *adj* left-handed

zurra (*thoo*-rrah) *f* spanking

Menu Reader

Food

a caballo steak topped with two eggs
acedera sorrel
aceite oil
aceituna olive
achicoria endive (US chicory)
(al) adobo marinated
aguacate avocado (pear)
ahumado smoked
ajiaceite garlic mayonnaise
ajiaco bogotano chicken soup with potatoes
(al) ajillo cooked in garlic and oil
ajo garlic
al, a la in the style of, with
albahaca basil
albaricoque apricot
albóndiga spiced meat- or fishball
alcachofa artichoke
alcaparra caper
aliñado seasoned
alioli garlic mayonnaise
almeja clam, cockle
almejas a la marinera cooked in hot, pimento sauce
almendra almond
   ~ garrapiñada sugared almond
almíbar syrup
almuerzo lunch
alubia bean

anchoa anchovy
anguila eel
angula baby eel
anticucho beef heart grilled on a skewer with green peppers
apio celery
a punto medium (done)
arenque herring
   ~ en escabeche marinated, pickled herring
arepa flapjack made of maize (corn)
arroz rice
   ~ blanco boiled, steamed
   ~ escarlata with tomatoes and prawns
   ~ a la española with chicken liver, pork, tomatoes, fish stock
   ~ con leche rice pudding
   ~ primavera with spring vegetables
   ~ a la valenciana with vegetables, chicken, shellfish (and sometimes eel)
asado roast
   ~ antiguo a la venezolana mechado roast beef stuffed with capers
asturias a strong, fermented cheese with a sharp flavour

146

atún tunny (US tuna)
avellana hazelnut
azafrán saffron
azúcar sugar
bacalao cod
 ~ **a la vizcaína** with green peppers, potatoes, tomato sauce
barbo barbel (fish)
batata sweet potato, yam
becada woodcock
berberecho cockle
berenjena aubergine (US eggplant)
berraza parsnip
berro cress
berza cabbage
besugo sea bream
bien hecho well-done
biftec, bistec beef steak
bizcocho sponge cake, sponge finger (US ladyfinger)
 ~ **borracho** cake steeped in rum (or wine) and syrup
bizcotela glazed biscuit (US cookie)
blando soft
bocadillo 1) sandwich 2) sweet (Colombia)
bollito, bollo roll, bun
bonito a kind of tunny (US tuna)
boquerón 1) anchovy 2) whitebait
(en) brocheta (on a) skewer
budín blancmange, custard
buey ox
buñuelo 1) doughnut 2) fritter with ham, mussels and prawns (sometimes flavoured with brandy)
burgos a popular, soft, creamy cheese named after the Spanish province of its origin
butifarra spiced sausage
caballa fish of the mackerel family
cabeza de ternera calf's head

cabra goat
cabrales blue-veined goat's-milk cheese
cabrito kid
cacahuete peanut
cachelos diced potatoes boiled with cabbage, paprika, garlic, bacon, *chorizo* sausage
calabacín vegetable marrow, courgette (US zucchini)
calabaza pumpkin
calamar squid
calamares a la romana squids fried in batter
caldereta de cabrito kid stew (often cooked in red wine)
caldillo de congrio conger-eel soup with tomatoes and potatoes
caldo consommé
 ~ **gallego** meat and vegetable broth
callos tripe (often served in pimento sauce)
 ~ **a la madrileña** in piquant sauce with *chorizo* sausage and tomatoes
camarón shrimp
canela cinnamon
cangrejo de mar crab
cangrejo de río crayfish
cantarela chanterelle mushroom
caracol snail
carbonada criolla baked pumpkin stuffed with diced beef
carne meat
 ~ **asada al horno** roast meat
 ~ **molida** minced beef
 ~ **a la parrilla** charcoal-grilled steak
 ~ **picada** minced beef
carnero mutton
carpa carp
casero home made

castaña chestnut

castañola sea perch

(a la) catalana with onions, parsley, tomatoes and herbs

caza game

(a la) cazadora with mushrooms, spring onions, herbs in wine

cazuela de cordero lamb stew with vegetables

cebolla onion

cebolleta chive

cebrero blue-veined cheese of creamy texture with a pale, yellow rind; sharp taste

cena dinner, supper

centolla spider-crab, served cold

cerdo pork

cereza cherry

ceviche fish marinated in lemon and lime juice

cigala Dublin Bay prawn

cincho a hard cheese made from sheep's milk

ciruela plum
   ~ pasa prune

cocido 1) cooked, boiled 2) stew of beef with ham, fowl, chick peas, potatoes and vegetables (the broth is eaten first)

cochifrito de cordero highly seasoned stew of lamb or kid

codorniz quail

col cabbage
   ~ de Bruselas brussels sprout

coliflor cauliflower

comida meal

compota stewed fruit

conejo rabbit

confitura jam

congrio conger eel

consomé al jerez chicken broth with sherry

copa nuria egg-yolk and egg-white, whipped and served with jam

corazón de alcachofa artichoke heart

corazonada heart stewed in sauce

cordero lamb
   ~ recental spring lamb

cortadillo small pancake with lemon

corzo deer

costilla chop

crema 1) cream or mousse
   ~ batida whipped cream
   ~ española dessert of milk, eggs, fruit jelly
   ~ nieve frothy egg-yolk, sugar, rum (or wine)

crema 2) soup

criadillas (de toro) glands (of bull)

(a la) criolla with green peppers, spices and tomatoes

croqueta croquette, fish or meat dumpling

crudo raw

cubierto cover charge

cuenta bill (US check)

curanto dish consisting of seafood, vegetables and suck(l)ing pig, all cooked in an earthen well, lined with charcoal

chabacano apricot

chalote shallot

champiñón mushroom

chancho adobado pork braised with sweet potatoes, orange and lemon juice

chanfaina goat's liver and kidney stew, served in a thick sauce

chanquete whitebait

chile chili pepper

chiles en nogada green peppers stuffed with whipped cream and nut sauce

chimichurri hot parsley sauce

chipirón small squid

chopa a kind of sea bream

chorizo pork sausage, highly seasoned with garlic and paprika

chuleta cutlet

chupe de mariscos scallops served with a creamy sauce and gratinéed with cheese

churro sugared tubular fritter

damasco variety of apricot

dátil date

desayuno breakfast

dorada gilt-head

dulce sweet
~ **de naranja** marmalade

durazno peach

embuchado stuffed with meat

embutido spicy sausage

empanada pie or tart with meat or fish filling
~ **de horno** dough filled with minced meat, similar to ravioli

empanadilla small patty stuffed with seasoned meat or fish

empanado breaded

emperador swordfish

encurtido pickle

enchilada a maizeflour (US cornmeal) pancake (*tortilla*) stuffed and usually served with vegetable garnish and sauce
~ **roja** sausage-filled maizeflour pancake dipped into a red sweet-pepper sauce
~ **verde** maizeflour pancake stuffed with meat or fowl and braised in a green-tomato sauce

endibia chicory (US endive)

eneldo dill

ensalada salad
~ **común** green
~ **de frutas** fruit salad
~ **(a la) primavera** spring
~ **valenciana** with green peppers, lettuce and oranges

ensaladilla rusa diced cold vegetables with mayonnaise

entremés appetizer, hors-d'oeuvre

erizo de mar sea urchin

(en) escabeche marinated, pickled
~ **de gallina** chicken marinated in vinegar

escarcho red gurnard (fish)

escarola endive (US chicory)

espalda shoulder

(a la) española with tomatoes

espárrago asparagus

especia spice

especialidad de la casa chef's speciality

espinaca spinach

esqueixada mixed fish salad

(al) estilo de in the style of

estofado stew(ed)

estragón tarragon

fabada (asturiana) stew of pork, beans, bacon and sausage

faisán pheasant

fiambres cold meat (US cold cuts)

fideo thin noodle

filete steak
~ **de lomo** fillet steak (US tenderloin)
~ **de res** beef steak
~ **de lenguado empanado** breaded fillet of sole

(a la) flamenca with onions, peas, green peppers, tomatoes and spiced sausage

flan caramel mould, custard

frambuesa raspberry

(a la) francesa sautéed in butter

fresa strawberry
~ **de bosque** wild

fresco fresh, chilled

fresón large strawberry

fricandó veal bird, thin slice of meat rolled in bacon and braised

frijol bean

frijoles refritos fried mashed beans

frío cold

frito 1) fried 2) fry
~ **de patata** deep-fried potato croquette

fritura fry
~ **mixta** meat, fish or vegetables deep-fried in batter

fruta fruit
~ **escarchada** crystallized (US candied) fruit

galleta salted or sweet biscuit (US cracker or cookie)
~ **de nata** cream biscuit (US sandwich cookie)

gallina hen
~ **de Guinea** guinea fowl

gallo cockerel

gamba shrimp
~ **grande** prawn

gambas con mayonesa shrimp cocktail

ganso goose

garbanzo chick pea

gazpacho seasoned broth made of raw onions, garlic, tomatoes, cucumber and green pepper; served chilled

(a la) gitanilla with garlic

gordo fatty, rich (of food)

granada pomegranate

grande large

(al) gratín gratinéed

gratinado gratinéed

grelo turnip greens

grosella currant
~ **espinosa** gooseberry
~ **negra** blackcurrant
~ **roja** redcurrant

guacamole a purée of avocado and spices used as a dip, in a salad, for a *tortilla* filling or as a garnish

guarnición garnish, trimming

guayaba guava (fruit)

guinda sour cherry

guindilla chili pepper

guisado stew(ed)

guisante green pea

haba broad bean

habichuela verde French bean (US green bean)

hamburguesa hamburger

hayaca central maizeflour (US cornmeal) pancake, usually with a minced-meat filling

helado ice-cream, ice

hervido 1) boiled 2) stew of beef and vegetables (Latin America)

hielo ice

hierba herb

hierbas finas finely chopped mixture of herbs

hígado liver

higo fig

hinojo fennel

hongo mushroom

(al) horno baked

hortaliza greens

hueso bone

huevo egg
~ **cocido** boiled
~ **duro** hard-boiled
~ **escalfado** poached
~ **a la española** stuffed with tomatoes and served with cheese sauce
~ **a la flamenca** baked with asparagus, peas, peppers, onions, tomatoes and sausage
~ **frito** fried
~ **al nido** egg-yolk placed into small, soft roll, fried, then covered with egg-white
~ **pasado por agua** soft-boiled
~ **revuelto** scrambled

~ **con tocino** bacon and egg

humita boiled maize (US corn) with tomatoes, green peppers, onions and cheese

(a la) inglesa 1) underdone (of meat) 2) boiled 3) served with boiled vegetables

jabalí wild boar

jalea jelly

jamón ham

~ **cocido** boiled (often referred to as *jamón de York*)

~ **en dulce** boiled and served cold

~ **gallego** smoked and cut thinly

~ **serrano** cured and cut thinly

(a la) jardinera with carrots, peas and other vegetables

jengibre ginger

(al) jerez braised in sherry

judía bean

~ **verde** French bean (US green bean)

jugo gravy, meat juice

en su ~ in its own juice

juliana with shredded vegetables

jurel variety of mackerel

lacón shoulder of pork

~ **curado** salted pork

lamprea lamprey

langosta spiny lobster

langostino Norway lobster, Dublin Bay prawn

laurel bay leaf

lechón suck(l)ing pig

lechuga lettuce

legumbre vegetable

lengua tongue

lenguado sole, flounder

~ **frito** fried fillet of sole on bed of vegetables

lenteja lentil

liebre hare

~ **estofada** jugged hare

lima 1) lime 2) sweet lime (Latin America)

limón lemon

lista de platos menu

lista de vinos wine list

lobarro a variety of bass

lombarda red cabbage

lomo loin

longaniza long, highly seasoned sausage

lonja slice of meat

lubina bass

macarrones macaroni

(a la) madrileña with *chorizo* sausage, tomatoes and paprika

magras al estilo de Aragón cured ham in tomato sauce

maíz maize (US corn)

(a la) mallorquina usually refers to highly seasoned fish and shellfish

manchego hard cheese from La Mancha, made from sheep's milk, white or golden-yellow in colour

maní peanut

mantecado 1) small butter cake 2) custard ice-cream

mantequilla butter

manzana apple

~ **en dulce** in honey

(a la) marinera usually with mussels, onions, tomatoes, herbs and wine

marisco seafood

matambre rolled beef stuffed with vegetables

mayonesa mayonnaise

mazapán marzipan, almond paste

mejillón mussel

mejorana marjoram

melaza treacle, molasses

melocotón peach

membrillo quince
menestra boiled green vegetable soup
  ~ **de pollo** chicken and vegetable soup
menta mint
menú menu
  ~ **del día** set menu
  ~ **turístico** tourist menu
menudillos giblets
merengue meringue
merienda snack
merluza hake
mermelada jam
mezclado mixed
miel honey
(a la) milanesa with cheese, generally baked
minuta menu
mixto mixed
mole poblano chicken served with a sauce of chili peppers, spices and chocolate
molusco mollusc (snail, mussel, clam)
molleja sweetbread
mora mulberry
morcilla black pudding (US blood sausage)
morilla morel mushroom
moros y cristianos rice and black beans with diced ham, garlic, green peppers and herbs
mostaza mustard
mújol mullet
nabo turnip
naranja orange
nata cream
  ~ **batida** whipped cream
natillas custard
  ~ **al limón** lemon cream
níspola medlar (fruit)
nopalito young cactus leaf served with salad dressing

nuez nut
  ~ **moscada** nutmeg
olla stew
  ~ **gitana** vegetable stew
  ~ **podrida** stew made of vegetables, meat, fowl and ham
ostra oyster
oveja ewe
pabellón criollo beef in tomato sauce garnished with beans, rice and bananas
paella consists basically of saffron rice with assorted seafood and sometimes meat
  ~ **alicantina** with green peppers, onions, tomatoes, artichokes and fish
  ~ **catalana** with sausages, pork, squid, tomatoes, red sweet peppers and peas
  ~ **marinera** with fish, shellfish and meat
  ~ **(a la) valenciana** with chicken, shrimps, peas, tomatoes, mussels and garlic
palmito palm heart
palta avocado (pear)
pan bread
panecillo roll
papa potato
papas a la huancaína with cheese and green peppers
(a la) parrilla grilled
parrillada mixta mixed grill
pasado done, cooked
  bien ~ well-done
  poco ~ underdone (US rare)
pastas noodles, macaroni, spaghetti
pastel cake, pie
  ~ **de choclo** maize with minced beef, chicken, raisins and olives
pastelillo small tart
pata trotter (US foot)

patatas potatoes
  ~ **fritas** fried; usually chips (US french fries)
  ~ **(a la) leonesa** with onions
  ~ **nuevas** new
pato duck, duckling
pavo turkey
pechuga breast (of fowl)
pepinillo gherkin (US pickle)
pepino cucumber
(en) pepitoria stewed with onions, green peppers and tomatoes
pera pear
perca perch
percebe barnacle (shellfish)
perdiz partridge
  ~ **en escabeche** cooked in oil with vinegar, onions, parsley, carrots and green pepper; served cold
  ~ **estofada** stewed and served with a white-wine sauce
perejil parsley
perifollo chervil
perilla a firm, bland cheese
pescadilla whiting
pescado fish
pez espada swordfish
picadillo minced meat, hash
picado minced
picante sharp, spicy, highly seasoned
picatoste deep-fried slice of bread
pichoncillo young pigeon (US squab)
pierna leg
pimentón chili pepper
pimienta pepper
pimiento sweet pepper
  ~ **morrón** red (sweet) pepper
pincho moruno grilled meat (often kidneys) on a skewer, sometimes served with spicy sauces
pintada guinea fowl

piña pineapple
pisto diced and sautéed vegetables: mainly aubergines, green peppers and tomatoes; served cold
(a la) plancha grilled on a girdle
plátano banana
plato plate, dish, portion
  ~ **típico de la región** regional speciality
pollito spring chicken
pollo chicken
  ~ **pibil** simmered in fruit juice and spices
polvorón hazelnut biscuit (US cookie)
pomelo grapefruit
porción portion
porotos granados shelled beans served with pumpkin and maize (US corn)
postre dessert, sweet
potaje vegetable soup
puchero stew
puerro leek
pulpo octopus
punta de espárrago asparagus tip
punto de nieve dessert of whipped cream with beaten egg-whites
puré de patatas mashed potatoes
queso cheese
quisquilla shrimp
rábano radish
  ~ **picante** horse-radish
raja slice or portion
rallado grated
rape angler fish
ravioles ravioli
raya skate, ray
rebanada slice
rebozado breaded or fried in batter
recargo extra charge
rehogada sautéed

elleno stuffed
emolacha beetroot
epollo cabbage
equesón a fresh-curd cheese
iñón kidney
óbalo haddock
odaballo turbot, flounder
a la) romana dipped in batter and fried
omero rosemary
oncal cheese made from sheep's milk; close grained and hard in texture with a few small holes; piquant flavour
opa vieja cooked, left-over meat and vegetables, covered with tomatoes and green peppers
osbif roast beef
osquilla doughnut
ubio red mullet
uibarbo rhubarb
al salt
alado salted, salty
alchicha small pork sausage for frying
alchichón salami
almón salmon
almonete red mullet
alsa sauce
~ **blanca** white
~ **española** brown sauce with herbs, spices and wine
~ **mayordoma** butter and parsley
~ **picante** hot pepper
~ **romana** bacon or ham, egg, cream (sometimes flavoured with nutmeg)
~ **tártara** tartar
~ **verde** parsley
alsifí salsify
alteado sauté(ed)
alvia sage
an simón a firm, bland cheese

resembling *perilla*; shiny yellow rind
sandía watermelon
sardina sardine, pilchard
sémola semolina
sencillo plain
sepia cuttlefish
servicio service
~ **(no) incluido** (not) included
sesos brains
seta mushroom
sobrasada salami
solomillo fillet steak (US tenderloin)
sopa soup
~ **(de) cola de buey** oxtail
~ **sevillana** a highly spiced fish soup
suave soft
suflé soufflé
suizo bun
surtido assorted
taco wheat or maizeflour (US cornmeal) pancake usually with a meat filling and garnished with a spicy sauce
tajada slice
tallarín noodle
tamal a pastry dough of coarsely ground maizeflour with meat or fruit filling, steamed in maizehusks (US corn husks)
tapa appetizer, snack
tarta cake, tart
~ **helada** ice-cream tart
ternera veal
tocino bacon
~ **de cielo** 1) caramel mould 2) custard-filled cake
tomate tomato
tomillo thyme
tordo thrush
toronja variety of grapefruit
tortilla 1) omelet 2) a type of

pancake made with maizeflour (US cornmeal)

~ **de chorizo** with pieces of a spicy sausage

~ **a la española** with onions, potatoes and seasoning

~ **a la francesca** plain

~ **gallega** potatoes with ham, red sweet peppers and peas

~ **a la jardinera** with mixed, diced vegetables

~ **al ron** rum

tortita waffle

tortuga turtle

tostada toast

tripas tripe

trucha trout

~ **frita a la asturiana** floured and fried in butter, garnished with lemon

trufa truffle

turrón nougat

ulloa a soft cheese from Galicia, rather like a mature camembert

uva grape

~ **pasa** raisin

vaca salada corned beef

vainilla vanilla

(a la) valenciana with rice, toma-

toes and garlic

variado varied, assorted

varios sundries

venado venison

venera scallop, coquille St Jacques

verdura greens

vieira scallop

villalón a cheese from sheep's milk

vinagre vinegar

vinagreta a piquant vinegar dressing (vinaigrette) to accompany salads

(a la) ~ marinated in oil and vinegar or lemon juice with mixed herbs

(a la) vizcaína with green peppers, tomatoes, garlic and paprika

yema egg-yolk

yemas a dessert of whipped egg-yolks and sugar

zanahoria carrot

zarzamora blackberry

zarzuela savoury stew of assorted fish and shellfish

~ **de mariscos** seafood stew

~ **de pescado** selection of fish served with a highly seasoned sauce

~ **de verduras** vegetable stew

Drinks

abocado sherry made from a blend of sweet and dry wines

agua water

aguardiente spirits

Alicante this region to the south

of Valencia produces a large quantity of red table wine and some good rosé, particularly from Yecla

Amontillado medium-dry sherry.

light amber in colour, with a nutty flavour

Andalucía a drink of dry sherry and orange juice

Angélica a Basque herb liqueur similar to yellow Chartreuse

anís aniseed liqueur

Anís del Mono a Calatonian aniseed liqueur

anís seco aniseed brandy

anisado an aniseed-based soft drink which may be slightly alcoholic

batido milk shake

bebida drink

Bobadilla Gran Reserva a wine-distilled brandy

botella bottle

media ~ half bottle

café coffee

~ **cortado** small cup of strong coffee with a dash of milk or cream

~ **descafeinado** coffeine-free

~ **exprés** espresso

~ **granizado** iced (white)

~ **con leche** white

~ **negro/solo** black

Calisay a quinine-flavoured liqueur

Carlos I a wine-distilled brandy

Cataluña Catalonia; this region southwest of Barcelona is known for its *xampañ*, bearing little resemblance to the famed French sparkling wine

Cazalla an aniseed liqueur

cerveza beer

~ **de barril** draught (US draft)

~ **dorada** light

~ **negra** dark

cola de mono a blend of coffee, milk, rum and *pisco*

coñac 1) French Cognac 2) term

applied to any Spanish wine-distilled brandy

Cordoníu a brand-name of Catalonian sparkling wine locally referred to as *xampañ* (champagne)

cosecha harvest; indicates the vintage of wine

crema de cacao cocoa liqueur, crème de cacao

Cuarenta y Tres an egg liqueur

Cuba libre rum and Coke

champán, champaña 1) French Champagne 2) term applied to any Spanish sparkling wine

chicha de manzana apple brandy

Chinchón an aniseed liqueur

chocolate chocolate drink

~ **con leche** hot chocolate with milk

Dulce dessert wine

Fino dry sherry wine, very pale and straw-coloured

Fundador a wine-distilled brandy

Galicia this Atlantic coastal region has good table wines

gaseosa fizzy (US carbonated) water

ginebra gin

gran vino term found on Chilean wine labels to indicate a wine of exceptional quality

granadina pomegranate syrup mixed with wine or brandy

horchata de almendra (or **de chufa**) drink made from ground almonds (or Jerusalem artichoke)

Jerez 1) sherry 2) the Spanish region near the Portuguese border, internationally renowned for its *Jerez*

jugo fruit juice

leche milk

limonada lemonade, lemon

squash

Málaga 1) dessert wine   2) the region in the south of Spain, is particularly noted for its dessert wine

Manzanilla dry sherry, very pale and straw-coloured

margarita *tequila* with lime juice

Montilla a dessert wine from near Cordoba, often drunk as an aperitif

Moscatel fruity dessert wine

naranjada orangeade

Oloroso sweet, dark sherry, drunk as dessert wine, resembles brown cream sherry

Oporto port (wine)

pisco grape brandy

ponche crema egg-nog liquor

Priorato the region south of Barcelona produces good quality red and white wine but also a dessert wine, usually called *Priorato* but renamed *Tarragona* when it is exported

refresco a soft drink

reservado term found on Chilean wine labels to indicate a wine of exceptional quality

Rioja the northern region near the French border is considered to produce Spain's best wines—especially red; some of the finest Rioja wines resemble good Bordeaux wines

ron rum

sangría a mixture of red wine, ice, orange, lemon, brandy and sugar

sangrita *tequila* with tomato, orange and lime juices

sidra cider

sol y sombra a blend of wine-distilled brandy and aniseed liqueur

sorbete (iced) fruit drink

té tea

tequila brandy made from agave (US aloe)

tinto 1) red wine   2) black coffee with sugar (Colombia)

Tío Pepe a brand-name sherry

Triple Seco an orange liqueur

Valdepeñas the region south of Madrid is an important wine-producing area

vermú vermouth

Veterano Osborne a wine-distilled brandy

vino wine

~ **blanco** white

~ **clarete** rosé

~ **común** table wine

~ **dulce** dessert

~ **espumoso** sparkling

~ **de mesa** table wine

~ **del país** local wine

~ **rosado** rosé

~ **seco** dry

~ **suave** sweet

~ **tinto** red

xampañ Catalonian sparkling wine

Yerba mate South American holly tea

zumo juice

Spanish Verbs

Below are some examples of Spanish verbs in the three regular conjugations, grouped by families according to their infinitive endings, -ar, -er and -ir. Verbs which do not follow the conjugations below are considered irregular (see irregular verb list). Note that there are some verbs which follow the regular conjugation of the category they belong to, but present some minor changes in spelling. Examples: *tocar, toque; cargar, cargue*. The personal pronoun is not generally expressed, since the verb endings clearly indicate the person.

		1st conj.	2nd conj.	3rd conj.
		am ar	**tem er**	**viv ir**
Infinitive		*(to love)*	*(to fear)*	*(to live)*
Present	(yo)	am **o**	tem **o**	viv **o**
	(tú)	am **as**	tem **es**	viv **es**
	(él)	am **a**	tem **e**	viv **e**
	(nosotros)	am **amos**	tem **emos**	viv **imos**
	(vosotros)	am **áis**	tem **éis**	viv **ís**
	(ellos)	am **an**	tem **en**	viv **en**
Imperfect	(yo)	am **ía**	tem **ía**	viv **ía**
	(tú)	am **abas**	tem **ías**	viv **ías**
	(él)	am **aba**	tem **ía**	viv **ía**
	(nosotros)	am **ábamos**	tem **íamos**	viv **íamos**
	(vosotros)	am **abais**	tem **íais**	viv **íais**
	(ellos)	am **aban**	tem **ían**	viv **ían**
Past. def.	(yo)	am **é**	tem **í**	viv **í**
	(tú)	am **aste**	tem **iste**	viv **iste**
	(él)	am **ó**	tem **ió**	viv **ió**
	(nosotros)	am **amos**	tem **imos**	viv **imos**
	(vosotros)	am **asteis**	tem **isteis**	viv **isteis**
	(ellos)	am **aron**	tem **ieron**	viv **ieron**
Future	(yo)	am **aré**	tem **eré**	viv **iré**
	(tú)	am **arás**	tem **erás**	viv **irás**
	(él)	am **ará**	tem **erá**	viv **irá**
	(nosotros)	am **aremos**	tem **eremos**	viv **iremos**
	(vosotros)	am **aréis**	tem **eréis**	viv **iréis**
	(ellos)	am **arán**	tem **erán**	viv **irán**
Conditional	(yo)	am **aría**	tem **ería**	viv **iría**
	(tú)	am **arías**	tem **erías**	viv **irías**
	(él)	am **aría**	tem **ería**	viv **iría**
	(nosotros)	am **aríamos**	tem **eríamos**	viv **iríamos**
	(vosotros)	am **aríais**	tem **eríais**	viv **iríais**
	(ellos)	am **arían**	tem **erían**	viv **irían**
Subj. Pres.	(yo)	am **e**	tem **a**	viv **a**
	(tú)	am **es**	tem **as**	viv **as**
	(él)	am **e**	tem **a**	viv **a**
	(nosotros)	am **emos**	tem **amos**	viv **amos**
	(vosotros)	am **éis**	tem **áis**	viv **áis**
	(ellos)	am **en**	tem **an**	viv **an**

Pres. Part./Gerund	am **ando**	tem **iendo**	viv **iendo**
Past. Part.	am **ado**	tem **ido**	viv **ido**

Auxiliary verbs

The verb **to have** is translated either by *haber* or by *tener*. *Haber* is the auxiliary (e.g. he has gone) and *tener* (see list of irregular verbs) is a transitive verb, which conveys the idea of possession (e.g. she has a house).

The verb **to be** is translated either by *ser* or *estar*. *Ser* is used as an auxiliary verb to form the passive (e.g. they are understood) and to express an intrinsic quality of a fundamental characteristic (e.g. man is mortal). *Estar* (see list of irregular verbs) expresses a state or an attitude, whether lasting or not, of a thing or a person (e.g. she is hungry).

	haber *(to have)*		**ser** *(to be)*	
	Present	*Imperfect*	*Present*	*Imperfect*
(yo)	he	había	soy	era
(tú)	has	habías	eres	eras
(él)	ha	había	es	era
(nosotros)	hemos	habíamos	somos	éramos
(vosotros)	habéis	habíais	sois	erais
(ellos)	han	habían	son	eran
	Future	*Conditional*	*Future*	*Conditional*
(yo)	habré	habría	seré	sería
(tú)	habrás	habrías	serás	serías
(él)	habrá	habría	será	sería
(nosotros)	habremos	habríamos	seremos	seríamos
(vosotros)	habréis	habríais	seréis	seríais
(ellos)	habrán	habrían	serán	serían
	Present subjunctive	*Present perfect*	*Present subjunctive*	*Present perfect*
(yo)	haya	he habido	sea	he sido
(tú)	hayas	has habido	seas	has sido
(él)	haya	ha habido	sea	ha sido
(nosotros)	hayamos	hemos habido	seamos	hemos sido
(vosotros)	hayáis	habéis habido	seáis	habéis sido
(ellos)	hayan	han habido	sean	han sido
	Present participle	*Past participle*	*Present participle*	*Past participle*
	habiendo	habido	siendo	sido

Irregular verbs

Below is a list of the verbs and tenses commonly used in spoken Spanish. In the listing, a) stands for the present tense, b) for the imperfect, c) for the past def., d) for the future, e) for the present participle and f) for the past participle. The only forms given below are the irregular ones commonly used. There can be other irregular forms, but they are considered rare. In tenses other than present, all persons can be regularly formed from the first person. Unless otherwise indicated, verbs with prefixes (*ad-, ante-, com-, con-, de-, des-, dis-, en-, ex-, im-, pos-, pre-, pro-, re-, sobre-, sub-, tras-*, etc.) are conjugated like the stem verb.

abstenerse *refrain*	→tener
acertar *guess*	→cerrar
acontecer *happen*	→agradecer
acordar *agree; decide*	→contar
acostarse *lie down*	→contar
acrecentar *increase; advance*	→cerrar
adormecer *put to sleep*	→agradecer
adquirir *acquire*	a) adquiero, adquieres, adquiere, adquirimos, adquirís, adquieren; b) adquiría; c) adquirí; d) adquiriré; e) adquiriendo; f) adquirido
advertir *notice*	→sentir
agradecer *thank*	a) agradezco, agradeces, agradece, agradecemos, agradecéis, agradecen; b) agradecía; c) agradecí; d) agradeceré; e) agradeciendo; f) agradecido
alentar *encourage*	→cerrar
almorzar *have lunch*	→contar
amanecer *dawn*	→agradecer
andar *walk*	a) ando, andas, anda, andamos, andáis, andan; b) andaba; c) anduve; d) andaré; e) andando; f) andado
anochecer *begin to get dark*	→agradecer
apetecer *want*	→agradecer
apostar *bet*	→contar
apretar *tighten, squeeze*	→cerrar

arrendar
let, lease, rent
→cerrar

arrepentirse
repent, regret
→sentir

ascender
climb, reach
→perder

atenerse
obey; rely on
→tener

atravesar
cross, pierce
→cerrar

atribuir
attribute
→instruir

aventar
fan, air
→cerrar

avergonzar
put to shame, embarrass
→contar

bendecir
bless
→decir

caber
contain; fit
a) quepo, cabes, cabe, cabemos, cabéis, caben; b) cabía; c) cupe; d) cabré; e) cabiendo; f) cabido

caer
fall
a) caigo, caes, cae, caemos, caéis, caen; b) caía; c) caí; d) caeré; e) cayendo; f) caído

calentar
heat
→cerrar

carecer
lack
→agradecer

cegar
blind
→cerrar

cerrar
close
a) cierro, cierras, cierra, cerramos, cerráis, cierran; b) cerraba; c) cerré; d) cerraré; e) cerrando; f) cerrado

cocer
boil
a) cuezo, cueces, cuece, cocemos, cocéis, cuecen; b) cocía; c) cocí; d) coceré; e) cociendo; f) cocido

colar
strain; filter
→contar

colgar
hang
→contar

comenzar
begin
→cerrar

competir
compete
→pedir

concebir
conceive
→pedir

concernir *concern*	→sentir
concluir *conclude, finish*	→instruir
concordar *agree, reconcile*	→contar
conducir *drive*	→traducir
conferir *confer*	→sentir
confesar *confess*	→cerrar
conocer *know*	a) conozco, conoces, conoce, conocemos, conocéis, conocen; b) conocía; c) conocí; d) conoceré; e) conociendo; f) conocido
consolar *console, comfort*	→contar
constituir *constitute, be*	→instruir
construir *build, erect*	→instruir
contar *count, bear in mind*	a) cuento, cuentas, cuenta, contamos, contáis, cuentan; b) contaba; c) conté; d) contaré; e) contando; f) contado
contribuir *contribute*	→instruir
convertir *convert*	→sentir
corregir *correct*	→pedir
costar *cost*	→contar
crecer *grow, rise*	→agradecer
dar *give*	a) doy, das, da, damos, dais, dan; b) daba; c) di; d) daré; e) dando; f) dado
decir *say*	a) digo, dices, dice, decimos, decís, dicen; b) decía; c) dije; d) diré e) diciendo; f) dicho
deducir *deduce*	→traducir
defender *defend*	→perder
derretir *melt*	→pedir

descender →perder
descend, let down

descollar →contar
be outstanding

desconcertar →cerrar
damage; upset

despertar →cerrar
awaken, revive

desterrar →cerrar
banish

destituir →instruir
deprive, dismiss

destruir →instruir
destroy

desvanecer →agradecer
make disappear,
take out

diferir →sentir
defer

digerir →sentir
digest

diluir →instruir
dilute

discernir →sentir
discern

disminuir →instruir
diminish

disolver →morder
dissolve

distribuir →instruir
distribute

divertir →sentir
entertain, distract

doler →morder
hurt

dormir a) duermo, duermes, duerme, dormimos, dormís
sleep duermen; b) dormía; c) dormí; d) dormiré;
e) durmiendo; f) dormido

elegir →pedir
elect, choose

embestir →pedir
assault

empezar →cerrar
begin, start

naltecer →agradecer
exalt, praise

nardecer →agradecer
excite; inflame

ncender →perder
light, ignite

ncomendar →cerrar
entrust

ncontrar →contar
find

ngrandecer →agradecer
enlarge, exaggerate

nloquecer →agradecer
madden

nmendar →cerrar
emend, correct

nmudecer →agradecer
silence

norgullecer →agradecer
fill with pride

nriquecer →agradecer
enrich

nsangrentar →cerrar
stain with blood

nsoberbecer →agradecer
make proud

nsordecer →agradecer
deafen

nternecer →agradecer
soften; affect

nterrar →cerrar
bury

ntristecer →agradecer
sadden

nvejecer →agradecer
age

rrar →cerrar
miss; wander

scarmentar →cerrar
chastise, punish

scarnecer →agradecer
scoff

stablecer →agradecer
establish

estar *be*	a) estoy, estás, está, estamos, estáis, están; b) estaba c) estuve; d) estaré; e) estando; f) estado
estremecer *shake*	→agradecer
excluir *exclude*	→instruir
fallecer *die*	→agradecer
favorecer *favour*	→agradecer
florecer *blossom*	→agradecer
fluir *flow*	→instruir
fortalecer *strengthen*	→agradecer
forzar *compel, force*	→contar
fregar *wash up; scrub*	→cerrar
freír *fry*	→reír
gemir *groan*	→pedir
gobernar *govern*	→cerrar
gruñir *grunt*	a) gruño, gruñes, gruñe, gruñimos, gruñís, gruñen; b) gruñía ;c) gruñí; d) gruñiré; e) gruñiendo; f) gruñid
haber *have*	a) he, has, ha, hemos, habéis, han; b) había; c) hube; d) habré; e) habiendo; f) habido
hacer *make*	a) hago, haces, hace, hacemos, hacéis, hacen; b) hacía c) hice; d) haré; e) haciendo; f) hecho
heder *stink*	→perder
helar *freeze*	→cerrar
hender *crack*	→perder
herir *injure*	→sentir
hervir *boil*	→sentir
huir *escape*	→instruir

humedecer *humidify*	→agradecer
incluir *include*	→instruir
inducir *induce*	→traducir
ingerir *swallow; consume*	→sentir
instituir *institute*	→instruir
instruir *instruct*	a) instruyo, instruyes, instruye, instruimos, instruís, instruyen; b) instruía; c) instruí; d) instruiré; e) instruyendo; f) instruido
introducir *introduce*	→traducir
invertir *invest*	→sentir
ir *go*	a) voy, vas, va, vamos, vais, van; b) iba; c) fui; d) iré; e) yendo; f) ido
jugar *play*	a) juego, juegas, juega, jugamos, jugáis, juegan; b) jugaba; c) jugué; d) jugaré; e) jugando; f) jugado
lucir *shine*	a) luzco, luces, luce, lucimos, lucís, lucen; b) lucía; c) lucí; d) luciré; e) luciendo; f) lucido
llover *rain*	a) llueve; b) llovía; c) llovió; d) lloverá; e) lloviendo; f) llovido
manifestar *manifest*	→cerrar
mantener *maintain*	→tener
medir *measure*	→pedir
mentir *tell a lie*	→sentir
merecer *deserve*	→agradecer
merendar *have tea, snack*	→cerrar
moler *grind*	→morder
morder *bite*	a) muerdo, muerdes, muerde, mordemos, mordéis, muerden; b) mordía; c) mordí; d) morderé; e) mordiendo; f) mordido
morir *die*	→dormir

mostrar *show*	→contar
mover *move*	→morder
nacer *be born*	a) nazco, naces, nace, nacemos, nacéis, nacen; b) nacía; c) nací; d) naceré; e) naciendo; f) nacido
negar *deny*	→cerrar
nevar *snow*	a) nieva; b) nevaba; c) nevó; d) nevará; e) nevando; f) nevado
obedecer *obey*	→agradecer
obscurecer *darken*	→agradecer
obstruir *obstruct*	→instruir
obtener *obtain*	→tener
ofrecer, *offer*	→agradecer
oír *hear, listen*	a) oigo, oyes, oye, oímos, oís, oyen; b) oía; c) oí; d) oiré; e) oyendo; f) oído
oler *smell*	→morder
pacer *graze*	→nacer
padecer *suffer*	→agradecer
parecer *seem*	→agradecer
pedir *ask for, request*	a) pido, pides, pide, pedimos, pedís, piden; b) pedía; c) pedí; d) pediré; e) pidiendo; f) pedido
pensar *think*	→cerrar
perder *lose*	a) pierdo, pierdes, pierde, perdemos, perdéis, pierden; b) perdía; c) perdí; d) perderé; e) perdiendo; f) perdido
perecer *perish*	→agradecer
permanecer *stay*	→agradecer
pertenecer *belong to*	→agradecer
pervertir *pervert*	→sentir

placer *please*	a) plazco, places, place, placemos, placéis, placen; b) placía; c) plací; d) placeré; e) placiendo; f) placido
plegar *fold*	→cerrar
poblar *populate*	→contar
poder *can, be able*	a) puedo, puedes, puede, podemos, podéis, pueden; b) podía; c) pude; d) podré; e) pudiendo; f) podido
poner *put*	a) pongo, pones, pone, ponemos, ponéis, ponen; b) ponía; c) puse; d) pondré; e) poniendo; f) puesto
preferir *prefer*	→sentir
probar *try*	→contar
producir *produce*	→traducir
proferir *utter*	→sentir
quebrar *break*	→cerrar
querer *want, wish*	a) quiero, quieres, quiere, queremos, queréis, quieren; b) quería; c) quise; d) querré; e) queriendo; f) querido
recomendar *recommend*	→cerrar
recordar *remember*	→contar
reducir *reduce*	→traducir
referir *refer, relate*	→sentir
regar *water*	→cerrar
regir *govern*	→pedir
reír *laugh*	a) río, ríes, ríe, reímos, reís, ríen; b) reía; c) reí; d) reiré; e) riendo; f) reído
remendar *mend*	→cerrar
rendir *produce; overcome*	→pedir
renovar *renew*	→contar
reñir *scold; quarrel*	→teñir

repetir	→pedir
repeat	
requerir	→sentir
request	
resolver	→morder
resolve	
resplandecer	→agradecer
shine	
restituir	→instruir
restore, return	
retribuir	→instruir
pay ; reward	
reventar	→cerrar
burst	
robustecer	→agradecer
strengthen	
rodar	→contar
drive ; roll	
rogar	→contar
beg, plead	
saber	a) sé, sabes, sabe, sabemos, sabéis, saben ;)b sabía ;
know	c) supe ; d) sabré ; e) sabiendo ; f) sabido
salir	a) salgo, sales, sale, salimos, salís, salen ; b) salía ;
go out	c) salí ; d) saldré ; e) saliendo ; f) salido
satisfacer	→hacer
satisfy	
seducir	→traducir
seduce	
seguir	→pedir
follow	
sembrar	→cerrar
sow	
sentar	→cerrar
sit, seat	
sentir	a) siento, sientes, siente, sentimos, sentís, sienten ;
feel	b) sentía ; c) sentí ; d) sentiré ; e) sintiendo ; f) sentido
ser.	a) soy, eres, es, somos, sois, son ; b) era c) fui ; d) seré ;
be	e) siendo ; f) sido
servir	→pedir
serve	
soldar	→contar
solder ; join	
soler	a) suelo, sueles, suele, solemos, soléis, suelen ; b) solía ;
be used to	c) solí ; e) soliendo ; f) solido

soltar	→contar
release ; loosen	
sonar	→contar
ring, sound	
soñar	→contar
dream	
sugerir	→sentir
suggest	
sustituir	→instruir
substitute	
temblar	→cerrar
tremble	
tender	→perder
stretch, extend	
tener	a) tengo, tienes, tiene, tenemos, tenéis, tienen; b) tenía;
have (got)	c) tuve; d) tendré; e) teniendo; f) tenido
tentar	→cerrar
touch ; try	
teñir	a) tiño, tiñes, tiñe, teñimos, teñís, tiñen; b) teñía;
dye	c) teñí; d) teñiré; e) tiñiendo; f) teñido
torcer	→cocer
twist	
tostar	→contar
roast	
traducir	a) traduzco, traduces, traduce, traducimos, traducís,
translate	traducen; b) traducía; c) traduje; d) traduciré;
	e) traduciendo; f) traducido
traer	a) traigo, traes, trae, traemos, traéis, traen; b) traía;
bring	c) traje; d) traeré; e) trayendo; f) traído
transferir	→sentir
transfer	
trocar	→contar
(ex)change	
tronar	a) trueno, truenas, truena, tronamos, tronáis, truenan;
thunder	b) tronaba; c) troné; d) tronaré; e) tronando; f) tronado
tropezar	→cerrar
stumble	
valer	a) valgo, vales, vale, valemos, valéis, valen; b) valía;
protect ; be worth	c) valí; d) valdré; e) valiendo; f) valido
venir	a) vengo, vienes, viene, venimos, venís, vienen; b) venía;
come	c) vine; d) vendré; e) viniendo; f) venido
ver	a) veo, ves, ve, vemos, veis, ven; b) veía; c) vi; d) veré;
see	e) viendo; f) visto

verter   →perder
  pour ; spill

vestir   →pedir
  dress

volar   →contar
  fly

volcar   →contar
  tip over

volver   →morder
  (re)turn

yacer   →nacer
  lie, rest

zambullir   a) zambullo, zambulles, zambulle, zambullimos,
  plunge   zambullís, zambullen; b) zambullía; c) zambullí;
                d) zambulliré; e) zambullendo; f) zambullido

Spanish Abbreviations

a.C.	*antes de Cristo*	B.C.
A.C.	*año de Cristo*	A.D.
admón.	*administración*	administration
A.L.A.L.C.	*Asociación Latino-Americana de Libre Comercio*	Latin American Free Trade Association
apdo.	*apartado de correos*	P.O. Box
Av./Avda.	*Avenida*	avenue
Barna.	*Barcelona*	Barcelona
C/	*Calle*	street, road
c/c.	*cuenta corriente*	current account
Cía.	*Compañía*	company
ct(s).	*céntimo(s)*	1/100 of a peseta
cta.	*cuenta*	account; bill
cte.	*corriente*	inst., of this month
CV	*caballos de vapor*	horsepower
D.	*Don*	courtesy title for gentlemen, only used together with the Christian name
D.ª	*Doña*	courtesy title for ladies, only used together with the Christian name
dcha.	*derecha*	right (direction)
D.N.I.	*Documento Nacional de Identidad*	identity card
d.v.	*días de visita*	open days
EE.UU.	*Estados Unidos*	USA
Exc.ª	*Excelencia*	Your Excellency
f.c.	*ferrocarril*	railway
G.C.	*Guardia Civil*	Spanish police force
gral.	*general*	general
h.	*hora*	hour
hab.	*habitantes*	inhabitants, population
hnos.	*hermanos*	brothers (in firms)
id.	*ídem*	ditto
igla.	*iglesia*	church
izq./izqda.	*izquierda*	left (direction)
lic.	*licenciado*	licentiate; lawyer
M.I.T.	*Ministerio de Información y Turismo*	Spanish Ministry of Information and Tourism
Mons.	*Monseñor*	Roman Catholic title (approx. Your Grace)

N.ª S.ª	*Nuestra Señora*	Our Lady, Virgin Mary
n.º/núm.	*número*	number
O.E.A.	*Organización de Estados Americanos*	Organization of American States
P.	*Padre*	Father (ecclesiastical title)
pág.	*página*	page
P.D.	*posdata*	P.S.
p.ej.	*por ejemplo*	e.g.
P.P.	*porte pagado*	postage paid
pta(s).	*peseta(s)*	peseta(s)
P.V.P.	*precio de venta al público*	retail price
R.A.C.E.	*Real Automóvil Club de España*	Royal Automobile Association of Spain
R.A.E.	*Real Academia Española*	Royal Academy of the Spanish Language
R.C.	*Real Club…*	Royal… Association
RENFE	*Red Nacional de los Ferrocarriles Españoles*	Spanish National Railways
R.M.	*Reverenda Madre*	Mother Superior, abbess
R.P.	*Reverendo Padre*	Reverend Father (title for Catholic priests and abbots)
Rte.	*Remite, Remitente*	sender (of a letter)
RTVE	*Radio Televisión Española*	Spanish Radio and Television Corporation
S./Sto./ Sta.	*San/Santo/Santa*	saint
S.A.	*Sociedad Anónima*	Ltd., Inc.
S.A.R.	*Su Alteza Real*	His/Her Royal Highness
s.a.s.s.	*su atento y seguro servidor*	approx. Yours faithfully
S.E.	*Su Excelencia*	His Excellency
sgte.	*siguiente*	following
S.M.	*Su Majestad*	His/Her Majesty
Sr.	*Señor*	Mr.
Sra.	*Señora*	Mrs.
S.R.C.	*se ruega contestación*	please reply
Sres./Srs.	*Señores*	Sirs, Gentlemen
Srta.	*Señorita*	Miss
S.S.	*Su Santidad*	His Holiness
Ud./Vd.	*Usted*	you (singular)
Uds./Vds.	*Ustedes*	you (plural)
Vda.	*viuda*	widow
v.g./v.gr.	*verbigracia*	e.g.

Numerals

Cardinal numbers		Ordinal numbers	
0	cero	1.°	primero
1	uno	2.°	segundo
2	dos	3.°	tercero
3	tres	4.°	cuarto
4	cuatro	5.°	quinto
5	cinco	6.°	sexto
6	seis	7.°	séptimo
7	siete	8.°	octavo
8	ocho	9.°	noveno (nono)
9	nueve	10.°	décimo
10	diez	11.°	undécimo
11	once	12.°	duodécimo
12	doce	13.°	decimotercero
13	trece	14.°	decimocuarto
14	catorce	15.°	decimoquinto
15	quince	16.°	decimosexto
16	dieciséis	17.°	decimoséptimo
17	diecisiete	18.°	decimoctavo
18	dieciocho	19.°	decimonoveno
19	diecinueve	20.°	vigésimo
20	veinte	21.°	vigésimo primero
21	veintiuno	22.°	vigésimo segundo
30	treinta	30.°	trigésimo
31	treinta y uno	40.°	cuadragésimo
40	cuarenta	50.°	quincuagésimo
50	cincuenta	60.°	sexagésimo
60	sesenta	70.°	septuagésimo
70	setenta	80.°	octogésimo
80	ochenta	90.°	nonagésimo
90	noventa	100.°	centésimo
100	ciento (cien)	230.°	ducentésimo trigésimo
101	ciento uno	300.°	tricentésimo
230	doscientos treinta	400.°	cuadringentésimo
500	quinientos	500.°	quingentésimo
700	setecientos	600.°	sexcentésimo
900	novecientos	700.°	septingentésimo
1.000	mil	800.°	octingentésimo
100.000	cien mil	900.°	noningentésimo
1.000.000	un millón	1.000.°	milésimo

Time

Although official time in Spain is based on the 24-hour clock, the 12-hour system is used in conversation.

In some Latin American countries you can specify *a.m.* or *p.m.* as in English, but it is far more common to add *de la mañana, de la tarde* or *de la noche* as in Spain.

Thus:

las ocho de la mañana	8 a.m.
la una de la tarde	1 p.m.
las ocho de la noche	8 p.m.

Days of the Week

domingo	Sunday	*jueves*	Thursday
lunes	Monday	*viernes*	Friday
martes	Tuesday	*sábado*	Saturday
miércoles	Wednesday		

Conversion tables/
Tablas de conversión

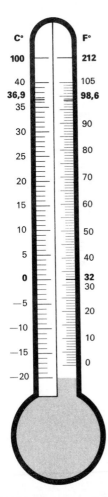

Metres and feet
The figure in the middle stands for both metres and feet, e.g. 1 metre = 3.281 ft. and 1 foot = 0.30 m.

Metros y pies
La columna del centro corresponde a metros y pies, por ejemplo 1 metro = 3,281 pies y 1 pie = 0,30 metros.

Metres/Metros		Feet/Pies
0.30	1	3.281
0.61	2	6.563
0.91	3	9.843
1.22	4	13.124
1.52	5	16.403
1.83	6	19.686
2.13	7	22.967
2.44	8	26.248
2.74	9	29.529
3.05	10	32.810
3.66	12	39.372
4.27	14	45.934
6.10	20	65.620
7.62	25	82.023
15.24	50	164.046
22.86	75	246.069
30.48	100	328.092

Temperature
To convert Centigrade to Fahrenheit, multiply by 1.8 and add 32.
To convert Fahrenheit to Centigrade, subtract 32 from Fahrenheit and divide by 1.8.

Temperatura
Para convertir grados centígrados en Fahrenheit multiplique los centígrados por 1,8 y sume 32 al resultado.
Para convertir grados Fahrenheit en centígrados reste 32 de los Fahrenheit y divida el resultado entre 1,8.

Some Basic Phrases	Algunas expresiones útiles
Please.	Por favor.
Thank you very much.	Muchas gracias.
Don't mention it.	No hay de qué.
Good morning.	Buenos días.
Good afternoon.	Buenas tardes.
Good evening.	Buenas noches.
Good night.	Buenas noches (despedida).
Good-bye.	Adiós.
See you later.	Hasta luego.
Where is/Where are…?	¿Dónde está/Dónde están…?
What do you call this?	¿Cómo se llama esto?
What does that mean?	¿Qué quiere decir eso?
Do you speak English?	¿Habla usted inglés?
Do you speak German?	¿Habla usted alemán?
Do you speak French?	¿Habla usted francés?
Do you speak Spanish?	¿Habla usted español?
Do you speak Italian?	¿Habla usted italiano?
Could you speak more slowly, please?	¿Puede usted hablar más despacio, por favor?
I don't understand.	No comprendo.
Can I have…?	¿Puede darme…?
Can you show me…?	¿Puede usted enseñarme…?
Can you tell me…?	¿Puede usted decirme…?
Can you help me, please?	¿Puede usted ayudarme, por favor?
I'd like…	Quisiera…
We'd like…	Quisiéramos…
Please give me…	Por favor, déme…
Please bring me…	Por favor, tráigame…
I'm hungry.	Tengo hambre.
I'm thirsty.	Tengo sed.
I'm lost.	Me he perdido.
Hurry up!	¡Dése prisa!

| There is/There are… | Hay… |
| There isn't/There aren't… | No hay… |

Arrival

	Llegada
Your passport, please.	Su pasaporte, por favor.
Have you anything to declare?	¿Tiene usted algo que declarar?
No, nothing at all.	No, nada en absoluto.
Can you help me with my luggage, please?	¿Puede usted ayudarme con mi equipaje, por favor?
Where's the bus to the centre of town, please?	¿Dónde está el autobús que va al centro, por favor?
This way, please.	Por aquí, por favor.
Where can I get a taxi?	¿Dónde puedo coger un taxi?
What's the fare to…?	¿Cuánto es la tarifa a…?
Take me to this address, please.	Lléveme a esta dirección, por favor.
I'm in a hurry.	Tengo mucha prisa.

Hotel

	Hotel
My name is…	Me llamo…
Have you a reservation?	¿Ha hecho usted una reserva?
I'd like a room with a bath.	Quisiera una habitación con baño.
What's the price per night?	¿Cuánto cuesta por noche?
May I see the room?	¿Puedo ver la habitación?
What's my room number, please?	¿Cuál es el número de mi habitación, por favor?
There's no hot water.	No hay agua caliente.
May I see the manager, please?	¿Puedo ver al director, por favor?
Did anyone telephone me?	¿Me ha llamado alguien?
Is there any mail for me?	¿Hay correo para mí?
May I have my bill (check), please?	¿Puede darme mi cuenta, por favor?

Eating out

Do you have a fixed-price menu?

May I see the menu?

May we have an ashtray, please?

Where's the toilet, please?

I'd like an hors d'œuvre (starter).

Have you any soup?

I'd like some fish.

What kind of fish do you have?

I'd like a steak.

What vegetables have you got?

Nothing more, thanks.

What would you like to drink?

I'll have a beer, please.

I'd like a bottle of wine.

May I have the bill (check), please?

Is service included?

Thank you, that was a very good meal.

Restaurante

¿Tiene usted un menú de precio fijo?

¿Puedo ver la carta?

¿Nos puede traer un cenicero, por favor?

¿Dónde están los servicios, por favor?

Quisiera un entremés.

¿Tiene usted sopa?

Quisiera pescado.

¿Qué clases de pescado tiene usted?

Quisiera un bistec.

¿Qué verduras tiene usted?

Nada más, gracias.

¿Qué le gustaría beber?

Tomaré una cerveza, por favor.

Quisiera una botella de vino.

¿Podría darme la cuenta, por favor?

¿Está incluido el servicio?

Gracias. Ha sido una comida muy buena.

Travelling

Where's the railway station, please?

Where's the ticket office, please?

I'd like a ticket to...

First or second class?

First class, please.

Single or return (one way or roundtrip)?

Viajes

¿Dónde está la estación de ferro-carril, por favor?

¿Dónde está la taquilla, por favor?

Quisiera un billete para...

¿Primera o segunda clase?

Primera clase, por favor.

¿Ida, o ida y vuelta?

have to change trains?	¿Tengo que transbordar?
What platform does the train for... leave from?	¿De qué andén sale el tren para...?
Where's the nearest underground (subway) station?	¿Dónde está la próxima estación de Metro?
Where's the bus station, please?	¿Dónde está la estación de autobuses, por favor?
When's the first bus to...?	¿Cuándo sale el primer autobús para...?
Please let me off at the next stop.	Por favor, deténgase en la próxima parada.

Relaxing

Diversiones

What's on at the cinema (movies)?	¿Qué dan en el cine?
What time does the film begin?	¿A qué hora empieza la película?
Are there any tickets for tonight?	¿Quedan entradas para esta noche?
Where can we go dancing?	¿Dónde se puede ir a bailar?

Meeting people

Presentaciones – Citas

How do you do.	Buenos días Señora/Señorita/Señor.
How are you?	¿Cómo está usted?
Very well, thank you. And you?	Muy bien, gracias. ¿Y usted?
May I introduce...?	¿Me permite presentarle a...?
My name is...	Me llamo...
I'm very pleased to meet you.	Tanto gusto (en conocerle).
How long have you been here?	¿Cuánto tiempo lleva usted aquí?
It was nice meeting you.	Ha sido un placer conocerle.
Do you mind if I smoke?	¿Le molesta si fumo?
Do you have a light, please?	¿Tiene usted fuego, por favor?
May I get you a drink?	¿Me permite invitarle a una bebida (una copa)?
May I invite you for dinner tonight?	¿Me permite invitarle a cenar esta noche?
Where shall we meet?	¿Dónde quedamos citados?

Shops, stores and services	**Comercios y servicios**
Where's the nearest bank, please?	Dónde está el banco más cercano, por favor?
Where can I cash some travellers' cheques?	¿Dónde puedo cambiar unos cheques de viaje?
Can you give me some small change, please?	¿Puede usted darme algún dinero suelto, por favor?
Where's the nearest chemist's (pharmacy)?	¿Dónde está la farmacia más cercana?
How do I get there?	¿Cómo podría ir hasta allí?
Is it within walking distance?	¿Se puede ir andando?
Can you help me, please?	¿Puede usted atenderme, por favor?
How much is this? And that?	¿Cuánto cuesta éste? ¿Y ése?
It's not quite what I want.	No es exactamente lo que quiero.
I like it.	Me gusta.
Can you recommend something for sunburn?	¿Podría recomendarme algo para las quemaduras del sol?
I'd like a haircut, please.	Quisiera cortarme el pelo, por favor.
I'd like a manicure, please.	Quisiera una manicura, por favor.

Street directions	**Direcciones**
Can you show me on the map where I am?	¿Puede enseñarme en el mapa dónde estoy?
You are on the wrong road.	Está usted equivocado de camino.
Go/Walk straight ahead.	Siga todo derecho.
It's on the left/on the right.	Está a la izquierda/a la derecha.

Emergencies	**Urgencias**
Call a doctor quickly.	Llame a un médico rápidamente.
Call an ambulance.	Llame a una ambulancia.
Please call the police.	Llame a la policía, por favor.

inglés-español

english-spanish

Abreviaturas

adj	adjetivo	*n*	nombre (sustantivo)
adv	adverbio		
Am	inglés americano	*nAm*	nombre (inglés americano)
art	artículo		
conj	conjunción	*num*	numeral
f	femenino	*p*	tiempo pasado
fMe	femenino (mexicano)	*pl*	plural
fpl	femenino plural	*plAm*	plural (inglés americano)
fplMe	femenino plural (mexicano)	*pp*	participio pasado
		pr	tiempo presente
m	masculino	*pref*	prefijo
Me	mexicano	*prep*	preposición
mMe	masculino (mexicano)	*pron*	pronombre
mpl	masculino plural	*v*	verbo
mplMe	masculino plural (mexicano)	*vAm*	verbo (inglés americano)
		vMe	verbo (mexicano)

Introducción

Este diccionario ha sido concebido para resolver de la mejor manera posible sus problemas prácticos de lenguaje. Se han suprimido las informaciones lingüísticas innecesarias. Los vocablos se suceden en un estricto orden alfabético, sin tener en cuenta si la palabra es simple o compuesta, o si se trata de una expresión formada por dos o más términos separados. Como única excepción, algunas expresiones idiomáticas están colocadas en orden alfabético, considerando para ello la palabra más característica. Cuando un término principal va seguido de otras palabras, expresiones o locuciones, éstas se hallan anotadas también en orden alfabético.

Cada palabra va seguida de una transcripción fonética (véase la guía de pronunciación). Después de la transcripción fonética se encuentra una indicación de la parte de la oración a la que pertenece el vocablo. Cuando una palabra puede desempeñar distintos oficios en la oración, las diferentes traducciones se dan una a continuación de la otra, precedidas de la indicación correspondiente.

Se indica el plural de los nombres cuando son irregulares y en algunos otros casos dudosos.

Cuando haya que repetir una palabra para formar el plural irregular o en las series de palabras se usa la tilde (~) para representar el vocablo principal.

En los plurales irregulares de las palabras compuestas sólo se escribe la parte que cambia, mientras que la parte invariable se representa por un guión (-).

Un asterisco (*) colocado antes de un verbo indica que dicho verbo es irregular. Para más detalles puede consultar la lista de los verbos irregulares.

Las palabras de este diccionario están escritas en su forma inglesa. La forma y significado americanos están señalados como tales (véase la lista de abreviaturas empleadas en el texto).

Guía de pronunciación

Cada vocablo principal de esta parte del diccionario va acompañado de una transcripción fonética destinada a indicar la pronunciación. Esta representación fonética debe leerse como si se tratara del idioma español hablado en Castilla. A continuación figuran tan solo las letras y los símbolos ambiguos o particularmente difíciles de comprender.

Cada sílaba está separada por un guión y la que lleva el acento está impresa en letra *bastardilla*.

Por supuesto, los sonidos de dos lenguas rara vez coinciden exactamente, pero siguiendo con atención nuestras explicaciones, el lector de habla española llegará a pronunciar las palabras extranjeras de manera que pueda ser comprendido. A fin de facilitar su tarea, algunas veces nuestras transcripciones simplifican ligeramente el sistema fonético del idioma, sin dejar por ello de reflejar·las diferencias de sonido esenciales.

Consonantes

b	como en **b**ueno
d	como en **d**ía
ð	como **d** en rui**d**o
dʒ	como la **ll** argentina, precedida por una **d**
gh	como **g** en **g**ato
h	sonido que es una espiración suave
ng	como **n** en bla**n**co
r	ponga la lengua en la misma posición que para pronunciar ʒ (véase más abajo), luego abra ligeramente la boca y baje la lengua
s	sonido siempre suave y sonoro como en mi**s**mo
ʃ	como **ch** en mu**ch**o, pero sin la **t** inicial que compone el sonido
v	más o menos como en la**v**a; sonido que se obtiene colocando los dientes incisivos superiores sobre el labio inferior y expulsando suavemente el aire
ʒ	como la **ll** argentina

Vocales y diptongos

æ	sonido que combina el de la **a** en c**a**so con el de la **e** en sab**e**r
ê	como **e** en sab**e**r
o	como **o** en p**o**r
ö	vocal neutra; sonido parecido al de la **a** española, pero con los labios extendidos

1) Las vocales largas están impresas a doble.

2) Las letras situadas más arriba que las otras (por ej.: **ᵘi, uᵒ**) deben pronunciarse con menor intensidad y rápidamente.

3) Algunas palabras inglesas toman del francés las vocales nasales, que están indicadas con un símbolo de vocal mas **ng** (por ej.: **ang**). Este signo **ng** *no* se debe pronunciar y sólo sirve para indicar la nasalidad de la vocal precedente. Las vocales nasales se pronuncian con la boca y la nariz simultáneamente.

Pronunciación americana

Nuestra transcripción representa la pronunciación de Gran Bretaña. Aunque existen notables variaciones regionales en la lengua americana, ésta presenta en general algunas diferencias importantes respecto al inglés de Gran Bretaña.

He aquí algunos ejemplos:

1) La **r**, delante de una consonante o al final de una palabra, siempre se pronuncia, lo cual es contrario a la costumbre inglesa.

2) En muchas palabras (por ej.: *ask, castle, laugh,* etc.) la **aa** se transforma en **ææ**.

3) El sonido inglés **o** se pronuncia **a** o también **oo**.

4) En palabras como *duty, tune, new,* etc., el sonido **y** se omite a menudo antes de **uu**.

5) Por último, el acento tónico de algunas palabras puede variar considerablemente.

A

a (ei,ö) *art* (an) un *art*

abbey (æ-bi) *n* abadía *f*

abbreviation (ö-brii-vi-*ei*-ʃön) *n* abreviatura *f*

aberration (æ-bö-*rei*-ʃön) *n* anomalía *f*

ability (ö-*bi*-lö-ti) *n* habilidad *f*

able (*ei*-böl) *adj* capaz; hábil; **be ~ to *ser capaz de; *saber, *poder

abnormal (æb-*noo*-möl) *adj* anormal

aboard (ö-*bood*) *adv* a bordo

abolish (ö-*bo*-liʃ) *v* abolir

abortion (ö-*boo*-ʃön) *n* aborto *m*

about (ö-*baut*) *prep* acerca de; respecto a; alrededor de; *adv* hacia, aproximadamente; en torno

above (ö-*bav*) *prep* encima de; *adv* encima

abroad (ö-*brood*) *adv* en el extranjero

abscess (æb-ssöss) *n* absceso *m*

absence (æb-ssönss) *n* ausencia *f*

absent (æb-ssönt) *adj* ausente

absolutely (æb-ssö-luut-li) *adv* absolutamente

abstain from (öb-*sstein*) *abstenerse de

abstract (æb-sstrækt) *adj* abstracto

absurd (öb-*ssööd*) *adj* absurdo

abundance (ö-*ban*-dönss) *n* abundancia *f*

abundant (ö-*ban*-dönt) *adj* abundante

abuse (ö-*byuuss*) *n* abuso *m*

abyss (ö-*biss*) *n* abismo *m*

academy (ö-*kæ*-dö-mi) *n* academia *f*

accelerate (ök-*ssê*-lö-reit) *v* acelerar

accelerator (ök-*ssê*-lö-rei-tö) *n* acelerador *m*

accent (æk-ssönt) *n* acento *m*

accept (ök-*ssêpt*) *v* aceptar

access (æk-ssêss) *n* acceso *m*

accessary (ök-*ssê*-ssö-ri) *n* cómplice *m*

accessible (ök-*ssê*-ssö-böl) *adj* accesible

accessories (ök-*ssê*-ssö-ris) *pl* accesorios *mpl*

accident (æk-ssi-dönt) *n* accidente *m*

accidental (æk-ssi-*dên*-töl) *adj* accidental

accommodate (ö-*ko*-mö-deit) *v* acomodar

accommodation (ö-ko-mö-*dei*-ʃön) *n* acomodación *f*, alojamiento *m*

accompany (ö-*kam*-pö-ni) *v* acompañar

accomplish (ö-*kam*-pliʃ) *v* terminar; cumplir

in accordance with (in ö-*koo*-dönss ⁱð) con arreglo a

according to (ö-*koo*-ding tuu) según; conforme a

account (ö-*kaunt*) *n* cuenta *f*; narra-

ción f; ~ **for** explicar; **on** ~ **of** a
causa de

accountable (ö-*kaun*-tö-böl) *adj* explicable

accurate (*æ*-kyu-röt) *adj* exacto

accuse (ö-*kyuus*) *v* acusar

accused (ö-*kyuusd*) *n* acusado *m*

accustom (ö-*ka*-sstöm) *v* acostumbrar; **accustomed** acostumbrado

ache (eik) *v* *doler; *n* dolor *m*

achieve (ö-*chiiv*) *v* alcanzar; lograr

achievement (ö-*chiiv*-mönt) *n* realización f

acid (*æ*-ssid) *n* ácido *m*

acknowledge (ök-*no*-lidʒ) *v* *reconocer; admitir; confirmar

acne (*æk*-ni) *n* acné *m*

acorn (*ei*-koon) *n* bellota f

acquaintance (ö-*kᵘein*-tönss) *n* conocido *m*

acquire (ö-*kᵘaiᵒ*) *v* *adquirir

acquisition (*æ*-kᵘi-*si*-ʃön) *n* adquisición f

acquittal (ö-*kᵘi*-töl) *n* absolución f

across (ö-*kross*) *prep* a través de; al
otro lado de; *adv* al otro lado

act (*æ*kt) *n* acto *m*; número *m*; *v* actuar, *hacer; comportarse

action (*æk*-ʃön) *n* acción f

active (*æk*-tiv) *adj* activo; vivaz

activity (*æk*-*ti*-vö-ti) *n* actividad f

actor (*æk*-tö) *n* actor *m*

actress (*æk*-triss) *n* actriz f

actual (*æk*-chu-öl) *adj* verdadero

actually (*æk*-chu-ö-li) *adv* en realidad

acute (ö-*kyuut*) *adj* agudo

adapt (ö-*dæpt*) *v* adaptar

add (*æd*) *v* sumar, adicionar; añadir

adding-machine (*æ*-ding-mö-ʃiin) *n*
calculadora f

addition (ö-*di*-ʃön) *n* adición f

additional (ö-*di*-ʃö-nöl) *adj* adicional;
accesorio

address (ö-*drêss*) *n* dirección f; *v*

destinar; dirigirse a

addressee (*æ*-drê-*ssii*) *n* destinatario
m

adequate (*æ*-di-kᵘöt) *adj* adecuado;
conveniente

adjective (*æ*-dʒik-tiv) *n* adjetivo *m*

adjourn (ö-*dʒöön*) *v* aplazar

adjust (ö-*dʒasst*) *v* ajustar

administer (öd-*mi*-ni-sstö) *v* administrar

administration (öd-mi-ni-*sstrei*-ʃön) *n*
administración f; gestión f

administrative (öd-*mi*-ni-sströ-tiv) *adj*
gerencial; administrativo; ~ **law**
derecho administrativo

admiral (*æd*-mö-röl) *n* almirante *m*

admiration (*æd*-mö-*rei*-ʃön) *n* admiración f

admire (öd-*maiᵒ*) *v* admirar

admission (öd-*mi*-ʃön) *n* entrada f;
admisión f

admit (öd-*mit*) *v* admitir; *reconocer

admittance (öd-*mi*-tönss) *n* admisión
f; **no** ~ prohibida la entrada

adopt (ö-*dopt*) *v* adoptar

adorable (ö-*doo*-rö-böl) *adj* adorable

adult (*æ*-dalt) *n* adulto *m*; *adj* adulto

advance (öd-*vaanss*) *n* adelanto *m*;
anticipo *m*; *v* avanzar; anticipar;
in ~ por adelantado

advanced (öd-*vaansst*) *adj* avanzado

advantage (öd-*vaan*-tidʒ) *n* ventaja f

advantageous (*æd*-vön-*tei*-dʒöss) *adj*
ventajoso

adventure (öd-*vên*-chö) *n* aventura f

adverb (*æd*-vööb) *n* adverbio *m*

advertisement (öd-*vöö*-tiss-mönt) *n*
anuncio *m*

advertising (*æd*-vö-tai-sing) *n* publicidad f

advice (öd-*vaiss*) *n* consejo *m*

advise (öd-*vais*) *v* aconsejar

advocate (*æd*-vö-köt) *n* abogado *m*

aerial (*êᵒ*-ri-öl) *n* antena f

aeroplane (*ê*ᵒ-rö-plein) *n* avión *m*

affair (ö-*fê*ᵒ) *n* asunto *m*; amorío *m*

affect (ö-*fêkt*) *v* afectar

affected (ö-*fêk*-tid) *adj* afectado

affection (ö-*fêk*-ſön) *n* afección *f*; cariño *m*

affectionate (ö-*fêk*-ſö-nit) *adj* cariñoso

affiliated (ö-*fi*-li-ei-tid) *adj* afiliado

affirmative (ö-*föö*-mö-tiv) *adj* afirmativo

affliction (ö-*flik*-ſön) *n* sufrimiento *m*

afford (ö-*food*) *v* permitirse

afraid (ö-*freid*) *adj* angustioso, asustado; *be ~ *tener miedo

Africa (*æ*-fri-kö) África *f*

African (*æ*-fri-kön) *adj* africano

after (*aaf*-tö) *prep* después de; detrás de; *conj* después de que

afternoon (aaf-tö-*nuun*) *n* tarde *f*

afterwards (*aaf*-tö-ᵘöds) *adv* después

again (ö-*ghên*) *adv* otra vez; de nuevo; *~ and again* repetidamente

against (ö-*ghênsst*) *prep* contra

age (eidȝ) *n* edad *f*; vejez *f*; *of ~* mayor de edad; *under ~* menor de edad

aged (*ei*-dȝid) *adj* viejo; anciano

agency (*ei*-dȝön-ssi) *n* agencia *f*; sección *f*

agenda (ö-*dȝên*-dö) *n* orden del día

agent (*ei*-dȝönt) *n* agente *m*, representante *m*

aggressive (ö-*ghrê*-ssiv) *adj* agresivo

ago (ö-*ghou*) *adv* hace

agrarian (ö-*ghrê*ᵒ-ri-ön) *adj* agrario, agrícola

agree (ö-*ghrii*) *v* *convenir, *concordar; *consentir; *acordar

agreeable (ö-*ghrii*-ö-böl) *adj* agradable

agreement (ö-*ghrii*-mönt) *n* contrato *m*; acuerdo *m*; conformidad *f*

agriculture (*æ*-ghri-kal-chö) *n* agricultura *f*

ahead (ö-*hêd*) *adv* adelante; *~ of* delante de; *go ~* continuar; *straight ~* todo seguido

aid (eid) *n* socorro *m*; *v* asistir, ayudar

ailment (*eil*-mönt) *n* enfermedad *f*

aim (eim) *n* fin *m*; *~ at* apuntar; aspirar a

air (ê*ᵒ*) *n* aire *m*; *v* airear

air-conditioning (*ê*ᵒ-kön-di-ſö-ning) *n* aire acondicionado; **air-conditioned** *adj* climatizado

aircraft (*ê*ᵒ-kraaft) *n* (pl ~) avión *m*

airfield (*ê*ᵒ-fiild) *n* campo de aviación

air-filter (*ê*ᵒ-fil-tö) *n* filtro de aire

airline (*ê*ᵒ-lain) *n* aerolínea *f*

airmail (*ê*ᵒ-meil) *n* correo aéreo

airplane (*ê*ᵒ-plein) *n*Am avión *m*

airport (*ê*ᵒ-poot) *n* aeropuerto *m*

air-sickness (*ê*ᵒ-ssik-nöss) *n* mal de las alturas

airtight (*ê*ᵒ-tait) *adj* hermético

airy (*ê*ᵒ-ri) *adj* airoso

aisle (ail) *n* nave lateral; pasillo *m*

alarm (ö-*laam*) *n* alarma *f*; *v* alarmar

alarm-clock (ö-*laam*-klok) *n* despertador *m*

album (*æl*-böm) *n* álbum *m*

alcohol (*æl*-kö-hol) *n* alcohol *m*

alcoholic (æl-kö-*ho*-lik) *adj* alcohólico

ale (eil) *n* cerveza *f*

algebra (*æl*-dȝi-brö) *n* álgebra *f*

Algeria (æl-*dȝi*ᵒ-ri-ö) Argelia *f*

Algerian (æl-*dȝi*ᵒ-ri-ön) *adj* argelino

alien (*ei*-li-ön) *n* extranjero *m*; *adj* extranjero

alike (ö-*laik*) *adj* igual, parecido; *adv* igualmente

alimony (*æ*-li-mö-ni) *n* pensión alimenticia

alive (ö-*laiv*) *adj* en vida, vivo

all (ool) *adj* todo; *~ in* todo incluido; *~ right!* ¡bien!; *at ~* en modo algunono

allergy (æ-lö-dʒi) *n* alergia *f*

alley (æ-li) *n* callejón *m*

alliance (ö-*lai*-önss) *n* alianza *f*

Allies (æ-lais) *pl* Aliados *mpl*

allot (ö-*lot*) *v* asignar

allow (ö-*lau*) *v* permitir, autorizar; ~ to autorizar a; *be allowed *estar autorizado

allowance (ö-*lau*-önss) *n* asignación *f*

all-round (ool-*raund*) *adj* polifacético

almanac (*ool*-mö-næk) *n* almanaque *m*

almond (*aa*-mönd) *n* almendra *f*

almost (*ool*-mousst) *adv* casi; cerca de

alone (ö-*loun*) *adv* sólo

along (ö-*long*) *prep* a lo largo de

aloud (ö-*laud*) *adv* en voz alta

alphabet (*æl*-fö-bêt) *n* abecedario *m*

already (ool-*rê*-di) *adv* ya

also (*ool*-ssou) *adv* también; asimismo

altar (*ool*-tö) *n* altar *m*

alter (*ool*-tö) *v* cambiar, alterar

alteration (ool-tö-*rei*-ſön) *n* cambio *m*, alteración *f*

alternate (ool-*töö*-nöt) *adj* alternativo

alternative (ool-*töö*-nö-tiv) *n* alternativa *f*

although (ool-*ðou*) *conj* aunque

altitude (*æl*-ti-tyuud) *n* altitud *f*

alto (*æl*-tou) *n* (pl ~s) contralto *m*

altogether (ool-tö-*ghê*-ðö) *adv* totalmente; en total

always (*ool*-ᵘeis) *adv* siempre

am (æm) *v* (pr be)

amaze (ö-*meis*) *v* extrañar, asombrar

amazement (ö-*meis*-mönt) *n* asombro *m*

ambassador (æm-*bæ*-ssö-dö) *n* embajador *m*

amber (*æm*-bö) *n* ámbar *m*

ambiguous (æm-*bi*-ghyu-öss) *adj* ambiguo; equívoco

ambitious (æm-*bi*-ſöss) *adj* ambicioso

ambulance (*æm*-byu-lönss) *n* ambulancia *f*

ambush (*æm*-buſ) *n* emboscada *f*

America (ö-*mê*-ri-kö) América *f*

American (ö-*mê*-ri-kön) *adj* americano

amethyst (*æ*-mi-zisst) *n* amatista *f*

amid (ö-*mid*) *prep* entre; en medio de

ammonia (ö-*mou*-ni-ö) *n* amoníaco *m*

amnesty (*æm*-ni-ssti) *n* amnistía *f*

among (ö-*mang*) *prep* entre; ~ other things entre otras cosas

amount (ö-*maunt*) *n* cantidad *f*; suma *f*; ~ to sumar

amuse (ö-*myuus*) *v* *divertir, *entretener

amusement (ö-*myuus*-mönt) *n* distracción *f*, entretenimiento *m*

amusing (ö-*myuu*-sing) *adj* divertido

anaemia (ö-*nii*-mi-ö) *n* anemia *f*

anaesthesia (æ-niss-*zii*-si-ö) *n* anestesia *f*

anaesthetic (æ-niss-*zê*-tik) *n* anestésico *m*

analyse (*æ*-nö-lais) *v* analizar

analysis (ö-*næ*-lö-ssiss) *n* (pl -ses) análisis *f*

analyst (*æ*-nö-lisst) *n* analista *m*; psicoanalista *m*

anarchy (*æ*-nö-ki) *n* anarquía *f*

anatomy (ö-*næ*-tö-mi) *n* anatomía *f*

ancestor (*æn*-ssê-sstö) *n* antepasado *m*

anchor (*æng*-kö) *n* ancla *f*

anchovy (*æn*-chö-vi) *n* anchoa *f*

ancient (*ein*-ſönt) *adj* viejo, antiguo; anticuado

and (ænd, önd) *conj* y

angel (*ein*-dʒöl) *n* ángel *m*

anger (*æng*-ghö) *n* cólera *f*, enojo *m*; furor *m*

angle (*æng*-ghöl) *v* pescar con caña; *n* ángulo *m*

angry (æng-ghri) *adj* enfadado, enoja-do

animal (æ-ni-möl) *n* animal *m*

ankle (æng-köl) *n* tobillo *m*

annex¹ (æ-nèkss) *n* anexo *m*

annex² (ö-nèkss) *v* anexar

anniversary (æ-ni-*vöö*-ssö-ri) *n* aniversario *m*

announce (ö-*naunss*) *v* anunciar

announcement (ö-*naunss*-mönt) *n* anuncio *m*

annoy (ö-*noi*) *v* irritar, fastidiar; aburrir

annoyance (ö-*noi*-önss) *n* aburrimiento *m*

annoying (ö-*noi*-ing) *adj* irritante, importuno

annual (æ-nyu-öl) *adj* anual; *n* anuario *m*

per annum (pör æ-nöm) al año

anonymous (ö-*no*-ni-möss) *adj* anónimo

another (ö-*na*-ðö) *adj* otro más; otro

answer (*aan*-ssö) *v* responder a; *n* respuesta *f*

ant (ænt) *n* hormiga *f*

anthology (æn-*zo*-lö-dʒi) *n* antología *f*

antibiotic (æn-ti-bai-*o*-tik) *n* antibiótico *m*

anticipate (æn-*ti*-ssi-peit) *v* *prever; *prevenir

antifreeze (æn-ti-friis) *n* anticongelante *m*

antipathy (æn-*ti*-pö-zi) *n* antipatía *f*

antique (æn-*tiik*) *adj* antiguo; *n* antigualla *f*; ~ **dealer** anticuario *m*

antiquity (æn-*ti*-kʷö-ti) *n* Antigüedad *f*; **antiquities** *pl* antigüedades *fpl*

antiseptic (æn-ti-*ssêp*-tik) *n* antiséptico *m*

antlers (*ænt*-lös) *pl* cornamenta *f*

anxiety (æng-*sai*-ö-ti) *n* preocupación *f*

anxious (*ængk*-ʃöss) *adj* ansioso; preocupado

any (*ê*-ni) *adj* alguno

anybody (*ê*-ni-bo-di) *pron* cualquiera

anyhow (*ê*-ni-hau) *adv* de cualquier modo

anyone (*ê*-ni-ᵘan) *pron* cualquiera

anything (*ê*-ni-zing) *pron* cualquier cosa

anyway (*ê*-ni-ᵘei) *adv* en todo caso

anywhere (*ê*-ni-ᵘê̂ᵒ) *adv* en donde sea; dondequiera

apart (ö-*paat*) *adv* por separado, separadamente; ~ **from** prescindiendo de

apartment (ö-*paat*-mönt) *nAm* apartamento *m*; piso *m*; ~ **house** *Am* casa de pisos

aperitif (ö-*pê*-ri-tiv) *n* aperitivo *m*

apologize (ö-*po*-lö-dʒais) *v* disculparse

apology (ö-*po*-lö-dʒi) *n* excusa *f*, disculpa *f*

apparatus (æ-pö-*rei*-töss) *n* aparato *m*

apparent (ö-*pæ*-rönt) *adj* aparente; obvio

apparently (ö-*pæ*-rönt-li) *adv* por lo visto; evidentemente

apparition (æ-pö-*ri*-ʃön) *n* aparición *f*

appeal (ö-*piil*) *n* apelación *f*

appear (ö-*piᵒ*) *v* *parecer; *salir; *aparecer

appearance (ö-*piᵒ*-rönss) *n* apariencia *f*; aspecto *m*; entrada *f*

appendicitis (ö-pên-di-*ssai*-tiss) *n* apendicitis *f*

appendix (ö-*pên*-dikss) *n* (pl -dices, -dixes) apéndice *m*

appetite (æ-pö-tait) *n* apetito *m*

appetizer (æ-pö-tai-sö) *n* tapa *f*

appetizing (æ-pö-tai-sing) *adj* apetitoso

applause (ö-*ploos*) *n* aplauso *m*

apple (æ-pöl) *n* manzana *f*

appliance (ö-*plai*-önss) *n* aparato *m*

application (æ-pli-*kei*-ſön) *n* aplicación *f*; demanda *f*; solicitud *f*

apply (ö-*plai*) *v* aplicar; solicitar un puesto; aplicarse a

appoint (ö-*point*) *v* designar, nombrar

appointment (ö-*point*-mönt) *n* cita *f*; nombramiento *m*

appreciate (ö-*prii*-ſi-eit) *v* valuar; apreciar

appreciation (ö-prii-ſi-*ei*-ſön) *n* aprecio *m*

approach (ö-*prouch*) *v* acercarse; *n* enfoque *m*; acceso *m*

appropriate (ö-*prou*-pri-öt) *adj* justo, apropiado, adecuado

approval (ö-*pruu*-völ) *n* aprobación *f*; consentimiento *m*, acuerdo *m*; on ~ a prueba

approve (ö-*pruuv*) *v* *aprobar; ~ **of** *estar de acuerdo con

approximate (ö-*prok*-ssi-möt) *adj* aproximado

approximately (ö-*prok*-ssi-möt-li) *adv* aproximadamente

apricot (*ei*-pri-kot) *n* albaricoque *m*; chabacano *mMe*

April (*ei*-pröl) abril

apron (*ei*-prön) *n* delantal *m*

Arab (*æ*-röb) *adj* árabe

arbitrary (*aa*-bi-trö-ri) *adj* arbitrario

arcade (aa-*keid*) *n* pórtico *m*, arcada *f*

arch (aach) *n* arco *m*; bóveda *f*

archaeologist (aa-ki-*o*-lö-dʒisst) *n* arqueólogo *m*

archaeology (aa-ki-*o*-lö-dʒi) *n* arqueología *f*

archbishop (aach-*bi*-ſöp) *n* arzobispo *m*

arched (aacht) *adj* arqueado

architect (*aa*-ki-têkt) *n* arquitecto *m*

architecture (*aa*-ki-têk-chö) *n* arquitectura *f*

archives (*aa*-kaivs) *pl* archivo *m*

are (aa) *v* (pr be)

area (*ê*ᵒ-ri-ö) *n* región *f*; zona *f*; superficie *f*; ~ **code** indicativo *m*

Argentina (aa-dʒön-*tii*-nö) Argentina *f*

Argentinian (aa-dʒön-*ti*-ni-ön) *adj* argentino

argue (*aa*-ghyuu) *v* argumentar, discutir; disputar

argument (*aa*-ghyu-mönt) *n* argumento *m*; discusión *f*; disputa *f*

arid (*æ*-rid) *adj* árido

*arise (ö-*rais*) *v* surgir

arithmetic (ö-*riz*-mö-tik) *n* aritmética *f*

arm (aam) *n* brazo *m*; arma *f*; *v* armar

armchair (*aam*-chêᵒ) *n* butaca *f*, sillón *m*

armed (aamd) *adj* armado; ~ **forces** fuerzas armadas

armour (*aa*-mö) *n* armadura *f*

army (*aa*-mi) *n* ejército *m*

aroma (ö-*rou*-mö) *n* aroma *m*

around (ö-*raund*) *prep* alrededor de, en torno de; *adv* en torno

arrange (ö-*reindʒ*) *v* clasificar, ordenar; organizar

arrangement (ö-*reindʒ*-mönt) *n* arreglo *m*

arrest (ö-*rêsst*) *v* arrestar; *n* arresto *m*

arrival (ö-*rai*-völ) *n* llegada *f*

arrive (ö-*raiv*) *v* llegar

arrow (*æ*-rou) *n* flecha *f*

art (aat) *n* arte *m/f*; habilidad *f*; ~ **collection** colección de arte; ~ **exhibition** exposición de arte; ~ **gallery** galería de arte; ~ **history** historia del arte; **arts and crafts** artes industriales; ~ **school** academia de bellas artes

artery (*aa*-tö-ri) *n* arteria *f*

artichoke (*aa*-ti-chouk) *n* alcachofa *f*

article (*aa*-ti-köl) *n* artículo *m*

artifice (*aa*-ti-fiss) n artificio m
artificial (aa-ti-*fi*-föl) adj artificial
artist (*aa*-tisst) n artista m/f
artistic (aa-*ti*-sstik) adj artístico
as (æs) conj como; tanto; que; ya que, porque; ~ **from** a partir de; ~ **if** como si
asbestos (æs-*bê*-sstoss) n asbesto m
ascend (ö-*ssênd*) v subir; escalar
ascent (ö-*ssênt*) n subida f
ascertain (æ-ssö-*tein*) v *comprobar; asegurarse de
ash (æʃ) n ceniza f
ashamed (ö-*ʃeimd*) adj avergonzado; *be ~ *avergonzarse
ashore (ö-*ʃoo*) adv en tierra
ashtray (*æʃ*-trei) n cenicero m
Asia (*ei*-ʃö) Asia f
Asian (*ei*-ʃön) adj asiático
aside (ö-*ssaid*) adv aparte
ask (aassk) v preguntar; *rogar; invitar
asleep (ö-*ssliip*) adj dormido
asparagus (ö-*sspæ*-rö-ghöss) n espárrago m
aspect (*æ*-sspêkt) n aspecto m
asphalt (*æss*-fælt) n asfalto m
aspire (ö-*sspaiⁿ*) v aspirar
aspirin (*æ*-sspö-rin) n aspirina f
ass (æss) n burro m
assassination (ö-ssæ-ssi-*nei*-ʃön) n asesinato m
assault (ö-*ssoolt*) v atacar; violar
assemble (ö-*ssêm*-böl) v reunir; montar
assembly (ö-*ssêm*-bli) n reunión f, asamblea f
assignment (ö-*ssain*-mönt) n encargo m
assign to (ö-*ssain*) asignar a; *atribuir a
assist (ö-*ssisst*) v asistir
assistance (ö-*ssi*-sstönss) n auxilio m; apoyo m, asistencia f

assistant (ö-*ssi*-sstönt) n asistente m
associate[1] (ö-*ssou*-ʃi-öt) n compañero m, asociado m; aliado m; socio m
associate[2] (ö-*ssou*-ʃi-eit) v asociar; ~ **with** frecuentar
association (ö-ssou-ssi-*ei*-ʃön) n asociación f
assort (ö-*ssoot*) v clasificar
assortment (ö-*ssoot*-mönt) n surtido m
assume (ö-*ssyuum*) v *suponer, presumir
assure (ö-*ʃuⁿ*) v asegurar
asthma (*æss*-mö) n asma f
astonish (ö-*ssto*-niʃ) v asombrar
astonishing (ö-*ssto*-ni-ʃing) adj asombroso
astonishment (ö-*ssto*-niʃ-mönt) n sorpresa f
astronomy (ö-*ssstro*-nö-mi) n astronomía f
asylum (ö-*ssai*-löm) n asilo m
at (æt) prep en, a; hacia
ate (êt) v (p eat)
atheist (*ei*-zi-isst) n ateo m
athlete (*æz*-liit) n atleta m
athletics (æz-*lê*-tikss) pl atletismo m
Atlantic (öt-*læn*-tik) Atlántico m
atmosphere (*æt*-möss-fiⁿ) n atmósfera f; esfera f, ambiente m
atom (*æ*-töm) n átomo m
atomic (ö-*to*-mik) adj atómico
atomizer (*æ*-tö-mai-sö) n vaporizador m; aerosol m, pulverizador m
attach (ö-*tæch*) v prender; fijar; juntar; **attached to** encariñado con
attack (ö-*tæk*) v atacar; n ataque m
attain (ö-*tein*) v llegar a
attainable (ö-*tei*-nö-böl) adj factible; alcanzable
attempt (ö-*têmpt*) v intentar; *probar; n tentativa f
attend (ö-*tênd*) v asistir a; ~ **on** *servir; ~ **to** cuidar de, *atender a;

prestar atención a

attendance (ö-*tên*-dönss) *n* asistencia *f*

attendant (ö-*tên*-dönt) *n* guardián *m*

attention (ö-*tên*-ʃön) *n* atención *f*; ***pay ~** prestar atención

attentive (ö-*tên*-tiv) *adj* atento

attic (*æ*-tik) *n* buhardilla *f*

attitude (*æ*-ti-tyuud) *n* actitud *f*

attorney (ö-*töö*-ni) *n* abogado *m*

attract (ö-*trækt*) *v* *atraer

attraction (ö-*træk*-ʃön) *n* atracción *f*

attractive (ö-*træk*-tiv) *adj* atractivo

auburn (*oo*-bön) *adj* castaño

auction (*ook*-ʃön) *n* subasta *f*

audible (*oo*-di-böl) *adj* audible

audience (*oo*-di-önss) *n* auditorio *m*

auditor (*oo*-di-tö) *n* oyente *m*

auditorium (oo-di-*too*-ri-öm) *n* aula *f*

August (*oo*-ghösst) agosto

aunt (aant) *n* tía *f*

Australia (o-*sstrei*-li-ö) Australia *f*

Australian (o-*sstrei*-li-ön) *adj* australiano

Austria (*o*-sstri-ö) Austria *f*

Austrian (*o*-sstri-ön) *adj* austríaco

authentic (oo-*zên*-tik) *adj* auténtico

author (*oo*-zö) *n* autor *m*

authoritarian (oo-zo-ri-*tê*ᵒ-ri-ön) *adj* autoritario

authority (oo-*zo*-rö-ti) *n* autoridad *f*; poder *m*

authorization (oo-zö-rai-*sei*-ʃön) *n* autorización *f*; permiso *m*

automatic (oo-tö-*mæ*-tik) *adj* automático

automation (oo-tö-*mei*-ʃön) *n* automatización *f*

automobile (*oo*-tö-mö-biil) *n* automóvil *m*; **~ club** automóvil club

autonomous (oo-*to*-nö-möss) *adj* autónomo

autopsy (*oo*-to-pssi) *n* autopsia *f*

autumn (*oo*-töm) *n* otoño *m*

available (ö-*vei*-lö-böl) *adj* adquirible, obtenible, disponible

avalanche (*æ*-vö-laanʃ) *n* avalancha *f*

avaricious (æ-vö-*ri*-ʃöss) *adj* avaro

avenue (*æ*-vö-nyuu) *n* avenida *f*

average (*æ*-vö-ridʒ) *adj* promedio; *n* promedio *m*; **on the ~** en promedio

averse (ö-*vööss*) *adj* opuesto

aversion (ö-*vöö*-ʃön) *n* aversión *f*

avert (ö-*vööt*) *v* desviar

avoid (ö-*void*) *v* evitar

await (ö-ᵘ*eit*) *v* esperar

awake (ö-ᵘ*eik*) *adj* despierto

*awake (ö-ᵘ*eik*) *v* *despertar

award (ö-ᵘ*ood*) *n* premio *m*; *v* conceder

aware (ö-ᵘ*ê*ᵒ) *adj* consciente

away (ö-ᵘ*ei*) *adv* fuera; ***go ~** *irse

awful (*oo*-föl) *adj* terrible, tremendo

awkward (*oo*-kᵘöd) *adj* embarazoso; torpe

awning (*oo*-ning) *n* toldo *m*

axe (ækss) *n* hacha *f*

axle (*æk*-ssöl) *n* eje *m*

B

baby (*bei*-bi) *n* bebé *m*; **~ carriage** *Am* cochecillo *m*

babysitter (*bei*-bi-ssi-tö) *n* babysitter *m*

bachelor (*bæ*-chö-lö) *n* soltero *m*

back (bæk) *n* espalda *f*; *adv* atrás; ***go ~** regresar

backache (*bæ*-keik) *n* dolor de espalda

backbone (*bæk*-boun) *n* espina dorsal *f*

background (*bæk*-ghraund) *n* fondo *m*; antecedentes *mpl*

backwards (*bæk*-ᵘöds) *adv* hacia atrás

bacon (*bei*-kön) *n* tocino *m*

bacterium (bæk-*tii*-ri-öm) *n* (pl -ria) bacteria *f*

bad (bæd) *adj* malo; grave; travieso

bag (bægh) *n* bolsa *f*; bolso *m*, cartera *f*; maleta *f*

baggage (*bæ*-ghidʒ) *n* equipaje *m*; **hand ~** *Am* equipaje de mano

bail (beil) *n* fianza *f*

bailiff (*bei*-lif) *n* ujier *m*

bait (beit) *n* cebo *m*

bake (beik) *v* hornear

baker (*bei*-kö) *n* panadero *m*

bakery (*bei*-kö-ri) *n* panadería *f*

balance (*bæ*-lönss) *n* equilibrio *m*; balance *m*; saldo *m*

balcony (*bæl*-kö-ni) *n* balcón *m*

bald (boold) *adj* calvo

ball (bool) *n* pelota *f*; baile *m*

ballet (*bæ*-lei) *n* ballet *m*

balloon (bö-*luun*) *n* globo *m*

ballpoint-pen (*bool*-point-pên) *n* bolígrafo *m*

ballroom (*bool*-ruum) *n* salón de baile

bamboo (bæm-*buu*) *n* (pl ~s) bambú *m*

banana (bö-*naa*-nö) *n* plátano *m*

band (bænd) *n* orquesta *f*; banda *f*

bandage (*bæn*-didʒ) *n* vendaje *m*

bandit (*bæn*-dit) *n* bandido *m*

bangle (*bæng*-ghöl) *n* pulsera *f*

banisters (*bæ*-ni-sstös) *pl* baranda *f*

bank (bængk) *n* orilla *f*; banco *m*; *v* depositar; **~ account** cuenta de banco

banknote (*bængk*-nout) *n* vale *m*, billete de banco

bank-rate (*bængk*-reit) *n* descuento bancario

bankrupt (*bængk*-rapt) *adj* en quiebra

banner (*bæ*-nö) *n* bandera *f*

banquet (*bæng*-kᵘit) *n* banquete *m*

banqueting-hall (*bæng*-kᵘi-ting-hool) *n* comedor de gala

baptism (*bæp*-ti-söm) *n* bautismo *m*, bautizo *m*

baptize (bæp-*tais*) *v* bautizar

bar (baa) *n* bar *m*; barra *f*; barrote *m*

barber (*baa*-bö) *n* barbero *m*

bare (bêᵒ) *adj* desnudo; raso

barely (*bêᵒ*-li) *adv* apenas

bargain (*baa*-ghin) *n* ganga *f*; *v* regatear

baritone (*bæ*-ri-toun) *n* barítono *m*

bark (baak) *n* corteza *f*; *v* ladrar

barley (*baa*-li) *n* cebada *f*

barmaid (*baa*-meid) *n* moza de taberna

barman (*baa*-mön) *n* (pl -men) barman *m*

barn (baan) *n* granero *m*

barometer (bö-*ro*-mi-tö) *n* barómetro *m*

baroque (bö-*rok*) *adj* barroco

barracks (*bæ*-rökss) *pl* cuartel *m*

barrel (*bæ*-röl) *n* tonel *m*, barril *m*

barrier (*bæ*-ri-ö) *n* barrera *f*

barrister (*bæ*-ri-sstö) *n* abogado *m*

bartender (*baa*-tên-dö) *n* barman *m*

base (beiss) *n* base *f*; fundamento *m*; *v* basar

baseball (*beiss*-bool) *n* béisbol *m*

basement (*beiss*-mönt) *n* sótano *m*

basic (*bei*-ssik) *adj* fundamental

basilica (bö-*si*-li-kö) *n* basílica *f*

basin (*bei*-ssön) *n* tazón *m*, palangana *f*

basis (*bei*-ssiss) *n* (pl bases) fundamento *m*, base *f*

basket (*baa*-sskit) *n* cesta *f*

bass¹ (beiss) *n* bajo *m*

bass² (bæss) *n* (pl ~) perca *f*

bastard (*baa*-sstöd) *n* bastardo *m*; descarado *m*

batch (bæch) *n* carga *f*

bath (baaz) *n* baño *m*; **~ salts** sales de baño; **~ towel** toalla de baño

bathe (beið) v bañarse

bathing-cap (*bei*-ðing-kæp) n gorro de baño

bathing-suit (*bei*-ðing-ssuut) n traje de baño

bathing-trunks (*bei*-ðing-trangkss) n bañador m

bathrobe (*baaz*-roub) n bata de baño

bathroom (*baaz*-ruum) n cuarto de baño; lavabos mpl; baño mMe

batter (*bæ*-tö) n masa f

battery (*bæ*-tö-ri) n batería f; acumulador m

battle (*bæ*-töl) n batalla f; pelea f, combate m; v combatir

bay (bei) n bahía f; v ladrar

***be** (bii) v *estar; *ser

beach (biich) n playa f; **nudist** ~ playa para nudistas

bead (biid) n cuenta f; **beads** pl collar m; rosario m

beak (biik) n pico m

beam (biim) n rayo m; viga f

bean (biin) n judía f; ejote mMe

bear (bêö) n oso m

***bear** (bêö) v llevar; aguantar; soportar

beard (biöd) n barba f

bearer (*bêö*-rö) n portador m

beast (biisst) n animal m; ~ **of prey** animal de presa

***beat** (biit) v batir, golpear

beautiful (*byuu*-ti-föl) adj hermoso

beauty (*byuu*-ti) n belleza f; ~ **parlour** salón de belleza; ~ **salon** salón de belleza; ~ **treatment** tratamiento de belleza

beaver (*bii*-vö) n castor m

because (bi-*kos*) conj porque; puesto que; ~ **of** a causa de

***become** (bi-*kam*) v *hacerse; *sentar bien

bed (bêd) n cama f; ~ **and board** pensión completa; ~ **and breakfast** cama y desayuno

bedding (*bê*-ding) n ropa de cama

bedroom (*bêd*-ruum) n dormitorio m

bee (bii) n abeja f

beech (bii-ch) n haya f

beef (biif) n carne de vaca

beehive (*bii*-haiv) n colmena f

been (biin) v (pp be)

beer (biö) n cerveza f

beet (biit) n remolacha f

beetle (*bii*-töl) n escarabajo m

beetroot (*biit*-ruut) n remolacha f

before (bi-*foo*) prep antes de; delante de; conj antes de que; adv antes

beg (bêgh) v mendigar; suplicar; *pedir

beggar (*bê*-ghö) n mendigo m

***begin** (bi-*ghin*) v *empezar; *comenzar

beginner (bi-*ghi*-nö) n principiante m

beginning (bi-*ghi*-ning) n comienzo m

on behalf of (on bi-*haaf*ov) en nombre de; a favor de

behave (bi-*heiv*) v comportarse

behaviour (bi-*hei*-vyö) n conducta f

behind (bi-*haind*) prep detrás de; adv detrás

beige (beiჳ) adj beige

being (*bii*-ing) n ser m

Belgian (*bêl*-dჳön) adj belga

Belgium (*bêl*-dჳöm) Bélgica f

belief (bi-*liif*) n creencia f

believe (bi-*liiv*) v *creer

bell (bêl) n campana f; timbre m

bellboy (*bêl*-boi) n botones mpl

belly (*bê*-li) n vientre m

belong (bi-*long*) v *pertenecer

belongings (bi-*long*-ings) pl pertenencias fpl

beloved (bi-*lavd*) adj querido

below (bi-*lou*) prep debajo de; bajo; adv debajo

belt (bêlt) n cinturón m

bench (bênch) n banco m

bend (bênd) *n* comba *f*, curva *f*

***bend** (bênd) *v* doblar; ~ **down** bajarse

beneath (bi-*niiz*) *prep* debajo de; *adv* debajo

benefit (*bê*-ni-fit) *n* beneficio *m*; ventaja *f*; *v* aprovechar

bent (bênt) *adj* (pp bend) curvo

beret (*bê*-rei) *n* boina *f*

berry (*bê*-ri) *n* baya *f*

berth (bööz) *n* litera *f*

beside (bi-*ssaid*) *prep* junto a

besides (bi-*ssaids*) *adv* además; por otra parte; *prep* además de

best (bêsst) *adj* óptimo

bet (bêt) *n* apuesta *f*; puesta *f*

***bet** (bêt) *v* *apostar

betray (bi-*trei*) *v* traicionar

better (*bê*-tö) *adj* mejor

between (bi-*t^uiin*) *prep* entre

beverage (*bê*-vö-ridʒ) *n* bebida *f*

beware (bi-*^uéô*) *v* precaverse, guardarse

bewitch (bi-*^uich*) *v* hechizar, encantar

beyond (bi-*yond*) *prep* más allá de; además de; *adv* más allá

bible (*bai*-böl) *n* biblia *f*

bicycle (*bai*-ssi-köl) *n* bicicleta *f*; biciclo *m*

big (bigh) *adj* grande; voluminoso; gordo; importante

bile (bail) *n* bilis *f*

bilingual (bai-*ling*-gh^uöl) *adj* bilingüe

bill (bil) *n* cuenta *f*; *v* facturar

billiards (*bil*-yöds) *pl* billar *m*

***bind** (baind) *v* atar

binding (*bain*-ding) *n* atadura *f*

binoculars (bi-*no*-kyö-lös) *pl* prismáticos *mpl*; gemelos *mpl*

biology (bai-*o*-lö-dʒi) *n* biología *f*

birch (bööch) *n* abedul *m*

bird (bööd) *n* pájaro *m*

Biro (*bai*-rou) *n* bolígrafo *m*

birth (bööz) *n* nacimiento *m*

birthday (*bööz*-dei) *n* cumpleaños *m*

biscuit (*biss*-kit) *n* galleta *f*

bishop (*bi*-ʃöp) *n* obispo *m*

bit (bit) *n* trozo *m*; poco *m*

bitch (bich) *n* perra *f*

bite (bait) *n* bocado *m*; mordedura *f*; picadura *f*

***bite** (bait) *v* *morder

bitter (*bi*-tö) *adj* amargo

black (blæk) *adj* negro; ~ **market** mercado negro

blackberry (*blæk*-bö-ri) *n* mora *f*

blackbird (*blæk*-bööd) *n* mirlo *m*

blackboard (*blæk*-bood) *n* pizarra *f*

black-currant (blæk-*ka*-rönt) *n* grosella negra

blackmail (*blæk*-meil) *n* chantaje *m*; *v* *hacer chantaje

blacksmith (*blæk*-ssmiz) *n* herrero *m*

bladder (*blæ*-dö) *n* vejiga *f*

blade (bleid) *n* hoja *f*; ~ **of grass** brizna de hierba

blame (bleim) *n* culpa *f*; reproche *m*; *v* echar la culpa, culpar

blank (blængk) *adj* blanco

blanket (*blæng*-kit) *n* manta *f*

blast (blaasst) *n* explosión *f*

blazer (*blei*-sö) *n* chaqueta de sport, chaqueta ligera

bleach (bliich) *v* blanquear

bleak (bliik) *adj* riguroso

***bleed** (bliid) *v* sangrar; chupar la sangre

bless (blêss) *v* *bendecir

blessing (*blê*-ssing) *n* bendición *f*

blind (blaind) *n* persiana *f*; *adj* ciego; *v* *cegar

blister (*bli*-sstö) *n* ampolla *f*

blizzard (*bli*-söd) *n* ventisca *f*

block (blok) *v* *obstruir, bloquear; *n* bloque *m*; ~ **of flats** casa de pisos

blonde (blond) *n* rubia *f*

blood (blad) *n* sangre *f*; ~ **pressure** tensión arterial

blood-poisoning (*blad*-poi-sö-ning) *n* septicemia *f*

blood-vessel (*blad*-vê-ssöl) *n* vaso sanguíneo

blot (blot) *n* borrón *m*; mancha *f*; **blotting paper** papel secante

blouse (blaus) *n* blusa *f*

blow (blou) *n* golpe *m*; ráfaga *f*

* **blow** (blou) *v* soplar

blow-out (*blou*-aut) *n* reventón *m*

blue (bluu) *adj* azul; deprimido

blunt (blant) *adj* desafilado; obtuso

blush (blaʃ) *v* ruborizarse

board (bood) *n* tabla *f*; tablero *m*; pensión *f*; consejo *m*; ~ **and lodging** pensión completa

boarder (*boo*-dö) *n* huésped *m*

boarding-house (*boo*-ding-hauss) *n* pensión *f*

boarding-school (*boo*-ding-sskuul) *n* internado *m*

boast (bousst) *v* presumir

boat (bout) *n* barco *m*, barca *f*

body (*bo*-di) *n* cuerpo *m*

bodyguard (*bo*-di-ghaad) *n* guardia personal

bog (bogh) *n* pantano *m*

boil (boil) *v* *hervir; *n* forúnculo *m*

bold (bould) *adj* audaz; impertinente, descarado

Bolivia (bö-*li*-vi-ö) Bolivia *f*

Bolivian (bö-*li*-vi-ön) *adj* boliviano

bolt (boult) *n* cerrojo *m*; perno *m*

bomb (bom) *n* bomba *f*; *v* bombardear

bond (bond) *n* obligación *f*

bone (boun) *n* hueso *m*; espina *f*; *v* deshuesar

bonnet (*bo*-nit) *n* capó *m*

book (buk) *n* libro *m*; *v* reservar; inscribir, registrar

booking (*bu*-king) *n* reservación *f*, reserva *f*

bookmaker (*buk*-mei-kö) *n* corredor *m*

bookseller (*buk*-ssê-lö) *n* librero *m*

bookstand (*buk*-sstænd) *n* puesto de libros

bookstore (*buk*-sstoo) *n* librería *f*

boot (buut) *n* bota *f*; portaequipajes *m*

booth (buuð) *n* puesto *m*; cabina *f*

border (*boo*-dö) *n* frontera *f*; borde *m*

bore¹ (boo) *v* aburrir; taladrar; *n* pelmazo *m*

bore² (boo) *v* (p bear)

boring (*boo*-ring) *adj* aburrido

born (boon) *adj* nacido

borrow (*bo*-rou) *v* tomar prestado; tomar

bosom (*bu*-söm) *n* pecho *m*; seno *m*

boss (boss) *n* jefe *m*, patrón *m*

botany (*bo*-tö-ni) *n* botánica *f*

both (bouz) *adj* ambos; **both ... and** tanto ... como

bother (*bo*-ðö) *v* fastidiar, molestar; *esforzarse; *n* molestia *f*

bottle (*bo*-töl) *n* botella *f*; ~ **opener** destapador de botellas; **hot-water** ~ calorífero *m*

bottleneck (*bo*-töl-nêk) *n* cuello de botella

bottom (*bo*-töm) *n* fondo *m*; trasero *m*; *adj* inferior

bough (bau) *n* rama *f*

bought (boot) *v* (p, pp buy)

boulder (*boul*-dö) *n* peña *f*

bound (baund) *n* frontera *f*; *be ~ to** deber de; ~ **for** camino de

boundary (*baun*-dö-ri) *n* límite *m*; frontera *f*

bouquet (bu-*kei*) *n* ramo *m*

bourgeois (*bu*ᵒ-ᵌᵘaa) *adj* burgués

boutique (bu-*tiik*) *n* boutique *f*

bow¹ (bau) *v* inclinar

bow² (bou) *n* arco *m*; ~ **tie** corbata de lazo, corbatín *m*

bowels (bau⁰ls) pl intestinos mpl

bowl (boul) n tazón m

bowling (bou-ling) n bowling m, juego de bolos; ~ **alley** bolera f

box¹ (bokss) v boxear; **boxing match** combate de boxeo

box² (bokss) n caja f

box-office (bokss-o-fiss) n taquilla f

boy (boi) n muchacho m; chico m, mozo m; sirviente m; ~ **scout** explorador m

bra (braa) n sujetador m, sostén m

bracelet (breiss-lit) n pulsera f

braces (brei-ssis) pl tirantes mpl

brain (brein) n cerebro m; inteligencia f

brain-wave (brein-ᵘeiv) n ocurrencia f

brake (breik) n freno m; ~ **drum** tambor del freno; ~ **lights** luces de freno

branch (braanch) n rama f; sucursal f

brand (brænd) n marca f

brand-new (brænd-nyuu) adj flamante

brass (braass) n latón m; cobre m, cobre amarillo; ~ **band** n charanga f

brassiere (bræ-si⁰) n sujetador m, sostén m

brassware (braass-ᵘê⁰) n cobres mpl

brave (breiv) adj valiente

Brazil (brö-sil) Brasil m

Brazilian (brö-sil-yön) adj brasileño

breach (briich) n brecha f

bread (brêd) n pan m; **wholemeal ~** pan integral

breadth (brêdz) n ancho m

break (breik) n fractura f; descanso m

*** break** (breik) v *quebrar, quebrantar; ~ **down** averiarse; analizar

breakdown (breik-daun) n avería f; descompostura fMe

breakfast (brêk-fösst) n desayuno m

bream (briim) n (pl ~) brema f

breast (brêsst) n seno m

breaststroke (brêsst-sstrouk) n braza f

breath (brêz) n aliento m; aire m

breathe (briið) v respirar

breathing (brii-ðing) n respiración f

breed (briid) n raza f; especie f

*** breed** (briid) v recriar

breeze (briis) n brisa f

brew (bruu) v fabricar cerveza

brewery (bruu-ö-ri) n cervecería f

bribe (braib) v sobornar

bribery (brai-bö-ri) n soborno m

brick (brik) n ladrillo m

bricklayer (brik-lei⁰) n albañil m

bride (braid) n novia f

bridegroom (braid-ghruum) n novio m

bridge (bridʒ) n puente m; bridge m

brief (briif) adj breve

briefcase (briif-keiss) n portafolio m

briefs (briifss) pl braga f, calzoncillos mpl

bright (brait) adj claro; reluciente; listo

brill (bril) n rodaballo m

brilliant (bril-yönt) adj brillante

brim (brim) n borde m

*** bring** (bring) v *traer; ~ **back** *devolver; ~ **up** educar; *introducir, levantar

brisk (brissk) adj vivo

Britain (bri-tön) Inglaterra f

British (bri-tiʃ) adj británico

Briton (bri-tön) n británico m; inglés m

broad (brood) adj ancho; amplio; general

broadcast (brood-kaasst) n transmisión f

*** broadcast** (brood-kaasst) v emitir

brochure (brou-ʃu⁰) n folleto m

broke¹ (brouk) v (p break)

broke² (brouk) adj arruinado

broken (brou-kön) adj (pp break) estropeado, roto

broker (*brou*-kö) *n* corredor *m*

bronchitis (brong-*kai*-tiss) *n* bronquitis *f*

bronze (brons) *n* bronce *m*; *adj* de bronce

brooch (brouch) *n* broche *m*

brook (bruk) *n* arroyo *m*

broom (bruum) *n* escoba *f*

brothel (*bro*-zöl) *n* burdel *m*

brother (*bra*-ðö) *n* hermano *m*

brother-in-law (*bra*-ðö-rin-loo) *n* (pl brothers-) cuñado *m*

brought (broot) *v* (p, pp bring)

brown (braun) *adj* moreno

bruise (bruus) *n* moretón *m*, magulladura *f*; *v* magullar

brunette (bruu-*nêt*) *n* morena *f*

brush (braʃ) *n* cepillo *m*; brocha *f*; *v* sacar brillo, cepillar

brutal (*bruu*-töl) *adj* brutal

bubble (*ba*-böl) *n* burbuja *f*

bucket (*ba*-kit) *n* balde *m*

buckle (*ba*-köl) *n* hebilla *f*

bud (bad) *n* capullo *m*

budget (*ba*-dʒit) *n* presupuesto *m*

buffet (*bu*-fei) *n* buffet *m*

bug (bagh) *n* chinche *f*; escarabajo *m*; *nAm* insecto *m*

*build (bild) *v* *construir

building (*bil*-ding) *n* edificio *m*

bulb (balb) *n* bulbo *m*; **light ~** bombilla *f*; foco *mMe*

Bulgaria (bal-*ghê*ô-ri-ö) Bulgaria *f*

Bulgarian (bal-*ghê*ô-ri-ön) *adj* búlgaro

bulk (balk) *n* bulto *m*; mayoría *f*

bulky (*bal*-ki) *adj* voluminoso

bull (bul) *n* toro *m*

bullet (*bu*-lit) *n* bala *f*

bullfight (*bul*-fait) *n* corrida de toros

bullring (*bul*-ring) *n* plaza de toros

bump (bamp) *v* topetar; chocar; *dar golpes; *n* golpe *m*, topetón *m*

bumper (*bam*-pö) *n* parachoques *m*

bumpy (*bam*-pi) *adj* lleno de baches

bun (ban) *n* bollo *m*

bunch (banch) *n* ramo *m*; grupo *m*

bundle (*ban*-döl) *n* paquete *m*; *v* atar, liar

bunk (bangk) *n* camastro *m*

buoy (boi) *n* boya *f*

burden (*böö*-dön) *n* peso *m*

bureau (*byu*ô-rou) *n* (pl ~x, ~s) escritorio *m*; *nAm* cómoda *f*

bureaucracy (byu*ô*-ro-krô-ssi) *n* burocracia *f*

burglar (*böö*-ghlö) *n* ladrón *m*

burgle (*böö*-ghöl) *v* robar

burial (*bê*-ri-öl) *n* entierro *m*

burn (böön) *n* quemadura *f*

*burn (böön) *v* quemar; pegarse

*burst (böösst) *v* *reventar; *quebrar

bury (*bê*-ri) *v* *enterrar

bus (bass) *n* autobús *m*

bush (buʃ) *n* matorral *m*

business (*bis*-nöss) *n* negocios *mpl*, comercio *m*; empresa *f*, negocio *m*; ocupación *f*; asunto *m*; **~ hours** horas hábiles, horas de oficina; **~ trip** viaje de negocios; **on ~** por asuntos de negocio

business-like (*bis*-niss-laik) *adj* práctico

businessman (*bis*-nöss-mön) *n* (pl -men) hombre de negocios

bust (basst) *n* busto *m*

bustle (*ba*-ssöl) *n* agitación *f*

busy (*bi*-si) *adj* ocupado; concurrido, atareado

but (bat) *conj* mas; pero; *prep* menos

butcher (*bu*-chö) *n* carnicero *m*

butter (*ba*-tö) *n* mantequilla *f*

butterfly (*ba*-tö-flai) *n* mariposa *f*; **~ stroke** braza de mariposa

buttock (*ba*-tök) *n* nalga *m*

button (*ba*-tön) *n* botón *m*; *v* abrochar

buttonhole (*ba*-tön-houl) *n* ojal *m*

*buy (bai) *v* comprar; *adquirir

buyer (*bai*-ö) *n* comprador *m*

by (bai) *prep* por; con; cerca de

by-pass (*bai*-paass) *n* cinturón *m*; *v* rodear

C

cab (kæb) *n* taxi *m*

cabaret (*kæ*-bö-rei) *n* cabaret *m*

cabbage (*kæ*-bidʒ) *n* col *m*

cab-driver (*kæb*-drai-vö) *n* taxista *m*

cabin (*kæ*-bin) *n* cabina *f*; cabaña *f*

cabinet (*kæ*-bi-nöt) *n* gabinete *m*

cable (*kei*-böl) *n* cable *m*; cablegrama *m*; *v* cablegrafiar

cadre (*kaa*-dö) *n* cuadro *m*

café (*kæ*-fei) *n* bar *m*

cafeteria (kæ-fö-*ti*º-ri-ö) *n* cafetería *f*

caffeine (*kæ*-fiin) *n* cafeína *f*

cage (keidʒ) *n* jaula *f*

cake (keik) *n* pastel *m*; pastelería *f*, tarta *f*, dulces

calamity (kö-*læ*-mö-ti) *n* desastre *m*, catástrofe *f*

calcium (*kæl*-ssi-öm) *n* calcio *m*

calculate (*kæl*-kyu-leit) *v* calcular

calculation (kæl-kyu-*lei*-ʃön) *n* cálculo *m*

calendar (*kæ*-lön-dö) *n* calendario *m*

calf (kaaf) *n* (pl calves) ternero *m*; pantorrilla *f*; ~ **skin** becerro *m*

call (kool) *v* llamar; *n* llamada *f*; visita *f*; *be called llamarse; ~ **names** insultar; ~ **on** visitar; ~ **up** *Am* telefonear

callus (*kæ*-löss) *n* callo *m*

calm (kaam) *adj* tranquilo; ~ **down** calmar

calorie (*kæ*-lö-ri) *n* caloría *f*

Calvinism (*kæl*-vi-ni-söm) *n* calvinismo *m*

came (keim) *v* (p come)

camel (*kæ*-möl) *n* camello *m*

cameo (*kæ*-mi-ou) *n* (pl ~s) camafeo *m*

camera (*kæ*-mö-rö) *n* cámara fotográfica; cámara *f*; ~ **shop** negocio fotográfico

camp (kæmp) *n* campamento *m*; *v* acampar

campaign (kæm-*pein*) *n* campaña *f*

camp-bed (kæmp-*bêd*) *n* catre de campaña, cama de tijera

camper (*kæm*-pö) *n* acampador *m*

camping (*kæm*-ping) *n* camping *m*; ~ **site** camping *m*, lugar de camping

camshaft (*kæm*-ʃaaft) *n* árbol de levas

can (kæn) *n* lata *f*; ~ **opener** abrelatas *m*

***can** (kæn) *v* *poder

Canada (*kæ*-nö-dö) Canadá *m*

Canadian (kö-*nei*-di-ön) *adj* canadiense

canal (kö-*næl*) *n* canal *m*

canary (kö-*nê*º-ri) *n* canario *m*

cancel (*kæn*-ssöl) *v* cancelar; anular

cancellation (kæn-ssö-*lei*-ʃön) *n* cancelación *f*

cancer (*kæn*-ssö) *n* cáncer *m*

candelabrum (kæn-dö-*laa*-bröm) *n* (pl -bra) candelabro *m*

candidate (*kæn*-di-döt) *n* candidato *m*, interesado *m*

candle (*kæn*-döl) *n* candela *f*

candy (*kæn*-di) *nAm* bombón *m*; dulces, golosinas

cane (kein) *n* caña *f*; bastón *m*

canister (*kæ*-ni-sstö) *n* caja metálica, lata *f*

canoe (kö-*nuu*) *n* canoa *f*

canteen (kæn-*tiin*) *n* cantina *f*

canvas (*kæn*-vöss) *n* lona *f*

cap (kæp) *n* gorra *f*, gorro *m*

capable (*kei*-pö-böl) *adj* capaz

capacity (kö-*pæ*-ssö-ti) *n* capacidad

f; potencia f; competencia f

cape (keip) n capa f; cabo m

capital (kæ-pi-töl) n capital f; capital m; adj importante, capital; ~ **letter** mayúscula f

capitalism (kæ-pi-tö-li-söm) n capitalismo m

capitulation (kö-pi-tyu-lei-ʃön) n capitulación f

capsule (kæp-ssyuul) n cápsula f

captain (kæp-tin) n capitán m; comandante m

capture (kæp-chö) v coger preso, capturar; conquistar; n captura f; conquista f

car (kaa) n coche m; carro mMe; ~ **hire** alquiler de coches; ~ **park** parque de estacionamiento

carafe (kö-ræf) n garrafa f

caramel (kæ-rö-möl) n caramelo m

carat (kæ-röt) n quilate m

caravan (kæ-rö-væn) n caravana f; carro de gitanos

carburettor (kaa-byu-ré-tö) n carburador m

card (kaad) n tarjeta f; tarjeta postal

cardboard (kaad-bood) n cartón m; adj de cartón

cardigan (kaa-di-ghön) n chaqueta f

cardinal (kaa-di-nöl) n cardenal m; adj cardinal, principal

care (kêᵒ) n cuidado m; ~ **about** preocuparse de; ~ **for** gustar; *take ~ **of** cuidar de

career (kö-riᵒ) n carrera f

carefree (kêᵒ-frii) adj despreocupado

careful (kêᵒ-föl) adj cuidadoso; escrupuloso

careless (kêᵒ-löss) adj indiferente, negligente

caretaker (kêᵒ-tei-kö) n guardián m

cargo (kaa-ghou) n (pl ~es) carga f

carnival (kaa-ni-völ) n carnaval m

carp (kaap) n (pl ~) carpa f

carpenter (kaa-pin-tö) n carpintero m

carpet (kaa-pit) n alfombra f

carriage (kæ-ridʒ) n vagón m; coche m, carruaje m

carriageway (kæ-ridʒ-ᵘei) n calzada f

carrot (kæ-röt) n zanahoria f

carry (kæ-ri) v llevar; *conducir; ~ **on** continuar; *proseguir; ~ **out** realizar

carry-cot (kæ-ri-kot) n cuna de viaje

cart (kaat) n carro m

cartilage (kaa-ti-lidʒ) n cartílago m

carton (kaa-tön) n caja de cartón; cartón m

cartoon (kaa-tuun) n dibujos animados

cartridge (kaa-tridʒ) n cartucho m

carve (kaav) v trinchar; entallar, tallar

carving (kaa-ving) n talla f

case (keiss) n caso m; causa f; valija f; estuche m; **attaché** ~ portafolio m; **in** ~ si; **in** ~ **of** en caso de

cash (kæʃ) n dinero contante, efectivo m; v cobrar, *hacer efectivo

cashier (kæ-fiᵒ) n cajero m; cajera f

cashmere (kæʃ-miᵒ) n casimir m

casino (kö-ssii-nou) n (pl ~s) casino m

cask (kaassk) n barril m, tonel m

cast (kaasst) n echada f

*cast (kaasst) v lanzar; **cast iron** hierro fundido

castle (kaa-ssöl) n castillo m

casual (kæ-ʒu-öl) adj informal; de paso, por casualidad

casualty (kæ-ʒu-öl-ti) n víctima f

cat (kæt) n gato m

catacomb (kæ-tö-koum) n catacumba f

catalogue (kæ-tö-logh) n catálogo m

catarrh (kö-taa) n catarro m

catastrophe (kö-tæ-sströ-fi) n catástrofe f

*catch (kæch) v coger; sorprender

category (kæ-ti-ghö-ri) n categoría f

cathedral (kö-zii-dröl) n catedral f

catholic (kæ-zö-lik) adj católico

cattle (kæ-töl) pl ganado m

caught (koot) v (p, pp catch)

cauliflower (ko-li-flau⁰) n coliflor f

cause (koos) v causar; provocar; n causa f; motivo m; ~ to *hacer

causeway (koos-ᵁei) n calzada f

caution (koo-∫ön) n cautela f; v *advertir

cautious (koo-∫öss) adj prudente

cave (keiv) n cueva f; grieta f

cavern (kæ-vön) n cueva f

caviar (kæ-vi-aa) n caviar m

cavity (kæ-vö-ti) n cavidad f

cease (ssiiss) v cesar

ceiling (ssii-ling) n cielo raso

celebrate (ssé-li-breit) v celebrar

celebration (ssé-li-brei-∫ön) n celebración f

celebrity (ssi-lê-brö-ti) n celebridad f

celery (ssé-lö-ri) n apio m

celibacy (ssé-li-bö-ssi) n celibato m

cell (ssél) n celda f

cellar (ssê-lö) n sótano m

cellophane (ssê-lö-fein) n celofán m

cement (ssi-mênt) n cemento m

cemetery (ssê-mi-tri) n cementerio m

censorship (ssên-ssö-∫ip) n censura f

centigrade (ssên-ti-ghreid) adj centígrado

centimetre (ssên-ti-mii-tö) n centímetro m

central (ssên-tröl) adj central; ~ heating calefacción central; ~ station estación central

centralize (ssên-trö-lais) v centralizar

centre (ssên-tö) n centro m

century (ssên-chö-ri) n siglo m

ceramics (ssi-ræ-mikss) pl cerámica f

ceremony (ssê-rö-mö-ni) n ceremonia f

certain (ssöö-tön) adj cierto

certificate (ssö-ti-fi-köt) n certificado m; certificación f, acta f, diploma m

chain (chein) n cadena f

chair (chê⁰) n silla f

chairman (chê⁰-mön) n (pl -men) presidente m

chalet (∫æ-lei) n chalet m

chalk (chook) n creta f

challenge (chæ-lönd3) v desafiar; n reto m

chamber (cheim-bö) n cuarto m

chambermaid (cheim-bö-meid) n doncella f

champagne (∫æm-pein) n champán m

champion (chæm-pyön) n campeón m; defensor m

chance (chaanss) n azar m; oportunidad f, ocasión f; riesgo m; suerte f; by ~ por casualidad

change (cheind3) v modificar, cambiar; mudarse; *hacer trasbordo; n modificación f, cambio m; moneda f

channel (chæ-nöl) n canal m; English Channel Canal de la Mancha

chaos (kei-oss) n caos m

chaotic (kei-o-tik) adj caótico

chap (chæp) n hombre m

chapel (chæ-pöl) n iglesia f, capilla f

chaplain (chæ-plin) n capellán m

character (kæ-rök-tö) n carácter m

characteristic (kæ-rök-tö-ri-sstik) adj típico, característico; n característica f; rasgo característico

characterize (kæ-rök-tö-rais) v caracterizar

charcoal (chaa-koul) n carbón de leña

charge (chaad3) v *pedir; cargar; acusar; n precio m; carga f; acusación f; ~ plate Am tarjeta de crédito; free of ~ gratuito; in ~ of encargado de; *take ~ of encargarse de

charity (*chæ*-rö-ti) *n* caridad *f*

charm (chaam) *n* encanto *m*; amuleto *m*

charming (*chaa*-ming) *adj* encantador

chart (chaat) *n* tabla *f*; gráfico *m*; carta marina; **conversion** ~ tabla de conversión

chase (cheiss) *v* cazar; expulsar, ahuyentar; *n* caza *f*

chasm (*kæ*-söm) *n* grieta *f*

chassis (*fæ*-ssi) *n* (pl ~) chasis *m*

chaste (cheisst) *adj* casto

chat (chæt) *v* charlar; *n* charla *f*

chatterbox (*chæ*-tö-bokss) *n* charlatán *m*

chauffeur (*fou*-fö) *n* chófer *m*

cheap (chiip) *adj* barato; económico

cheat (chiit) *v* engañar; estafar

check (chêk) *v* controlar, verificar; *n* escaque *m*; *nAm* cuenta *f*; cheque *m*; **check!** ¡jaque!; ~ **in** inscribirse; ~ **out** *despedirse

check-book (*chêk*-buk) *nAm* talonario *m*

checkerboard (*chê*-kö-bood) *nAm* tablero de ajedrez

checkroom (*chêk*-ruum) *nAm* guardarropa *m*

check-up (*chê*-kap) *n* reconocimiento *m*

cheek (chiik) *n* mejilla *f*

cheek-bone (*chiik*-boun) *n* pómulo *m*

cheer (chi⁰) *v* aclamar; ~ **up** alegrar

cheerful (*chi⁰*-föl) *adj* alegre

cheese (chiis) *n* queso *m*

chef (fêf) *n* jefe de cocina

chemical (*kê*-mi-köl) *adj* químico

chemist (*kê*-misst) *n* farmacéutico *m*; **chemist's** farmacia *f*; droguería *f*

chemistry (*kê*-mi-sstri) *n* química *f*

cheque (chêk) *n* cheque *m*

cheque-book (*chêk*-buk) *n* talonario *m*

chequered (*chê*-köd) *adj* a cuadros, cuadriculado

cherry (*chê*-ri) *n* cereza *f*

chess (chêss) *n* ajedrez *m*

chest (chêsst) *n* pecho *m*; arca *f*; ~ **of drawers** cómoda *f*

chestnut (*chêss*-nat) *n* castaña *f*

chew (chuu) *v* masticar

chewing-gum (*chuu*-ing-gham) *n* goma de mascar, chicle *m*

chicken (*chi*-kin) *n* pollo *m*

chickenpox (*chi*-kin-pokss) *n* varicela *f*

chief (chiif) *n* jefe *m*; *adj* principal

chieftain (*chiif*-tön) *n* jefe *m*

chilblain (*chil*-blein) *n* sabañón *m*

child (chaild) *n* (pl children) niño *m*

childbirth (*chaild*-bööz) *n* parto *m*

childhood (*chaild*-hud) *n* infancia *f*

Chile (*chi*-li) Chile *m*

Chilean (*chi*-li-ön) *adj* chileno

chill (chil) *n* escalofrío *m*

chilly (*chi*-li) *adj* fresco

chimes (chaims) *pl* carillón *m*

chimney (*chim*-ni) *n* chimenea *f*

chin (chin) *n* barbilla *f*

China (*chai*-nö) China *f*

china (*chai*-nö) *n* porcelana *f*

Chinese (chai-*niis*) *adj* chino

chink (chingk) *n* hendidura *f*

chip (chip) *n* astilla *f*; ficha *f*; *v* cortar, astillar; **chips** patatas fritas

chiropodist (ki-*ro*-pö-disst) *n* pedicuro *m*

chisel (*chi*-söl) *n* cincel *m*

chives (chaivs) *pl* cebollino *m*

chlorine (*kloo*-riin) *n* cloro *m*

chock-full (chok-*ful*) *adj* de bote en bote, repleto

chocolate (*cho*-klöt) *n* chocolate *m*; bombón *m*

choice (choiss) *n* elección *f*; selección *f*

choir (kᵘai⁰) *n* coro *m*

choke (chouk) v sofocarse; estrangular; n starter m

* choose (chuus) v escoger

chop (chop) n chuleta f; v tajar

Christ (kraisst) Cristo

christen (kri-ssön) v bautizar

christening (kri-ssö-ning) n bautizo m

Christian (kriss-chön) adj cristiano; ~ **name** nombre de pila

Christmas (kriss-möss) Navidad f

chromium (krou-mi-öm) n cromo m

chronic (kro-nik) adj crónico

chronological (kro-nö-lo-dʒi-köl) adj cronológico

chuckle (cha-köl) v *reírse entre dientes

chunk (changk) n trozo m

church (chööch) n iglesia f

churchyard (chööch-yaad) n cementerio m

cigar (ssi-ghaa) n puro m; ~ **shop** estanco m

cigarette (ssi-ghö-rêt) n cigarrillo m; ~ **tobacco** picadura f

cigarette-case (ssi-ghö-rêt-keiss) n pitillera f

cigarette-holder (ssi-ghö-rêt-houl-dö) n boquilla f

cigarette-lighter (ssi-ghö-rêt-lai-tö) n encendedor m

cinema (ssi-nö-mö) n cinematógrafo m

cinnamon (ssi-nö-mön) n canela f

circle (ssöö-köl) n círculo m; balcón m; v rodear, circundar

circulation (ssöö-kyu-lei-ʃön) n circulación f; circulación de la sangre

circumstance (ssöö-köm-sstænss) n circunstancia f

circus (ssöö-köss) n circo m

citizen (ssi-ti-sön) n ciudadano m

citizenship (ssi-ti-sön-ʃip) n ciudadanía f

city (ssi-ti) n ciudad f

civic (ssi-vik) adj cívico

civil (ssi-völ) adj civil; cortés; ~ **law** derecho civil; ~ **servant** funcionario m

civilian (ssi-vil-yön) adj civil; n paisano m

civilization (ssi-vö-lai-sei-ʃön) n civilización f

civilized (ssi-vö-laisd) adj civilizado

claim (kleim) v reivindicar, reclamar; afirmar; n reivindicación f, pretensión f

clamp (klæmp) n mordaza f; grapa f

clap (klæp) v aplaudir

clarify (klæ-ri-fai) v aclarar, clarificar

class (klaass) n clase f

classical (klæ-ssi-köl) adj clásico

classify (klæ-ssi-fai) v clasificar

class-mate (klaass-meit) n compañero de clase

classroom (klaass-ruum) n clase f

clause (kloos) n cláusula f

claw (kloo) n garra f

clay (klei) n arcilla f

clean (kliin) adj puro, limpio; v limpiar

cleaning (klii-ning) n limpieza f; ~ **fluid** quitamanchas m

clear (kliö) adj claro; v limpiar

clearing (kliö-ring) n claro m

cleft (klêft) n grieta f

clergyman (klöö-dʒi-mön) n (pl -men) pastor m; clérigo m

clerk (klaak) n empleado de oficina, oficinista m; escribano m; secretario m

clever (klê-vö) adj inteligente; astuto, listo

client (klai-önt) n cliente m

cliff (klif) n acantilado m, farallón m

climate (klai-mit) n clima m

climb (klaim) v trepar; n subida f

clinic (kli-nik) n clínica f

cloak (klouk) n capa f

cloakroom (*klouk*-ruum) *n* guardarropa *m*

clock (klok) *n* reloj *m*; **at ... o'clock** a las ...

cloister (*kloi*-sstö) *n* convento *m*

close¹ (klous) *v* *cerrar

close² (klouss) *adj* cercano

closet (*klo*-sit) *n* armario *m*

cloth (kloz) *n* tela *f*; paño *m*

clothes (klouðs) *pl* ropa *f*, vestidos *mpl*

clothes-brush (*klouðs*-braf) *n* cepillo de la ropa

clothing (*klou*-ðing) *n* vestido *m*

cloud (klaud) *n* nube *f*

cloud-burst (*klaud*-böösst) *n* chaparrón *m*

cloudy (*klau*-di) *adj* cubierto, nublado

clover (*klou*-vö) *n* trébol *m*

clown (klaun) *n* payaso *m*

club (klab) *n* club *m*; círculo *m*, asociación *f*; porra *f*, garrote *m*

clumsy (*klam*-si) *adj* torpe

clutch (klach) *n* embrague *m*; apretón *m*

coach (kouch) *n* autobús *m*; vagón *m*; carroza *f*; entrenador *m*

coachwork (*kouch*-ᵁöök) *n* carrocería *f*

coagulate (kou-æ-ghyu-leit) *v* coagularse

coal (koul) *n* carbón *m*

coarse (kooss) *adj* burdo; grosero

coast (kousst) *n* costa *f*

coat (kout) *n* sobretodo *m*, abrigo *m*

coat-hanger (*kout*-hæng-ö) *n* percha *f*

cobweb (*kob*-ᵁêb) *n* tela de araña

cocaine (kou-*kein*) *n* cocaína *f*

cock (kok) *n* gallo *m*

cocktail (*kok*-teil) *n* cóctel *m*

coconut (*kou*-kö-nat) *n* coco *m*

cod (kod) *n* (pl ~) bacalao *m*

code (koud) *n* código *m*

coffee (*ko*-fi) *n* café *m*

cognac (*ko*-nyæk) *n* coñac *m*

coherence (kou-*hi*ᵒ-rönss) *n* coherencia *f*

coin (koin) *n* moneda *f*

coincide (kou-in-*ssaid*) *v* coincidir

cold (kould) *adj* frío; *n* frío *m*; resfriado *m*; **catch a ~** resfriarse

collapse (kö-*læpss*) *v* desplomarse, derrumbarse

collar (*ko*-lö) *n* collar *m*; cuello *m*; **~ stud** botón del cuello

collarbone (*ko*-lö-boun) *n* clavícula *f*

colleague (*ko*-liigh) *n* colega *m*

collect (kö-*lêkt*) *v* juntar; recoger; *hacer una colecta

collection (kö-*lêk*-fön) *n* colección *f*; recogida *f*

collective (kö-*lêk*-tiv) *adj* colectivo

collector (kö-*lêk*-tö) *n* coleccionista *m*; colector *m*

college (*ko*-lidʒ) *n* colegio *m*

collide (kö-*laid*) *v* chocar

collision (kö-*li*-ʒön) *n* colisión *f*

Colombia (kö-*lom*-bi-ö) Colombia *f*

Colombian (kö-*lom*-bi-ön) *adj* colombiano

colonel (*köö*-nöl) *n* coronel *m*

colony (*ko*-lö-ni) *n* colonia *f*

colour (*ka*-lö) *n* color *m*; *v* colorear; **~ film** película en colores

colourant (*ka*-lö-rönt) *n* colorante *m*

colour-blind (*ka*-lö-blaind) *adj* daltoniano

coloured (*ka*-löd) *adj* de color

colourful (*ka*-lö-föl) *adj* colorado, lleno de color

column (*ko*-löm) *n* columna *f*

coma (*kou*-mö) *n* coma *m*

comb (koum) *v* peinar; *n* peine *m*

combat (*kom*-bæt) *n* lucha *f*, combate *m*; *v* combatir

combination (kom-bi-*nei*-fön) *n* combinación *f*

combine (köm-*bain*) *v* combinar; unir

*come (kam) v *venir; ~ **across** *encontrar; hallar

comedian (kö-*mii*-di-ön) n comediante m; cómico m

comedy (*ko*-mö-di) n comedia f; **musical** ~ comedia musical

comfort (kam-föt) n comodidad f, confort m; consuelo m; v *consolar

comfortable (kam-fö-tö-böl) adj confortable

comic (*ko*-mik) adj cómico

comics (*ko*-mikss) pl tebeo m

coming (*ka*-ming) n llegada f

comma (*ko*-mö) n coma f

command (kö-*maand*) v mandar; n orden f

commander (kö-*maan*-dö) n comandante m

commemoration (kö-mê-mö-*rei*-ſön) n conmemoración f

commence (kö-*mênss*) v *comenzar

comment (*ko*-mênt) n comentario m; v comentar

commerce (*ko*-mööss) n comercio m

commercial (kö-*möö*-ſöl) adj comercial; n anuncio publicitario; ~ **law** derecho comercial

commission (kö-*mi*-ſön) n comisión f

commit (kö-*mit*) v confiar, entregar; cometer

committee (kö-*mi*-ti) n comisión f, comité m

common (*ko*-mön) adj común; usual; ordinario

commune (*ko*-myuun) n comuna f

communicate (kö-*myuu*-ni-keit) v comunicar

communication (kö-myuu-ni-*kei*-ſön) n comunicación f

communiqué (kö-*myuu*-ni-kei) n comunicado m

communism (*ko*-myu-ni-söm) n comunismo m

communist (*ko*-myu-nisst) n comunista m

community (kö-*myuu*-nö-ti) n sociedad f, vecindario m

commuter (kö-*myuu*-tö) n suburbano m

compact (kom-pækt) adj compacto

companion (köm-*pæ*-nyön) n compañero m

company (kam-pö-ni) n compañía f; sociedad f

comparative (köm-*pæ*-rö-tiv) adj relativo

compare (köm-*pê*ᵒ) v comparar

comparison (köm-*pæ*-ri-ssön) n comparación f

compartment (köm-*paat*-mönt) n compartimento m

compass (kam-pöss) n brújula f

compel (köm-*pêl*) v compeler

compensate (kom-pön-sseit) v compensar

compensation (kom-pön-*ssei*-ſön) n compensación f; indemnización f

compete (köm-*piit*) v *competir

competition (kom-pö-*ti*-ſön) n concurso m; competencia f

competitor (köm-*pê*-ti-tör) n competidor m

compile (köm-*pail*) v compilar

complain (köm-*plein*) v quejarse

complaint (köm-*pleint*) n queja f; **complaints book** libro de reclamaciones

complete (köm-*pliit*) adj completo; v completar

completely (köm-*pliit*-li) adv enteramente, totalmente, completamente

complex (kom-plêkss) n complejo m; adj complejo

complexion (köm-*plêk*-ſön) n tez f

complicated (kom-pli-kei-tid) adj complicado

compliment (kom-pli-mönt) n cumplimiento m; v cumplimentar

compose (köm-*pous*) v *componer

composer (köm-*pou*-sö) n compositor m

composition (kom-pö-*si*-ʃön) n composición f

comprehensive (kom-pri-*hên*-ssiv) adj extenso

comprise (köm-*prais*) v comprender

compromise (*kom*-prö-mais) n compromiso m

compulsory (köm-*pal*-ssö-ri) adj obligatorio

comrade (*kom*-reid) n camarada m

conceal (kön-*ssiil*) v disimular

conceited (kön-*ssii*-tid) adj presuntuoso

conceive (kön-*ssiiv*) v *concebir, *entender; imaginar

concentrate (*kon*-ssön-treit) v concentrarse

concentration (kon-ssön-*trei*-ʃön) n concentración f

conception (kön-*ssêp*-ʃön) n entendimiento m; concepción f

concern (kön-*ssöön*) v *concernir, atañer; n preocupación f; asunto m; empresa f, consorcio m

concerned (kön-*ssöönd*) adj preocupado; interesado

concerning (kön-*ssöö*-ning) prep en lo que se refiere a, concerniente a

concert (*kon*-ssöt) n concierto m; ~ **hall** sala de conciertos

concession (kön-*ssê*-ʃön) n concesión f

concierge (kong-ssi-ê⁰ʒ) n conserje m

concise (kön-*ssaiss*) adj conciso

conclusion (köng-*kluu*-ʒön) n conclusión f

concrete (*kong*-kriit) adj concreto; n hormigón m

concurrence (köng-*ka*-rönss) n coincidencia f

concussion (köng-*ka*-ʃön) n conmoción cerebral

condition (kön-*di*-ʃön) n condición f; estado m; circunstancia f

conditional (kön-*di*-ʃö-nöl) adj condicional

conduct[1] (*kon*-dakt) n conducta f

conduct[2] (kön-*dakt*) v *conducir; acompañar

conductor (kön-*dak*-tö) n cobrador m; director m; conductor mMe

confectioner (kön-*fêk*-ʃö-nö) n confitero m

conference (*kon*-fö-rönss) n conferencia f

confess (kön-*fêss*) v *reconocer; *confesarse; profesar

confession (kön-*fê*-ʃön) n confesión f

confidence (*kon*-fi-dönss) n confianza f

confident (*kon*-fi-dönt) adj lleno de confianza

confidential (kon-fi-*dên*-ʃöl) adj confidencial

confirm (kön-*fööm*) v confirmar

confirmation (kon-fö-*mei*-ʃön) n confirmación f

confiscate (*kon*-fi-sskeit) v embargar, confiscar

conflict (*kon*-flikt) n conflicto m

confuse (kön-*fyuus*) v confundir; **confused** adj confuso

confusion (kön-*fyuu*-ʒön) n confusión f

congratulate (köng-*ghræ*-chu-leit) v felicitar

congratulation (köng-ghræ-chu-*lei*-ʃön) n felicitación f

congregation (kong-ghri-*ghei*-ʃön) n comunidad f, congregación f

congress (*kong*-ghrêss) n congreso m

connect (kö-*nêkt*) v conectar

connection (kö-*nêk*-ʃön) n relación f; conexión f; enlace m connoisseur (ko-nö-*ssöö*) n perito m

connotation (ko-nö-*tei*-[ön) n connotación f

conquer (*kong*-kö) v conquistar; vencer

conqueror (*kong*-kö-rö) n conquistador m

conquest (*kong*-k^{u}ĕsst) n conquista f

conscience (*kon*-[önss) n conciencia f

conscious (*kon*-[öss) adj consciente

consciousness (*kon*-[öss-nöss) n conciencia f

conscript (*kon*-sskript) n quinto m

consent (kön-*ssĕnt*) v *consentir; n consentimiento m

consequence (*kon*-ssi-k^{u}önss) n consecuencia f

consequently (*kon*-ssi-k^{u}önt-li) adv por consiguiente

conservative (kön-*ssöö*-vö-tiv) adj conservador

consider (kön-*ssi*-dö) v considerar; opinar

considerable (kön-*ssi*-dö-rö-böl) adj considerable; importante, notable

considerate (kön-*ssi*-dö-röt) adj considerado

consideration (kön-ssi-dö-*rei*-[ön) n consideración f; atención f

considering (kön-*ssi*-dö-ring) prep considerando

consignment (kön-*ssain*-mönt) n envío m

consist of (kön-*ssisst*) constar de

conspire (kön-*sspai*^{ö}) v conspirar

constant (*kon*-sstönt) adj constante

constipated (*kon*-ssti-pei-tid) adj estreñido

constipation (kon-ssti-*pei*-[ön) n estreñimiento m

constituency (kön-*ssti*-chu-ön-ssi) n distrito electoral

constitution (kon-ssti-*tyuu*-[ön) n constitución f

construct (kön-*sstrakt*) v *construir; edificar

construction (kön-*sstrak*-[ön) n construcción f; edificio m

consul (*kon*-ssöl) n cónsul m

consulate (*kon*-ssyu-löt) n consulado m

consult (kön-*ssalt*) v consultar

consultation (kön-ssöl-*tei*-[ön) n consulta f; ~ hours n horas de consulta

consumer (kön-*ssyuu*-mö) n consumidor m

contact (*kon*-tækt) n contacto m; v *ponerse en contacto con; ~ lenses lentillas fpl

contagious (kön-*tei*-dʒöss) adj contagioso

contain (kön-*tein*) v *contener; comprender

container (kön-*tei*-nö) n receptáculo m; contenedor m

contemporary (kön-*têm*-pö-rö-ri) adj contemporáneo; de entonces; n contemporáneo m

contempt (kön-*têmpt*) n desprecio m, menosprecio m

content (kön-*tênt*) adj contento

contents (*kon*-têntss) pl contenido m

contest (*kon*-tĕsst) n lucha f; concurso m

continent (*kon*-ti-nönt) n continente m

continental (kon-ti-*nĕn*-töl) adj continental

continual (kön-*ti*-nyu-öl) adj continuo

continue (kön-*ti*-nyuu) v continuar; *proseguir, durar

continuous (kön-*ti*-nyu-öss) adj continuo, ininterrumpido

contour (*kon*-tu^ö) n contorno m

contraceptive (kon-trö-*ssĕp*-tiv) n anticonceptivo m

contract[1] (*kon*-trækt) n contrato m

contract² (kön-*trækt*) *v* atrapar

contractor (kön-*træk*-tö) *n* contratista *m*

contradict (kon-trö-*dikt*) *v* *contradecir

contradictory (kon-trö-*dik*-tö-ri) *adj* contradictorio

contrary (*kon*-trö-ri) *n* contrario *m*; *adj* contrario; **on the ~** al contrario

contrast (*kon*-traasst) *n* contraste *m*; diferencia *f*

contribution (kon-tri-*byuu*-fön) *n* contribución *f*

control (kön-*troul*) *n* control *m*; *v* controlar

controversial (kon-trö-*vöö*-föl) *adj* controvertido, controvertible

convenience (kön-*vii*-nyönss) *n* comodidad *f*

convenient (kön-*vii*-nyönt) *adj* cómodo; adecuado, conveniente

convent (*kon*-vönt) *n* convento *m*

conversation (kon-vö-*ssei*-fön) *n* conversación *f*

convert (kön-*vööt*) *v* *convertir

convict¹ (kön-*vikt*) *v* convencer

convict² (*kon*-vikt) *n* condenado *m*

conviction (kön-*vik*-fön) *n* convencimiento *m*; condena *f*

convince (kön-*vinss*) *v* convencer

convulsion (kön-*val*-fön) *n* convulsión *f*

cook (kuk) *n* cocinero *m*; *v* cocinar; guisar, preparar

cooker (*ku*-kö) *n* cocina *f*; **gas ~** cocina de gas

cookery-book (*ku*-kö-ri-buk) *n* libro de cocina

cookie (*ku*-ki) *nAm* bizcocho *m*

cool (kuul) *adj* fresco; **cooling system** sistema de refrigeración

co-operation (kou-o-pö-*rei*-fön) *n* cooperación *f*; colaboración *f*

co-operative (kou-*o*-pö-rö-tiv) *adj*

cooperativo; cooperador; *n* cooperativa *f*

co-ordinate (kou-*oo*-di-neit) *v* coordinar

co-ordination (kou-oo-di-*nei*-fön) *n* coordinación *f*

copper (*ko*-pö) *n* cobre *m*

copy (*ko*-pi) *n* copia *f*; ejemplar *m*; *v* copiar; imitar; **carbon ~** copia *f*

coral (*ko*-röl) *n* coral *m*

cord (kood) *n* cuerda *f*; cordón *m*

cordial (*koo*-di-öl) *adj* cordial

corduroy (*koo*-dö-roi) *n* pana *f*

core (koo) *n* núcleo *m*; corazón *m*

cork (kook) *n* corcho *m*; tapón *m*

corkscrew (*kook*-sskruu) *n* sacacorchos *mpl*

corn (koon) *n* grano *m*; cereales *mpl*, trigo *m*; callo *m*; **~ on the cob** maíz en la mazorca

corner (*koo*-nö) *n* esquina *f*

cornfield (*koon*-fiild) *n* trigal *m*

corpse (koopss) *n* cadáver *m*

corpulent (*koo*-pyu-lönt) *adj* corpulento; grueso, obeso

correct (kö-*rêkt*) *adj* correcto, justo; *v* *corregir

correction (kö-*rêk*-fön) *n* corrección *f*; rectificación *f*

correctness (kö-*rêkt*-nöss) *n* exactitud *f*

correspond (ko-ri-*sspond*) *v* corresponderse; corresponder

correspondence (ko-ri-*sspon*-dönss) *n* correspondencia *f*

correspondent (ko-ri-*sspon*-dönt) *n* corresponsal *m*

corridor (*ko*-ri-doo) *n* pasillo *m*

corrupt (kö-*rapt*) *adj* corrupto; *v* corromper

corruption (kö-*rap*-fön) *n* corrupción *f*

corset (*koo*-ssit) *n* corsé *m*

cosmetics (kos-*mê*-tikss) *pl* productos

cosméticos, cosméticos *mpl*

cost (kosst) *n* coste *m*; precio *m*

* **cost** (kosst) *v* *costar

cosy (kou-si) *adj* íntimo, confortable

cot (kot) *nAm* cama de tijera

cottage (ko-tidʒ) *n* casa de campo

cotton (ko-tön) *n* algodón *m*; de algodón

cotton-wool (ko-tön-ᵘul) *n* algodón *m*

couch (kauch) *n* diván *m*

cough (kof) *n* tos *f*; *v* toser

could (kud) *v* (p can)

council (kaun-ssöl) *n* consejo *m*

councillor (kaun-ssö-lö) *n* consejero *m*

counsel (kaun-ssöl) *n* consejo *m*

counsellor (kaun-ssö-lö) *n* consejero *m*

count (kaunt) *v* *contar; adicionar; *incluir; considerar; *n* conde *m*

counter (kaun-tö) *n* mostrador *m*; barra *f*

counterfeit (kaun-tö-fiit) *v* falsificar

counterfoil (kaun-tö-foil) *n* talón *m*

counterpane (kaun-tö-pein) *n* colcha *f*

countess (kaun-tiss) *n* condesa *f*

country (kan-tri) *n* país *m*; campo *m*; región *f*; ~ **house** quinta *f*

countryman (kan-tri-mön) *n* (pl -men) compatriota *m*

countryside (kan-tri-ssaid) *n* campo *m*

county (kaun-ti) *n* condado *m*

couple (ka-pöl) *n* pareja *f*

coupon (kuu-pon) *n* cupón *m*

courage (ka-ridʒ) *n* valor *m*

courageous (kö-rei-dʒöss) *adj* valiente

course (kooss) *n* rumbo *m*; plato *m*; curso *m*; **intensive** ~ curso intensivo; **of** ~ por supuesto

court (koot) *n* tribunal *m*; corte *f*

courteous (köö-ti-öss) *adj* cortés

cousin (ka-sön) *n* prima *f*, primo *m*

cover (ka-vö) *v* cubrir; *n* refugio *m*;

tapa *f*; cubierta *f*; ~ **charge** precio del cubierto

cow (kau) *n* vaca *f*

coward (kau-öd) *n* cobarde *m*

cowardly (kau-öd-li) *adj* cobarde

cow-hide (kau-haid) *n* cuero vacuno

crab (kræb) *n* cangrejo *m*

crack (kræk) *n* crujido *m*; hendidura *f*; *v* crujir; *quebrar, *reventar

cradle (krei-döl) *n* cuna *f*

cramp (kræmp) *n* calambre *m*

crane (krein) *n* grúa *f*

crankcase (krængk-keiss) *n* cárter *m*

crankshaft (krængk-ʃaaft) *n* cigüeñal *m*

crash (kræʃ) *n* choque *m*; *v* chocar; precipitarse; ~ **barrier** barrera de protección

crate (kreit) *n* caja *f*

crater (krei-tö) *n* cráter *m*

crawl (krool) *v* arrastrarse; *n* crawl *m*

craze (kreis) *n* manía *f*

crazy (krei-si) *adj* loco

creak (kriik) *v* crujir

cream (kriim) *n* crema *f*; nata *f*; *adj* de color crema

creamy (krii-mi) *adj* cremoso

crease (kriiss) *v* *plegar; *n* raya *f*; pliegue *m*

create (kri-eit) *v* crear

creature (krii-chö) *n* criatura *f*; ser *m*

credible (krê-di-böl) *adj* verosímil

credit (krê-dit) *n* crédito *m*; *v* acreditar; ~ **card** tarjeta de crédito

creditor (krê-di-tö) *n* acreedor *m*

credulous (krê-dyu-löss) *adj* crédulo

creek (kriik) *n* ensenada *f*

* **creep** (kriip) *v* gatear

creepy (krii-pi) *adj* lúgubre, espeluznante

cremate (kri-meit) *v* incinerar

cremation (kri-mei-ʃön) *n* incineración *f*

crew (kruu) *n* equipo *m*

cricket (*kri*-kit) *n* cricquet *m*; grillo *m*

crime (kraim) *n* crimen *m*

criminal (*kri*-mi-nöl) *n* delincuente *m*, criminal *m*; *adj* criminal; ~ **law** derecho penal

criminality (kri-mi-*næ*-lö-ti) *n* criminalidad *f*

crimson (*krim*-sön) *adj* carmesí

crippled (*kri*-pöld) *adj* estropeado

crisis (*krai*-ssiss) *n* (pl crises) crisis *f*

crisp (krissp) *adj* crujiente, quebradizo

critic (*kri*-tik) *n* crítico *m*

critical (*kri*-ti-köl) *adj* crítico; precario

criticism (*kri*-ti-ssi-söm) *n* crítica *f*

criticize (*kri*-ti-ssais) *v* criticar

crochet (krou-*fei*) *v* *hacer croché

crockery (*kro*-kö-ri) *n* cerámica *f*, loza *f*

crocodile (*kro*-kö-dail) *n* cocodrilo *m*

crooked (*kru*-kid) *adj* torcido, curvo; deshonesto

crop (krop) *n* cosecha *f*

cross (kross) *v* *atravesar; *adj* enojado, enfadado; *n* cruz *f*

cross-eyed (*kross*-aid) *adj* bizco

crossing (*kro*-ssing) *n* travesía *f*; encrucijada *f*; paso *m*; paso a nivel

crossroads (*kross*-rouds) *n* cruce *m*

crosswalk (*kross*-ᵘook) *nAm* cruce para peatones

crow (krou) *n* corneja *f*

crowbar (*krou*-baa) *n* pie de cabra

crowd (kraud) *n* masa *f*, muchedumbre *f*

crowded (*krau*-did) *adj* animado; repleto

crown (kraun) *n* corona *f*; *v* coronar

crucifix (*kruu*-ssi-fikss) *n* crucifijo *m*

crucifixion (kruu-ssi-*fik*-fön) *n* crucifixión *f*

crucify (*kruu*-ssi-fai) *v* crucificar

cruel (kru-öl) *adj* cruel

cruise (kruus) *n* crucero *m*

crumb (kram) *n* migaja *f*

crusade (kruu-*sseid*) *n* cruzada *f*

crust (krasst) *n* corteza *f*

crutch (krach) *n* muleta *f*

cry (krai) *v* llorar; gritar; llamar; *n* grito *m*; voz *f*

crystal (*kri*-sstöl) *n* cristal *m*; *adj* de cristal

Cuba (*kyuu*-bö) Cuba *f*

Cuban (*kyuu*-bön) *adj* cubano

cube (kyuub) *n* cubo *m*

cuckoo (*ku*-kuu) *n* cuclillo *m*

cucumber (*kyuu*-köm-bö) *n* pepino *m*

cuddle (*ka*-döl) *v* acariciar

cudgel (*ka*-dʒöl) *n* garrote *m*

cuff (kaf) *n* puño *m*

cuff-links (*kaf*-lingkss) *pl* gemelos *mpl*; mancuernillas *fplMe*

cul-de-sac (*kal*-dö-ssæk) *n* callejón sin salida

cultivate (*kal*-ti-veit) *v* cultivar

culture (*kal*-chö) *n* cultura *f*

cultured (*kal*-chöd) *adj* culto

cunning (*ka*-ning) *adj* astuto

cup (kap) *n* taza *f*; copa *f*

cupboard (*ka*-böd) *n* armario *m*

curb (kööb) *n* bordillo *m*; *v* refrenar

cure (kyu ͦ) *v* curar; *n* cura *f*; curación *f*

curio (*kyu* ͦ-ri-ou) *n* (pl ~s) curiosidad *f*

curiosity (kyu ͦ-ri-*o*-ssö-ti) *n* curiosidad *f*

curious (*kyu* ͦ-ri-öss) *adj* curioso

curl (kööl) *v* rizar; *n* rizo *m*

curler (*köö*-lö) *n* rulo *m*

curling-tongs (*köö*-ling-tongs) *pl* rizador *m*

curly (*köö*-li) *adj* crespo; chino *adjMe*

currant (*ka*-rönt) *n* pasa de Corinto; grosella *f*

currency (*ka*-rön-ssi) *n* moneda *f*; **foreign** ~ moneda extranjera

current (*ka*-rönt) *n* corriente *f*; *adj* corriente; **alternating** ~ corriente alterna; **direct** ~ corriente continua

curry (*ka*-ri) *n* cari *m*

curse (kööss) *v* *maldecir; *n* maldición *f*

curtain (*köö*-tön) *n* cortina *f*; telón *m*

curve (kööv) *n* curva *f*

curved (köövd) *adj* curvado, encorvado

cushion (*ku*-fön) *n* almohadón *m*

custodian (ka-*sstou*-di-ön) *n* guarda *m*

custody (*ka*-sstö-di) *n* detención *f*; custodia *f*; tutela *f*

custom (*ka*-stöm) *n* costumbre *f*

customary (*ka*-sstö-mö-ri) *adj* usual, corriente, acostumbrado

customer (*ka*-sstö-mö) *n* cliente *m*

Customs (*ka*-sstöms) *pl* aduana *f*; ~ **duty** impuesto *m*; ~ **officer** oficial de aduanas

cut (kat) *n* incisión *f*; cortadura *f*

***cut** (kat) *v* cortar; *reducir; ~ **off** cortar

cutlery (*kat*-lö-ri) *n* cubiertos *mpl*

cutlet (*kat*-löt) *n* chuleta *f*

cycle (*ssai*-köl) *n* biciclo *m*; bicicleta *f*; ciclo *m*

cyclist (*ssai*-klisst) *n* ciclista *m*

cylinder (*ssi*-lin-dö) *n* cilindro *m*; ~ **head** culata del cilindro

cystitis (ssi-*sstai*-tiss) *n* cistitis *f*

Czech (chêk) *adj* checo

Czechoslovakia (chê-kö-sslö-*vaa*-ki-ö) Checoslovaquia *f*

D

dad (dæd) *n* papá *m*

daddy (*dæ*-di) *n* papaíto *m*

daffodil (*dæ*-fö-dil) *n* narciso *m*

daily (*dei*-li) *adj* diario; *n* diario *m*

dairy (*dê*ᵒ-ri) *n* lechería *f*

dam (dæm) *n* presa *f*; dique *m*

damage (*dæ*-midʒ) *n* perjuicio *m*; *v* dañar

damp (dæmp) *adj* húmedo; mojado; *n* humedad *f*; *v* *humedecer

dance (daanss) *v* bailar; *n* baile *m*

dandelion (*dæn*-di-lai-ön) *n* diente de león

dandruff (*dæn*-dröf) *n* caspa *f*

Dane (dein) *n* danés *m*

danger (*dein*-dʒö) *n* peligro *m*

dangerous (*dein*-dʒö-röss) *adj* peligroso

Danish (*dei*-nif) *adj* danés

dare (dêᵒ) *v* atreverse, osar; desafiar

daring (*dê*ᵒ-ring) *adj* atrevido

dark (daak) *adj* oscuro, obscuro; *n* oscuridad *f*

darling (*daa*-ling) *n* amor *m*, querido *m*

darn (daan) *v* zurcir

dash (dæf) *v* correr; *n* guión *m*

dashboard (*dæf*-bood) *n* tablero de instrumentos

data (*dei*-tö) *pl* dato *m*

date¹ (deit) *n* fecha *f*; cita *f*; *v* datar; **out of** ~ anticuado

date² (deit) *n* dátil *m*

daughter (*doo*-tö) *n* hija *f*

dawn (doon) *n* alba *f*; aurora *f*

day (dei) *n* día *m*; **by** ~ de día; ~ **trip** jornada *f*; **per** ~ a diario; **the** ~ **before yesterday** anteayer

daybreak (*dei*-breik) *n* amanecer *m*

daylight (*dei*-lait) *n* luz del día

dead (dêd) *adj* muerto; difunto

deaf (dêf) *adj* sordo

deal (diil) *n* transacción *f*

***deal** (diil) *v* repartir; ~ **with** *v* tratar con; *hacer negocios con

dealer (*dii*-lö) *n* negociante *m*, comerciante *m*

dear (diᵒ) *adj* querido; caro; amado

death (dêz) *n* muerte *f*; ~ **penalty** pena de muerte

debate (di-*beit*) *n* debate *m*

debit (*dé*-bit) *n* debe *m*

debt (dêt) *n* deuda *f*

decaffeinated (dii-kæ-fi-nei-tid) *adj* descafeinado

deceit (di-*ssiit*) *n* engaño *m*

deceive (di-*ssiiv*) *v* engañar

December (di-*ssêm*-bö) diciembre

decency (*dii*-ssön-ssi) *n* decencia *f*

decent (*dii*-ssönt) *adj* decente

decide (di-*ssaid*) *v* decidir

decision (di-*ssi*-ʒön) *n* decisión *f*

deck (dêk) *n* cubierta *f*; ~ **cabin** camarote en cubierta; ~ **chair** silla de tijera

declaration (dê-klö-*rei*-ʃön) *n* declaración *f*

declare (di-*klêö*) *v* declarar; indicar

decoration (dê-kö-*rei*-ʃön) *n* decoración *f*

decrease (dii-*kriss*) *v* *reducir; *disminuir; *n* disminución *f*

dedicate (*dé*-di-keit) *v* dedicar

deduce (di-*dyuuss*) *v* *deducir

deduct (di-*dakt*) *v* *deducir

deed (diid) *n* acción *f*, acto *m*

deep (diip) *adj* hondo

deep-freeze (diip-*friis*) *n* congelador *m*

deer (diö) *n* (pl ~) ciervo *m*

defeat (di-*fiit*) *v* derrotar; *n* derrota *f*

defective (di-*fêk*-tiv) *adj* defectuoso

defence (di-*fênss*) *n* defensa *f*

defend (di-*fênd*) *v* *defender

deficiency (di-*fi*-ʃön-ssi) *n* deficiencia *f*

deficit (*dé*-fi-ssit) *n* déficit *m*

define (di-*fain*) *v* definir, determinar

definite (*dé*-fi-nit) *adj* determinado; definido

definition (dê-fi-*ni*-ʃön) *n* definición *f*

deformed (di-*foomd*) *adj* contrahecho, deforme

degree (di-*ghrii*) *n* grado *m*; título *m*

delay (di-*lei*) *v* retardar; *diferir; *n* retraso *m*, tardanza *f*; dilación *f*

delegate (*dé*-li-ghöt) *n* delegado *m*

delegation (dê-li-*ghei*-ʃön) *n* delegación *f*

deliberate[1] (di-*li*-bö-reit) *v* discutir, deliberar

deliberate[2] (di-*li*-bö-röt) *adj* deliberado

deliberation (di-li-bö-*rei*-ʃön) *n* deliberación *f*

delicacy (*dé*-li-kö-ssi) *n* golosina *f*

delicate (*dé*-li-köt) *adj* delicado; fino

delicatessen (dê-li-kö-*tê*-ssön) *n* gollerías *fpl*; tienda de comestibles finos

delicious (di-*li*-ʃöss) *adj* exquisito, delicioso

delight (di-*lait*) *n* delicia *f*, deleite *m*; *v* encantar

delightful (di-*lait*-föl) *adj* delicioso, deleitoso

deliver (di-*li*-vö) *v* entregar; librar

delivery (di-*li*-vö-ri) *n* entrega *f*, reparto *m*; parto *m*; liberación *f*; ~ **van** furgoneta *f*

demand (di-*maand*) *v* *requerir, exigir; *n* exigencia *f*; demanda *f*

democracy (di-*mo*-krö-ssi) *n* democracia *f*

democratic (dê-mö-*kræ*-tik) *adj* democrático

demolish (di-*mo*-liʃ) *v* *demoler

demolition (dê-mö-*li*-ʃön) *n* demolición *f*

demonstrate (*dê*-mön-sstreit) *v* *demostrar; *hacer una manifestación

demonstration (dê-mön-*sstrei*-ʃön) *n* manifestación *f*; demostración *f*

den (dên) *n* madriguera *f*

Denmark (*dên*-maak) Dinamarca *f*

denomination (di-no-mi-*nei*-ʃön) *n* nominación *f*

dense (dênss) *adj* denso

dent (dênt) *n* abolladura *f*

dentist (dên-tisst) *n* dentista *m*

denture (dên-chö) *n* dentadura postiza

deny (di-*nai*) *v* *negar; *denegar

deodorant (dii-*ou*-dö-rönt) *n* desodorante *m*

depart (di-*paat*) *v* partir; *fallecer

department (di-*paat*-mönt) *n* departamento *m*; ~ **store** grandes almacenes

departure (di-*paa*-chö) *n* despedida *f*, partida *f*

dependant (di-*pên*-dönt) *adj* dependiente

depend on (di-*pênd*) depender de

deposit (di-*po*-sit) *n* depósito *m*; fianza *f*; capa *f*, yacimiento *m*; *v* ingresar

depository (di-*po*-si-tö-ri) *n* almacén *m*

depot (*dê*-pou) *n* almacén *m*; *nAm* estación *f*

depress (di-*prêss*) *v* deprimir

depression (di-*prê*-fön) *n* desánimo *m*; depresión *f*

deprive of (di-*praiv*) privar de

depth (dêpz) *n* profundidad *f*

deputy (*dê*-pyu-ti) *n* diputado *m*; sustituto *m*

descend (di-*sênd*) *v* *descender

descendant (di-*sên*-dönt) *n* descendiente *m*

descent (di-*sênt*) *n* bajada *f*

describe (di-*sskraib*) *v* describir

description (di-*sskrip*-fön) *n* descripción *f*; señas personales

desert¹ (*dê*-söt) *n* desierto *m*; *adj* salvaje, desierto

desert² (di-*söt*) *v* desertar; dejar

deserve (di-*sööv*) *v* *merecer

design (di-*sain*) *v* diseñar; *n* diseño *m*; objetivo *m*

designate (*dê*-sigh-neit) *v* designar

desirable (di-*sai*ö-rö-böl) *adj* deseable

desire (di-*sai*ö) *n* deseo *m*; ganas *fpl*; *v* anhelar, desear

desk (dêssk) *n* escritorio *m*; pupitre *m*

despair (di-*sspê*ö) *n* desesperación *f*; *v* *estar desesperado

despatch (di-*sspaech*) *v* despachar

desperate (*dê*-sspö-röt) *adj* desesperado

despise (di-*sspais*) *v* despreciar

despite (di-*sspait*) *prep* a pesar de

dessert (di-*sööt*) *n* postre *m*

destination (dê-ssti-*nei*-fön) *n* destino *m*

destine (*dê*-sstin) *v* destinar

destiny (*dê*-ssti-ni) *n* destino *m*

destroy (di-*sstroi*) *v* *destruir

destruction (di-*sstrak*-fön) *n* destrucción *f*; ruina *f*

detach (di-*taech*) *v* separar

detail (*dii*-teil) *n* particularidad *f*, detalle *m*

detailed (*dii*-teild) *adj* detallado

detect (di-*têkt*) *v* descubrir

detective (di-*têk*-tiv) *n* detective *m*; ~ **story** novela policíaca

detergent (di-*töö*-dзönt) *n* detergente *m*

determine (di-*töö*-min) *v* determinar

determined (di-*töö*-mind) *adj* resuelto

detour (*dii*-tu°) *n* desvío *m*

devaluation (dii-væl-yu-*ei*-fön) *n* desvalorización *f*

devalue (dii-*væl*-yuu) *v* desvalorizar

develop (di-*vê*-löp) *v* desarrollar; revelar

development (di-*vê*-löp-mönt) *n* desarrollo *m*

deviate (*dii*-vi-eit) *v* desviarse

devil (*dê*-völ) *n* diablo *m*

devise (di-*vais*) *v* idear

devote (di-*vout*) *v* dedicar

dew (dyuu) *n* rocío *m*
diabetes (dai-ö-*bii*-tiis) *n* diabetes *f*
diabetic (dai-ö-*bê*-tik) *n* diabético *m*
diagnose (dai-ögh-*nous*) *v* diagnosticar; *comprobar
diagnosis (dai-ögh-*nou*-ssiss) *n* (pl -ses) diagnosis *f*
diagonal (dai-æ-ghö-nöl) *n* diagonal *f*; *adj* diagonal
diagram (*dai*-ö-ghræm) *n* esquema *m*; gráfico *m*
dialect (*dai*-ö-lêkt) *n* dialecto *m*
diamond (*dai*-ö-mönd) *n* diamante *m*
diaper (*dai*-ö-pö) *nAm* pañal *m*
diaphragm (*dai*-ö-fræm) *n* membrana *f*
diarrhoea (dai-ö-*ri*-ö) *n* diarrea *f*
diary (*dai*-ö-ri) *n* agenda *f*; diario *m*
dictaphone (*dik*-tö-foun) *n* dictáfono *m*
dictate (dik-*teit*) *v* dictar
dictation (dik-*tei*-fön) *n* dictado *m*
dictator (dik-*tei*-tö) *n* dictador *m*
dictionary (*dik*-fö-nö-ri) *n* diccionario *m*
did (did) *v* (p do)
die (dai) *v* *morir
diesel (*dii*-söl) *n* diesel *m*
diet (*dai*-öt) *n* régimen *m*
differ (*di*-fö) *v* *diferir
difference (*di*-fö-rönss) *n* diferencia *f*; distinción *f*
different (*di*-fö-rönt) *adj* diferente; otro'
difficult (*di*-fi-költ) *adj* difícil; fastidioso
difficulty (*di*-fi-köl-ti) *n* dificultad *f*; trabajo *m*
*dig (digh) *v* cavar
digest (di-*dzêsst*) *v* *digerir
digestible (di-*dzê*-sstö-böl) *adj* digerible
digestion (di-*dzêss*-chön) *n* digestión *f*

digit (*di*-dzit) *n* número *m*
dignified (*digh*-ni-faid) *adj* distinguido
dike (daik) *n* dique *m*
dilapidated (di-*læ*-pi-dei-tid) *adj* ruinoso
diligence (*di*-li-dzönss) *n* celo *m*, diligencia *f*
diligent (*di*-li-dzönt) *adj* celoso, cuidadoso
dilute (dai-*lyuut*) *v* *diluir
dim (dim) *adj* deslucido, mate; oscuro, vago, difuso
dine (dain) *v* cenar
dinghy (*ding*-ghi) *n* chinchorro *m*
dining-car (*dai*-ning-kaa) *n* coche comedor
dining-room (*dai*-ning-ruum) *n* comedor *m*
dinner (*di*-nö) *n* comida principal; cena *f*
dinner-jacket (*di*-nö-dzæ-kit) *n* smoking *m*
dinner-service (*di*-nö-ssöö-viss) *n* servicio de mesa
diphtheria (dif-*zi*^{ö}-ri-ö) *n* difteria *f*
diploma (di-*plou*-mö) *n* diploma *m*
diplomat (*di*-plö-mæt) *n* diplomático *m*
direct (di-*rêkt*) *adj* directo; *v* dirigir; administrar
direction (di-*rêk*-fön) *n* dirección *f*; instrucción *f*; dirección de escena; administración *f*; **directions for use** modo de empleo
directive (di-*rêk*-tiv) *n* directriz *f*
director (di-*rêk*-tö) *n* director *m*; director de escena
dirt (dööt) *n* suciedad *f*
dirty (*döö*-ti) *adj* sucio
disabled (di-*ssei*-böld) *adj* minusválido, inválido
disadvantage (di-ssöd-*vaan*-tidz) *n* desventaja *f*
disagree (di-ssö-*ghrii*) *v* no *estar de

acuerdo, *disentir

disagreeable (di-ssö-ghrii-ö-böl) *adj*
desagradable

disappear (di-ssö-*piö*) *v* *desaparecer

disappoint (di-ssö-*point*) *v* decepcionar

disappointment (di-ssö-*point*-mönt) *n*
desengaño *m*

disapprove (di-ssö-*pruuv*) *v* *desaprobar

disaster (di-saa-sstö) *n* desastre *m*;
catástrofe *f*, calamidad *f*

disastrous (di-saa-sströss) *adj* desastroso

disc (dissk) *n* disco *m*; **slipped** ~ hernia intervertebral

discard (di-*sskaad*) *v* desechar

discharge (diss-*chaadʒ*) *v* descargar;
~ **of** dispensar de

discipline (*di*-ssi-plin) *n* disciplina *f*

discolour (di-*sska*-lö) *v* *desteñirse;
discoloured descolorido

disconnect (di-sskö-*nêkt*) *v* desconectar

discontented (di-sskön-*tên*-tid) *adj*
descontento

discontinue (di-sskön-*ti*-nyuu) *v* suprimir, cesar

discount (*di*-sskaunt) *n* descuento *m*

discover (di-*sska*-vö) *v* descubrir

discovery (di-*sska*-vö-ri) *n* descubrimiento *m*

discuss (di-*sskass*) *v* discutir; debatir

discussion (di-*sska*-ʃön) *n* discusión
f; conversación *f*, debate *m*

disease (di-*siis*) *n* enfermedad *f*

disembark (di-ssim-*baak*) *v* desembarcar

disgrace (diss-*ghreiss*) *n* deshonor *m*

disguise (diss-*ghais*) *v* disfrazarse; *n*
disfraz *m*

disgusting (diss-*gha*-ssting) *adj* repugnante, asqueroso

dish (diʃ) *n* plato *m*; fuente *f*; guiso
m

dishonest (di-*sso*-nisst) *adj* improbo

disinfect (di-ssin-*fêkt*) *v* desinfectar

disinfectant (di-ssin-*fêk*-tönt) *n* desinfectante *m*

dislike (di-*sslaik*) *v* detestar, no gustar; *n* repugnancia *f*, aversión *f*, antipatía *f*

dislocated (*di*-sslö-kei-tid) *adj* dislocado

dismiss (diss-*miss*) *v* *despedir

disorder (di-*ssoo*-dö) *n* desorden *m*

dispatch (di-*sspæch*) *v* enviar, despachar

display (di-*ssplei*) *v* exhibir; *mostrar; *n* exposición *f*

displease (di-*sspliis*) *v* disgustar, desagradar

disposable (di-*sspou*-sö-böl) *adj* desechable

disposal (di-*sspou*-söl) *n* disposición *f*

dispose of (di-*sspous*) *disponer de

dispute (di-*sspyuut*) *n* disputa *f*; riña
f, contienda *f*; *v* *reñir, disputar

dissatisfied (di-*ssæ*-tiss-faid) *adj* insatisfecho

dissolve (di-*solv*) *v* *disolver

dissuade from (di-*ssᵘeid*) disuadir

distance (*di*-sstönss) *n* distancia *f*; ~
in kilometres kilometraje *m*

distant (*di*-sstönt) *adj* lejano

distinct (di-*sstingkt*) *adj* claro; distinto

distinction (di-*sstingk*-ʃön) *n* distinción *f*, diferencia *f*

distinguish (di-*ssting*-ghᵘiʃ) *v* distinguir

distinguished (di-*ssting*-ghᵘiʃt) *adj*
distinguido

distress (di-*sstrêss*) *n* peligro *m*; ~
signal señal de alarma

distribute (di-*sstri*-byuut) *v* *distribuir

distributor (di-*sstri*-byu-tö) *n* distribuidor *m*

district (*di*-sstrikt) *n* distrito *m*; comarca *f*; barrio *m*

disturb (di-*sstööb*) *v* estorbar, molestar

disturbance (di-*sstöö*-bönss) *n* disturbio *m*; confusión *f*

ditch (dich) *n* zanja *f*, cuneta *f*

dive (daiv) *v* bucear

diversion (dai-*vöö*-ßön) *n* desvío *m*; diversión *f*

divide (di-*vaid*) *v* dividir; repartir; separar

divine (di-*vain*) *adj* divino

division (di-*vi*-ßön) *n* división *f*; separación *f*; departamento *m*

divorce (di-*vooss*) *n* divorcio *m*; *v* divorciar

dizziness (*di*-si-nöss) *n* vértigo *m*

dizzy (*di*-si) *adj* mareado

****do** (duu) *v* *hacer; *ser suficiente

dock (dok) *n* dock *m*; muelle *m*; *v* atracar

docker (*do*-kö) *n* obrero portuario

doctor (*dok*-tö) *n* médico *m*; doctor *m*

document (*do*-kyu-mönt) *n* documento *m*

dog (dogh) *n* perro *m*

dogged (*do*-ghid) *adj* obstinado

doll (dol) *n* muñeca *f*

dome (doum) *n* cúpula *f*

domestic (dö-*mê*-sstik) *adj* doméstico; interior; *n* sirviente *m*

domicile (*do*-mi-ssail) *n* domicilio *m*

domination (do-mi-*nei*-ßön) *n* dominación *f*

dominion (dö-*mi*-nyön) *n* dominio *m*

donate (dou-*neit*) *v* donar

donation (dou-*nei*-ßön) *n* donación *f*

done (dan) *v* (pp do)

donkey (*dong*-ki) *n* burro *m*

donor (*dou*-nö) *n* donante *m*

door (doo) *n* puerta *f*; **revolving** ~ puerta giratoria; **sliding** ~ puerta

corrediza

doorbell (*doo*-bêl) *n* timbre *m*

door-keeper (*doo*-kii-pö) *n* portero *m*

doorman (*doo*-mön) *n* (pl -men) portero *m*

dormitory (*doo*-mi-tri) *n* dormitorio *m*

dose (douss) *n* dosis *f*

dot (dot) *n* punto *m*

double (*da*-böl) *adj* doble

doubt (daut) *v* dudar; *n* duda *f*; **without** ~ sin duda

doubtful (*daut*-föl) *adj* dudoso; inseguro

dough (dou) *n* masa *f*

down¹ (daun) *adv* abajo; hacia abajo; *adj* abatido; *prep* a lo largo de, debajo de; ~ **payment** primer pago

down² (daun) *n* flojel *m*

downpour (*daun*-poo) *n* aguacero *m*

downstairs (daun-*sstê*ᵒs) *adv* abajo

downstream (daun-*sstriim*) *adv* río abajo

down-to-earth (daun-tu-*ööz*) *adj* sensato

downwards (daun-ᵘöds) *adv* hacia abajo

dozen (*da*-sön) *n* (pl ~, ~s) docena *f*

draft (draaft) *n* giro *m*

drag (drægh) *v* arrastrar

dragon (*dræ*-ghön) *n* dragón *m*

drain (drein) *v* desecar; drenar; *n* desagüe *m*

drama (*draa*-mö) *n* drama *m*; tragedia *f*; teatro *m*

dramatic (drö-*mæ*-tik) *adj* dramático

dramatist (*dræ*-mö-tisst) *n* dramaturgo *m*

drank (drængk) *v* (p drink)

draper (*drei*-pö) *n* pañero *m*

drapery (*drei*-pö-ri) *n* pañería *f*

draught (draaft) *n* corriente de aire; **draughts** juego de damas

draught-board (*draaft*-bood) *n* tablero

de damas

draw (droo) n sorteo m

***draw** (droo) v dibujar; arrastrar; sacar; jalar vMe; ~ **up** redactar

drawbridge (droo-bridȝ) n puente levadizo

drawer (droo-ö) n cajón m; **drawers** calzoncillos mpl

drawing (droo-ing) n dibujo m

drawing-pin (droo-ing-pin) n chinche f

drawing-room (droo-ing-ruum) n salón m

dread (drêd) v temer; n temor m

dreadful (drêd-fŏl) adj terrible, espantoso

dream (driim) n sueño m

***dream** (driim) v *soñar

dress (drêss) v *vestir; *vestirse; vendar; n vestido m

dressing-gown (drê-ssing-ghaun) n bata f

dressing-room (drê-ssing-ruum) n vestuario m

dressing-table (drê-ssing-tei-böl) n tocador m

dressmaker (drêss-mei-kö) n modista f

drill (dril) v taladrar; entrenar; n taladro m

drink (dringk) n aperitivo m, bebida f

***drink** (dringk) v beber

drinking-water (dring-king-ᵘoo-tö) n agua potable

drip-dry (drip-drai) adj no precisa plancha

drive (draiv) n calzada f; paseo en coche

***drive** (draiv) v *conducir

driver (drai-vö) n conductor m

drizzle (dri-söl) n llovizna f

drop (drop) v dejar caer; n gota f

drought (draut) n sequía f

drown (draun) v ahogar; ***be**

drowned ahogarse

drug (dragh) n estupefaciente m; medicamento m

drugstore (dragh-sstoo) nAm droguería f, farmacia f; almacén m

drum (dram) n tambor m

drunk (drangk) adj (pp drink) borracho

dry (drai) adj seco; v secar

dry-clean (drai-kliin) v limpiar en seco

dry-cleaner's (drai-klii-nös) n tintorería f

dryer (drai-ö) n secadora f

duchess (da-chiss) n duquesa f

duck (dak) n pato m

due (dyuu) adj aguardado; adeudado; debido

dues (dyuus) pl derechos mpl

dug (dagh) v (p, pp dig)

duke (dyuuk) n duque m

dull (dal) adj aburrido; pálido, mate; embotado

dumb (dam) adj mudo; atontado, estúpido

dune (dyuun) n duna f

dung (dang) n abono m

dunghill (dang-hil) n estercolero m

duration (dyu-rei-ʃön) n duración f

during (dyuᵒ-ring) prep durante

dusk (dassk) n crepúsculo m

dust (dasst) n polvo m

dustbin (dasst-bin) n cubo de la basura

dusty (da-ssti) adj polvoriento

Dutch (dach) adj holandés

Dutchman (dach-mön) n (pl -men) holandés m

dutiable (dyuu-ti-ö-böl) adj imponible

duty (dyuu-ti) n deber m; tarea f; arancel m; **Customs** ~ impuesto de aduana

duty-free (dyuu-ti-frii) adj exento de impuestos

dwarf (dᵘoof) n enano m

dye (dai) v *teñir; n tintura f
dynamo (dai-nö-mou) n (pl ~s) dínamo f
dysentery (di-ssön-tri) n disentería f

E

each (iich) adj cada; ~ **other** el uno al otro
eager (ii-ghö) adj ansioso, impaciente
eagle (ii-ghöl) n águila m
ear (iö) n oreja f
earache (iö-reik) n dolor de oídos
ear-drum (iö-dram) n tímpano m
earl (ööl) n conde m
early (öö-li) adj temprano
earn (öön) v ganar
earnest (öö-nisst) n seriedad f
earnings (öö-nings) pl ingresos mpl, ganancias fpl
earring (iö-ring) n pendiente m
earth (ööz) n tierra f; suelo m
earthenware (öö-zön-uêö) n loza f
earthquake (ööz-kueik) n terremoto m
ease (iis) n desenvoltura f, facilidad f; bienestar m
east (iisst) n este m
Easter (ii-sstö) Pascua
easterly (ii-sstö-li) adj oriental
eastern (ii-sstön) adj oriental
easy (ii-si) adj fácil; cómodo; ~ **chair** butaca f
easy-going (ii-si-ghou-ing) adj relajado
***eat** (iit) v comer; cenar
eavesdrop (iivs-drop) v escuchar
ebony (ê-bö-ni) n ébano m
eccentric (ik-ssên-trik) adj excéntrico
echo (ê-kou) n (pl ~es) eco m
eclipse (i-klipss) n eclipse m
economic (ii-kö-no-mik) adj económico

economical (ii-kö-no-mi-köl) adj parsimonioso, económico
economist (i-ko-nö-misst) n economista m
economize (i-ko-nö-mais) v economizar
economy (i-ko-nö-mi) n economía f
ecstasy (êk-sstö-si) n éxtasis m
Ecuador (ê-kuö-doo) Ecuador m
Ecuadorian (ê-kuö-doo-ri-ön) n ecuatoriano m
eczema (êk-ssi-smö) n eczema m
edge (êdʒ) n borde m
edible (ê-di-böl) adj comestible
edition (i-di-ʃön) n edición f; **morning ~** edición de mañana
editor (ê-di-tö) n redactor m
educate (ê-dʒu-keit) v formar, educar
education (ê-dʒu-kei-ʃön) n educación f
eel (iil) n anguila f
effect (i-fêkt) n resultado m, efecto m; v efectuar; **in ~** en realidad
effective (i-fêk-tiv) adj eficaz
efficient (i-fi-ʃönt) adj eficiente
effort (ê-föt) n esfuerzo m
egg (êgh) n huevo m
egg-cup (êgh-kap) n huevera f
eggplant (êgh-plaant) n berenjena f
egg-yolk (êgh-youk) n yema de huevo
egoistic (ê-ghou-i-sstik) adj egoísta
Egypt (ii-dʒipt) Egipto m
Egyptian (i-dʒip-ʃön) adj egipcio
eiderdown (ai-dö-daun) n edredón m
eight (eit) num ocho
eighteen (ei-tiin) num dieciocho
eighteenth (ei-tiinz) num decimoctavo
eighth (eitz) num octavo
eighty (ei-ti) num ochenta
either (ai-ðö) pron cualquiera de los dos; **either ... or** o ... o, bien ... bien

laborate (i-*læ*-bö-reit) *v* elaborar

lastic (i-*læ*-sstik) *adj* elástico; flexible; ~ **band** cinta de goma

lasticity (è-læ-*ssti*-ssö-ti) *n* elasticidad *f*

lbow (*él*-bou) *n* codo *m*

lder (*él*-dö) *adj* mayor

lderly (*él*-dö-li) *adj* anciano

ldest (*él*-disst) *adj* mayor

lect (i-*lèkt*) *v* *elegir

lection (i-*lèk*-fön) *n* elección *f*

lectric (i-*lèk*-trik) *adj* eléctrico; ~ **razor** afeitadora eléctrica

lectrician (i-lèk-*tri*-fön) *n* electricista *m*

lectricity (i-lèk-*tri*-ssö-ti) *n* electricidad *f*

lectronic (i-lèk-*tro*-nik) *adj* electrónico

legance (*è*-li-ghönss) *n* elegancia *f*

legant (*è*-li-ghönt) *adj* elegante

lement (*è*-li-mönt) *n* elemento *m*

lephant (*è*-li-fönt) *n* elefante *m*

levator (*è*-li-vei-tö) *nAm* ascensor *m*; elevador *mMe*

leven (i-*lè*-vön) *num* once

leventh (i-*lè*-vönz) *num* onceno

lf (èlf) *n* (pl elves) duende *m*

liminate (i-*li*-mi-neit) *v* eliminar

lm (èlm) *n* olmo *m*

lse (èlss) *adv* si no

lsewhere (èl-ss*u*ę*ö*) *adv* otra parte

lucidate (i-*luu*-ssi-deit) *v* elucidar

mancipation (i-mæn-ssi-*pei*-fön) *n* emancipación *f*

mbankment (im-*bæ̊ngk*-mönt) *n* terraplén *m*

mbargo (êm-*baa*-ghou) *n* (pl ~es) embargo *m*

mbark (im-*baak*) *v* embarcar

mbarkation (êm-baa-*kei*-fön) *n* embarcación *f*

mbarrass (im-*bæ*-röss) *v* turbar; *desconcertar; estorbar; **embar**-

rassed tímido

embassy (*êm*-bö-ssi) *n* embajada *f*

emblem (*êm*-blöm) *n* emblema *m*

embrace (im-*breiss*) *v* abrazar; *n* abrazo *m*

embroider (im-*broi*-dö) *v* bordar

embroidery (im-*broi*-dö-ri) *n* bordado *m*

emerald (*ê*-mö-röld) *n* esmeralda *f*

emergency (i-*möö*-dзön-ssi) *n* caso de urgencia, urgencia *f*; emergencia *f*; ~ **exit** salida de emergencia

emigrant (*ê*-mi-ghrönt) *n* emigrante *m*

emigrate (*ê*-mi-ghreit) *v* emigrar

emigration (è-mi-*ghrei*-fön) *n* emigración *f*

emotion (i-*mou*-fön) *n* emoción *f*

emperor (*êm*-pö-rö) *n* emperador *m*

emphasize (*êm*-fö-ssais) *v* enfatizar, acentuar

empire (*êm*-pai*ö*) *n* imperio *m*

employ (im-*ploi*) *v* emplear

employee (êm-ploi-*ii*) *n* empleado *m*

employer (im-*ploi*-ö) *n* patrón *m*

employment (im-*ploi*-mönt) *n* empleo *m*; ~ **exchange** oficina de colocación

empress (*êm*-priss) *n* emperatriz *f*

empty (*êmp*-ti) *adj* vacío; *v* vaciar

enable (i-*nei*-böl) *v* permitir

enamel (i-*næ*-möl) *n* esmalte *m*

enamelled (i-*næ*-möld) *adj* esmaltado

enchanting (in-*chaan*-ting) *adj* espléndido, encantador

encircle (in-*ssöö*-köl) *v* *circuir, cercar; *encerrar

enclose (ing-*klous*) *v* *incluir

enclosure (ing-*klou*-зö) *n* anexo *m*

encounter (ing-*kaun*-tö) *v* *encontrarse con; *n* encuentro *m*

encourage (ing-ka-ridз) *v* *alentar

encyclopaedia (ên-ssai-klô-*pii*-di-ö) *n* enciclopedia *f*

end (énd) *n* fin *m*, extremo *m*; final *m*; *v* terminar, acabar; terminarse

ending (*én*-ding) *n* conclusión *f*

endless (*énd*-löss) *adj* infinito

endorse (in-*dooss*) *v* visar, endosar

endure (in-*dyu*⁰) *v* soportar

enemy (*ê*-nö-mi) *n* enemigo *m*

energetic (ê-nö-*dzê*-tik) *adj* enérgico

energy (*ê*-nö-dzi) *n* energía *f*; fuerza *f*

engage (ing-*gheidz*) *v* emplear; reservar; comprometerse; **engaged** prometido; ocupado

engagement (ing-*gheidz*-mönt) *n* noviazgo *m*; compromiso *m*; ~ **ring** anillo de esponsales

engine (*én*-dzin) *n* máquina *f*, motor *m*; locomotora *f*

engineer (ên-dzi-*ni*⁰) *n* ingeniero *m*

England (*ing*-ghlönd) Inglaterra *f*

English (*ing*-ghlif) *adj* inglés

Englishman (*ing*-ghlif-mön) *n* (pl - men) inglés *m*

engrave (ing-*ghreiv*) *v* grabar

engraver (ing-*ghrei*-vö) *n* grabador *m*

engraving (ing-*ghrei*-ving) *n* estampa *f*; grabado *m*

enigma (i-*nigh*-mö) *n* enigma *m*

enjoy (in-*dzoi*) *v* disfrutar, gozar

enjoyable (in-*dzoi*-ö-böl) *adj* agradable, grato, deleitable; rico

enjoyment (in-*dzoi*-mönt) *n* goce *m*

enlarge (in-*laadz*) *v* ampliar

enlargement (in-*laadz*-mönt) *n* ampliación *f*

enormous (i-*noo*-möss) *adj* gigantesco, enorme

enough (i-*naf*) *adv* bastante; *adj* suficiente

enquire (ing-*k*ᵘ*ai*⁰) *v* preguntar; investigar

enquiry (ing-*k*ᵘ*ai*⁰-ri) *n* información *f*; investigación *f*; encuesta *f*

enter (*én*-tö) *v* entrar; inscribir

enterprise (*ên*-tö-prais) *n* empresa *f*

entertain (ên-tö-*tein*) *v* *divertir, *entretener; hospedar

entertainer (ên-tö-*tei*-nö) *n* cómico *m*

entertaining (ên-tö-*tei*-ning) *adj* divertido, entretenido

entertainment (ên-tö-*tein*-mönt) *n* diversión *f*, entretenimiento *m*

enthusiasm (in-*zyuu*-si-æ-söm) *n* entusiasmo *m*

enthusiastic (in-zyuu-si-æ-*sstik*) *adj* entusiasta

entire (in-*tai*⁰) *adj* todo, entero

entirely (in-*tai*⁰-li) *adv* enteramente

entrance (*ên*-trönss) *n* entrada *f*; acceso *m*

entrance-fee (*ên*-trönss-fii) *n* entrada *f*

entry (*én*-tri) *n* entrada *f*, ingreso *m*; anotación *f*; **no** ~ prohibido el paso

envelope (*ên*-vö-loup) *n* sobre *m*

envious (*ên*-vi-öss) *adj* envidioso, celoso

environment (in-*vai*⁰-rön-mönt) *n* medio ambiente; alrededores *mpl*

envoy (*ên*-voi) *n* enviado *m*

envy (*ên*-vi) *n* envidia *f*; *v* envidiar

epic (*ê*-pik) *n* poema épico; *adj* épico

epidemic (ê-pi-*dê*-mik) *n* epidemia *f*

epilepsy (*ê*-pi-lêp-ssi) *n* epilepsia *f*

epilogue (*ê*-pi-logh) *n* epílogo *m*

episode (*ê*-pi-ssoud) *n* episodio *m*

equal (*ii*-kᵘöl) *adj* igual; *v* igualar

equality (i-*k*ᵘ*o*-lö-ti) *n* igualdad *f*

equalize (*ii*-kᵘö-lais) *v* igualar

equally (*ii*-kᵘö-li) *adv* igualmente

equator (i-*k*ᵘ*ei*-tö) *n* ecuador *m*

equip (i-*k*ᵘ*ip*) *v* equipar

equipment (i-*k*ᵘ*ip*-mönt) *n* equipo *m*

equivalent (i-*k*ᵘ*i*-vö-lönt) *adj* equivalente

eraser (i-*rei*-sö) *n* goma de borrar

erect (i-*rêkt*) *v* erigir; *adj* erguido, recto; parado *adjMe*

err (öö) *v* *errar

errand (*ê*-rönd) *n* recado *m*

error (*ê*-rö) *n* falta *f*, error *m*

escalator (*ê*-sskö-lei-tö) *n* escalera móvil

escape (i-*sskeip*) *v* escaparse; *huir, escapar; *n* evasión *f*

escort[1] (*ê*-sskoot) *n* escolta *f*

escort[2] (i-*sskoot*) *v* escoltar

especially (i-*sspê*-fö-li) *adv* sobre todo, especialmente

esplanade (ê-ssplö-*neid*) *n* explanada *f*

essay (*ê*-ssei) *n* ensayo *m*; tratado *m*, composición *f*

essence (*ê*-ssönss) *n* esencia *f*; núcleo *m*

essential (i-*ssên*-föl) *adj* indispensable; esencial

essentially (i-*ssên*-fö-li) *adv* sobre todo

establish (i-*sstæ*-blif) *v* *establecer; *comprobar

estate (i-*ssteit*) *n* propiedad *f*

esteem (i-*sstiim*) *n* respeto *m*, estima *f*; *v* estimar

estimate[1] (*ê*-ssti-meit) *v* evaluar, estimar

estimate[2] (*ê*-ssti-möt) *n* estimación *f*

estuary (*êss*-chu-ö-ri) *n* estuario *m*

etcetera (êt-*ssê*-tö-rö) etcétera

etching (*ê*-ching) *n* aguafuerte *f*

eternal (i-*töö*-nöl) *adj* eterno

eternity (i-*töö*-nö-ti) *n* eternidad *f*

ether (*ii*-zö) *n* éter *m*

Ethiopia (i-zi-*ou*-pi-ö) Etiopía *f*

Ethiopian (i-zi-*ou*-pi-ön) *adj* etíope

Europe (*yu*ᵒ-röp) Europa *f*

European (yuᵒ-rö-*pii*-ön) *adj* europeo

evacuate (i-*væ*-kyu-eit) *v* evacuar

evaluate (i-*væl*-yu-eit) *v* evaluar

evaporate (i-*væ*-pö-reit) *v* evaporar

even (*ii*-vön) *adj* llano, plano, igual; constante; par; *adv* aun

evening (*iiv*-ning) *n* tarde *f*; ~ **dress** traje de etiqueta

event (i-*vênt*) *n* acontecimiento *m*; caso *m*

eventual (i-*vên*-chu-öl) *adj* eventual; final

ever (*ê*-vö) *adv* jamás; siempre

every (*êv*-ri) *adj* cada

everybody (*êv*-ri-bo-di) *pron* todos

everyday (*êv*-ri-dei) *adj* cotidiano

everyone (*êv*-ri-ᵘan) *pron* cada uno, todo el mundo

everything (*êv*-ri-zing) *pron* todo

everywhere (*êv*-ri-ᵘêᵒ) *adv* por todas partes

evidence (*ê*-vi-dönss) *n* prueba *f*

evident (*ê*-vi-dönt) *adj* evidente

evil (*ii*-völ) *n* mal *m*; *adj* malo, malvado

evolution (ii-vö-*luu*-fön) *n* evolución *f*

exact (igh-*sækt*) *adj* exacto

exactly (igh-*sækt*-li) *adv* exactamente

exaggerate (igh-*sæ*-dʒö-reit) *v* exagerar

examination (igh-sæ-mi-*nei*-fön) *n* examen *m*; interrogatorio *m*

examine (igh-*sæ*-min) *v* examinar

example (igh-*saam*-pöl) *n* ejemplo *m*; **for** ~ por ejemplo

excavation (êkss-kö-*vei*-fön) *n* excavación *f*

exceed (ik-*ssiid*) *v* exceder; superar

excel (ik-*ssêl*) *v* distinguirse

excellent (*êk*-ssö-lönt) *adj* excelente

except (ik-*ssêpt*) *prep* excepto

exception (ik-*ssêp*-fön) *n* excepción *f*

exceptional (ik-*ssêp*-fö-nöl) *adj* extraordinario, excepcional

excerpt (*êk*-ssööpt) *n* extracto *m*

excess (ik-*ssêss*) *n* exceso *m*

excessive (ik-*ssê*-ssiv) *adj* excesivo

exchange (ikss-*cheindʒ*) *v* intercambiar, cambiar; *n* cambio *m*; bolsa *f*; ~ **office** oficina de cambio; ~

rate cambio *m*
excite (ik-*ssait*) *v* excitar
excitement (ik-*ssait*-mönt) *n* agitación *f*, excitación *f*
exciting (ik-*ssai*-ting) *adj* excitante
exclaim (ik-*sskleim*) *v* exclamar
exclamation (êk-ssklö-*mei*-[ön) *n* exclamación *f*
exclude (ik-*sskluud*) *v* *excluir
exclusive (ik-*sskluu*-ssiv) *adj* exclusivo
exclusively (ik-*sskluu*-ssiv-li) *adv* exclusivamente, únicamente
excursion (ik-*ssköö*-[ön) *n* excursión *f*
excuse[1] (ik-*sskyuuss*) *n* excusa *f*
excuse[2] (ik-*sskyuus*) *v* excusar, disculpar
execute (*êk*-ssi-kyuut) *v* ejecutar
execution (êk-ssi-*kyuu*-[ön) *n* ejecución *f*
executioner (êk-ssi-*kyuu*-[ö-nö) *n* verdugo *m*
executive (igh-*sê*-kyu-tiv) *adj* ejecutivo; *n* poder ejecutivo; ejecutivo *m*
exempt (igh-ʒêmpt) *v* dispensar, eximir; *adj* exento
exemption (igh-*sêmp*-[ön) *n* exención *f*
exercise (*êk*-ssö-ssais) *n* ejercicio *m*; *v* ejercitar; ejercer
exhale (êkss-*heil*) *v* exhalar
exhaust (igh-*soosst*) *n* tubo de escape, escape *m*; *v* extenuar; ~ **gases** gases de escape
exhibit (igh-*si*-bit) *v* *exponer; exhibir
exhibition (êk-ssi-*bi*-[ön) *n* exposición *f*
exile (*êk*-ssail) *n* exilio *m*; exiliado *m*
exist (igh-*sisst*) *v* existir
existence (igh-*si*-sstönss) *n* existencia *f*
exit (*êk*-ssit) *n* salida *f*
exotic (igh-*so*-tik) *adj* exótico
expand (ik-*sspænd*) *v* *extender;

*desplegar
expect (ik-*sspêkt*) *v* aguardar, esperar
expectation (êk-sspêk-*tei*-[ön) *n* esperanza *f*
expedition (êk-sspö-*di*-[ön) *n* envío *m*; expedición *f*
expel (ik-*sspêl*) *v* expulsar
expenditure (ik-*sspên*-di-chö) *n* gasto *m*
expense (ik-*sspênss*) *n* gasto *m*
expensive (ik-*sspên*-ssiv) *adj* caro; costoso
experience (ik-*sspi*[ö]-ri-önss) *n* experiencia *f*; *v* experimentar, vivir; **experienced** experimentado
experiment (ik-*sspê*-ri-mönt) *n* prueba *f*, experimento *m*; *v* experimentar
expert (*êk*-sspööt) *n* perito *m*, experto *m*; *adj* competente
expire (ik-*sspai*[ö]) *v* expirar, terminarse; espirar; **expired** caducado
expiry (ik-*sspai*[ö]-ri) *n* vencimiento *m*
explain (ik-*sspein*) *v* explicar
explanation (êk-ssplö-*nei*-[ön) *n* aclaración *f*, explicación *f*
explicit (ik-*sspli*-ssit) *adj* expreso, explícito
explode (ik-*ssploud*) *v* estallar
exploit (ik-*ssploit*) *v* abusar de, explotar
explore (ik-*ssploo*) *v* explorar
explosion (ik-*ssplou*-ʒön) *n* explosión *f*
explosive (ik-*ssplou*-ssiv) *adj* explosivo; *n* explosivo *m*
export[1] (ik-*sspoot*) *v* exportar
export[2] (*êk*-sspoot) *n* exportación *f*
exportation (êk-sspoo-*tei*-[ön) *n* exportación *f*
exports (*êk*-sspootss) *pl* exportación *f*
exposition (êk-sspö-*si*-[ön) *n* exposición *f*
exposure (ik-*sspou*-ʒö) *n* exposición *f*; ~ **meter** exposímetro *m*

express (ik-*sprêss*) v expresar; adj
expreso; explícito; ~ **train** tren expreso

expression (ik-*ssprê*-∫ön) n expresión
f

exquisite (ik-*ssk*ᵘ*i*-sit) adj exquisito

extend (ik-*sstênd*) v prolongar; ampliar; conceder

extension (ik-*sstên*-∫ön) n prórroga f;
ampliación f; extensión f; ~ **cord**
cordón de extensión

extensive (ik-*sstên*-ssiv) adj extenso;
vasto

extent (ik-*sstênt*) n dimensión f

exterior (êk-*ssti*ᵒ-ri-ö) adj exterior; n
exterior m

external (êk-*sstöö*-nöl) adj exterior

extinguish (ik-*ssting*-gh*i*∫) v extinguir, apagar

extort (ik-*sstoot*) v extorsionar

extortion (ik-*sstoo*-∫ön) n extorsión f

extra (*êk*-sströ) adj extra

extract¹ (ik-*ssträkt*) v *extraer

extract² (*êk*-sssträkt) n fragmento m

extradite (*êk*-sströ-dait) v entregar

extraordinary (ik-*sstroo*-dön-ri) adj extraordinario

extravagant (ik-*ssträ*-vö-ghönt) adj
exagerado, extravagante

extreme (ik-*sstriim*) adj extremo; n
extremo m

exuberant (igh-*syuu*-bö-rönt) adj exuberante

eye (ai) n ojo m

eyebrow (*ai*-brau) n ceja f

eyelash (*ai*-læ∫) n pestaña f

eyelid (*ai*-lid) n párpado m

eye-pencil (*ai*-pên-ssöl) n lápiz para
las cejas

eye-shadow (*ai*-∫æ-dou) n sombra para los ojos

eye-witness (*ai*-ᵘit-nöss) n testigo de
vista

F

fable (*fei*-böl) n fábula f

fabric (*fæ*-brik) n tejido m; estructura
f

façade (fö-*ssaad*) n fachada f

face (feiss) n cara f; v enfrentarse
con; ~ **massage** masaje facial;
facing enfrente de

face-cream (*feiss*-kriim) n crema facial

face-pack (*feiss*-pæk) n máscara facial

face-powder (*feiss*-pau-dö) n polvo
facial

facility (fö-*ssi*-lö-ti) n facilidad f

fact (fækt) n hecho m; **in** ~ efectivamente

factor (*fæk*-tö) n factor m

factory (*fæk*-tö-ri) n fábrica f

factual (*fæk*-chu-öl) adj real

faculty (*fæ*-köl-ti) n facultad f; don
m, aptitud f

fad (fæd) n antojo m

fade (feid) v *desteñirse

faience (fai-*angss*) n loza f

fail (feil) v fallar; faltar; omitir; *ser
suspendido; **without** ~ sin falta

failure (*feil*-yö) n fracaso m; fiasco m

faint (feint) v desmayarse; adj débil,
vago

fair (fê°) n feria f; adj justo; rubio;
bonito

fairly (*fê*°-li) adv bastante, medianamente

fairy (*fê*°-ri) n hada f

fairytale (*fê*°-ri-teil) n cuento de hadas

faith (feiz) n fe f; confianza f

faithful (*feiz*-ful) adj fiel

fake (feik) n falsificación f

fall (fool) n caída f; nAm otoño m

*fall (fool) v *caer

false (foolss) adj falso; inexacto; ~

teeth dentadura postiza

falter (*fool-*tö) v vacilar; balbucear

fame (feim) n fama f; reputación f

familiar (fö-*mil-*yö) adj familiar

family (*fæ-*mö-li) n familia f; ~ **name** apellido m

famous (*fei-*möss) adj famoso

fan (fæn) n ventilador m; abanico m; admirador m; ~ **belt** correa del ventilador

fanatical (fö-*næ-*ti-köl) adj fanático

fancy (*fæn-*ssi) v gustar, antojarse; imaginarse; n capricho m; imaginación f

fantastic (fæn-*tæ-*sstik) adj fantástico

fantasy (*fæn-*tö-si) n fantasía f

far (faa) adj lejano; adv mucho; **by ~** con mucho; **so ~** hasta ahora

far-away (*faa-*rö-ᵘei) adj remoto

farce (faass) n sainete m, farsa f

fare (fêö) n gastos de viaje, precio del billete; alimento m

farm (faam) n granja f

farmer (*faa-*mö) n granjero m; **farmer's wife** granjera f

farmhouse (*faam-*hauss) n cortijo m; rancho mMe

far-off (*faa-*rof) adj remoto

fascinate (*fæ-*ssi-neit) v cautivar

fascism (*fæ-*ʃi-söm) n fascismo m

fascist (*fæ-*ʃisst) adj fascista

fashion (*fæ-*ʃön) n moda f; modo m

fashionable (*fæ-*ʃö-nö-böl) adj a la moda

fast (faasst) adj rápido; firme

fast-dyed (faasst-*daid*) adj lavable, no destiñe

fasten (*faa-*ssön) v atar; *cerrar

fastener (*faa-*ssö-nö) n cierre m

fat (fæt) adj graso, gordo; n grasa f

fatal (*fei-*töl) adj fatal, mortal

fate (feit) n destino m

father (*faa-*ðö) n padre m

father-in-law (*faa-*ðö-rin-loo) n (pl fathers-) suegro m

fatherland (*faa-*ðö-lönd) n patria f

fatness (*fæt-*nöss) n obesidad f

fatty (*fæ-*ti) adj grasiento

faucet (*foo-*ssit) nAm grifo m

fault (foolt) n culpa f; imperfección f, defecto m

faultless (*foolt-*löss) adj impecable; perfecto

faulty (*fool-*ti) adj defectuoso

favour (*fei-*vö) n favor m; v *favorecer

favourable (*fei-*vö-rö-böl) adj favorable

favourite (*fei-*vö-rit) n favorito m; adj preferido

fawn (foon) adj marrón claro; n cervato m, corcino m

fear (fiö) n temor m, miedo m; v temer

feasible (*fii-*sö-böl) adj realizable

feast (fiisst) n fiesta f

feat (fiit) n gran trabajo

feather (*fê-*ðö) n pluma f

feature (*fii-*chö) n característica f; rasgo m

February (*fê-*bru-ö-ri) febrero

federal (*fê-*dö-röl) adj federal

federation (fê-dö-*rei-*jön) n federación f

fee (fii) n honorarios mpl

feeble (*fii-*böl) adj débil

*feed (fiid) v alimentar; **fed up with** harto de

*feel (fiil) v *sentir; palpar; ~ **like** antojarse

feeling (*fii-*ling) n sensación f

fell (fêl) v (p fall)

fellow (*fê-*lou) n tipo m

felt¹ (fêlt) n fieltro m

felt² (fêlt) v (p, pp feel)

female (*fii-*meil) adj femenino

feminine (*fê-*mi-nin) adj femenino

fence (fênss) n cerca f; reja f; v esgrimir

fender (fén-dö) *n* parachoques *m*; defensa *fMe*

ferment (föö-mênt) *v* fermentar

ferry-boat (fé-ri-bout) *n* transbordador *m*

fertile (föö-tail) *adj* fértil

festival (fé-ssti-völ) *n* festival *m*

festive (fé-sstiv) *adj* festivo

fetch (fêch) *v* *ir por; *ir a buscar

feudal (fyuu-döl) *adj* feudal

fever (fii-vö) *n* fiebre *f*

feverish (fii-vö-rif) *adj* febril

few (fyuu) *adj* pocos

fiancé (fi-*ang*-ssei) *n* novio *m*

fiancée (fi-*ang*-ssei) *n* novia *f*

fibre (fai-bö) *n* fibra *f*

fiction (fik-fön) *n* ficción *f*

field (fiild) *n* campo *m*; terreno *m*; ~ **glasses** gemelos de campaña

fierce (fiöss) *adj* fiero; salvaje, violento

fifteen (fif-tiin) *num* quince

fifteenth (fif-tiinz) *num* quinceno

fifth (fifz) *num* quinto

fifty (fif-ti) *num* cincuenta

fig (figh) *n* higo *m*

fight (fait) *n* combate *m*, lucha *f*

*fight (fait) *v* combatir, luchar

figure (fi-ghö) *n* estatura *f*, figura *f*; cifra *f*

file (fail) *n* lima *f*; expediente *m*; cola *f*

Filipino (fi-li-pii-nou) *n* filipino *m*

fill (fil) *v* llenar; ~ **in** completar, llenar; **filling station** estación de servicio; ~ **out** *Am* completar, llenar; ~ **up** llenar

filling (fi-ling) *n* empaste *m*; relleno *m*

film (film) *n* película *f*; *v* filmar

filter (fil-tö) *n* filtro *m*

filthy (fil-zi) *adj* sórdido, inmundo

final (fai-nöl) *adj* final

finance (fai-*næns*) *v* financiar

finances (fai-*næn*-ssis) *pl* finanzas *fpl*

financial (fai-*næn*-föl) *adj* financiero

finch (finch) *n* pinzón *m*

*find (faind) *v* *encontrar

fine (fain) *n* multa *f*; *adj* fino; bello; excelente, maravilloso; ~ **arts** bellas artes

finger (fing-ghö) *n* dedo *m*; **little** ~ dedo auricular

fingerprint (fing-ghö-print) *n* impresión digital

finish (fi-nif) *v* terminar; *n* terminación *f*; meta *f*; **finished** acabado

Finland (fin-lönd) Finlandia *f*

Finn (fin) *n* finlandés *m*

Finnish (fi-nif) *adj* finlandés

fire (faiö) *n* fuego *m*; incendio *m*; *v* disparar; *despedir

fire-alarm (faiö-rö-laam) *n* alarma de incendio

fire-brigade (faiö-bri-gheid) *n* bomberos *mpl*

fire-escape (faiö-ri-sskeip) *n* escala de incendios

fire-extinguisher (faiö-rik-ssting-ghᵘi-fö) *n* extintor *m*

fireplace (faiö-pleiss) *n* chimenea *f*

fireproof (faiö-pruuf) *adj* incombustible; refractario

firm (fööm) *adj* firme; sólido; *n* firma *f*

first (föösst) *num* primero; **at** ~ antes; al principio; ~ **name** nombre de pila

first-aid (föösst-*eid*) *n* primeros auxilios; ~ **kit** botiquín de urgencia; ~ **post** puesto de socorro

first-class (föösst-*klaass*) *adj* de primera calidad

first-rate (föösst-*reit*) *adj* de primer orden, de primera clase

fir-tree (föö-trii) *n* pino *m*

fish¹ (fif) *n* (pl ~, ~es) pez *m*; ~

shop pescadería f

fish² (fiʃ) v pescar; **fishing gear** avíos de pesca; **fishing fly** mosca artificial; **fishing hook** anzuelo m; **fishing licence** permiso de pesca; **fishing line** línea de pesca; **fishing net** red de pescar; **fishing rod** caña de pescar; **fishing tackle** aparejo de pesca

fishbone (fiʃ-boun) n espina f

fisherman (fi-ʃö-mön) n (pl -men) pescador m

fist (fisst) n puño m

fit (fit) adj apropiado; n ataque m; v *convenir; **fitting room** probador m

five (faiv) num cinco

fix (fikss) v arreglar

fixed (fiksst) adj fijo

fizz (fis) n efervescencia f

fjord (fyood) n fiordo m

flag (flægh) n bandera f

flame (fleim) n llama f

flamingo (flö-ming-ghou) n (pl ~s, ~es) flamenco m

flannel (flæ-nöl) n franela f

flash (flæʃ) n relámpago m

flash-bulb (flæʃ-balb) n bombilla de flash

flash-light (flæʃ-lait) n linterna f

flask (flaassk) n frasco m; **thermos ~** termo m

flat (flæt) adj llano; n piso m; **~ tyre** neumático desinflado

flavour (flei-vö) n sabor m; v sazonar

fleet (fliit) n flota f

flesh (fleʃ) n carne f

flew (fluu) v (p fly)

flex (flêkss) n cordón flexible

flexible (flêk-ssi-böl) adj flexible

flight (flait) n vuelo m; **charter ~** vuelo fletado

flint (flint) n pedernal m

float (flout) v flotar; n flotador m

flock (flok) n rebaño m

flood (flad) n inundación f; riada f

floor (floo) n suelo m; piso m; **~ show** espectáculo de variedades

florist (flo-risst) n florista m

flour (flauⁿ) n harina f

flow (flou) v correr, *fluir

flower (flauⁿ) n flor f

flowerbed (flauⁿ-bêd) n arriate m

flower-shop (flauⁿ-ʃop) n floristería f

flown (floun) v (pp fly)

flu (fluu) n gripe f

fluent (fluu-önt) adj con soltura

fluid (fluu-id) adj fluido; n fluido m

flute (fluut) n flauta f

fly (flai) n mosca f; bragueta f

*fly (flai) v *volar

foam (foum) n espuma f; v espumar

foam-rubber (foum-ra-bö) n goma espumada

focus (fou-köss) n foco m

fog (fogh) n niebla f

foggy (fo-ghi) adj brumoso

foglamp (fogh-læmp) n faro de niebla

fold (fould) v doblar; n pliegue m

folk (fouk) n gente f; **~ song** canción popular

folk-dance (fouk-daanss) n danza popular

folklore (fouk-loo) n folklore m

follow (fo-lou) v *seguir; **following** adj siguiente

*be fond of (bii fond ov) *querer

food (fuud) n comida f; alimento m; **~ poisoning** intoxicación alimentaria

foodstuffs (fuud-sstafss) pl artículos alimenticios

fool (fuul) n idiota m, tonto m; v engañar

foolish (fuu-liʃ) adj necio, tonto; absurdo

foot (fut) n (pl feet) pie m; **~ powder** polvo para los pies; **on ~** a pie

football (*fut*-bool) *n* fútbol *m*; ~ **match** partido de fútbol

foot-brake (*fut*-breik) *n* freno de pie

footpath (*fut*-paaz) *n* senda *f*

footwear (*fut*-ᵘêᵒ) *n* calzado *m*

for (foo, fö) *prep* para; durante; a causa de, por; *conj* porque

***forbid** (fö-*bid*) *v* prohibir

force (fooss) *v* obligar, *forzar; *n* fuerza *f*; **by** ~ forzosamente; **driving** ~ fuerza motriz

ford (food) *n* vado *m*

forecast (*foo*-kaasst) *n* previsión *f*; *v* pronosticar

foreground (*foo*-ghraund) *n* primer plano

forehead (*fo*-rêd) *n* frente *f*

foreign (*fo*-rin) *adj* extranjero; extraño

foreigner (*fo*-ri-nö) *n* extranjero *m*; forastero *m*

foreman (*foo*-mön) *n* (pl -men) capataz *m*

foremost (*foo*-mousst) *adj* primero

foresail (*foo*-sseil) *n* foque *m*

forest (*fo*-risst) *n* selva *f*, bosque *m*

forester (*fo*-ri-sstö) *n* guardabosques *m*

forge (foodʒ) *v* falsificar

***forget** (fö-*ghêt*) *v* olvidar

forgetful (fö-*ghêt*-föl) *adj* olvidadizo

***forgive** (fö-*ghiv*) *v* perdonar

fork (fook) *n* tenedor *m*; bifurcación *f*; *v* bifurcarse

form (foom) *n* forma *f*; formulario *m*; clase *f*; *v* formar

formal (*foo*-möl) *adj* formal

formality (foo-*mæ*-lö-ti) *n* formalidad *f*

former (*foo*-mö) *adj* antiguo; anterior; **formerly** antes

formula (*foo*-myu-lö) *n* (pl ~e, ~s) fórmula *f*

fort (foot) *n* fortaleza *f*

fortnight (*foot*-nait) *n* quincena *f*

fortress (*foo*-triss) *n* fortaleza *f*

fortunate (*foo*-chö-nöt) *adj* afortunado

fortune (*foo*-chuun) *n* fortuna *f*; suerte *f*

forty (*foo*-ti) *num* cuarenta

forward (*foo*-ᵘöd) *adv* hacia adelante, adelante; *v* reexpedir

foster-parents (*fo*-sstö-pêᵒ-röntss) *pl* padres adoptivos

fought (foot) *v* (p, pp fight)

foul (faul) *adj* sucio; vil

found¹ (faund) *v* (p, pp find)

found² (faund) *v* fundar

foundation (faun-*dei*-ʃön) *n* fundación *f*; ~ **cream** crema de base

fountain (*faun*-tin) *n* fuente *f*

fountain-pen (*faun*-tin-pên) *n* estilográfica *f*

four (foo) *num* cuatro

fourteen (foo-*tiin*) *num* catorce

fourteenth (foo-*tiinz*) *num* catorceno

fourth (fooz) *num* cuarto

fowl (faul) *n* (pl ~s, ~) volatería *f*

fox (fokss) *n* zorro *m*

foyer (*foi*-ei) *n* vestíbulo *m*

fraction (*fræk*-ʃön) *n* fracción *f*

fracture (*fræk*-chö) *v* fracturar; *n* fractura *f*

fragile (*fræ*-dʒail) *adj* frágil

fragment (*frægh*-mönt) *n* fragmento *m*; trozo *m*

frame (freim) *n* marco *m*; armadura *f*

France (fraanss) Francia *f*

franchise (*fræn*-chais) *n* derecho electoral

fraternity (frö-*töö*-nö-ti) *n* fraternidad *f*

fraud (frood) *n* fraude *m*

fray (frei) *v* deshilacharse

free (frii) *adj* libre; gratuito; ~ **of charge** gratis; ~ **ticket** billete gratuito

freedom (*frii*-döm) *n* libertad *f*

***freeze** (friis) *v* *helar; congelar

freezing (*frii*-sing) *adj* helado

freezing-point (*frii*-sing-point) *n* punto de congelación

freight (freit) *n* carga *f*, cargo *m*

French (frênch) *adj* francés

Frenchman (*frênch*-mön) *n* (pl -men) francés *m*

frequency (*frii*-kᵘön-ssi) *n* frecuencia *f*

frequent (*frii*-kᵘönt) *adj* frecuente

fresh (frêʃ) *adj* fresco; ~ **water** agua dulce

friction (*frik*-ʃön) *n* fricción *f*

Friday (*frai*-di) *n* viernes *m*

fridge (fridʒ) *n* frigorífico *m*, refrigerador *m*

friend (frênd) *n* amigo *m*; amiga *f*

friendly (*frênd*-li) *adj* amable; amistoso

friendship (*frênd*-ʃip) *n* amistad *f*

fright (frait) *n* miedo *m*, espanto *m*

frighten (*frai*-tön) *v* espantar

frightened (*frai*-tönd) *adj* espantado; ***be** ~ asustarse

frightful (*frait*-föl) *adj* terrible

fringe (frindʒ) *n* franja *f*

frock (frok) *n* vestido *m*

frog (frogh) *n* rana *f*

from (from) *prep* desde; de; a partir de

front (frant) *n* frente *m*; **in** ~ **of** delante de

frontier (*fran*-tiᵒ) *n* frontera *f*

frost (frosst) *n* escarcha *f*

froth (froz) *n* espuma *f*

frozen (*frou*-sön) *adj* congelado; ~ **food** alimento congelado

fruit (fruut) *n* fruta *f*; fruto *m*

fry (frai) *v* *freír

frying-pan (*frai*-ing-pæn) *n* sartén *f*

fuel (*fyuu*-öl) *n* combustible *m*; ~ **pump** *Am* bomba de gasolina

full (ful) *adj* lleno; ~ **board** pensión completa; ~ **stop** punto *m*; ~ **up** completo

fun (fan) *n* diversión *f*

function (*fangk*-ʃön) *n* función *f*

fund (fand) *n* fondos *mpl*

fundamental (fan-dö-*mên*-töl) *adj* fundamental

funeral (*fyuu*-nö-röl) *n* funerales *mpl*

funnel (*fa*-nöl) *n* embudo *m*

funny (*fa*-ni) *adj* gracioso, cómico; extraño

fur (föö) *n* piel *f*; ~ **coat** abrigo de pieles; **furs** piel *f*

furious (*fyu*-ö-ri-öss) *adj* furioso

furnace (*föö*-niss) *n* horno *m*

furnish (*föö*-niʃ) *v* suministrar, procurar; instalar, amueblar; ~ **with** *proveer de

furniture (*föö*-ni-chö) *n* muebles *mpl*

furrier (*fa*-ri-ö) *n* peletero *m*

further (*föö*-ðö) *adj* más lejos; ulterior

furthermore (*föö*-ðö-moo) *adv* además

furthest (*föö*-ðisst) *adj* el más alejado

fuse (fyuus) *n* fusible *m*; mecha *f*

fuss (fass) *n* bulla *f*; ostentación *f*, alharaca *f*

future (*fyuu*-chö) *n* porvenir *m*; *adj* futuro

G

gable (*ghei*-böl) *n* faldón *m*

gadget (*ghæ*-dʒit) *n* accesorio *m*

gaiety (*ghei*-ö-ti) *n* alegría *f*

gain (ghein) *v* ganar; *n* ganancia *f*

gait (gheit) *n* paso *m*

gale (gheil) *n* ventarrón *m*

gall (ghool) *n* bilis *f*; ~ **bladder** vesícula biliar

gallery (*ghæ*-lö-ri) *n* galería *f*

gallop (*ghæ*-löp) *n* galope *m*

gallows (*ghæ*-lous) *pl* horca *f*

gallstone (*ghool*-sstoun) *n* cálculo biliar

game (gheim) *n* juego *m*; caza *f*; ~ **reserve** parque de reserva zoológica

gang (ghæng) *n* banda *f*; equipo *m*

gangway (*ghæng*-ᵁei) *n* pasarela *f*

gaol (dzeil) *n* cárcel *f*

gap (ghæp) *n* hueco *m*

garage (*ghæ*-raaʒ) *n* garaje *m*; *v* dejar en garaje

garbage (*ghaa*-bidʒ) *n* basura *f*

garden (*ghaa*-dön) *n* jardín *m*; **public** ~ jardín público; **zoological gardens** jardín zoológico

gardener (*ghaa*-dö-nö) *n* jardinero *m*

gargle (*ghaa*-ghöl) *v* *hacer gárgaras

garlic (*ghaa*-lik) *n* ajo *m*

gas (ghæss) *n* gas *m*; *nAm* gasolina *f*; ~ **cooker** cocina de gas; ~ **station** *Am* puesto de gasolina; ~ **stove** estufa de gas

gasoline (*ghæ*-ssö-liin) *nAm* gasolina *f*

gastric (*ghæ*-sstrik) *adj* gástrico; ~ **ulcer** úlcera gástrica

gasworks (*ghæss*-ᵁöökss) *n* fábrica de gas

gate (gheit) *n* portón *m*; reja *f*

gather (*ghæ*-ðö) *v* coleccionar; juntarse; recoger

gauge (gheidʒ) *n* medidor *m*

gauze (ghoos) *n* gasa *f*

gave (gheiv) *v* (p give)

gay (ghei) *adj* alegre; gaitero

gaze (gheis) *v* mirar

gazetteer (ghæ-sö-*ti*ᵒ) *n* diccionario geográfico

gear (ghiᵒ) *n* velocidad *f*; aparejo *m*; **change** ~ cambiar de marcha; ~ **lever** palanca de cambios

gear-box (*ghiᵒ*-bokss) *n* caja de veloci-

dades

gem (dʒêm) *n* joya *f*, gema *f*; alhaja *f*

gender (*dʒên*-dö) *n* género *m*

general (*dʒê*-nö-röl) *adj* general; *n* general *m*; ~ **practitioner** médico de cabecera; **in** ~ en general

generate (*dʒê*-nö-reit) *v* generar

generation (dʒê-nö-*rei*-ʃön) *n* generación *f*

generator (*dʒê*-nö-rei-tör) *n* generador *m*

generosity (dʒê-nö-*ro*-ssö-ti) *n* generosidad *f*

generous (*dʒê*-nö-röss) *adj* generoso

genital (*dʒê*-ni-töl) *adj* genital

genius (*dʒii*-ni-öss) *n* genio *m*

gentle (*dʒên*-töl) *adj* gentil; tierno, suave; prudente

gentleman (*dʒên*-töl-mön) *n* (pl -men) caballero *m*

genuine (*dʒê*-nyu-in) *adj* genuino

geography (dʒi-*o*-ghrö-fi) *n* geografía *f*

geology (dʒi-*o*-lö-dʒi) *n* geología *f*

geometry (dʒi-*o*-mö-tri) *n* geometría *f*

germ (dʒööm) *n* germen *m*

German (*dʒöö*-mön) *adj* alemán

Germany (*dʒöö*-mö-ni) Alemania *f*

gesticulate (dʒi-*ssti*-kyu-leit) *v* gesticular

****get** (ghêt) *v* *conseguir; *ir a buscar; *hacerse; ~ **back** regresar; ~ **off** apearse; ~ **on** subir, montar; adelantar; ~ **up** levantarse

ghost (ghousst) *n* fantasma *m*; espíritu *m*

giant (*dʒai*-önt) *n* gigante *m*

giddiness (*ghi*-di-nöss) *n* mareo *m*

giddy (*ghi*-di) *adj* mareado

gift (ghift) *n* regalo *m*; talento *m*

gifted (*ghif*-tid) *adj* talentoso

gigantic (dʒai-*ghæn*-tik) *adj* gigantesco

giggle (*ghi*-ghöl) *v* *soltar risitas

gill (ghil) n branquia f

gilt (ghilt) adj dorado

ginger (dʒin-dʒö) n jengibre m

gipsy (dʒip-ssi) n gitano m

girdle (ghöö-döl) n faja f

girl (ghööl) n muchacha f; ~ **guide** exploradora f

***give** (ghiv) v *dar; entregar; ~ **away** revelar; ~ **in** ceder; ~ **up** renunciar

glacier (ghlæ-ssi-ö) n glaciar m

glad (ghlæd) adj alegre, contento; **gladly** con mucho gusto, gustosamente

gladness (ghlæd-nöss) n alegría f

glamorous (ghlæ-mö-röss) adj encantador

glamour (ghlæ-mö) n encanto m

glance (ghlaanss) n ojeada f; v ojear

gland (ghlænd) n glándula f

glare (ghlêˆ) n destello m; resplandor m

glaring (ghlêˆ-ring) adj deslumbrador

glass (ghlaass) n vaso m; vidrio m; de vidrio; **glasses** anteojos mpl; **magnifying** ~ lente de aumento

glaze (ghleis) v esmaltar

glen (ghlên) n cañada f

glide (ghlaid) v resbalar

glider (ghlai-dö) n planeador m

glimpse (ghlimpss) n vislumbre m; ojeada f; v vislumbrar

global (ghlou-böl) adj mundial

globe (ghloub) n globo m

gloom (ghluum) n obscuridad f

gloomy (ghluu-mi) adj sombrío

glorious (ghloo-ri-öss) adj espléndido

glory (ghloo-ri) n gloria f; honor m, elogio m

gloss (ghloss) n brillo m

glossy (ghlo-ssi) adj lustroso

glove (ghlav) n guante m

glow (ghlou) v brillar; n brillo m

glue (ghluu) n cola f

***go** (ghou) v *ir; caminar; *hacerse; ~ **ahead** continuar; ~ **away** *irse; ~ **back** regresar; ~ **home** *volver a casa; ~ **in** entrar; ~ **on** continuar; ~ **out** *salir; ~ **through** pasar

goal (ghoul) n meta f; gol m

goalkeeper (ghoul-kii-pö) n portero m

goat (ghout) n cabrón m, cabra f

god (ghod) n dios m

goddess (gho-diss) n diosa f

godfather (ghod-faa-ðö) n padrino m

goggles (gho-ghöls) pl gafas fpl

gold (ghould) n oro m; ~ **leaf** hojas de oro

golden (ghoul-dön) adj dorado

goldmine (ghould-main) n mina de oro

goldsmith (ghould-ssmiz) n orfebre m

golf (gholf) n golf m

golf-club (gholf-klab) n palo de golf

golf-course (gholf-kooss) n campo de golf

golf-links (gholf-lingkss) n campo de golf

gondola (ghon-dö-lö) n góndola f

gone (ghon) adv (pp go) ido

good (ghud) adj bueno

good-bye! (ghud-bai) ¡adiós!

good-humoured (ghud-hyuu-möd) adj de buen humor

good-looking (ghud-lu-king) adj bien parecido

good-natured (ghud-nei-chöd) adj bondadoso

goods (ghuds) pl mercancías fpl, bienes mpl; ~ **train** tren de mercancías

good-tempered (ghud-têm-pöd) adj de buen humor

goodwill (ghud-ᵁil) n buena voluntad f

goose (ghuuss) n (pl geese) oca f

gooseberry (ghus-bö-ri) n grosella espinosa

goose-flesh (ghuuss-fIêʃ) n carne de

gallina

gorge (ghoodȝ) n cañón m

gorgeous (ghoo-dȝöss) adj magnífico

gospel (gho-sspöl) n evangelio m

gossip (gho-ssip) n chisme m; v *contar chismes

got (ghot) v (p, pp get)

gourmet (ghuᵒ-mei) n gastrónomo m

gout (ghaut) n gota f

govern (gha-vön) v *regir

governess (gha-vö-niss) n aya f

government (gha-vön-mönt) n régimen m, gobierno m

governor (gha-vö-nö) n gobernador m

gown (ghaun) n traje m

grace (ghreiss) n gracia f; perdón m

graceful (ghreiss-föl) adj gracioso

grade (ghreid) n grado m; v graduar

gradient (ghrei-di-önt) n pendiente f

gradual (ghræ-dȝu-öl) adj gradual; **gradually** adv paulatinamente

graduate (ghræ-dȝu-eit) v graduarse

grain (ghrein) n grano m, trigo m

gram (ghræm) n gramo m

grammar (ghræ-mö) n gramática f

grammatical (ghrö-mæ-ti-köl) adj gramatical

gramophone (ghræ-mö-foun) n gramófono m

grand (ghrænd) adj imponente

granddad (ghræn-dæd) n abuelo m

granddaughter (ghræn-doo-tö) n nieta f

grandfather (ghræn-faa-ðö) n abuelo m

grandmother (ghræn-ma-ðö) n abuela f

grandparents (ghræn-pêᵒ-röntss) pl abuelos mpl

grandson (ghræn-ssan) n nieto m

granite (ghræ-nit) n granito m

grant (ghraant) v conceder; n subvención f, beca f

grapefruit (ghreip-fruut) n pomelo m; toronja fMe

grapes (ghreipss) pl uvas fpl

graph (ghræf) n gráfico m

graphic (ghræ-fik) adj gráfico

grasp (ghraassp) v agarrar; n agarre m

grass (ghraass) n césped m

grasshopper (ghraass-ho-pö) n saltamontes m

grate (ghreit) n reja f; v rallar

grateful (ghreit-föl) adj agradecido

grater (ghrei-tö) n rayador m

gratis (ghræ-tiss) adj gratuito

gratitude (ghræ-ti-tyuud) n gratitud f

gratuity (ghrö-tyuu-ö-ti) n propina f

grave (ghreiv) n sepultura f; adj grave

gravel (ghræ-völ) n grava f

gravestone (ghreiv-sstoun) n lápida f

graveyard (ghreiv-yaad) n cementerio m

gravity (ghræ-vö-ti) n gravedad f; seriedad f

gravy (ghrei-vi) n salsa f

graze (ghreis) v *pacer; n rozadura f

grease (ghriiss) n grasa f; v engrasar

greasy (ghrii-ssi) adj grasiento, grasoso

great (ghreit) adj grande; **Great Britain** Gran Bretaña

Greece (ghriiss) Grecia f

greed (ghriid) n codicia f

greedy (ghrii-di) adj codicioso; glotón

Greek (ghriik) adj griego

green (ghriin) adj verde; ~ **card** tarjeta verde

greengrocer (ghriin-ghrou-ssö) n verdulero m

greenhouse (ghriin-hauss) n invernadero m, invernáculo m

greens (ghriins) pl legumbres fpl

greet (ghriit) v saludar

greeting (ghrii-ting) n saludo m

grey (ghrei) *adj* gris
greyhound (*ghrei*-haund) *n* galgo *m*
grief (ghriif) *n* pesadumbre *f*; aflicción *f*, dolor *m*
grieve (ghriiv) *v* *estar afligido
grill (ghril) *n* parrilla *f*; *v* asar en parrilla
grill-room (*ghril*-ruum) *n* parrilla *f*
grin (ghrin) *v* *sonreír; *n* sonrisa sardónica
*grind (ghraind) *v* *moler; triturar
grip (ghrip) *v* *asir; *n* agarradero *m*, agarre *m*; *nAm* maletín *m*
grit (ghrit) *n* polvo *m*
groan (ghroun) *v* *gemir
grocer (*ghrou*-ssö) *n* abacero *m*; abarrotero *mMe*; **grocer's** abacería *f*; abarrotería *fMe*
groceries (*ghrou*-ssö-ris) *pl* comestibles *mpl*
groin (ghroin) *n* ingle *f*
groove (ghruuv) *n* surco *m*
gross¹ (ghrouss) *n* (pl ~) gruesa *f*
gross² (ghrouss) *adj* grosero; bruto *f*
grotto (*ghro*-tou) *n* (pl ~es, ~s) gruta *f*
ground¹ (ghraund) *n* fondo *m*, tierra *f*; ~ **floor** piso bajo; **grounds** terreno *m*
ground² (ghraund) *v* (p, pp grind)
group (ghruup) *n* grupo *m*
grouse (ghrauss) *n* (pl ~) gallo de bosque
grove (ghrouv) *n* soto *m*
*grow (ghrou) *v* *crecer; cultivar; *hacerse
growl (ghraul) *v* *gruñir
grown-up (*ghroun*-ap) *adj* adulto; *n* adulto *m*
growth (ghrouz) *n* crecimiento *m*; tumor *m*
grudge (ghradʒ) *v* envidiar
grumble (*ghram*-böl) *v* refunfuñar
guarantee (ghæ-rön-*tii*) *n* garantía *f*;

v garantizar
guarantor (ghæ-rön-*too*) *n* garante *m*
guard (ghaad) *n* guardia *f*; *v* guardar
guardian (*ghaa*-di-ön) *n* tutor *m*
guess (ghêss) *v* adivinar; *creer, conjeturar; *n* conjetura *f*
guest (ghêsst) *n* huésped *m*, invitado *m*
guest-house (*ghêsst*-hauss) *n* pensión *f*
guest-room (*ghêsst*-ruum) *n* habitación para huéspedes
guide (ghaid) *n* guía *m*; *v* guiar
guidebook (*ghaid*-buk) *n* guía *f*
guide-dog (*ghaid*-dogh) *n* perro lazarillo
guilt (ghilt) *n* culpa *f*
guilty (*ghil*-ti) *adj* culpable
guinea-pig (*ghi*-ni-pigh) *n* conejillo de Indias
guitar (ghi-*taa*) *n* guitarra *f*
gulf (ghalf) *n* golfo *m*
gull (ghal) *n* gaviota *f*
gum (gham) *n* encía *f*; goma *f*; cola *f*
gun (ghan) *n* fusil *m*, revólver *m*; cañón *m*
gunpowder (*ghan*-pau-dö) *n* pólvora *f*
gust (ghasst) *n* ráfaga *f*
gusty (*gha*-ssti) *adj* borrascoso
gut (ghat) *n* intestino *m*; **guts** coraje *m*
gutter (*gha*-tö) *n* cuneta *f*
guy (ghai) *n* tipo *m*
gymnasium (dʒim-*nei*-si-öm) *n* (pl ~s, -sia) gimnasio *m*
gymnast (*dʒim*-næsst) *n* gimnasta *m*
gymnastics (dʒim-*næ*-sstikss) *pl* gimnasia *f*
gynaecologist (ghai-nö-*ko*-lö-dʒisst) *n* ginecólogo *m*

H

haberdashery (*hæ-bö-dæ-ʃö-ri*) *n* mercería *f*

habit (*hæ-bit*) *n* hábito *m*

habitable (*hæ-bi-tö-böl*) *adj* habitable

habitual (*hö-bi-chu-öl*) *adj* habitual

had (*hæd*) *v* (p, pp have)

haddock (*hæ-dök*) *n* (pl ~) bacalao *m*

haemorrhage (*hê-mö-ridʒ*) *n* hemorragia *f*

haemorrhoids (*hê-mö-roids*) *pl* hemorroides *fpl*

hail (*heil*) *n* granizo *m*

hair (*hêᵒ*) *n* cabello *m*; ~ **cream** brillantina *f*; ~ **piece** postizo *m*; ~ **rollers** rizadores *mpl*; ~ **tonic** tónico para el cabello

hairbrush (*hêᵒ-braʃ*) *n* cepillo para el cabello

haircut (*hêᵒ-kat*) *n* corte de pelo

hair-do (*hêᵒ-duu*) *n* peinado *m*

hairdresser (*hêᵒ-drê-ssö*) *n* peluquero *m*

hair-dryer (*hêᵒ-drai-ö*) *n* secador para el pelo

hair-grip (*hêᵒ-ghrip*) *n* horquilla *f*

hair-net (*hêᵒ-nêt*) *n* redecilla *f*

hair-oil (*hêᵒ-roil*) *n* aceite para el pelo

hairpin (*hêᵒ-pin*) *n* horquilla *f*

hair-spray (*hêᵒ-ssprei*) *n* laca para el cabello

hairy (*hêᵒ-ri*) *adj* cabelludo

half¹ (*haaf*) *adj* medio

half² (*haaf*) *n* (pl halves) mitad *f*

half-time (*haaf-taim*) *n* descanso *m*

halfway (*haaf-ᵘei*) *adv* a mitad de camino

halibut (*hæ-li-böt*) *n* (pl ~) halibut *m*

hall (*hool*) *n* vestíbulo *m*; sala *f*

halt (*hoolt*) *v* pararse

halve (*haav*) *v* partir por la mitad

ham (*hæm*) *n* jamón *m*

hamlet (*hæm-löt*) *n* aldea *f*

hammer (*hæ-mö*) *n* martillo *m*

hammock (*hæ-mök*) *n* hamaca *f*

hamper (*hæm-pö*) *n* cesto *m*

hand (*hænd*) *n* mano *f*; *v* alargar; ~ **cream** crema para las manos

handbag (*hænd-bægh*) *n* bolso *m*

handbook (*hænd-buk*) *n* manual *m*

hand-brake (*hænd-breik*) *n* freno de mano

handcuffs (*hænd-kafss*) *pl* esposas *fpl*

handful (*hænd-ful*) *n* puñado *m*

handicraft (*hæn-di-kraaft*) *n* trabajo manual; artesanía *f*

handkerchief (*hæng-kö-chif*) *n* pañuelo *m*

handle (*hæn-döl*) *n* mango *m*; *v* manejar; tratar

hand-made (hænd-*meid*) *adj* hecho a mano

handshake (*hænd-ʃeik*) *n* apretón de manos

handsome (*hæn-ssöm*) *adj* guapo

handwork (*hænd-ᵘöök*) *n* obra hecha a mano

handwriting (*hænd-rai-ting*) *n* escritura *f*

handy (*hæn-di*) *adj* manejable

*hang (*hæng*) *v* *colgar

hanger (*hæng-ö*) *n* percha *f*

hangover (*hæng-ou-vö*) *n* resaca *f*

happen (*hæ-pön*) *v* suceder, pasar

happening (*hæ-pö-ning*) *n* acontecimiento *m*

happiness (*hæ-pi-nöss*) *n* felicidad *f*

happy (*hæ-pi*) *adj* contento, feliz

harbour (*haa-bö*) *n* puerto *m*

hard (*haad*) *adj* duro; difícil; **hardly** apenas

hardware (*haad-ᵘêᵒ*) *n* quincalla *f*; ~ **store** ferretería *f*

hare (*hêᵒ*) *n* liebre *f*

harm (*haam*) *n* perjuicio *m*; mal *m*,

daño m; v perjudicar

harmful (haam-föl) adj perjudicial, dañoso

harmless (haam-löss) adj inocuo

harmony (haa-mö-ni) n armonía f

harp (haap) n arpa f

harpsichord (haap-ssi-kood) n clavicémbalo m

harsh (haaʃ) adj áspero; severo; cruel

harvest (haa-visst) n cosecha f

has (hæs) v (pr have)

haste (heisst) n prisa f

hasten (hei-ssön) v apresurarse

hasty (hei-ssti) adj apresurado

hat (hæt) n sombrero m; ~ **rack** percha f

hatch (hæch) n trampa f

hate (heit) v detestar; odiar; n odio m

hatred (hei-trid) n odio m

haughty (hoo-ti) adj altivo

haul (hool) v arrastrar

*have (hæv) v *haber, *tener; *hacer; ~ **to** deber

haversack (hæ-vö-ssæk) n morral m

hawk (hook) n azor m; halcón m

hay (hei) n heno m; ~ **fever** fiebre del heno

hazard (hæ-söd) n riesgo m

haze (heis) n calina f; niebla f

hazelnut (hei-söl-nat) n avellana f

hazy (hei-si) adj calinoso; brumoso

he (hii) pron él

head (hêd) n cabeza f; v dirigir; ~ **of state** jefe de Estado; ~ **teacher** director de escuela

headache (hê-deik) n dolor de cabeza

heading (hê-ding) n título m

headlamp (hêd-læmp) n fanal m

headland (hêd-lönd) n promontorio m

headlight (hêd-lait) n faro m

headline (hêd-lain) n titular m

headmaster (hêd-maa-sstö) n director

de escuela

headquarters (hêd-kᵘoo-tös) pl cuartel general

head-strong (hêd-sstrong) adj cabezudo

head-waiter (hêd-ᵘei-tö) n jefe de camareros

heal (hiil) v curar

health (hêlz) n salud f; ~ **centre** dispensario m; ~ **certificate** certificado de salud

healthy (hêl-zi) adj sano

heap (hiip) n montón m

*hear (hiᵒ) v *oír

hearing (hiᵒ-ring) n oído m

heart (haat) n corazón m; núcleo m; **by** ~ de memoria; ~ **attack** ataque cardíaco

heartburn (haat-böön) n acidez f

hearth (haaz) n hogar m

heartless (haat-löss) adj insensible

hearty (haa-ti) adj cordial

heat (hiit) n calor m; v *calentar; **heating pad** almohada eléctrica

heater (hii-tö) n calefactor m; **immersion** ~ calentador de inmersión

heath (hiiz) n landa f

heathen (hii-ðön) n pagano m

heather (hê-ðö) n brezo m

heating (hii-ting) n calefacción f

heaven (hê-vön) n cielo m

heavy (hê-vi) adj pesado

Hebrew (hii-bruu) n hebreo m

hedge (hêdʒ) n seto m

hedgehog (hêdʒ-hogh) n erizo m

heel (hiil) n talón m; tacón m

height (hait) n altura f; colmo m, apogeo m

hell (hêl) n infierno m

hello! (hê-lou) ¡hola!; ¡buenos días!

helm (hêlm) n timón m

helmet (hêl-mit) n casco m

helmsman (hêlms-mön) n timonero m

help (hêlp) v ayudar; n ayuda f

helper (*hêl*-pö) *n* ayudante *m*
helpful (*hêlp*-föl) *adj* servicial
helping (*hêl*-ping) *n* porción *f*
hem (hêm) *n* dobladillo *m*
hemp (hêmp) *n* cáñamo *m*
hen (hên) *n* gallina *f*
henceforth (hênss-*fooz*) *adv* de ahora en adelante
her (höö) *pron* la, le; *adj* su
herb (hööb) *n* hierba *f*
herd (hööd) *n* manada *f*
here (hi⁶) *adv* acá; ~ **you are** tenga usted
hereditary (hi-*rê*-di-tö-ri) *adj* hereditario
hernia (*höö*-ni-ö) *n* hernia *f*
hero (*hi⁶*-rou) *n* (pl ~es) héroe *m*
heron (*hê*-rön) *n* garza *f*
herring (*hê*-ring) *n* (pl ~, ~s) arenque *m*
herself (höö-*ssêlf*) *pron* se; ella misma
hesitate (*hê*-si-teit) *v* vacilar
heterosexual (hê-tö-rö-*ssêk*-ʃu-öl) *adj* heterosexual
hiccup (*hi*-kap) *n* hipo *m*
hide (haid) *n* piel *f*
*****hide** (haid) *v* esconder
hideous (*hi*-di-öss) *adj* horrible
hierarchy (*hai⁶*-raa-ki) *n* jerarquía *f*
high (hai) *adj* alto
highway (*hai*-ᵘei) *n* carretera *f*; *nAm* autopista *f*
hijack (*hai*-dʒæk) *v* apresar
hijacker (*hai*-dʒæ-kö) *n* secuestrador *m*
hike (haik) *v* caminar
hill (hil) *n* colina *f*
hillside (*hil*-ssaid) *n* ladera *f*
hilltop (*hil*-top) *n* cima *f*
hilly (*hi*-li) *adj* montuoso
him (him) *pron* le
himself (him-*ssêlf*) *pron* se; él mismo
hinder (*hin*-dö) *v* *impedir

hinge (hindʒ) *n* bisagra *f*
hip (hip) *n* cadera *f*
hire (hai⁶) *v* alquilar; **for ~** de alquiler
hire-purchase (hai⁶-*pöö*-chöss) *n* compra a plazos
his (his) *adj* su
historian (hi-*sstoo*-ri-ön) *n* historiador *m*
historic (hi-*ssto*-rik) *adj* histórico
historical (hi-*ssto*-ri-köl) *adj* histórico
history (*hi*-sstö-ri) *n* historia *f*
hit (hit) *n* éxito *m*
*****hit** (hit) *v* pegar; tocar, *acertar
hitchhike (*hich*-haik) *v* *hacer autostop
hitchhiker (*hich*-hai-kö) *n* autoestopista *m*
hoarse (hooss) *adj* ronco
hobby (*ho*-bi) *n* afición *f*
hobby-horse (*ho*-bi-hooss) *n* comidilla *f*
hockey (*ho*-ki) *n* hockey *m*
hoist (hoisst) *v* izar
hold (hould) *n* bodega *f*
*****hold** (hould) *v* *tener; *retener; ~ **on** agarrarse; ~ **up** *sostener
hold-up (*houl*-dap) *n* atraco *m*
hole (houl) *n* bache *m*, agujero *m*
holiday (*ho*-lö-di) *n* vacaciones *fpl*; fiesta *f*; ~ **camp** colonia veraniega; ~ **resort** lugar de descanso; **on ~** de vacaciones
Holland (*ho*-lönd) Holanda *f*
hollow (*ho*-lou) *adj* hueco
holy (*hou*-li) *adj* santo
homage (*ho*-midʒ) *n* homenaje *m*
home (houm) *n* casa *f*; hospicio *m*; *adv* en casa, a casa; **at ~** en casa
home-made (houm-*meid*) *adj* casero
homesickness (*houm*-ssik-nöss) *n* nostalgia *f*
homosexual (hou-mö-*ssêk*-ʃu-öl) *adj* homosexual

honest (*o*-nisst) *adj* honesto; sincero
honesty (*o*-ni-ssti) *n* honradez *f*
honey (*ha*-ni) *n* miel *f*
honeymoon (*ha*-ni-muun) *n* luna de miel
honour (*o*-nö) *n* honor *m*; *v* honrar, *rendir homenaje
honourable (*o*-nö-rö-böl) *adj* honorable; honesto
hood (hud) *n* capucha *f*; *nAm* capó *m*
hoof (huuf) *n* casco *m*
hook (huk) *n* gancho *m*
hoot (huut) *v* tocar la bocina
hooter (*huu*-tö) *n* bocina *f*
hoover (*huu*-vö) *v* pasar el aspirador
hop¹ (hop) *v* brincar; *n* salto *m*
hop² (hop) *n* lúpulo *m*
hope (houp) *n* esperanza *f*; *v* esperar
hopeful (*houp*-föl) *adj* esperanzado
hopeless (*houp*-löss) *adj* desesperado
horizon (hö-*rai*-sön) *n* horizonte *m*
horizontal (ho-ri-*son*-töl) *adj* horizontal
horn (hoon) *n* cuerno *m*; bocina *f*
horrible (*ho*-ri-böl) *adj* horrible; terrible, atroz
horror (*ho*-rö) *n* espanto *m*, horror *m*
hors-d'œuvre (oo-*döövr*) *n* entremeses *mpl*
horse (hooss) *n* caballo *m*
horseman (*hooss*-mön) *n* (pl -men) jinete *m*
horsepower (*hooss*-pau⁶) *n* caballo de vapor
horserace (*hooss*-reiss) *n* carrera de caballos
horseradish (*hooss*-ræ-diʃ) *n* rábano picante
horseshoe (*hooss*-ʃuu) *n* herradura *f*
horticulture (*hoo*-ti-kal-chö) *n* horticultura *f*
hosiery (*hou*-ʒö-ri) *n* géneros de punto

hospitable (*ho*-sspi-tö-böl) *adj* hospitalario
hospital (*ho*-sspi-töl) *n* hospital *m*
hospitality (ho-sspi-*tæ*-lö-ti) *n* hospitalidad *f*
host (housst) *n* anfitrión *m*
hostage (*ho*-sstidʒ) *n* rehén *m*
hostel (*ho*-sstöl) *n* hospedería *f*
hostess (*hou*-sstiss) *n* azafata *f*
hostile (*ho*-sstail) *adj* hostil
hot (hot) *adj* caliente
hotel (hou-*têl*) *n* hotel *m*
hot-tempered (hot-*têm*-pöd) *adj* colérico
hour (au⁶) *n* hora *f*
hourly (*au⁶*-li) *adj* a cada hora
house (hauss) *n* casa *f*; vivienda *f*; inmueble *m*; ~ agent corredor de casas; ~ block *Am* manzana de casas; public ~ café *m*
houseboat (*hauss*-bout) *n* casa flotante
household (*hauss*-hould) *n* menaje *m*
housekeeper (*hauss*-kii-pö) *n* ama de llaves
housekeeping (*hauss*-kii-ping) *n* gobierno de la casa
housemaid (*hauss*-meid) *n* criada *f*
housewife (*hauss*-ᵘaif) *n* ama de casa
housework (*hauss*-ᵘöök) *n* faenas domésticas
how (hau) *adv* cómo; qué; ~ many cuánto; ~ much cuánto
however (hau-ê-vö) *conj* todavía, sin embargo
hug (hagh) *v* abrazar; *n* abrazo *m*
huge (hyuudʒ) *adj* formidable, enorme
hum (ham) *v* tararear
human (*hyuu*-mön) *adj* humano; ~ being ser humano
humanity (hyu-*mæ*-nö-ti) *n* humanidad *f*
humble (*ham*-böl) *adj* humilde

humid (*hyuu*-mid) *adj* húmedo

humidity (hyu-*mi*-dö-ti) *n* humedad *f*

humorous (*hyuu*-mö-röss) *adj* chistoso, gracioso, humorístico

humour (*hyuu*-mö) *n* humor *m*

hundred (*han*-dröd) *n* ciento

Hungarian (hang-*ghê*ö-ri-ön) *adj* húngaro

Hungary (*hang*-ghö-ri) Hungría *m*

hunger (*hang*-ghö) *n* hambre *f*

hungry (*hang*-ghri) *adj* hambriento

hunt (hant) *v* cazar; *n* caza *f*; ~ **for** buscar

hunter (*han*-tö) *n* cazador *m*

hurricane (*ha*-ri-kön) *n* huracán *m*; ~ **lamp** lámpara sorda

hurry (*ha*-ri) *v* *darse prisa, apresurarse; *n* prisa *f*; **in a** ~ de prisa

***hurt** (hööt) *v* *hacer daño, dañar; ofender

hurtful (*hööt*-föl) *adj* perjudicial

husband (*has*-bönd) *n* esposo *m*, marido *m*

hut (hat) *n* cabaña *f*

hydrogen (*hai*-drö-dʒön) *n* hidrógeno *m*

hygiene (*hai*-dʒiin) *n* higiene *f*

hygienic (hai-*dʒii*-nik) *adj* higiénico

hymn (him) *n* himno *m*

hyphen (*hai*-fön) *n* guión *m*

hypocrisy (hi-*po*-krö-ssi) *n* hipocresía *f*

hypocrite (*hi*-pö-krit) *n* hipócrita *m*

hypocritical (hi-pö-*kri*-ti-köl) *adj* hipócrita, mojigato

hysterical (hi-*sstê*-ri-köl) *adj* histérico

I

I (ai) *pron* yo

ice (aiss) *n* hielo *m*

ice-bag (*aiss*-bægh) *n* bolsa de hielo

ice-cream (*aiss*-kriim) *n* helado *m*

Iceland (*aiss*-lönd) Islandia *f*

Icelander (*aiss*-lön-dö) *n* islandés *m*

Icelandic (aiss-*læn*-dik) *adj* islandés

icon (*ai*-kon) *n* icono *m*

idea (ai-*di*ö) *n* idea *f*; pensamiento *m*; noción *f*, concepto *m*

ideal (ai-*di*öl) *adj* ideal; *n* ideal *m*

identical (ai-*dên*-ti-köl) *adj* idéntico

identification (ai-dên-ti-fi-*kei*-fön) *n* identificación *f*

identify (ai-*dên*-ti-fai) *v* identificar

identity (ai-*dên*-tö-ti) *n* identidad *f*; ~ **card** carnet de identidad

idiom (*i*-di-öm) *n* modismo *m*

idiomatic (i-di-ö-*mæ*-tik) *adj* idiomático

idiot (*i*-di-öt) *n* idiota *m*

idiotic (i-di-*o*-tik) *adj* idiota

idle (*ai*-döl) *adj* ocioso; vago; vano

idol (*ai*-döl) *n* ídolo *m*

if (if) *conj* si

ignition (igh-*ni*-fön) *n* encendido *m*; ~ **coil** bobina del encendido

ignorant (*igh*-nö-rönt) *adj* ignorante

ignore (igh-*noo*) *v* ignorar

ill (il) *adj* enfermo; malo; maligno

illegal (i-*lii*-ghöl) *adj* ilegal

illegible (i-*lê*-dʒö-böl) *adj* ilegible

illiterate (i-*li*-tö-röt) *n* analfabeto *m*

illness (*il*-nöss) *n* enfermedad *f*

illuminate (i-*luu*-mi-neit) *v* iluminar

illumination (i-luu-mi-*nei*-fön) *n* iluminación *f*

illusion (i-*luu*-ʒön) *n* ilusión *f*

illustrate (*i*-lö-sstreit) *v* ilustrar

illustration (i-lö-*sstrei*-fön) *n* ilustración *f*

image (*i*-midʒ) *n* imagen *f*

imaginary (i-*mæ*-dʒi-nö-ri) *adj* imaginario

imagination (i-mæ-dʒi-*nei*-fön) *n* imaginación *f*

imagine (i-*mæ*-dʒin) *v* imaginarse; figurarse

imitate (*i*-mi-teit) *v* imitar

imitation (i-mi-*tei*-∫ön) *n* imitación *f*

immediate (i-*mii*-dyöt) *adj* inmediato

immediately (i-*mii*-dyöt-li) *adv* inmediatamente, de inmediato

immense (i-*mênss*) *adj* inmenso, enorme

immigrant (*i*-mi-ghrönt) *n* inmigrante *m*

immigrate (*i*-mi-ghreit) *v* inmigrar

immigration (i-mi-*ghrei*-∫ön) *n* inmigración *f*

immodest (i-*mo*-disst) *adj* inmodesto

immunity (i-*myuu*-nö-ti) *n* inmunidad *f*

immunize (*i*-myu-nais) *v* inmunizar

impartial (im-*paa*-∫öl) *adj* imparcial

impassable (im-*paa*-ssö-böl) *adj* intransitable

impatient (im-*pei*-∫önt) *adj* impaciente

impede (im-*piid*) *v* *impedir

impediment (im-*pê*-di-mönt) *n* impedimento *m*

imperfect (im-*pöö*-fikt) *adj* imperfecto

imperial (im-*pi⁰*-ri-öl) *adj* imperial

impersonal (im-*pöö*-ssö-nöl) *adj* impersonal

impertinence (im-*pöö*-ti-nönss) *n* impertinencia *f*

impertinent (im-*pöö*-ti-nönt) *adj* grosero, descarado, impertinente

implement[1] (*im*-pli-mönt) *n* herramienta *f*

implement[2] (*im*-pli-mênt) *v* efectuar

imply (im-*plai*) *v* implicar

impolite (im-pö-*lait*) *adj* descortés

import[1] (im-*poot*) *v* importar

import[2] (*im*-poot) *n* importación *f*; ~ **duty** impuestos de importación

importance (im-*poo*-tönss) *n* importancia *f*

important (im-*poo*-tönt) *adj* impor-

tante

importer (im-*poo*-tö) *n* importador *m*

imposing (im-*pou*-sing) *adj* imponente

impossible (im-*po*-ssö-böl) *adj* imposible

impotence (*im*-pö-tönss) *n* impotencia *f*

impotent (*im*-pö-tönt) *adj* impotente

impound (im-*paund*) *v* confiscar

impress (im-*prêss*) *v* impresionar

impression (im-*prê*-∫ön) *n* impresión *f*

impressive (im-*prê*-ssiv) *adj* impresionante

imprison (im-*pri*-sön) *v* encarcelar

imprisonment (im-*pri*-sön-mönt) *n* encarcelamiento *m*

improbable (im-*pro*-bö-böl) *adj* improbable

improper (im-*pro*-pö) *adj* impropio

improve (im-*pruuv*) *v* mejorar

improvement (im-*pruuv*-mönt) *n* mejora *f*

improvise (*im*-prö-vais) *v* improvisar

impudent (*im*-pyu-dönt) *adj* impudente

impulse (*im*-palss) *n* impulso *m*; estímulo *m*

impulsive (im-*pal*-ssiv) *adj* impulsivo

in (in) *prep* en; dentro de; *adv* adentro

inaccessible (i-næk-*ssê*-ssö-böl) *adj* inaccesible

inaccurate (i-*næ*-kyu-röt) *adj* inexacto

inadequate (i-*næ*-di-k⁰öt) *adj* inadecuado

incapable (ing-*kei*-pö-böl) *adj* incapaz

incense (*in*-ssênss) *n* incienso *m*

incident (*in*-ssi-dönt) *n* incidente *m*

incidental (in-ssi-*dên*-töl) *adj* imprevisto

incite (in-*ssait*) *v* incitar

inclination (ing-kli-*nei*-∫ön) *n* inclinación *f*

incline (ing-*klain*) *n* inclinación *f*

inclined (ing-*klaind*) *adj* dispuesto, inclinado; ***be ~ to** *v* inclinarse

include (ing-*kluud*) *v* *incluir

inclusive (ing-*kluu*-ssiv) *adj* incluso

income (*ing*-köm) *n* ingresos *mpl*

income-tax (*ing*-köm-tækss) *n* impuesto sobre los ingresos

incompetent (ing-*kom*-pö-tönt) *adj* incompetente

incomplete (in-köm-*pliit*) *adj* incompleto

inconceivable (ing-kön-*ssii*-vö-böl) *adj* inconcebible

inconspicuous (ing-kön-*sspi*-kyu-öss) *adj* discreto

inconvenience (ing-kön-*vii*-nyönss) *n* incomodidad *f*, inconveniencia *f*

inconvenient (ing-kön-*vii*-nyönt) *adj* inoportuno; molesto

incorrect (ing-kö-*rêkt*) *adj* inexacto, incorrecto

increase[1] (ing-*kriiss*) *v* aumentar; incrementar, *acrecentarse

increase[2] (*ing*-kriiss) *n* aumento *m*

incredible (ing-*krê*-dö-böl) *adj* increíble

incurable (ing-*kyuᵒ*-rö-böl) *adj* incurable

indecent (in-*dii*-ssönt) *adj* indecente

indeed (in-*diid*) *adv* por cierto

indefinite (in-*dê*-fi-nit) *adj* indefinido

indemnity (in-*dêm*-nö-ti) *n* indemnización *f*

independence (in-di-*pên*-dönss) *n* independencia *f*

independent (in-di-*pên*-dönt) *adj* independiente; autónomo

index (*in*-dêkss) *n* índice *m*; **~ finger** índice *m*

India (*in*-di-ö) India *f*

Indian (*in*-di-ön) *adj* indio; *n* indio *m*

indicate (*in*-di-keit) *v* señalar, indicar

indication (in-di-*kei*-ʃön) *n* señal *f*, indicación *f*

indicator (*in*-di-kei-tö) *n* indicador *m*

indifferent (in-*di*-fö-rönt) *adj* indiferente

indigestion (in-di-*dʒêss*-chön) *n* indigestión *f*

indignation (in-digh-*nei*-ʃön) *n* indignación *f*

indirect (in-di-*rêkt*) *adj* indirecto

individual (in-di-*vi*-dʒu-öl) *adj* aparte, individual; *n* individuo *m*

Indonesia (in-dö-*nii*-si-ö) Indonesia *f*

Indonesian (in-dö-*nii*-si-ön) *adj* indonesio

indoor (*in*-doo) *adj* en casa

indoors (in-*doos*) *adv* en casa

indulge (in-*daldʒ*) *v* ceder

industrial (in-*da*-sstri-öl) *adj* industrial; **~ area** zona industrial

industrious (in-*da*-sstri-öss) *adj* diligente

industry (*in*-dö-sstri) *n* industria *f*

inedible (i-*nê*-di-böl) *adj* incomible

inefficient (i-ni-*fi*-ʃönt) *adj* ineficiente

inevitable (i-*nê*-vi-tö-böl) *adj* inevitable

inexpensive (i-nik-*sspên*-ssiv) *adj* barato

inexperienced (i-nik-*sspiᵒ*-ri-önsst) *adj* inexperto

infant (*in*-fönt) *n* criatura *f*

infantry (*in*-fön-tri) *n* infantería *f*

infect (in-*fêkt*) *v* infectar

infection (in-*fêk*-ʃön) *n* infección *f*

infectious (in-*fêk*-föss) *adj* contagioso

infer (in-*föö*) *v* *deducir

inferior (in-*fiᵒ*-ri-ö) *adj* inferior

infinite (*in*-fi-nöt) *adj* infinito

infinitive (in-*fi*-ni-tiv) *n* infinitivo *m*

infirmary (in-*föö*-mö-ri) *n* enfermería *f*

inflammable (in-*flæ*-mö-böl) *adj* inflamable

inflammation (in-flö-*mei*-ʃön) *n* inflamación *f*

inflatable (in-*flei*-tö-böl) *adj* inflable
inflate (in-*fleit*) *v* hinchar
inflation (in-*flei*-jön) *n* inflación *f*
influence (*in*-flu-önss) *n* influencia *f*; *v* *influir
influential (in-flu-*ên*-jöl) *adj* influyente
influenza (in-flu-*ên*-sö) *n* gripe *f*
inform (in-*foom*) *v* informar; comunicar
informal (in-*foo*-möl) *adj* informal
information (in-fö-*mei*-jön) *n* información *f*; informes *mpl*, comunicado *m*; ~ **bureau** oficina de informaciones
infra-red (in-frö-*rêd*) *adj* infrarrojo
infrequent (in-*frii*-kʷönt) *adj* infrecuente
ingredient (ing-*ghrii*-di-önt) *n* ingrediente *m*
inhabit (in-*hæ*-bit) *v* habitar
inhabitable (in-*hæ*-bi-tö-böl) *adj* habitable
inhabitant (in-*hæ*-bi-tönt) *n* habitante *m*
inhale (in-*heil*) *v* inhalar
inherit (in-*hê*-rit) *v* heredar
inheritance (in-*hê*-ri-tönss) *n* herencia *f*
initial (i-*ni*-jöl) *adj* inicial; *n* inicial *f*; *v* rubricar
initiative (i-*ni*-jö-tiv) *n* iniciativa *f*
inject (in-*dʒêkt*) *v* inyectar
injection (in-*dʒêk*-jön) *n* inyección *f*
injure (*in*-dʒö) *v* *herir; ofender
injury (*in*-dʒö-ri) *n* herida *f*; lesión *f*
injustice (in-*dʒa*-sstiss) *n* injusticia *f*
ink (ingk) *n* tinta *f*
inlet (*in*-lêt) *n* ensenada *f*
inn (in) *n* posada *f*
inner (*i*-nö) *adj* interior; ~ **tube** cámara de aire
inn-keeper (*in*-kii-pö) *n* posadero *m*
innocence (*i*-nö-ssönss) *n* inocencia *f*

innocent (*i*-nö-ssönt) *adj* inocente
inoculate (i-*no*-kyu-leit) *v* vacunar
inoculation (i-no-kyu-*lei*-jön) *n* inoculación *f*
inquire (ing-kʷ*aiᵒ*) *v* informarse, *pedir informes
inquiry (ing-kʷ*aiᵒ*-ri) *n* pregunta *f*, indagación *f*; encuesta *f*; ~ **office** oficina de informaciones
inquisitive (ing-kʷ*i*-sö-tiv) *adj* curioso
insane (in-*ssein*) *adj* lunático
inscription (in-*sskrip*-jön) *n* inscripción *f*
insect (*in*-ssêkt) *n* insecto *m*; ~ **repellent** insectífugo *m*
insecticide (in-*ssêk*-ti-ssaid) *n* insecticida *m*
insensitive (in-*ssên*-sso-tiv) *adj* insensible
insert (in-*ssööt*) *v* insertar
inside (in-*ssaid*) *n* interior *m*; *adj* interior; *adv* adentro; dentro; *prep* en, dentro de; ~ **out** al revés; **insides** entrañas *fpl*
insight (*in*-ssait) *n* entendimiento *m*
insignificant (in-ssigh-*ni*-fi-könt) *adj* insignificante; irrelevante; baladí
insist (in-*ssisst*) *v* insistir; persistir
insolence (*in*-ssö-lönss) *n* insolencia *f*
insolent (*in*-ssö-lönt) *adj* insolente
insomnia (in-*ssom*-ni-ö) *n* insomnio *m*
inspect (in-*sspêkt*) *v* inspeccionar
inspection (in-*sspêk*-jön) *n* inspección *f*; control *m*
inspector (in-*sspêk*-tö) *n* inspector *m*
inspire (in-sspai*ᵒ*) *v* inspirar
install (in-*sstool*) *v* instalar
installation (in-sstö-*lei*-jön) *n* instalación *f*
instalment (in-*sstool*-mönt) *n* plazo *m*
instance (*in*-sstönss) *n* ejemplo *m*; caso *m*; **for ~** por ejemplo
instant (*in*-sstönt) *n* instante *m*

instantly (*in*-sstönt-li) *adv* instantáneamente, inmediatamente, al instante

instead of (in-*ssted* ov) en lugar de

instinct (*in*-sstingkt) *n* instinto *m*

institute (*in*-ssti-tyuut) *n* instituto *m*; institución *f*; *v* *instituir

institution (*in*-ssti-*tyuu*-ʃön) *n* instituto *m*, institución *f*

instruct (in-*sstrakt*) *v* *instruir

instruction (in-*sstrak*-ʃön) *n* instrucción *f*

instructive (in-*sstrak*-tiv) *adj* instructivo

instructor (in-*sstrak*-tö) *n* instructor *m*

instrument (*in*-sstru-mönt) *n* instrumento *m*; **musical** ~ instrumento músico

insufficient (in-ssö-*fi*-ʃönt) *adj* insuficiente

insulate (*in*-ssyu-leit) *v* aislar

insulation (in-ssyu-*lei*-ʃön) *n* aislamiento *m*

insulator (*in*-ssyu-lei-tö) *n* aislador *m*

insult¹ (in-*ssalt*) *v* insultar

insult² (*in*-ssalt) *n* insulto *m*

insurance (in-*ʃuᵒ*-rönss) *n* seguro *m*; ~ **policy** póliza de seguro

insure (in-*ʃuᵒ*) *v* asegurar

intact (in-*tækt*) *adj* intacto

intellect (*in*-tö-lêkt) *n* intelecto *m*

intellectual (in-tö-*lêk*-chu-öl) *adj* intelectual

intelligence (in-*tê*-li-dʒönss) *n* inteligencia *f*

intelligent (in-*tê*-li-dʒönt) *adj* inteligente

intend (in-*tênd*) *v* intentar, *tener la intención de

intense (in-*tênss*) *adj* intenso

intention (in-*tên*-ʃön) *n* intención *f*

intentional (in-*tên*-ʃö-nöl) *adj* intencional

intercourse (*in*-tö-kooss) *n* trato *m*

interest (*in*-trösst) *n* interés *m*; rédito *m*; *v* interesar

interesting (*in*-trö-ssting) *adj* interesante

interfere (in-tö-*fiᵒ*) *v* interferir; ~ **with** mezclarse en

interference (in-tö-*fiᵒ*-rönss) *n* interferencia *f*

interim (*in*-tö-rim) *n* interin *m*

interior (in-*tiᵒ*-ri-ö) *n* interior *m*

interlude (*in*-tö-luud) *n* intermedio *m*

intermediary (in-tö-*mii*-dyö-ri) *n* intermediario *m*

intermission (in-tö-*mi*-ʃön) *n* entreacto *m*

internal (in-*töö*-nöl) *adj* interno

international (in-tö-*næ*-ʃö-nöl) *adj* internacional

interpret (in-*töö*-prit) *v* interpretar

interpreter (in-*töö*-pri-tö) *n* intérprete *m*

interrogate (in-*tê*-rö-gheit) *v* interrogar

interrogation (in-tê-rö-*ghei*-ʃön) *n* interrogatorio *m*

interrogative (in-tö-*ro*-ghö-tiv) *adj* interrogativo

interrupt (in-tö-*rapt*) *v* interrumpir

interruption (in-tö-*rap*-ʃön) *n* interrupción *f*

intersection (in-tö-*ssêk*-ʃön) *n* intersección *f*

interval (*in*-tö-völ) *n* intervalo *m*

intervene (in-tö-*viin*) *v* *intervenir

interview (*in*-tö-vyuu) *n* entrevista *f*

intestine (in-*tê*-sstin) *n* intestino *m*

intimate (*in*-ti-möt) *adj* íntimo

into (*in*-tu) *prep* dentro de

intolerable (in-*to*-lö-rö-böl) *adj* insoportable

intoxicated (in-*tok*-ssi-kei-tid) *adj* embriagado

intrigue (in-*triigh*) *n* intriga *f*

introduce (in-trö-*dyuuss*) *v* presentar; *introducir

introduction (in-trö-*dak*-ſön) *n* presentación *f*; introducción *f*

invade (in-*veid*) *v* invadir

invalid[1] (in-*vö*-liid) *n* inválido *m*; *adj* inválido

invalid[2] (in-*væ*-lid) *adj* nulo

invasion (in-*vei*-ʒön) *n* irrupción *f*, invasión *f*

invent (in-*vênt*) *v* inventar

invention (in-*vên*-ſön) *n* invención *f*

inventive (in-*vên*-tiv) *adj* inventivo

inventor (in-*vên*-tö) *n* inventor *m*

inventory (*in*-vön-tri) *n* inventario *m*

invert (in-*vööt*) *v* *invertir

invest (in-*vêsst*) *v* *invertir

investigate (in-*vê*-ssti-gheit) *v* investigar

investigation (in-vê-ssti-*ghei*-ſön) *n* investigación *f*

investment (in-*vêsst*-mönt) *n* inversión *f*

investor (in-*vê*-sstö) *n* inversionista *m*

invisible (in-*vi*-sö-böl) *adj* invisible

invitation (in-vi-*tei*-ſön) *n* invitación *f*

invite (in-*vait*) *v* invitar, convidar

invoice (*in*-voiss) *n* factura *f*

involve (in-*volv*) *v* *envolver; **involved** implicado

inwards (*in*-ᵁöds) *adv* hacia adentro

iodine (*ai*-ö-diin) *n* yodo *m*

Iran (i-*raan*) Irán *m*

Iranian (i-*rei*-ni-ön) *adj* iraní

Iraq (i-*raak*) Irak *m*

Iraqi (i-*raa*-ki) *adj* iraquí

irascible (i-*ræ*-ssi-böl) *adj* irascible

Ireland (*ai*ᵒ-lönd) Irlanda *f*

Irish (*ai*ᵒ-riſ) *adj* irlandés

Irishman (*ai*ᵒ-riſ-mön) *n* (pl -men) irlandés *m*

iron (*ai*-ön) *n* hierro *m*; plancha *f*; de hierro; *v* planchar

ironical (ai-*ro*-ni-köl) *adj* irónico

ironworks (*ai*-ön-ᵁöökss) *n* herrería *f*

irony (*ai*ᵒ-rö-ni) *n* ironía *f*

irregular (i-*rê*-ghyu-lö) *adj* irregular

irreparable (i-*rê*-pö-rö-böl) *adj* irreparable

irrevocable (i-*rê*-vö-kö-böl) *adj* irrevocable

irritable (*i*-ri-tö-böl) *adj* irritable

irritate (*i*-ri-teit) *v* irritar

is (is) *v* (pr be)

island (*ai*-lönd) *n* isla *f*

isolate (*ai*-ssö-leit) *v* aislar

isolation (ai-ssö-*lei*-ſön) *n* aislamiento *m*

Israel (*is*-reil) Israel *m*

Israeli (is-*rei*-li) *adj* israelí

issue (*i*-ſuu) *v* *distribuir; *n* emisión *f*, tirada *f*, edición *f*; cuestión *f*, punto *m*; consecuencia *f*, resultado *m*, conclusión *f*, término *m*; salida *f*

isthmus (*iss*-möss) *n* istmo *m*

it (it) *pron* lo

Italian (i-*tæl*-yön) *adj* italiano

italics (i-*tæ*-likss) *pl* cursiva *f*

Italy (*i*-tö-li) Italia *f*

itch (ich) *n* picazón *f*; prurito *m*; *v* picar

item (*ai*-töm) *n* ítem *m*; punto *m*

itinerant (ai-*ti*-nö-rönt) *adj* ambulante

itinerary (ai-*ti*-nö-rö-ri) *n* itinerario *m*

ivory (*ai*-vö-ri) *n* marfil *m*

ivy (*ai*-vi) *n* hiedra *f*

J

jack (dʒæk) *n* gato *m*

jacket (*dʒæ*-kit) *n* americana *f*, chaqueta *f*; sobrecubierta *f*; saco *m*Me

jade (dʒeid) *n* jade *m*

jail (dʒeil) *n* cárcel *f*

jailer (*dʒei*-lö) *n* carcelero *m*

jam (dʒæm) n mermelada f; congestión f

janitor (dʒæ-ni-tö) n conserje m

January (dʒæ-nyu-ö-ri) enero

Japan (dʒö-pæn) Japón m

Japanese (dʒæ-pö-niis) adj japonés

jar (dʒaa) n jarra f

jaundice (dʒoon-diss) n ictericia f

jaw (dʒoo) n mandíbula f

jealous (dʒê-löss) adj celoso

jealousy (dʒê-lö-ssi) n celos

jeans (dʒiins) pl vaqueros mpl

jelly (dʒê-li) n jalea f

jelly-fish (dʒê-li-fiʃ) n medusa f

jersey (dʒöö-si) n jersey m

jet (dʒêt) n chorro m; avión a reacción

jetty (dʒê-ti) n muelle m

Jew (dʒuu) n judío m

jewel (dʒuu-öl) n joya f

jeweller (dʒuu-ö-lö) n joyero m

jewellery (dʒuu-öl-ri) n joyería f

Jewish (dʒuu-iʃ) adj judío

job (dʒob) n tarea f; puesto m, empleo m

jockey (dʒo-ki) n jockey m

join (dʒoin) v juntar; unirse a, asociarse a; ensamblar, reunir

joint (dʒoint) n articulación f; soldadura f; adj unido, en común

jointly (dʒoint-li) adv juntamente

joke (dʒouk) n broma f

jolly (dʒo-li) adj jovial

Jordan (dʒoo-dön) Jordania f

Jordanian (dʒoo-dei-ni-ön) adj jordano

journal (dʒöö-nöl) n revista f

journalism (dʒöö-nö-li-söm) n periodismo m

journalist (dʒöö-nö-lisst) n periodista m

journey (dʒöö-ni) n viaje m

joy (dʒoi) n delicia f, regocijo m

joyful (dʒoi-föl) adj contento, alegre

jubilee (dʒuu-bi-lii) n aniversario m

judge (dʒadʒ) n juez m; v juzgar

judgment (dʒadʒ-mönt) n juicio m

jug (dʒagh) n cántaro m

Jugoslav (yuu-ghö-sslaav) adj yugoslavo

Jugoslavia (yuu-ghö-sslaa-vi-ö) Yugoslavia f

juice (dʒuuss) n zumo m

juicy (dʒuu-ssi) adj zumoso

July (dʒu-lai) julio

jump (dʒamp) v saltar; n salto m

jumper (dʒam-pö) n jersey m

junction (dʒangk-ʃön) n encrucijada f; empalme m

June (dʒuun) junio

jungle (dʒang-ghöl) n selva f, jungla f

junior (dʒuu-nyö) adj menor

junk (dʒangk) n cachivache m

jury (dʒuⁿ-ri) n jurado m

just (dʒasst) adj justo; adv apenas; justamente

justice (dʒa-sstiss) n derecho m; justicia f

juvenile (dʒuu-vö-nail) adj juvenil

K

kangaroo (kæng-ghö-ruu) n canguro m

keel (kiil) n quilla f

keen (kiin) adj entusiasta; agudo

***keep** (kiip) v *tener; guardar; continuar; ~ **away from** *mantenerse alejado de; ~ **off** no tocar; ~ **on** continuar; ~ **quiet** *estarse quieto; ~ **up** perseverar; ~ **up with** *seguir el paso

keg (kêgh) n barrilete m

kennel (kê-nöl) n perrera f; perrera m

Kenya (kê-nyö) Kenya m

kerosene (*kê*-rö-ssiin) *n* petróleo lampante

kettle (*kê*-töl) *n* olla *f*

key (kii) *n* llave *f*

keyhole (*kii*-houl) *n* ojo de la cerradura

khaki (*kaa*-ki) *n* caqui *m*

kick (kik) *v* patear; *n* patada *f*

kick-off (ki-*kof*) *n* saque inicial

kid (kid) *n* niño *m*, chico *m*; cabritilla *f*; *v* embromar

kidney (*kid*-ni) *n* riñón *m*

kill (kil) *v* matar

kilogram (*ki*-lö-ghræm) *n* kilogramo *m*

kilometre (*ki*-lö-mii-tö) *n* kilómetro *m*

kind (kaind) *adj* amable, bondadoso; bueno; *n* género *m*

kindergarten (*kin*-dö-ghaa-tön) *n* escuela de párvulos, jardín de infancia

king (king) *n* rey *m*

kingdom (*king*-döm) *n* reino *m*

kiosk (*kii*-ossk) *n* quiosco *m*

kiss (kiss) *n* beso *m*; *v* besar

kit (kit) *n* avíos *mpl*

kitchen (*ki*-chin) *n* cocina *f*; ~ **garden** huerto *m*

Kleenex® (*klii*-nêkss) *n* pañuelo de papel

knapsack (*næp*-ssæk) *n* mochila *f*

knave (neiv) *n* sota *f*

knee (nii) *n* rodilla *f*

kneecap (*nii*-kæp) *n* rótula *f*

*****kneel** (niil) *v* arrodillarse

knew (nyuu) *v* (p know)

knickers (*ni*-kös) *pl* braga *f*

knife (naif) *n* (pl knives) cuchillo *m*

knight (nait) *n* caballero *m*

*****knit** (nit) *v* *hacer punto

knob (nob) *n* botón *m*

knock (nok) *v* golpear; *n* golpe *m*; ~ **against** chocar contra; ~ **down** derribar

knot (not) *n* nudo *m*; *v* anudar

*****know** (nou) *v* *saber, *conocer

knowledge (*no*-lidʒ) *n* conocimiento *m*

knuckle (*na*-köl) *n* nudillo *m*

L

label (*lei*-böl) *n* rótulo *m*; *v* rotular

laboratory (lö-*bo*-rö-tö-ri) *n* laboratorio *m*

labour (*lei*-bö) *n* trabajo *m*, labor *f*; dolores *mpl*; *v* ajetrearse, bregar; **labor permit** *Am* permiso de trabajo

labourer (*lei*-bö-rö) *n* obrero *m*

labour-saving (*lei*-bö-ssei-ving) *adj* economizador de trabajo

labyrinth (*læ*-bö-rinz) *n* laberinto *m*

lace (leiss) *n* puntilla *f*; cordón *m*

lacquer (*læ*-kö) *n* laca *f*

lad (læd) *n* joven *m*, muchacho *m*

ladder (*læ*-dö) *n* escalera de mano

lady (*lei*-di) *n* señora *f*; **ladies' room** lavabos para señoras

lagoon (lö-*ghuun*) *n* laguna *f*

lake (leik) *n* lago *m*

lamb (læm) *n* cordero *m*

lame (leim) *adj* paralítico, cojo

lamentable (*læ*-mön-tö-böl) *adj* lamentable

lamp (læmp) *n* lámpara *f*

lamp-post (*læmp*-pousst) *n* poste de farol

lampshade (*læmp*-ʃeid) *n* pantalla *f*

land (lænd) *n* país *m*, tierra *f*; *v* aterrizar; desembarcar

landlady (*lænd*-lei-di) *n* patrona *f*

landlord (*lænd*-lood) *n* propietario *m*, dueño *m*; patrón *m*

landmark (*lænd*-maak) *n* punto de re-

ferencia; mojón *m*
landscape (*lænd*-sskeip) *n* paisaje *m*
lane (lein) *n* callejón *m*; pista *f*
language (*læng*-gh^uidʒ) *n* lengua *f*; ~ **laboratory** laboratorio de lenguas
lantern (*læn*-tön) *n* linterna *f*
lapel (lö-*pêl*) *n* solapa *f*
larder (*laa*-dö) *n* despensa *f*
large (laadʒ) *adj* grande; espacioso
lark (laak) *n* alondra *f*
laryngitis (læ-rin-*dʒai*-tiss) *n* laringitis *f*
last (laasst) *adj* último; precedente; *v* durar; **at ~** al fin; al final
lasting (*laa*-ssting) *adj* duradero
latchkey (*læch*-kii) *n* llave de la casa
late (leit) *adj* tardío; retrasado
lately (*leit*-li) *adv* últimamente, recientemente
lather (*laa*-ðö) *n* espuma *f*
Latin America (*læ*-tin ö-*mê*-ri-kö) América Latina
Latin-American (*læ*-tin-ö-*mê*-ri-kön) *adj* latinoamericano
latitude (*læ*-ti-tyuud) *n* latitud *f*
laugh (laaf) *v* *reír; *n* risa *f*
laughter (*laaf*-tö) *n* risa *f*
launch (loonch) *v* lanzar; *n* buque a motor
launching (*loon*-ching) *n* botadura *f*
launderette (loon-dö-*rêt*) *n* lavandería de autoservicio
laundry (*loon*-dri) *n* lavandería *f*; ropa sucia
lavatory (*læ*-vö-tö-ri) *n* cuarto de aseo
lavish (*læ*-viʃ) *adj* pródigo
law (loo) *n* ley *f*; derecho *m*; ~ **court** tribunal *m*
lawful (*loo*-fôl) *adj* lícito
lawn (loon) *n* césped *m*
lawsuit (*loo*-ssuut) *n* proceso *m*, causa *f*
lawyer (*loo*-yö) *n* abogado *m*; jurista *m*

laxative (*læk*-ssö-tiv) *n* laxante *m*
*lay (lei) *v* colocar, *poner; ~ **bricks** mampostear
layer (lei^ö) *n* capa *f*
layman (*lei*-mön) *n* profano *m*
lazy (*lei*-si) *adj* perezoso
lead[1] (liid) *n* ventaja *f*; dirección *f*; trailla *f*
lead[2] (lêd) *n* plomo *m*
*lead (liid) *v* *conducir
leader (*lii*-dö) *n* jefe *m*, líder *m*
leadership (*lii*-dö-ʃip) *n* dirección *f*
leading (*lii*-ding) *adj* dominante, principal
leaf (liif) *n* (pl leaves) hoja *f*
league (liigh) *n* liga *f*
leak (liik) *v* gotear; *n* goteo *m*
leaky (*lii*-ki) *adj* que tiene escapes
lean (liin) *adj* magro
*lean (liin) *v* apoyarse
leap (liip) *n* salto *m*
*leap (liip) *v* saltar
leap-year (*liip*-yi^ö) *n* año bisiesto
*learn (löön) *v* aprender
learner (*löö*-nö) *n* principiante *m*
lease (liiss) *n* contrato de arrendamiento; arrendamiento *m*; *v* *arrendar, alquilar
leash (liiʃ) *n* correa *f*
least (liisst) *adj* mínimo, menos; **at ~** por lo menos
leather (*lê*-ðö) *n* cuero *m*; de piel
leave (liiv) *n* licencia *f*
*leave (liiv) *v* partir, dejar; ~ **out** omitir
Lebanese (lê-bö-*niis*) *adj* libanés
Lebanon (*lê*-bö-nön) Líbano *m*
lecture (*lêk*-chö) *n* curso *m*, conferencia *f*
left[1] (lêft) *adj* izquierdo
left[2] (lêft) *v* (p, pp leave)
left-hand (*lêft*-hænd) *adj* izquierdo, de izquierda
left-handed (lêft-*hæn*-did) *adj* zurdo

leg (lêgh) *n* pata *f*, pierna *f*

legacy (*lê*-ghö-ssi) *n* herencia *f*

legal (*lii*-ghöl) *adj* legítimo, legal; jurídico

legalization (lii-ghö-lai-*sei*-[ʃön) *n* legalización *f*

legation (li-*ghei*-[ʃön) *n* legación *f*

legible (*lê*-dʒi-böl) *adj* legible

legitimate (li-*dʒi*-ti-möt) *adj* legítimo

leisure (*lê*-ʒö) *n* ocio *m*; comodidad *f*

lemon (*lê*-mön) *n* limón *m*

lemonade (lê-mö-*neid*) *n* limonada *f*

***lend** (lênd) *v* prestar

length (lêngʒ) *n* longitud *f*

lengthen (*lêng*-zön) *v* alargar

lengthways (*lêngz*-ᵘeis) *adv* longitudinalmente

lens (lêns) *n* lente *m/f*; **telephoto ~** teleobjetivo *m*; **zoom ~** lente de foco regulable

leprosy (*lê*-prö-ssi) *n* lepra *f*

less (lêss) *adv* menos

lessen (*lê*-ssön) *v* *disminuir

lesson (*lê*-ssön) *n* lección *f*

***let** (lêt) *v* dejar; alquilar; **~ down** decepcionar

letter (*lê*-tö) *n* carta *f*; letra *f*; **~ of credit** carta de crédito; **~ of recommendation** carta de recomendación

letter-box (*lê*-tö-bokss) *n* buzón *m*

lettuce (*lê*-tiss) *n* lechuga *f*

level (*lê*-völ) *adj* igual; plano, llano; *n* nivel *m*; *v* igualar, nivelar; **~ crossing** paso a nivel

lever (*lii*-vö) *n* palanca *f*

Levis (*lii*-vais) *pl* jeans *mpl*

liability (lai-ö-*bi*-lö-ti) *n* responsabilidad *f*

liable (*lai*-ö-böl) *adj* responsable; **~ to** sujeto a

liberal (*li*-bö-röl) *adj* liberal; generoso, dadivoso

liberation (li-bö-*rei*-[ʃön) *n* liberación *f*

Liberia (lai-*biᵒ*-ri-ö) Liberia *f*

Liberian (lai-*biᵒ*-ri-ön) *adj* liberiano

liberty (*li*-bö-ti) *n* libertad *f*

library (*lai*-brö-ri) *n* biblioteca *f*

licence (*lai*-ssönss) *n* licencia *f*; permiso *m*; **driving ~** permiso de conducir

license (*lai*-ssönss) *v* autorizar

lick (lik) *v* lamer

lid (lid) *n* tapa *f*

lie (lai) *v* *mentir; *n* mentira *f*

***lie** (lai) *v* *yacer; **~ down** *tenderse

life (laif) *n* (pl lives) vida *f*; **~ insurance** seguro de vida

lifebelt (*laif*-bêlt) *n* chaleco salvavidas

lifetime (*laif*-taim) *n* vida *f*

lift (lift) *v* levantar; *n* ascensor *m*; elevador *mMe*

light (lait) *n* luz *f*; *adj* ligero; pálido; **~ bulb** bulbo *m*

***light** (lait) *v* *encender

lighter (*lai*-tö) *n* encendedor *m*

lighthouse (*lait*-hauss) *n* faro *m*

lighting (*lai*-ting) *n* alumbrado *m*

lightning (*lait*-ning) *n* relámpago *m*

like (laik) *v* *querer; gustar; *adj* semejante; *conj* como

likely (*lai*-kli) *adj* probable

like-minded (laik-*main*-did) *adj* unánime

likewise (*laik*-ᵘais) *adv* así también, asimismo

lily (*li*-li) *n* azucena *f*

limb (lim) *n* miembro *m*

lime (laim) *n* cal *f*; tilo *m*; lima *f*

limetree (*laim*-trii) *n* tilo *m*

limit (*li*-mit) *n* límite *m*; *v* limitar

limp (limp) *v* cojear; *adj* inerte

line (lain) *n* renglón *m*; raya *f*; cordón *m*; línea *f*; cola *f*

linen (*li*-nin) *n* lino *m*; ropa blanca

liner (*lai*-nö) *n* vapor de línea

lingerie (*long*-ʒö-rii) *n* ropa interior de

mujer

lining (*lai*-ning) *n* forro *m*

link (lingk) *v* enlazar; *n* enlace *m*; eslabón *m*

lion (*lai*-ön) *n* león *m*

lip (lip) *n* labio *m*

lipsalve (*lip*-ssaav) *n* manteca de cacao

lipstick (*lip*-sstik) *n* lápiz labial

liqueur (li-*kyu⁰*) *n* licor *m*

liquid (*li*-kᵘid) *adj* líquido; *n* líquido *m*

liquor (*li*-kö) *n* bebidas alcohólicas

liquorice (*li*-kö-riss) *n* regaliz *m*

list (lisst) *n* lista *f*; *v* inscribir

listen (*li*-ssön) *v* escuchar

listener (*liss*-nö) *n* oyente *m*

literary (*li*-trö-ri) *adj* literario

literature (*li*-trö-chö) *n* literatura *f*

litre (*lii*-tö) *n* litro *m*

litter (*li*-tö) *n* desperdicio *m*; trastos *mpl*; lechigada *f*

little (*li*-töl) *adj* pequeño; poco

live¹ (liv) *v* vivir

live² (laiv) *adj* vivo

livelihood (*laiv*-li-hud) *n* sustento *m*

lively (*laiv*-li) *adj* vivo

liver (*li*-vö) *n* hígado *m*

living-room (*li*-ving-ruum) *n* sala de estar, living *m*

load (loud) *n* carga *f*; fardo *m*; *v* cargar

loaf (louf) *n* (pl loaves) pan *m*

loan (loun) *n* préstamo *m*

lobby (*lo*-bi) *n* vestíbulo *m*

lobster (*lob*-sstö) *n* langosta *f*

local (*lou*-köl) *adj* local; ~ **call** llamada local; ~ **train** tren ómnibus

locality (lou-*kæ*-lö-ti) *n* localidad *f*

locate (lou-*keit*) *v* localizar

location (lou-*kei*-jön) *n* ubicación *f*

lock (lok) *v* *cerrar con llave; *n* cerradura *f*; esclusa *f*; ~ **up** guardar con llave

locomotive (lou-kö-*mou*-tiv) *n* locomotora *f*

lodge (lodʒ) *v* alojar; *n* apeadero de caza

lodger (*lo*-dʒö) *n* huésped *m*

lodgings (*lo*-dʒīngs) *pl* alojamiento *m*

log (logh) *n* madero *m*

logic (*lo*-dʒik) *n* lógica *f*

logical (*lo*-dʒi-köl) *adj* lógico

lonely (*loun*-li) *adj* solitario

long (long) *adj* largo; ~ **for** anhelar; **no longer** ya no

longing (*long*-ing) *n* anhelo *m*

longitude (*lon*-dʒi-tyuud) *n* longitud *f*

look (luk) *v* mirar; *parecer, *tener aires de; *n* ojeada *f*, mirada *f*; aspecto *m*; ~ **after** ocuparse de, cuidar de; ~ **at** mirar; ~ **for** buscar; ~ **out** prestar atención, *tener cuidado; ~ **up** buscar

looking-glass (*lu*-king-ghlaass) *n* espejo *m*

loop (luup) *n* nudo corredizo

loose (luuss) *adj* suelto

loosen (*luu*-ssön) *v* *soltar

lord (lood) *n* lord *m*

lorry (*lo*-ri) *n* camión *m*

***lose** (luus) *v* *perder

loss (loss) *n* pérdida *f*

lost (losst) *adj* perdido; desaparecido; ~ **and found** objetos perdidos; ~ **property office** oficina de objetos perdidos

lot (lot) *n* suerte *f*, destino *m*; masa *f*, cantidad *f*

lotion (*lou*-jön) *n* loción *f*; **aftershave** ~ loción para después de afeitarse

lottery (*lo*-tö-ri) *n* lotería *f*

loud (laud) *adj* fuerte

loud-speaker (laud-*sspii*-kö) *n* altavoz *m*

lounge (laundʒ) *n* salón *m*

louse (lauss) *n* (pl lice) piojo *m*

love (lav) v amar; n amor m; in ~ enamorado

lovely (lav-li) adj delicioso, precioso, bonito

lover (la-vö) n amante m

love-story (lav-sstoo-ri) n historia de amor

low (lou) adj bajo; profundo; deprimido; ~ tide bajamar f

lower (lou-ö) v bajar; rebajar; arriar; adj inferior

lowlands (lou-lönds) pl tierra baja

loyal (loi-öl) adj leal

lubricate (luu-bri-keit) v lubrificar, lubricar

lubrication (luu-bri-kei-ſön) n lubricación f; ~ oil aceite lubricante; ~ system sistema de lubricación

luck (lak) n éxito m, suerte f; azar m

lucky (la-ki) adj afortunado; ~ charm talismán m

ludicrous (luu-di-kröss) adj ridículo, grotesco

luggage (la-ghidʒ) n equipaje m; hand ~ equipaje de mano; left ~ office consigna f; ~ rack portabagajes m, rejilla f; ~ van furgón de equipajes

lukewarm (luuk-ᵘoom) adj tibio

lumbago (lam-bei-ghou) n lumbago m

luminous (luu-mi-nöss) adj luminoso

lump (lamp) n nudo m, grumo m, terrón m; chichón m; ~ of sugar terrón de azúcar; ~ sum suma global

lumpy (lam-pi) adj apelmazado

lunacy (luu-nö-ssi) n locura f

lunatic (luu-nö-tik) adj lunático; n alienado m

lunch (lanch) n almuerzo m

luncheon (lan-chön) n almuerzo m

lung (lang) n pulmón m

lust (lasst) n concupiscencia f

luxurious (lagh-ʒuᵒ-ri-öss) adj lujoso

luxury (lak-ſö-ri) n lujo m

M

machine (mö-ſiin) n aparato m, máquina f

machinery (mö-ſii-nö-ri) n maquinaria f; mecanismo m

mackerel (mæ-kröl) n (pl ~) escombro m

mackintosh (mæ-kin-toſ) n impermeable m

mad (mæd) adj loco; rabioso

madam (mæ-döm) n señora f

madness (mæd-nöss) n locura f

magazine (mæ-ghö-siin) n revista f

magic (mæ-dʒik) n magia f; adj mágico

magician (mö-dʒi-ſön) n prestidigitador m

magistrate (mæ-dʒi-sstreit) n magistrado m

magnetic (mægh-nê-tik) adj magnético

magneto (mægh-nii-tou) n (pl ~s) magneto m

magnificent (mægh-ni-fi-ssönt) adj magnífico; grandioso, espléndido

magpie (mægh-pai) n urraca f

maid (meid) n muchacha f

maiden name (mei-dön neim) apellido de soltera

mail (meil) n correo m; v enviar por correo

mailbox (meil-bokss) nAm buzón m

main (mein) adj principal; mayor; ~ deck puente superior; ~ line línea principal; ~ road camino principal; ~ street calle mayor

mainland (mein-lönd) n tierra firme

mainly (mein-li) adv principalmente

mains (meins) pl conducción principal

maintain (mein-*tein*) v *mantener

maintenance (*mein*-tö-nönss) n mantenimiento m

maize (meis) n maíz m

major (*mei*-dʒö) adj grande; mayor; n mayor m

majority (mö-*dʒo*-rö-ti) n mayoría f

***make** (meik) v *hacer; ganar; *conseguir; ~ **do with** arreglarse con; ~ **good** compensar; ~ **up** redactar

make-up (*mei*-kap) n maquillaje m

malaria (mö-*lê^ö*-ri-ö) n malaria f

Malay (mö-*lei*) n malayo m

Malaysia (mö-*lei*-si-ö) Malasia f

Malaysian (mö-*lei*-si-ön) adj malayo

male (meil) adj macho

malicious (mö-*li*-jöss) adj malicioso

malignant (mö-*ligh*-nönt) adj maligno

mallet (*mæ*-lit) n mazo m

malnutrition (mæl-nyu-*tri*-jön) n desnutrición f

mammal (*mæ*-möl) n mamífero m

mammoth (*mæ*-möz) n mamut m

man (mæn) n (pl men) hombre m; **men's room** lavabos para caballeros

manage (*mæ*-nidʒ) v administrar; *tener éxito

manageable (*mæ*-ni-dʒö-böl) adj manejable

management (*mæ*-nidʒ-mönt) n manejo m; gestión f

manager (*mæ*-ni-dʒö) n jefe m, director m

mandarin (*mæn*-dö-rin) n mandarina f

mandate (*mæn*-deit) n mandato m

manger (*mein*-dʒö) n pesebre m

manicure (*mæ*-ni-kyu^ö) n manicura f; v *hacer la manicura

mankind (mæn-*kaind*) n humanidad f

mannequin (*mæ*-nö-kin) n maniquí m

manner (*mæ*-nö) n modo m, manera f; **manners** pl modales mpl

man-of-war (mæ-növ-*^uoo*) n buque de guerra

manor-house (*mæ*-nö-hauss) n casa señorial

mansion (*mæn*-jön) n mansión f

manual (*mæ*-nyu-öl) adj manual

manufacture (mæ-nyu-*fæk*-chö) v fabricar

manufacturer (mæ-nyu-*fæk*-chö-rö) n fabricante m

manure (mö-*nyu^ö*) n abono m

manuscript (*mæ*-nyu-sskript) n manuscrito m

many (*mê*-ni) adj muchos

map (mæp) n carta f; mapa m; plano m

maple (*mei*-pöl) n arce m

marble (*maa*-böl) n mármol m; canica f

March (maach) marzo

march (maach) v marchar; n marcha f

mare (mê^ö) n yegua f

margarine (maa-dʒö-*riin*) n margarina f

margin (*maa*-dʒin) n margen m

maritime (*mæ*-ri-taim) adj marítimo

mark (maak) v marcar; caracterizar; n marca f; nota f; blanco m

market (*maa*-kit) n mercado m

market-place (*maa*-kit-pleiss) n plaza de mercado

marmalade (*maa*-mö-leid) n confitura f

marriage (*mæ*-ridʒ) n matrimonio m

marrow (*mæ*-rou) n médula f

marry (*mæ*-ri) v casarse; **married couple** cónyuges mpl

marsh (maaj) n pantano m

marshy (*maa*-ji) adj pantanoso

martyr (*maa*-tö) n mártir m

marvel (*maa*-völ) n maravilla f; v maravillarse

marvellous (*maa*-vö-löss) adj maravilloso

mascara (mæ-sskaa-rö) n rímel m

masculine (mæ-sskyu-lin) adj masculino

mash (mæʃ) v machacar

mask (maassk) n máscara f

Mass (mæss) n misa f

mass (mæss) n masa f; ~ **production** producción en serie

massage (mæ-ssaaʒ) n masaje m; v *dar masaje

masseur (mæ-ssöö) n masajista m

massive (mæ-ssiv) adj macizo

mast (maasst) n mástil m

master (maa-sstö) n maestro m; patrón m; profesor m; v dominar

masterpiece (maa-sstö-piiss) n obra maestra

mat (mæt) n estera f; adj mate, apagado

match (mæch) n cerilla f; partido m; cerillo mMe; v *hacer juego con

match-box (mæch-bokss) n caja de cerillas

material (mö-tiᵒ-ri-öl) n material m; tejido m; adj material

mathematical (mæ-zö-mæ-ti-köl) adj matemático

mathematics (mæ-zö-mæ-tikss) n matemáticas fpl

matrimonial (mæ-tri-mou-ni-öl) adj matrimonial

matrimony (mæ-tri-mö-ni) n matrimonio m

matter (mæ-tö) n materia f; asunto m, cuestión f; v *tener importancia; **as a ~ of fact** efectivamente, en realidad

matter-of-fact (mæ-tö-röv-fækt) adj desapasionado

mattress (mæ-tröss) n colchón m

mature (mö-tyuᵒ) adj maduro

maturity (mö-tyuᵒ-rö-ti) n madurez f

mausoleum (moo-ssö-lii-öm) n mausoleo m

mauve (mouv) adj malva

May (mei) mayo

***may** (mei) v *poder

maybe (mei-bii) adv quizás

mayor (mêᵒ) n alcalde m

maze (meis) n laberinto m

me (mii) pron me

meadow (mê-dou) n prado m

meal (miil) n comida f

mean (miin) adj mezquino; n promedio m

***mean** (miin) v significar; *querer decir

meaning (mii-ning) n significado m

meaningless (mii-ning-löss) adj sin sentido

means (miins) n medio m; **by no ~** en ningún caso, de ningún modo

in the meantime (in ðö miin-taim) entretanto

meanwhile (miin-ᵘail) adv entretanto

measles (mii-sölss) n sarampión m

measure (mê-ʒö) v *medir; n medida f

meat (miit) n carne f

mechanic (mi-kæ-nik) n mecánico m

mechanical (mi-kæ-ni-köl) adj mecánico

mechanism (mê-kö-ni-söm) n mecanismo m

medal (mê-döl) n medalla f

mediaeval (mê-di-ii-völ) adj medieval

mediate (mii-di-eit) v mediar

mediator (mii-di-ei-tö) n mediador m

medical (mê-di-köl) adj médico

medicine (mêd-ssin) n medicamento m; medicina f

meditate (mê-di-teit) v meditar

Mediterranean (mê-di-tö-rei-ni-ön) Mediterráneo

medium (mii-di-öm) adj mediano, medio

***meet** (miit) v *encontrarse con

meeting (*mii*-ting) *n* asamblea *f*, reunión *f*; encuentro *m*

meeting-place (*mii*-ting-pleiss) *n* lugar de reunión

melancholy (*mê*-löng-kö-li) *n* melancolía *f*

mellow (*mê*-lou) *adj* suave

melodrama (*mê*-lö-draa-mö) *n* melodrama *m*

melody (*mê*-lö-di) *n* melodía *f*

melon (*mê*-lön) *n* melón *m*

melt (mêlt) *v* fundir

member (*mêm*-bö) *n* miembro *m*;
Member of Parliament diputado *m*

membership (*mêm*-bö-fip) *n* afiliación *f*

memo (*mê*-mou) *n* (pl ~s) apunte *m*

memorable (*mê*-mö-rö-böl) *adj* memorable

memorial (mö-*moo*-ri-öl) *n* monumento *m*

memorize (*mê*-mö-rais) *v* aprenderse de memoria

memory (*mê*-mö-ri) *n* memoria *f*; recuerdo *m*

mend (mênd) *v* reparar, *remendar

menstruation (mên-sstru-*ei*-fön) *n* menstruación *f*

mental (*mên*-töl) *adj* mental

mention (*mên*-fön) *v* nombrar, mencionar; *n* mención *f*

menu (*mê*-nyuu) *n* menú *m*

merchandise (*möö*-chön-dais) *n* mercancía *f*

merchant (*möö*-chönt) *n* comerciante *m*

merciful (*möö*-ssi-föl) *adj* misericordioso

mercury (*möö*-kyu-ri) *n* mercurio *m*

mercy (*möö*-ssi) *n* misericordia *f*, clemencia *f*

mere (mi^ö) *adj* puro

merely (*mi^ö*-li) *adv* solamente

merger (*möö*-dʒö) *n* fusión *f*

merit (*mê*-rit) *v* *merecer; *n* mérito *m*

mermaid (*möö*-meid) *n* sirena *f*

merry (*mê*-ri) *adj* alegre

merry-go-round (*mê*-ri-ghou-raund) *n* caballitos *mpl*

mesh (mêʃ) *n* malla *f*

mess (mêss) *n* desorden *m*; ~ **up** estropear

message (*mê*-ssidʒ) *n* mensaje *m*

messenger (*mê*-ssin-dʒö) *n* mensajero *m*

metal (*mê*-töl) *n* metal *m*; metálico

meter (*mii*-tö) *n* contador *m*

method (*mê*-zöd) *n* método *m*; orden *m*

methodical (mö-*zo*-di-köl) *adj* metódico

methylated spirits (*mê*-zö-lei-tid *sspi*-ritss) alcohol de quemar

metre (*mii*-tö) *n* metro *m*

metric (*mê*-trik) *adj* métrico

Mexican (*mêk*-ssi-kön) *adj* mejicano; *n* mejicano *m*

Mexico (*mêk*-ssi-kou) Méjico *m*

mezzanine (*mê*-sö-niin) *n* entresuelo *m*

microphone (*mai*-krö-foun) *n* micrófono *m*

midday (*mid*-dei) *n* mediodía *m*

middle (*mi*-döl) *n* medio *m*; *adj* medio; **Middle Ages** Edad Media; ~ **class** clase media; **middle-class** *adj* burgués

midnight (*mid*-nait) *n* medianoche *f*

midst (midsst) *n* medio *m*

midsummer (*mid*-ssa-mö) *n* pleno verano

midwife (*mid*-^uaif) *n* (pl -wives) comadrona *f*

might (mait) *n* fuerza *f*

***might** (mait) *v* *poder

mighty (*mai*-ti) *adj* fuerte

migraine (*mi*-ghrein) *n* migraña *f*

mild (maild) *adj* suave

mildew (*mil*-dyu) *n* moho *m*

mile (mail) *n* milla *f*

mileage (*mai*-lidȝ) *n* millaje *m*

milepost (*mail*-pousst) *n* cipo *m*

milestone (*mail*-sstoun) *n* piedra miliar

milieu (*mii*-lyöö) *n* medio ambiente

military (*mi*-li-tö-ri) *adj* militar; ~ force fuerzas armadas

milk (milk) *n* leche *f*

milkman (*milk*-mön) *n* (pl -men) lechero *m*

milk-shake (*milk*-ʃeik) *n* batido de leche

milky (*mil*-ki) *adj* lechoso

mill (mil) *n* molino *m*; fábrica *f*

miller (*mi*-lö) *n* molinero *m*

milliner (*mi*-li-nö) *n* sombrerera *f*

million (*mil*-yön) *n* millón *m*

millionaire (mil-yö-*nêᵒ*) *n* millonario *m*

mince (minss) *v* picar

mind (maind) *n* mente *f*; *v* *hacer objeción a; fijarse en, *tener cuidado con

mine (main) *n* mina *f*

miner (*mai*-nö) *n* minero *m*

mineral (*mi*-nö-röl) *n* mineral *m*; ~ water agua mineral

miniature (*min*-yö-chö) *n* miniatura *f*

minimum (*mi*-ni-möm) *n* mínimum *m*

mining (*mai*-ning) *n* minería *f*

minister (*mi*-ni-sstö) *n* ministro *m*; clérigo *m*; Prime Minister Presidente de Consejo de ministros

ministry (*mi*-ni-sstri) *n* ministerio *m*

mink (mingk) *n* visón *m*

minor (*mai*-nö) *adj* pequeño, escaso, menor; secundario; *n* menor de edad

minority (mai-*no*-rö-ti) *n* minoría *f*

mint (mint) *n* menta *f*

minus (*mai*-nöss) *prep* menos

minute¹ (*mi*-nit) *n* minuto *m*; minutes actas

minute² (mai-*nyuut*) *adj* menudo

miracle (*mi*-rö-köl) *n* milagro *m*

miraculous (mi-*ræ*-kyu-löss) *adj* milagroso

mirror (*mi*-rö) *n* espejo *m*

misbehave (miss-bi-*heiv*) *v* portarse mal

miscarriage (miss-*kæ*-ridȝ) *n* aborto *m*

miscellaneous (mi-ssö-*lei*-ni-öss) *adj* misceláneo

mischief (*miss*-chif) *n* diabluras *fpl*; mal *m*, daño *m*, malicia *f*

mischievous (*miss*-chi-vöss) *adj* travieso

miserable (*mi*-sö-rö-böl) *adj* miserable

misery (*mi*-sö-ri) *n* miseria *f*; necesidad *f*

misfortune (miss-*foo*-chên) *n* contratiempo *m*, infortunio *m*

*mislay (miss-*lei*) *v* extraviar

misplaced (miss-*pleisst*) *adj* inoportuno; fuera de lugar

mispronounce (miss-prö-*naunss*) *v* pronunciar mal

miss¹ (miss) señorita *f*

miss² (miss) *v* *perder

missing (*mi*-ssing) *adj* que falta; ~ person desaparecido *m*

mist (misst) *n* niebla *f*

mistake (mi-*ssteik*) *n* error *m*, equivocación *f*

*mistake (mi-*ssteik*) *v* confundir

mistaken (mi-*sstei*-kön) *adj* equivocado; *be ~ equivocarse

mister (*mi*-sstö) *n* señor *m*

mistress (*mi*-sströss) *n* señora *f*; dueña *f*; querida *f*

mistrust (miss-*trasst*) *v* desconfiar de

misty (*mi*-ssti) *adj* nebuloso

*misunderstand (mi-ssan-dö-*sstænd*)

v comprender mal

misunderstanding (mi-ssan-dö-*sstæn*-ding) *n* equivocación *f*

misuse (miss-*yuuss*) *n* abuso *m*

mittens (*mi*-töns) *pl* guantes *mpl*

mix (mikss) *v* mezclar; ~ **with** alternar con

mixed (miksst) *adj* mezclado

mixer (*mik*-ssö) *n* batidora *f*

mixture (*mikss*-chö) *n* mezcla *f*

moan (moun) *v* *gemir

moat (mout) *n* foso *m*

mobile (*mou*-bail) *adj* móvil

mock (mok) *v* burlarse de

mockery (*mo*-kö-ri) *n* burla *f*

model (*mo*-döl) *n* modelo *m*; maniquí *m*; *v* modelar

moderate (*mo*-dö-röt) *adj* moderado; mediocre

modern (*mo*-dön) *adj* moderno

modest (*mo*-disst) *adj* modesto

modesty (*mo*-di-ssti) *n* modestia *f*

modify (*mo*-di-fai) *v* modificar

mohair (*mou*-hê⁶) *n* mohair *m*

moist (moisst) *adj* mojado, húmedo

moisten (*moi*-ssön) *v* *humedecer

moisture (*moiss*-chö) *n* humedad *f*; **moisturizing cream** crema hidratante

molar (*mou*-lö) *n* muela *f*

moment (*mou*-mönt) *n* momento *m*

momentary (*mou*-mön-tö-ri) *adj* momentáneo

monarch (*mo*-nök) *n* monarca *f*

monarchy (*mo*-nö-ki) *n* monarquía *f*

monastery (*mo*-nö-sstri) *n* monasterio *m*

Monday (*man*-di) lunes *m*

monetary (*ma*-ni-tö-ri) *adj* monetario; ~ **unit** unidad monetaria

money (*ma*-ni) *n* dinero *m*; ~ **exchange** oficina de cambio; ~ **order** libranza *f*

monk (mangk) *n* monje *m*

monkey (*mang*-ki) *n* mono *m*

monologue (*mo*-no-logh) *n* monólogo *m*

monopoly (mö-*no*-pö-li) *n* monopolio *m*

monotonous (mö-*no*-tö-nöss) *adj* monótono

month (manz) *n* mes *m*

monthly (*manz*-li) *adj* mensual; ~ **magazine** revista mensual

monument (*mo*-nyu-mönt) *n* monumento *m*

mood (muud) *n* humor *m*

moon (muun) *n* luna *f*

moonlight (*muun*-lait) *n* luz de la luna

moor (mu⁶) *n* brezal *m*, turbera *f*

moose (muuss) *n* (pl ~, ~s) alce *m*

moped (*mou*-pêd) *n* bicimotor *m*

moral (*mo*-röl) *n* moral *f*; *adj* moral; **morals** costumbres

morality (mö-*ræ*-lö-ti) *n* moralidad *f*

more (moo) *adj* más; **once** ~ otra vez

moreover (moo-*rou*-vö) *adv* además

morning (*moo*-ning) *n* mañana *f*; ~ **paper** diario matutino

Moroccan (mö-*ro*-kön) *adj* marroquí

Morocco (mö-*ro*-kou) Marruecos *m*

morphia (*moo*-fi-ö) *n* morfina *f*

morphine (*moo*-fiin) *n* morfina *f*

morsel (*moo*-ssöl) *n* trozo *m*

mortal (*moo*-töl) *adj* fatal, mortal

mortgage (*moo*-ghidʒ) *n* hipoteca *f*

mosaic (mö-*sei*-ik) *n* mosaico *m*

mosque (mossk) *n* mezquita *f*

mosquito (mö-*sskii*-tou) *n* (pl ~es) mosquito *m*

mosquito-net (mö-*sskii*-tou-nêt) *n* mosquitero *m*

moss (moss) *n* musgo *m*

most (mousst) *adj* el más; **at** ~ a lo sumo, como máximo; ~ **of all** sobre todo

mostly (*mousst*-li) *adv* generalmente

motel (mou-*têl*) *n* motel *m*

moth (moz) *n* polilla *f*

mother (ma-ðö) *n* madre *f*; ~ **tongue** lengua materna

mother-in-law (ma-ðö-rin-loo) *n* (pl mothers-) suegra *f*

mother-of-pearl (ma-ðö-röv-*pööl*) *n* nácar *m*

motion (mou-ʃön) *n* movimiento *m*; moción *f*

motive (mou-tiv) *n* motivo *m*

motor (mou-tö) *n* motor *m*; *v* *ir en coche; **starter** ~ motor de arranque

motorbike (mou-tö-baik) *nAm* motocicleta *f*

motor-boat (mou-tö-bout) *n* bote a motor

motor-car (mou-tö-kaa) *n* automóvil *m*

motor-cycle (mou-tö-ssai-köl) *n* motocicleta *f*

motoring (mou-tö-ring) *n* automovilismo *m*

motorist (mou-tö-risst) *n* automovilista *m*

motorway (mou-tö-ᵘei) *n* autopista *f*

motto (mo-tou) *n* (pl ~es, ~s) lema *m*

mouldy (moul-di) *adj* enmohecido

mound (maund) *n* montículo *m*

mount (maunt) *v* montar; *n* monte *m*

mountain (maun-tin) *n* montaña *f*; ~ **pass** paso *m*; ~ **range** cordillera *f*

mountaineering (maun-ti-*ni*ᵒ-ring) *n* montañismo *m*

mountainous (maun-ti-nöss) *adj* montañoso

mourning (moo-ning) *n* luto *m*

mouse (mauss) *n* (pl mice) ratón *m*

moustache (mö-*sstaaʃ*) *n* bigote *m*

mouth (mauz) *n* boca *f*; hocico *m*; desembocadura *f*

mouthwash (mauz-ᵘoʃ) *n* enjuague bucal

movable (muu-vö-böl) *adj* movible

move (muuv) *v* *mover; trasladar; mudarse; *conmover; *n* jugada *f*, paso *m*; mudanza *f*

movement (muuv-mönt) *n* movimiento *m*

movie (muu-vi) *n* filme *m*

much (mach) *adj* mucho; **as** ~ tanto

muck (mak) *n* suciedad *f*

mud (mad) *n* lodo *m*

muddle (ma-döl) *n* dédalo *m*, embrollo *m*; *v* embrollar

muddy (ma-di) *adj* lodoso

mud-guard (mad-ghaad) *n* guardabarros *m*; salpicadera *fMe*

mug (magh) *n* vaso *m*, taza *f*

mulberry (mal-bö-ri) *n* mora *f*

mule (myuul) *n* mulo *m*

mullet (ma-lit) *n* mújol *m*

multiplication (mal-ti-pli-*kei*-ʃön) *n* multiplicación *f*

multiply (mal-ti-plai) *v* multiplicar

mumps (mampss) *n* paperas *fpl*

municipal (myuu-*ni*-ssi-pöl) *adj* municipal

municipality (myuu-ni-ssi-*pæ*-lö-ti) *n* municipalidad *f*

murder (möö-dö) *n* asesinato *m*; *v* asesinar

murderer (möö-dö-rö) *n* asesino *m*

muscle (ma-ssöl) *n* músculo *m*

muscular (ma-sskyu-lö) *adj* musculoso

museum (myuu-*sii*-öm) *n* museo *m*

mushroom (maʃ-ruum) *n* seta *f*; hongo *m*

music (myuu-sik) *n* música *f*; ~ **academy** conservatorio *m*

musical (myuu-si-köl) *adj* musical; comedia musical

music-hall (myuu-sik-hool) *n* teatro de variedades

musician (myuu-*si*-ʃön) *n* músico *m*

muslin (mas-lin) *n* muselina *f*

mussel (ma-ssöl) *n* mejillón *m*

*must (masst) *v* *tener que

mustard (ma-sstöd) *n* mostaza *f*

mute (myuut) *adj* mudo

mutiny (*myuu*-ti-ni) *n* amotinamiento *m*

mutton (*ma*-tön) *n* carnero *m*

mutual (*myuu*-chu-öl) *adj* mutuo, recíproco

my (mai) *adj* mi

myself (mai-*ssélf*) *pron* me; yo mismo

mysterious (mi-*ssti°*-ri-öss) *adj* misterioso

mystery (*mi*-sstö-ri) *n* enigma *m*, misterio *m*

myth (miz) *n* mito *m*

N

nail (neil) *n* uña *f*; clavo *m*

nailbrush (*neil*-braʃ) *n* cepillo para las uñas

nail-file (*neil*-fail) *n* lima para las uñas

nail-polish (*neil*-po-liʃ) *n* barniz para las uñas

nail-scissors (*neil*-ssi-sös) *pl* tijeras para las uñas

naïve (naa-*iiv*) *adj* ingenuo

naked (*nei*-kid) *adj* desnudo

name (neim) *n* nombre *m*; *v* nombrar; **in the ~ of** en nombre de

namely (*neim*-li) *adv* a saber

nap (næp) *n* siesta *f*

napkin (*næp*-kin) *n* servilleta *f*

nappy (*næ*-pi) *n* pañal *m*

narcosis (naa-*kou*-ssiss) *n* (pl -ses) narcosis *f*

narcotic (naa-*ko*-tik) *n* narcótico *m*

narrow (*næ*-rou) *adj* angosto, estrecho

narrow-minded (næ-rou-*main*-did) *adj* mezquino

nasty (*naa*-ssti) *adj* antipático, desagradable

nation (*nei*-ʃön) *n* nación *f*; pueblo *m*

national (*næ*-ʃö-nöl) *adj* nacional; del Estado; **~ anthem** himno nacional; **~ dress** traje del país; **~ park** parque nacional

nationality (næ-ʃö-*næ*-lö-ti) *n* nacionalidad *f*

nationalize (*næ*-ʃö-nö-lais) *v* nacionalizar

native (*nei*-tiv) *n* indígena *m*; *adj* nativo; **~ country** patria *f*, país natal; **~ language** lengua materna

natural (*næ*-chö-röl) *adj* natural; innato

naturally (*næ*-chö-rö-li) *adv* naturalmente, por supuesto

nature (*nei*-chö) *n* naturaleza *f*; natural *m*

naughty (*noo*-ti) *adj* travieso

nausea (*noo*-ssi-ö) *n* náusea *f*

naval (*nei*-völ) *adj* naval

navel (*nei*-völ) *n* ombligo *m*

navigable (*næ*-vi-ghö-böl) *adj* navegable

navigate (*næ*-vi-gheit) *v* navegar

navigation (næ-vi-*ghei*-ʃön) *n* navegación *f*

navy (*nei*-vi) *n* marina *f*

near (ni°) *prep* cerca de; *adj* cercano

nearby (ni°-bai) *adj* cercano

nearly (ni°-li) *adv* casi

neat (niit) *adj* pulcro; puro

necessary (*né*-ssö-ssö-ri) *adj* necesario

necessity (nö-*ssé*-ssö-ti) *n* necesidad *f*

neck (nêk) *n* cuello *m*; **nape of the ~** nuca *f*

necklace (*nêk*-löss) *n* collar *m*

necktie (*nêk*-tai) *n* corbata *f*

need (niid) *v* deber, necesitar; *n* necesidad *f*; **~ to** deber

needle (*nii*-döl) *n* aguja *f*

needlework (*nii*-döl-ᵘöök) *n* labor de aguja

negative (*nê*-ghö-tiv) *adj* negativo; *n*

negativo *m*

neglect (ni-*ghlêkt*) *v* descuidar; *n* negligencia *f*

neglectful (ni-*ghlêkt*-föl) *adj* negligente

negligee (*nê*-ghli-ʒei) *n* bata suelta

negotiate (ni-*ghou*-ʃi-eit) *v* negociar

negotiation (ni-ghou-ʃi-*ei*-ʃön) *n* negociación *f*

Negro (*nii*-ghrou) *n* (pl ~es) negro *m*

neighbour (*nei*-bö) *n* vecino *m*

neighbourhood (*nei*-bö-hud) *n* vecindad *f*

neighbouring (*nei*-bö-ring) *adj* contiguo, vecino

neither (*nai*-ðö) *pron* ninguno de los dos; **neither ... nor** ni ... ni

neon (*nii*-on) *n* neón *m*

nephew (*nê*-fyuu) *n* sobrino *m*

nerve (nööv) *n* nervio *m*; audacia *f*

nervous (*nöö*-vöss) *adj* nervioso

nest (nêsst) *n* nido *m*

net (nêt) *n* red *f*; *adj* neto

the Netherlands (*nê*-ðö-lönds) Países Bajos *mpl*

network (*nêt*-ᵁöök) *n* red *f*

neuralgia (nyu-ᵒ-*ræl*-dʒö) *n* neuralgia *f*

neurosis (nyu-ᵒ-*rou*-ssiss) *n* neurosis *f*

neuter (*nyuu*-tö) *adj* neutro

neutral (*nyuu*-tröl) *adj* neutral

never (*nê*-vö) *adv* nunca

nevertheless (nê-vö-ðö-*lêss*) *adv* no obstante

new (nyuu) *adj* nuevo; **New Year** año nuevo

news (nyuus) *n* noticiario *m*, noticia *f*; noticias *fpl*

newsagent (*nyuu*-sei-dʒönt) *n* vendedor de periódicos

newspaper (*nyuus*-pei-pö) *n* diario *m*

newsreel (*nyuus*-riil) *n* noticiario *m*

newsstand (*nyuus*-sstænd) *n* quiosco de periódicos

New Zealand (nyuu *sii*-lönd) Nueva Zelanda

next (nêksst) *adj* próximo; ~ **to** junto a

next-door (nêksst-*doo*) *adv* al lado

nice (naiss) *adj* agradable, bonito, ameno; rico; simpático

nickel (*ni*-köl) *n* níquel *m*

nickname (*nik*-neim) *n* mote *m*

nicotine (*ni*-kö-tiin) *n* nicotina *f*

niece (niiss) *n* sobrina *f*

Nigeria (nai-*dʒi*-ri-ö) Nigeria *f*

Nigerian (nai-*dʒi*-ri-ön) *adj* nigeriano

night (nait) *n* noche *f*; **by** ~ de noche; ~ **flight** vuelo nocturno; ~ **rate** tarifa nocturna; ~ **train** tren nocturno

nightclub (*nait*-klab) *n* cabaret *m*

night-cream (*nait*-kriim) *n* crema de noche

nightdress (*nait*-drêss) *n* camisón *m*

nightingale (*nai*-ting-gheil) *n* ruiseñor *m*

nightly (*nait*-li) *adj* nocturno

nil (nil) nada

nine (nain) *num* nueve

nineteen (nain-*tiin*) *num* diecinueve

nineteenth (nain-*tiinz*) *num* decimonono

ninety (*nain*-ti) *num* noventa

ninth (nainz) *num* noveno

nitrogen (*nai*-trö-dʒön) *n* nitrógeno *m*

no (nou) no; *adj* ninguno; ~ **one** nadie

nobility (nou-*bi*-lö-ti) *n* nobleza *f*

noble (*nou*-böl) *adj* noble

nobody (*nou*-bo-di) *pron* nadie

nod (nod) *n* cabeceo *m*; *v* cabecear

noise (nois) *n* ruido *m*; alboroto *m*

noisy (*noi*-si) *adj* ruidoso

nominal (*no*-mi-nöl) *adj* nominal

nominate (*no*-mi-neit) *v* nombrar

nomination (no-mi-*nei*-ʃön) *n* nominación *f*; nombramiento *m*

none (nan) *pron* ninguno

nonsense (*non*-ssönss) *n* tontería *f*

noon (nuun) *n* mediodía *m*

normal (*noo*-möl) *adj* normal

north (nooz) *n* norte *m*; *adj* septentrional; **North Pole** polo norte

north-east (nooz-*iisst*) *n* nordeste *m*

northerly (*noo*-ðö-li) *adj* del norte

northern (*noo*-ðön) *adj* norteño

north-west (nooz-*ᵘêsst*) *n* noroeste *m*

Norway (*noo*-ᵘei) Noruega *f*

Norwegian (noo-ᵘii-dʒön) *adj* noruego

nose (nous) *n* nariz *f*

nosebleed (*nous*-bliid) *n* hemorragia nasal

nostril (*no*-sstril) *n* ventana de la nariz

not (not) *adv* no

notary (*nou*-tö-ri) *n* notario *m*

note (nout) *n* apunte *m*, esquela *f*; nota *f*; tono *m*; *v* notar; observar, *comprobar

notebook (*nout*-buk) *n* libreta de apuntes

noted (*nou*-tid) *adj* afamado

notepaper (*nout*-pei-pö) *n* papel de escribir, papel para cartas

nothing (*na*-zing) *n* nada *f*, nada

notice (*nou*-tiss) *v* observar, notar, *advertir; *ver; *n* aviso *m*, noticia *f*; atención *f*

noticeable (*nou*-ti-ssö-böl) *adj* perceptible; notable

notify (*nou*-ti-fai) *v* notificar

notion (*nou*-ʃön) *n* noción *f*

notorious (nou-*too*-ri-öss) *adj* de mala fama

nougat (*nuu*-ghaa) *n* turrón *m*

nought (noot) *n* cero *m*

noun (naun) *n* nombre *m*, substantivo *m*

nourishing (*na*-ri-ʃing) *adj* nutritivo

novel (*no*-völ) *n* novela *f*

novelist (*no*-vö-lisst) *n* novelista *m*

November (nou-*vêm*-bö) noviembre

now (nau) *adv* ahora; actualmente; ~ **and then** de vez en cuando

nowadays (*nau*-ö-deis) *adv* hoy en día

nowhere (*nou*-ᵘêô) *adv* en ninguna parte

nozzle (*no*-söl) *n* tobera *f*

nuance (nyuu-*angss*) *n* matiz *m*

nuclear (*nyuu*-kli-ö) *adj* nuclear; ~ **energy** energía nuclear

nucleus (*nyuu*-kli-öss) *n* núcleo *m*

nude (nyuud) *adj* desnudo; *n* desnudo *m*

nuisance (*nyuu*-ssönss) *n* molestia *f*

numb (nam) *adj* entumecido; aterido

number (*nam*-bö) *n* número *m*; cifra *f*; cantidad *f*

numeral (*nyuu*-mö-röl) *n* numeral *m*

numerous (*nyuu*-mö-röss) *adj* numeroso

nun (nan) *n* monja *f*

nunnery (*na*-nö-ri) *n* convento *m*

nurse (nööss) *n* enfermera *f*; niñera *f*; *v* *atender a; amamantar

nursery (*nöö*-ssö-ri) *n* cuarto de niños; guardería *f*; vivero *m*

nut (nat) *n* nuez *f*; tuerca *f*

nutcrackers (*nat*-kræ-kös) *pl* cascanueces *m*

nutmeg (*nat*-mêgh) *n* nuez moscada

nutritious (nyuu-*tri*-ʃöss) *adj* nutritivo

nutshell (*nat*-ʃêl) *n* cáscara de nuez

nylon (*nai*-lon) *n* nylon *m*

O

oak (ouk) *n* roble *m*

oar (oo) *n* remo *m*

oasis (ou-*ei*-ssiss) *n* (pl oases) oasis *f*

oath (ouz) *n* juramento *m*

oats (outss) *pl* avena *f*

obedience (ö-*bii*-di-önss) *n* obediencia *f*

obedient (ö-*bii*-di-önt) *adj* obediente

obey (ö-*bei*) *v* *obedecer

object¹ (*ob*-dʒikt) *n* objeto *m*

object² (öb-*dʒêkt*) *v* objetar; ~ **to** *oponerse a

objection (öb-*dʒêk*-ʃön) *n* objeción *f*

objective (öb-*dʒêk*-tiv) *adj* objetivo; *n* objetivo *m*

obligatory (ö-*bli*-ghö-tö-ri) *adj* obligatorio

oblige (ö-*blaidʒ*) *v* obligar; *be obliged to* *estar obligado a; *tener que

obliging (ö-*blai*-dʒing) *adj* simpático

oblong (*ob*-long) *adj* oblongo; *n* rectángulo *m*

obscene (öb-*ssiin*) *adj* obsceno

obscure (öb-*sskyuᵒ*) *adj* obscuro, misterioso, oscuro

observation (ob-sö-*vei*-ʃön) *n* observación *f*

observatory (öb-*söö*-vö-tri) *n* observatorio *m*

observe (öb-*sööv*) *v* observar

obsession (öb-*ssê*-ʃön) *n* obsesión *f*

obstacle (*ob*-sstö-köl) *n* obstáculo *m*

obstinate (*ob*-ssti-nöt) *adj* obstinado; pertinaz

obtain (öb-*tein*) *v* *conseguir, *obtener

obtainable (öb-*tei*-nö-böl) *adj* adquirible

obvious (*ob*-vi-öss) *adj* obvio

occasion (ö-*kei*-ʒön) *n* ocasión *f*; motivo *m*

occasionally (ö-*kei*-ʒö-nö-li) *adv* de vez en cuando, ocasionalmente

occupant (*o*-kyu-pönt) *n* ocupante *m*

occupation (o-kyu-*pei*-ʃön) *n* ocupación *f*

occupy (*o*-kyu-pai) *v* ocupar

occur (ö-*köö*) *v* suceder, ocurrir, *acontecer

occurrence (ö-*ka*-rönss) *n* acontecimiento *m*

ocean (*ou*-ʃön) *n* océano *m*

October (ok-*tou*-bö) octubre

octopus (*ok*-tö-pöss) *n* pulpo *m*

oculist (*o*-kyu-lisst) *n* oculista *m*

odd (od) *adj* raro; impar

odour (*ou*-dö) *n* olor *m*

of (ov, öv) *prep* de

off (of) *adv* fuera; *prep* de

offence (ö-*fênss*) *n* falta *f*; ofensa *f*, escándalo *m*

offend (ö-*fênd*) *v* ofender; transgredir

offensive (ö-*fên*-ssiv) *adj* ofensivo; insultante; *n* ofensivo *m*

offer (*o*-fö) *v* *ofrecer; presentar; *n* oferta *f*

office (*o*-fiss) *n* oficina *f*; cargo *m*; ~ **hours** horas de oficina

officer (*o*-fi-ssö) *n* oficial *m*

official (ö-*fi*-ʃöl) *adj* oficial

off-licence (*of*-lai-ssönss) *n* almacén de licores

often (*o*-fön) *adv* a menudo, frecuentemente

oil (oil) *n* aceite *m*; petróleo *m*; **fuel** ~ combustible líquido; ~ **filter** filtro del aceite; ~ **pressure** presión del aceite

oil-painting (oil-*pein*-ting) *n* pintura al óleo

oil-refinery (*oil*-ri-fai-nö-ri) *n* refinería de petróleo

oil-well (*oil*-ᵘêl) *n* pozo de petróleo

oily (*oi*-li) *adj* aceitoso

ointment (*oint*-mönt) *n* ungüento *m*

okay! (ou-*kei*) ¡de acuerdo!

old (ould) *adj* viejo; ~ **age** vejez *f*

old-fashioned (ould-*fæ*-ʃönd) *adj* anticuado

olive (*o*-liv) *n* aceituna *f*; ~ **oil** aceite de oliva

omelette (*om*-löt) *n* tortilla *f*

ominous (*o*-mi-nöss) *adj* siniestro

omit (ö-*mit*) *v* omitir

omnipotent (om-*ni*-pö-tönt) *adj* omnipotente

on (on) *prep* sobre; a

once (^uanss) *adv* una vez; **at ~** en seguida; **~ more** otra vez

oncoming (on-ka-ming) *adj* venidero

one (^uan) *num* uno; *pron* uno

oneself (^uan-*ssêlf*) *pron* uno mismo

onion (a-nyön) *n* cebolla *f*

only (oun-li) *adj* solo; *adv* sólo, solamente; *conj* pero

onwards (on-^uöds) *adv* adelante

onyx (o-nikss) *n* ónix *m*

opal (ou-pöl) *n* ópalo *m*

open (ou-pön) *v* abrir; *adj* abierto; sincero

opening (ou-pö-ning) *n* abertura *f*

opera (o-pö-rö) *n* ópera *f*; **~ house** teatro de la ópera

operate (o-pö-reit) *v* operar, funcionar

operation (o-pö-*rei*-ʃön) *n* funcionamiento *m*; operación *f*

operator (o-pö-rei-tö) *n* telefonista *f*

operetta (o-pö-rê-tö) *n* opereta *f*

opinion (ö-*pi*-nyön) *n* parecer *m*, opinión *f*

opponent (ö-*pou*-nönt) *n* contrincante *m*

opportunity (o-pö-*tyuu*-nö-ti) *n* oportunidad *f*

oppose (ö-*pous*) *v* *oponerse

opposite (o-pö-sit) *prep* enfrente de; *adj* contrario, opuesto

opposition (o-pö-*si*-ʃön) *n* oposición *f*

oppress (ö-*prêss*) *v* oprimir

optician (op-*ti*-ʃön) *n* óptico *m*

optimism (*op*-ti-mi-söm) *n* optimismo *m*

optimist (*op*-ti-misst) *n* optimista *m*

optimistic (op-ti-*mi*-sstik) *adj* optimista

optional (*op*-ʃö-nöl) *adj* opcional

or (oo) *conj* o

oral (oo-röl) *adj* oral

orange (o-rindʒ) *n* naranja *f*; *adj* de color naranja

orchard (oo-chöd) *n* vergel *m*

orchestra (oo-ki-sströ) *n* orquesta *f*; **~ seat** *Am* butaca *f*

order (oo-dö) *v* ordenar; *pedir; *n* orden *m*; orden *f*, mandato *m*; pedido *m*; **in ~** en regla; **in ~ to** para; **made to ~** hecho a la medida; **out of ~** averiado; **postal ~** giro postal

order-form (oo-dö-foom) *n* hoja de pedido

ordinary (oo-dön-ri) *adj* común, ordinario

ore (oo) *n* mineral *m*

organ (oo-ghön) *n* órgano *m*

organic (oo-*ghæ*-nik) *adj* orgánico

organization (oo-ghö-nai-*sei*-ʃön) *n* organización *f*

organize (oo-ghö-nais) *v* organizar

Orient (oo-ri-önt) *n* oriente *m*

oriental (oo-ri-*ên*-töl) *adj* oriental

orientate (oo-ri-ön-teit) *v* orientarse

origin (o-ri-dʒin) *n* origen *m*; descendencia *f*, procedencia *f*

original (ö-*ri*-dʒi-nöl) *adj* auténtico, original

originally (ö-*ri*-dʒi-nö-li) *adv* originalmente

orlon (oo-lon) *n* orlón *m*

ornament (oo-nö-mönt) *n* adorno *m*

ornamental (oo-nö-*mên*-töl) *adj* ornamental

orphan (oo-fön) *n* huérfano *m*

orthodox (oo-zö-dokss) *adj* ortodoxo

ostrich (o-sstrich) *n* avestruz *m*

other (a-ðö) *adj* otro

otherwise (a-ðö-^uais) *conj* si no; *adv* de otra manera

*ought to (oot) *tener que

our (au^ö) *adj* nuestro

ourselves (au^ö-*ssêlvs*) *pron* nos; nosotros mismos

out (aut) *adv* fuera; ~ **of** fuera de, de

outbreak (*aut*-breik) *n* explosión *f*

outcome (*aut*-kam) *n* resultado *m*

*outdo (aut-*duu*) *v* superar

outdoors (aut-*doos*) *adv* afuera

outer (*au*-tö) *adj* exterior

outfit (*aut*-fit) *n* equipo *m*

outline (*aut*-lain) *n* contorno *m*; *v* bosquejar

outlook (*aut*-luk) *n* previsión *f*; punto de vista

output (*aut*-put) *n* producción *f*

outrage (*aut*-reidʒ) *n* ultraje *m*

outside (aut-*ssaid*) *adv* afuera; *prep* fuera de; *n* exterior *m*

outsize (*aut*-ssais) *n* tamaño extraordinario

outskirts (*aut*-ssköötss) *pl* afueras *fpl*

outstanding (aut-*sstæn*-ding) *adj* eminente, destacado

outward (*aut*-ᵘöd) *adj* externo

outwards (*aut*-ᵘöds) *adv* hacia afuera

oval (*ou*-völ) *adj* ovalado

oven (*a*-vön) *n* horno *m*

over (*ou*-vö) *prep* encima de; más de; *adv* encima; abajo; *adj* acabado; ~ **there** allá

overall (*ou*-vö-rool) *adj* total

overalls (*ou*-vö-rools) *pl* mono *m*; overol *mMe*

overcast (*ou*-vö-kaasst) *adj* nublado

overcoat (*ou*-vö-kout) *n* abrigo *m*

*overcome (ou-vö-*kam*) *v* vencer

overdue (ou-vö-*dyuu*) *adj* atrasado

overgrown (ou-vö-*ghroun*) *adj* cubierto de verdor

overhaul (ou-vö-*hool*) *v* revisar

overhead (ou-vö-*hêd*) *adv* en alto

overlook (ou-vö-*luk*) *v* pasar por alto

overnight (ou-vö-*nait*) *adv* de noche

overseas (ou-vö-*ssiis*) *adj* ultramar

oversight (*ou*-vö-ssait) *n* descuido *m*

*oversleep (ou-vö-*ssliip*) *v* quedarse

dormido

overstrung (ou-vö-*sstrang*) *adj* sobreexcitado

*overtake (ou-vö-*teik*) *v* recoger; **no overtaking** prohibido adelantar

over-tired (ou-vö-*tai*ᵒd) *adj* exhausto

overture (*ou*-vö-chö) *n* obertura *f*

overweight (*ou*-vö-ᵘeit) *n* sobrepeso *m*

overwhelm (ou-vö-ᵘ*êlm*) *v* *desconcertar, subyugar

overwork (ou-vö-ᵘ*öök*) *v* trabajar demasiado

owe (ou) *v* deber; **owing to** a causa de, debido a

owl (aul) *n* buho *m*

own (oun) *v* *poseer; *adj* propio

owner (*ou*-nö) *n* propietario *m*

ox (okss) *n* (pl oxen) buey *m*

oxygen (*ok*-ssi-dʒön) *n* oxígeno *m*

oyster (*oi*-sstö) *n* ostra *f*

P

pace (peiss) *n* andares *mpl*; paso *m*; ritmo *m*

Pacific Ocean (pö-*ssi*-fik ou-*ʃ*ön) Océano Pacífico

pacifism (*pæ*-ssi-fi-söm) *n* pacifismo *m*

pacifist (*pæ*-ssi-fisst) *n* pacifista *m*

pack (pæk) *v* embalar; ~ **up** empaquetar

package (*pæ*-kidʒ) *n* paquete *m*

packet (*pæ*-kit) *n* paquete *m*

packing (*pæ*-king) *n* embalaje *m*

pad (pæd) *n* almohadilla *f*; bloque *m*

paddle (*pæ*-döl) *n* remo *m*

padlock (*pæd*-lok) *n* candado *m*

pagan (*pei*-ghön) *adj* pagano; *n* pagano *m*

page (peidʒ) *n* página *f*

page-boy (*peidʒ*-boi) *n* paje *m*

pail (peil) *n* balde *m*

pain (pein) *n* dolor *m*; **pains** pena *f*

painful (*pein*-föl) *adj* dolorido

painless (*pein*-löss) *adj* sin dolor

paint (peint) *n* pintura *f*; *v* pintar

paint-box (*peint*-bokss) *n* caja de colores

paint-brush (*peint*-braʃ) *n* pincel *m*

painter (*pein*-tö) *n* pintor *m*

painting (*pein*-ting) *n* pintura *f*

pair (pê^ö) *n* par *m*

Pakistan (paa-ki-*staan*) Paquistán *m*

Pakistani (paa-ki-*sstaa*-ni) *adj* paquistaní

palace (*pæ*-löss) *n* palacio *m*

pale (peil) *adj* pálido

palm (paam) *n* palma *f*

palpable (*pæl*-pö-böl) *adj* palpable

palpitation (pæl-pi-*tei*-ʃön) *n* palpitación *f*

pan (pæn) *n* sartén *f*

pane (pein) *n* cristal *m*

panel (*pæ*-nöl) *n* painel *m*, cuarterón *m*

panelling (*pæ*-nö-ling) *n* enmaderado *m*

panic (*pæ*-nik) *n* pánico *m*

pant (pænt) *v* jadear

panties (*pæn*-tis) *pl* braga *f*

pants (pæntss) *pl* calzoncillos *mpl*; *plAm* pantalones *mpl*

pant-suit (*pænt*-ssuut) *n* traje pantalón

panty-hose (*pæn*-ti-hous) *n* media pantalón

paper (*pei*-pö) *n* papel *m*; periódico *m*; de papel; **carbon ~** papel carbón; **~ bag** bolsa de papel; **~ napkin** servilleta de papel; **typing ~** papel para mecanografiar; **wrapping ~** papel de envolver

paperback (*pei*-pö-bæk) *n* libro de bolsillo

paper-knife (*pei*-pö-naif) *n* abrecartas *m*

parade (pö-*reid*) *n* parada *f*, desfile *m*

paraffin (*pæ*-rö-fin) *n* parafina *f*

paragraph (*pæ*-rö-ghraaf) *n* párrafo *m*

parakeet (*pæ*-rö-kiit) *n* cotorra *f*

paralise (*pæ*-rö-lais) *v* paralizar

parallel (*pæ*-rö-lêl) *adj* paralelo; *n* paralelo *m*

parcel (*paa*-ssöl) *n* paquete *m*

pardon (*paa*-dön) *n* perdón *m*; indulto *m*

parents (*pê^ö*-röntss) *pl* padres *mpl*

parents-in-law (*pê^ö*-röntss-in-loo) *pl* padres políticos

parish (*pæ*-riʃ) *n* parroquia *f*

park (paak) *n* parque *m*; *v* estacionar

parking (*paa*-king) *n* aparcamiento *m*; **no ~** prohibido estacionarse; **~ fee** derechos de estacionamiento; **~ light** luz de estacionamiento; **~ lot** *Am* estacionamiento *m*; **~ meter** parquímetro *m*; **~ zone** zona de aparcamiento

parliament (*paa*-lö-mönt) *n* parlamento *m*

parliamentary (paa-lö-*mên*-tö-ri) *adj* parlamentario

parrot (*pæ*-röt) *n* loro *m*

parsley (*paa*-ssli) *n* perejil *m*

parson (*paa*-ssön) *n* pastor *m*

parsonage (*paa*-ssö-nidʒ) *n* curato *m*

part (paat) *n* parte *f*; pieza *f*; *v* separar; **spare ~** recambio *m*

partial (*paa*-ʃöl) *adj* parcial

participant (paa-*ti*-ssi-pönt) *n* participante *m*

participate (paa-*ti*-ssi-peit) *v* participar

particular (pö-*ti*-kyu-lö) *adj* especial, particular; exigente; **in ~** en particular

parting (*paa*-ting) *n* despedida *f*; raya *f*

partition (paa-*ti*-fön) *n* tabique *m*

partly (*paat*-li) *adv* en parte

partner (*paat*-nö) *n* pareja *f*; socio *m*

partridge (*paa*-tridʒ) *n* perdiz *f*

party (*paa*-ti) *n* partido *m*; guateque *m*, fiesta *f*; grupo *m*

pass (paass) *v* transcurrir, pasar; *aprobar; ~ **by** pasar de largo; ~ **through** *atravesar

passage (*pæ*-ssidʒ) *n* pasaje *m*; travesía *f*; trozo *m*

passenger (*pæ*-ssön-dʒö) *n* pasajero *m*; ~ **train** tren de pasajeros

passer-by (paa-ssö-*bai*) *n* transeúnte *m*

passion (*pæ*-fön) *n* pasión *f*; cólera *f*

passionate (*pæ*-fö-nöt) *adj* apasionado

passive (*pæ*-ssiv) *adj* pasivo

passport (*paass*-poot) *n* pasaporte *m*; ~ **control** inspección de pasaportes; ~ **photograph** fotografía de pasaporte

password (*paass*-ᵁööd) *n* santo y seña

past (paasst) *n* pasado *m*; *adj* pasado; transcurrido; *prep* a lo largo de, más allá de

paste (peisst) *n* pasta *f*; *v* pegar

pastry (*pei*-sstri) *n* pastelería *f*; ~ **shop** pastelería *f*

pasture (*paass*-chö) *n* prado *m*

patch (pæch) *v* *remendar

patent (*pei*-tönt) *n* patente *f*

path (paaz) *n* senda *f*

patience (*pei*-fönss) *n* paciencia *f*

patient (*pei*-fönt) *adj* paciente; *n* paciente *m*

patriot (*pei*-tri-öt) *n* patriota *m*

patrol (pö-*troul*) *n* patrulla *f*; *v* patrullar; vigilar

pattern (*pæ*-tön) *n* diseño *m*

pause (poos) *n* pausa *f*; *v* *hacer una pausa

pave (peiv) *v* pavimentar

pavement (*peiv*-mönt) *n* acera *f*; pavimento *m*

pavilion (pö-*vil*-yön) *n* pabellón *m*

paw (poo) *n* pata *f*

pawn (poon) *v* empeñar; *n* peón *m*

pawnbroker (*poon*-brou-kö) *n* prestamista *m*

pay (pei) *n* salario *m*, sueldo *m*

*****pay** (pei) *v* pagar; *rendir; ~ **attention to** prestar atención a; **paying** rentable; ~ **off** amortizar; ~ **on account** pagar a plazos

pay-desk (*pei*-dèssk) *n* caja *f*

payee (pei-*ii*) *n* favorecido *m*

payment (*pei*-mönt) *n* pago *m*

pea (pii) *n* guisante *m*

peace (piiss) *n* paz *f*

peaceful (*piiss*-föl) *adj* tranquilo

peach (piich) *n* melocotón *m*

peacock (*pii*-kok) *n* pavo *m*

peak (piik) *n* pico *m*; cumbre *f*; ~ **hour** hora punta; ~ **season** apogeo de la temporada

peanut (*pii*-nat) *n* cacahuete *m*; cacahuate *mMe*

pear (pèᵒ) *n* pera *f*

pearl (pööl) *n* perla *f*

peasant (*pê*-sönt) *n* campesino *m*

pebble (*pê*-böl) *n* guijarro *m*

peculiar (pi-*kyuul*-yö) *adj* extraño; especial, peculiar

peculiarity (pi-kyuu-li-æ-rö-ti) *n* particularidad *f*

pedal (*pê*-döl) *n* pedal *m*

pedestrian (pi-*dê*-sstri-ön) *n* peatón *m*; **no pedestrians** prohibido para los peatones; ~ **crossing** cruce para peatones

pedicure (*pê*-di-kyuᵒ) *n* pedicuro *m*

peel (piil) *v* pelar; *n* piel *f*

peep (piip) *v* espiar

peg (pêgh) *n* percha *f*

pelican (*pê*-li-kön) *n* pelícano *m*

pelvis (*pêl*-viss) *n* pelvis *m*

pen (pên) n pluma f

penalty (pê-nöl-ti) n pena f; castigo m; ~ **kick** penalty m

pencil (pên-ssöl) n lápiz m

pencil-sharpener (pên-ssöl-ʃaap-nö) n sacapuntas m

pendant (pên-dönt) n pendiente m

penetrate (pê-ni-treit) v penetrar

penguin (pêng-ghⁱin) n pingüino m

penicillin (pê-ni-ssi-lin) n penicilina f

peninsula (pö-nin-ssyu-lö) n península f

penknife (pên-naif) n (pl -knives) cortaplumas m

pension¹ (pang-ssi-ong) n pensión f

pension² (pên-ʃön) n pensión f

people (pii-pöl) pl gente f; n pueblo m

pepper (pê-pö) n pimienta f

peppermint (pê-pö-mint) n menta f

perceive (pö-ssiiv) v percibir

percent (pö-ssênt) n por ciento

percentage (pö-ssên-tidʒ) n porcentaje m

perceptible (pö-ssêp-ti-böl) adj perceptible

perception (pö-ssêp-ʃön) n percepción f

perch (pööch) (pl ~) perca f

percolator (pöö-kö-lei-tö) n cafetera filtradora

perfect (pöö-fikt) adj perfecto

perfection (pö-fêk-ʃön) n perfección f

perform (pö-foom) v ejecutar, desempeñar

performance (pö-foo-mönss) n representación f

perfume (pöö-fyuum) n perfume m

perhaps (pö-hæpss) adv quizás

peril (pê-ril) n peligro m

perilous (pê-ri-löss) adj peligroso

period (piⁱ-ri-öd) n época f, período m; punto m

periodical (piⁱ-ri-o-di-köl) n periódico

m; adj periódico

perish (pê-riʃ) v *perecer

perishable (pê-ri-ʃö-böl) adj perecedero

perjury (pöö-dʒö-ri) n perjurio m

permanent (pöö-mö-nönt) adj duradero, permanente; estable, fijo; ~ **press** planchado permanente; ~ **wave** ondulación permanente

permission (pö-mi-ʃön) n permiso m, autorización f; licencia f

permit¹ (pö-mit) v permitir

permit² (pöö-mit) n permiso m

peroxide (pö-rok-ssaid) n peróxido m

perpendicular (pöö-pön-di-kyu-lö) adj perpendicular

Persia (pöö-ʃö) Persia f

Persian (pöö-ʃön) adj persa

person (pöö-ssön) n persona f; **per** ~ por persona

personal (pöö-ssö-nöl) adj personal

personality (pöö-ssö-næ-lö-ti) n personalidad f

personnel (pöö-ssö-nêl) n personal m

perspective (pö-sspêk-tiv) n perspectiva f

perspiration (pöö-ssppö-rei-ʃön) n transpiración f, sudor m

perspire (pö-sspaiⁱ) v transpirar, sudar

persuade (pö-ssⁱeid) v persuadir; convencer

persuasion (pö-ssⁱei-ʒön) n convicción f

pessimism (pê-ssi-mi-söm) n pesimismo m

pessimist (pê-ssi-misst) n pesimista m

pessimistic (pê-ssi-mi-sstik) adj pesimista

pet (pêt) n animal doméstico; cariño m; favorito

petal (pê-töl) n pétalo m

petition (pi-ti-ʃön) n petición f

petrol (pê-tröl) n gasolina f; ~ **pump**

bomba de gasolina; ~ **station** puesto de gasolina; ~ **tank** depósito de gasolina

petroleum (pi-*trou*-li-öm) n petróleo m

petty (pê-ti) adj pequeño, fútil, insignificante; ~ **cash** calderilla f

pewit (pii-ᵘit) n avefría f

pewter (pyuu-tö) n estaño m

phantom (fæn-töm) n fantasma m

pharmacology (faa-mö-*ko*-lö-dʒi) n farmacología f

pharmacy (*faa*-mö-ssi) n farmacia f; droguería f

phase (feis) n fase f

pheasant (fê-sönt) n faisán m

Philippine (fi-li-pain) adj filipino

Philippines (fi-li-piins) pl Filipinas fpl

philosopher (fi-*lo*-ssö-fö) n filósofo m

philosophy (fi-*lo*-ssö-fi) n filosofía f

phone (foun) n teléfono m; v llamar por teléfono, telefonear

phonetic (fö-*nê*-tik) adj fonético

photo (fou-tou) n (pl ~s) foto f

photograph (fou-tö-ghraaf) n fotografía f; v fotografiar

photographer (fö-*to*-ghrö-fö) n fotógrafo m

photography (fö-*to*-ghrö-fi) n fotografía f

photostat (fou-tö-sstæt) n fotocopia f

phrase (freis) n frase f

phrase-book (*freis*-buk) n manual de conversación

physical (fi-si-köl) adj físico

physician (fi-si-jön) n médico m

physicist (fi-si-ssist) n físico m

physics (fi-sikss) n física f

physiology (fi-si-*o*-lö-dʒi) n fisiología f

pianist (*pii*-ö-nisst) n pianista m

piano (pi-æ-nou) n piano m; **grand** ~ piano de cola

pick (pik) v recoger; escoger; n elec-

ción f; ~ **up** recoger; *ir a buscar; **pick-up van** camioneta de reparto

pick-axe (*pi*-kækss) n pico m

pickles (*pi*-köls) pl encurtidos mpl

picnic (*pik*-nik) n día de campo; v *hacer un día de campo

picture (*pik*-chö) n cuadro m; ilustración f, grabado m; imagen f; ~ **postcard** tarjeta postal ilustrada, postal ilustrada; **pictures** cine m

picturesque (pik-chö-*ressk*) adj pintoresco

piece (piiss) n fragmento m, pedazo m

pier (piᵒ) n muelle m

pierce (piᵒss) v punzar

pig (pigh) n cerdo m

pigeon (*pi*-dʒön) n paloma f

pig-headed (pigh-*hê*-did) adj testarudo

piglet (*pigh*-löt) n cochinillo m

pigskin (*pigh*-sskin) n piel de cerdo

pike (paik) (pl ~) lucio m

pile (pail) n montón m; v amontonar; **piles** pl hemorroides fpl

pilgrim (*pil*-ghrim) n peregrino m

pilgrimage (*pil*-ghri-midʒ) n peregrinación f

pill (pil) n píldora f

pillar (*pi*-lö) n columna f, pilar m

pillar-box (*pi*-lö-bokss) n buzón m

pillow (*pi*-lou) n almohadón m, almohada f

pillow-case (*pi*-lou-keiss) n funda de almohada

pilot (*pai*-löt) n piloto m; práctico m

pimple (*pim*-pöl) n grano m

pin (pin) n alfiler m; v clavar; **bobby** ~ Am horquilla f

pincers (*pin*-ssös) pl tenazas fpl

pinch (pinch) v pellizcar

pineapple (*pai*-næ-pöl) n piña f

ping-pong (*ping*-pong) n tenis de mesa

pink (pingk) *adj* rosado

pioneer (pai-ö-*ni*ö) *n* pionero *m*

pious (*pai*-öss) *adj* pío

pip (pip) *n* pepita *f*

pipe (paip) *n* pipa *f*; conducto *m*; ~ **cleaner** limpiapipas *m*; ~ **tobacco** tabaco de pipa

pirate (*pai*ö-röt) *n* pirata *m*

pistol (*pi*-sstöl) *n* pistola *f*

piston (*pi*-sstön) *n* pistón *m*; ~ **ring** aro de émbolo

piston-rod (*pi*-sstön-rod) *n* biela *f*

pit (pit) *n* hoyo *m*; mina *f*

pitcher (*pi*-chö) *n* cántaro *m*

pity (*pi*-ti) *n* piedad *f*; *v* *tener piedad de, compadecerse de; **what a pity!** ¡qué lástima!

placard (*plæ*-kaad) *n* cartel *m*

place (pleiss) *n* lugar *m*; *v* *poner, colocar; ~ **of birth** lugar de nacimiento; ***take** ~ *tener lugar

plague (pleigh) *n* plaga *f*

plaice (pleiss) (pl ~) platija *f*

plain (plein) *adj* claro; corriente, sencillo; *n* llano *m*

plan (plæn) *n* plan *m*; plano *m*; *v* planear

plane (plein) *adj* plano; *n* avión *m*; ~ **crash** accidente aéreo

planet (*plæ*-nit) *n* planeta *m*

planetarium (plæ-ni-*tê*ö-ri-öm) *n* planetario *m*

plank (plængk) *n* tablón *m*

plant (plaant) *n* planta *f*; instalación *f*; *v* plantar

plantation (plæn-*tei*-∫ön) *n* plantación *f*

plaster (*plaa*-sstö) *n* estuco *m*, yeso *m*; esparadrapo *m*

plastic (*plæ*-sstik) *adj* de plástico; *n* plástico *m*

plate (pleit) *n* plato *m*; chapa *f*

plateau (*plæ*-tou) *n* (pl ~x, ~s) meseta *f*

platform (*plæt*-foom) *n* andén *m*; ~ **ticket** billete de andén

platinum (*plæ*-ti-nöm) *n* platino *m*

play (plei) *v* *jugar; tocar; *n* juego *m*; obra de teatro; **one-act** ~ pieza en un acto; ~ **truant** *hacer novillos

player (*plei*ö) *n* jugador *m*

playground (*plei*-ghraund) *n* patio de recreo

playing-card (*plei*-ing-kaad) *n* naipe *m*

playwright (*plei*-rait) *n* dramaturgo *m*

plea (plii) *n* defensa *f*

plead (pliid) *v* informar

pleasant (*plê*-sönt) *adj* agradable, simpático

please (pliis) por favor; *v* *placer; **pleased** contento; **pleasing** agradable

pleasure (*plê*-зö) *n* placer *m*, diversión *f*

plentiful (*plên*-ti-föl) *adj* abundante

plenty (*plên*-ti) *n* abundancia *f*

pliers (*plai*ös) *pl* alicates *mpl*

plimsolls (*plim*-ssöls) *pl* zapatos de gimnasia

plot (plot) *n* conjuración *f*, complot *m*; trama *f*; parcela *f*

plough (plau) *n* arado *m*; *v* arar

plucky (*pla*-ki) *adj* valiente

plug (plagh) *n* enchufe *m*; ~ **in** enchufar

plum (plam) *n* ciruela *f*

plumber (*pla*-mö) *n* plomero *m*

plump (plamp) *adj* regordete

plural (*plu*ö-röl) *n* plural *m*

plus (plass) *prep* más

pneumatic (nyuu-*mæ*-tik) *adj* neumático

pneumonia (nyuu-*mou*-ni-ö) *n* neumonía *f*

poach (pouch) *v* cazar en vedado

pocket (*po*-kit) *n* bolsillo *m*

pocket-book (*po*-kit-buk) *n* bolsa *f*

pocket-comb (*po*-kit-koum) *n* peine de bolsillo

pocket-knife (*po*-kit-naif) *n* (pl -knives) navaja *f*

pocket-watch (*po*-kit-ᵘoch) *n* reloj de bolsillo

poem (*pou*-im) *n* poema *m*

poet (*pou*-it) *n* poeta *m*

poetry (*pou*-i-tri) *n* poesía *f*

point (point) *n* punto *m*; punta *f*; *v* señalar con el dedo; ~ **of view** punto de vista; ~ **out** apuntar

pointed (*poin*-tid) *adj* puntiagudo

poison (*poi*-sön) *n* veneno *m*; *v* envenenar

poisonous (*poi*-sö-nöss) *adj* venenoso

Poland (*pou*-lönd) Polonia *f*

Pole (poul) *n* polaco *m*

pole (poul) *n* poste *m*

police (pö-*liiss*) *pl* policía *f*

policeman (pö-*liiss*-mön) *n* (pl -men) agente de policía, guardia *m*

police-station (pö-*liiss*-sstei-ʃön) *n* comisaría *f*

policy (*po*-li-ssi) *n* política *f*; póliza *f*

polio (*pou*-li-ou) *n* polio *f*, poliomielitis *f*

Polish (*pou*-liʃ) *adj* polaco

polish (*po*-liʃ) *v* pulir

polite (pö-*lait*) *adj* cortés

political (pö-*li*-ti-köl) *adj* político

politician (po-li-*ti*-ʃön) *n* político *m*

politics (*po*-li-tikss) *n* política *f*

pollution (pö-*luu*-ʃön) *n* contaminación *f*, polución *f*

pond (pond) *n* estanque *m*

pony (*pou*-ni) *n* pony *m*

poor (puᵒ) *adj* pobre; mediocre

pope (poup) *n* Papa *m*

poplin (*po*-plin) *n* popelín *m*

pop music (pop *myuu*-sik) música pop

poppy (*po*-pi) *n* amapola *f*; adormidera *f*

popular (*po*-pyu-lö) *adj* popular

population (po-pyu-*lei*-ʃön) *n* población *f*

populous (*po*-pyu-löss) *adj* populoso

porcelain (*poo*-ssö-lin) *n* porcelana *f*

porcupine (*poo*-kyu-pain) *n* puerco espín

pork (pook) *n* carne de cerdo

port (poot) *n* puerto *m*; babor *m*

portable (*poo*-tö-böl) *adj* portátil

porter (*poo*-tö) *n* mozo *m*; portero *m*

porthole (*poot*-houl) *n* portilla *f*

portion (*poo*-ʃön) *n* porción *f*

portrait (*poo*-trit) *n* retrato *m*

Portugal (*poo*-tyu-ghöl) Portugal *m*

Portuguese (poo-tyu-*ghiis*) *adj* portugués

position (pö-*si*-ʃön) *n* posición *f*; actitud *f*; puesto *m*

positive (*po*-sö-tiv) *adj* positivo; *n* positiva *f*

possess (pö-*sêss*) *v* *poseer; possessed *adj* poseído

possession (pö-*sê*-ʃön) *n* posesión *f*; possessions bienes *mpl*

possibility (po-ssö-*bi*-lö-ti) *n* posibilidad *f*

possible (*po*-ssö-böl) *adj* posible; eventual

post (pousst) *n* poste *m*; puesto *m*; correo *m*; *v* echar al correo; post-office casa de correos

postage (*pou*-sstidʒ) *n* franqueo *m*; ~ **paid** franco; ~ **stamp** sello de correos; timbre *mMe*

postcard (*pousst*-kaad) *n* tarjeta postal; tarjeta postal ilustrada

poster (*pou*-sstö) *n* cartel *m*, poster *m*

poste restante (pousst rê-*sstangt*) lista de correos

postman (*pousst*-mön) *n* (pl -men) cartero *m*

post-paid (pousst-*peid*) *adj* franco

postpone (pö-*sspoun*) *v* aplazar

pot (pot) *n* olla *f*

potato (pö-*tei*-tou) *n* (pl ~es) patata *f*; papa *fMe*

pottery (*po*-tö-ri) *n* cerámica *f*; loza *f*

pouch (pauch) *n* petaca *f*

poulterer (*poul*-tö-rö) *n* pollero *m*

poultry (*poul*-tri) *n* aves de corral

pound (paund) *n* libra *f*

pour (poo) *v* *verter

poverty (*po*-vö-ti) *n* pobreza *f*

powder (*pau*-dö) *n* polvo *m*; ~ **compact** polvera *f*; **talc** ~ talco *m*

powder-puff (*pau*-dö-paf) *n* borla para empolvarse

powder-room (*pau*-dö-ruum) *n* tocador *m*

power (pau⁰) *n* fuerza *f*, energía *f*; poder *m*; potencia *f*

powerful (*pau⁰*-föl) *adj* poderoso; fuerte

powerless (*pau⁰*-löss) *adj* impotente

power-station (*pau⁰*-sstei-∫ön) *n* central eléctrica

practical (*præk*-ti-köl) *adj* práctico

practically (*præk*-ti-kli) *adv* prácticamente

practice (*præk*-tiss) *n* práctica *f*

practise (*præk*-tiss) *v* practicar; ensayarse

praise (preis) *v* alabar; *n* elogio *m*

pram (præm) *n* cochecillo *m*

prawn (proon) *n* gamba *f*

pray (prei) *v* orar

prayer (prê⁰) *n* oración *f*

preach (priich) *v* predicar

precarious (pri-*kê⁰*-ri-öss) *adj* precario

precaution (pri-*koo*-∫ön) *n* precaución *f*

precede (pri-*ssiid*) *v* preceder

preceding (pri-*ssii*-ding) *adj* precedente

precious (*prê*-∫öss) *adj* precioso; querido

precipice (*prê*-ssi-piss) *n* precipicio *m*

precipitation (pri-ssi-pi-*tei*-∫ön) *n* precipitación *f*

precise (pri-*ssaiss*) *adj* preciso, exacto; meticuloso

predecessor (*prii*-di-ssê-ssö) *n* predecesor *m*

predict (pri-*dikt*) *v* *predecir

prefer (pri-*föö*) *v* *preferir

preferable (*prê*-fö-rö-böl) *adj* preferible

preference (*prê*-fö-rönss) *n* preferencia *f*

prefix (*prii*-fikss) *n* prefijo *m*

pregnant (*prêgh*-nönt) *adj* encinta, embarazada

prejudice (*prê*-dʒö-diss) *n* prejuicio *m*

preliminary (pri-*li*-mi-nö-ri) *adj* preliminar

premature (*prê*-mö-chu⁰) *adj* prematuro

premier (*prêm*-i⁰) *n* jefe de gobierno

premises (*prê*-mi-ssis) *pl* finca *f*

premium (*prii*-mi-öm) *n* prima *f*

prepaid (prii-*peid*) *adj* pagado por adelantado

preparation (prê-pö-*rei*-∫ön) *n* preparación *f*

prepare (pri-*pê⁰*) *v* preparar

preposition (prê-pö-*si*-∫ön) *n* preposición *f*

prescribe (pri-*sskraib*) *v* prescribir

prescription (pri-*sskrip*-∫ön) *n* prescripción *f*

presence (*prê*-sönss) *n* presencia *f*

present[1] (*prê*-sönt) *n* regalo *m*, presente *m*; *adj* actual; presente

present[2] (pri-*sênt*) *v* presentar

presently (*prê*-sönt-li) *adv* en seguida, dentro de poco

preservation (prê-sö-*vei*-∫ön) *n* conservación *f*

preserve (pri-*sööv*) *v* preservar; conservar

president (*prê*-si-dönt) *n* presidente *m*

press (prêss) *n* prensa *f*; *v* empujar, *apretar; planchar; ~ **conference** conferencia de prensa

pressing (prê-ssing) *adj* urgente

pressure (prê-ʃö) *n* presión *f*; tensión *f*; **atmospheric** ~ presión atmosférica

pressure-cooker (prê-ʃö-ku-kö) *n* olla a presión

prestige (prê-sstiiʒ) *n* prestigio *m*

presumable (pri-syuu-mö-böl) *adj* presumible

presumptuous (pri-samp-ʃöss) *adj* presuntuoso; presumido

pretence (pri-têuss) *n* pretexto *m*

pretend (pri-tênd) *v* fingir

pretext (prii-têksst) *n* pretexto *m*

pretty (pri-ti) *adj* bonito; *adv* bastante

prevent (pri-vênt) *v* *impedir; *prevenir

preventive (pri-vên-tiv) *adj* preventivo

previous (prii-vi-öss) *adj* precedente, anterior, previo

pre-war (prii-ᵘoo) *adj* de la preguerra

price (praiss) *n* precio *m*; *v* fijar el precio

priceless (praiss-löss) *adj* inapreciable

price-list (praiss-lisst) *n* lista de precios

prick (prik) *v* pinchar

pride (praid) *n* orgullo *m*

priest (priisst) *n* cura *m*

primary (prai-mö-ri) *adj* primario; primero, primordial; elemental

prince (prinss) *n* príncipe *m*

princess (prin-ssêss) *n* princesa *f*

principal (prin-ssö-pöl) *adj* principal; *n* director de escuela, principal *m*

principle (prin-ssö-pöl) *n* principio *m*

print (print) *v* *imprimir; *n* positiva *f*; grabado *m*; **printed matter** impreso *m*

prior (prai⁰) *adj* anterior

priority (prai-o-rö-ti) *n* prioridad *f*

prison (pri-sön) *n* prisión *f*

prisoner (pri-sö-nö) *n* preso *m*, prisionero *m*; ~ **of war** prisionero de guerra

privacy (prai-vö-ssi) *n* intimidad *f*, vida privada

private (prai-vit) *adj* particular, privado; personal

privilege (pri-vi-lidʒ) *n* privilegio *m*

prize (prais) *n* premio *m*; recompensa *f*

probable (pro-bö-böl) *adj* probable

probably (pro-bö-bli) *adv* probablemente

problem (pro-blöm) *n* problema *m*

procedure (prö-ssii-dʒö) *n* procedimiento *m*

proceed (prö-ssiid) *v* *proseguir; proceder

process (prou-ssêss) *n* procedimiento *m*, proceso *m*

procession (prö-ssê-ʃön) *n* procesión *f*, comitiva *f*

proclaim (prö-kleim) *v* proclamar

produce¹ (prö-dyuuss) *v* *producir

produce² (prod-yuuss) *n* producto *m*

producer (prö-dyuu-ssö) *n* productor *m*

product (pro-dakt) *n* producto *m*

production (prö-dak-ʃön) *n* producción *f*

profession (prö-fê-ʃön) *n* profesión *f*

professional (prö-fê-ʃö-nöl) *adj* profesional

professor (prö-fê-ssö) *n* profesor *m*

profit (pro-fit) *n* beneficio *m*, ganancia *f*; ventaja *f*; *v* aprovechar

profitable (pro-fi-tö-böl) *adj* provechoso

profound (prö-faund) *adj* profundo

programme (prou-ghræm) *n* programa *m*

progress¹ (prou-ghrêss) *n* progreso *m*

progress² (prö-*ghrêss*) *v* progresar

progressive (prö-*ghrê*-ssiv) *adj* progresista; progresivo

prohibit (prö-*hi*-bit) *v* prohibir

prohibition (prou-i-*bi*-∫ön) *n* prohibición *f*

prohibitive (prö-*hi*-bi-tiv) *adj* exorbitante

project (*pro*-dʒêkt) *n* plan *m*, proyecto *m*

promenade (pro-mö-*naad*) *n* paseo *m*

promise (*pro*-miss) *n* promesa *f*; *v* prometer

promote (prö-*mout*) *v* *promover

promotion (prö-*mou*-∫ön) *n* promoción *f*

prompt (prompt) *adj* inmediato, pronto

pronoun (*prou*-naun) *n* pronombre *m*

pronounce (prö-*naunss*) *v* pronunciar

pronunciation (prö-nan-ssi-*ei*-∫ön) *n* pronunciación *f*

proof (pruuf) *n* prueba *f*

propaganda (pro-pö-*ghæn*-dö) *n* propaganda *f*

propel (prö-*pêl*) *v* impeler

propeller (prö-*pê*-lö) *n* hélice *f*

proper (*pro*-pö) *adj* justo; debido, conveniente, apropiado

property (*pro*-pö-ti) *n* propiedad *f*; cualidad *f*

prophet (*pro*-fit) *n* profeta *m*

proportion (prö-*poo*-∫ön) *n* proporción *f*

proportional (prö-*poo*-∫ö-nöl) *adj* proporcional

proposal (prö-*pou*-söl) *n* propuesta *f*

propose (prö-*pous*) *v* *proponer

proposition (pro-pö-*si*-∫ön) *n* propuesta *f*

proprietor (prö-*prai*-ö-tö) *n* propietario *m*

prospect (*pro*-sspêkt) *n* perspectiva *f*

prospectus (prö-*sspêk*-töss) *n* prospecto *m*

prosperity (pro-*sspê*-rö-ti) *n* prosperidad *f*

prosperous (*pro*-sspö-röss) *adj* próspero

prostitute (*pro*-ssti-tyuut) *n* prostituta *f*

protect (prö-*têkt*) *v* proteger

protection (prö-*têk*-∫ön) *n* protección *f*

protein (*prou*-tiin) *n* proteína *f*

protest¹ (*prou*-têsst) *n* protesta *f*

protest² (prö-*têsst*) *v* protestar

Protestant (*pro*-ti-sstönt) *adj* protestante

proud (praud) *adj* orgulloso

prove (pruuv) *v* *demostrar, *comprobar; resultar

proverb (*pro*-vööb) *n* proverbio *m*

provide (prö-*vaid*) *v* *proveer; **provided that** con tal que

province (*pro*-vinss) *n* provincia *f*

provincial (prö-*vin*-∫öl) *adj* provincial

provisional (prö-*vi*-ʒö-nöl) *adj* provisional

provisions (prö-*vi*-ʒöns) *pl* provisiones *fpl*

prune (pruun) *n* ciruela pasa

psychiatrist (ssai-*kai*-ö-trisst) *n* psiquiatra *m*

psychic (*ssai*-kik) *adj* psíquico

psychoanalyst (ssai-kou-*æ*-nö-lisst) *n* psicoanalista *m*

psychological (ssai-ko-*lo*-dʒi-köl) *adj* psicológico

psychologist (ssai-*ko*-lö-dʒisst) *n* psicólogo *m*

psychology (ssai-*ko*-lö-dʒi) *n* psicología *f*

pub (pab) *n* taberna *f*

public (*pa*-blik) *adj* público; general; *n* público *m*; ~ **garden** jardín público; ~ **house** taberna *f*

publication (pa-bli-*kei*-∫ön) *n* publicación f

publicity (pa-*bli*-ssö-ti) n publicidad f

publish (pa-blíʃ) v publicar

publisher (pa-bli-ʃö) n editor m

puddle (pa-döl) n charco m

pull (pul) v tirar; ~ **out** partir; ~ **up** pararse

pulley (pu-li) n (pl ~s) polea f

Pullman (pul-mön) n coche Pullman

pullover (pu-lou-vö) n pulóver m

pulpit (pul-pit) n púlpito m

pulse (palss) n pulso m

pump (pamp) n bomba f; v bombear

punch (panch) v *dar puñetazos; n puñetazo m

punctual (pangk-chu-öl) adj puntual

puncture (pangk-chö) n pinchazo m

punctured (pangk-chöd) adj pinchado

punish (pa-niʃ) v castigar

punishment (pa-niʃ-mönt) n castigo m

pupil (pyuu-pöl) n alumno m

puppet-show (pa-pit-ʃou) n teatro guiñol

purchase (pöö-chöss) v comprar; n compra f; ~ **price** precio de compra; ~ **tax** impuesto sobre la venta

purchaser (pöö-chö-ssö) n comprador m

pure (pyuö) adj casto, puro

purple (pöö-pöl) adj purpúreo

purpose (pöö-pöss) n propósito m, fin m, intención f; **on** ~ intencionado

purse (pööss) n bolsa f, monedero m

pursue (pö-ssyuu) v *perseguir

pus (pass) n pus f

push (puʃ) n empujón m; v empujar

push-button (puʃ-ba-tön) n botón m

*****put** (put) v colocar, *poner; meter; plantear; ~ **away** guardar; ~ **off** aplazar; ~ **on** *ponerse; ~ **out** apagar

puzzle (pa-söl) n rompecabezas m;

enigma m; v confundir; **jigsaw** ~ rompecabezas m

puzzling (pas-ling) adj embarazoso

pyjamas (pö-dʒaa-mös) pl pijama m

Q

quack (kᵘæk) n curandero m, charlatán m

quail (kᵘeil) n (pl ~, ~s) codorniz f

quaint (kᵘeint) adj curioso; anticuado

qualification (kᵘo-li-fi-kei-ʃön) n aptitud f; reserva f, restricción f

qualified (kᵘo-li-faid) adj calificado; competente

qualify (kᵘo-li-fai) v *ser capaz de, *ser apto para

quality (kᵘo-lö-ti) n calidad f; característica f

quantity (kᵘon-tö-ti) n cantidad f; número m

quarantine (kᵘo-rön-tiin) n cuarentena f

quarrel (kᵘo-röl) v disputar, *reñir; n disputa f

quarry (kᵘo-ri) n cantera f

quarter (kᵘoo-tö) n cuarto m; trimestre m; barrio m; ~ **of an hour** cuarto de hora

quarterly (kᵘoo-tö-li) adj trimestral

quay (kii) n muelle m

queen (kᵘiin) n reina f

queer (kᵘiö) adj singular, extraño

query (kᵘiö-ri) n pregunta f; v indagar; *poner en duda

question (kᵘêss-chön) n pregunta f; cuestión f, problema m; v interrogar; *poner en duda; ~ **mark** signo de interrogación

queue (kyuu) n cola f; v *hacer cola

quick (kᵘik) adj rápido

quick-tempered (kᵘik-têm-pöd) adj

irascible

quiet (kᵘai-öt) adj quieto, tranquilo; n silencio m, paz f

quilt (kᵘilt) n colcha f

quinine (kᵘi-niin) n quinina f

quit (kᵘit) v cesar

quite (kᵘait) adv enteramente, completamente; bastante; muy

quiz (kᵘis) n (pl ~zes) concurso m

quota (kᵘou-tö) n cuota f

quotation (kᵘou-tei-ʃön) n cita f; ~ **marks** comillas fpl

quote (kᵘout) v citar

R

rabbit (ræ-bit) n conejo m

rabies (rei-bis) n rabia f

race (reiss) n carrera f; raza f

race-course (reiss-kooss) n pista para carreras, hipódromo m

race-horse (reiss-hooss) n caballo de carrera

race-track (reiss-træk) n pista para carreras

racial (rei-ʃöl) adj racial

racket (ræ-kit) n alboroto m

racquet (ræ-kit) n raqueta f

radiator (rei-di-ei-tö) n radiador m

radical (ræ-di-köl) adj radical

radio (rei-di-ou) n radio f

radish (ræ-diʃ) n rábano m

radius (rei-di-öss) n (pl radii) radio m

raft (raaft) n zatara f

rag (rægh) n trapo m

rage (reidʒ) n furor m, rabia f; v rabiar

raid (reid) n irrupción f

rail (reil) n barandilla f, barrera f

railing (rei-ling) n barandilla f

railroad (reil-roud) nAm vía del tren, ferrocarril m

railway (reil-ᵘei) n ferrocarril m

rain (rein) n lluvia f; v *llover

rainbow (rein-bou) n arco iris

raincoat (rein-kout) n impermeable m

rainproof (rein-pruuf) adj impermeable

rainy (rei-ni) adj lluvioso

raise (reis) v alzar; aumentar; educar, cultivar, criar; recaudar; nAm aumento de sueldo

raisin (rei-sön) n pasa f

rake (reik) n rastrillo m

rally (ræ-li) n reunión f

ramp (ræmp) n rampa f

ramshackle (ræm-ʃæ-köl) adj destartalado

rancid (ræn-ssid) adj rancio

rang (ræng) v (p ring)

range (reindʒ) n alcance m

range-finder (reindʒ-fain-dö) n telémetro m

rank (rængk) n rango m; fila f

ransom (ræn-ssöm) n rescate m

rape (reip) v violar

rapid (ræ-pid) adj rápido

rapids (ræ-pids) pl rápidos de río

rare (rêᵒ) adj raro

rarely (rêᵒ-li) adv raras veces

rascal (raa-ssköl) n pícaro m, pillo m

rash (ræʃ) n erupción f; adj precipitado, irreflexivo

raspberry (raas-bö-ri) n frambuesa f

rat (ræt) n rata f

rate (reit) n precio m, tarifa f; velocidad f; **at any** ~ de todos modos, en todo caso; ~ **of exchange** cambio m

rather (raa-ðö) adv bastante; más bien

ration (ræ-ʃön) n ración f

rattan (ræ-tæn) n rota f

raven (rei-vön) n cuervo m

raw (roo) adj crudo; ~ **material** materia prima

ray (rei) n rayo m
rayon (rei-on) n rayón m
razor (rei-sö) n máquina de afeitar
razor-blade (rei-sö-bleid) n hoja de afeitar
reach (riich) v alcanzar; n alcance m
reaction (ri-æk-ſön) n reacción f
*read (riid) v *leer
reading (rii-ding) n lectura f
reading-lamp (rii-ding-læmp) n lámpara para lectura
reading-room (rii-ding-ruum) n sala de lectura
ready (rê-di) adj preparado, listo
ready-made (rê-di-meid) adj confeccionado
real (ri⁰l) adj verdadero
reality (ri-æ-lö-ti) n realidad f
realizable (ri⁰-lai-sö-böl) adj realizable
realize (ri⁰-lais) v *reconocer; realizar
really (ri⁰-li) adv verdaderamente, en realidad; de veras
rear (ri⁰) n parte posterior; v criar
rear-light (ri⁰-lait) n luz trasera
reason (rii-sön) n causa f, razón f; sentido m; v razonar
reasonable (rii-sö-nö-böl) adj razonable
reassure (rii-ö-fu⁰) v tranquilizar
rebate (rii-beit) n reducción f, rebaja f
rebellion (ri-bêl-yön) n sublevación f, rebelión f
recall (ri-kool) v *acordarse; llamar; revocar
receipt (ri-ssiit) n recibo m
receive (ri-ssiiv) v recibir
receiver (ri-ssii-vö) n receptor m
recent (rii-ssönt) adj reciente
recently (rii-ssönt-li) adv el otro día, recientemente
reception (ri-ssêp-ſön) n recepción f; acogida f; ~ office oficina de recibo

receptionist (ri-ssêp-ſö-nisst) n recepcionista f
recession (ri-ssê-ſön) n retroceso m
recipe (rê-ssi-pi) n receta f
recital (ri-ssai-töl) n recital m
reckon (rê-kön) v calcular; considerar; *creer
recognition (rê-kögh-ni-ſön) n reconocimiento m
recognize (rê-kögh-nais) v *reconocer
recollect (rê-kö-lêkt) v *acordarse
recommence (rii-kö-mênss) v *recomenzar
recommend (rê-kö-mênd) v *recomendar; aconsejar
recommendation (rê-kö-mên-dei-ſön) n recomendación f
reconciliation (rê-kön-ssi-li-ei-ſön) n reconciliación f
record¹ (rê-kood) n disco m; récord m; registro m; long-playing ~ microsurco m
record² (ri-kood) v registrar
recorder (ri-koo-dö) n magnetófono m
recording (ri-koo-ding) n grabación f
record-player (rê-kood-plei⁰) n tocadiscos m
recover (ri-ka-vö) v recuperar; *restablecerse, curarse
recovery (ri-ka-vö-ri) n curación f, restablecimiento m
recreation (rê-kri-ei-ſön) n recreación f, recreo m; ~ centre centro de recreo; ~ ground terreno de recreo público
recruit (ri-kruut) n recluta m
rectangle (rêk-tæng-ghöl) n rectángulo m
rectangular (rêk-tæng-ghyu-lö) adj rectangular
rector (rêk-tö) n pastor m, rector m
rectory (rêk-tö-ri) n rectoría f

rectum (rêk-töm) *n* intestino recto

red (rêd) *adj* rojo

redeem (ri-diim) *v* redimir

reduce (ri-*dyuuss*) *v* *reducir, *disminuir, rebajar

reduction (ri-*dak*-ʃön) *n* rebaja *f*, reducción *f*

redundant (ri-*dan*-dönt) *adj* superfluo

reed (riid) *n* junquillo *m*

reef (riif) *n* arrecife *m*

reference (*rêf*-rönss) *n* referencia *f*; relación *f*; **with ~ to** con respecto a

refer to (ri-*föö*) remitir a

refill (*rii*-fil) *n* repuesto *m*

refinery (ri-*fai*-nö-ri) *n* refinería *f*

reflect (ri-*flêkt*) *v* reflejar

reflection (ri-*flêk*-ʃön) *n* reflejo *m*; imagen reflejada

reflector (ri-*flêk*-tö) *n* reflector *m*

reformation (rê-fö-*mei*-ʃön) *n* Reforma *f*

refresh (ri-*frêʃ*) *v* refrescar

refreshment (ri-*frêʃ*-mönt) *n* refresco *m*

refrigerator (ri-*fri*-dʒö-rei-tö) *n* refrigerador *m*

refund[1] (ri-*fand*) *v* reintegrar

refund[2] (*rii*-fand) *n* reintegro *m*

refusal (ri-*fyuu*-söl) *n* negativa *f*

refuse[1] (ri-*fyuus*) *v* rehusar

refuse[2] (*rê*-fyuus) *n* desecho *m*

regard (ri-*ghaad*) *v* considerar; *n* respeto *m*; **as regards** en cuanto a, por lo que se refiere a

regarding (ri-*ghaa*-ding) *prep* relativo a, tocante a; respecto a

regatta (ri-*ghæ*-tö) *n* regata *f*

régime (rei-*ʒiim*) *n* régimen *m*

region (*rii*-dʒön) *n* región *f*

regional (*rii*-dʒö-nöl) *adj* regional

register (*rê*-dʒi-sstö) *v* inscribirse; certificar; **registered letter** carta certificada

registration (rê-dʒi-*sstrei*-ʃön) *n* inscripción *f*; **~ form** formulario de matriculación; **~ number** matrícula *f*; **~ plate** placa *f*

regret (ri-*ghrêt*) *v* *sentir; *n* arrepentimiento *m*

regular (*rê*-ghyu-lö) *adj* regular; corriente, normal

regulate (*rê*-ghyu-leit) *v* regular

regulation (rê-ghyu-*lei*-ʃön) *n* reglamento *m*, regulación *f*; regla *f*

rehabilitation (rii-hö-bi-li-*tei*-ʃön) *n* rehabilitación *f*

rehearsal (ri-*höö*-ssöl) *n* ensayo *m*

rehearse (ri-*hööss*) *v* ensayar

reign (rein) *n* reinado *m*; *v* *gobernar

reimburse (rii-im-*bööss*) *v* reembolsar

reindeer (*rein*-di°) *n* (pl ~) reno *m*

reject (ri-*dʒêkt*) *v* rehusar, rechazar; *reprobar

relate (ri-*leit*) *v* *contar

related (ri-*lei*-tid) *adj* emparentado

relation (ri-*lei*-ʃön) *n* relación *f*; pariente *m*

relative (*rê*-lö-tiv) *n* pariente *m*; *adj* relativo

relax (ri-*lækss*) *v* descansar

relaxation (ri-læk-*ssei*-ʃön) *n* relajación *f*

reliable (ri-*lai*-ö-böl) *adj* fiable

relic (*rê*-lik) *n* reliquia *f*

relief (ri-*liif*) *n* alivio *m*; ayuda *f*; relieve *m*

relieve (ri-*liiv*) *v* relevar

religion (ri-*li*-dʒön) *n* religión *f*

religious (ri-*li*-dʒöss) *adj* religioso

rely on (ri-*lai*) *contar con

remain (ri-*mein*) *v* quedarse; quedar

remainder (ri-*mein*-dö) *n* resto *m*

remaining (ri-*mei*-ning) *adj* demás, restante

remark (ri-*maak*) *n* observación *f*; *v* *hacer una observación

remarkable (ri-*maa*-kö-böl) *adj* notable

remedy (rê-mö-di) *n* remedio *m*

remember (ri-*mêm*-bö) *v* *acordarse

remembrance (ri-*mêm*-brönss) *n* recuerdo *m*

remind (ri-*maind*) *v* *recordar

remit (ri-*mit*) *v* remitir

remittance (ri-*mi*-tönss) *n* remesa *f*

remnant (*rêm*-nönt) *n* resto *m*, residuo *m*, remanente *m*

remote (ri-*mout*) *adj* remoto, lejano

removal (ri-*muu*-völ) *n* remoción *f*

remove (ri-*muuv*) *v* *remover

remunerate (ri-*myuu*-nö-reit) *v* remunerar

remuneration (ri-myuu-nö-*rei*-fön) *n* remuneración *f*

renew (ri-*nyuu*) *v* *renovar; alargar

rent (rênt) *v* alquilar; *n* alquiler *m*

repair (ri-*pê*ö) *v* arreglar, reparar; *n* reparación *f*

reparation (rê-pö-*rei*-fön) *n* reparación *f*

*repay (ri-*pei*) *v* reintegrar

repayment (ri-*pei*-mönt) *n* reintegro *m*

repeat (ri-*piit*) *v* *repetir

repellent (ri-*pê*-lönt) *adj* repugnante, repelente

repentance (ri-*pên*-tönss) *n* arrepentimiento *m*

repertory (*rê*-pö-tö-ri) *n* repertorio *m*

repetition (rê-pö-*ti*-fön) *n* repetición *f*

replace (ri-*pleiss*) *v* reemplazar

reply (ri-*plai*) *v* responder; *n* respuesta *f*; **in ~** en contestación

report (ri-*poot*) *v* relatar; informar; presentarse; *n* relación *f*, informe *m*

reporter (ri-*poo*-tö) *n* reportero *m*

represent (rê-pri-*sênt*) *v* representar

representation (rê-pri-sên-*tei*-fön) *n* representación *f*

representative (rê-pri-*sên*-tö-tiv) *adj* representativo

reprimand (*rê*-pri-maand) *v* reprender

reproach (ri-*prouch*) *n* reproche *m*; *v* reprochar

reproduce (rii-prö-*dyuuss*) *v* *reproducir

reproduction (rii-prö-*dak*-fön) *n* reproducción *f*

reptile (*rêp*-tail) *n* reptil *m*

republic (ri-*pa*-blik) *n* república *f*

republican (ri-*pa*-bli-kön) *adj* republicano

repulsive (ri-*pal*-ssiv) *adj* repulsivo

reputation (rê-pyu-*tei*-fön) *n* reputación *f*; renombre *m*

request (ri-k^u*êsst*) *n* ruego *m*; demanda *f*; *v* solicitar

require (ri-k^u*ai*ö) *v* *requerir

requirement (ri-k^u*ai*ö-mönt) *n* requerimiento *m*

requisite (*rê*-k^{u}i-sit) *adj* necesario

rescue (*rê*-sskyuu) *v* rescatar; *n* rescate *m*

research (ri-*ssööch*) *n* investigación *f*

resemblance (ri-*sêm*-blönss) *n* semejanza *f*

resemble (ri-*sêm*-böl) *v* asemejarse

resent (ri-*sênt*) *v* *resentirse por

reservation (rê-sö-*vei*-fön) *n* reservación *f*

reserve (ri-*sööv*) *v* reservar; *n* reserva *f*

reserved (ri-*söövd*) *adj* reservado

reservoir (*rê*-sö-v^{u}aa) *n* embalse *m*

reside (ri-*said*) *v* residir

residence (*rê*-si-dönss) *n* residencia *f*; **~ permit** permiso de residencia

resident (*rê*-si-dönt) *n* residente *m*; *adj* residente; interno

resign (ri-*sain*) *v* resignar

resignation (rê-sigh-*nei*-fön) *n* resignación *f*

resin (*rê*-sin) *n* resina *f*

resist (ri-*sisst*) *v* resistir

resistance (ri-*si*-sstönss) *n* resistencia

f

resolute (rê-sö-luut) *adj* resuelto, decidido

respect (ri-sspêkt) *n* respeto *m*; estimación *f*, reverencia *f*; *v* respetar

respectable (ri-sspêk-tö-böl) *adj* respetable

respectful (ri-sspêkt-föl) *adj* respetuoso

respective (ri-sspêk-tiv) *adj* respectivo

respiration (rê-sspö-rei-ʃön) *n* respiración *f*

respite (rê-sspait) *n* dilación *f*

responsibility (ri-sspon-ssö-bi-lö-ti) *n* responsabilidad *f*

responsible (ri-sspon-ssö-böl) *adj* responsable

rest (rêsst) *n* descanso *m*; resto *m*; *v* *hacer reposo, descansar

restaurant (rê-sstö-rong) *n* restaurante *m*

restful (rêsst-föl) *adj* reposado

rest-home (rêsst-houm) *n* casa de reposo

restless (rêsst-löss) *adj* inquieto

restrain (ri-sstrein) *v* *contener, *impedir

restriction (ri-sstrik-ʃön) *n* restricción *f*

result (ri-salt) *n* resultado *m*; consecuencia *f*; *v* resultar

resume (ri-syuum) *v* reemprender

résumé (rê-syu-mei) *n* resumen *m*

retail (rii-teil) *v* vender al detalle; ~ **trade** comercio al por menor

retailer (rii-tei-lö) *n* comerciante al por menor, minorista *m*; revendedor *m*

retina (rê-ti-nö) *n* retina *f*

retired (ri-taiᵒd) *adj* jubilado

return (ri-töön) *v* *volver; *n* regreso *m*; ~ **flight** vuelo de regreso; ~ **journey** vuelta *f*, viaje de regreso

reunite (rii-yuu-nait) *v* reunir

reveal (ri-viil) *v* *manifestar, revelar

revelation (rê-vö-lei-ʃön) *n* revelación *f*

revenge (ri-vêndʒ) *n* venganza *f*

revenue (rê-vö-nyuu) *n* ingresos *mpl*, renta *f*

reverse (ri-vööss) *n* contrario *m*; reverso *m*; marcha atrás; revés *m*; *adj* inverso; *v* *dar marcha atrás

review (ri-vyuu) *n* reseña *f*; revista *f*

revise (ri-vais) *v* revisar

revision (ri-vi-ʒön) *n* revisión *f*

revival (ri-vai-völ) *n* recuperación *f*

revolt (ri-voult) *v* sublevarse; *n* rebelión *f*, revuelta *f*

revolting (ri-voul-ting) *adj* repugnante, chocante, repelente

revolution (rê-vö-luu-ʃön) *n* revolución *f*

revolutionary (rê-vö-luu-ʃö-nö-ri) *adj* revolucionario

revolver (ri-vol-vö) *n* revólver *m*

revue (ri-vyuu) *n* revista *f*

reward (ri-ᵘood) *n* recompensa *f*; *v* recompensar

rheumatism (ruu-mö-ti-söm) *n* reumatismo *m*

rhinoceros (rai-no-ssö-röss) *n* (pl ~, ~es) rinoceronte *m*

rhubarb (ruu-baab) *n* ruibarbo *m*

rhyme (raim) *n* rima *f*

rhythm (ri-ðöm) *n* ritmo *m*

rib (rib) *n* costilla *f*

ribbon (ri-bön) *n* cinta *f*

rice (raiss) *n* arroz *m*

rich (rich) *adj* rico

riches (ri-chis) *pl* riqueza *f*

riddle (ri-döl) *n* adivinanza *f*

ride (raid) *n* paseo *m*

* **ride** (raid) *v* *ir en coche; montar

rider (rai-dö) *n* jinete *m*

ridge (ridʒ) *n* cresta *f*

ridicule (ri-di-kyuul) *v* ridiculizar

ridiculous (ri-di-kyu-löss) *adj* ridículo

riding (*rai*-ding) *n* equitación *f*
riding-school (*rai*-ding-sskuul) *n* picadero *m*
rifle (*rai*-föl) *v* rifle *m*
right (rait) *n* derecho *m*; *adj* correcto; derecho; justo; **all right!** ¡de acuerdo!; * **be ~** *tener razón; **~ of way** prioridad de paso
righteous (*rai*-chöss) *adj* justo
right-hand (*rait*-hænd) *adj* derecho
rightly (*rait*-li) *adv* justamente
rim (rim) *n* llanta *f*; borde *m*
ring (ring) *n* anillo *m*; círculo *m*; pista *f*
* **ring** (ring) *v* *sonar; **~ up** llamar por teléfono
rinse (rinss) *v* enjuagar; *n* enjuague *m*
riot (*rai*-öt) *n* motín *m*
rip (rip) *v* rasgar
ripe (raip) *adj* maduro
rise (rais) *n* aumento de sueldo, aumento *m*; levantamiento *m*; subida *f*; nacimiento *m*
* **rise** (rais) *v* levantarse; subir
rising (*rai*-sing) *n* levantamiento *m*
risk (rissk) *n* riesgo *m*; peligro *m*; *v* arriesgar
risky (*ri*-sski) *adj* arriesgado
rival (*rai*-völ) *n* rival *m*; competidor *m*; *v* rivalizar
rivalry (*rai*-völ-ri) *n* rivalidad *f*; competencia *f*
river (*ri*-vö) *n* río *m*; **~ bank** ribera *f*
riverside (*ri*-vö-ssaid) *n* ribera *f*
roach (rouch) *n* (pl ~) escarcho *m*
road (roud) *n* calle *f*, camino *m*; **~ fork** *n* bifurcación *f*; **~ map** mapa de carreteras; **~ system** red de carreteras; **~ up** camino en obras
roadhouse (*roud*-hauss) *n* parador *m*
roadside (*roud*-ssaid) *n* borde del camino
roam (roum) *v* vagabundear

roar (roo) *v* mugir, rugir; *n* rugido *m*, retumbo *m*
roast (rousst) *v* asar, asar en parrilla
rob (rob) *v* robar
robber (*ro*-bö) *n* ladrón *m*
robbery (*ro*-bö-ri) *n* robo *m*
robe (roub) *n* traje largo
robin (*ro*-bin) *n* petirrojo *m*
robust (rou-*basst*) *adj* robusto
rock (rok) *n* roca *f*; *v* mecer
rocket (*ro*-kit) *n* cohete *m*
rocky (*ro*-ki) *adj* rocoso
rod (rod) *n* barra *f*
roe (rou) *n* huevos de los peces, hueva *f*
roll (roul) *v* *rodar; *n* rollo *m*; panecillo *m*
roller-skating (*rou*-lö-sskei-ting) *n* patinaje de ruedas
Roman Catholic (*rou*-mön *kæ*-zö-lik) católico
romance (rö-*mænss*) *n* amorío *m*
romantic (rö-*mæn*-tik) *adj* romántico
roof (ruuf) *n* techo *m*; **thatched ~** techo de paja
room (ruum) *n* habitación *f*; espacio *m*, sitio *m*; **~ and board** pensión completa; **~ service** servicio de habitación; **~ temperature** temperatura ambiente
roomy (*ruu*-mi) *adj* espacioso
root (ruut) *n* raíz *f*
rope (roup) *n* soga *f*
rosary (*rou*-sö-ri) *n* rosario *m*
rose (rous) *n* rosa *f*; *adj* rosa
rotten (*ro*-tön) *adj* podrido
rouge (ruuჳ) *n* colorete *m*
rough (raf) *adj* áspero
roulette (ruu-*lêt*) *n* ruleta *f*
round (raund) *adj* redondo; *prep* alrededor de, en torno de; *n* vuelta *f*; **~ trip** *Am* ida y vuelta
roundabout (*raun*-dö-baut) *n* glorieta *f*

rounded (*raun*-did) *adj* redondeado

route (ruut) *n* ruta *f*

routine (ruu-*tiin*) *n* rutina *f*

row¹ (rou) *n* fila *f*; *v* remar

row² (rau) *n* bronca *f*

rowdy (*rau*-di) *adj* alborotador

rowing-boat (*rou*-ing-bout) *n* bote *m*

royal (*roi*-öl) *adj* real

rub (rab) *v* frotar

rubber (*ra*-bö) *n* caucho *m*; goma de borrar; hule *mMe*; ~ **band** elástico *m*

rubbish (*ra*-biʃ) *n* basura *f*; habladuría *f*, tontería *f*; **talk** ~ *decir tonterías

rubbish-bin (*ra*-biʃ-bin) *n* cubo de la basura

ruby (*ruu*-bi) *n* rubí *m*

rucksack (*rak*-ssæk) *n* mochila *f*

rudder (*ra*-dö) *n* timón *m*

rude (ruud) *adj* grosero

rug (ragh) *n* alfombrilla *f*

ruin (*ruu*-in) *v* arruinar; *n* ruina *f*

ruination (ruu-i-*nei*-ʃön) *n* hundimiento *m*

rule (ruul) *n* regla *f*; régimen *m*, gobierno *m*, dominio *m*; *v* *gobernar, *regir; **as a** ~ generalmente, por regla general

ruler (*ruu*-lö) *n* monarca *m*, gobernante *m*; regla *f*

Rumania (ruu-*mei*-ni-ö) Rumania *f*

Rumanian (ruu-*mei*-ni-ön) *adj* rumano

rumour (*ruu*-mö) *n* rumor *m*

***run** (ran) *v* correr; ~ **into** *encontrarse con

runaway (*ra*-nö-ᵘei) *n* fugitivo *m*

rung (ran) *v* (pp ring)

runway (*ran*-ᵘei) *n* pista de aterrizaje

rural (*ruᵒ*-röl) *adj* rural

ruse (ruus) *n* astucia *f*

rush (raʃ) *v* precipitarse; *n* junco *m*

rush-hour (*raʃ*-auᵒ) *n* hora de afluencia

Russia (*ra*-ʃö) Rusia *f*

Russian (*ra*-ʃön) *adj* ruso

rust (rasst) *n* herrumbre *f*

rustic (*ra*-sstik) *adj* rústico

rusty (*ra*-ssti) *adj* oxidado

S

saccharin (*ssæ*-kö-rin) *n* sacarina *f*

sack (ssæk) *n* saco *m*

sacred (*ssei*-krid) *adj* sagrado

sacrifice (*ssæ*-kri-faiss) *n* sacrificio *m*; *v* sacrificar

sacrilege (*ssæ*-kri-lidʒ) *n* sacrilegio *m*

sad (ssæd) *adj* triste; afligido, melancólico

saddle (*ssæ*-döl) *n* silla *f*

sadness (*ssæd*-nöss) *n* tristeza *f*

safe (sseif) *adj* seguro; *n* caja fuerte, caja de caudales

safety (*sseif*-ti) *n* seguridad *f*

safety-belt (*sseif*-ti-bêlt) *n* cinturón de seguridad

safety-pin (*sseif*-ti-pin) *n* imperdible *m*

safety-razor (*sseif*-ti-rei-sö) *n* máquina de afeitar

sail (sseil) *v* navegar; *n* vela *f*

sailing-boat (*ssei*-ling-bout) *n* buque velero

sailor (*ssei*-lö) *n* marinero *m*

saint (sseint) *n* santo *m*

salad (*ssæ*-löd) *n* ensalada *f*

salad-oil (*ssæ*-löd-oil) *n* aceite de mesa

salary (*ssæ*-lö-ri) *n* sueldo *m*

sale (sseil) *n* venta *f*; **clearance** ~ liquidación *f*; **for** ~ de venta; **sales** rebajas *fpl*

saleable (*ssei*-lö-böl) *adj* vendible

salesgirl (*sseils*-ghööl) *n* vendedora *f*

salesman (*sseils*-mön) *n* (pl -men)

vendedor *m*

salmon (*ssæ*-mön) *n* (pl ~) salmón *m*

salon (*ssæ*-long) *n* salón *m*

saloon (ssö-*luun*) *n* bar *m*; cantina *fMe*

salt (ssoolt) *n* sal *f*

salt-cellar (*ssoolt*-ssê-lö) *n* salero *m*

salty (*ssool*-ti) *adj* salado

salute (ssö-*luut*) *v* saludar

salve (ssaav) *n* ungüento *m*

same (sseim) *adj* mismo

sample (*ssaam*-pöl) *n* muestra *f*

sanatorium (ssæ-nö-*too*-ri-öm) *n* (pl ~s, -ria) sanatorio *m*

sand (ssænd) *n* arena *f*

sandal (*ssæn*-döl) *n* sandalia *f*

sandpaper (*ssænd*-pei-pö) *n* papel de lija

sandwich (*ssæn*-ᵘidʒ) *n* bocadillo *m*; emparedado *m*

sandy (*ssæn*-di) *adj* arenoso

sanitary (*ssæ*-ni-tö-ri) *adj* sanitario; ~ **towel** paño higiénico

sapphire (*ssæ*-faiᵒ) *n* zafiro *m*

sardine (ssaa-*diin*) *n* sardina *f*

satchel (*ssæ*-chöl) *n* cartera *f*

satellite (*ssæ*-tö-lait) *n* satélite *m*

satin (*ssæ*-tin) *n* raso *m*

satisfaction (ssæ-tiss-*fæk*-ʃön) *n* satisfacción *f*

satisfy (*ssæ*-tiss-fai) *v* *satisfacer

Saturday (*ssæ*-tö-di) sábado *m*

sauce (ssooss) *n* salsa *f*

saucepan (*ssooss*-pön) *n* cacerola *f*

saucer (*ssoo*-ssö) *n* platillo *m*

Saudi Arabia (ssau-di-ö-*rei*-bi-ö) Arabia Saudí

Saudi Arabian (ssau-di-ö-*rei*-bi-ön) *adj* saudí

sauna (*ssoo*-nö) *n* sauna *f*

sausage (*sso*-ssidʒ) *n* salchicha *f*

savage (*ssæ*-vidʒ) *adj* salvaje

save (sseiv) *v* salvar; ahorrar

savings (*ssei*-vings) *pl* ahorros *mpl*;

~ **bank** caja de ahorros

saviour (*ssei*-vyö) *n* salvador *m*

savoury (*ssei*-vö-ri) *adj* sabroso; picante

saw[1] (ssoo) *v* (p see)

saw[2] (ssoo) *n* sierra *f*

sawdust (*ssoo*-dasst) *n* serrín *m*

saw-mill (*ssoo*-mil) *n* serrería de maderas

*say (ssei) *v* *decir

scaffolding (*sskæ*-föl-ding) *n* andamio *m*

scale (sskeil) *n* escala *f*; escala musical; escama *f*; **scales** *pl* balanza *f*

scandal (*sskæn*-döl) *n* escándalo *m*

Scandinavia (sskæn-di-*nei*-vi-ö) Escandinavia *f*

Scandinavian (sskæn-di-*nei*-vi-ön) *adj* escandinavo

scapegoat (*sskeip*-ghout) *n* cabeza de turco

scar (sskaa) *n* cicatriz *f*

scarce (sskêᵒss) *adj* escaso

scarcely (*sskêᵒ*-ssli) *adv* apenas

scarcity (*sskêᵒ*-ssö-ti) *n* escasez *f*

scare (sskêᵒ) *v* asustar; *n* susto *m*

scarf (sskaaf) *n* (pl ~s, scarves) bufanda *f*

scarlet (*sskaa*-löt) *adj* escarlata

scary (*sskêᵒ*-ri) *adj* alarmante

scatter (*sskæ*-tö) *v* esparcir

scene (ssiin) *n* escena *f*

scenery (*ssii*-nö-ri) *n* paisaje *m*

scenic (*ssii*-nik) *adj* pintoresco

scent (ssênt) *n* perfume *m*

schedule (/ʃê-dyuul) *n* horario *m*

scheme (sskiim) *n* esquema *m*; proyecto *m*

scholar (*ssko*-lö) *n* erudito *m*; alumno *m*

scholarship (*ssko*-lö-ʃip) *n* beca *f*

school (sskuul) *n* escuela *f*

schoolboy (*sskuul*-boi) *n* alumno *m*

schoolgirl (*sskuul*-ghööl) *n* alumna *f*

schoolmaster (*sskuul*-maa-sstö) *n* maestro *m*

schoolteacher (*sskuul*-tii-chö) *n* maestro *m*

science (*ssai*-önss) *n* ciencia *f*

scientific (ssai-ön-*ti*-fik) *adj* científico

scientist (*ssai*-ön-tisst) *n* científico *m*

scissors (*ssi*-sös) *pl* tijeras *fpl*

scold (sskould) *v* reprender; insultar

scooter (*sskuu*-tö) *n* motoneta *f*; patín *m*

score (sskoo) *n* tanteo *m*; *v* marcar

scorn (sskoon) *n* escarnio *m*, desprecio *m*; *v* despreciar

Scot (sskot) *n* escocés *m*

Scotch (sskoch) *adj* escocés; **scotch tape** cinta adhesiva

Scotland (*sskot*-lönd) Escocia *f*

Scottish (*ssko*-tiſ) *adj* escocés

scout (sskaut) *n* explorador *m*

scrap (sskræp) *n* pedazo *m*

scrap-book (*sskræp*-buk) *n* álbum *m*

scrape (sskreip) *v* raspar

scrap-iron (*sskræ*-pai ön) *n* chatarra *f*

scratch (sskræch) *v* *hacer raeduras, rascar; *n* raedura *f*, rasguño *m*

scream (sskriim) *v* gritar, chillar; *n* grito *m*, chillido *m*

screen (sskriin) *n* mampara *f*; pantalla *f*

screw (sskruu) *n* tornillo *m*; *v* atornillar

screw-driver (*sskruu*-drai-vö) *n* destornillador *m*

scrub (sskrab) *v* *fregar; *n* matorral *m*

sculptor (*sskalp*-tö) *n* escultor *m*

sculpture (*sskalp*-chö) *n* escultura *f*

sea (ssii) *n* mar *m*

sea-bird (*ssii*-bööd) *n* ave marina

sea-coast (*ssii*-kousst) *n* litoral *m*

seagull (*ssii*-ghal) *n* gaviota *f*

seal (ssiil) *n* sello *m*; foca *f*

seam (ssiim) *n* costura *f*

seaman (*ssii*-mön) *n* (pl -men) marino *m*

seamless (*ssiim*-löss) *adj* sin costura

seaport (*ssii*-poot) *n* puerto de mar

search (ssööch) *v* buscar; cachear; *n* búsqueda *f*

searchlight (*ssööch*-lait) *n* reflector *m*

seascape (*ssii*-sskeip) *n* marina *f*

sea-shell (*ssii*-ſêl) *n* concha *f*

seashore (*ssii*-ſoo) *n* orilla del mar

seasick (*ssii*-ssik) *adj* mareado

seasickness (*ssii*-ssik-nöss) *n* mareo *m*

seaside (*ssii*-ssaid) *n* orilla del mar; ~ **resort** playa de veraneo

season (*ssii*-sön) *n* temporada *f*, estación *f*; **high** ~ apogeo de la temporada; **low** ~ temporada baja; **off** ~ fuera de temporada

season-ticket (*ssii*-sön-ti-kit) *n* tarjeta de temporada

seat (ssiit) *n* asiento *m*; sitio *m*, localidad *f*; sede *f*

seat-belt (*ssiit*-bêlt) *n* cinturón de seguridad

sea-urchin (*ssii*-öö-chin) *n* erizo de mar

sea-water (*ssii*-ᵘoo-tö) *n* agua de mar

second (*ssê*-könd) *num* segundo; *n* segundo *m*; instante *m*

secondary (*ssê*-kön-dö-ri) *adj* secundario; ~ **school** escuela secundaria

second-hand (ssê-könd-*hænd*) *adj* de segunda mano

secret (*ssii*-kröt) *n* secreto *m*; *adj* secreto

secretary (*ssê*-krö-tri) *n* secretaria *f*; secretario *m*

section (*ssêk*-ſön) *n* sección *f*; división *f*, departamento *m*

secure (ssi-*kyu*ö) *adj* firme; *v* lograr

security (ssi-*kyu*ö-rö-ti) *n* seguridad *f*; fianza *f*

sedate (ssi-*deit*) *adj* sosegado

sedative (ssĕ-dö-tiv) n calmante m
seduce (ssi-dyuuss) v *seducir
*see** (ssii) v *ver; comprender, *darse cuenta; ~ **to** *atender a
seed (ssiid) n semilla f
*seek** (ssiik) v buscar
seem (ssiim) v *parecer
seen (ssiin) v (pp see)
seesaw (ssii-ssoo) n columpio m
seize (ssiis) v agarrar
seldom (ssĕl-döm) adv pocas veces
select (ssi-lĕkt) v seleccionar, *elegir; adj seleccionado, selecto
selection (ssi-lĕk-ʃön) n elección f, selección f
self-centred (ssĕlf-ssĕn-töd) adj egocéntrico
self-employed (ssĕl-fim-ploid) adj independiente
self-evident (ssĕl-fĕ-vi-dönt) adj evidente
self-government (ssĕlf-gha-vö-mönt) n autonomía f
selfish (ssĕl-fiʃ) adj egoísta
selfishness (ssĕl-fiʃ-nöss) n egoísmo m
self-service (ssĕlf-ssöö-viss) n autoservicio m
*sell** (ssĕl) v vender
semblance (ssĕm-blönss) n apariencia f
semi- (ssĕ-mi) semi-
semicircle (ssĕ-mi-ssöö-köl) n semicírculo m
semi-colon (ssĕ-mi-kou-lön) n punto y coma
senate (ssĕ-nöt) n senado m
senator (ssĕ-nö-tö) n senador m
*send** (ssĕnd) v enviar, mandar; ~ **back** *devolver; ~ **for** mandar a buscar; ~ **off** despachar
senile (ssii-nail) adj senil
sensation (ssĕn-ssei-ʃön) n sensación f

sensational (ssĕn-ssei-ʃö-nöl) adj sensacional
sense (ssĕnss) n sentido m; juicio m, razón f; v *sentir; ~ **of honour** sentido del honor
senseless (ssĕnss-löss) adj insensato
sensible (ssĕn-ssö-böl) adj sensato
sensitive (ssĕn-ssi-tiv) adj sensitivo
sentence (ssĕn-tönss) n frase f; sentencia f; v sentenciar
sentimental (ssĕn-ti-mĕn-töl) adj sentimental
separate¹ (ssĕ-pö-reit) v separar
separate² (ssĕ-pö-röt) adj separado
separately (ssĕ-pö-röt-li) adv por separado
September (ssĕp-tĕm-bö) septiembre
septic (ssĕp-tik) adj séptico; *become** ~ infectarse
sequel (ssii-kⁱöl) n continuación f
sequence (ssii-kⁱönss) n sucesión f; serie f
serene (ssö-riin) adj sereno; claro
serial (ssiⁱö-ri-öl) n novela por entregas
series (ssiⁱö-riis) n (pl ~) serie f
serious (ssiⁱö-ri-öss) adj serio
seriousness (ssiⁱö-ri-öss-nöss) n seriedad f
sermon (ssöö-mön) n sermón m
serum (ssiⁱö-röm) n suero m
servant (ssöö-vönt) n criado m
serve (ssööv) v *servir
service (ssöö-viss) n servicio m; ~ **charge** servicio m; ~ **station** puesto de gasolina
serviette (ssöö-vi-ĕt) n servilleta f
session (ssĕ-ʃön) n sesión f
set (ssĕt) n juego m, grupo m
*set** (ssĕt) v *poner; ~ **menu** cubierto a precio fijo; ~ **out** partir
setting (ssĕ-ting) n escena f; ~ **lotion** fijador m
settle (ssĕ-töl) v arreglar; ~ **down**

arraigarse

settlement (*ssê*-töl-mönt) *n* acuerdo *m*, arreglo *m*, convenio *m*

seven (*ssê*-vön) *num* siete

seventeen (ssê-vön-*tiin*) *num* diecisiete

seventeenth (ssê-vön-*tiinz*) *num* decimoséptimo

seventh (*ssê*-vönz) *num* séptimo

seventy (*ssê*-vön-ti) *num* setenta

several (*ssê*-vö-röl) *adj* varios

severe (ssi-*vi*ᵒ) *adj* violento, rigoroso, severo

sew (ssou) *v* coser; ~ **up** *hacer una sutura

sewer (*ssuu*-ö) *n* desagüe *m*

sewing-machine (*ssou*-ing-mö-ʃiin) *n* máquina de coser

sex (ssêkss) *n* sexo *m*; sexualidad *f*

sexton (*ssêk*-sstön) *n* sacristán *m*

sexual (*ssêk*-ʃu-öl) *adj* sexual

sexuality (ssêk-ʃu-æ-lö-ti) *n* sexualidad *f*

shade (ʃeid) *n* sombra *f*; tono *m*

shadow (*ʃæ*-dou) *n* sombra *f*

shady (*ʃei*-di) *adj* sombreado

*shake (ʃeik) *v* sacudir

shaky (*ʃei*-ki) *adj* vacilante

*shall (ʃæl) *v* *tener que

shallow (*ʃæ*-lou) *adj* poco profundo

shame (ʃeim) *n* vergüenza *f*; deshonra *f*; **shame!** ¡qué vergüenza!

shampoo (ʃæm-*puu*) *n* champú *m*

shamrock (*ʃæm*-rok) *n* trébol *m*

shape (ʃeip) *n* forma *f*; *v* formar

share (ʃêᵒ) *v* compartir; *n* parte *f*; acción *f*

shark (ʃaak) *n* tiburón *m*

sharp (ʃaap) *adj* afilado

sharpen (*ʃaa*-pön) *v* afilar

shave (ʃeiv) *v* rasurarse, afeitarse

shaver (*ʃei*-vö) *n* máquina de afeitar

shaving-brush (*ʃei*-ving-braʃ) *n* brocha de afeitar

shaving-cream (*ʃei*-ving-kriim) *n* crema de afeitar

shaving-soap (*ʃei*-ving-ssoup) *n* jabón de afeitar

shawl (ʃool) *n* chal *m*

she (ʃii) *pron* ella

shed (ʃêd) *n* cobertizo *m*

*shed (ʃêd) *v* derramar; esparcir

sheep (ʃiip) *n* (pl ~) oveja *f*

sheer (ʃiᵒ) *adj* absoluto, puro; fino, traslúcido

sheet (ʃiit) *n* sábana *f*; hoja *f*; chapa *f*

shelf (ʃêlf) *n* (pl shelves) estante *m*

shell (ʃêl) *n* concha *f*; cáscara *f*

shellfish (*ʃêl*-fiʃ) *n* marisco *m*

shelter (*ʃêl*-tö) *n* refugio *m*; *v* abrigar

shepherd (*ʃê*-pöd) *n* pastor *m*

shift (ʃift) *n* turno *m*

*shine (ʃain) *v* *relucir; brillar, *resplandecer

ship (ʃip) *n* buque *m*; *v* transportar; **shipping line** línea de navegación

shipowner (*ʃi*-pou-nö) *n* armador *m*

shipyard (*ʃip*-yaad) *n* astillero *m*

shirt (ʃööt) *n* camisa *f*

shiver (*ʃi*-vö) *v* *temblar, tiritar; *n* escalofrío *m*

shivery (*ʃi*-vö-ri) *adj* estremecido

shock (ʃok) *n* choque *m*; *v* chocar; ~ **absorber** amortiguador *m*

shocking (*ʃo*-king) *adj* chocante

shoe (ʃuu) *n* zapato *m*; **gym shoes** sandalias de gimnasia; ~ **polish** betún *m*; grasa *fMe*

shoe-lace (*ʃuu*-leiss) *n* cordón *m*

shoemaker (*ʃuu*-mei-kö) *n* zapatero *m*

shoe-shop (*ʃuu*-ʃop) *n* zapatería *f*

shook (ʃuk) *v* (p shake)

*shoot (ʃuut) *v* tirar

shop (ʃop) *n* tienda *f*; *v* *ir de compras; ~ **assistant** dependiente *m*; **shopping bag** saco de compras; **shopping centre** centro comercial

shopkeeper (*ʃop*-kii-pö) *n* tendero *m*

shop-window (*ʃop*-*u in*-dou) *n* escaparate *m*

shore (ʃoo) *n* ribera *f*, orilla *f*

short (ʃoot) *adj* corto; bajo; ~ **circuit** cortocircuito *m*

shortage (*ʃoo*-tidʒ) *n* carencia *f*, escasez *f*

shortcoming (*ʃoo*-ka-ming) *n* deficiencia *f*

shorten (*ʃoo*-tön) *v* acortar

shorthand (*ʃoot*-hænd) *n* taquigrafía *f*

shortly (*ʃoot*-li) *adv* pronto, próximamente

shorts (ʃootss) *pl* pantalones cortos; *plAm* calzoncillos *mpl*

short-sighted (ʃoot-*ssai*-tid) *adj* miope

shot (ʃot) *n* disparo *m*; inyección *f*; secuencia *f*

*should (ʃud) *v* *tener que

shoulder (*ʃoul*-dö) *n* hombro *m*

shout (ʃaut) *v* gritar; *n* grito *m*

shovel (*ʃa*-völ) *n* pala *f*

show (ʃou) *n* representación *f*, espectáculo *m*; exposición *f*

*show (ʃou) *v* *mostrar; enseñar; *demostrar

show-case (*ʃou*-keiss) *n* vitrina *f*

shower (ʃauô) *n* ducha *f*; aguacero *m*

showroom (*ʃou*-ruum) *n* salón de demostraciones

shriek (ʃriik) *v* chillar; *n* chillido *m*

shrimp (ʃrimp) *n* camarón *m*

shrine (ʃrain) *n* santuario *m*

*shrink (ʃringk) *v* encogerse

shrinkproof (*ʃringk*-pruuf) *adj* no encoge

shrub (ʃrab) *n* arbusto *m*

shudder (*ʃa*-dö) *n* estremecimiento *m*

shuffle (*ʃa*-föl) *v* barajar

*shut (ʃat) *v* *cerrar; ~ **in** *encerrar

shutter (*ʃa*-tö) *n* persiana *f*

shy (ʃai) *adj* esquivo, tímido

shyness (*ʃai*-nöss) *n* timidez *f*

Siam (ssai-*æm*) Siam *m*

Siamese (ssai-ö-*miis*) *adj* siamés

sick (ssik) *adj* enfermo; que tiene náuseas

sickness (*ssik*-nöss) *n* enfermedad *f*; náusea *f*

side (ssaid) *n* lado *m*; partido *m*; **one-sided** *adj* unilateral

sideburns (*ssaid*-bööns) *pl* patillas *fpl*

sidelight (*ssaid*-lait) *n* luz lateral

side-street (*ssaid*-sstriit) *n* calle lateral

sidewalk (*ssaid*-u ook) *nAm* acera *f*

sideways (*ssaid*-u eis) *adv* lateralmente

siege (ssiidʒ) *n* sitio *m*

sieve (ssiv) *n* tamiz *m*; *v* tamizar

sift (ssift) *v* tamizar

sight (ssait) *n* vista *f*; aspecto *m*; curiosidad *f*

sign (ssain) *n* signo *m*, señal *f*; gesto *m*, seña *f*; *v* suscribir, firmar

signal (*ssigh*-nöl) *n* señal *f*; *v* *hacer señales

signature (*ssigh*-nö-chö) *n* firma *f*

significant (ssigh-*ni*-fi-könt) *adj* significativo

signpost (*ssain*-pousst) *n* poste de indicador

silence (*ssai*-lönss) *n* silencio *m*; *v* acallar

silencer (*ssai*-lön-ssö) *n* silenciador *m*

silent (*ssai*-lönt) *adj* callado; *be ~ callarse

silk (ssilk) *n* seda *f*

silken (*ssil*-kön) *adj* sedoso

silly (*ssi*-li) *adj* necio, bobo

silver (*ssil*-vö) *n* plata *f*; de plata

silversmith (*ssil*-vö-ssmiz) *n* platero *m*

silverware (*ssil*-vö-u ê ô) *n* plata labrada

similar (*ssi*-mi-lö) *adj* similar

similarity (ssi-mi-*læ*-rö-ti) *n* semejanza *f*

simple (*ssim*-pöl) *adj* ingenuo, simple; ordinario

simply (*ssim*-pli) *adv* simplemente

simulate (*ssi*-myu-leit) *v* simular

simultaneous (ssi-möl-*tei*-ni-öss) *adj* simultáneo

sin (ssin) *n* pecado *m*

since (ssinss) *prep* desde; *adv* desde entonces; *conj* desde que; puesto que

sincere (ssin-*ssiⁱ*ⁿ) *adj* sincero

sinew (*ssi*-nyuu) *n* tendón *m*

*sing (ssing) *v* cantar

singer (*ssing*-ö) *n* cantante *m*; cantadora *f*

single (*ssing*-ghöl) *adj* solo; soltero

singular (*ssing*-ghyu-lö) *n* singular *m*; *adj* singular

sinister (*ssi*-ni-sstö) *adj* siniestro

sink (ssingk) *n* pileta *f*

*sink (ssingk) *v* hundirse

sip (ssip) *n* sorbo *m*

siphon (*ssai*-fön) *n* sifón *m*

sir (ssöö) *n* señor *m*

siren (*ssaiⁱ*ⁿ-rön) *n* sirena *f*

sister (*ssi*-sstö) *n* hermana *f*

sister-in-law (*ssi*-sstö-rin-loo) *n* (pl sisters-) cuñada *f*

*sit (ssit) *v* *estar sentado; ~ **down** *sentarse

site (ssait) *n* sitio *m*

sitting-room (*ssi*-ting-ruum) *n* sala de estar

situated (*ssi*-chu-ei-tid) *adj* situado

situation (ssi-chu-ei-ʃön) *n* situación *f*; ubicación *f*

six (ssiks) *num* seis

sixteen (ssiks-*tiin*) *num* dieciséis

sixteenth (ssiks-*tiinz*) *num* decimosexto

sixth (ssikssz) *num* sexto

sixty (*ssikss*-ti) *num* sesenta

size (ssais) *n* tamaño *m*, número *m*; dimensión *f*; formato *m*

skate (sskeit) *v* patinar; *n* patín *m*

skating (*sskei*-ting) *n* patinaje *m*

skating-rink (*sskei*-ting-ringk) *n* pista de patinaje

skeleton (*sskê*-li-tön) *n* esqueleto *m*

sketch (sskêch) *n* dibujo *m*, bosquejo *m*; *v* dibujar, bosquejar

sketch-book (*sskêch*-buk) *n* cuaderno de diseño

ski¹ (sskii) *v* esquiar

ski² (sskii) *n* (pl ~, ~s) esquí *m*; ~ **boots** botas de esquí; ~ **pants** pantalones de esquí; ~ **sticks** bastones de esquí

skid (sskid) *v* patinar

skier (*sskii*-ö) *n* esquiador *m*

skiing (*sskii*-ing) *n* esquí *m*

ski-jump (*sskii*-dʒamp) *n* salto de esquí

skilful (*sskil*-föl) *adj* hábil, diestro

ski-lift (*sskii*-lift) *n* telesilla *m*

skill (sskil) *n* habilidad *f*

skilled (sskild) *adj* hábil; especializado

skin (sskin) *n* piel *f*; cáscara *f*; ~ **cream** crema para la piel

skip (sskip) *v* saltar; brincar

skirt (sskööt) *n* falda *f*

skull (sskal) *n* cráneo *m*

sky (sskai) *n* cielo *m*; aire *m*

skyscraper (*sskai*-sskrei-pö) *n* rascacielos *m*

slack (sslæk) *adj* lento

slacks (sslækss) *pl* pantalones *mpl*

slam (sslæm) *v* *dar un portazo

slander (*sslaan*-dö) *n* calumnia *f*

slant (sslaant) *v* inclinarse

slanting (*sslaan*-ting) *adj* oblicuo, pendiente, inclinado

slap (sslæp) *v* pegar; *n* bofetada *f*

slate (ssleit) *n* pizarra *f*

slave (ssleiv) *n* esclavo *m*

sledge (sslêdʒ) *n* trineo *m*

sleep (ssliip) *n* sueño *m*

*sleep (ssliip) *v* *dormir

sleeping-bag (*sslii*-ping-bægh) *n* saco de dormir

sleeping-car (*sslii*-ping-kaa) *n* coche cama

sleeping-pill (*sslii*-ping-pil) *n* somnífero *m*

sleepless (*ssliip*-löss) *adj* desvelado

sleepy (*sslii*-pi) *adj* soñoliento

sleeve (ssliiv) *n* manga *f*; funda *f*

sleigh (sslei) *n* trineo *m*

slender (*sslên*-dö) *adj* esbelto

slice (sslaiss) *n* tajada *f*

slide (sslaid) *n* desliz *m*; tobogán *m*; diapositiva *f*

***slide** (sslaid) *v* deslizarse

slight (sslait) *adj* ligero; leve

slim (sslim) *adj* esbelto; *v* adelgazar

slip (sslip) *v* deslizarse, resbalar; *n* desliz *m*; combinación *f*; fondo *mMe*

slipper (*sslii*-pö) *n* zapatilla *f*

slippery (*sslii*-pö-ri) *adj* resbaladizo

slogan (*sslou*-ghön) *n* lema *m*, slogan *m*

slope (ssloup) *n* pendiente *f*; *v* inclinarse

sloping (*sslou*-ping) *adj* inclinado

sloppy (*sslo*-pi) *adj* chapucero

slot (sslot) *n* ranura *f*

slot-machine (*sslot*-mö-ʃiin) *n* máquina tragamonedas

slovenly (*sslʌ*-vön-li) *adj* descuidado

slow (sslou) *adj* lerdo, lento; ~ **down** desacelerar, *ir más despacio; frenar

sluice (ssluuss) *n* compuerta *f*

slum (sslam) *n* barrio bajo

slump (sslamp) *n* baja *f*

slush (sslaʃ) *n* aguanieve *f*

sly (sslai) *adj* astuto

smack (ssmæk) *v* pegar; *n* bofetada *f*

small (ssmool) *adj* pequeño; menudo

smallpox (*ssmool*-pokss) *n* viruelas *fpl*

smart (ssmaat) *adj* elegante; inteli-gente, listo

smell (ssmêl) *n* olor *m*

***smell** (ssmêl) *v* *oler; *heder

smelly (*ssmê*-li) *adj* hediondo

smile (ssmail) *v* sonreír; *n* sonrisa *f*

smith (ssmiz) *n* herrero *m*

smoke (ssmouk) *v* fumar; *n* humo *m*; **no smoking** prohibido fumar

smoker (*ssmou*-kö) *n* fumador *m*; compartimento para fumadores

smoking-compartment (*ssmou*-king-köm-paat-mönt) *n* compartimento para fumadores

smoking-room (*ssmou*-king-ruum) *n* sala para fumar

smooth (ssmuuð) *adj* llano, liso; dulce

smuggle (*ssma*-ghöl) *v* contrabandear

snack (ssnæk) *n* tentempié *m*

snack-bar (*ssnæk*-baa) *n* cafetería *f*

snail (ssneil) *n* caracol *m*

snake (ssneik) *n* culebra *f*

snapshot (*ssnæp*-ʃot) *n* instantánea *f*

sneakers (*ssnii*-kös) *plAm* zapatos de gimnasia

sneeze (ssniis) *v* estornudar

sniper (*ssnai*-pö) *n* francotirador *m*

snooty (*ssnuu*-ti) *adj* arrogante

snore (ssnoo) *v* roncar

snorkel (*ssnoo*-köl) *n* esnórquel *m*

snout (ssnaut) *n* hocico *m*

snow (ssnou) *n* nieve *f*; *v* *nevar

snowstorm (*ssnou*-sstoom) *n* nevasca *f*

snowy (*ssnou*-i) *adj* nevoso

so (ssou) *conj* por tanto; *adv* así; a tal grado, tan; **and** ~ **on** etcétera; ~ **far** hasta ahora; ~ **that** así que, a fin de

soak (ssouk) *v* empapar, remojar

soap (ssoup) *n* jabón *m*; ~ **powder** jabón en polvo

sober (*ssou*-bö) *adj* sobrio; ponderado

so-called (ssou-*koold*) *adj* así llamado

soccer (*sso*-kö) *n* fútbol *m*; ~ **team** equipo *m*

social (*ssou*-ʃöl) *adj* social

socialism (*ssou*-ʃó-li-söm) *n* socialismo *m*

socialist (*ssou*-ʃö-lisst) *adj* socialista; *n* socialista *m*

society (ssö-*ssai*-ö-ti) *n* sociedad *f*; asociación *f*; compañía *f*

sock (ssok) *n* calcetín *m*

socket (*sso*-kit) *n* casquillo *m*; sóquet *mMe*

soda-water (*ssou*-dö-ᵘoo-tö) *n* agua de soda, soda *f*

sofa (*ssou*-fó) *n* sofá *m*

soft (ssoft) *adj* blando; ~ **drink** bebida no alcohólica

soften (*sso*-fön) *v* ablandar

soil (ssoil) *n* suelo *m*; tierra *f*

soiled (ssoild) *adj* manchado

sold (ssould) *v* (p, pp sell); ~ **out** agotado

solder (*ssol*-dö) *v* *soldar

soldering-iron (*ssol*-dö-ring-aiᵒn) *n* soldador *m*

soldier (*ssoul*-dʒö) *n* militar *m*, soldado *m*

sole[1] (ssoul) *adj* único

sole[2] (ssoul) *n* suela *f*; lenguado *m*

solely (*ssoul*-li) *adv* exclusivamente

solemn (*sso*-löm) *adj* solemne

solicitor (ssö-*li*-ssi-tö) *n* procurador *m*, abogado *m*

solid (*sso*-lid) *adj* robusto, sólido; macizo; *n* sólido *m*

soluble (*sso*-lyu-böl) *adj* soluble

solution (ssö-*luu*-ʃön) *n* solución *f*

solve (ssolv) *v* *resolver

sombre (*ssom*-bö) *adj* sombrío

some (ssam) *adj* algunos, unos; *pron* algunos, unos; un poco; ~ **day** uno u otro día; ~ **more** algo más; ~ **time** alguna vez

somebody (*ssam*-bö-di) *pron* alguien

somehow (*ssam*-hau) *adv* de un modo u otro

someone (*ssam*-ᵘan) *pron* alguien

something (*ssam*-zing) *pron* algo

sometimes (*ssam*-taims) *adv* a veces

somewhat (*ssam*-ᵘot) *adv* algo

somewhere (*ssam*-ᵘêᵒ) *adv* en alguna parte

son (ssan) *n* hijo *m*

song (ssong) *n* canción *f*

son-in-law (*ssa*-nin-loo) *n* (pl sons-) yerno *m*

soon (ssuun) *adv* rápidamente, pronto, en breve; **as** ~ **as** tan pronto como

sooner (*ssuu*-nö) *adv* más bien

sore (ssoo) *adj* doloroso; *n* llaga *f*; úlcera *f*; ~ **throat** dolor de garganta

sorrow (*sso*-rou) *n* tristeza *f*, sufrimiento *m*, pena *f*

sorry (*sso*-ri) *adj* apenado; **sorry!** ¡dispense usted!, ¡disculpe!, ¡perdón!

sort (ssoot) *v* clasificar, *disponer; *n* clase *f*; **all sorts of** toda clase de

soul (ssoul) *n* alma *f*

sound (ssaund) *n* sonido *m*; *v* *sonar, *resonar; *adj* bueno

soundproof (*ssaund*-pruuf) *adj* insonorizado

soup (ssuup) *n* sopa *f*

soup-plate (*ssuup*-pleit) *n* plato para sopa

soup-spoon (*ssuup*-sspuun) *n* cuchara *f*

sour (ssauᵒ) *adj* agrio

source (ssooss) *n* fuente *f*

south (ssaus) *n* sur *m*; **South Pole** polo sur

South Africa (ssaus æ-fri-kö) África del Sur

south-east (ssaus-*iisst*) *n* sudeste *m*

southerly (*ssa*-ðö-li) *adj* meridional
southern (*ssa*-ðön) *adj* meridional
south-west (ssauz-*u ésst*) *n* sudoeste *m*
souvenir (*ssuu*-vö-niº) *n* recuerdo *m*
sovereign (*ssov*-rin) *n* soberano *m*
Soviet (*ssou*-vi-öt) *adj* soviético
Soviet Union (*ssou*-vi-öt *yuu*-nyön) Unión Soviética
* **sow** (ssou) *v* *sembrar
spa (sspaa) *n* balneario *m*
space (sspeiss) *n* espacio *m* ; distancia *f* ; *v* espaciar
spacious (*sspei*-föss) *adj* espacioso
spade (sspeid) *n* azada *f*, pala *f*
Spain (sspein) España *f*
Spaniard (*sspæ*-nyöd) *n* español *m*
Spanish (*sspæ*-nif) *adj* español
spanking (*sspæng*-king) *n* zurra *f*
spanner (*sspæ*-nö) *n* llave inglesa
spare (sspêº) *adj* de reserva, disponible ; *v* pasarse sin ; ~ **part** pieza de repuesto ; ~ **room** cuarto para huéspedes ; ~ **time** tiempo libre ; ~ **tyre** neumático de repuesto ; ~ **wheel** rueda de repuesto
spark (sspaak) *n* chispa *f*
sparking-plug (*sspaa*-king-plagh) *n* bujía *f*
sparkling (*sspaa*-kling) *adj* centelleante ; espumante
sparrow (*sspæ*-rou) *n* gorrión *m*
* **speak** (sspiik) *v* hablar
spear (sspiº) *n* lanza *f*
special (*sspê*-föl) *adj* especial ; ~ **delivery** por expreso
specialist (*sspê*-fö-lisst) *n* especialista *m*
speciality (*sspê*-fi-æ-lö-ti) *n* especialidad *f*
specialize (*sspê*-fö-lais) *v* especializarse
specially (*sspê*-fö-li) *adv* en particular
species (*sspii*-fiis) *n* (pl ~) especie *f*

specific (sspö-*ssi*-fik) *adj* específico
specimen (*sspê*-ssi-mön) *n* espécimen *m*
speck (sspêk) *n* mancha *f*
spectacle (*sspêk*-tö-köl) *n* espectáculo *m* ; **spectacles** anteojos *mpl*
spectator (sspêk-*tei*-tö) *n* espectador *m*
speculate (*sspê*-kyu-leit) *v* especular
speech (sspiich) *n* habla *f* ; discurso *m* ; lenguaje *m*
speechless (*sspiich*-löss) *adj* atónito
speed (sspiid) *n* velocidad *f* ; rapidez *f*, prisa *f* ; **cruising** ~ velocidad de cruce ; ~ **limit** límite de velocidad
* **speed** (sspiid) *v* *dar prisa ; correr demasiado
speeding (*sspii*-ding) *n* exceso de velocidad
speedometer (sspii-*do*-mi-tö) *n* velocímetro *m*
spell (sspêl) *n* encanto *m*
* **spell** (sspêl) *v* deletrear
spelling (*sspê*-ling) *n* deletreo *m*
* **spend** (sspênd) *v* gastar ; pasar
sphere (ssfiº) *n* esfera *f*
spice (sspaiss) *n* especia *f*
spiced (sspaisst) *adj* condimentado
spicy (*sspai*-ssi) *adj* picante
spider (*sspai*-dö) *n* araña *f* ; **spider's web** telaraña *f*
* **spill** (sspil) *v* *verter
* **spin** (sspin) *v* hilar ; *hacer girar
spinach (*sspi*-nidʒ) *n* espinacas *fpl*
spine (sspain) *n* espinazo *m*
spinster (*sspin*-sstö) *n* solterona *f*
spire (sspaiº) *n* aguja *f*
spirit (*sspi*-rit) *n* espíritu *m* ; humor *m* ; **spirits** bebidas espirituosas ; moral *f* ; ~ **stove** calentador de alcohol
spiritual (*sspi*-ri-chu-öl) *adj* espiritual
spit (sspit) *n* esputo *m*, saliva *f* ; espetón *m*

*spit (sspit) v escupir

in spite of (in sspait ov) a pesar de

spiteful (sspait-föl) adj malévolo

splash (ssplæʃ) v salpicar

splendid (ssplên-did) adj magnífico, espléndido

splendour (ssplên-dö) n esplendor m

splint (ssplint) n tablilla f

splinter (ssplin-tö) n astilla f

*split (ssplit) v *hender

*spoil (sspoil) v echar a perder; mimar

spoke¹ (sspouk) v (p speak)

spoke² (sspouk) n radio m

sponge (sspandʒ) n esponja f

spook (sspuuk) n fantasma m

spool (sspuul) n bobina f

spoon (sspuun) n cuchara f

spoonful (sspuun-ful) n cucharada f

sport (sspoot) n deporte m

sports-car (sspootss-kaa) n coche de carreras

sports-jacket (sspootss-dʒæ-kit) n chaqueta de deporte

sportsman (sspootss-mön) n (pl -men) deportista m

sportswear (sspootss-ᵘêᵒ) n conjunto de deporte

spot (sspot) n mancha f; lugar m, puesto m

spotless (sspot-löss) adj inmaculado

spotlight (sspot-lait) n proyector m

spotted (sspo-tid) adj moteado

spout (sspaut) n chorro m

sprain (ssprein) v *torcerse; n torcedura f

*spread (ssprêd) v *extender

spring (sspring) n primavera f; muelle m; manantial m

springtime (sspring-taim) n primavera f

sprouts (ssprautss) pl col de Bruselas

spy (sspai) n espia m

squadron (sskᵘo-drön) n escuadrilla f

square (sskᵘêᵒ) adj cuadrado; n cuadrado m; plaza f

squash (sskᵘoʃ) n zumo m

squirrel (sskᵘi-röl) n ardilla f

squirt (sskᵘööt) n chisguete m

stable (sstei-böl) adj estable; n establo m

stack (sstæk) n montón m

stadium (sstei-di-öm) n estadio m

staff (sstaaf) n personal m

stage (ssteidʒ) n escenario m; fase f; etapa f

stain (sstein) v manchar; n mancha f; stained glass vidrio de color; ~ remover quitamanchas m

stainless (sstein-löss) adj inmaculado; ~ steel acero inoxidable

staircase (sstêᵒ-keiss) n escalera f

stairs (sstêᵒs) pl escalera f

stale (ssteil) adj viejo

stall (sstool) n puesto m; butaca f

stamina (sstæ-mi-nö) n vigor m

stamp (sstæmp) n sello m; v sellar; patear; n estampilla fMe; ~ machine máquina expendedora de sellos

stand (sstænd) n puesto m; tribuna f

*stand (sstænd) v *estar de pie

standard (sstæn-död) n norma f; normal; ~ of living nivel de vida

stanza (sstæn-sö) n estrofa f

staple (sstei-pöl) n grapa f

star (sstaa) n estrella f

starboard (sstaa-böd) n estribor m

starch (sstaach) n almidón m; v almidonar

stare (sstêᵒ) v mirar

starling (sstaa-ling) n estornino m

start (sstaat) v *empezar; n comienzo m; starter motor arranque m

starting-point (sstaa-ting-point) n punto de partida

state (ssteit) n Estado m; estado m; v declarar; the States Estados Unidos

statement (*ssteit*-mönt) *n* declaración *f*

statesman (*ssteitss*-mön) *n* (pl -men) estadista *m*

station (*sstei*-ʃön) *n* estación *f*; puesto *m*

stationary (*sstei*-ʃö-nö-ri) *adj* estacionario

stationer's (*sstei*-ʃö-nös) *n* papelería *f*

stationery (*sstei*-ʃö-nö-ri) *n* papelería *f*

station-master (*sstei*-ʃön-maa-sstö) *n* jefe de estación

statistics (sstö-*ti*-sstikss) *pl* estadística *f*

statue (*sstæ*-chuu) *n* estatua *f*

stay (sstei) *v* quedarse; hospedarse; *n* estancia *f*

steadfast (*sstêd*-faasst) *adj* constante

steady (*sstê*-di) *adj* firme

steak (ssteik) *n* bistec *m*

*steal (sstiil) *v* hurtar

steam (sstiim) *n* vapor *m*

steamer (*sstii*-mö) *n* vapor *m*

steel (sstiil) *n* acero *m*

steep (sstiip) *adj* abrupto

steeple (*sstii*-pöl) *n* campanario *m*

steering-column (*sstiⁱ*ö-ring-ko-löm) *n* columna del volante

steering-wheel (*sstiⁱ*ö-ring-ᵘiil) *n* volante *m*

steersman (*sstiⁱ*ös-mön) *n* (pl -men) timonel *m*

stem (sstêm) *n* tallo *m*

stenographer (sstê-*no*-ghrö-fö) *n* taquígrafo *m*

step (sstêp) *n* paso *m*; peldaño *m*; *v* pisar

stepchild (*sstêp*-chaild) *n* (pl -children) hijastro *m*

stepfather (*sstêp*-faa-ðö) *n* padrastro *m*

stepmother (*sstêp*-ma-ðö) *n* madras-

tra *f*

sterile (*sstê*-rail) *adj* estéril

sterilize (*sstê*-ri-lais) *v* esterilizar

steward (*sstyuu*-öd) *n* camarero *m*

stewardess (*sstyuu*-ö-dêss) *n* azafata *f*

stick (sstik) *n* palo *m*

*stick (sstik) *v* pegar

sticky (*ssti*-ki) *adj* pegajoso

stiff (sstif) *adj* tieso

still (sstil) *adv* todavía; sin embargo; *adj* quieto

stillness (*sstil*-nöss) *n* silencio *m*

stimulant (*ssti*-myu-lönt) *n* estimulante *m*

stimulate (*ssti*-myu-leit) *v* estimular

sting (ssting) *n* picadura *f*

*sting (ssting) *v* picar

stingy (*sstin*-dʒi) *adj* mezquino

*stink (sstingk) *v* apestar

stipulate (*ssti*-pyu-leit) *v* estipular

stipulation (ssti-pyu-*lei*-ʃön) *n* estipulación *f*

stir (sstöö) *v* *mover; *revolver

stirrup (*ssti*-röp) *n* estribo *m*

stitch (sstich) *n* punto *m*, punzada *f*; sutura *f*

stock (sstok) *n* existencias *fpl*; *v* *tener en existencia; ~ **exchange** bolsa de valores, bolsa *f*; ~ **market** bolsa *f*; **stocks and shares** acciones *fpl*

stocking (*ssto*-king) *n* media *f*

stole¹ (sstoul) *v* (p steal)

stole² (sstoul) *n* estola *f*

stomach (*ssta*-mök) *n* estómago *m*

stomach-ache (*ssta*-mö-keik) *n* dolor de estómago

stone (sstoun) *n* piedra *f*; piedra preciosa; hueso *m*; de piedra; **pumice** ~ piedra pómez

stood (sstud) *v* (p, pp stand)

stop (sstop) *v* cesar; dejar de; *n* parada *f*; **stop!** ¡alto!

stopper (*ssto*-pö) *n* tapón *m*

storage (*sstoo*-ridʒ) *n* almacenaje *m*

store (sstoo) *n* repuesto *m*; almacén *m*; *v* almacenar

store-house (*sstoo*-hauss) *n* almacén *m*

storey (*sstoo*-ri) *n* piso *m*

stork (sstook) *n* cigüeña *f*

storm (sstoom) *n* tormenta *f*

stormy (*sstoo*-mi) *adj* tempestuoso

story (*sstoo*-ri) *n* cuento *m*

stout (sstaut) *adj* gordo, corpulento

stove (sstouv) *n* estufa *f*; cocina *f*

straight (sstreit) *adj* derecho; honesto; *adv* directamente; ~ **ahead** todo seguido; ~ **away** directamente, en seguida; ~ **on** todo seguido

strain (sstrein) *n* esfuerzo *m*; tensión *f*; *v* *forzar; filtrar

strainer (*sstrei*-nö) *n* escurridor *m*

strange (sstreindʒ) *adj* extraño; raro

stranger (*sstrein*-dʒö) *n* extranjero *m*; forastero *m*

strangle (*sstræng*-ghöl) *v* estrangular

strap (sstræp) *n* correa *f*

straw (sstroo) *n* paja *f*

strawberry (*sstroo*-bö-ri) *n* fresa *f*

stream (sstriim) *n* arroyo *m*; corriente *f*; *v* *fluir

street (sstriit) *n* calle *f*

streetcar (*sstriit*-kaa) *nAm* tranvía *m*

street-organ (*sstrii*-too-ghön) *n* organillo *m*

strength (sstrengz) *n* fuerza *f*, vigor *m*

stress (sstrèss) *n* esfuerzo *m*; énfasis *m*; *v* acentuar

stretch (sstrêch) *v* estirar; *n* trecho *m*

strict (sstrikt) *adj* estricto; severo

strife (sstraif) *n* lucha *f*

strike (sstraik) *n* huelga *f*

*strike (sstraik) *v* golpear; atacar; impresionar; *estar en huelga; arriar

striking (*sstrai*-king) *adj* impresionante, notable, vistoso

string (sstring) *n* cordel *m*; cuerda *f*

strip (sstrip) *n* faja *f*

stripe (sstraip) *n* raya *f*

striped (sstraipt) *adj* rayado

stroke (sstrouk) *n* ataque *m*

stroll (sstroul) *v* pasear; *n* paseo *m*

strong (sstrong) *adj* fuerte

stronghold (*sstrong*-hould) *n* plaza fuerte

structure (*sstrak*-chö) *n* estructura *f*

struggle (*sstra*-ghöl) *n* combate *m*, lucha *f*; *v* luchar

stub (sstab) *n* talón *m*

stubborn (*ssta*-bön) *adj* testarudo

student (*sstyuu*-dönt) *n* estudiante *m*; estudiante *f*

study (*ssta*-di) *v* estudiar; *n* estudio *m*; despacho *m*

stuff (sstaf) *n* substancia *f*; cachivache *m*

stuffed (sstaft) *adj* rellenado

stuffing (*ssta*-fing) *n* relleno *m*

stuffy (*ssta*-fi) *adj* sofocante

stumble (*sstam*-böl) *v* *tropezarse

stung (sstang) *v* (p, pp sting)

stupid (*sstyuu*-pid) *adj* estúpido

style (sstail) *n* estilo *m*

subject¹ (*ssab*-dʒikt) *n* sujeto *m*; súbdito *m*; ~ **to** sujeto a

subject² (ssöb-*dʒèkt*) *v* someter

submit (ssöb-*mit*) *v* someterse

subordinate (ssö-*boo*-di-nöt) *adj* subalterno; subordinado

subscriber (ssöb-*sskrai*-bö) *n* abonado *m*

subscription (ssöb-*sskrip*-[ö]n) *n* suscripción *f*

subsequent (*ssab*-ssi-kᵘönt) *adj* posterior

subsidy (*ssab*-ssi-di) *n* subsidio *m*

substance (*ssab*-sstönss) *n* sustancia *f*

substantial (ssöb-*sstæn*-[öl) *adj* material; real; sustancial

substitute (*ssab*-ssti-tyuut) *v* *sustituir; *n* sustituto *m*

subtitle (*ssab*-tai-töl) *n* subtítulo *m*

subtle (*ssa*-töl) *adj* sutil

subtract (ssöb-*trækt*) *v* restar

suburb (*ssa*-bööb) *n* suburbio *m*

suburban (ssö-*böö*-bön) *adj* suburbano

subway (*ssab*-ᵘei) *nAm* metro *m*

succeed (ssök-*ssiid*) *v* *tener éxito; suceder

success (ssök-*ssêss*) *n* éxito *m*

successful (ssök-*ssêss*-föl) *adj* de éxito

succumb (ssö-*kam*) *v* sucumbir

such (ssach) *adj* tal; *adv* tan; ~ **as** tal como

suck (ssak) *v* chupar

sudden (*ssa*-dön) *adj* súbito

suddenly (*ssa*-dön-li) *adv* repentinamente

suede (ssᵘeid) *n* gamuza *f*

suffer (*ssa*-fö) *v* sufrir

suffering (*ssa*-fö-ring) *n* sufrimiento *m*

suffice (ssö-*faiss*) *v* bastar

sufficient (ssö-*fi*-fönt) *adj* suficiente, bastante

suffrage (*ssa*-fridʒ) *n* derecho electoral, sufragio *m*

sugar (*ʃu*-ghö) *n* azúcar *m/f*

suggest (ssö-*dʒêsst*) *v* *sugerir

suggestion (ssö-*dʒêss*-chön) *n* sugestión *f*

suicide (*ssuu*-i-ssaid) *n* suicidio *m*

suit (ssuut) *v* *convenir; adaptar; *ir bien; *n* traje *m*

suitable (*ssuu*-tö-böl) *adj* apropiado, apto

suitcase (*ssuut*-keiss) *n* maleta *f*

suite (ssᵘiit) *n* apartamento *m*

sum (ssam) *n* suma *f*

summary (*ssa*-mö-ri) *n* resumen *m*, sumario *m*

summer (*ssa*-mö) *n* verano *m*; ~ **time** horario de verano

summit (*ssa*-mit) *n* cima *f*

summons (*ssa*-möns) *n* (pl ~es) citación *f*

sun (ssan) *n* sol *m*

sunbathe (*ssan*-beið) *v* tomar el sol

sunburn (*ssan*-böön) *n* quemadura del sol

Sunday (*ssan*-di) *n* domingo *m*

sun-glasses (*ssan*-ghlaa-ssis) *pl* gafas de sol

sunlight (*ssan*-lait) *n* luz del sol

sunny (*ssa*-ni) *adj* soleado

sunrise (*ssan*-rais) *n* amanecer *m*

sunset (*ssan*-ssêt) *n* ocaso *m*

sunshade (*ssan*-feid) *n* quitasol *m*

sunshine (*ssan*-fain) *n* sol *m*

sunstroke (*ssan*-sstrouk) *n* insolación *f*

suntan oil (*ssan*-tæn-oil) aceite bronceador

superb (ssu-*pööb*) *adj* grandioso, soberbio

superficial (ssuu-pö-*fi*-föl) *adj* superficial

superfluous (ssu-*pöö*-flu-öss) *adj* superfluo

superior (ssu-*piᵒ*-ri-ö) *adj* mejor, mayor, superior

superlative (ssu-*pöö*-lö-tiv) *adj* superlativo; *n* superlativo *m*

supermarket (*ssuu*-pö-maa-kit) *n* supermercado *m*

superstition (ssuu-pö-*ssti*-fön) *n* superstición *f*

supervise (*ssuu*-pö-vais) *v* supervisar

supervision (ssuu-pö-*vi*-ʒön) *n* supervisión *f*

supervisor (*ssuu*-pö-vai-sö) *n* supervisor *m*

supper (*ssa*-pö) *n* cena *f*

supple (*ssa*-pöl) *adj* flexible, ágil

supplement (*ssa*-pli-mönt) *n* suplemento *m*

supply (ssö-*plai*) *n* abastecimiento *m*, suministro *m*; existencias *fpl*; oferta *f*; *v* suministrar

support (ssö-*poot*) *v* apoyar, *sostener, soportar; *n* apoyo *m*; ~ **hose** medias elásticas

supporter (ssö-*poo*-tö) *n* aficionado *m*

suppose (ssö-*pous*) *v* *suponer; **supposing that** dado que

suppository (ssö-*po*-si-tö-ri) *n* supositorio *m*

suppress (ssö-*prêss*) *v* reprimir

surcharge (*ssöö*-chaad3) *n* sobretasa *f*

sure (ʃuᵒ) *adj* seguro

surely (ʃuᵒ-li) *adv* seguramente

surface (*ssöö*-fiss) *n* superficie *f*

surf-board (*ssööf*-bood) *n* tabla para surf

surgeon (*ssöö*-dʒön) *n* cirujano *m*; **veterinary** ~ veterinario *m*

surgery (*ssöö*-dʒö-ri) *n* operación *f*; consultorio *m*

surname (*ssöö*-neim) *n* apellido *m*

surplus (*ssöö*-plöss) *n* sobra *f*

surprise (ssö-*prais*) *n* sorpresa *f*; *v* sorprender; extrañar

surrender (ssö-*rên*-dö) *v* *rendirse; *n* rendición *f*

surround (ssö-*raund*) *v* rodear, cercar

surrounding (ssö-*raun*-ding) *adj* circundante

surroundings (ssö-*raun*-dings) *pl* alrededores *mpl*

survey (*ssöö*-vei) *n* resumen *m*

survival (ssö-*vai*-völ) *n* supervivencia *f*

survive (ssö-*vaiv*) *v* sobrevivir

suspect¹ (ssö-*sspêkt*) *v* sospechar

suspect² (ssa-sspêkt) *n* persona sospechosa

suspend (ssö-*sspênd*) *v* suspender

suspenders (ssö-*sspên*-dös) *plAm* tirantes *mpl*; **suspender belt** portaligas *m*

suspension (ssö-*sspên*-ʃön) *n* suspensión *f*; ~ **bridge** puente colgante

suspicion (ssö-*sspi*-ʃön) *n* sospecha *f*; suspicacia *f*, desconfianza *f*

suspicious (ssö-*sspi*-ʃöss) *adj* sospechoso; suspicaz, desconfiado

sustain (ssö-*sstein*) *v* soportar

Swahili (ssᵘö-*hii*-li) *n* suahili *m*

swallow (*ssᵘo*-lou) *v* tragar; *n* golondrina *f*

swam (ssᵘæm) *v* (p swim)

swamp (ssᵘomp) *n* marisma *f*

swan (ssᵘon) *n* cisne *m*

swap (ssᵘop) *v* *trocar

***swear** (ssᵘêᵒ) *v* jurar

sweat (ssᵘêt) *n* sudor *m*; *v* sudar

sweater (*ssᵘê*-tö) *n* suéter *m*

Swede (ssᵘiid) *n* sueco *m*

Sweden (*ssᵘii*-dön) *n* Suecia *f*

Swedish (*ssᵘii*-diʃ) *adj* sueco

***sweep** (ssᵘiip) *v* barrer

sweet (ssᵘiit) *adj* dulce; lindo; *n* caramelo *m*; dulce *m*

sweeten (*ssᵘii*-tön) *v* endulzar

sweetheart (*ssᵘiit*-haat) *n* amor *m*, querida *f*

sweetshop (*ssᵘiit*-ʃop) *n* confitería *f*

swell (ssᵘêl) *adj* magnífico

***swell** (ssᵘêl) *v* hincharse

swelling (*ssᵘê*-ling) *n* hinchazón *f*

swift (ssᵘift) *adj* veloz

***swim** (ssᵘim) *v* nadar

swimmer (*ssᵘi*-mö) *n* nadador *m*

swimming (*ssᵘi*-ming) *n* natación *f*; ~ **pool** piscina *f*

swimming-trunks (*ssᵘi*-ming-trangkss) *n* calzón de baño

swim-suit (*ssᵘim*-ssuut) *n* traje de baño

swindle (*ssᵘin*-döl) *v* estafar; *n* estafa *f*

swindler (*ssᵘin*-dlö) *n* estafador *m*

swing (ss^uing) *n* columpio *m*

***swing** (ss^uing) *v* oscilar; columpiarse

Swiss (ss^uiss) *adj* suizo

switch (ss^uich) *n* interruptor *m*; *v* cambiar; ~ **off** apagar; ~ **on** *encender

switchboard (ss^uich-bood) *n* cuadro de distribución

Switzerland (ss^uit-ssö-lönd) Suiza *f*

sword (ssood) *n* espada *f*

swum (ss^uam) *v* (pp swim)

syllable (ssi-lö-böl) *n* sílaba *f*

symbol (ssim-böl) *n* símbolo *m*

sympathetic (ssim-pö-zê-tik) *adj* cordial, compasivo

sympathy (ssim-pö-zi) *n* simpatía *f*; compasión *f*

symphony (ssim-fö-ni) *n* sinfonía *f*

symptom (ssim-töm) *n* síntoma *m*

synagogue (ssi-nö-ghogh) *n* sinagoga *f*

synonym (ssi-nö-nim) *n* sinónimo *m*

synthetic (ssin-zê-tik) *adj* sintético

syphon (ssai-fön) *n* sifón *m*

Syria (ssi-ri-ö) Siria *f*

Syrian (ssi-ri-ön) *adj* sirio

syringe (ssi-rindʒ) *n* jeringa *f*

syrup (ssi-röp) *n* jarabe *m*

system (ssi-sstöm) *n* sistema *m*; **decimal** ~ sistema decimal

systematic (ssi-sstö-mæ-tik) *adj* sistemático

T

table (tei-böl) *n* mesa *f*; tabla *f*; ~ **of contents** índice *m*; ~ **tennis** tenis de mesa

table-cloth (tei-böl-kloz) *n* mantel *m*

tablespoon (tei-böl-sspuun) *n* cuchara *f*

tablet (tæ-blit) *n* pastilla *f*

taboo (tö-buu) *n* tabú *m*

tactics (tæk-tikss) *pl* táctica *f*

tag (tægh) *n* etiqueta *f*

tail (teil) *n* cola *f*

tail-light (teil-lait) *n* farol trasero

tailor (tei-lö) *n* sastre *m*

tailor-made (tei-lö-meid) *adj* hecho a la medida

***take** (teik) *v* coger; tomar; llevar; comprender, *entender; ~ **away** quitar; llevarse; ~ **off** despegar; ~ **out** sacar; ~ **over** encargarse de; ~ **place** *tener lugar; ~ **up** ocupar

take-off (tei-kof) *n* despegue *m*

tale (teil) *n* cuento *m*

talent (tæ-lönt) *n* talento *m*

talented (tæ-lön-tid) *adj* dotado

talk (took) *v* hablar; *n* conversación *f*

talkative (too-kö-tiv) *adj* locuaz

tall (tool) *adj* alto

tame (teim) *adj* manso, domesticado; *v* domesticar

tampon (tæm-pön) *n* tapón *m*

tangerine (tæn-dʒö-riin) *n* mandarina *f*

tangible (tæn-dʒi-böl) *adj* tangible

tank (tængk) *n* tanque *m*

tanker (tæng-kö) *n* buque cisterna

tanned (tænd) *adj* tostado

tap (tæp) *n* grifo *m*; golpecito *m*; *v* golpear

tape (teip) *n* cinta *f*; **adhesive** ~ cinta adhesiva; esparadrapo *m*

tape-measure (teip-mê-ʒö) *n* centímetro *m*, cinta métrica

tape-recorder (teip-ri-koo-dö) *n* magnetófono *m*

tapestry (tæ-pi-sstri) *n* tapiz *m*

tar (taa) *n* brea *f*

target (taa-ghit) *n* objetivo *m*, blanco *m*

tariff (tæ-rif) *n* arancel *m*

tarpaulin (taa-poo-lin) *n* lona impermeable

task (taassk) *n* tarea *f*

taste (teisst) *n* gusto *m*; *v* *saber a; *probar

tasteless (*teisst*-löss) *adj* insípido

tasty (*tei*-ssti) *adj* rico, sabroso

taught (toot) *v* (p, pp teach)

tavern (*tæ*-vön) *n* taberna *f*

tax (tækss) *n* impuesto *m*; *v* *imponer contribuciones

taxation (tæk-*ssei*-∫ön) *n* impuesto *m*

tax-free (*tækss*-frii) *adj* libre de impuestos

taxi (*tæk*-ssi) *n* taxi *m*; ~ **rank** parada de taxis; ~ **stand** *Am* parada de taxis

taxi-driver (*tæk*-ssi-drai-vö) *n* taxista *m*

taxi-meter (*tæk*-ssi-mii-tö) *n* taxímetro *m*

tea (tii) *n* té *m*; merienda *f*

***teach** (tiich) *v* enseñar

teacher (*tii*-chö) *n* profesor *m*, maestro *m*; profesora *f*; institutor *m*

teachings (*tii*-chings) *pl* enseñanza *f*

tea-cloth (*tii*-kloz) *n* trapo de cocina

teacup (*tii*-kap) *n* taza de té

team (tiim) *n* equipo *m*

teapot (*tii*-pot) *n* tetera *f*

tear¹ (ti°) *n* lágrima *f*

tear² (tê°) *n* rasgón *m*; ***tear** *v* desgarrar

tear-jerker (*ti°*-d3öö-kö) *n* cuplé lacrimoso

tease (tiis) *v* tomar el pelo

tea-set (*tii*-ssêt) *n* juego de té

tea-shop (*tii*-∫op) *n* salón de té

teaspoon (*tii*-sspuun) *n* cucharilla *f*

teaspoonful (*tii*-sspuun-ful) *n* cucharadita *f*

technical (*têk*-ni-köl) *adj* técnico

technician (têk-*ni*-∫ön) *n* técnico *m*

technique (têk-*niik*) *n* técnica *f*

technology (têk-*no*-lö-d3i) *n* tecnolo-

gía *f*

teenager (*tii*-nei-d3ö) *n* jovencito *m*

teetotaller (tii-*tou*-tö-lö) *n* abstemio *m*

telegram (*tê*-li-ghræm) *n* telegrama *m*

telegraph (*tê*-li-ghraaf) *v* telegrafiar

telepathy (ti-*lê*-pö-zi) *n* telepatía *f*

telephone (*tê*-li-foun) *n* teléfono *m*; ~ **book** *Am* listín telefónico, guía telefónica; ~ **booth** cabina telefónica; ~ **call** llamada telefónica; ~ **directory** guía telefónica, listín telefónico; directorio telefónico *Me*; ~ **exchange** central telefónica; ~ **operator** telefonista *f*

telephonist (ti-*lê*-fö-nisst) *n* telefonista *f*

television (*tê*-li-vi-3ön) *n* televisión *f*; ~ **set** televisor *m*

telex (*tê*-lêkss) *n* télex *m*

***tell** (têl) *v* *decir; *contar

temper (*têm*-pö) *n* cólera *f*

temperature (*têm*-prö-chö) *n* temperatura *f*

tempest (*têm*-pisst) *n* tempestad *f*

temple (*têm*-pöl) *n* templo *m*; sien *f*

temporary (*têm*-pö-rö-ri) *adj* provisional, temporal

tempt (têmpt) *v* *tentar

temptation (têmp-*tei*-∫ön) *n* tentación *f*

ten (tên) *num* diez

tenant (*tê*-nönt) *n* inquilino *m*

tend (tênd) *v* *tender a; cuidar de; ~ **to** *tender a

tendency (*tên*-dön-ssi) *n* inclinación *f*, tendencia *f*

tender (*tên*-dö) *adj* tierno, delicado

tendon (*tên*-dön) *n* tendón *m*

tennis (*tê*-niss) *n* tenis *m*; ~ **shoes** zapatos de tenis

tennis-court (*tê*-niss-koot) *n* campo de tenis, cancha *f*

tense (tênss) *adj* tenso

tension (tên-[ʃ]ön) n tensión m

tent (tênt) n tienda f

tenth (tênz) num décimo

tepid (té-pid) adj tibio

term (tööm) n término m; período m, plazo m; condición f

terminal (töö-mi-nöl) n estación terminal

terrace (tê-röss) n terraza f

terrain (tê-rein) n terreno m

terrible (tê-ri-böl) adj tremendo, terrible, pésimo

terrific (tö-ri-fik) adj tremendo

terrify (tê-ri-fai) v aterrorizar; **terrifying** aterrador

territory (tê-ri-tö-ri) n territorio m

terror (tê-rö) n terror m

terrorism (tê-rö-ri-söm) n terrorismo m, terror m

terrorist (tê-rö-risst) n terrorista m

terylene (tê-rö-liin) n terilene m

test (têsst) n prueba f, ensayo m; v *probar, ensayar

testify (tê-ssti-fai) v testimoniar

text (têksst) n texto m

textbook (têkss-buk) n libro de texto

textile (têk-sstail) n textil m

texture (têkss-chö) n textura f

Thai (tai) adj tailandés

Thailand (tai-lænd) Tailandia f

than (ðæn) conj que

thank (zængk) v *agradecer; ~ you gracias

thankful (zængk-föl) adj agradecido

that (ðæt) adj aquel, ese; pron aquél, eso; que; conj que

thaw (zoo) v descongelarse; n deshielo m

the (ðö,ði) art el art; **the ... the** cuanto más ... más

theatre (ziⁿ-tö) n teatro m

theft (zêft) n robo m

their (ðêⁿ) adj su

them (ðêm) pron les

theme (ziim) n tema m, sujeto m

themselves (ðöm-sssêlvs) pron se; ellos mismos

then (ðên) adv entonces; después; en tal caso

theology (zi-o-lö-dʒi) n teología f

theoretical (ziⁿ-rê-ti-köl) adj teórico

theory (ziⁿ-ri) n teoría f

therapy (zê-rö-pi) n terapia f

there (ðêⁿ) adv allí; hacia allá

therefore (ðêⁿ-foo) conj por lo tanto

thermometer (zö-mo-mi-tö) n termómetro m

thermostat (zöö-mö-sstæt) n termostato m

these (ðiis) adj éstos

thesis (zii-ssiss) n (pl theses) tesis f

they (ðei) pron ellos

thick (zik) adj espeso; denso

thicken (zi-kön) v espesar

thickness (zik-nöss) n espesor m

thief (ziif) n (pl thieves) ladrón m

thigh (zai) n muslo m

thimble (zim-böl) n dedal m

thin (zin) adj delgado; flaco

thing (zing) n cosa f

***think** (zingk) v *pensar; reflexionar; ~ of *pensar en; *recordar; ~ over considerar

thinker (zing-kö) n pensador m

third (zööd) num tercero

thirst (zöösst) n sed f

thirsty (zöö-ssti) adj sediento

thirteen (zöö-tiin) num trece

thirteenth (zöö-tiinz) num treceno

thirtieth (zöö-ti-öz) num treintavo

thirty (zöö-ti) num treinta

this (ðiss) adj este, esto; pron éste

thistle (zi-ssöl) n cardo m

thorn (zoon) n espina f

thorough (za-rö) adj minucioso

thoroughbred (za-rö-brêd) adj purasangre

thoroughfare (za-rö-fêⁿ) n ruta principal, arteria principal

those (ðous) *adj* aquellos; *pron* aquéllos

though (ðou) *conj* si bien, aunque;
adv sin embargo

thought[1] (zoot) *v* (p, pp think)

thought[2] (zoot) *n* pensamiento *m*

thoughtful (zoot-föl) *adj* pensativo;
atento

thousand (zau-sönd) *num* mil

thread (zrêd) *n* hilo *m*; *v* enhebrar

threadbare (zrêd-bêô) *adj* gastado

threat (zrêt) *n* amenaza *f*

threaten (zrê-tön) *v* amenazar;
threatening amenazador

three (zrii) *num* tres

three-quarter (zrii-kʷoo-tö) *adj* tres
cuartos

threshold (zrê-ʃould) *n* umbral *m*

threw (zruu) *v* (p throw)

thrifty (zrif-ti) *adj* económico

throat (zrout) *n* garganta *f*

throne (zroun) *n* trono *m*

through (zruu) *prep* a través de

throughout (zruu-aut) *adv* por todas
partes

throw (zrou) *n* lanzamiento *m*

*****throw** (zrou) *v* tirar, arrojar

thrush (zraʃ) *n* tordo *m*

thumb (zam) *n* pulgar *m*

thumbtack (zam-tæk) *nAm* chinche *f*

thump (zamp) *v* golpear

thunder (zan-dö) *n* trueno *m*; *v* *tronar

thunderstorm (zan-dö-sstoom) *n* tronada *f*

thundery (zan-dö-ri) *adj* tormentoso

Thursday (zöös-di) *n* jueves *m*

thus (ðass) *adv* así

thyme (taim) *n* tomillo *m*

tick (tik) *n* señal *f*; ~ **off** señalar

ticket (ti-kit) *n* billete *m*; multa *f*;
boleto *mMe*; ~ **collector** revisor
m; ~ **machine** máquina de billetes

tickle (ti-köl) *v* cosquillear

tide (taid) *n* marea *f*; **high** ~ pleamar
f; **low** ~ bajamar *f*

tidings (tai-dings) *pl* noticias *fpl*

tidy (tai-di) *adj* aseado; ~ **up** arreglar

tie (tai) *v* anudar, atar; *n* corbata *f*

tiger (tai-ghö) *n* tigre *m*

tight (tait) *adj* estrecho; angosto,
apretado; *adv* fuertemente

tighten (tai-tön) *v* estrechar, *apretar; estrecharse

tights (taitss) *pl* traje de malla

tile (tail) *n* azulejo *m*; teja *f*

till (til) *prep* hasta; *conj* hasta que

timber (tim-bö) *n* madera de construcción

time (taim) *n* tiempo *m*; vez *f*; **all
the** ~ continuamente; **in** ~ a tiempo; ~ **of arrival** hora de llegada; ~
of departure hora de salida

time-saving (taim-ssei-ving) *adj* que
economiza tiempo

timetable (taim-tei-böl) *n* horario *m*

timid (ti-mid) *adj* tímido

timidity (ti-mi-dö-ti) *n* timidez *f*

tin (tin) *n* estaño *m*; lata *f*; **tinned
food** conservas *fpl*

tinfoil (tin-foil) *n* papel de estaño

tin-opener (ti-nou-pö-nö) *n* abrelatas
m

tiny (tai-ni) *adj* menudo

tip (tip) *n* punta *f*; propina *f*

tire[1] (taiô) *n* neumático *m*; llanta
fMe

tire[2] (taiô) *v* cansar

tired (taiôd) *adj* cansado; ~ **of** harto
de

tissue (ti-ʃuu) *n* tejido *m*; pañuelo de
papel

title (tai-töl) *n* título *m*

to (tuu) *prep* hasta; a, para, en, hacia

toad (toud) *n* sapo *m*

toadstool (toud-sstuul) *n* hongo *m*

toast (tousst) *n* pan tostado; brindis

m

tobacco (tö-*bæ*-kou) *n* (pl ~s) tabaco *m*; ~ **pouch** petaca *f*

tobacconist (tö-*bæ*-kö-nisst) *n* estanquero *m*; **tobacconist's** estanco *m*

today (tö-*dei*) *adv* hoy

toddler (*tod*-lö) *n* párvulo *m*

toe (tou) *n* dedo del pie

toffee (*to*-fi) *n* caramelo *m*

together (tö-*ghê*-ðö) *adv* juntos

toilet (*toi*-löt) *n* retrete *m*; ~ **case** neceser *m*

toilet-paper (*toi*-löt-pei-pö) *n* papel higiénico

toiletry (*toi*-lö-tri) *n* artículos de tocador

token (*tou*-kön) *n* señal *f*; prueba *f*; ficha *f*

told (tould) *v* (p, pp tell)

tolerable (*to*-lö-rö-böl) *adj* tolerable

toll (toul) *n* peaje *m*

tomato (tö-*maa*-tou) *n* (pl ~es) tomate *m*; jitomate *mMe*

tomb (tuum) *n* tumba *f*

tombstone (*tuum*-sstoun) *n* lápida *f*

tomorrow (tö-*mo*-rou) *adv* mañana

ton (tan) *n* tonelada *f*

tone (toun) *n* tono *m*; timbre *m*

tongs (tongs) *pl* tenazas *f*

tongue (tang) *n* lengua *f*

tonic (*to*-nik) *n* tónico *m*

tonight (tö-*nait*) *adv* esta noche

tonsilitis (ton-ssö-*lai*-tiss) *n* amigdalitis *f*

tonsils (*ton*-ssöls) *pl* amígdalas *fpl*

too (tuu) *adv* demasiado; también

took (tuk) *v* (p take)

tool (tuul) *n* herramienta *f*; ~ **kit** bolsa de herramientas

tooth (tuuz) *n* (pl teeth) diente *m*

toothache (*tuu*-zeik) *n* dolor de muelas

toothbrush (*tuuz*-braʃ) *n* cepillo de dientes

toothpaste (*tuuz*-peisst) *n* pasta dentífrica

toothpick (*tuuz*-pik) *n* palillo *m*

toothpowder (*tuuz*-pau-dö) *n* polvo para los dientes

top (top) *n* cima *f*; parte superior; tapa *f*; superior; **on** ~ **of** encima de; ~ **side** parte superior

topcoat (*top*-kout) *n* sobretodo *m*

topic (*to*-pik) *n* asunto *m*

topical (*to*-pi-köl) *adj* actual

torch (tooch) *n* antorcha *f*; linterna *f*

torment[1] (too-*mênt*) *v* atormentar

torment[2] (*too*-mênt) *n* tormento *m*

torture (*too*-chö) *n* tortura *f*; *v* torturar

toss (toss) *v* echar

tot (tot) *n* niño pequeño

total (*tou*-töl) *adj* total; completo, absoluto; *n* total *m*

totalitarian (tou-tæ-li-*tê*ô-ri-ön) *adj* totalitario

totalizator (*tou*-tö-lai-sei-tö) *n* totalizador *m*

touch (tach) *v* tocar; *concernir; *n* contacto *m*, toque *m*; tacto *m*

touching (*ta*-ching) *adj* conmovedor

tough (taf) *adj* duro

tour (tuᵒ) *n* vuelta *f*

tourism (*tu*ᵒ-ri-söm) *n* turismo *m*

tourist (*tu*ᵒ-risst) *n* turista *m*; ~ **class** clase turista; ~ **office** oficina para turistas

tournament (*tu*ᵒ-nö-mönt) *n* torneo *m*

tow (tou) *v* remolcar

towards (tö-ᵘ*oods*) *prep* hacia; para con

towel (tauᵒl) *n* toalla *f*

towelling (*tau*ᵒ-ling) *n* tela para toallas

tower (tauᵒ) *n* torre *f*

town (taun) *n* ciudad *f*; ~ **centre** centro de la ciudad; ~ **hall** ayuntamiento *m*

townspeople (*tauns*-pii-pöl) *pl* ciudadanos *mpl*

toxic (*tok*-ssik) *adj* tóxico

toy (toi) *n* juguete *m*

toyshop (*toi*-ʃop) *n* juguetería *f*

trace (treiss) *n* huella *f*; *v* rastrear

track (træk) *n* vía *f*; pista *f*

tractor (*træk*-tö) *n* tractor *m*

trade (treid) *n* comercio *m*; oficio *m*; *v* comerciar

trademark (*treid*-maak) *n* marca de fábrica

trader (*trei*-dö) *n* comerciante *m*

tradesman (*treids*-mön) *n* (pl -men) tendero *m*

trade-union (treid-*yuu*-nyön) *n* sindicato *m*

tradition (trö-*di*-ʃön) *n* tradición *f*

traditional (trö-*di*-ʃö-nöl) *adj* tradicional

traffic (*træ*-fik) *n* tránsito *m*; ~ **jam** embotellamiento *m*; ~ **light** semáforo *m*

trafficator (*træ*-fi-kei-tö) *n* indicador *m*

tragedy (*træ*-dʒö-di) *n* tragedia *f*

tragic (*træ*-dʒik) *adj* trágico

trail (treil) *n* rastro *m*, sendero *m*

trailer (*trei*-lö) *n* remolque *m*; *nAm* caravana *f*

train (trein) *n* tren *m*; *v* amaestrar, entrenar; **stopping** ~ tren de cercanías; **through** ~ tren directo; ~ **ferry** transbordador de trenes

training (*trei*-ning) *n* entrenamiento *m*

trait (treit) *n* rasgo *m*

traitor (*trei*-tö) *n* traidor *m*

tram (træm) *n* tranvía *m*

tramp (træmp) *n* vagabundo *m*; *v* vagabundear

tranquil (*træng*-kᵘil) *adj* tranquilo

tranquillizer (*træng*-kᵘi-lai-sö) *n* cal-

mante *m*

transaction (træn-*sæk*-ʃön) *n* transacción *f*

transatlantic (træn-söt-*læn*-tik) *adj* transatlántico

transfer (trænss-*föö*) *v* *transferir

transform (trænss-*foom*) *v* transformar

transformer (trænss-*foo*-mö) *n* transformador *m*

transition (træn-*ssi*-ʃön) *n* transición *f*

translate (trænss-*leit*) *v* *traducir

translation (trænss-*lei*-ʃön) *n* traducción *f*

translator (trænss-*lei*-tö) *n* traductor *m*

transmission (træns-*mi*-ʃön) *n* transmisión *f*

transmit (træns-*mit*) *v* transmitir

transmitter (træns-*mi*-tö) *n* emisor *m*

transparent (træn-*sspê*ᵒ-rönt) *adj* transparente

transport¹ (*træn*-sspoot) *n* transporte *m*

transport² (træn-*sspoot*) *v* transportar

transportation (træn-sspoo-*tei*-ʃön) *n* transporte *m*

trap (træp) *n* trampa *f*

trash (træʃ) *n* basura *f*

travel (*træ*-völ) *v* viajar; ~ **agency** agencia de viajes; ~ **agent** agente de viajes; ~ **insurance** seguro de viaje; **travelling expenses** gastos de viaje

traveller (*træ*-vö-lö) *n* viajero *m*; **traveller's cheque** cheque de viajero

tray (trei) *n* bandeja *f*; charola *fMe*

treason (*trii*-sön) *n* traición *f*

treasure (*trê*-ʒö) *n* tesoro *m*

treasurer (*trê*-ʒö-rö) *n* tesorero *m*

treasury (*trê*-ʒö-ri) *n* Tesorería *f*

treat (triit) *v* tratar

treatment (*triit*-mönt) *n* tratamiento

m

treaty (*trii*-ti) *n* tratado *m*

tree (trii) *n* árbol *m*

tremble (*trêm*-böl) *v* *temblar; vibrar

tremendous (tri-*mên*-döss) *adj* tremendo

trespass (*tréss*-pöss) *v* infringir

trespasser (*tréss*-pö-ssö) *n* intruso *m*

trial (trai⁰l) *n* proceso *m*; prueba *f*

triangle (*trai*-æng-ghöl) *n* triángulo *m*

triangular (trai-*æng*-ghyu-lö) *adj* triangular

tribe (traib) *n* tribu *m*

tributary (*tri*-byu-tö-ri) *n* afluente *m*

tribute (*tri*-byuut) *n* homenaje *m*

trick (trik) *n* truco *m*

trigger (*tri*-ghö) *n* gatillo *m*

trim (trim) *v* recortar

trip (trip) *n* excursión *f*, viaje *m*

triumph (*trai*-ömf) *n* triunfo *m*; *v* triunfar

triumphant (trai-*am*-fönt) *adj* triunfante

trolley-bus (*tro*-li-bass) *n* trolebús *m*

troops (truupss) *pl* tropas *fpl*

tropical (*tro*-pi-köl) *adj* tropical

tropics (*tro*-pikss) *pl* trópicos *mpl*

trouble (*tra*-böl) *n* preocupación *f*, molestia *f*; *v* molestar

troublesome (*tra*-böl-ssöm) *adj* molesto

trousers (*trau*-sös) *pl* pantalones *mpl*

trout (traut) *n* (pl ~) trucha *f*

truck (trak) *nAm* camión *m*

true (truu) *adj* verdadero; real, auténtico; leal, fiel

trumpet (*tram*-pit) *n* trompeta *f*

trunk (trangk) *n* baúl *m*; tronco *m*; *nAm* portaequipajes *m*; **trunks** *pl* pantalones de gimnasia

trunk-call (*trangk*-kool) *n* conferencia interurbana

trust (trasst) *v* confiar en; *n* confianza *f*

trustworthy (*trasst*-ᵁöö-ði) *adj* confiable

truth (truuz) *n* verdad *f*

truthful (*truuz*-föl) *adj* verídico

try (trai) *v* intentar; *esforzarse; *n* tentativa *f*; ~ **on** *probarse

tube (tyuub) *n* tubo *m*

tuberculosis (tyuu-böö-kyu-*lou*-ssiss) *n* tuberculosis *f*

Tuesday (*tyuus*-di) martes *m*

tug (tagh) *v* remolcar; *n* remolcador *m*; estirón *m*

tuition (tyuu-*i*-ʃön) *n* enseñanza *f*

tulip (*tyuu*-lip) *n* tulipán *m*

tumbler (*tam*-blö) *n* vaso *m*

tumour (*tyuu*-mö) *n* tumor *m*

tuna (*tyuu*-nö) *n* (pl ~, ~s) atún *m*

tune (tyuun) *n* tonada *f*; ~ **in** sintonizar

tuneful (*tyuun*-föl) *adj* melodioso

tunic (*tyuu*-nik) *n* túnica *f*

Tunisia (tyuu-*ni*-si-ö) Túnez *m*

Tunisian (tyuu-*ni*-si-ön) *adj* tunecino

tunnel (*ta*-nöl) *n* túnel *m*

turbine (*töö*-bain) *n* turbina *f*

turbojet (töö-bou-*dʒêt*) *n* avión turborreactor

Turk (töök) *n* turco *m*

Turkey (*töö*-ki) Turquía *f*

turkey (*töö*-ki) *n* pavo *m*

Turkish (*töö*-kiʃ) *adj* turco; ~ **bath** baño turco

turn (töön) *v* girar; *volver; *n* cambio *m*, vuelta *f*; curva *f*; turno *m*; ~ **back** *volver; ~ **down** rechazar; ~ **into** *convertirse en; ~ **off** *cerrar; ~ **on** *encender; abrir; ~ **over** *volver; ~ **round** *volver; *volverse

turning (*töö*-ning) *n* vuelta *f*

turning-point (*töö*-ning-point) *n* punto decisivo

turnover (*töö*-nou-vö) *n* volumen de transacciones; ~ **tax** impuesto sobre la venta

turnpike (*töön*-paik) *nAm* autopista de peaje

turpentine (*töö*-pön-tain) *n* trementina *f*

turtle (*töö*-töl) *n* tortuga *f*

tutor (*tyuu*-tö) *n* maestro particular; tutor *m*

tuxedo (tak-*ssii*-dou) *nAm* (pl ~s, ~es) smoking *m*

tweed (t^uiid) *n* lana tweed

tweezers (*t^uii*-sös) *pl* pinzas *fpl*

twelfth (t^uêlfz) *num* duodécimo

twelve (t^uêlv) *num* doce

twentieth (*t^uên*-ti-öz) *num* vigésimo

twenty (*t^uên*-ti) *num* veinte

twice (t^uaiss) *adv* dos veces

twig (t^uigh) *n* ramita *f*

twilight (*t^uai*-lait) *n* crepúsculo *m*

twine (t^uain) *n* trenza *f*

twins (t^uins) *pl* gemelos *mpl*; **twin beds** camas gemelas

twist (t^uisst) *v* *torcer; *n* torsión *f*

two (tuu) *num* dos

two-piece (tuu-*piiss*) *adj* de dos piezas

type (taip) *v* escribir a máquina, mecanografiar; *n* tipo *m*

typewriter (*taip*-rai-tö) *n* máquina de escribir

typewritten (*taip*-ri-tön) mecanografiado

typhoid (*tai*-foid) *n* tifus *m*

typical (*ti*-pi-köl) *adj* característico, típico

typist (*tai*-pisst) *n* dactilógrafa *f*

tyrant (*tai^ö*-rönt) *n* tirano *m*

tyre (tai^ö) *n* neumático *m*; ~ **pressure** presión del neumático

U

ugly (*a*-ghli) *adj* feo

ulcer (*al*-ssö) *n* úlcera *f*

ultimate (*al*-ti-möt) *adj* último

ultraviolet (al-trö-*vai^ö*-löt) *adj* ultravioleta

umbrella (am-*brê*-lö) *n* paraguas *m*

umpire (*am*-pai^ö) *n* árbitro *m*

unable (a-*nei*-böl) *adj* incapaz

unacceptable (a-nök-*ssêp*-tö-böl) *adj* inaceptable

unaccountable (a-nö-*kaun*-tö-böl) *adj* inexplicable

unaccustomed (a-nö-*ka*-sstömd) *adj* desacostumbrado

unanimous (yuu-*næ*-ni-möss) *adj* unánime

unanswered (a-*naan*-ssöd) *adj* sin contestación

unauthorized (a-*noo*-zö-raisd) *adj* desautorizado

unavoidable (a-nö-*voi*-dö-böl) *adj* inevitable

unaware (a-nö-*^uê^ö*) *adj* inconsciente

unbearable (an-*bê^ö*-rö-böl) *adj* insufrible

unbreakable (an-*brei*-kö-böl) *adj* irrompible

unbroken (an-*brou*-kön) *adj* intacto

unbutton (an-*ba*-tön) *v* desabotonar

uncertain (an-*ssöö*-tön) *adj* incierto

uncle (*ang*-köl) *n* tío *m*

unclean (an-*kliin*) *adj* sucio

uncomfortable (an-*kam*-fö-tö-böl) *adj* incómodo

uncommon (an-*ko*-mön) *adj* insólito, raro

unconditional (an-kön-*di*-jö-nöl) *adj* incondicional

unconscious (an-*kon*-jöss) *adj* inconsciente

uncork (an-*kook*) *v* descorchar

uncover (an-*ka*-vö) *v* destapar

uncultivated (an-*kal*-ti-vei-tid) *adj* inculto

under (*an*-dö) *prep* debajo de, bajo

undercurrent (*an*-dö-ka-rönt) *n* resaca *f*

underestimate (an-dö-*rê*-ssti-meit) *v* subestimar

underground (*an*-dö-ghraund) *adj* subterráneo; *n* metro *m*

underline (an-dö-*lain*) *v* subrayar

underneath (an-dö-*niiz*) *adv* debajo

undershirt (*an*-dö-ʃööt) *n* camiseta *f*

undersigned (*an*-dö-ssaind) *n* suscrito *m*

*****understand** (an-dö-*sstænd*) *v* comprender

understanding (an-dö-*sstæn*-ding) *n* comprensión *m*

*****undertake** (an-dö-*teik*) *v* emprender

undertaking (an-dö-*tei*-king) *n* empresa *f*

underwater (*an*-dö-ᵘoo-tö) *adj* subacuático

underwear (*an*-dö-ᵘêᵒ) *n* ropa interior

undesirable (an-di-*saiᵒ*-rö-böl) *adj* indeseable

*****undo** (an-*duu*) *v* desatar

undoubtedly (an-*dau*-tid-li) *adv* sin duda

undress (an-*drêss*) *v* desnudarse

undulating (*an*-dyu-lei-ting) *adj* ondulante

unearned (a-*nöönd*) *adj* inmerecido

uneasy (a-*nii*-si) *adj* inquieto

uneducated (a-*nê*-dyu-kei-tid) *adj* inculto

unemployed (a-nim-*ploid*) *adj* desocupado

unemployment (a-nim-*ploi*-mönt) *n* desempleo *m*

unequal (a-*nii*-kᵘöl) *adj* desigual

uneven (a-*nii*-vön) *adj* desigual; irregular

unexpected (a-nik-*sspêk*-tid) *adj* imprevisto, inesperado

unfair (an-*fêᵒ*) *adj* improbo, injusto

unfaithful (an-*feiz*-föl) *adj* infiel

unfamiliar (an-fö-*mil*-yö) *adj* desconocido

unfasten (an-*faa*-ssön) *v* desatar

unfavourable (an-*fei*-vö-rö-böl) *adj* desfavorable

unfit (an-*fit*) *adj* inadecuado

unfold (an-*fould*) *v* *desplegar

unfortunate (an-*foo*-chö-nöt) *adj* desafortunado

unfortunately (an-*foo*-chö-nöt-li) *adv* por desgracia, desgraciadamente

unfriendly (an-*frênd*-li) *adj* poco amistoso

unfurnished (an-*föö*-niʃt) *adj* desamueblado

ungrateful (an-*ghreit*-föl) *adj* ingrato

unhappy (an-*hæ*-pi) *adj* desdichado

unhealthy (an-*hêl*-zi) *adj* insalubre

unhurt (an-*hööt*) *adj* ileso

uniform (*yuu*-ni-foom) *n* uniforme *m*; *adj* uniforme

unimportant (a-nim-*poo*-tönt) *adj* insignificante

uninhabitable (a-nin-*hæ*-bi-tö-böl) *adj* inhabitable

uninhabited (a-nin-*hæ*-bi-tid) *adj* inhabitado

unintentional (a-nin-*tên*-ʃö-nöl) *adj* no intencional

union (*yuu*-nyön) *n* unión *f*; liga *f*, confederación *f*

unique (yuu-*niik*) *adj* único

unit (*yuu*-nit) *n* unidad *f*

unite (yuu-*nait*) *v* unir

United States (yuu-*nai*-tid ssteitss) Estados Unidos

unity (*yuu*-nö-ti) *n* unidad *f*

universal (yuu-ni-*vöö*-ssöl) *adj* general, universal

universe (yuu-ni-vööss) *n* universo *m*

university (yuu-ni-vöö-ssö-ti) *n* universidad *f*

unjust (an-dʒasst) *adj* injusto

unkind (an-kaind) *adj* desagradable, arisco

unknown (an-noun) *adj* desconocido

unlawful (an-loo-föl) *adj* ilegal

unlearn (an-löön) *v* desacostumbrar

unless (ön-léss) *conj* a menos que

unlike (an-laik) *adj* diferente

unlikely (an-lai-kli) *adj* improbable

unlimited (an-li-mi-tid) *adj* ilimitado

unload (an-loud) *v* descargar

unlock (an-lok) *v* abrir

unlucky (an-la-ki) *adj* desafortunado

unnecessary (an-nê-ssö-ssö-ri) *adj* innecesario

unoccupied (a-no-kyu-paid) *adj* desocupado

unofficial (a-nö-fi-jöl) *adj* extraoficial

unpack (an-pæk) *v* desempaquetar

unpleasant (an-plé-sönt) *adj* desagradable; antipático

unpopular (an-po-pyu-lö) *adj* impopular

unprotected (an-prö-têk-tid) *adj* indefenso

unqualified (an-kᵘo-li-faid) *adj* incompetente

unreal (an-riⁱöl) *adj* irreal

unreasonable (an-rii-sö-nö-böl) *adj* irrazonable

unreliable (an-ri-lai-ö-böl) *adj* no confiable

unrest (an-rêsst) *n* desasosiego *m*; inquietud *f*

unsafe (an-sseif) *adj* inseguro

unsatisfactory (an-ssæ-tiss-fæk-tö-ri) *adj* poco satisfactorio

unscrew (an-sskruu) *v* destornillar

unselfish (an-ssêl-fiʃ) *adj* desinteresado

unskilled (an-sskild) *adj* no especializado

unsound (an-ssaund) *adj* enfermizo

unstable (an-sstei-böl) *adj* inestable

unsteady (an-sstê-di) *adj* vacilante, inestable

unsuccessful (an-ssök-ssêss-föl) *adj* fracasado

unsuitable (an-ssuu-tö-böl) *adj* inadecuado

unsurpassed (an-ssö-paasst) *adj* sin igual

untidy (an-tai-di) *adj* desaliñado

untie (an-tai) *v* desatar

until (ön-til) *prep* hasta

untrue (an-truu) *adj* falso

untrustworthy (an-trasst-ᵘöö-ði) *adj* indigno de confianza

unusual (an-yuu-ʒu-öl) *adj* inusitado, insólito

unwell (an-ᵘêl) *adj* indispuesto

unwilling (an-ᵘi-ling) *adj* desinclinado

unwise (an-ᵘais) *adj* imprudente

unwrap (an-ræp) *v* *desenvolver

up (ap) *adv* hacia arriba, arriba

upholster (ap-houl-sstö) *v* tapizar

upkeep (ap-kiip) *n* manutención *f*

uplands (ap-lönds) *pl* altiplano *m*

upon (ö-pon) *prep* sobre

upper (a-pö) *adj* superior

upright (ap-rait) *adj* derecho; *adv* de pie

upset (ap-ssêt) *v* trastornar; *adj* trastornado

upside-down (ap-ssaid-daun) *adv* al revés

upstairs (ap-sstêᵒs) *adv* arriba

upstream (ap-sstriim) *adv* río arriba

upwards (ap-ᵘöds) *adv* hacia arriba

urban (öö-bön) *adj* urbano

urge (öödʒ) *v* estimular; *n* impulso *m*

urgency (öö-dʒön-ssi) *n* urgencia *f*

urgent (öö-dʒönt) *adj* urgente

urine (*yu⁰*-rin) *n* orina *f*
Uruguay (*yu⁰*-rö-gh*u*ai) Uruguay *m*
Uruguayan (yu⁰-rö-*gh*u*ai-ön) *adj* uruguayo
us (ass) *pron* nosotros
usable (*yuu*-sö-böl) *adj* utilizable
usage (*yuu*-sidʒ) *n* uso *m*
use¹ (yuus) *v* usar; *be used to* *estar acostumbrado a; ~ up* consumir
use² (yuuss) *n* uso *m*; utilidad *f*; *be of ~* *servir
useful (*yuuss*-föl) *adj* útil
useless (*yuuss*-löss) *adj* inútil
user (*yuu*-sö) *n* usuario *m*
usher (*a*-ʃö) *n* acomodador *m*
usherette (a-ʃö-*rêt*) *n* acomodadora *f*
usual (*yuu*-ʒu-öl) *adj* usual
usually (*yuu*-ʒu-ö-li) *adv* habitualmente
utensil (yuu-*tên*-ssöl) *n* herramienta *f*, utensilio *m*
utility (yuu-*ti*-lö-ti) *n* utilidad *f*
utilize (*yuu*-ti-lais) *v* utilizar
utmost (*at*-mousst) *adj* extremo
utter (*a*-tö) *adj* completo, total; *v* emitir

V

vacancy (*vei*-kön-ssi) *n* vacante *f*
vacant (*vei*-könt) *adj* vacante
vacate (vö-*keit*) *v* vaciar
vacation (vö-*kei*-ʃön) *n* vacaciones *fpl*
vaccinate (*væk*-ssi-neit) *v* vacunar
vaccination (væk-ssi-*nei*-ʃön) *n* vacunación *f*
vacuum (*væ*-kyu-öm) *n* vacío *m*; ~ **cleaner** aspirador *m*; ~ **flask** termo *m*
vagrancy (*vei*-ghrön-ssi) *n* vagancia *f*
vague (veigh) *adj* vago
vain (vein) *adj* vanidoso; vano; *in ~*

inútilmente, en vano
valet (*væ*-lit) *n* ayuda de cámara
valid (*væ*-lid) *adj* vigente
valley (*væ*-li) *n* valle *m*
valuable (*væ*-lyu-böl) *adj* valioso; **valuables** *pl* objetos de valor
value (*væ*-lyuu) *n* valor *m*; *v* valuar
valve (vælv) *n* válvula *f*
van (væn) *n* camioneta *f*
vanilla (vö-*ni*-lö) *n* vainilla *f*
vanish (*væ*-niʃ) *v* *desaparecer
vapour (*vei*-pö) *n* vapor *m*
variable (*vê⁰*-ri-ö-böl) *adj* variable
variation (vê⁰-ri-*ei*-ʃön) *n* variación *f*; cambio *m*
varied (*vê⁰*-rid) *adj* variado
variety (vö-*rai*-ö-ti) *n* variedad *f*; ~ **show** espectáculo de variedades; ~ **theatre** teatro de variedades
various (*vê⁰*-ri-öss) *adj* varios
varnish (vaa-niʃ) *n* barniz *m*; *v* barnizar
vary (*vê⁰*-ri) *v* variar; cambiar; *diferir
vase (vaas) *n* vaso *m*
vaseline (*væ*-ssö-liin) *n* vaselina *f*
vast (vaasst) *adj* vasto
vault (voolt) *n* bóveda *f*; caja de caudales
veal (viil) *n* carne de ternera
vegetable (*vê*-dʒö-tö-böl) *n* legumbre *f*
vegetarian (vê-dʒi-*tê⁰*-ri-ön) *n* vegetariano *m*
vegetation (vê-dʒi-*tei*-ʃön) *n* vegetación *f*
vehicle (*vii*-ö-köl) *n* vehículo *m*
veil (veil) *n* velo *m*
vein (vein) *n* vena *f*; **varicose** ~ varice *f*
velvet (*vêl*-vit) *n* terciopelo *m*
velveteen (vêl-vi-*tiin*) *n* pana *f*
venerable (*vê*-nö-rö-böl) *adj* venerable

venereal disease (vi-*ni*ᵒ-ri-öl di-*siis*) enfermedad venérea

Venezuela (vê-ni-s*u*ei-lö) Venezuela *f*

Venezuelan (vê-ni-s*u*ei-lön) *adj* venezolano

ventilate (*vên*-ti-leit) *v* ventilar; airear

ventilation (vên-ti-*lei*-ʃön) *n* ventilación *f*; aireo *m*

ventilator (*vên*-ti-lei-tö) *n* ventilador *m*

venture (*vên*-chö) *v* arriesgar

veranda (vö-*ræn*-dö) *n* veranda *f*

verb (vööb) *n* verbo *m*

verbal (*vöö*-böl) *adj* verbal

verdict (*vöö*-dikt) *n* sentencia *f*, veredicto *m*

verge (vöödʒ) *n* borde *m*

verify (*vê*-ri-fai) *v* verificar

verse (vööss) *n* verso *m*

version (*vöö*-ʃön) *n* versión *f*

versus (*vöö*-ssöss) *prep* contra

vertical (*vöö*-ti-köl) *adj* vertical

vertigo (*vöö*-ti-ghou) *n* vértigo *m*

very (*vê*-ri) *adv* mucho, muy; *adj* preciso, verdadero; extremo

vessel (*vê*-ssöl) *n* embarcación *f*, buque *m*; vasija *f*

vest (vêsst) *n* camiseta *f*; *nAm* chaleco *m*

veterinary surgeon (*vê*-tri-nö-ri *ssöö*-dʒön) veterinario *m*

via (vaiᵒ) *prep* por

viaduct (*vai*ᵒ-dakt) *n* viaducto *m*

vibrate (vai-*breit*) *v* vibrar

vibration (vai-*brei*-ʃön) *n* vibración *f*

vicar (*vi*-kö) *n* vicario *m*

vicarage (*vi*-kö-ridʒ) *n* casa del párroco

vice-president (vaiss-*prê*-si-dönt) *n* vicepresidente *m*

vicinity (vi-*ssi*-nö-ti) *n* vecindad *f*

vicious (*vi*-ʃöss) *adj* vicioso

victim (*vik*-tim) *n* víctima *f*

victory (*vik*-tö-ri) *n* victoria *f*

view (vyuu) *n* vista *f*; parecer *m*, opinión *f*; *v* mirar

view-finder (*vyuu*-fain-dö) *n* visor *m*

vigilant (*vi*-dʒi-lönt) *adj* despierto

villa (*vi*-lö) *n* villa *f*

village (*vi*-lidʒ) *n* pueblo *m*

villain (*vi*-lön) *n* villano *m*

vine (vain) *n* vid *f*

vinegar (*vi*-ni-ghö) *n* vinagre *m*

vineyard (*vin*-yöd) *n* viña *f*

vintage (*vin*-tidʒ) *n* vendimia *f*

violation (vaiᵒ-*lei*-ʃön) *n* violación *f*

violence (*vai*ᵒ-lönss) *n* violencia *f*

violent (*vai*ᵒ-lönt) *adj* violento; impetuoso

violet (*vai*ᵒ-löt) *n* violeta *f*; *adj* morado

violin (vaiᵒ-*lin*) *n* violín *m*

virgin (*vöö*-dʒin) *n* virgen *f*

virtue (*vöö*-chuu) *n* virtud *f*

visa (*vii*-sö) *n* visado *m*

visibility (vi-sö-*bi*-lö-ti) *n* visibilidad *f*

visible (*vi*-sö-böl) *adj* visible

vision (*vi*-ʒön) *n* visión *f*

visit (*vi*-sit) *v* visitar; *n* visita *f*; **visiting hours** horas de visita

visiting-card (*vi*-si-ting-kaad) *n* tarjeta de visita

visitor (*vi*-si-tö) *n* visitante *m*

vital (*vai*-töl) *adj* esencial

vitamin (*vi*-tö-min) *n* vitamina *f*

vivid (*vi*-vid) *adj* vivo

vocabulary (vö-*kæ*-byu-lö-ri) *n* vocabulario *m*; glosario *m*

vocal (*vou*-köl) *adj* vocal

vocalist (*vou*-kö-lisst) *n* vocalista *m*

voice (voiss) *n* voz *f*

void (void) *adj* nulo

volcano (vol-*kei*-nou) *n* (pl ~es, ~s) volcán *m*

volt (voult) *n* voltio *m*

voltage (*voul*-tidʒ) *n* voltaje *m*

volume (*vo*-lyum) *n* volumen *m*; tomo *m*

voluntary (*vo*-lön-tö-ri) *adj* voluntario

volunteer (vo-lön-*ti*ŏ) *n* voluntario *m*

vomit (*vo*-mit) *v* vomitar

vote (vout) *v* votar; *n* voto *m*; votación *f*

voucher (*vau*-chö) *n* recibo *m*, comprobante *m*

vow (vau) *n* voto *m*, juramento *m*; *v* prestar juramento

vowel (vau^ŏl) *n* vocal *f*

voyage (*voi*-idʒ) *n* viaje *m*

vulgar (*val*-ghö) *adj* vulgar; popular, ordinario

vulnerable (*val*-nö-rö-böl) *adj* vulnerable

vulture (*val*-chö) *n* buitre *m*

W

wade (^ueid) *v* vadear

wafer (*^uei*-fö) *n* oblea *f*

waffle (*^uo*-föl) *n* barquillo *m*

wages (*^uei*-dʒis) *pl* paga *f*

waggon (*^uæ*-ghön) *n* vagón *m*

waist (^ueisst) *n* cintura *f*

waistcoat (*^ueiss*-kout) *n* chaleco *m*

wait (^ueit) *v* esperar; ~ **on** *servir

waiter (*^uei*-tö) *n* camarero *m*; mesero *mMe*

waiting *n* espera *f*

waiting-list (*^uei*-ting-lisst) *n* lista de espera

waiting-room (*^uei*-ting-ruum) *n* sala de espera

waitress (*^uei*-triss) *n* camarera *f*; mesera *fMe*

***wake** (^ueik) *v* *despertar; ~ **up** *despertarse

walk (^uook) *v* *andar; pasear; *n* caminata *f*; andadura *f*; **walking** a pie

walker (*^uoo*-kö) *n* paseante *m*

walking-stick (*^uoo*-king-sstik) *n* bastón *m*

wall (^uool) *n* muro *m*; pared *f*

wallet (*^uo*-lit) *n* cartera *f*

wallpaper (*^uool*-pei-pö) *n* papel pintado

walnut (*^uool*-nat) *n* nogal *m*

waltz (^uoolss) *n* vals *m*

wander (*^uon*-dö) *v* vagar, *errar

want (^uont) *v* *querer; desear; *n* necesidad *f*; carencia *f*, falta *f*

war (^uoo) *n* guerra *f*

warden (*^uoo*-dön) *n* guardián *m*

wardrobe (*^uoo*-droub) *n* guardarropa *m*, vestuario *m*

warehouse (*^uê</sup>ŏ*-hauss) *n* almacén *m*

wares (^uê^ŏs) *pl* mercancías *fpl*

warm (^uoom) *adj* caliente; *v* *calentar

warmth (^uoomz) *n* calor *m*

warn (^uoon) *v* *advertir

warning (*^uoo*-ning) *n* advertencia *f*

wary (*^uê</sup>ŏ*-ri) *adj* prudente

was (^uos) *v* (p be)

wash (^uoʃ) *v* lavar; ~ **and wear** no precisa plancha; ~ **up** *fregar

washable (*^uo*-ʃö-böl) *adj* lavable

wash-basin (*^uoʃ*-bei-ssön) *n* palangana *f*

washing (*^uo*-ʃing) *n* lavado *m*; ropa sucia

washing-machine (*^uo*-ʃing-mö-ʃiin) *n* máquina de lavar

washing-powder (*^uo*-ʃing-pau-dö) *n* jabón en polvo

washroom (*^uoʃ*-ruum) *nAm* cuarto de aseo

wash-stand (*^uoʃ*-sstænd) *n* lavabo *m*

wasp (^uossp) *n* avispa *f*

waste (^ueisst) *v* *perder; *n* desperdicio *m*; *adj* baldío

wasteful (*^ueisst*-föl) *adj* derrochador

wastepaper-basket (*^ueisst*-*pei*-pö-baa-sskit) *n* cesto para papeles

watch (ᵘoch) v mirar, observar; vigilar; n reloj m; ~ **for** acechar; ~ **out** *tener cuidado

watch-maker (ᵘoch-mei-kö) n relojero m

watch-strap (ᵘoch-sstræp) n correa de reloj

water (ᵘoo-tö) n agua f; **iced** ~ agua helada; **running** ~ agua corriente; ~ **pump** bomba de agua; ~ **ski** esqui acuático

water-colour (ᵘoo-tö-ka-lö) n color de aguada; acuarela f

watercress (ᵘoo-tö-krêss) n berro m

waterfall (ᵘoo-tö-fool) n cascada f

watermelon (ᵘoo-tö-mê-lön) n sandía f

waterproof (ᵘoo-tö-pruuf) adj impermeable

water-softener (ᵘoo-tö-ssof-nö) n ablandador m

waterway (ᵘoo-tö-ᵘei) n vía navegable

watt (ᵘot) n vatio m

wave (ᵘeiv) n ondulación f, ola f; v *hacer señales

wave-length (ᵘeiv-lêngz) n longitud de onda

wavy (ᵘei-vi) adj ondulado

wax (ᵘækss) n cera f

waxworks (ᵘækss-ᵘöökss) pl museo de figuras de cera

way (ᵘei) n manera f; camino m; lado m, dirección f; distancia f; **any** ~ de todos modos; **by the** ~ a propósito; **one-way traffic** dirección única; **out of the** ~ apartado; **the other** ~ **round** al revés; ~ **back** vuelta f; ~ **in** entrada f; ~ **out** salida f

wayside (ᵘei-ssaid) n borde del camino

we (ᵘii) pron nosotros

weak (ᵘiik) adj débil; flojo

weakness (ᵘiik-nöss) n debilidad f

wealth (ᵘêlz) n riqueza f

wealthy (ᵘêl-zi) adj rico

weapon (ᵘê-pön) n arma f

*wear (ᵘêⁿ) v llevar; ~ **out** gastar

weary (ᵘiⁿ-ri) adj cansado

weather (ᵘê-öö) n tiempo m; ~ **forecast** boletín meteorológico

*weave (ᵘiiv) v tejer

weaver (ᵘii-vö) n tejedor m

wedding (ᵘê-ding) n matrimonio m, boda f

wedding-ring (ᵘê-ding-ring) n anillo de boda

wedge (ᵘêdʒ) n cuña f

Wednesday (ᵘêns-di) miércoles m

weed (ᵘiid) n mala hierba

week (ᵘiik) n semana f

weekday (ᵘiik-dei) n día laborable

weekend (ᵘii-kênd) n fin de semana

weekly (ᵘii-kli) adj semanal

*weep (ᵘiip) v llorar

weigh (ᵘei) v pesar

weighing-machine (ᵘei-ing-mö-ʃiin) n báscula f

weight (ᵘeit) n peso m

welcome (ᵘêl-köm) adj bienvenido; n bienvenida f; v *dar la bienvenida

weld (ᵘêld) v *soldar

welfare (ᵘêl-fêⁿ) n bienestar m

well¹ (ᵘêl) adv bien; adj sano; **as** ~ también; **as** ~ **as** así como; **well!** ¡bueno!

well² (ᵘêl) n pozo m

well-founded (ᵘêl-faun-did) adj fundamentado

well-known (ᵘêl-noun) adj notorio

well-to-do (ᵘêl-tö-duu) adj acomodado

went (ᵘênt) v (p go)

were (ᵘöö) v (p be)

west (ᵘêsst) n occidente m, oeste m

westerly (ᵘê-sstö-li) adj occidental

western (ᵘê-sstön) adj occidental

wet (ᵘêt) *adj* mojado; húmedo
whale (ᵘeil) *n* ballena *f*
wharf (ᵘoof) *n* (pl ~s, wharves) muelle *m*
what (ᵘot) *pron* qué; lo que; ~ **for** para que
whatever (ᵘo-tê-vö) *pron* cualquier cosa que
wheat (ᵘiit) *n* trigo *m*
wheel (ᵘiil) *n* rueda *f*
wheelbarrow (ᵘiil-bæ-rou) *n* carretilla *f*
wheelchair (ᵘiil-chêᵒ) *n* silla de ruedas
when (ᵘên) *adv* cuándo; *conj* cuando
whenever (ᵘê-nê-vö) *conj* cuando quiera que
where (ᵘêᵒ) *adv* dónde; *conj* donde
wherever (ᵘêᵒ-rê-vö) *conj* dondequiera que
whether (ᵘê-ðö) *conj* si; **whether ... or** si ... o
which (ᵘich) *pron* cuál; que
whichever (ᵘi-chê-vö) *adj* cualquiera
while (ᵘail) *conj* mientras; *n* rato *m*
whilst (ᵘailsst) *conj* mientras
whim (ᵘim) *n* antojo *m*, capricho *m*
whip (ᵘip) *n* azote *m*; *v* batir
whiskers (ᵘi-sskös) *pl* patillas *fpl*
whisper (ᵘi-sspö) *v* susurrar; *n* susurro *m*
whistle (ᵘi-ssöl) *v* silbar; *n* silbato *m*
white (ᵘait) *adj* blanco
whitebait (ᵘait-beit) *n* boquerón *m*
whiting (ᵘai-ting) *n* (pl ~) merluza *f*
Whitsun (ᵘit-ssön) Pentecostés *m*
who (huu) *pron* quien; que
whoever (huu-ê-vö) *pron* quienquiera
whole (houl) *adj* completo, entero; intacto; *n* total *m*
wholesale (houl-sseil) *n* venta al por mayor; ~ **dealer** mayorista *m*
wholesome (houl-ssöm) *adj* saludable
wholly (houl-li) *adv* totalmente

whom (huum) *pron* a quien
whore (hoo) *n* puta *f*
whose (huus) *pron* cuyo; de quien
why (ᵘai) *adv* por qué
wicked (ᵘi-kid) *adj* malvado
wide (ᵘaid) *adj* vasto, ancho
widen (ᵘai-dön) *v* ensanchar
widow (ᵘi-dou) *n* viuda *f*
widower (ᵘi-dou-ö) *n* viudo *m*
width (ᵘidz) *n* anchura *f*
wife (ᵘaif) *n* (pl wives) esposa *f*, mujer *f*
wig (ᵘigh) *n* peluca *f*
wild (ᵘaild) *adj* salvaje; feroz
will (ᵘil) *n* voluntad *f*; testamento *m*
***will** (ᵘil) *v* *querer
willing (ᵘi-ling) *adj* dispuesto
willingly (ᵘi-ling-li) *adv* gustosamente
will-power (ᵘil-pauᵒ) *n* fuerza de voluntad
***win** (ᵘin) *v* vencer
wind (ᵘind) *n* viento *m*
***wind** (ᵘaind) *v* serpentear; *dar cuerda, enrollar
winding (ᵘain-ding) *adj* tortuoso
windmill (ᵘind-mil) *n* molino de viento
window (ᵘin-dou) *n* ventana *f*
window-sill (ᵘin-dou-ssil) *n* antepecho *m*
windscreen (ᵘind-sskriin) *n* parabrisas *m*; ~ **wiper** limpiaparabrisas *m*
windshield (ᵘind-fiild) *nAm* parabrisas *m*
windy (ᵘin-di) *adj* ventoso
wine (ᵘain) *n* vino *m*
wine-cellar (ᵘain-ssê-lö) *n* cueva *f*
wine-list (ᵘain-lisst) *n* carta de vinos
wine-merchant (ᵘain-möö-chönt) *n* vinatero *m*
wine-waiter (ᵘain-ᵘei-tö) *n* camarero *m*
wing (ᵘing) *n* ala *f*
winkle (ᵘing-köl) *n* caracol marino

winner (ᵘi-nö) n vencedor m

winning (ᵘi-ning) adj ganador; **winnings** pl ganancias fpl

winter (ᵘin-tö) n invierno m; ~ **sports** deportes de invierno

wipe (ᵘaip) v enjugar

wire (ᵘaiö) n alambre m

wireless (ᵘaiö-löss) n radio f

wisdom (ᵘis-döm) n sabiduría f

wise (ᵘais) adj sabio

wish (ᵘiʃ) v desear; n deseo m

witch (ᵘich) n bruja f

with (ᵘið) prep con; de

***withdraw** (ᵘið-droo) v retirar

within (ᵘi-ðin) prep dentro de; adv de dentro

without (ᵘi-ðaut) prep sin

witness (ᵘit-nöss) n testigo m

wits (ᵘitss) pl razón f

witty (ᵘi-ti) adj chistoso

wolf (ᵘulf) n (pl wolves) lobo m

woman (ᵘu-mön) n (pl women) mujer f

womb (ᵘuum) n matriz f

won (ᵘan) v (p, pp win)

wonder (ᵘan-dö) v milagro m; asombro m; v preguntarse

wonderful (ᵘan-dö-föl) adj estupendo, maravilloso; delicioso

wood (ᵘud) n madera f; bosque m

wood-carving (ᵘud-kaa-ving) n talla f

wooded (ᵘu-did) adj selvoso

wooden (ᵘu-dön) adj de madera; ~ **shoe** zueco m

woodland (ᵘud-lönd) n arbolado m

wool (ᵘul) n lana f; **darning** ~ hilo de zurcir

woollen (ᵘu-lön) adj de lana

word (ᵘööd) n palabra f

wore (ᵘoo) v (p wear)

work (ᵘöök) n obra f; trabajo m; v trabajar; funcionar; **working day** día de trabajo; ~ **of art** obra de arte; ~ **permit** permiso de trabajo

worker (ᵘö-kö) n obrero m

working (ᵘöö-king) n funcionamiento m

workman (ᵘöök-mön) n (pl -men) obrero m

works (ᵘöökss) pl fábrica f

workshop (ᵘöök-ʃop) n taller m

world (ᵘööld) n mundo m; ~ **war** guerra mundial

world-famous (ᵘööld-fei-möss) adj de fama mundial

world-wide (ᵘööld-ᵘaid) adj mundial

worm (ᵘööm) n gusano m

worn (ᵘoon) adj (pp wear) gastado

worn-out (ᵘoon-aut) adj gastado

worried (ᵘa-rid) adj inquieto

worry (ᵘa-ri) v inquietarse; n preocupación f, inquietud f

worse (ᵘööss) adj peor; adv peor

worship (ᵘöö-ʃip) v venerar; n culto m

worst (ᵘöösst) adj pésimo; adv peor

worsted (ᵘu-sstid) n estambre m/f

worth (ᵘööz) n valor m; ***be** ~ *valer; ***be worth-while** *valer la pena

worthless (ᵘööz-löss) adj sin valor

worthy of (ᵘöö-ði öv) digno de

would (ᵘud) v (p will) *soler

wound¹ (ᵘuund) n herida f; v ofender, *herir

wound² (ᵘaund) v (p, pp wind)

wrap (ræp) v *envolver

wreck (rêk) n pecio m; v *destruir

wrench (rênch) n llave f; tirón m; v dislocar

wrinkle (ring-köl) n arruga f

wrist (risst) n muñeca f

wrist-watch (risst-ᵘoch) n reloj de pulsera

***write** (rait) v escribir; **in writing** por escrito; ~ **down** anotar

writer (rai-tö) n escritor m

writing-pad (rai-ting-pæd) n bloque m; bloc mMe

writing-paper (*rai*-ting-pei-pö) *n* papel de escribir

written (*ri*-tön) *adj* (pp write) por escrito

wrong (rong) *adj* impropio, erróneo; *n* mal *m*; *v* agraviar; *be* ~ no *tener razón

wrote (rout) *v* (p write)

X

Xmas (*kriss*-möss) Navidad *f*

X-ray (*êkss*-rei) *n* radiografía *f*; *v* radiografiar

Y

yacht (yot) *n* yate *m*

yacht-club (*yot*-klab) *n* club de yates

yachting (*yo*-ting) *n* deporte de vela

yard (yaad) *n* corral *m*

yarn (yaan) *n* hilo *m*

yawn (yoon) *v* bostezar

year (yi⁰) *n* año *m*

yearly (*yi⁰*-li) *adj* anual

yeast (yiisst) *n* levadura *f*

yell (yêl) *v* gritar; *n* grito *m*

yellow (*yê*-lou) *adj* amarillo

yes (yêss) sí

yesterday (*yê*-sstö-di) *adv* ayer

yet (yêt) *adv* aun; *conj* pero, sin embargo

yield (yiild) *v* producir; ceder

yoke (youk) *n* yugo *m*

yolk (youk) *n* yema *f*

you (yuu) *pron* tú; a ti; usted; a usted; vosotros; os; ustedes

young (yang) *adj* joven

your (yoo) *adj* de usted; tu; vuestro, tuyos

yourself (yoo-*ssêlf*) *pron* te; tú mismo; usted mismo

yourselves (yoo-*ssêlvs*) *pron* se; vosotros mismos; ustedes mismos

youth (yuuz) *n* juventud *f*; ~ **hostel** albergue para jóvenes

Yugoslav (yuu-ghö-*sslaav*) *n* yugoslavo *m*

Yugoslavia (yuu-ghö-*sslaa*-vi-ö) Yugoslavia *f*

Z

zeal (siil) *n* celo *m*

zealous (*sê*-löss) *adj* celoso

zebra (*sii*-brö) *n* cebra *f*

zenith (*sê*-niz) *n* cenit *m*; apogeo *m*

zero (*si⁰*-rou) *n* (pl ~s) cero *m*

zest (sêsst) *n* energía *f*

zinc (singk) *n* cinc *m*

zip (sip) *n* cremallera *f*; ~ **code** *Am* código postal

zipper (*si*-pö) *n* cierre relámpago

zodiac (*sou*-di-æk) *n* zodíaco *m*

zone (soun) *n* zona *f*; región *f*

zoo (suu) *n* (pl ~s) jardín zoológico

zoology (sou-*o*-lö-dʒi) *n* zoología *f*

Léxico gastronómico

Comidas

almond almendra
anchovy anchoa
angel food cake pastel confeccionado con clara de huevo
angels on horseback ostras envueltas en tocino, asadas y servidas en pan tostado
appetizer entremés
apple manzana
~ **charlotte** pastel de compota de manzanas y pan rallado
~ **dumpling** pastel de manzanas
~ **sauce** puré de manzanas
apricot albaricoque
Arbroath smoky róbalo ahumado
artichoke alcachofa
asparagus espárrago
~ **tip** punta de espárrago
aspic (en) gelatina
assorted variado
aubergine berenjena
avocado (pear) aguacate
bacon tocino
~ **and eggs** huevos con tocino
bagel panecillo en forma de corona
baked al horno
~ **Alaska** helado cubierto con merengue, dorado en el horno;

se sirve flameado como postre
~ **beans** judías blancas en salsa de tomates
~ **potato** patata sin pelar cocida al horno
Bakewell tart pastel de almendras con mermelada de frambuesas
baloney especie de mortadela
banana plátano
~ **split** dos mitades de plátano servidas con helado y nueces, rociadas con almíbar o crema de chocolate
barbecue 1) carne picada de ternera en una salsa a base de tomates, servida en un panecillo 2) comida al aire libre
~ **sauce** salsa de tomates muy picante
barbecued asado a la parrilla con carbón de leña
basil albahaca
bass lubina (pescado)
bean judía, haba, fríjol
beef carne de ternera
~ **olive** rollo de carne de ternera
beefburger bistec de carne picada, asado y a veces servido en un panecillo

beet, beetroot remolacha
bilberry arándano
bill cuenta
  ~ **of fare** lista de platos
biscuit 1) galleta (GB) 2) panecillo (US)
black pudding morcilla
blackberry zarzamora
blackcurrant grosella negra
bloater arenque salado, ahumado
blood sausage morcilla
blueberry arándano
boiled hervido
Bologna (sausage) especie de mortadela
bone hueso
boned deshuesado
Boston baked beans judías blancas con tocino y melaza
Boston cream pie torta rellena de nata en capas superpuestas, cubierta de chocolate
brains sesos
braised asado
bramble pudding pudín de zarzamoras (a menudo con manzanas)
braunschweiger salchichón de hígado ahumado
bread pan
breaded empanado
breakfast desayuno
bream brema (pescado)
breast pecho, pechuga
brisket pecho
broad bean haba
broth caldo
brown Betty especie de compota de manzanas, con especias y cubierta de pan rallado
brunch comida que reemplaza el desayuno y el almuerzo
brussels sprout col de Bruselas
bubble and squeak patatas y coles

picadas que se fríen, mezcladas a veces con trozos de carne de ternera (especie de tortilla)
bun 1) panecillo dulce confeccionado con frutas secas 2) especie de panecillo (US)
butter mantequilla
buttered con mantequilla
cabbage col, repollo
Caesar salad ensalada verde con ajo, anchoas, cuscurro y queso rallado
cake pastel, torta
cakes galletas, pastelillos
calf ternera
Canadian bacon lomo de cerdo ahumado que se corta en lonchas finas
cantaloupe melón
caper alcaparra
capercaillie, capercailzie urogallo grande
caramel caramelo
carp carpa
carrot zanahoria
cashew anacardo
casserole cacerola
catfish siluro (pescado)
catsup salsa de tomate
cauliflower coliflor
celery apio
cereal cereal
  hot ~ gachas
chateaubriand solomillo de ternera
check cuenta
Cheddar (cheese) queso de textura firme y de sabor ligeramente ácido
cheese queso
  ~ **board** bandeja de quesos
  ~ **cake** pastel de queso doble crema, ligeramente azucarado
cheeseburger bistec de carne pica-

da, asado con una loncha de queso, servido en un panecillo

chef's salad ensalada de jamón, pollo, huevos cocidos, tomates, lechuga y queso

cherry cereza

chestnut castaña

chicken pollo

chicory 1) endibia (GB) 2) escarola, achicoria (US)

chili pepper chile, ají

chips 1) patatas fritas (GB) 2) chips (US)

chitt(er)lings tripas de cerdo

chive cebolleta

choice elección, surtido

chop costilla

~ **suey** plato hecho con carne picada de cerdo o de pollo, arroz y legumbres

chopped picado

chowder sopa espesa a base de mariscos

Christmas pudding pudín inglés hecho con frutas secas, a veces flameado, muy nutritivo y que se sirve en Navidad

chutney condimento indio muy sazonado, con sabor agridulce

cinnamon canela

clam almeja

club sandwich bocadillo doble con tocino, pollo, tomates, lechuga y mayonesa

cobbler compota de frutas cubierta con una capa de pasta

cock-a-leekie soup sopa de pollo y puerros

coconut coco

cod bacalao

Colchester oyster ostra inglesa muy afamada

cold cuts/meat fiambres

coleslaw ensalada de col

compote compota

condiment condimento

cooked cocido

cookie galleta

corn 1) trigo (GB) 2) maíz (US)
~ **on the cob** mazorca de maíz

cornflakes copos de maíz

corned beef carne de ternera sazonada

cottage cheese requesón

cottage pie carne picada que se cuece con cebollas y se cubre con puré de patatas

course plato

cover charge precio del cubierto

crab cangrejo de mar

cracker galletita salada

cranberry arándano agrio
~ **sauce** mermelada de arándanos agrios

crawfish, crayfish 1) cangrejo de río 2) langosta (GB) 3) langostino (US)

cream 1) nata 2) crema (sopa) 3) crema (postre)
~ **cheese** queso doble crema
~ **puff** pastelillo con nata

creamed potatoes patatas cortadas en forma de dados en salsa blanca

creole plato muy condimentado con tomates, pimientos y cebollas; suele servirse con arroz blanco

cress berro

crisps patatas a la inglesa, chips

croquette croqueta

crumpet especie de panecillo redondo, asado y untado de mantequilla

cucumber pepino

Cumberland ham jamón ahumado, muy conocido

Cumberland sauce jalea de grosellas sazonada de vino, jugo de naranja y especias

cupcake pastellillo, hojaldre

cured salado y ahumado

currant 1) pasa de Corinto 2) grosella

curried con curry

custard 1) crema 2) flan

cutlet 1) chuleta 2) escalope 3) fina lonja de carne

dab lenguado

Danish pastry pastellillos hojaldrados

date dátil

Derby cheese queso blando picante, de color amarillo claro

dessert postre

devilled con aliño muy fuerte

devil's food cake torta de chocolate muy nutritiva

devils on horseback ciruelas pasas cocidas en vino tinto, rellenas de almendras y anchoas, envueltas en tocino, asadas y servidas en una tostada

Devonshire cream crema doble muy espesa

diced cortado en daditos

diet food alimento dietético

dill eneldo

dinner cena

dish plato

donut, doughnut buñuelo en forma de anillo, rosquilla

double cream doble crema, nata

Dover sole lenguado de Dover, muy afamado

dressing 1) salsa para ensalada 2) relleno para aves (US)

Dublin Bay prawn langostino

duck pato

duckling anadón

dumpling albóndiga de pasta

Dutch apple pie tarta de manzanas, cubierta con una capa de azúcar negra y mantequilla

éclair pastellillo relleno de crema de chocolate o de café

eel anguila

egg huevo
    boiled ～ pasado por agua
    fried ～ frito
    hard-boiled ～ duro
    poached ～ escalfado
    scrambled ～ revuelto
    soft-boiled ～ poco pasado por agua

eggplant berenjena

endive 1) escarola, achicoria (GB) 2) endibia (US)

entrecôte solomo de ternera

entrée 1) entrada (GB) 2) plato principal (US)

fennel hinojo

fig higo

filet mignon solomillo

fillet filete de carne o de pescado

finnan haddock róbalo ahumado

fish pescado
    ～ **and chips** filetes de pescado y patatas fritas
    ～ **cake** albóndigas, galleta de pescado y patatas

flan tarta de frutas

flapjack hojuela espesa

flounder fleso (pescado)

forcemeat relleno, picadillo

fowl ave

frankfurter salchicha de Francfort

French bean judía verde

French bread pan francés

French dressing 1) vinagreta (GB) 2) salsa cremosa de ensalada con salsa de tomates (US)

french fries patatas fritas

French toast rebanada de pan, mojada en huevos batidos, frita en una sartén y servida con

mermelada o azúcar
fresh fresco
fried frito, asado
fritter buñuelo
frogs' legs ancas de rana
frosting capa de azúcar garrapiñado
fruit fruta
fry fritura
galantine trozos de carne y picadillo cocidos en gelatina
game caza
gammon jamón ahumado
garfish anguila de mar
garlic ajo
garnish aderezo
gherkin pepinillo
giblets menudillos de ave
ginger jengibre
goose ganso
 ∼ **berry** grosella espinosa
grape uva
 ∼ **fruit** pomelo, toronja
grated rallado
gravy jugo de carne, salsa
grayling pescado de la familia del salmón
green bean judía verde
green pepper pimiento verde
green salad ensalada verde
greens verduras
grilled asado a la parrilla
grilse salmón joven
grouse urogallo
gumbo 1) legumbre de origen africano 2) plato criollo a base de *okra*, con carne o pescado y tomates
haddock róbalo
haggis panza de cordero rellena de copos de avena
hake merluza
half mitad, semi
ham jamón

 ∼ **and eggs** huevos con jamón
hamburger hamburguesa
hare liebre
haricot bean alubia blanca
hash 1) carne picada 2) picadillo de carne de ternera cubierto con patatas y legumbres
hazelnut avellana
heart corazón
herb hierba aromática
herring arenque
home-made de confección casera
hominy grits crema espesa de harina de maíz, especie de polenta
honey miel
 ∼ **dew melon** tipo de melón cuya carne es de color verde amarillento
hors-d'œuvre entremeses
horse-radish rábano picante
hot 1) caliente 2) con especias
 ∼ **cross bun** bollito con pasas (que se come durante la Cuaresma)
 ∼ **dog** salchicha caliente en un panecillo
huckleberry especie de arándano
hush puppy buñuelo a base de harina de maíz
ice-cream helado
iced helado
icing capa de azúcar garrapiñado
Idaho baked potato patata sin pelar cocida al horno
Irish stew guisado de cordero con cebollas y patatas
Italian dressing vinagreta
jam confitura
jellied en gelatina
Jell-O postre a la gelatina
jelly gelatina o jalea de frutas
Jerusalem artichoke aguaturma
John Dory especie de dorada
jugged hare estofado de liebre

juice jugo, zumo
juniper berry baya de enebro
junket leche cuajada azucarada
kale col rizada
kedgeree migajas de pescado aderezadas con arroz, huevos y mantequilla
ketchup salsa de tomates
kidney riñón
kipper arenque ahumado
lamb cordero
Lancashire hot pot guisado de chuletas y riñones de cordero, con patatas y cebollas
larded mechado
lean magro
leek puerro
leg pierna, muslo, corvejón
lemon limón
  ~ **sole** especie de platija
lentil lenteja
lettuce lechuga, ensalada verde
lima bean haba grande
lime lima (limón verde)
liver hígado
loaf pan, hogaza
lobster bogavante
loin lomo
Long Island duck pato de Long Island, muy afamado
low-calorie pobre en calorías
lox salmón ahumado
lunch almuerzo
macaroni macarrones
macaroon macarrón (almendrado)
mackerel caballa
maize maíz
mandarin mandarina
maple syrup jarabe de arce
marinade escabeche
marinated en escabeche
marjoram mejorana
marmalade mermelada de naranja

u otros sabores
marrow tuétano
  ~ **bone** hueso con tuétano
marshmallow dulce de malvavisco
marzipan mazapán
mashed potatoes puré de patatas
mayonnaise mayonesa
meal comida
meat carne
  ~**ball** albóndiga de carne
  ~ **loaf** carne picada preparada en forma de un pan y que se cuece al horno
medium (done) a punto
melted derretido
Melton Mowbray pie especie de empanada de carne
menu lista de platos
meringue merengue
milk leche
mince picadillo
  ~ **pie** tarta de frutas confitadas cortadas en daditos, con manzanas y especias (con o sin carne)
minced picado
  ~ **meat** carne picada
mint menta
mixed mezclado, surtido
  ~ **grill** brocheta de carne
molasses melaza
morel morilla
mousse postre de nata aromatizada
mulberry mora
mullet mújol (pescado)
mulligatawny soup sopa de pollo muy picante de origen indio
mushroom champiñón
muskmelon tipo de melón
mussel mejillón
mustard mostaza
mutton carnero
noodle tallarín
nut nuez

oatmeal (porridge) gachas de avena

oil aceite

okra fruto del *gumbo* utilizado generalmente para espesar las sopas y guisados

olive aceituna

omelet tortilla

onion cebolla

orange naranja

ox tongue lengua de buey

oxtail cola de buey (sopa)

oyster ostra

pancake hojuela espesa, torta de sartén

paprika pimiento

Parmesan (cheese) queso parmesano

parsley perejil

parsnip chirivía

partridge perdiz

pastry pastel, pastellilo

pasty empanadilla de carne

pea guisante

peach melocotón

peanut cacahuete, maní
  ~ **butter** manteca de cacahuete

pear pera

pearl barley cebada perlada

pepper pimienta

peppermint menta

perch perca

persimmon caqui

pheasant faisán

pickerel lucio pequeño (pescado)

pickle 1) legumbre o fruta en vinagre 2) pepinillo (US)

pickled conservado en salmuera o vinagre

pie torta a menudo cubierta con una capa de pasta, rellena de carne, legumbres, frutas o crema inglesa

pig cerdo

pigeon pichón

pike lucio

pineapple piña

plaice platija, acedía

plain natural

plate plato

plum ciruela, ciruela pasa
  ~ **pudding** pudín inglés hecho con frutas secas, a veces flameado, muy nutritivo y que se sirve en Navidad

poached escalfado

popcorn palomitas de maíz

popover panecillo esponjoso cocido en el horno

pork cerdo

porridge gachas

porterhouse steak lonja espesa de solomillo de res

pot roast carne de ternera asada y legumbres

potato patata, papa
  ~ **chips** 1) patatas fritas (GB) 2) chips (US)
  ~ **in its jacket** patata sin pelar

potted shrimps mantequilla sazonada, derretida y enfriada, servida con camarones

poultry ave de corral

prawn camarón grande

prune ciruela seca

ptarmigan perdiz blanca

pudding pudín blando o consistente hecho con harina, relleno de carne, pescado, legumbres o frutas

pumpernickel pan hecho con harina gruesa de centeno

pumpkin calabaza

quail codorniz

quince membrillo

rabbit conejo

radish rábano

rainbow trout trucha arco iris

raisin pasa
rare poco hecho
raspberry frambuesa
raw crudo
red mullet salmonete
red (sweet) pepper pimiento morrón
redcurrant grosella roja
relish condimento hecho con trocitos de legumbres y vinagre
rhubarb ruibarbo
rib (of beef) costilla (de ternera)
rib-eye steak solomillo
rice arroz
rissole croqueta de pescado o carne
river trout trucha de río
roast(ed) asado
Rock Cornish hen pollo tomatero
roe huevos de pescado
roll panecillo
rollmop herring filete de arenque escabechado con vino blanco, enrollado con un pepinillo en medio
round steak filete de pierna de ternera
Rubens sandwich carne de ternera en pan tostado, con col fermentada, queso suizo y salsa para ensalada; se sirve caliente
rump steak filete de lomo de ternera
rusk rebanadas tostadas de pan de molde
rye bread pan de centeno
saddle cuarto trasero
saffron azafrán
sage salvia
salad ensalada
  ~ **bar** surtido de ensaladas
  ~ **cream** salsa cremosa para ensalada, ligeramente azucarada

  ~ **dressing** salsa para ensalada
salmon salmón
  ~ **trout** trucha asalmonada
salt(ed) sal(ado)
sandwich bocadillo, emparedado
sardine sardina
sauce salsa
sauerkraut col fermentada
sausage salchicha
sauté(ed) salteado
scallop 1) venera 2) escalope de ternera
scampi langostino
scone panecillo tierno hecho con harina de avena o cebada
Scotch broth caldo a base de carne de carnero o de buey y legumbres
Scotch woodcock pan tostado con huevos revueltos y crema de anchoas
sea bass róbalo, lubina
sea kale col marina
seafood mariscos y peces marinos
(in) season (en su) época (estación del año)
seasoning condimento, sazón
service servicio
  ~ **charge** importe que se paga por el servicio
  ~ **(not) included** servicio (no) incluido
set menu menú fijo
shad alosa, sábalo
shallot chalote
shellfish marisco
sherbet sorbete
shoulder espalda
shredded wheat hojuelas de trigo en croquetas (se sirven en el desayuno)
shrimp camarón, gamba
silverside (of beef) codillo (de ternera)

sirloin steak bistec del solomillo
skewer brocheta
slice loncha, rodaja
sliced cortado en lonchas
sloppy Joe carne picada de ternera con una salsa picante de tomates, se sirve en un panecillo
smelt eperlano
smoked ahumado
snack comida ligera
sole lenguado
soup sopa, crema
sour agrio
soused herring arenque conservado en vinagre y especias
spaghetti espaguetis
spare rib costilla de cerdo casi descarnada
spice especia
spinach espinaca
spiny lobster langosta
(on a) spit (en un) espetón
sponge cake bizcocho ligero y esponjoso
sprat arenque pequeño, sardineta
squash calabaza
starter entrada
steak and kidney pie empanada de carne de ternera y riñones
steamed cocido al vapor
stew guisado
Stilton (cheese) queso inglés afamado (blanco o con mohos azules)
strawberry fresa
string bean judía verde
stuffed relleno
stuffing (el) relleno
suck(l)ing pig lechón
sugar azúcar
sugarless sin azúcar
sundae copa de helado con frutas, nueces, nata batida y a veces jarabe

supper comida ligera de la noche, cena
swede naba de Suecia
sweet 1) dulce 2) postre
~ **corn** maíz blanco
~ **potato** patata dulce
sweetbread lechecillas
Swiss cheese queso suizo (Emmenthal)
Swiss roll bizcocho enrollado y relleno de mermelada
Swiss steak lonja de ternera asada con legumbres y especias
T-bone steak bistec y filete de ternera separados por un hueso en forma de T
table d'hôte menú fijo
tangerine especie de mandarina
tarragon estragón
tart tarta de frutas
tenderloin filete de carne
Thousand Island dressing salsa para ensalada, sazonada, hecha de mayonesa y pimientos
thyme tomillo
toad-in-the-hole carne de ternera (o salchicha) cubierta de pasta y cocida al horno
toast pan tostado, tostada
toasted tostado
~ **cheese** pan tostado con queso derretido
tomato tomate
tongue lengua
tournedos bistec espeso del filete (ternera)
treacle melaza
trifle pastel con jerez o aguardiente, hecho con almendras, mermelada y crema batida o natillas y crema de vainilla
tripe tripas, callos
trout trucha
truffle trufa

tuna, tunny atún
turbot rodaballo, rombo
turkey pavo
turnip nabo
turnover pastelillo relleno de compota o mermelada
turtle tortuga
underdone poco hecho
vanilla vainilla
veal ternera
  ~ **bird** pulpeta de ternera
vegetable legumbre
  ~ **marrow** calabacín
venison caza, corzo
vichyssoise sopa fría preparada con puerros, patatas y crema
vinegar vinagre
Virginia baked ham jamón cocido al horno, adornado con clavos de especia, rebanadas de piña y cerezas; se le baña con el jugo de las frutas
vol-au-vent pastel de hojaldre relleno de salsa con crema, trozos de carne y champiñones
wafer barquillo
waffle especie de barquillo caliente
walnut nuez
water ice sorbete
watercress berro de agua
watermelon sandía
well-done bastante hecho
Welsh rabbit/rarebit queso derretido sobre una tostada
whelk buccino (molusco)
whipped cream nata batida
whitebait boquerón
Wiener schnitzel escalope de ternera empanado
wine list lista de vinos
woodcock becada
Worcestershire sauce condimento líquido picante a base de vinagre, soja y ajo
yoghurt yogur
York ham jamón de York (ahumado)
Yorkshire pudding especie de pasta de hojuelas que se sirve con el rosbif
zucchini calabacín
zwieback rebanadas tostadas de pan de molde

Bebidas

ale cerveza negra, ligeramente azucarada, fermentada a elevada temperatura
  bitter ~ negra, amarga y más bien pesada
  brown ~ negra de botella, ligeramente azucarada
  light ~ dorada de botella
  mild ~ negra de barril, bastante fuerte
  pale ~ dorada de botella
angostura esencia aromática amarga que se añade a los cócteles
applejack aguardiente de manzanas

Athol Brose bebida escocesa hecha con whisky, miel, agua y a veces copos de avena

Bacardi cocktail cóctel de ron con ginebra, jarabe de granadina y jugo de limón

barley water bebida refrescante a base de cebada y aromatizada con limón

barley wine cerveza negra muy alcoholizada

beer cerveza
   bottled ~ de botella
   draft, draught ~ de barril

bitters aperitivos y digestivos a base de raíces, corteza o hierbas

black velvet champán mezclado con *stout* (acompaña con frecuencia las ostras)

bloody Mary vodka, jugo de tomate y especias

bourbon whisky americano, a base de maíz

brandy 1) denominación genérica de los aguardientes de uvas y otras frutas 2) coñac
   ~ **Alexander** mezcla de aguardiente, crema de cacao y nata

British wines vino fermentado en Gran Bretaña, fabricado a base de uvas o jugo de uvas importadas

cherry brandy licor de cerezas

cider sidra
   ~ **cup** mezcla de sidra, especias, azúcar y hielo

claret vino tinto de Burdeos

cobbler *long drink* helado a base de frutas, al que se añade vino o licor

coffee café
   ~ **with cream** con nata
   black ~ solo
   caffeine-free ~ descafeinado

   white ~ con leche, cortado

cordial licor estimulante y digestivo

cream nata

cup bebida refrescante a base de vino helado, sifón, un espirituoso y adornada con una raja de naranja, de limón o de pepino

daiquiri cóctel de ron con jugo de limón y de piña

double doble porción

Drambuie licor a base de whisky y miel

dry martini 1) vermú seco (GB) 2) cóctel de ginebra con algo de vermú seco (US)

egg-nog bebida de ron u otro licor fuerte con yemas de huevos batidas y azúcar

gin ginebra

gin and it mezcla de ginebra y vermú italiano

gin-fizz mezcla de ginebra, jugo de limón, sifón y azúcar

ginger ale bebida sin alcohol, perfumada con extracto de jengibre

ginger beer bebida ligeramente alcohólica, a base de jengibre y azúcar

grasshopper mezcla de crema de menta, crema de cacao y nata

Guinness (stout) cerveza negra, con gusto muy pronunciado y algo dulce, con mucha malta y lúpulo

half pint aproximadamente 3 decilitros

highball whisky o aguardiente diluido con agua, soda o *ginger ale* helado

iced helado

Irish coffee café con azúcar y whisky irlandés, cubierto con nata batida (Chantilly)

Irish Mist licor irlandés a base de whisky y miel

Irish whiskey whisky irlandés menos áspero que el whisky escocés *(scotch);* además de cebada contiene centeno, avena y trigo

juice jugo, zumo

lager cerveza dorada ligera

lemon squash zumo de limón

lemonade limonada

lime juice zumo de lima (limón verde)

liqueur licor, poscafé

liquor aguardiente

long drink licor diluido en agua o tónica y servido con cubitos de hielo

madeira vino de Madera

Manhattan whisky americano, vermú y *angostura*

milk leche

~ **shake** batido

mineral water agua mineral

mulled wine vino caliente con especias

neat bebida pura, sola, sin hielo y sin agua

old-fashioned whisky, *angostura*, cerezas con marrasquino y azúcar

on the rocks con cubitos de hielo

Ovaltine Ovomaltina

Pimm's cup(s) bebida alcohólica compuesta por alguno de los siguientes licores; se mezcla con zumo de fruta y algunas veces con agua de Seltz

~ **No. 1** a base de ginebra

~ **No. 2** a base de whisky

~ **No. 3** a base de ron

~ **No. 4** a base de aguardiente

pink champagne champán rosado

pink lady mezcla de clara de huevo, Calvados, zumo de limón, jarabe de granadina y ginebra

pint aproximadamente 6 decilitros

port (wine) (vino de) Oporto

porter cerveza negra y amarga

punch ponche

quart 1,14 litro (US 0,95 litro)

root beer bebida edulcorada efervescente, aromatizada con hierbas y raíces

rum ron

rye (whiskey) whisky de centeno, más pesado y más áspero que el *bourbon*

scotch (whisky) whisky escocés, mezcla de whisky de trigo y de whisky de cebada

screwdriver vodka y zumo de naranja

shandy *bitter ale* mezclada con zumo de limón o con una *ginger beer*

sherry jerez

short drink todo licor no diluido, puro

shot dosis de cualquier licor espirituoso

sloe gin-fizz licor de endrina con sifón y zumo de limón

soda water agua gaseosa

soft drink bebida sin alcohol

spirits aguardientes

stinger coñac y crema de menta

stout cerveza negra con mucho lúpulo y alcohol

straight alcohol que se bebe seco, sin mezcla

tea té

toddy ponche hecho de ron, agua, limón y azúcar

Tom Collins ginebra, zumo de limón, sifón y azúcar

tonic (water) (agua) tónica, agua gaseosa, a base de quinina

vermouth vermú
water agua
whisky sour whisky, zumo de
  limón, azúcar y sifón
wine vino
  dessert ~ de postre

dry ~ seco
red ~ tinto
rosé ~ clarete, rosado
sparkling ~ espumoso
sweet ~ dulce (de postre)
white ~ blanco

Verbos irregulares ingleses

En la siguiente lista damos los verbos irregulares ingleses. Los verbos compuestos o los que llevan un prefijo se conjugan como los verbos simples, por ej.: *mistake* y *overdrive* se conjugan como *take* y *drive*.

Infinitivo	Pret. indefinido	Participio pasado	
arise	arose	arisen	*levantarse*
awake	awoke	awoken	*despertarse*
be	was	been	*ser, estar*
bear	bore	borne	*soportar*
beat	beat	beaten	*batir*
become	became	become	*llegar a ser*
begin	began	begun	*comenzar*
bend	bent	bent	*doblar*
bet	bet	bet	*apostar*
bid	bade/bid	bidden/bid	*pedir*
bind	bound	bound	*atar*
bite	bit	bitten	*morder*
bleed	bled	bled	*sangrar*
blow	blew	blown	*soplar*
break	broke	broken	*romper*
breed	bred	bred	*criar*
bring	brought	brought	*traer*
build	built	built	*construir*
burn	burnt/burned	burnt/burned	*quemar*
burst	burst	burst	*reventar*
buy	bought	bought	*comprar*
can*	could	—	*poder*
cast	cast	cast	*arrojar*
catch	caught	caught	*coger*
choose	chose	chosen	*escoger*
cling	clung	clung	*adherirse*
clothe	clothed/clad	clothed/clad	*vestir*
come	came	come	*venir*
cost	cost	cost	*costar*
creep	crept	crept	*arrastrar*
cut	cut	cut	*cortar*
deal	dealt	dealt	*distribuir*
dig	dug	dug	*cavar*
do (he does)	did	done	*hacer*
draw	drew	drawn	*dibujar*
dream	dreamt/dreamed	dreamt/dreamed	*soñar*
drink	drank	drunk	*beber*
drive	drove	driven	*conducir*
dwell	dwelt	dwelt	*habitar*
eat	ate	eaten	*comer*
fall	fell	fallen	*caer*

* presente de indicativo

feed	fed	fed	*alimentar*
feel	felt	felt	*sentir*
fight	fought	fought	*luchar*
find	found	found	*encontrar*
flee	fled	fled	*huir*
fling	flung	flung	*lanzar*
fly	flew	flown	*volar*
forsake	forsook	forsaken	*renunciar*
freeze	froze	frozen	*helar*
get	got	got	*obtener*
give	gave	given	*dar*
go	went	gone	*ir*
grind	ground	ground	*moler*
grow	grew	grown	*crecer*
hang	hung	hung	*colgar*
have	had	had	*tener*
hear	heard	heard	*oír*
hew	hewed	hewed/hewn	*cortar*
hide	hid	hidden	*esconder*
hit	hit	hit	*golpear*
hold	held	held	*sostener*
hurt	hurt	hurt	*herir*
keep	kept	kept	*guardar*
kneel	knelt	knelt	*arrodillarse*
knit	knitted/knit	knitted/knit	*juntar*
know	knew	known	*saber*
lay	laid	laid	*acostar*
lead	led	led	*dirigir*
lean	leant/leaned	leant/leaned	*apoyarse*
leap	leapt/leaped	leapt/leaped	*saltar*
learn	learnt/learned	learnt/learned	*aprender*
leave	left	left	*marcharse*
lend	lent	lent	*prestar*
let	let	let	*permitir*
lie	lay	lain	*acostarse*
light	lit/lighted	lit/lighted	*encender*
lose	lost	lost	*perder*
make	made	made	*hacer*
may*	might	—	*poder*
mean	meant	meant	*significar*
meet	met	met	*encontrar (personas)*
mow	mowed	mowed/mown	*segar*
must*	—	—	*tener que*
ought (to)*	—	—	*deber*
pay	paid	paid	*pagar*
put	put	put	*poner*
read	read	read	*leer*
rid	rid	rid	*desembarazar*
ride	rode	ridden	*cabalgar*

* presente de indicativo

ring	rang	rung	*sonar*
rise	rose	risen	*ascender*
run	ran	run	*correr*
saw	sawed	sawn	*aserrar*
say	said	said	*decir*
see	saw	seen	*ver*
seek	sought	sought	*buscar*
sell	sold	sold	*vender*
send	sent	sent	*enviar*
set	set	set	*poner*
sew	sewed	sewed/sewn	*coser*
shake	shook	shaken	*agitar*
shall*	should	—	*deber*
shed	shed	shed	*desprenderse*
shine	shone	shone	*brillar*
shoot	shot	shot	*tirar*
show	showed	shown	*mostrar*
shrink	shrank	shrunk	*encogerse*
shut	shut	shut	*cerrar*
sing	sang	sung	*cantar*
sink	sank	sunk	*hundir*
sit	sat	sat	*sentarse*
sleep	slept	slept	*dormir*
slide	slid	slid	*resbalar*
sling	slung	slung	*lanzar*
slink	slunk	slunk	*escabullirse*
slit	slit	slit	*rajar*
smell	smelled/smelt	smelled/smelt	*oler*
sow	sowed	sown/sowed	*sembrar*
speak	spoke	spoken	*hablar*
speed	sped/speeded	sped/speeded	*apresurarse*
spell	spelt/spelled	spelt/spelled	*deletrear*
spend	spent	spent	*gastar*
spill	spilt/spilled	spilt/spilled	*derramar*
spin	spun	spun	*girar*
spit	spat	spat	*escupir*
split	split	split	*rajar*
spoil	spoilt/spoiled	spoilt/spoiled	*estropear*
spread	spread	spread	*extender*
spring	sprang	sprung	*saltar*
stand	stood	stood	*estar de pie*
steal	stole	stolen	*robar*
stick	stuck	stuck	*hundir*
sting	stung	stung	*picar*
stink	stank/stunk	stunk	*apestar*
strew	strewed	strewed/strewn	*esparcir*
stride	strode	stridden	*andar a pasos largos*
strike	struck	struck/stricken	*golpear*
string	strung	strung	*atar*

* presente de indicativo

strive	strove	striven	*esforzarse*
swear	swore	sworn	*jurar*
sweep	swept	swept	*barrer*
swell	swelled	swollen	*hinchar*
swim	swam	swum	*nadar*
swing	swung	swung	*balancearse*
take	took	taken	*tomar*
teach	taught	taught	*enseñar*
tear	tore	torn	*desgarrar*
tell	told	told	*decir*
think	thought	thought	*pensar*
throw	threw	thrown	*arrojar*
thrust	thrust	thrust	*impeler*
tread	trod	trodden	*pisotear*
wake	woke/waked	woken/waked	*despertar*
wear	wore	worn	*llevar puesto*
weave	wove	woven	*tejer*
weep	wept	wept	*llorar*
will*	would	—	*querer*
win	won	won	*ganar*
wind	wound	wound	*enrollar*
wring	wrung	wrung	*torcer*
write	wrote	written	*escribir*

---

* presente de indicativo

Abreviaturas inglesas

AA	*Automobile Association*	Asociación Automovilística
AAA	*American Automobile Association*	Asociación Automovilística de los Estados Unidos
ABC	*American Broadcasting Company*	Sociedad Privada de Radio-difusión y Televisión (EE.UU.)
A.D.	*anno Domini*	año de Cristo
Am.	*America; American*	América; americano
a.m.	*ante meridiem (before noon)*	de la mañana (de 00.00 a 12.00 h.)
Amtrak	*American railroad corporation*	Sociedad Privada de Compañías de Ferrocarriles Americanos
AT & T	*American Telephone and Telegraph Company*	Compañía Americana de Teléfonos y Telégrafos
Ave.	*avenue*	avenida
BBC	*British Broadcasting Corporation*	Sociedad Británica de Radio-difusión y Televisión
B.C.	*before Christ*	antes de Cristo
bldg.	*building*	edificio
Blvd.	*boulevard*	bulevar
B.R.	*British Rail*	Ferrocarriles Británicos
Brit.	*Britain; British*	Gran Bretaña; británico
Bros.	*brothers*	hermanos
¢	*cent*	1/100 de dólar
Can.	*Canada; Canadian*	Canadá; canadiense
CBS	*Columbia Broadcasting System*	Sociedad Privada de Radio-difusión y Televisión (EE.UU.)
CID	*Criminal Investigation Department*	Oficina de Investigación Criminal
CNR	*Canadian National Railway*	Ferrocarriles Canadienses
c/o	*(in) care of*	al cuidado de
Co.	*company*	compañía
Corp.	*corporation*	compañía
CPR	*Canadian Pacific Railways*	Compañía Privada de Ferrocarriles Canadienses
D.C.	*District of Columbia*	Distrito de Columbia (Washington, D.C.)
DDS	*Doctor of Dental Science*	Dentista

dept.	*department*	departamento, división administrativa
EEC	*European Economic Community*	Comunidad Económica Europea
e.g.	*for instance*	por ejemplo, verbigracia
Eng.	*England; English*	Inglaterra; inglés
excl.	*excluding; exclusive*	no incluido
ft.	*foot/feet*	pie/pies (medida: 30,5 cm.)
GB	*Great Britain*	Gran Bretaña
H.E.	*His/Her Excellency; His Eminence*	Su Excelencia; Su Eminencia
H.H.	*His Holiness*	Su Santidad
H.M.	*His/Her Majesty*	Su Majestad
H.M.S.	*Her Majesty's ship*	navío de guerra británico
hp	*horsepower*	caballos de vapor
Hwy	*highway*	carretera principal
i.e.	*that is to say*	a saber, es decir
in.	*inch*	pulgada (medida: 2,54 cm.)
Inc.	*incorporated*	Sociedad Anónima
incl.	*including, inclusive*	incluido
£	*pound sterling*	libra esterlina
L.A.	*Los Angeles*	Los Angeles
Ltd.	*limited*	Sociedad Anónima
M.D.	*Doctor of Medicine*	médico
M.P.	*Member of Parliament*	Miembro del Parlamento
mph	*miles per hour*	millas por hora
Mr.	*Mister*	Señor
Mrs.	*Missis*	Señora
Ms.	*Missis/Miss*	Señora/Señorita
nat.	*national*	nacional
NBC	*National Broadcasting Company*	Sociedad Privada de Radiodifusión y Televisión (EE.UU.)
No.	*number*	número
N.Y.C.	*New York City*	Ciudad de Nueva York
O.B.E.	*Officer (of the Order) of the British Empire*	Caballero de la Orden del Imperio Británico
p.	*page; penny/pence*	página; 1/100 de libra
p.a.	*per annum*	por año
Ph.D.	*Doctor of Philosophy*	Doctor en Filosofía
p.m.	*post meridiem (after noon)*	de la tarde/noche (de 12.00 a 24.00 h.)
PO	*Post Office*	Oficina de Correos
POO	*post office order*	giro postal

pop.	*population*	población
P.T.O.	*please turn over*	vuelva la página, por favor
RAC	*Royal Automobile Club*	Real Club Autómovil (Gran Bretaña)
RCMP	*Royal Canadian Mounted Police*	Policía Montada de Canadá
Rd.	*road*	carretera
ref.	*reference*	referencia
Rev.	*reverend*	Reverendo (pastor de la Iglesia Anglicana)
RFD	*rural free delivery*	distribución del correo en el campo
RR	*railroad*	ferrocarril
RSVP	*please reply*	se ruega contestación
$	*dollar*	dólar
Soc.	*society*	sociedad
St.	*saint ; street*	santo(a); calle
STD	*Subscriber Trunk Dialling*	teléfono automático
UN	*United Nations*	Organización de las Naciones Unidas
UPS	*United Parcel Service*	Compañía Privada de Expedición de Paquetes (EE.UU.)
US	*United States*	Estados Unidos de América
USS	*United States Ship*	navío de guerra (EE.UU.)
VAT	*value added tax*	tasa al valor añadido
VIP	*very important person*	persona importante que beneficia de ventajas particulares
Xmas	*Christmas*	Navidad
yd.	*yard*	yarda (medida: 91,44 cm.)
YMCA	*Young Men's Christian Association*	Asociación Cristiana de Muchachos
YWCA	*Young Women's Christian Association*	Asociación Cristiana de Muchachas
ZIP	*ZIP code*	número de distrito postal

Numerales

Cardinales		**Ordinales**	
0	zero	1st	first
1	one	2nd	second
2	two	3rd	third
3	three	4th	fourth
4	four	5th	fifth
5	five	6th	sixth
6	six	7th	seventh
7	seven	8th	eighth
8	eight	9th	ninth
9	nine	10th	tenth
10	ten	11th	eleventh
11	eleven	12th	twelfth
12	twelve	13th	thirteenth
13	thirteen	14th	fourteenth
14	fourteen	15th	fifteenth
15	fifteen	16th	sixteenth
16	sixteen	17th	seventeenth
17	seventeen	18th	eighteenth
18	eighteen	19th	nineteenth
19	nineteen	20th	twentieth
20	twenty	21st	twenty-first
21	twenty-one	22nd	twenty-second
22	twenty-two	23rd	twenty-third
23	twenty-three	24th	twenty-fourth
24	twenty-four	25th	twenty-fifth
25	twenty-five	26th	twenty-sixth
30	thirty	27th	twenty-seventh
40	forty	28th	twenty-eighth
50	fifty	29th	twenty-ninth
60	sixty	30th	thirtieth
70	seventy	40th	fortieth
80	eighty	50th	fiftieth
90	ninety	60th	sixtieth
100	a/one hundred	70th	seventieth
230	two hundred and thirty	80th	eightieth
1,000	a/one thousand	90th	ninetieth
10,000	ten thousand	100th	hundredth
100,000	a/one hundred thousand	230th	two hundred and thirtieth
1,000,000	a/one million	1,000th	thousandth

La hora

Los británicos y los americanos utilizan el sistema de 12 horas. La abreviatura *a.m. (ante meridiem)* designa las horas anteriores al mediodía, *p.m. (post meridiem)* las de la tarde o de la noche. Sin embargo, en Gran Bretaña existe la tendencia, cada vez más acentuada, a indicar los horarios como en el continente.

I'll come at seven a.m.	Vendré a las 7 de la mañana.
I'll come at two p.m.	Vendré a las 2 de la tarde.
I'll come at eight p.m.	Vendré a las 8 de la noche.

Los días de la semana

Sunday	domingo	*Thursday*	jueves
Monday	lunes	*Friday*	viernes
Tuesday	martes	*Saturday*	sábado
Wednesday	miércoles		

MANUALES DE CONVERSACION BERLITZ

Estos libros ofrecen, además de abundancia de frases y de un vocabulario muy útil acompañado de pronunciación, interesantes detalles relativos a propinas, datos útiles y sugerencias. Manejables y eficaces, son una ayuda valiosa para darse a entender.

Francés

Inglés
  (Edición Británica)

Inglés
  (Edición
  Norteamericana)

CASSETTES BERLITZ

La mayoría de los Manuales de Conversación pueden combinarse con una cassette que le ayudará a mejorar su acento. Cada cassette, grabada en alta fidelidad, va acompañada de un folleto de 32 páginas impresas con el texto completo de la grabación.